FUZZY LOGIC FOR THE MANAGEMENT OF UNCERTAINTY

EDITED BY

Lotfi A. Zadeh
Computer Science Division
University of California, Berkeley

Janusz Kacprzyk
Systems Research Institute
Polish Academy of Sciences, Warsaw

John Wiley & Sons, Inc.
New York · Chichester · Brisbane · Toronto · Singapore

Library of Congress Cataloging-in-Publication Data

Fuzzy logic for the management of uncertainty / edited by Lotfi A. Zadeh, Janusz Kacprzyk.
   p. cm.
   Includes bibliographical references and index.
   ISBN 0-471-54799-9 (cloth)
   1. Artificial intelligence. 2. Fuzzy systems. I. Zadeh, Lotfi Asker. II. Kacprzyk, Janusz.
   Q335.F89 1992
   006.3-dc20   91-38839
                                                 CIP

Printed in the United States of America

10 9 8 7 6 5 4 3 2 1

Printed and bound by Courier Companies, Inc.

CONTRIBUTORS

Helena Rasiowa, Institute of Mathematics, University of Warsaw, ul. Banacha 2, 00-325 Warsaw, POLAND

Raj Bhatnagar, University of Cincinnati, Cincinnati, OH 45221, USA

Laveen N. Kanal, University of Maryland, College Park, MD 20742, USA

Richard E. Neapolitan, Dept. of Computer Science, Northeastern University, Chicago, IL 60625, USA

Prakash P. Shenoy, School of Business, University of Kansas, Lawrence, KS 66045-2003, USA

Zdzisław Pawlak, Institute of Computer Science, Warsaw Technical University, ul. Nowowiejska 15/19, 00-665 Warsaw, POLAND

Nguyen Cat Ho, National Center for Scientific Research of Vietnam, Center for System and Management Research, Lieugiai-Badinh-Hanoi, P.O. Box 626 Bo Ho, VIETNAM

James R. Kenevan, Dept. of Computer Science, Illinois Institute of Technology, Chicago, IL 60616, USA

Esko Turunen, Lappeenranta University of Technology, SF-53851 Lappeenranta, FINLAND

Dimiter Driankov, Dept. of Computer and Information Science, Linköping University, S-58183 Linköping, SWEDEN

Patrick Doherty, Dept. of Computer and Information Science, Linköping University, S-58183 Linköping, SWEDEN

Jorma K. Mattila, Dept. of Information Tech., Lappeenranta University of Technology, SF-53851 Lappeenranta, FINLAND

Hiroyuki Watanabe, Dept. of Computer Science, University of North Carolina, Chapel Hill, NC 27514-3175, USA

James R. Symon, Dept. of Computer Science, University of North Carolina, Chapel Hill, NC 27514-3175, USA

Wayne D. Dettloff, MCNC, Research Triangle Park, NC 27709, USA

Kathy E. Yount, MCNC, Research Triangle Park, NC 27709, USA

Vilem Novák, Czechoslovak Academy of Sciences, Mining Institute, Studentska 1768, 708-00 Ostrava-Poruba, CZECHOSLOVAKIA

Thomas Whalen, Dept. of Decision Sciences, Georgia State University, Atlanta, GA 30303, USA

Brian Schott, Dept. of Decision Sciences, Georgia State University, Atlanta, GA 30303, USA

Etienne E. Kerre, Seminar for Mathematical Analysis, State University of Gent, Galglaan, 2, B-9000 Gent, BELGIUM

Lászlo T. Kóczy, Communication Electronics, Technical University of Budapest, Sztoczek u. 2, Budapest, H-1111 HUNGARY

Kaoru Hirota, Dept. of Instrument & Control Eng., College of Engineering, Hosei University, Kajino-cho, Koganei-shi, Tokyo 184, JAPAN

Henri Farreny, Institut de Recherche en Informatique de Toulouse, Université Paul Sabatier, 118, route de Narbonne, 31062 Toulouse Cédex, FRANCE

Henri Prade, Institut de Recherche en Informatique de Toulouse, Université Paul Sabatier, 118, route de Narbonne, 31062 Toulouse Cédex, FRANCE

Didier Dubois, Institut de Recherche en Informatique de Toulouse, Université Paul Sabatier, 118, route de Narbonne, 31062 Toulouse Cédex, FRANCE

Jerôme Lang, Institut de Recherche en Informatique de Toulouse, Universite Paul Sabatier, 118 route de Narbonne, 31062 Toulouse Cédex, FRANCE

J. F. Baldwin, Engineering Mathematics Dept., University of Bristol, Bristol BS8 1TR, ENGLAND

P. Torasso, Dipartimento di Informatica, Universitá di Torino, Corso Svizzera, 185, 10149 Torino, ITALY

L. Portinale, Dipartimento di Informatica, Universitá di Torino, Corso Svizzera, 185, 10149 Torino, ITALY

L. Console, Dipartimento di Informatica, Universitá di Torino, Corso Svizzera, 185, 10149 Torino, ITALY

M. Cassasa Mont, Dipartimento di Informatica, Università di Torino, Corso Svizzera, 185, 10149 Torino ITALY

Bernadette Bouchon-Meunier, LAFORIA, Université Paris VI, Tour 46, 4 place Jussieu, 75252 Paris Cédex 05, FRANCE

Ladislav J. Kohout, Institute for Cognitive Sciences, Institute for Expert Systems & Robotics, Florida State University, Tallahassee, FL 32306, USA

Wyllis Bandler, Dept. of Computer Science, Florida State University, Tallahassee, FL 32306, USA

A. F. Rocha, RANI – Research on Artificial and Natural Intelligence, Rua Tenente Ary Aps 172, 13200 Jundiai, BRAZIL

M. Theoto, RANI – Research on Artificial and Natural Intelligence, Rua Tenente Ary Aps 172, 13200 Jundiai, BRAZIL

C. A. C. Oliveira, Superintedencia Geral de Automação e Instrumentacão, Companhia Siderurgica Nacional, 27180 Volta Redonda, BRAZIL

F. Gomide, Faculty of Electric Engineering, UNICAMP, 13081 Campinas, BRAZIL

James J. Buckley, Dept. of Mathematics, University of Alabama at Birmingham, Birmingham, AL 35294, USA

Cezary Iwański, Systems Research Institute, Polish Academy of Sciences, ul. Newelska 6, 01-447 Warsaw, POLAND

Janusz Kacprzyk, Systems Research Institute, Polish Academy of Sciences, ul. Newelska 6, 01-447 Warsaw, POLAND

M. M. Gupta, Intelligent Systems Research Laboratory, College of Engineering, University of Saskatchewan, Saskatoon, Saskatchewan, CANADA S7N 0W0

J. Qi, Intelligent Systems Research Laboratory, College of Engineering, University of Saskatchewan, Saskatoon, Saskatchewan, CANADA S7N 0W0

Zenon A. Sosnowski, Knowledge Systems Laboratory, Institute for Information Tech., National Research Council of Canada, Ottawa, CANADA K1A 0R6

Witold Pedrycz, Electrical & Computer Eng. Dept., University of Manitoba, Winnipeg, CANADA R3T 2N2

J. Agustí, Institut d'Investigacion en Intelligencia Artificial, Centre d'Estudis Avançats de Blanes, CSIC, Blanes, SPAIN

F. Esteva, Institut d'Investigacion en Intelligencia Artificial, Centre d'Estudis Avançats de Blanes, CSIC, Blanes, SPAIN

P. Garcia, Institut d'Investigacion en Intelligencia Artificial, Centre d'Estudis Avançats de Blanes, CSIC, Blanes, SPAIN

L. Godo, Institut d'Investigacion en Intelligencia Artificial, Centre d'Estudis Avançats de Blanes, CSIC, Blanes, SPAIN

R. López de Mántaras, Institut d'Investigacion en Intelligencia Artificial, Centre d'Estudis Avançats de Blanes, CSIC, Blanes, SPAIN

J. Puyol, Institut d'Investigacion en Intelligencia Artificial, Centre d'Estudis Avançats de Blanes, CSIC, Blanes, SPAIN

L. Murguí, Aliança Mataronina Hospital, Mataró, SPAIN

C. Sierra, Institut d'Investigacion en Intelligencia Artificial, Centre d'Estudis Avançats de Blanes, CSIC, Blanes, SPAIN

M. E. Cohen, Department of Mathematics, California State University, Fresno, CA 93740, USA

D. L. Hudson, School of Medicine, University of California at San Francisco, Fresno, CA 93793, USA

Abraham Kandel, Dept. of Computer Science & Engineering, University of South Florida, Tampa, FL 33620, USA

Moti Schneider, Dept. of Computer Science, Florida Inst. of Technology, Melbourne, FL 32901, USA

Gideon Langholz, Dept. of Electrical Engineering, FAMU/FSU College of Engineering, Tallahassee, FL 32306, USA

Ana M. Chang, Honeywell Inc., MavD, 11601 Roosevelt Blvd., St. Petersburg, FL 33716-2202, USA

Lawrence O. Hall, Dept. of Computer Science & Eng., University of South Florida, Tampa, FL 33620, USA

A. Yazici, Center for Intelligent & Knowledge-Based Applications, Dept. of Computer Science, Tulane University, New Orleans, LA 70118, USA

R. George, Center for Intelligent & Knowledge-Based Applications, Dept. of Computer Science, Tulane University, New Orleans, LA 70118, USA

B. P. Buckles, Center for Intelligent & Knowledge-Based Applications, Dept. of Computer Science, Tulane University, New Orleans, LA 70118, USA

F. E. Petry, Center for Intelligent & Knowledge-Based Applications, Dept. of Computer Science, Tulane University, New Orleans, LA 70118, USA

P. Bosc, IRISA/ENSSAT, BP 447, 22305 Lannion Cédex, FRANCE

O. Pivert, IRISA/ENSSAT, BP 447, 22305 Lannion Cédex, FRANCE

CONTENTS

Preface

There has been a dramatic change in uncertainty paradigms during the last 25 years: until the 1960s, uncertainty, vagueness, and inexactness were features with rather negative meanings. Nobody wanted to be called a "vague decision maker"; a scientist that could not make precise and definite statements was not regarded as a "true" scientist, and uncertainty was considered to be something disturbing that should, if at all possible, be avoided in models, theories, and statements. The only theory that dealt with uncertainty was probability theory, and this—predominantly in its frequentistic interpretation—was restricted to situations in which the law of large numbers was valid and uncertainty could be attributed to randomness.

Since the 1960s this has changed. One increasingly accepts the fact that uncertainty in a generic sense is a part of reality, which we cannot change. Therefore, more and more it seems not only desirable but even necessary to include it in our models rather than to neglect its existence. One also realizes that human beings have dealt quite well in the past with uncertainty in their daily language. By contrast to formal, scientific languages, such as mathematics, logics, and computer languages, our daily language is anything but crisp, certain, or unequivocal in its meaning. People, however, can cope with this by deriving the exact meanings of words from the context.

Computers cannot do this and hence we always face problems when humans want either to communicate with computers or if we expect computers to behave like human beings. This has led to an increasing number of uncertainty theories during the last two decades and to numerous attempts to modify existing formal methods such that they correspond more to reality and human mental behavior.

A pioneer in this direction was and is, without any doubt, Lotfi A. Zadeh, who proposed fuzzy set theory in 1965. It is, therefore, justified that the title of this book uses the term "fuzzy logic" not in a narrow sense as a name for a specific logic, but rather generically for logics of this spirit: rough sets, possibility ditributions or neural systems, as included in this book, are formally not fuzzy sets but focus also on uncertainty and vagueness. This becomes particularly obvious when considering terms such as "fuzzy intuitionistic logic," "nonmonotonic fuzzy logic," "modifier logic," and the like.

Issues of the type described above become particularly relevant when either human knowledge is to be used on computers or when databanks are to answer human queries and store data and knowledge. This is particularly true in two areas: "knowledge-based systems" and "fuzzy databank systems," and these are the two areas this book concentrates on.

Three essential functions in knowledge-based systems are knowledge representation, knowledge acquisition, and inference. The first five parts of this book lead gradually to a coverage of these areas: Parts 1 and 2 survey different approaches for approximate reasoning, Part 3 focuses on specific aspects of fuzzy inference, Part 4 concentrates on knowledge representation and elicitation, and Part 5 presents the implementation of these methods in specific knowledge-based systems. Finally, Part 6 is dedicated to fuzzy database systems.

The editors of the book have managed to obtain contributions from leading scientists in all these areas. Thus, for scientists and practitioners in related fields this volume will remain one of the most important references for years to come!

H.-J. Zimmermann
RWTH Aachen (Germany)

About the Editors

Lotfi A. Zadeh is an alumnus of the University of Teheran, Massachusetts Institute of Technology, and Columbia University. Prior to the publication of his first paper on fuzzy sets in 1965, his work was centered on information processing and systems analysis. In 1963 he coauthored with Professor C. A. Desoer a basic text in linear system theory that laid foundations for the state space approach.

Since 1969 Dr. Zadeh's work has been focused on the theory of fuzzy sets and its applications. He has written extensively on issues related to knowledge representation, management of uncertainty in expert systems, decision analysis, and approximate reasoning.

Dr. Zadeh joined the faculty of the University of California, Berkeley in 1959 and served as chairman of the Department of Electrical Engineering and Computer Science from 1963 to 1968. He is currently serving as director of the Berkeley Initiative on Soft Computing.

Dr. Zadeh has been awarded the IEEE Medal of Education and the Honda Foundation Prize. He is a member of the National Academy of Engineering and a fellow of the Institute of Electrical and Electronics Engineers and American Association for Artificial Intelligence.

Janusz Kacprzyk is an alumnus of Warsaw University of Technology. He holds an M.S. degree in automatic control and computer science, a Ph.D. degree in systems analysis, and a Dr. Sc. degree in computer science.

Since 1973, Dr. Kacprzyk's work has concentrated on application of fuzzy sets and fuzzy logic, primarily in modeling socioeconomic systems, multistage decision making and control, group decision making and consensus formation, and knowledge-based systems.

Dr. Kacprzyk is a research associate at the Systems Research Institute, Polish Academy of Sciences in Warsaw, Poland. He holds various positions as visiting professor in management information systems and computer science in the United States.

Dr. Kacprzyk is the author of three books, coeditor of at least ten edited volumes, and author or coauthor of more than a hundred papers. He has been awarded the Prize of Scientific Secretary of the Polish Academy of Sciences. He is currently a vice president of the International Fuzzy Systems Association (IFSA).

1 Toward fuzzy logic

Helena RASIOWA
Institute of Mathematics
University of Warsaw
ul. Banacha 2
02-097 Warsaw, POLAND

Abstract. The purpose of the present paper is to show, within the framework of a cursory survey of certain results concerning an algebraic approach to various first-order logics as, e.g., classical (Rasiowa and Sikorski, 1950), intuitionistic (Mostowski, 1948; Rasiowa, 1951; Rasiowa and Sikorski, 1953), modal S4 (Rasiowa, 1951; Rasiowa and Sikorski, 1953), Post's m-valued (Rasiowa, 1969), Post's ω^+-valued (Rasiowa, 1973), and poset-based approximation logics (Rasiowa, 1987, 1988), that there is a strict connection between this area and that of fuzzy sets (Zadeh, 1965), especially of L-fuzzy sets (Goguen, 1967). Formulas in the above-mentioned logics have been algebraically interpreted as functions from a universe under consideration into certain complete lattices, that is, as L-fuzzy sets, which were introduced by Goguen (1967). A concept of LT-fuzzy sets (Rasiowa and Cat Ho, 1992), being a modification of L-fuzzy sets, is also considered as a basis for a formulation of first-order LT-fuzzy logics (Rasiowa and Cat Ho, Chapter 6 in this volume).

1. INTRODUCTION

The present paper is a short introduction to the classical and certain nonclassical predicate calculi from the point of view of their connections with fuzzy set theory as initiated by Zadeh (1965), and

L-fuzzy sets introduced by Goguen (1967). For that purpose a consideration of an algebraic treatment of predicate calculi will be presented.

In an *algebraic approach to logics,* predicates are interpreted as functions from the domain of an interpretation into appropriate (for these logics) complete lattices. Notice that a fuzzy set over a domain U is any function from U into the interval $[0, 1]$ of the real line, and an L-fuzzy set is any function from a given domain U into a partially ordered set L, particularly into a complete lattice L. It will be shown that by our approach all formulas are treated in a similar way and that this leads to complete characterizations of these logics (i.e., completeness theorems hold). Aside from the classical predicate calculi, the following ones will be considered: the intuitionistic predicate calculi, modal predicate calculi of Lewis's S4 logic, many-valued and ω^+-valued Post's predicate calculi, and poset-based approximation logics. The last of these can be treated as a kind of fuzzy logic.

Historically, until the end of the nineteenth century, mathematical theories were built in an intuitive or axiomatic way. In other words, they were constructed either on intuitive ideas concerning their primitive notions or on the basis of properties of primitive notions established in a set of axioms. The discovery of *paradoxes* in the Cantor intuitive set theory as, e.g., Russell's paradox of 1903 (for more details on paradoxes, see, e.g., Fraenkel, 1958), strongly implied the need of constructing *axiomatic mathematical theories.* The paradoxes of set theory can be eliminated in axiomatic systems of set theory.

The first axiom system for set theory was proposed by Zermelo (1908) – see also, e.g., Fraenkel (1922) or Bernays (1937). However, the axiomatic method does not preclude the appearance of other kinds of paradoxes, the so-called *semantic paradoxes* (see, e.g., Beth, 1959 or Kleene, 1952). This inspired the introduction of an even greater precision in the construction of mathematical theories leading to the concept of a *formalized theory* in which not only properties of primitive notions are formulated by a set of axioms but the language of a theory is also precisely described, and logical tools allowed in any process of deduction are exactly defined. This point of view regarding the foundations of mathematics corresponds to that of the Hilbert school of formalism (see, e.g., Kleene, 1952). Mathematical ways of reasoning are based on the principle that any mathematical statement is either true or false, that is, on two-valued logic, and are usually formalized within the framework of classical (two-valued) first-order predicate calculi (see, e.g., Hilbert and Ackerman, 1928; Kleene, 1952; Rasiowa and Sikorski 1963; Mendelson, 1964).

A close connection between classical logic and the theory of Boolean algebras has been known for a long time. Boole's research in logic led to a concept that is now called Boolean algebra. Stone's (1936) results on the representation of Boolean algebras by fields of sets extended this relationship on fields of sets. The interpretation of formulas of classical propositional calculus as functions over any Boolean algebra (field of sets) is a generalization of the well-known truth-table method. An extension of this method to classical predicate calculi through the work of Rasiowa and Sikorski (1950) permitted an interpretation of formulas as functions from a universe of an interpretation into complete Boolean algebras, and into fields of all subsets of a space. This method was applied to an algebraic proof of the Gödel completeness theorem. For a comprehensive exposition of this approach and its applications, see Rasiowa and Sikorski (1963).

In 1908, Brouwer (1908) formulated principles of a philosophical view on the foundations of mathematics, known as *intuitionism*. This trend, anticipated by Kant and such mathematicians as Kronecker and Poincaré, has been developed by Brouwer and his school as a radical form of constructivism. The purpose of intuitionism is to prevent paradoxes in mathematics. An exposition of the principles of intuitionism can be found, e.g., in Heyting (1956), Beth (1959), and Kleene (1952). The basic difference between the viewpoint of most mathematicians and that of the intuitionists on the meaning of fundamental logical and set-theoretic concepts lies in a different understanding of the notion of an infinite set and of the word "exists." For example, "there exists a positive integer x satisfying condition $A(x)$" is considered by the intuitionists as true if there exists a method of constructing a positive integer x satisfying condition $A(x)$, that is if such an x can be indicated. In general, however, the mathematicians consider this as true if there exists a proof from axioms of arithmetic on the basis of classical logic, in particular by first proving that "not for every x not $A(x)$," i.e., that the assumption "for every x not $A(x)$" leads to a contradiction. Hence, applying a law of classical logic that "if not for every x, not $A(x)$, then there exists an x such that $A(x)$" and the modus ponens rule, we infer that there exists an x satisfying $A(x)$. This proof by reducing to a contradiction does not give any method for constructing a positive integer x satisfying $A(x)$, and is rejected by the intuitionists. The elimination of nonconstructive proofs from mathematical reasoning caused the rejection of all laws of classical logic that can lead to such proofs. In particular, the law of the excluded middle, establishing the bivalence of classical logic, was rejected by intuitionism.

Propositional calculi and predicate calculi of intuitionistic logic were formalized by Heyting (1930), and investigated by many authors from different points of view. In this paper, only algebraic investigations will be considered.

Research by Stone (1937), Tarski (1938), and McKinsey and Tarski (1946, 1948) established a relation between intuitionistic propositional calculi and algebras of open subsets of topological spaces (in particular of the real line or the unit interval of the real line) as well as pseudo-Boolean algebras. Especially interesting is McKinsey and Tarski's (1946, 1948) result establishing that the algebra of all open subsets of any dense-in-itself metric space $X \neq \emptyset$, for example, of Euclidean space, of the real line or of the interval $[0, 1]$ is adequate for intuitionistic propositional calculi. This allowed the interpretation of formulas of intuitionistic propositional calculi as functions defined on pseudo-Boolean algebras and algebras of open subsets of topological spaces. The idea of extending this method of interpretation to intuitionistic predicate calculi was proposed by Mostowski (1948) for problems of nondeducibility of formulas. It was undertaken by Henkin (1950) and Rasiowa (1951), and developed in several papers by Rasiowa and Sikorski, as, e.g., in Rasiowa and Sikorski (1953), and Rasiowa (1954a, 1954b) — for a comprehensive exposition, see. e.g., Rasiowa and Sikorski (1963). This approach permitted the interpretation of formulas of intuitionistic predicate calculi as functions from a universe of an interpretation into complete pseudo-Boolean algebras, and into algebras of all open subsets of topological spaces, particularly of the real line. It was shown by Sikorski (1958) that there exists a set of irrational numbers such that the algebra of all open subsets of this set is adequate for predicate formulas deducible in the intuitionistic predicate calculi.

It is surprising that algebraic investigations concerning intuitionistic logic, which was devised to formalize constructive reasoning, led to interpretations, e.g., in the algebra of all open subsets of the real line or the interval $[0, 1]$, that suggest interpretations in the algebra of fuzzy truth-values, if open subsets of $[0, 1]$ are treated as fuzzy truth values.

A philosophical criticism concerning the classical ("material") implication resulted in the formulation of Lewis's *modal logics* S1 — S5, in which the modal propositional connectives — "it is necessary that" and "it is possible that"— occur besides propositional connectives of classical logic. These modal logics were introduced as formalized deductive systems of propositional calculi in Lewis and Langford (1932). Philosophical aspects of these logics are discussed in the same book (Lewis and Langford, 1932) and in Beth (1959). Other modal logics were constructed by other authors, playing an increasing role in theoretical computer science and artificial intelligence, for instance, in logics of programs, nonmonotonic logics, and logic of knowledge (cf. Chellas, 1980; Turner, 1964). Lewis's modal propositional calculi have been examined by many authors from various points of view. In this paper only algebraic investigations concerning logic S4 will be considered.

McKinsey's (1941) and McKinsey and Tarski's (1946, 1948) research established connections between modal propositional calculus S4 and topological Boolean algebras as well as topological fields of sets. Formulas of this calculus can be interpreted as functions defined on any such algebra. Especially interesting is the result concerning the adequacy of such an interpretation in the algebra of all subsets of the real line or the [0, 1] interval, treated as a topological field of sets. An algebraic treatment of *modal predicate calculi*, a generalization of the method mentioned above, was initiated and developed by Rasiowa (1951, 1954a, 1963), and Rasiowa and Sikorski (1953). An exposition of results is given in Rasiowa and Sikorski (1963). This approach permitted an interpretation of formulas of modal predicate calculi as functions from a universe of an interpretation into complete topological Boolean algebras and into topological fields of all subsets of topological spaces.

Commonsense reasoning takes uncertainty into consideration, particularly concerning statements about events in the future. The idea that there are statements that are neither true nor false led to the formulation by Łukasiewicz (1920) of his three-valued propositional calculus, and later to *m*-valued and even uncountably valued generalizations (Łukasiewicz and Tarski, 1930). Independently, Post (1921) introduced his *m*-valued propositional calculus. All of these calculi were constructed not as formalized axiomatic deductive systems but by means of the truth-table method.

In *many-valued logics* of Łukasiewicz, the propositional connectives ¬, ∪, ∩ and ⇒ are based on arithmetical rules. A three-valued system can be developed from the three logical values: 0, 1/2 and 1, where 0 and 1 correspond to falsehood and truth, respectively, using the following equations, for each $x, y, z \in \{0, 1/2, 1\}$:

$$\neg x = 1 - x, \quad x \cup y = \max(x, y), \quad x \cap y = \min(x, y)$$

$$x \Rightarrow y = \begin{cases} 1 & \text{if } x \leqslant y \\ 1 - x + y & \text{if } x > y \end{cases} \tag{1}$$

The same equations are used to develop *m*-valued systems, in which the logical values are: $1 = (m - 1)/(m - 1)$, $(m - 2/(m - 1)$, ..., $1/(m - 1), 0/(m - 1) = 0$. In infinitely valued Łukasiewicz's propositional calculi with a denumerable set of logical values, it is assumed that they are rational numbers in the interval $[0, 1]$, and in the case of an uncountable set of logical values they are real numbers in $[0, 1]$. The propositional connectives are defined by the same equations (1).

Łukasiewicz's uncountably valued logic is considered by specialists in the foundations of fuzzy sets theory (e.g., Gaines, 1977) as a basic logic for *fuzzy reasoning*. The logics of Łukasiewicz will not, however, be considered in this paper. A comprehensive exposition can be found in Rescher (1969).

The first axiomatic system for algebras corresponding to Post's *m*-valued logics was given by Rosenbloom (1942). Epstein's (1960) paper initiated an intensive development of the theory of these algebras (called *Post algebras of order* $m = 2$, 3, ...). The first equational axiom system was proposed by Traczyk (1964). Another important equational axiom system was given by Rousseau (1969, 1970). A comprehensive exposition of the theory of Post algebras can be found in Rasiowa (1974).

The Post many-valued predicate calculi, based on Post algebras of order $m \geqslant 2$, were formalized in Rasiowa (1969). Formulas of these predicate calculi are interpreted as functions from a universe of an interpretation into a chain $e_0 \leqslant e_1 \leqslant ... \leqslant e_{m-1}$ where e_0 and e_{m-1} play the role of falsehood and truth, respectively. A generalization of Post algebras of order m to Post algebras of order ω^+, and predicate calculi of order ω^+ based on these algebras were introduced and investigated in Rasiowa (1973). Formulas of these predicate calculi are interpreted as functions from a universe of an interpretation into an infinite chain $e_0 \leqslant e_1 \leqslant ... \leqslant e_\omega$.

Although there are many other generalizations of Post algebras known in the literature, we will mention only *plain semi-Post algebras of any poset type* $\mathbf{T} = (T, \leqslant)$. By a poset we mean any partially ordered set. These algebras, introduced and investigated by Cat Ho and Rasiowa (1989), constitute a poset-based generalization of Post algebras and are a simplification of those in Cat Ho and Rasiowa (1987). This concept turned out to be stimulating for logics of approximate reasoning (Rasiowa, 1987, 1988). On the other hand, the algebraic semantics of the poset-based approximation logics suggested a notion of *LT*-fuzzy sets being a modification of *L*-fuzzy sets. A theory of *LT*-fuzzy sets was introduced by Rasiowa and Cat Ho (1992a), and will be applied later in this volume to the formulation of *LT*-fuzzy predicate logics, which may be conceived as logics for fuzzy reasoning.

2. LATTICE-THEORETIC CONCEPTS AND $L\,T$-FUZZY SETS

The aim of this section is to establish the terminology and notation concerning certain notions of *lattice theory*, and to introduce some concepts that will be applied later.

By a *poset* we mean any partially ordered set $T = (T, \leqslant)$. A *greatest element* and a *least element* in a poset, provided they exist, are denoted by 1 and 0 (or by v and ʌ), respectively. A *least upper bound* and a *greatest lower bound* of a set $(t_j)_{j \in J}$ of elements in a poset, provided they exist, are denoted by $\cup_{j \in J} t_j$ and $\cap_{j \in J} t_j$, respectively.

A *lattice* is a poset $T = (T, \leqslant)$ such that for any two elements t, w in T there exists their least upper bound, denoted by $t \cup w$, and their greatest lower bound, denoted by $t \cap w$. A lattice is said to be *distributive* if for all its elements s, t, w, $(s \cup t) \cap w = (s \cap w) \cup (t \cap w)$. A lattice is said to be *complete* if for every set $(t_j)_{j \in J}$ of its elements there exists $\cup_{j \in J} t_j$ and $\cap_{j \in J} t_j$.

A Boolean algebra is a distributive lattice with 1 and 0 such that for every element t there exists its complement $-t$ satisying $t \cup -t = 1$ and $t \cap -t = 0$. In every Boolean algebra we define operation $\Rightarrow$ as follows: $t \Rightarrow w = -t \cup w$.

The simplest example is offered by the well-known two-element Boolean algebra $\mathbf{B}_0 = (\{1, 0\}, \cup, \cap, \Rightarrow, -)$, where $0 \cup 0 = 0$, $1 \cup 0 = 0 \cup 1 = 1 \cup 1 = 1$, $1 \cap 1 = 1$, $0 \cap 0 = 0 \cap 1 = 1 \cap 0 = 0$, $-1 = 0$, $-0 = 1$, $(0 \Rightarrow 0) = (0 \Rightarrow 1) = (1 \Rightarrow 1) = 1$, $(1 \Rightarrow 0) = 0$. Examples of complete Boolean algebras are fields $B(X)$ of all subsets of any space $X \neq \emptyset$ under the set-theoretic operations $\cup$ of union, $\cap$ of intersection, and $-$ of complementation.

A topological space is any space $X \neq \emptyset$, in which with every subset $Y \subseteq X$ there is associated $IY \subseteq X$, called the *interior* of Y, such that: $I(Y \cap Z) = IY \cap IZ, IY \subseteq Y, IIY = IY$, and $IX = X$. A subset $Y \subseteq X$ is said to be *open* if $Y = IY$.

A lattice $\mathbf{P} = (P, \cup, \cap)$ with 1 and 0 is said to be a *pseudo-Boolean algebra* if for any elements a, b in P there exists the pseudocomplement of a relative to b, denoted by $a \Rightarrow b$, such that for any $c \in P$, $c \leqslant a \Rightarrow b$ if and only if $a \cap c \leqslant b$. For any a in such a lattice there exists its pseudocomplement $\neg a$ defined by $\neg a = a \Rightarrow 0$. Every chain with a greatest and least element, for instance the interval $[0, 1]$ of the real line, is an example of a pseudo-Boolean algebra, where:

$$x \cup y = \max(x, y), \; x \cap y = \min(x, y), \; x \Rightarrow y = \begin{cases} 1 \text{ if } x \leqslant y \\ y \text{ if } x > y \end{cases}, \text{ and}$$

$$\neg x = x \Rightarrow 0$$

For any topological space $X \neq \emptyset$, the family $G(X)$ of all open subsets of X is a complete pseudo-Boolean algebra under the set-theoretic operations of union, intersection, and operation $\Rightarrow$ defined by

$$Y \Rightarrow Z = I((X - Y) \cup Z) \text{ and } \neg Y = I(X - Y) \tag{2}$$

They are called *pseudofields* of open subsets of X. Every pseudo-Boolean algebra is isomorphic with a subalgebra of a pseudofield $G(X)$ (McKinsey and Tarski, 1946).

A *topological Boolean algebra* is any Boolean algebra with an additional unary operation I, satisfying the following conditions for any elements a, b of this algebra: $I(a \cap b) = Ia \cap Ib$, $Ia \leqslant a$, $IIa = Ia$, and $I1 = 1$; these conditions are analogous to those for a topological space.

Fields of all subsets of any topological space X, called topological fields of sets, under the set-theoretic operations of union, intersection, complementation, and interior operation are examples of complete topological Boolean algebras. Every topological Boolean algebra is isomorphic with a subalgebra of a topological field $B(X)$ of all subsets of a topological space X (see McKinsey and Tarski, 1944).

An exposition of Boolean, pseudo-Boolean, and topological Boolean algebras can be found in, e.g., Rasiowa and Sikorski (1963) or Rasiowa (1974).

Let $T = (T, \leqslant)$ be any poset, in particular any chain or a set T with the identity relation on T. By a T-ideal we mean any nonempty subset $I \subseteq T$, such that if $w \leqslant t$ and $t \in I$, then $w \in I$. Let LT be the family of subsets of T consisting of the empty set $\emptyset$ and of all the T-ideals. Clearly, $(LT, \leqslant)$ is a poset with respect to the inclusion relation. It is easy to see that for any family of sets in LT their union and intersection belong to LT, too. Thus LT is a complete set lattice with $\wedge = \emptyset$ and $\vee = T$. Moreover, for any I_1, I_2 in LT, there exists their pseudocomplement of I_1 relative to I_2, defined as the union of all $I \in LT$ such that $I_1 \cap I \leqslant I_2$, that is

$$I_1 \Rightarrow I_2 = \cup \{I \in LT: I_1 \cap I \leqslant I_2\} \text{ and } \neg I = I \Rightarrow \emptyset \tag{3}$$

Thus LT is a complete pseudo-Boolean algebra of sets.

Define for every $t \in T$ a unary operation d_t as follows:

$$d_t I = \begin{cases} \vee = T \text{ if } t \in I \\ \wedge = \emptyset \text{ if } t \notin I \end{cases} \tag{4}$$

The algebra $LT = (LT, \cup, \cap, \Rightarrow, \neg, (d_t)_{t \in T}, (e_I)_{I \in LT})$, where $e_I = I$ for every $I \in LT$ are considered to be zero-argument operations, is said to be a *basic plain semi-Post algebra* (or, briefly, a *basic psP-algebra*) of type T (Rasiowa, 1987; Cat Ho and Rasiowa, 1989).

For every $t \in T$, let $I(t) = \{w \in T : w \leqslant t\}$. Clearly, $I(t)$ is a T-ideal generated by t, and may be identified with t.

After such an identification, $(T, \leqslant)$ may be treated as a subposet of $(LT, \leqslant)$. In particular, if $(T, \leqslant)$ is a chain $e_1 \leqslant ... \leqslant e_{m-1}$, then LT is isomorphic with the m-element Post algebra of order m. If $(T, \leqslant)$ is an infinite chain of order ω, $e_1 \leqslant e_2 \leqslant ...$, then LT is isomorphic with the generalized linear Post algebra of order ω^+.

Especially interesting is the case when $T = Q(0, 1)$, where $Q(0, 1)$ is the set of all rational numbers x such that $0 < x < 1$. Then LT consists of $\varnothing$, $Q(0, 1)$, all $I(q)$ for $q \in Q(0, 1)$, all sets $I_q = \{x \in Q(0, 1) : x < q\}$, for $q \in Q(0, 1)$, and all sets $I_{ir} = \{x \in Q(0, 1) : x < ir\}$, for every irrational number $ir \in [0, 1]$. Identifying each $q \in Q(0, 1)$ with $I(q)$, and every $ir \in [0, 1]$ with I_{ir}, the integer 0 with the empty set $\varnothing$, and the integer 1 with $T = Q(0, 1)$, we can treat the interval $[0, 1]$ of the real line with the relation $\leqslant$ as a subposet of LT.

If a poset $T = (T, \leqslant)$ is symmetric (self-dual), that is if there exists a symmetry mapping (an involution on T, that is a mapping $-: T \to T$ satisfying $--t = t$, and moreover such that $t \leqslant w$ if and only if $-w \leqslant -t$), then an operation $\sim$ of quasi-complementation (cf. Rasiowa, 1974) is defined as follows:

$$\sim I = \{t \in T : -t \notin I\} \tag{5}$$

This implies $d_t \sim I = \neg d_{-t} I$, for $t \in T$. It has the following properties: $\sim \wedge = \vee$, $\sim \vee = \wedge$, $\sim \sim I = I$, $\sim(I_1 \cup I_2) = \sim I_1 \cap \sim I_2$, $\sim(I_1 \cap I_2) = \sim I_1 \cup \sim I_2$, analogous to the operation of complementation on Boolean algebras (Rasiowa and Cat Ho, 1992a).

Any poset $T = (T, \leqslant)$ determines uniquely (up to an isomorphism) not only a basic psP-algebra of type T but also a class of psP-algebras of type T by a system of axioms. The theory of these algebras is developed in Cat Ho and Rasiowa (1989). This theory inspired a notion of *LT-fuzzy sets* that were introduced and investigated in Rasiowa and Cat Ho (1992a).

Recall that a fuzzy set over a universe $U \neq \varnothing$ is any function $f : U \to [0, 1]$ (Zadeh, 1965), and an L-fuzzy set over U is any function $f : U \to L$, where L is a poset (Goguen, 1967).

Given any poset $T = (T, \leqslant)$, by an *LT-fuzzy set* over U we understand any function $f : U \to LT$, and more generally, by an n-ary *LT-fuzzy relation* over U we mean any function $f : U^n \to LT$.

Note that for every poset T, LT is a poset and hence any LT-fuzzy set is an L-fuzzy set for $L = LT$. On the other hand, for any poset $L = T$, L-fuzzy sets, that is, mappings $f: U \to T$, are mappings from U into LT if T is treated as a subset of LT by the identification of each $t \in T$ with $I(t)$. Moreover, any fuzzy set $f: U \to [0, 1]$ is an LT-fuzzy set for $T = Q(0, 1)$ if the poset $([0, 1], \leqslant)$ is treated as a subposet of $(LT, \leqslant)$, as we saw earlier.

3. AN ALGEBRAIC TREATMENT OF CLASSICAL PREDICATE CALCULI

We should remember that in order to construct a *formalized language* L we have first to establish a set of signs that will form its *alphabet*. We assume in this section that an alphabet of L contains a denumerable set *Var* of individual variables to be denoted by $x, y, z, x_1, y_1, z_1, ...$, and finite sets $Pred_n$, $n = 1, 2, ...$, (maybe empty) of n-ary predicates. At least one of $Pred_n$, $n = 1, 2, ...$, is nonempty. Predicates in $Pred_n$ are interpreted as n-ary relations. Moreover, an alphabet of L contains the propositional connectives viz. the disjunction sign $\cup$, conjunction sign $\cap$, implication sign $\Rightarrow$, negation sign $-$, and quantifiers $\cup$ and $\cap$. We use the same symbols: $\cup, \cap, -, \Rightarrow, \cup, \cap$ to stand for set theoretic operations, lattice theoretic operations, and the corresponding propositional connectives and quantifiers, in order to emphasize a close reciprocal relationship between them.

Atomic formulas in L are expressions $p(x_1, ..., x_n)$, where $p \in Pred_n$ and $x_1, ..., x_n \in Var$. The set of all formulas in L is the least set containing the atomic formulas, and such that if A and B are formulas, then $A \cup B$, $A \cap B$, $A \Rightarrow B$, $-A$, $\cup_x A$ and $\cap_x A$ are formulas too. They are read "A or B," "A and B," "if A then B," "not A," "there exists an x such that A," and "for every x, A," respectively. An individual variable x in a formula A is said to be *free* if it is not in the scope of any quantifier $\cup_x$ or $\cap_x$. A formula A is said to be *open* if no quantifier occurs in A.

Given a formalized language L, nonempty set U and a complete Boolean algebra $\mathbf{B} = (B, \cup, \cap, \Rightarrow, -)$, in particular the two-element Boolean algebra, or a field of all subsets of a space X, we understand by a *realization of language* L in $\mathbf{B}$ and U any mapping R assigning to every predicate $p \in Pred_n$ a function $p_R: U^n \to B$. Let $Val(R)$ be the set of all valuations in U, that is of all functions $v: Val \to U$ assigning to every individual variable x an element $v(x)$ in U.

Every realization R of a language L in U and $\mathbf{B}$ determines for each formula A in L the realization A_R of this formula, which for technical reasons is a mapping $A_R : U^{Val} \to \mathbf{B}$, but the value of A_R for any valuation v depends in fact on values of free individual variables in A. Thus A_R is an L-fuzzy set, where $L = \mathbf{B}$. We define the value of A_R for every valuation v by induction with respect to the length of A as follows:

$$p(x_1, \ldots, x_n)_R(v) = p_R(v(x_1), \ldots, v(x_n)) \tag{6}$$

$$(A \cup B)_R(v) = A_R(v) \cup B_R(v) \tag{7}$$

$$(A \cap B)_R(v) = A_R(v) \cap B_R(v) \tag{8}$$

$$(A \Rightarrow B)_R(v) = A_R(v) \Rightarrow B_R(v) \tag{9}$$

$$(-A)_R(v) = -(A_R(v)) \tag{10}$$

$$(\cup_x A)_R(v) = \cup_{u \in U} A_R(v_u) \tag{11}$$

$$(\cap_x A))_R(v) = \cap_{u \in U} A_R(v_u) \tag{12}$$

where in (11) and (12), v_u is a valuation defined by assuming that $v_u(x) = u$ and $v_u(y) = v(y)$, for each $y \neq x$, $y \in Val$.

The symbols $\cup, \cap, \Rightarrow, -, \cup$ and $\cap$ on the right-hand sides of (6)–(12) denote operations in the complete Boolean algebra $\mathbf{B}$.

Realizations in U and the two-element Boolean algebra $\mathbf{B}_0$ are called *semantic realizations*. They realize any n-ary predicate p as a mapping $p_R : U^n \to \{0, 1\}$, which may be treated as a characteristic function of n-ary relation r_p over U, such that $(u_1, \ldots, u_n)$ bears relation r_p if and only if $p_R(u_1, \ldots, u_n) = 1$.

A valuation v is said to satisfy a formula A in realization R if $A_R(v) = 1$. This is written $Rv \models A$. A formula A is said to be *valid* in realization R if every valuation v in $Val(R)$ satisfies A in R. Formulas valid in every semantic realization are called *tautologies*. A realization R is said to be a *model* for a set Σ of formulas in L if every formula in Σ is valid in R. A formula A is said to be a *semantic consequence* of a set Σ of formulas in L, written $\Sigma \models A$, if A is valid in every semantic model R for the set Σ. In particular, if Σ is empty, we write $\models A$, denoting that A is a tautology.

The notion of a semantic realization and of the satisfiability in semantic realizations is an equivalent formulation of the Tarski satisfiability notion in semantic interpretations of a language L under consideration. This yields the equivalent definition of a tautology and of a semantic consequence in a language L .

Given a formalized language L we will construct an axiomatic deductive system of classical predicate calculus by distinguishing a set of tautologies as a set of logical axioms, and establishing rules of inference. A formula A is said to be *deducible* from a set Σ of formulas if there is a formal proof from these formulas and logical axioms by means of rules of inference. This is written $\Sigma \vdash A$. In particular, if Σ is empty, we write $\vdash A$, meaning that A is deducible from logical axioms only, by means of rules of inference. A set Σ of formulas is said to be *consistent* in the deductive system, if there is a formula A such that not $(\Sigma \vdash A)$. The deductive system is said to be *sound* with respect to semantic realizations, if for every consistent set Σ, $\Sigma \vdash A$ implies $\Sigma \models A$.

For any formulas A, B, C in language L the following formulas, being tautologies, are assumed to be the logical axioms: (ax1) $A \Rightarrow (B \Rightarrow A)$, (ax2) $(A \Rightarrow (B \Rightarrow C)) \Rightarrow ((A \Rightarrow B) \Rightarrow (A \Rightarrow C))$, (ax3) $A \Rightarrow (A \cup B)$, (ax4) $B \Rightarrow (A \cup B)$, (ax5) $(A \Rightarrow C) \Rightarrow ((B \Rightarrow C) \Rightarrow \Rightarrow ((A \cup B) \Rightarrow C))$, (ax6) $(A \cap B) \Rightarrow A$, (ax7) $(A \cap B) \Rightarrow B$, (ax8) $(A \Rightarrow B) \Rightarrow ((A \Rightarrow C) \Rightarrow (A \Rightarrow (B \cap C)))$, (ax9) $(A \Rightarrow -B) \Rightarrow (B \Rightarrow -A)$, (ax10) $-(A \Rightarrow A) \Rightarrow B$, and (ax11) $A \cup -A$.

The following well-known *rules of inference* are allowed: modus ponens, the rule of substitution for free individual variables, and four rules concerning the quantifiers, viz. the rules of elimination and of introduction of a universal and an existential quantifier (cf. Rasiowa and Sikorski, 1963). There are several other deductive systems of classical predicate calculi equivalent to the system presented above, based on simpler axiomatization. The choice of this one is motivated by a relationship with the axiomatization of intuitionistic predicate calculi.

The following theorem holds (Rasiowa and Sikorski, 1953; see also Rasiowa and Sikorski, 1963, Ch. 8, 5.5):

(c) For every consistent set Σ of formulas in L, and any formula A, the following conditions are equivalent:

  (i) $\Sigma \vdash A$ (i.e., A is deducible from Σ)
  (ii) A is valid in every model for Σ in every complete Boolean algebra
  (iii) A is valid in every model for Σ in the field $B(X)$ of all subsets of any space $X \neq \varnothing$
  (iv) $\Sigma \models A$ (i.e., A is valid in every semantic model for Σ), in any denumerable universe $U \neq \varnothing$

The equivalence of (i) and (iv) is the Gödel completeness theorem (Gödel, 1930). An algebraic proof was given in Rasiowa and Sikorski

(1950), and other proofs were given, for example, by Herbrand in 1933, Henkin in 1949, Beth in 1951, and Łoś in 1955.

Observe that on the basis of the above theorem, classical predicate calculi may be conceived as formalizing "L-fuzzy reasonings" if all subsets of any space X are considered as L-fuzzy truth-values.

4. AN ALGEBRAIC APPROACH TO PREDI-CATE CALCULI OF INTUITIONISTIC AND MODAL S4 LOGICS

4.1. Intuitionistic Predicate Calculi

A formalized language L_i of intuitionistic predicate calculus is obtained from a language L of classical predicate calculus, as described in Section 3, replacing in its alphabet the sign – of the classical negation with the sign ⌐ of the intuitionistic negation.

An axiomatic deductive system of intuitionistic predicate calculus can be obtained from that of classical predicate calculus (see Section 3), by the elimination of axiom (ax11), that is admitting (ax1) – (ax10) and the same rules of inference.

Algebraic and topological models will now be introduced, based on realizations in complete pseudo-Boolean algebras and pseudofields of all subsets of any topological space. Algebraic realizations are credited to Mostowski (1942), whereas topological ones were introduced by Rasiowa and Sikorski (1953). Well-known Beth's (1959) models and Kripke's (1965) models are special cases of topological models (cf. Troelstra, 1977).

Given a formalized language L_i, a complete pseudo-Boolean algebra **P** (a pseudofield $G(X)$ of all open subsets of any topological space X) and a universe $U \neq \emptyset$, we understand by a realization of L_i in **P** (in $G(X)$) and U any mapping R assigning to every predicate $p \in Pred_n$ a function $p_R : U^n \to \mathbf{P} \, (p_R : U^n \to G(X))$. Realization R determines for each formula A in L_i a realization A_R of A, being a mapping $A_R : U^{Val} \to \mathbf{P} \, (A_R : U^{Val} \to G(X))$, by means of equations (6) – (12) from Section 3 (in which any symbol "–" is replaced by "⌐", and in the case of a realization in $G(X)$, symbol ∩ on the right-hand side of (12) is replaced by I∩) where ∪, ∩, ⇒, ⌐, ∪, and ∩ on the right-hand sides of (6) – (12) denote operations in **P** (in $G(X)$). A formula A is said to be valid in a realization R if $A_R(v) = \vee$ for every valuation $v \in Val(R)$. A realization R in $\mathbf{P}$ (in $G(X)$) is said to be an *algebraic model* (a *topological model*) for a set Σ of formulas if every formula in Σ is valid in R.

The following theorem (ci) (for a proof see Rasiowa and Sikorski 1963) characterizes formulas deducible from any consistent set Σ (in particular $\Sigma = \emptyset$) of formulas in L_i by means of algebraic and topological models:

(ci) For every consistent set Σ of formulas in L_i and every formula A the following conditions are equivalent:

    (i) $\Sigma \vdash A$ (i.e., A is deducible from Σ)
    (ii) A is valid in every algebraic model for Σ in every complete pseudo-Boolean algebra
    (iii) A is valid in every topological model for Σ in the pseudofield $G(X)$ of all open subsets of any topological space X
    (iv) A is valid in every topological model for Σ in a denumerable set U_o and the pseudofield $G(X)$ of all open subsets of X_o, where X_o is a set of irrational numbers

Implication (i) $\Rightarrow$ (ii) was proved by Mostowski (1948), (ii) $\Rightarrow$ (i) in Rasiowa (1951), (iii) $\Rightarrow$ (ii) in Rasiowa and Sikorski (1953), and (iv) $\Rightarrow$ (i) in Sikorski (1958). This theorem for $\Sigma = \emptyset$ yields a completeness theorem for intuitionistic predicate calculi. It follows from Beth's (1959) findings that intuitionistic predicate calculi are complete, even when the realizations are restricted to realizations in pseudofields over topological spaces that are closed subsets of Cantor's discontinuum (for a proof, see Dyson and Kreisel, 1961).

Theorem (ci) proves the soundness for intuitionistic predicate calculi of realizations of formulas as L-fuzzy sets for every complete pseudo-Boolean algebra L, and in particular for $L = G([0, 1])$. Operations on L-fuzzy sets should be understood as defined by means of (6)–(12) with a suitable modification.

4.2. Modal Predicate Calculi

A formalized language L_M of a modal predicate calculus is obtained from a language L of classical predicate calculus, as described in Section 3, adjoining to its alphabet the sign I of a necessity connective. An axiomatic deductive system of modal S4 predicate calculus can be obtained by adjoining to the axiom schemes (ax1)–(ax11) for classical predicate calculi (see Section 3) the following axiom schemes: (m_1) $(IA \cap IB) \Rightarrow I(A \cap B)$, (m_2) $IA \Rightarrow A$, (m_3) $IA \Rightarrow IIA$, and (m_4) $I(A \cup -A)$; and adjoining to the rules of inference for classical predicate calculi (see Section 3) the following rule of inference: $\dfrac{A \Rightarrow B}{IA \Rightarrow IB}$. A possibility propositional connective C is defined by $CA = -I - A$.

Algebraic and topological models will now be introduced, based on realizations in complete topological Boolean algebras and topological fields of all subsets of any topological space. Algebraic realizations were introduced in Rasiowa (1951), whereas topological ones were introduced in Rasiowa and Sikorski (1953).

By an *algebraic* (*topological*) *realization* of a language L_M in a complete topological Boolean algebra B (the topological field $B(X)$ of all subsets of any topological space X) and in a universe $U \neq \emptyset$ we understand any mapping R assigning to every predicate $p \in Pred_n$ a function $p_R : U^n \to B$ $(p_R : U^n \to B(X))$. Realization R is extended on the set of all formulas in L_M by means of equations (6) – (12) in Section 3 and the following one: $(IA)_R(v) = I(A_R(v))$. Symbols $\cup, \cap, \Rightarrow, -, I, \cup,$ and $\cap$ on the right – hand sides of these equations denote corresponding operations in B (or $B(X)$).

Admitting the analogy of an algebraic (topological) model of a set Σ of formulas in L_M to that in the case of intuitionistic predicate calculi (see Section 4.1), the following completeness theorem (cM) holds (Rasiowa and Sikorski, 1963):

(cM) For every consistent set Σ of formulas in L_M and every formula A the following conditions are equivalent:

   (i) $\Sigma \vdash A$ (i.e., A is deducible from Σ)
   (ii) A is valid in every algebraic model for Σ
   (iii) A is valid in every topological model for Σ
   (iv) A is valid in every topological model for Σ in a denumerable set U_0 and the topological field of all subsets of a set X_0 of irrational numbers

Equivalence of (i) and (ii) was proved in Rasiowa (1951), implication (iii) $\Rightarrow$ (ii) in Rasiowa and Sikorski (1953), and implication (iv) $\Rightarrow$ (i) in Sikorski (1958).

This theorem shows the soundness for modal predicate calculi of realizations of formulas as L-fuzzy sets for every complete topological Boolean algebra L, in particular the topological field $B(X)$ of all subsets of $[0, 1]$.

5. APPROXIMATION LOGICS OF POSET TYPES AND POST'S m-VALUED AND ω^+-VALUED PREDICATE CALCULI

Approximation logics of any poset type $T = (T, \leqslant)$, as introduced in Rasiowa (1987), were intended to be logics for *approximation reasoning*. They have various interpretations. We will briefly describe a semantic interpretation (Rasiowa and Marek, 1989; Rasiowa, 1991) and semantic models, as well as algebraic models.

Let $T = (T, \leqslant)$ be any denumerable poset (perhaps symmetric with a symmetry mapping - and $LT = (LT, \cup, \cap, \Rightarrow, \neg, (d_t)_{t \in T}, (e_I)_{I \in LT})$ be a basic psP–algebra of type T (perhaps with a quasi-complementation $\sim$) (see Section 2). A formalized language L_T of any approximation predicate calculus of type T is obtained from a language L_i of an intuitionistic predicate calculus (see Section 4) by adjoining (a quasi-negation connective $\sim$ if T is symmetric) unary approximation connectives d_t for $t \in T$, and propositional constants e_I for $I \in LT$.

Considering a semantic realization of L_T, the poset T may be interpreted as a poset of (fully communicating) intelligent agents (Rasiowa and Marek, 1989; Rasiowa 1991). The intended meaning of $t \leqslant w$ for $t, w \in T$, is that abilities of agent t are less than or equal to those of agent w. We assume that all agents observe the same reality and each of them approximates any predicate in his or her own way, according to his or her perception of this reality.

Condition $t \leqslant w$ implies that for any predicate p a relation implementing the approximation of p by agent w is contained in the relation implementing approximation of p by agent t. Moreover, we assume that each agent is aware of other agents' approximations of predicates and does not attempt to modify their viewpoints. We consider any I in LT as a T-group of agents in T. According to such an interpretation we read $d_t A$ as "agent t approximates A," for every $t \in T$, and e_I as "true from the viewpoint of the T-group I," particularly $e_\emptyset$ as "true from the viewpoint of T-group ø."

A semantic realization of L_T in a universe $U \neq \emptyset$ is any mapping M associating with each predicate $p \in Pred_n$ a family $(p_{tM})_{t \in T}$ of n-ary relations $p_{tM} \subseteq U^n$ (implementing approximations of predicate p by agents t from T) such that if $t \leqslant w$, then $p_{wM} \subseteq p_{tM}$ for $w, t \in T$.

The satisfiability of any formula A by a valuation $v: Var \to U$ in semantic realization M is defined first for formulas having d_t for some $t \in T$ in front. We assume:

$Mv \vdash d_t e_I$ if and only if $t \in I$

$Mv \vdash d_t p(x_1, \ldots, x_n)$ if and only if $(v(x_1), \ldots, v(x_n)) \in p_{tM}$

$Mv \vdash d_t(A \cup B)$ if and only if $Mv \vdash d_t A$ or $Mv \vdash d_t B$

$Mv \vdash d_t(A \cap B)$ if and only if $Mv \vdash d_t A$ and $Mv \vdash d_t B$

$Mv \vdash d_t d_w A$ if and only if $Mv \vdash d_w A$

$Mv \vdash d_t(A \Rightarrow B)$ if and only if for each $w \leqslant t$: not $Mv \vdash d_w A$ or
$\quad Mv \vdash d_w B$

$Mv \vdash d_t \neg A$ if and only if for each $w \leqslant t$: not $Mv \vdash d_w A$

$Mv \vdash d_t \sim A$ if and only if not $Mv \vdash d_{-t} A$ (if T is symmetric)

$Mv \vdash d_t \bigcup_x A$ if and only if there exists $u \in U$ such that $Mv_u \vdash d_t A$

$Mv \vdash d_t \bigcap_x A$ if and only if for every $u \in U$, $Mv_u \vdash A$
$\quad$ where $v_u(x) = u$ and $v_u(y) = v(y)$ for every $y \neq x$, $y \in \mathrm{Var}$

$Mv \vdash A$ if and only if for every $t \in T$, $Mv \vdash d_t A$

A formula A is said to be *valid* in M if $Mv \vdash A$ for every valuation v: $Var \rightarrow U$. A formula A is said to be a *tautology* if it is valid in every semantic realization of L_T. A semantic realization M is a *semantic model* for a set Σ of formulas in L_T if every formula A in Σ is valid in M. A formula A is said to be a *semantic consequence* of a set Σ of formulas in L_T if A is valid in every semantic model M for Σ.

An *algebraic realization* of L_T in any universe $U \neq \emptyset$ is any mapping R assigning to every e_I, $e_{IR} = e_I$, $I \in LT$, and to every predicate $p \in Pred_n$ an n-ary LT-fuzzy relation $p_R: U^n \rightarrow LT$ over U (see Section 2). Realization R is extended on the set of all formulas analogously to extending any realization in the case of intuitionistic predicate calculi (see Section 4), adjoining equations $(d_t A)_R(v) = d_t(A_R(v))$, for $t \in T$, and $(\sim A)_R(v) = \sim(A_R(v))$ if T is symmetric. The signs $\cup, \cap, \Rightarrow, \neg, \sim, d_t$ for $t \in T$ and e_I for $I \in LT$ are considered to be operations in the basic psP-algebra LT (with the quasi-complementation operation $\sim$ in the case of a symmetric T).

An axiomatic deductive system of approximation predicate calculus of type T can be obtained from that of intuitionistic predicate calculus (see Section 4) by adjoining to the axioms (ax1)–(ax10) (where sign $-$ is replaced by $\neg$) the following axiom schemes: (ap1) $d_t(A \cup B) \Leftrightarrow (d_t A \cup d_t B)$, (ap2) $d_t(A \cap B) \Leftrightarrow (d_t A \cap d_t B)$, (ap3) $d_t e_I$ if $t \in I$, $\neg d_t e_I$ if $t \notin I$, (ap4) $d_t d_w A \Leftrightarrow d_w A$, (ap5) $d_t A \cup \neg d_t A$, (ap6) $(d_t A \cap e_t) \Rightarrow A$, (ap7) $d_t \sim A \Leftrightarrow \neg d_{-t} A$, if T is symmetric, where $t \in T$, $I \in LT$ and $A \Leftrightarrow B$ is an abbreviation of $(A \Rightarrow B) \cap (B \Rightarrow A)$, and the additional inference rules are: (ri) $\dfrac{A \Rightarrow B}{d_t A \Rightarrow d_t B}$ for $t \in T$, and (re)

$$\dfrac{\{d_t A \Rightarrow d_t B\}_{t \in T}}{A \Rightarrow B}.$$

The following completeness theorem (Rasiowa, 1989) characterizes formulas that are semantic consequences of any set Σ of formulas in L_T:

If poset T is enumerable and well founded or LT is enumerable, then for every consistent set Σ of formulas in L_T and every formula A the following conditions are equivalent:

(i) $\Sigma \vdash A$ (i.e., A is deducible from Σ)
(ii) A is valid in every semantic model for Σ
(iii) $d_t A$ is valid in every semantic model for Σ, for every $t \in T$
(iv) $d_t A$ is valid in every semantic model for Σ, for every maximal t in T
(v) A is valid in every algebraic model for Σ

The case when poset T is $(Q(0, 1), \leqslant)$, where $Q(0, 1)$ is the set of all rational numbers q such that $0 < q < 1$ (see Section 2), is not included in the above theorem. It will be considered separately in Rasiowa (1992).

If $(T, \leqslant)$ is a chain $e_1 \leqslant \ldots \leqslant e_{m-1}$ for some $m \geqslant 2$, then LT is isomorphic with the m-element Post algebra, and the above theorem gives a completeness theorem for Post m-valued predicate calculi (Rasiowa, 1969). If poset $(T, \leqslant)$ is an infinite chain of order ω, $e_1 \leqslant e_2 \leqslant \ldots$, then LT is isomorphic with the generalized linear Post algebra of order ω^+ and this theorem gives a completeness theorem for ω^+-valued predicate calculi (Rasiowa, 1973). In both cases these predicate calculi have two interpretations. Under algebraic models they have been considered in Rasiowa (1969, 1973), but it is easy to see that algebraic interpretations correspond to interpretations by LT-fuzzy sets. Under semantic realizations they are approximation predicate calculi.

Algebraic realizations of approximation logics seemed to imply LT-fuzzy sets and LT-fuzzy logics. LT-fuzzy sets were introduced and investigated by Rasiowa and Cat Ho (1992a). This concept and LT-fuzzy logics will be discussed in Rasiowa and Cat Ho (1992b) later in this volume.

It is worth mentioning that in case of finite posets T there are mechanical proof systems of the Gentzen style and of the resolution style for approximation logics of type T and for LT-fuzzy logics (Rasiowa, 1991).

Keywords: poset, complete lattice, Boolean algebra, pseudo-Boolean algebra, topological Boolean algebra, Post algebra of order

$m \geqslant 2$ (order ω^+), basic plain semi-Post algebra of a poset type, fuzzy set, L-fuzzy set, $L\,T$-fuzzy set

BIBLIOGRAPHY

Bernays, P. (1937–1954). A system of axiomatic set theory. *Journal of Symbolic Logic,* **2** (1937), 65–77; **6** (1941), 1–17; **7** (1942), 65–89, 133–145; **8** (1943), 89–106; **13** (1948), 65–79; **19** (1954), 81–96.

Beth, E. W. (1959). *The Foundations of Mathematics.* Amsterdam: North-Holland.

Brouwer, L.E.J. (1908). De onbetrouwbaarheid der logische principes. *Tijdschrift voor Wijsbegeerte,* **2,** 152–158.

Chellas, B. F. (1980). *Modal Logic.* Cambridge University Press.

Cat Ho, Ng. and Rasiowa, H. (1987). Semi-Post algebras. *Studia Logica,* **46,** 147–158.

Cat Ho, Ng. and Rasiowa, H. (1989). Plain semi-Post algebras as a poset-based generalization of Post algebras and their representability. *Studia Logica,* **48,** 509–530.

Dyson, V. H. and Kreisel, G. (1961). Analysis of Beth's semantic construction of intuitionistic logic. Applied Mathematics and Statistics Laboratories, Stanford University, Tech. Rep. no. 3.

Epstein, G. (1960). The lattice theory of Post algebras. *Transactions Amer. Math. Soc.,* **95,** 300–317.

Fraenkel, A. (1922). Zu den Grundlagen der Cantor-Zermeloschen Mengenlehre, *Math. Annalen,* **86,** 230–237.

Fraenkel, A. (1958). *Foundations of Set Theory.* Amsterdam: North-Holland.

Gaines, B. R. (1977). Foundations of fuzzy reasoning. In Gupta M. M., Saridis, G. N., and Gaines, B. R. (eds.): *Fuzzy Automata and Decision Processes.* Amsterdam: North-Holland, pp. 19–75.

Goguen, J. A. (1967). L-fuzzy sets. *Journ, Math. Anal. and Appls.,* **18,** 145–174.

Gödel, K. (1930). Die Vollständigkeit der Axiome des logischen Funktionenkalküls. *Monatshefte für Mathematik und Physik,* **37,** 349–360.

Hilbert, D. and Ackerman, W. (1928). *Grundzüge der theoretischen Logic.* Berlin. (3rd edition: Berlin, Göttingen, Heidelberg, 1949).

Henkin, L. (1950). An algebraic characterization of quantifiers. *Fundamenta Mathematicae,* **37,** 63–74.

Heyting, A. (1930). Die formalen Regeln der intuitionistischen Logik. *Sitzungsberichte der Preussischen Akademie der Wissenschaften, Phys. math. Klasse,* 42–56. Die formalen Regeln der intuitionistischen Mathematik, *ibid.,* 57–71, 158–169.

Heyting, A. (1956). *Intuitionism, an Introduction. Studies in Logic and the Foundations of Mathematics.* Amsterdam: North-Holland.

Kleene, S. C. (1952). *Introduction to Metamathematics.* New York – Toronto: Van Nostrand.

Kripke, S. A. (1963). Semantical considerations on modal logic. *Acta Phil. Fennica,* Fasc. 16, 83–94.

Kripke, S. A. (1965). Semantical analysis of intuitionistic logic I. In J.M. Crossley and M.K.A. Dummet (eds.): *Formal Systems and Recursive Functions,* Amsterdam: North-Holland, pp. 92–130.

Lewis, C. I. and Langford, C. H. (1932). *Symbolic Logic*. New York: The Century Co.

Łukasiewicz, J. (1920). O logice trójwartościowej. *Ruch Filozoficzny*, **5**, 169–170.

Łukasiewicz, J. and Tarski, A. (1930). Untersuchungen über den Aussagen-kalkül. *Comptes-rendus des séances de la Societé des Sciences et des Lettres de Varsovie, Cl III*, **23**, 30–50.

McKinsey, J.C.C. (1941). A solution of the decision problem for the Lewis system S.2 and S.4 with an application to topology. *Journal of Symbolic Logic*, **6**, 117–134.

McKinsey, J. C. C. and Tarski, A. (1944). On the algebra of topology. *Annals of Mathematics*, **45**, 141–191.

McKinsey, J. C. C. and Tarski, A. (1946). On the closed elements in closure algebras. *Annals of Mathematics*, **47**, 122–162.

McKinsey J. C. C. and Tarski, A. (1948). Some theorems about the sentential calculi of Lewis and Heyting. *Journal of Symbolic Logic*, **13**, 1–15.

Mendelson, E. (1964). *An Introduction to Mathematical Logic*. Princeton: Van Nostrand Reinhold.

Mostowski, A. (1948). Proofs of non-deducibility in intuitionistic functional calculus. *Journal of Symbolic Logic*, **13**, 204–207.

Post, E. I. (1921). Introduction to a general theory of elementary propositions. *American Journal of Mathematics*, **43**, 165–185.

Rasiowa, H. (1951). Algebraic treatment of the functional calculi of Heyting and Lewis. *Fundamenta Mathematicae*, **38**, 99–126.

Rasiowa, H. (1954). Algebraic models of axiomatic theories. *Fundamenta Mathematicae*, **41**, 291–310.

Rasiowa, H. (1954). Constructive theories, *Bull. Acad. Pol. Sci., Cl III*, **2**, 121–124.

Rasiowa, H. (1963). On modal theories. *Acta Phil. Fennica*, **16**, 201–214.

Rasiowa, H. (1969). A theorem on the existence of prime filters in Post algebras and the completeness theorem for some many valued predicate calculi. *Bull. Acad. Pol. Sci., Ser. Sci. Math. Astr. Phys.*, **17**, 347–354.

Rasiowa, H. (1973). On generalized Post algebras of order ω^+ and ω^+-valued predicate calculi. *Ibid.*, **21**, 209–219.

Rasiowa, H. (1974). *An Algebraic Approach to Non-classical Logics*. Amsterdam: North-Holland.

Rasiowa, H. (1987). An algebraic approach to some approximate reasoning. Invited lecture, *Proc. ISMVL '87, Boston;* IEEE Comp. Soc. Press, 324–347.

Rasiowa, H. (1988). Logic of approximation reasoning. *Proc. First Workshop on Comp. Sci. Logic (CSL'87)*, Karlsruhe, Germany. LNCS 329, Berlin: Springer-Verlag, pp. 188–210.

Rasiowa, H. (1989). Logics of approximation reasoning, semantically based on partially ordered sets. *Notes of Invited Lecture, ASL Logic Colloquium 89, Berlin*.

Rasiowa, H. (1991). Mechanical proof systems for logic: reaching consensus by groups of intelligent agents. *Int. Journal of Approximate Reasoning*, **5**, 415–432.

Rasiowa, H. (1992). Axiomatization and completeness of uncountably valued approximation logic. In press.

Rasiowa, H. and Ng. Cat Ho. (1992a). *LT*-fuzzy sets. *Fuzzy Sets and Systems.* In press.

Rasiowa, H. and Ng. Cat Ho. (1992b). *LT*-fuzzy logics. In L.A. Zadeh, and J. Kacprzyk, (eds.): *Fuzzy Logic for the Management of Uncertainty* (later in this volume).

Rasiowa, H. and M. Marek. (1989). On reaching consensus by groups of intelligent agents. In Z.W. Ras, (ed.): *Methodologies for Intelligent Systems.* Amsterdam: North-Holland, pp. 234–243.

Rasiowa, H. and R. Sikorski. (1950). A proof of the completeness theorem of Gödel. *Fundamenta Mathematicae,* **37**, 193–200.

Rasiowa, H. and R. Sikorski. (1953). Algebraic treatment of the notion of satisfiability. *Fundamenta Mathematicae,* **40**, 62–95.

Rasiowa, H. and R. Sikorski. (1963). *The Mathematics of Metamathematics.* Warsaw: PWN Sci. Publ. (3rd ed., 1970).

Rescher, N. (1969). *Many-Valued Logics.* New York: McGraw-Hill.

Rosenbloom, P. C. (1942). Post algebras I. Postulates and general theory. *American Journal of Mathematics,* **64**, 167–188.

Rousseau, G. (1969). Logical systems with finitely many truth-values. *Bull. Acad. Pol. Sci., Ser. Math. Astr. Phys.,* **17**, 189–194.

Rousseau, G. (1970). Post algebras and pseudo-Post algebras. *Fundamenta Mathematicae,* **67**, 133–145.

Sikorski, R. (1958). Some applications of interior mappings. *Fundamenta Mathematicae,* **45**, 62–95.

Stone, M. H. (1936). The theory of representation for Boolean algebras. *Trans. Amer. Math. Soc.,* **40**, 37–111.

Stone, M. H. (1937). Topological representation of distributive lattices and Brouwerian logic. *Čas. Mat. Fiz.,* **67**, 1–25.

Tarski, A. (1938). Der Aussagenkalkül und die Topologie. *Fundamenta Mathematicae,* **31**, 104–134.

Traczyk, T. (1964). An equational definition of a class of Post algebras. *Bull. Acad. Pol. Sci., CIIII,* **12**, 147–149.

Troelstra, A. S. (1977). Aspects of constructive mathematics. In J. Barwise, (ed.): *Handbook of Mathematical Logic.* Amsterdam: North-Holland.

Turner, R. (1984). *Logics for Artificial Intelligence.* Chichester: Ellis Horwood; New York: Wiley.

Zadeh, L. A. (1965). Fuzzy sets. *Information and Control,* **6**, 338–353.

Zadeh, L. A. (1974). Fuzzy logic and approximate reasoning. Memo. ERL–M479, Nov., 1974, Electronics Research Laboratory, University of California, Berkeley.

Zermelo, E. (1908). Untersuchungen über die Grundlagen der Mengenlehre. *Mathematische Annalen,* **65**, 261–281.

1

INTRODUCTION:

ISSUES IN THE MANAGEMENT OF UNCERTAINTY

2 Models of enquiry and formalisms for approximate reasoning

Raj BHATNAGAR
University of Cincinnati
Cincinnati, OH 45221
USA

Laveen N. KANAL
University of Maryland
College Park, MD 20742
USA

Abstract. In this paper we present an overview of the methodologies for approximate reasoning from the perspective of designing intelligent enquiring systems. Leibnizian, Kantian, and Hegelian models of enquiry are presented and then various reasoning methodologies are examined for their relevance to these modes of enquiry.

1. THE TASK OF REASONING

When we attempt either to solve a problem or to make a decision an essential part of the effort can be called *reasoning*. Informally speaking, reasoning is the exercise of inferring information about some unobservable aspect of a situation based on the information about the observed parts of the situation. For example, reasoning is performed to infer some information about a patient's internal subsystems based on the observable external symptoms; to infer an accused's role in a crime based on the available evidence; and to determine the possible intentions of an enemy force based on available intelligence. A number of formalisms for automated reasoning have been developed and these are based on a wide spectrum of theoretical frameworks, ranging from formal logics to theories of probability. In this paper we examine various types of objectives a reasoner might be trying to achieve and then examine the usefulness of various reasoning formalisms for attaining these objectives.

1.1. Types of Reasoning

As stated above, for a particular problem the reasoning exercise can be viewed in a very general form:

- Given:
    - Information about the observable aspects of a particular problem.
    - Knowledge about the domain to which the problem belongs.
- Determine:
    - Some information about some unobserved aspect of the problem.

Depending on the nature and type of the observable information and the objective of the reasoner the reasoning task can be stated in a more refined manner. For example, when first order predicate calculus is used for representing knowledge, the reasoning task may be specified as follows:

- Given:
    - Observed aspect of the problem situation in terms of truth values of some predicates.
    - Domain knowledge in the form of wff's of first order predicate calculus.
- Determine:
    - Truth value of some other wff's of interest.

Many decision-making tasks demand more than a mere inference about an unobserved aspect of the situation. These tasks demand that the reasoning exercise generate either a hypothesis or an explanation to justify the observed events. For example, given some symptoms, a reasoner may be asked to hypothesize a set of physiological processes to explain the symptoms. Based on the available information, a battlefield planner may be interested in hypothesizing an enemy's plan of attack. These hypothesizations can sometimes be more useful than knowing just the probability of the patient suffering from a particular disease, or the probability of being attacked by the enemy.

2. MODELS OF ENQUIRY

In his book, Churchman (1971) presents a detailed discussion of various types of enquiring systems and their relevance to various reasoning situations. When viewed in the context of these models of enquiry, the above formulation of the reasoning exercise provides a better insight into the reasoning process. We present here a brief summary of Churchman's classification.

The two primitives Churchman uses are the concepts of *innate ideas,* and *inputs.* Innate ideas refers to some principles or theoretical truths about nature in which the reasoner believes. The inputs are the experimental observations made by the observer. A *fact-net* is an interconnection of inputs and innate ideas constructed by means of a given set of *relations* and *operators.* A fact-net is therefore a network of contingent truths.

2.1. Leibnizian Enquirer

A *Leibnizian enquiring system (enquirer)* aims at constructing an optimal fact-net for a situation. Optimality becomes relevant because for any given set of inputs, it may be possible to construct a number of different fact-nets. The Leibnizian enquirer assumes that there is an optimal network and the process of building the network would converge with it because of the abilities inherent in the net building process. Leibnizian enquirers represent a very general class of enquiring systems. The practice of science can be viewed as Leibnizian enquiry. Every new scientific result is an "input" that can be linked into the network of older results, especially when the field is governed by a theory. The theory provides the relations and the operators for tying together the results in the form of a fact-net and corresponds to the innate ideas of the enquirer. A result, or input, that lies outside the largest net will often be ignored, whereas a result that enables the researchers to connect two hitherto unconnected nets will be acclaimed. These enquirers therefore do not discard the theories but look for networks containing all the inputs. Another example of such an enquirer is theorem proving and problem-solving machines where the primitives, axioms, and inference rules of the logic are the innate ideas and the various wff's are the inputs. The objective of the enquirer (theorem prover) is to make a network containing the wffs in order to determine if the desired wff is consistent with all the others.

A Leibnizian enquirer assumes the existence of an a priori model of the situation (the innate ideas or the theory), and attempts to configure the inputs of the situation according to this model.

2.2. Kantian Enquirer

A *Kantian enquirer* does not presuppose the existence of an a priori model of the situation. The only a priori model assumed is for the basics, such as a clock-event, to enable the enquirer to observe the inputs. A Kantian enquirer initially contains a set of models. Each model is an independent set of innate ideas and may contain its primitives, axioms, and rules of inference, etc. An enquirer then selects a model from the set and builds a Leibnizian fact-net using the inputs and the innate ideas of this model. The enquirer then determines the extent to which this fact-net is "satisfactory" according to some criterion. The model that generates the most "satisfactory" fact-net is the solution the enquiry. An example of such an enquirer is encountered in the social sciences, where often the search is for a theoretical model in which all the observed data can be shown to fit properly.

2.3. Hegelian Enquirer

The *Hegelian model of enquiry* seeks to develop the ability to see the same inputs from different points of view. The enquirer possesses a number of models, each of which is an independent set of innate ideas and may contain primitives, axioms, and rules of inference. Let us denote this set of models by W. Let I be a set of propositions that can possibly be true of the situation under consideration. Let D denote the set of inputs $d_1, d_2, ...d_k$. Let X be an operator conjoining an element of D with an element of W, such that for every d_i in D and every W_i in W there corresponds one and only one element of the set I. That is, X maps elements of D for a given W onto the set I in a many-to-one correspondence. The set I is called the "information set" of a given set of models W and the operator X is called the interpretive operator. Thus, for each element of W there corresponds an information subset, represented by $I(W_j)$.

Consider a set T of "theses," that is, sentences stating something about the world, such that no element of T implies or is implied by any element of D, W, or I. C is a two-place function that transforms a T_i and a W_j into elements of the real number system. C represents the "degree of confidence" in T_i given the information in $I(W_j)$. This represents the credence of a thesis given that the world is accurately described by model W_j.

The enquirer selects a thesis A from the set T and undertakes to construct a "case" for supporting A, in effect, a defense of thesis "A." This is achieved by selecting a W_{th} such that $W_{th} = \max_j [C(A, I(W_j))]$. That is, the enquirer sets about showing that there is a way to look at reality, given by W_{th}, such that the inputs can be interpreted to support thesis A.

The next thing a Hegelian enquirer does is to find a thesis B that is an antithesis of A, and also find the model that supports B. B does not have to be a logical negation of A. For example, in the context of some battlefield intelligence information, if the thesis is that a "target will be destroyed," the antithesis may be "the attacking army will be destroyed" instead of "target will *not* be destroyed."

The next act of a Hegelian enquirer is to look at the two models of the world, the W_i's that support the thesis and the antithesis and examine the sources of conflict beteen them. It is hoped that the attempts to understand or resolve these conflicts would lead one toward the truth about the situation. The bigger model of the situation in the context of which the conflict can be understood is called the "synthesis" model of the situation.

2.4. Choosing a Model of Enquiry

The importance of Churchman's categorization is that it helps us see that different models of enquiry are more natural or useful in different problem domains. The choice depends on our knowledge and on our view of where the truth is likely to reside. If we think that "truth is in the model" and a good model (theory) is at hand, the Leibnizian model of enquiry, much used in the physical sciences, is most appropriate. This might also be called a top-down or model-directed approach. On the other hand, if in our view "truth is partially in a model and partially in data," then one may pursue the Kantian model, which is the case in most social sciences. The Hegelian or dialectical model of enquiry is more appropriate to those domains where, in our view, the truth is likely to emerge from a clash between a thesis and an antithesis." Relatively ill-structured problem domains such as management, economics, law, politics, marketing, battlefield planning, and some poorly understood areas of medicine are examples where the Hegelian model of enquiry may be more appropriate.

The main point that one can conclude is that there are many approaches to enquiry, and depending on the problem domain, one approach may be more useful than the other. When we perform a reasoning exercise in some particular situation, it must be done in the context of the model of enquiry being pursued for the problem at hand.

In view of the above categorization, our earlier view of the reasoning can be refined as follows:

- Given:
  - Observed aspects of the problem situations in terms of the observed events (inputs).
  - Domain knowledge that provides basic facts for constructing models for various situations possible in the domain.
- Determine:
  - Some model that is in accordance with the observed events and satisfies some specified criterion of interestingness. This model may be obtained according to Leibnizian, Kantian, or Hegelian models of enquiry.
  - An inference about some unobserved aspect of the problem situation in the context of the above model.

3. APPROXIMATE REASONING

A problem faced in most reasoning situations is that all the information that may be relevant is not available and that which is available is confusing and not necessarily relevant.

3.1. Reasons for Approximation

Incompleteness of relevant knowledge is faced by reasoners in most reasoning situations. For example, the knowledge of only a few symptoms may not enable a reasoner to pinpoint a unique causal chain of physiological processes responsible for causing the observed symptoms. Similarly, the limited amount of available battlefield intelligence may fail to point toward a unique hypothesis about an enemy's plan. In situations of incomplete observed knowledge a number of hypotheses or explanations may be generated such that each of them is capable of explaining most if not all the observed symptoms. A reasoner now faces the problem of handling the multiplicity of hypotheses that explain a situation.

Another problem encountered by reasoners is *uncertainty of knowledge*. In many situations we are often not in a position to insist that a statement about either an input or about an innate idea is absolutely true, but are willing to admit that it carries a degree of uncertainty. A number of attempts have been made to model this uncertainty either with or without using numbers.

Another problem encountered by reasoners is *imprecision of knowledge*. The problem is encountered when the inputs and innate ideas may be imprecise in nature. For example, a Leibnizian enquirer may fail to include the input "economy has an inflation rate of 3.87%" in a fact-net consisting of very precise inputs but may be able to connect the input "economy has a low inflation rate" in the same fact-net. The former input is very precise and the latter is less precise. In many situations of enquiry in our everyday life the fact-nets or models are constructed by choosing less precise predicates or propositions. That is, instead of discarding some input, we sometimes try to find a less precise version of the model in which the inputs can be included. This is one aspect that Churchman's discourse on models of enquiry has not addressed. The only calculus that has systematically addressed the issue of imprecision of statements is the theory of fuzzy sets.

3.2. Approximate Enquirers

If a reasoner working according to the Leibnizian model of enquiry is interested in determining the "truth value" of some proposition by trying to form a fact-net containing it, then an approximate reasoner is interested in determining:

- either the uncertainty associated with the proposition of interest, given the uncertainties associated with the inputs and the innate ideas,

- or an imprecise version of the proposition and the model such that the proposition can be proved to be "true" given the imprecisions associated with the inputs and the innate ideas.

An approximate reasoner working according to the Kantian model of enquiry is interested in determining an ordered list of a few models that best explain the inputs. The imprecision associated with some propositions included in a model may be a criterion for preferring it over another model.

An approximate reasoner working according to the Hegelian model of enquiry would be interested in determining pairs of models that support the thesis and the antithesis. Precision of the propositions in models may be a part of the criterion for preferring one model over the other.

In the preceding discussion we have used the idea of a model of a situation. We now look at the nature of models of a situation that may be used by various types of reasoners.

4. CAUSAL MODELS

In the preceding section we used the idea of models of a situation without going into the details of what a model may look like, that is, how the innate ideas about a situation, including its primitives, axioms, and rules of inference, etc., may be represented. For example, in the domain of medical diagnosis one knows the effects of various types of physiological processes and this knowledge should be included in any model of a patient's situation. What we need is some relationship operations between the physiological processes so that they may be interconnected to constitute a meaningful explanation of the observed symptoms.

The knowledge of causality relationships provides a basis for relating various events and thus providing a causal structure for a situation. Causal information appears to be the most convincing basis for relating various events. Tversky and Kahneman (1982) state:

It is a psychological commonplace that people strive to achieve a coherent interpretation of the events that surround them, and that the organization of events by schemas of cause–effect relations serves to achieve this goal.

The authors go on to show that in the context of human behavior, data that are given causal interpretation affect judgments, while data that do not fit into causal schemas are dominated by causally relevant data. A number of reasoning systems that seek to deal with the structures of situations have used causality information for interconnecting various events. In the domain of situations have used causality information for interconnecting various events. In the domain of medical diagnosis the systems presented in Long et al. (1986), Coopes (1984), and Kuipers (1984) are some that use causal modeling of situations. The cause–effect structures for devices have also been used by Davis and Hamschur (1988) for the model-based approach to reasoning. Methods for constructing causal models for devices have been presented in Iwasaki and Simon (1986) and de Kleer and Brown (1986). Philosophically there have been many problems with the idea of causality. Many have argued against our being ever able to establish the relationships of causality between various events. However, in this discussion, by causality we refer to the perceived notion of causality as experienced by humans. Such notions of perceived causality are the innate ideas from which our models of situations are constructed. And we use these innate ideas of perceived causality without questioning the validity of these perceived causality relationships.

In the following discussion we examine various systems for reasoning and their capabilities in various types of reasoning situations. We classify the systems in two categories – those based on formal logic and those based on numeric calculi.

5. FORMAL LOGIC

Most of the early reasoning frameworks developed in artificial intelligence were based on formal logic and almost completely ignored the problems of approximate reasoning. Probability theory has been advanced as one framework best suited for handling uncertainty (Cheeseman, 1985) but some nonnumeric systems for handling uncertainty within the framework of formal logics have also been presented. Examples of such works include Halpern and Rabin (1987) and Poole (1988). Let us first look at some simple exercises of reasoning based on formal logic.

A formal *theorem-proving* system is a Leibnizian enquirer (Churchman, 1971). The mechanism of theorem-proving activity is the same as the construction of a network of wff's to possibly derive the null clause – the activity similar to that of constructing a fact-net. The wff's and the axioms constitute a unique model of the situation and the attempt to prove a "theorem" is to determine whether the "theorem" can be deduced from the knowledge contained in the model.

Kantian and Hegelian models of enquiry require that more than one model of the situation be available to the enquirer. It is possible that the axioms corresponding to two different models of a situation may be inconsistent; therefore the framework of theorem proving does not belong to the Kantian and Hegelian models of enquiry.

Default logics present a framework that can possibly be used for implementing Kantian and Hegelian enquirers. In the framework of these logics, the reasoner possesses two types of knowledge: *facts,* and *defaults*. The facts are those pieces of information that are known to be always true in the world. The defaults are those pieces of information that may or may not be true in any particular situation. For example, "Birds fly" is not always "true" in the world and is therefore not a fact. Since some birds fly and some don't this piece of information may be assumed to be true in some descriptions of the world and not in others. This is thus a possible piece of default knowledge. An example demonstrating the use of such knowledge taken from Poole (1988) is as follows:

default 1 $\neg$flies (X) $\leftarrow$ mammal (X)
default 2 flies (X) $\leftarrow$ bat (X)
default 3 $\neg$flies (X) $\leftarrow$ dead (X)
fact 1 mammal (X) $\leftarrow$ bat (X)
fact 2 bat (dracula)
fact 3 dead (dracula)

Now let us say the input available to us is:

$\neg$flies (dracula)

We can construct a theory that includes all three facts and default 1 and according to this theory we can explain the input. However, if the input available to us is:

flies(dracula)

then we can construct a theory with all three facts and default 2 to explain this input. The point is that logical inferences can be used within a theory, but when a number of theories may be possible the selection of an appropriate theory is of paramount concern. The exercise of reasoning concerns as much the task of inferencing as that of selecting a suitable theory. David Poole (1988) states:

> Rather than expecting reasoning to be just deduction (in any logic) from our knowledge, we examine the consequences of viewing reasoning as a very simple case of theory formation.

The basic components used for constructing a theory are the facts and the defaults. In any theory, all the facts and some of the defaults are included in such a way that the theory remains consistent. In many situations it may be possible to construct a number of theories to explain some particular set of inputs. If the theory is to serve as a model of some situation and the reasoner is planning on taking some action based on this assumed model, then it may be required that only one of these models is selected. An alternative for handling such a situation is to determine all the theories that explain the evidence and then determine the utility of each possible action in the context of each theory. The framework of decision theory may then be used to select the optimal action. In this approach we would need to know the relative chances of each of the theories being the actual model of the situation. The other alternative is to order various possible theories according to some criterion of interestingness and select the most interesting theory. Such an approach is suitable during a hypthesize-and-test cycle where we may want to determine the most interesting hypothesis and then verify it.

The inability of a reasoner to obtain all those inputs that may be needed to unravel the actual theory may have to be dealt with in one of the above two ways. The first option is closer to a Leibnizian enquirer and the second to a Kantian or Hegelian enquirer. In the first option numeric measures are used to indicate the uncertainty, and in the second the uncertainty is represented by accepting more than one model as the possible candidate.

The problem of representing uncertainty associated with a proposition, without having to use numeric measures, has been presented in many works. Most of this work has been done in the domain of modal logics. Segerberg (1971) and Gärdenfors (1975) have presented modal logics using formulas of the form $p \geqslant q$, interpreted as p *is more likely than q*. Halpern and Rabin (1987) have presented a modal logic LL to reason about the likelihood. In this logic the modal operator

L captures the notion of being likely. That is, the formula L_p represents the notion "*p is likely to be true.*" A model M for this logic can be viewed as a tree structure of states s. Each state s consists of a set of hypotheses that are taken to be "true for now." A state s_2 is a child of state s_1 if assuming s_1 to be true, an expert with his knowledge of the domain may call s_2 a likely state. Each state represents a set of consistent hypotheses. Also, a state does not represent a causal model of the situation being described, which in our view would be a desirable feature of any reasoner.

The problem of handling the level of imprecision has not been addressed within the framework of formal logics. It is possible to have two predicates for indicating "economy has low inflation" and "economy has an inflation rate between 2% and 3%," but there is no formalism that would automatically attempt to prove the former, a less precise statement, if the latter cannot be proved. That is, an attempt to form a fact-net with less precise statements would not be made automatically if the attempt with the more precise statements fails.

6. THE NUMERICAL APPROACHES

For every situation there is a causal structure underlying the observed symptoms. In cases of incomplete observable knowledge, it is difficult to uniquely identify the underlying causal model, and one may have to consider a number of causal models as possible candidates. If we are interested in the probability of some event, it may be determined by finding the fraction of possible causal models in which the event occurs.

6.1. Theories of Probability

A more useful probabilistic relationship from the point of view of reasoning is that of conditional probability. Let us consider two variables A and b with associated sets of discrete possible values $(a_1, a_2, ..., a_k)$, and (b_1, b_2, b_n). Let us say a reasoner knows the conditional probability values $P(a_i|b_j)$. Now, whenever some event $B = b_l$ is observed, the probability values for the unobserved events $A = a_m$ can be computed by the reasoner.

In a reasoning situation where relationships among various aspects of a situation are known only in terms of conditional probabilities, the knowledge of observed events can in general be used to infer the probabilities of other unobserved events. The work done in the area of Bayesian networks by Pearl (1986) has resulted in a framework for such reasoning. Some related work has also been presented in Lauritzen and Spiegelhalter (1988) and Schachter (1986).

Bayesian networks (Pearl, 1986) are directed acyclic graphs (DAGs) in which the nodes correspond to propositional variables, the edges represent the conditional probability relationships between the linked propositions, and the edges also signify causal relationships. In the network the causal relationships are quantified by the conditional probabilities of each variable given the state of its parent nodes. An example of a typical Bayesian network taken from Pearl (1986) is shown in Figure 2.1. A Bayesian network is a graphical representation for the independence relationships embedded in the known joint probability distribution for the variables included in the network. This means that the joint probability distribution for variables $x_1, ..., x_6$ of Figure 2.1 can be written as:

$$P(x_6|x_5)P(x_5|x_2,x_3)P(x_4|x_1,x_2)P(x_3|x_1)P(x_2|x_1)P(x_1)$$

Each term in the above product can be associated with the set of edges incident at various nodes of the network. Such a network represents a reasoner's complete knowledge about the domain. In any

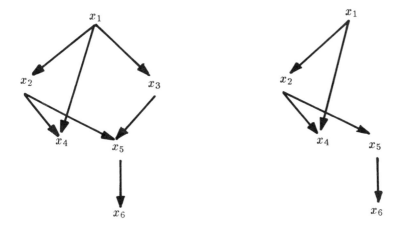

Figure 2.1   Figure 2.2

particular instance of reasoning when some events (inputs) are observed, this network and the associated conditional probabilities can be used to determine the resultant probability values at all the other unobserved nodes of the network. An elegant and computationally tractable algorithm for updating the beliefs at the nodes of a singly connected network has been presented in Pearl (1986). A singly connected network is one in which there is only one undirected path between any two nodes. The mechanism for updating the probability values at the unobserved nodes is based on local computations, wherein each node performs some computation and sends messages to its parent and child nodes. When this process stabilizes we obtain the updated values at all the unobserved nodes. When the network is not singly connected, it has been shown in Cooper (1990) that the problem of inference using belief networks is NP-hard. If we work with the restriction of networks being singly connected only, then we would not be capturing the knowledge in problem domains in their entirety. Some work has been presented in Chang and Fung (1990) to design special-case, average-case, and approximation algorithms for computations in Bayesian networks.

Let us look at probabilistic reasoning in Bayesian networks from the point of view of Churchman's classification. In Figure 2.1, let us say that x_1 represents a disease, x_2 and x_3 represent possible physiological reactions initiated by the disease, x_5 represents the functioning level of some body organ, and x_4 and x_6 represent observable symptoms in a patient's body. Now let us say that in some case an x_6 event is observed and the reasoner is interested in knowing about some particular x_4 event. After performing the Bayesian computations, let us say we can find out the probability of the relevant x_4 event may be obtained when using the network of Figure 2.2. The network shown in Figure 2.3 is another alternative model of the world and may result in another inference about the x_4 event.

Let us consider the differences between the models of the situation represented by the three different networks. The network shown in Figure 2.2 considers x_2 to be the only possible cause of x_5; that of Figure 2.3 considers x_3 to be the only cause of x_5; and the network of Figure 2.1 includes both x_2 and x_3 as the possible causes of x_5. There may be still more possible causes of x_5 not included in any of these networks. In the context of network 2 we consider x_2 to be the only cause of x_5. That is, we are hypothesizing that all other causes are absent. In case of network 1 we do not know which of the two may have been the cause of x_5 and in the inference for x_4 we reflect the possibility of either of the two causes.

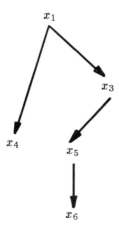

Figure 2.3

In any model of the situation it is sufficient to include only one cause for each such effect for which we need to know a cause. When two individual causes may be present, we can view the effect as being caused by the interaction of the two individual causes, and then this interaction is the sole cause responsible for the effect. So we can say that a Bayesian network that includes all the known causes for each effect variable is a combination of all individual models that may be possible for the situation. An inference using such a network can be said to be based on the following: a number of models for the situation are known, and considering each of them to be possible, the inference reflects the effects of each possible model.

The Bayesian networks represent the knowledge of a causal relationship by means of conditional probabilities associated with the edges of the network. It has, however, been demonstrated in Hunter (1980) that conditional probabilities fail to capture the important information about the direction of causal influence and this information may be crucial in some instances of reasoning.

This type of reasoner is then closest to a Leibnizian enquirer. This enquirer, given a model of the situation, determines its logical consequences. The Bayesian network is then a model of the situation incorporating all known probabilistic relationships among the aspects of interest. The Bayesian networks cannot be used to construct a Kantian or a Hegelian type of enquirer where the reasoner needs to identify a suitable model from among all known models.

The use of probability theory for reasoning has also been explored by Lauritzen and Spiegelhalter (1988). Their techniques are also developed for a context in which a graphical structure represents the dependence relationships among propositions. Their method seeks to update probability information at all the other nodes when evidence is obtained at one of the nodes. Successive updates are performed when evidence at more than one node is available. Regarding the model of the situation (the graph structure) the authors state:

> We assume a fixed model is currently being entertained and the numerical assessments are precisely specified, and our objective is to draw conclusions valid within this current structure, without any claim that the model is "true."

Therefore their techniques can also be used only by a Leibnizian enquirer; Kantian and Hegelian enquirers, in their search for suitable models, would have to look for other techniques.

6.2. Theory of Evidence

Numerical calculi other than the traditional probability theories have also been developed and used in many reasoning systems. A popular calculus among these has been Shafer's (1976) theory of evidence.

If S is the universal set of events, then in probability theory the uncertainty information consists of a *probability density* p on the elements of S such that $p: S \rightarrow [0,1]$ and

$$\sum_{s \in S} p(s) = 1$$

In the theory of evidence we define a *mass function* which, it is postulated, is induced in us by the available evidence and assigns parts of finite amount of belief to subsets of S. Each assignment of a mass to a subset s of S represents that part of our belief that supports s without being able to allocate this belief among strict subsets of s.

The *degree of belief* in a subset A of S, bel (A), is defined as the sum of all masses that support either A or any of its strict subsets. That is,

$$\text{bel}(A) = \sum_{X \in A, X \neq \emptyset} m(X)$$

The *degree of plausibility* of a subset A of S, $Pl(A)$ is defined as the sum of all those masses that can possibly support A. The possibility of a subset s supporting A means that the mass assigned to s can possibly gravitate to that strict subset of s which is also a subset of A. That is,

$$Pl(A) = \sum_{X \cap A \neq \emptyset} m(X)$$

When more than one mass function is available for a set S, they are combined using Dempster's rule, which performs an orthogonal sum of the two mass functions. The process of updating belief functions has been looked at from two different perspectives. There are some researchers who look at the belief and plausibility functions as the lower and upper envelopes of a family of probability distributions (Fagin and Halpern, 1990). The techniques for updating with this perspective have been presented in Fagin and Halpern (1990). In the view of some researchers, the attempts to relate the theory of evidence to probability theory, as either a generalization or as a specialization, are not in the right direction and belief functions should be viewed in the light of their own framework. The ideas that view the updating process as only a transfer of belief in the light of new evidence are discussed in Smets (1990).

6.3. Theory of Fuzzy Sets

The theory of fuzzy sets was originally developed by Zadeh in 1965 to capture and represent notions that are imprecise, such as "tall," "long," "young," etc. Systems for performing operations with these imprecise notions as operands, and to yield imprecise notions as results, have also been developed and examined (Zadeh, 1978; Zadeh, 1981; Smets, 1982). From the point of view of a reasoner, this calculus provides a powerful formalism, and the only available one, for handling imprecise notions in any of the three types of enquirers. For a brief introduction, let us consider the predicate *Low-Infl* *(Low-inflation)*. Instead of evaluating to "True" or "False" for real-valued parameters, the predicate acts as an elastic constraint on the acceptable values for the parameter. For each x belonging to the set of real numbers, one can define $\mu_{Low-Infl}(x) \in [0,1]$ as the extent of membership of the number x in the acceptable values for low-inflation.

The grade of membership $\mu_{Low-Infl}(x)$ is also interpreted by Zadeh to be the possibility, $\pi_{Low-Infl}(x)$, that the proposition is true with the value x. Necessity and possibility measures have been defined for each proposition and can be easily computed.

This theory is very useful when one wants to make transitions between a very precise but uncertain proposition and a fuzzified and less precise but strictly true proposition. Magrez and Smets (1989) present methods for computing the modalities (possibility and necessity) of a more precise statement from the knowledge of a strictly true proposition. They also present a method for computing a strictly true proposition B from a proposition A qualified by necessity and possibility modalities.

A Leibnizian enquirer that fails to form a fact-net can attempt to construct another fact-net after making some of its propositions less precise. This is an aspect of reasoning we perform in our daily life but there is no formalism yet in artificial intelligence systems to simulate this capability. That is, our inability to precisely assess an enemy's strategy, based on incomplete and uncertain data, leads us to at least infer that an attack somewhere is imminent. The techniques presented by the theory of possibility for making transitions between related statements of varying precision are extremely useful for the Leibnizian enquirers.

For example, if it is not possible to construct a model to infer that the inflation in the economy would be below 3 percent, we may try to find a less precise version of the proposition that can be supported by a model containing the available evidence. It may turn out that the available evidence within some model can let us infer the proposition "the inflation in the economy would be low" with complete certainty, that is with necessity equal to one. To determine the least imprecise version of a proposition that can be inferred with certainty is a type of reasoning that we perform very often. The framework of possibility theory helps us in designing such reasoners.

The same techniques can also be employed by the Kantian and Hegelian enquirers for constructing less precise or more precise models. This can be very useful in systems that perform adversarial arguments. In these situations one may want to advance a less precise proposition as argument instead of a proposition that can be countered as being not "true" in at least some cases. To this end the theories of possibility and fuzzy sets provide a unique tool for the three types of enquirers.

7. THE MECHANICAL REASONER

A Leibnizian enquirer is suitable for well-structured domains but one strongly feels the need for a Hegelian type of enquirer in most other situations. Let us study a few examples. In problems of medical diagnosis the reasoner must proceed from an initial knowledge about the patient consisting of some observable symptoms and the medical history of the patient. The reasoner may then perform the following two steps:

1. Perform more tests, etc., to determine a causal model of the physiological processes in the patient's body that explains the observed symptoms.
2. The above model being the diagnosis, determine a treatment that attenuates or removes the causes of undesirable effects.

The first task can be performed by a number of iterations of hypothesize-and-test steps. That is, given the knowledge about the symptoms, one hypothesizes one or more models and then performs tests to check the hypotheses. Information gained by performing the tests can be included in the next iteration to hypothesize new models. In the preceding section, Figure 2.2 and Figure 2.3 represent two possible models of the situation. Tests can be performed in the context of each model to verify the inferences for the unobserved nodes of the models.

The numeric approaches, in being consistent with their axioms and semantics, may not be applicable in many situations. For example, when dealing with the Iraqi threat to Saudi Arabia, President Bush declared that he has "drawn a line in sand" and implied that Iraqi forces must not cross it. In this situation there is no sound probabilistic basis for quantifying the uncertainty associated with various events that may possibly be encountered if this "line in sand" is crossed or not crossed. The logic LL of Halpern and Rabin (1987) can determine the *likelihood* of a proposition p and we can find out if it is L^2p, or L^3p, or L^kp, where L^2p stands for LLp meaning that it is likely that p is likely. According to the semantics of this logic L^kp holds if a state along a sequence of states representing "likely successors of states" can be found in which L^kp is consistent. But the model for the logic represented by a tree of states must be made available before the reasoning can begin. For a new situation, such as the one above, one needs a model in which all possible consistent states have already been included. The experts of the domain are expected to make this state-structure available to the reasoner who can then enquire if a proposition is likely or not, and if yes, in which state.

According to the semantics of LL (Halpern and Rabin, 1987) the knowledge of the expert that links various possible states of the world in the tree structure is her knowledge about various extralogical axioms, rules, and hunches embodying her past experience. Such an approach may be useful for domains where a manageable number of possible states of the situation is sufficient to handle most instances of the reasoning exercise. In a domain like medical diagnosis, or automobile fault diagnosis, it may be possible to construct the set of frequently occurring states. But it is not possible to maintain an enumerated set of all conceivable states that a situation may evolve into. For example, the situation created by the Iraqi invasion of Kuwait, and possible ways of dealing with it, could not have been enumerated and kept ready for a reasoner.

The task of an intelligent reasoner is also to enumerate that subset of conceivable states of the world which may become very likely due to some observed developments. It is this capability to construct the hypothetical states that become relevant that we want the reasoner to possess. The enumeration of hypotheses can be done by constructing them from the very primitive innate ideas about the world. The primitives available for constructing possible states are the reasoner's knowledge of the axioms and rules governing the domain and his past knowledge. A Kantian and Hegelian enquirer is expected to select the optimal model when given some evidence, but if the number of possible models is so large that it is impossible to explicitly store each possible model then one must implicitly store these models by storing the basic components from which these models may be constructed.

The primitive knowledge that is useful for constructing causal models is the knowledge regarding individual causal relationships. Figure 2.4 shows an example where a hypergraph structure has been used to represent the knowledge of known causal relationships. A hypergraph structure is suitable because a hyperedge can easily capture the notion of some effect being caused by an interaction of two or more other aspects of the situation. A hyperedge can include more than two nodes of a graph in it and is represented in Figure 2.4 by either a closed curve or a polygon. For example, hyperedge 3 includes nodes S, C and H and the arrow pointing to N signifies that an interaction between S and C causally affects H. Each subgraph of this hypergraph, such that only one cause is included for each effect, represents one possible causal model of some situation. The hyper-

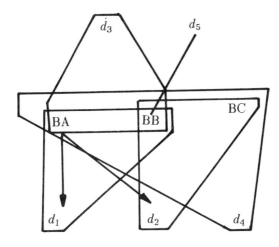

Figure 2.4

graph consisting of hyperedges for all known causal relationships about a domain implicitly includes in it all possible models of various situations in that domain.

Consider the situation in which the presence of three types of bacteria, BA, BB, and BC is of interest. Also consider some organ C that can be found to be defective in one of five different ways, d_1, d_2, etc. Now let us say the known causal links between the bacteria and the defects are the following:

BA when present alone is highly likely to cause d_1 but may also sometimes cause d_2.

BA and BB when present together, interact, and this interaction is highly likely to cause d_3, and may also sometimes cause d_1.

BA, BB, and BC, when present together, interact, and this interaction is highly likely to cause d_2 and may sometime cause d_4.

BB when present alone is highly likely to cause d_5 but may also sometimes cause d_2.

The hypergraph in Figure 2.5 includes a hyperedge for each of these possible causal relationships. Which defect is being caused is

H: Headache (severe, mild, none)
C: Common-Cold (infctn, chrnc)
M: Meningitis (viral, bactrl)
T: Temprtr (high, low, normal(
    F: Fatal (yes, no)
    A: Age (¿60, ¿40, ¿20, ¡20)
    S: Sinus-Condtn *s1, s2, s3)
J: Bctria-Prsnt (b1, b2, b3, b4, b5)
    E: Hrdtry-Fctrl (h1, h2, h3)
    K: Disease1 (present, absent)
    D: Smoker (no, light, heavy)
    G: Symptom1 (p1, p2, p3, p4)

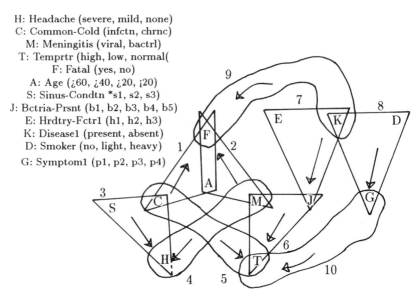

Figure 2.5

determined not by the presence of a particular bacteria, but by the presence of one or the other causal relationship. A model of the situation should therefore hypothesize the set of causal relationships that are present and not that of individual bacteria. That is, when one of the d_i's is observed, the reasoner should hypothesize by selecting one of the hyperedges and not by selecting an individual bacteria.

When we use the joint probability distribution of all the bacteria and all the defects and use it to constrct a Bayesian network as shown in Figure 2.6, we lose all knowledge about individual causal relationships. Each edge between a bacteria and the defects represents a relationship summed up over all possible causal relationships according to which the bacteria could have affected the organ. Each edge therefore does not represent a single causal relationship, but a sum total of all those causal relationships of which the two connected nodes are a constituent, and is therefore not suitable when the objective of creating a model is to identify the active causal relationships.

A reasoner that constructs suitable causal models by finding appropriate subgraphs of the hypergraph has been presented in Bhatnagar (1989). Each hyperedge in this methodology also stores a joint probability distribution of all the nodes included in the

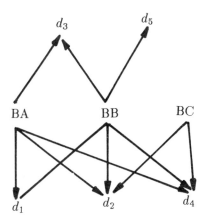

Figure 2.6

hyperedge. This reasoner needs to know the criterion for preferring a model and the observed events. For example, the preference criterion could be "maximum probability for the event that the patient would die." The reasoner would then find that subgraph of the hypergraph that includes all the observed symptoms and is such that among all other possible models it satisfies the preference criterion. The algorithm is based on a heuristic search in the space of all possible subgraphs of the hypergraph. This reasoner can construct causal models and can work as a Hegelian or Kantian enquirer. This type of reasoner can be called a "constructive reasoner" because the capability to determine the suitable model is like constructing an argument to support a suitable thesis. This type of reasoner can also be called a hypothetical reasoner because it can be used for hypothesizing suitable models of the world that may be of interest to the reasoner. For example, hypothetical models of the world in which an army may achieve victory may be needed to plan its offensive strategy and hypothetical models in which an army faces defeat may be used to plan its defensive strategy.

Any one of the various uncertainty calculi can be incorporated into such a mechanical reasoner. For example, if the preference criterion for hypotheses is in terms of the preciseness of inferred propositions then we can adopt the possibility calculus or the calculus of the fuzzy sets, whereas if uncertainty of one of the many options is of concern we may adopt the probability calculus.

8. CONCLUSION

We have examined various types of uncertainty calculi, reasoners, and reasoning framework. A mechanical reasoner in our view should be able to act like a Leibnizian, a Kantian, or a Hegelian enquirer. Most existing formalisms are closer to Leibnizian reasoners; in our view a significant amount of work needs to be done to develop the latter two types of reasoners. These latter two types of reasoners capture many of the intelligent aspects of our day-to-day reasoning.

BIBLIOGRAPHY

Bhatnagar, R. (1989). *Construction of preferred causal hypotheses for reasoning with uncertain knowledge*. Ph.D. Dissertation, Computer Science Department, University of Maryland, College Park.

Chang K.-C. and R. Fung. (1990). Refinement and coarsening of bayesian networks. *Proceedings of the Sixth Conference on Uncertainty in Artificial Intelligence*, pp. 475–482.

Cheeseman, P. (1985). In defense of probability. *Proceedings of IJCAI*, pp. 1002–1009.

Churchman, C. W. (1971). *The Design of Inquiring Systems: Basic Concepts of Systems and Organization*. New York: Basic Books.

Cooper, G. F. (1984). *NESTOR: A Computer-based Medical Diagnostic Aid that Integrates Causal and Probabilistic Knowledge*. Ph.D. Dissertation. Department of Computer Science, Stanford University.

Cooper, G. F. (1990). The computational complexity of probabilistic inference using bayesian belief networks. *Artificial Intelligence*, **42**, 393–405.

Davis, R. and W. C. Hamscher. (1988). Model-based reasoning: Troubleshooting. A.I. Memo no. 1059, MIT AI Laboratory, July.

de Kleer, J. (1986). An assumption-based TMS. *Artificial Intelligence*, **28**, 127–162.

de Kleer, J. and J.S. Brown. (1986). Theories of causal ordering. *Artificial Intelligence*, **29**, 33–61.

Fagin R. and J. Y. Halpern. (1990). A New approach to updating beliefs. *Proceedings of the Sixth Conference on Uncertainty in Artificial Intelligence, 1990*, pp. 317–325.

Gärdenfors, P. (1975). Qualitative probability as intensional logic. *J. Philos. Logic*, **4**, 171–185.

Halpern, J.Y. and M.O. Rabin. (1987). A Logic to reason about likelihood. *Artificial Intelligence*, **32**, 379–405.

Hunter, D. (1989). Causality and maximum entropy updating. *International Journal of Approximate Reasoning*, **3**, 87–114.

Iwasaki, Y. and H. A. Simon. (1986). Causality in device behaviour. *Artificial Intelligence*, **29**, 3–32

Kanal, L. and D. Perlis. (1988). Uniform accountability for multiple modes of Reasoning. *International Journal of Approximate Reasoning*, **2**, 233–246.

Kanal, L. and V. Kumar (eds.). (1988). *Search in Artificial Intelligence*. Berlin: Springer-Verlag.

Kuipers, B. (1984). Causal reasoning in medicine: Analysis of a protocol. *Cognitive Science*, **8**, 363–385.

Lauritzen, S. L. and D. J. Spiegelhalter. (1988). Local computations with probabilities on graphical structures and their application to expert Systems. *The Journal of the Royal Statistical Society*, series B, vol. 50, no. 2, 157–224.

Long, W. J. S. Naimi, M. G. Criscitiello, and S. Kurzrok. (1986). Reasoning about therapy from a physiological model. In R. Salamon, B. Blum, and M. Jorgensen (eds.): *MEDINFD'86*. Amsterdam: Elsevier (North-Holland), pp. 756–760.

Magrez, P. and P. Smets. (1989). Epistemic necessity, possibility, and truth. Tools for dealing with imprecision and uncertainty in fuzzy knowledge based systems. *International Journal of Approximate Reasoning*, **3**, 35–57.

McCarthy, J. (1980). Circumscription – A form of non-monotonic reasoning. *Artificial Intelligence*, **13**, 27–39.

Pearl, J. (1986). Fusion, propagation and structuring in belief networks. *Artificial Intelligence*, **29**, 241–288.

Pearl, J. (1987). Evidential reasoning using stochastic simulation of causal models. *Artificial Intelligence*, **32**, 245–257.

Poole, D. (1988). A logical framework for default reasoning. *Artificial Intelligence*, **36**, 27–47.

Segerberg, K. (1971). Qualitative probability in a modal setting. *Proceedings of the 2nd Scandinavian Logic Symposium*, E. Fenstad (ed.). Amsterdam: North-Holland.

Shachter, R. D. (1986). Intelligent probabilistic inference. In L. N. Kanal and J. F. Lammer (eds.): *Uncertainty in Artificial Intelligence*. Englewood Cliffs, NJ: Prentice Hall, pp. 371–382.

Shafer, G. (1976). *A. Mathematical Theory of Evidence*. Princeton University Press.

Smets, P. (1987). Elementary semantic operators. In R. R. Yager (ed.). *Recent Advances in Fuzzy Set and Possibility Theory*. New York: Pergamon Press, pp. 247–256.

Smets, P. (1990). The transferable belief model and other interpretations of Dempster-Shafer's model. *Proceedings of the Sixth Conference on Uncertainty in Artificial Intelligence*, 1990, pp. 326–333.

Tversky, A., and D. Kahneman. (1982). *Judgement under Uncertainty: Heuristics and Biases*. Cambridge University Press.

Zadeh, L. A. (1978). Fuzzy sets as a basis for a theory of possibility. *Fuzzy Sets and Systems*, 1, 3–28.
Zadeh, L. A. (1981). PRUF: A meaning representation language for natural languages. In E. H. Mamdani and B. R. Gaines (eds.), *Fuzzy Reasoning and its Applications*. New York: Academic Press, pp. 1–66.

3 A survey of uncertain and approximate inference

Richard E. NEAPOLITAN
Computer Science Department
Northeastern Illinois University
Chicago, IL 60625, USA

Abstract. This paper concerns the inference performed by computer programs that make judgments in a complex area. Such programs are called expert systems. A number of alternative approaches to handling uncertainty have been developed and used in expert systems. A new type of inference, called fuzzy inference, has also been applied to expert systems. There is a distinct difference between uncertain and fuzzy inference. In what follows, this difference is clarified, and various methods for performing uncertain and fuzzy inference are briefly described. Furthermore, it is shown that the use of probability theory is compelling for performing uncertain inference in expert systems, and that the Dempster-Shafer theory uses probability theory in a legitimate fashion. Finally, an example is given for which the use of the Dempster-Shafer theory is the most appropriate, and an example for which the use of fuzzy inference is the most appropriate.

1. INTRODUCTION

This paper examines the inference performed by "intelligent" computer programs. By an intelligent computer program we mean one that makes judgments or gives assistance in a complex area. Such programs are often called expert systems.

The early expert systems of the 1960s used probability theory and a simple Bayes model to perform uncertain inference. A number of researchers (Gorry, 1973; Shortliffe, 1976; Norusis and Jacquez, 1975) noted the shortcomings of this model. At that time, the use of a full-scale decision theoretic model appeared intractable. Furthermore, in the early 1970s researchers were beginning to successfully use cognitive modeling to create rule-based expert systems that performed categorical (certain) inference. (See, e.g., McDermott, 1982). It therefore seemed that such an approach could be used to create systems that needed to perform uncertain inference. Buchanan and Shortliffe (1984) describe MYCIN, one of the best known of these systems. Because many researchers at this time did not feel that probability theory offered a descriptive model of human uncertain inference, a number of alternative approaches flourished. These approaches included the use of certainty factors (Buchanan and Shortliffe, 1984), the Dempster-Shafer theory of evidence (Shafer, 1976), fuzzy set theory and fuzzy logic (Yager et al., 1987), nonmonotonic reasoning including nonmonotonic logic (McDermott and Doyle, 1980) and default logic (Reiter, 1987), and the theory of endorsements (Cohen, 1985). A controversy eventually arose as to whether probability theory alone is adequate for handling uncertainty or whether these alternative methods are sometimes more appropriate. The perspectives of various authors on this controversy can be found in Kanal and Lemmer (1986) and in Cheeseman (1988).

The development of the influence diagram (Howard and Matheson, 1981) and methods for performing tractable inference in influence diagrams (Pearl, 1986; Lauritzen and Spiegelhalter, 1988) enabled researchers to build "normative" expert systems. Unlike the systems of the 1970s, such systems are not meant to descriptively model human reasoning. Rather probability and utility theory are used in these systems to model the way a human ideally should reason (Savage, 1954).

I take the position that the fundamental goal of an expert system is to make the best possible judgments, not to descriptively model human reasoning. If expert consensus and the results of an autopsy were different, I would want the system to agree with the results of the autopsy. I would not want the system to agree with the experts, much less model the way the experts reason. If this view is taken, the normative approach of the 1980s is appropriate in expert systems, which must perform uncertain inference. Heckerman (1990) discusses why this is the case and also elaborates on the ideas presented in this introduction.

There is, however, a distinct difference between uncertain and approximate (fuzzy) inference. The goal of this paper is to survey both and to clarify the difference between them. In Section 2 I discuss uncertain inference and probability theory and show that the use of probability theory is compelling for performing uncertain inference in expert systems. I note, however, that the Dempster-Shafer theory is based on probability theory and can sometimes be used to obtain meaningful results in cases where the use of Bayesian probabilistic inference fails to do so. In Section 3 I discuss approximate inference and show that fuzzy set theory and fuzzy logic are appropriate disciplines for this type of inference.

2. UNCERTAIN INFERENCE

Uncertain inference is illustrated in the following situation. A set of possibilities exist such that pricisely one of them is true or will turn out to be true. That is, the possibilities are mutually exclusive and exhaustive. Certain information arrives that is supportive of one or more of the possibilities; however, the information does not confirm any of the possibilities for certain. Uncertain inference is the process of ranking the possibilities by likelihood based on this information.

In order to clarify the different meanings of the term "probability," I will first briefly discuss three of the major approaches to probability theory. Then I will show how probability theory is used to perform uncertain inference in expert systems. I discuss this topic in much greater detail in Neapolitan (1990).

2.1. Probability Theory

2.1.1. The Classical Approach to Probability

The *classical approach* is the term used to denote the *logical approach to probability* adopted by Laplace (1749–1827). At its heart we find Laplace's classical definition of *probability* (Laplace, 1820):

> The theory of chance consists in reducing all the events of some kind to a certain number of cases equally possible, that is to say, such as we may be equally undecided about in

regard to their existence, and in determining the number of cases favorable to the event whose probability is sought. The ratio of this number to that of all cases possible is the measure of the probability.

Probabilities are assigned within the framework of the classical approach by using the principle of indifference (a term first used by Keynes in 1921). The idea in the principle is that "alternatives are to be judged equiprobable if we have no reason to expect or prefer one over the other" (Weatherford, 1982). The classical approach is commonly used to assign probabilities in games of chance. For example, we say that the probability of drawing a king from a deck of cards is 4/52 because there are 4 equipossible alternatives, which yield a king, out of a total of 52 equipossible alternatives.

It is a simple matter to derive the following results from the classical definition of probability: Let Ω be the set of equipossible alternatives, a subset E of Ω denote the event that one of the alternatives in E occurs, and $P(E)$ stand for the probability of E. Then

$$P(E) \geqslant 0 \tag{1}$$
$$P(\Omega) = 1 \tag{2}$$
$$\text{If } E_1 \cap E_2 = \varnothing, \text{ then } P(E_1) \cup E_2) = P(E_1) + P(E_2) \tag{3}$$

For example, (3) is obtained as follows. Suppose E_1 contains m equipossible alternatives, E_2 contains k equipossible alternatives, $E_1 \cap E_2 = \varnothing$, and there are n equipossible alternatives. Then, according to the classical definition,

$$P(E_1) + P(E_2) = \frac{m}{n} + \frac{k}{n} = \frac{m+k}{n} = P(E_1 \cup E_2)$$

A set of events can be represented by the proposition that describes the set. For example, the set of all kings can be represented by the proposition "king is drawn" or simply "king." Thus, in probability theory, some authors (e.g., Cox, 1979) represent intersection by conjunction and union by disjunction. For example, $E \cap F$ is represented by $E \wedge F$ or $E \cdot F$. Such a treatment is justified by the well-known correspondence between a Boolean algebra and a set of propositions.

The above three results are the first three axioms of probability theory. That is, in a standard probability text, they, and not the classical definition of probability, are assumed. A fourth axiom in probability theory concerns conditional probability. Except perhaps in the case of quantum mechanical phenomena, all probabilities are conditional on information. They are not a property of the event. For example, suppose that the top card was drawn from a well-shuffled deck, and one person happened to get enough of a glimpse of the card at the end of the shuffeing process that he knew for certain that it was a royal card; however, he had no idea as to which royal card it was. For that person the probability of a king would be 1/3 rather than 1/13, and he would bet according to this probability. For anyone who was not privy to this fellow's information the probability would still be 1/13. Even this value of 1/13, however, is relative to information. That is, it is relative to the information that the card is drawn from a well-shuffled deck. Probabilities relative to this initial information are called prior probabilities and are denoted by $P(E)$, where E is the event in question. Probabilities relative to additional information are called *conditional probabilities* and are denoted by $P(E|F)$, where F is the additional information. Since all probabilities are relative to information, many authors (e.g., Lindley, 1965) prefer to denote all probabilities as conditional probabilities and use a symbol such as ξ for the prior information. A prior probability is then denoted by $P(E|\xi)$ while a conditional probability is denoted by $P(E|F,\xi)$.

The fourth axiom of probability theory is the following definition of conditional probability:

$$\text{If } P(F) \neq 0, \text{ then } P(E|F) = \frac{P(E \cap F)}{P(F)} \tag{4}$$

This axiom can also be easily derived from the classical definition if one assumes that the alternatives in E remain equipossible when it is known for certain that F has occurred.

The classical approach fell into disfavor due to a number of criticisms. One of these criticisms is that applications of the principle of indifference can lead to paradoxical results. However, as I show in Neapolitan (1990), these paradoxes can be resolved by distinguishing two interpretations of the principle. The first interpretation is that there is a uniform, random process that generates the alternative, such as in the case of the well-shuffled deck. The fact that the process is uniform means that all the alternatives are treated equitably, and therefore we assume that they are equipossible. Such reasoning appears circular. However, when the process apparently treats all the alternatives the same, we take that as the *definition* of being equipossible. The second interpretation of the principle is that we should apply it whenever the information gives us no reason to choose one alternative over the other. (See Neapolitan, 1990 for a discussion of these two interpretations and the paradoxes.)

The real problem with the classical approach is that the principle of indifference is not applicable in many of the most important applications of probability theory. For example, an insurance company would decide on the insurance rate of a thirty-year-old man based partly on the probability of the man dying in his thirty-first year. To access this probability, they would observe perhaps 10,000 men, who are in the same insurance class as the man under consideration, during their thirty-first year. The insurance class is the information on which the probability is based. An example of such a class is the class of all thirty-year-old men who are white-collar workers in the United States in 1990. If 20 of the men died in their thirty-first year, the insurance company would compute the probability of the new thirty-year-old prospect dying in the coming year to be approximately .002. In this example, there is not a set of equipossible alternatives from which the new prospect is selected. Some stretch the classical approach by saying that if we take the set of all men in this class who ever lived or who will ever live, then the probability of picking a man who dies in his thirty-first year is the number who die divided by the number of all such men. The probability obtained from the 10,000 men is then a statistical estimate of the true probability. However, even this stretch of the classical approach cannot be applied to the simple situation of tossing a coin. Even if the coin is never tossed, many feel that there is a probability of heads associated with the coin's composition. Often it is assumed the coin is fair and that the value is .5. However, what probability value should we use in the case where a thumbtack is tossed? Even here many assume that there is a probability associated with the event that the tack lands on its head. However, how do we determine that probability? All these cases are addressed by the limiting frequency approach to probability, which is discussed in the next subsection.

The classical approach is called a logical approach to probability, and probabilities obtained using the principle of indifference are called *objective probabilities* because their values are thought to be a logical property of the information and therefore independent of subjective judgment. Carnap (1950) and Keynes (1921) developed logical approaches that are extensions of the classical approach. (See Fine, 1979 for a discussion of these and other approaches to probability.)

2.2.2. The Limiting Frequency Approach

Von Mises (1919) says that numerical probability only has meaning in the case of an experiment that can be repeated. Specifically, von Mises defines a *collective* as follows:

> This term is "the collective," and it denotes a sequence of uniform events or processes which differ by certain observable attributes, say colors, numbers, or anything else.

Examples of collectives include the class of all thirty-year-old men who are white-collar workers in the United States in 1990, and the set of all tosses of a specific coin or thumbtack.

If the experiment is repeated n times and $S^n(E)$ is the number of times an event E occurs (an attribute is observed), then von Mises defines the probability of E as $\lim_{n \to \infty} S^n(E)/n$. The argument is that if, for example, the thumbtack were tossed 100 times it might land on its head 67 times, after 1000 tosses there might be 681 heads, and after 10,000 tosses 6813 heads. The point is that as the number of repetitions of the experiment increases, the number of stable decimal digits in the frequency increases. Therefore there is a *limiting value* and that value is the *probability*. Of course this assumption cannot be proved for any experiment since we can never proceed indefinitely. However, von Mises (1919) says that it is applicable whenever we have "sufficient reason to believe that the relative frequency of the observed attribute would tend to a fixed limit if the observations were indefinitely continued." Kerrich (1946) has actually carried out numerous experiments in order to demonstrate the stability of the success ratio. For example, he spun a coin 10,000 times and demonstrated that the ratio for heads kept very close to .5.

Von Mises' second assumption is that the class of events for which probability theory is applicable includes only random processes. Von Mises considers a random process one which, when repeated indefinitely, does not allow a successful gambling strategy. That is, a gambler cannot obtain profit in the long run by using a strategy to choose when to bet instead of betting every time. (See van Lambalgen, 1987 for a discussion of random sequences.) With these two assumptions, it is possible to prove the axioms of probability theory.

Note that the limiting frequency definition of probability is still relative to information. That is, according to von Mises, there is no probability of Joe Smith dying in his thirty-first year since Joe Smith will definitely die or definitely not die. The probability is only relative to a collective (information) of which Joe Smith is a member. If we consider Joe Smith a member of all thirty-year-old white-collar workers, that probability may be .001. If we learned that Joe Smith had lung cancer, then we would compute the probability relative to the collective of thirty-year-old white-collar workers who have lung cancer. This probability may be .1. When we toss a coin, the probability is usually relative only to the information that the coin is tossed and we know nothing of the nature of the toss. If we knew the distance from the ground, the torque placed on the coin, etc., the probability would change.

Von Mises' theory has been criticized due to the claim that his definition of probability depends on future events that might never occur. Many feel that there is still a probability associated with a coin's composition (propensity) even if the coin is never tossed. This criticism is contrary to von Mises' intentions as he states (von Mises, 1919) "the probability of a 6 is a physical property of a given die and is a property analogous to its mass, specific heat, or electrical resistance. The probability of a 6 then determines what would happen if the experiment were repeated. It is not necessary to repeat the experiment for the probability to exist.

As a result of the above criticism and others elaborated in van Lambalgen (1987), von Mises' theory was essentially abandoned after a conference on the theory of probability in Geneva in 1937. The popular limiting frequency approach to probability theory became the *measure theoretic approach* termed the *propensity interpretation* (Popper, 1935). Although Kolmogorov himself was not a proponent of this approach, it is based on his (1933) axiomatic development of probability theory. The propensity interpretation assumes the axioms of probability theory rather than deriving them from a theoretical counterpart to observable physical phenomena, and therefore, as discussed in van Lambalgen (1987), is not philosophically or physically compelling.

The real problem I see in von Mises' theory is that his basic assumption is that the relative frequency will *definitely* converge to the probability. The primary objection today of many modern probabilists, who have adopted the propensity interpretation, to von Mises' theory is that they simply do not accept the fact that the relative frequency definitely converges. Consider the following quote from an introductory probability text (Lindley, 1965):

The limit here is not a mathematical limit. That is to say, given a small positive ε, it is not possible to find a value N such that $|m/n-p| < \varepsilon$ for all $n > N$, where $p = $ "$\lim_{n\to\infty}$" m/n as would be required of a mathematical limit. For there is nothing impossible in m/n differing from p by as much as 2ε, it is merely rather unlikely. And the word unlikely involves probability ideas so that the attempt at a definition of "limit" using the mathematical limit becomes circular. The axiomatic approach avoids this difficulty and the empirical observations will not be used to define probability, but only to suggest the axioms.

In spite of the aforementioned results in Kerrich (1946), these probabilists do not accept that the relative frequency will definitely converge. Von Mises' assumption of strict convergence is in no way inconsistent with the results of probability theory such as the laws of large numbers. Rather strict convergence is just too much for many probabilists to accept on philosophical grounds. Unfortunately, these probabilists must therefore adopt the "propensity" interpretation and assume the axioms of probability theory. However, as already noted, doing this is not compelling. To solve this dilemma, in Neapolitan (1991a) I do what Lindley (above) felt to be circular. I derive the axioms of probability theory by assuming convergence only in the sense of the weak law of large numbers.

There is still a problem with making the limiting frequency approach the sole foundation of probability theory. That is, the approach is not applicable to many useful applications of probability theory. For example, I gamble routinely on football and baseball games. If the Las Vegas bookmaker offers me 7 to 5 odds against the Yankees winning a certain game, this means that, if I bet on the Yankees winning, I will pay him $5 dollars if they lose while he will pay me $7 if they win. To determine whether this is a good bet, I attempt to analyze the probability of the Yankees winning. However, since this game could never be repeated under the same conditions (actually with my having the same information about the conditions), this probability has nothing to do with limiting relative frequencies. (Reichenbach [1949] did stretch the limiting frequency interpretation to include such situations.) We address such probabilities with the subjectivistic approach, which is described in the next subsection.

Probabilities assigned within the framework of the limiting freqency approach are called physical probabilities because they are thought to be a physical property of reality just as is mass or specific heat. This is evident in the above quote of von Mises concerning the probability of 6 on a die.

2.2.3. The Subjectivistic Approach

De Finetti (1972) defines the probability $P(E)$ of an event E as the fraction of a whole unit value that one would feel is the fair amount to exchange for the promise that one would receive a whole unit value if E ends up occurring and zero units if E does not occur. If there are n mutually exclusive and exhaustive events E_i, and a person assigned probability $P(E_i)$ to each of them respectively, then he would agree that all n exchanges are fair and thus agree that it is fair to exchange $\sum_{i=1}^{n} P(E_i)$ units for 1 unit. Therefore if $\sum_{i=1}^{n} P(E_1) \neq 1$, the person would have to agree to a bet that he is sure to lose. This has been called the Dutch book theorem (de Finetti, 1964). A set of probability values that do not allow a Dutch book are said to be coherent. Based on the assumption of coherency, de Finetti was able to deduce the axioms of probability theory. De Finetti's definition of probability is called a *subjectivistic approach* because the rule for assigning probabilities is merely that the sum of the probabilities of mutually exclusive and exhaustive events must add up to 1. Within the confinement of that restriction, an individual is free to use his subjective judgment. One individual may say the probability of the Yankees winning is .4 while another may say it is .5.

Notice that the subjectivistic approach makes probability theory not only applicable to gambling, but also to many practical inference problems. For example (Shachter, 1988), a firm may set its price for a product based on its projected sales, the price that a competitor will set, and other uncertain information. The uncertainties in this problem cannot be represented by relative frequencies. Yet the subjectivistic argument implies that the firm should still use probability theory to analyze the problem whenever real numbers are used to represent the uncertainty.

A problem with de Finetti's definition is that it demands that the probability assessor must wager and be willing to exchange monetary units. Furthermore, one's willingness to gamble does not necessarily reflect one's subjective probabilities. For example, based on symptoms my neighbor described to me, I was almost certain (a probability of .99) that he had a herniated disc. However, I was only willing to offer him odds of 9 to 1 in favor of a herniated disc. This is because I would value winning $10 sufficiently that I would risk $90 for that opportunity. However, $1 has essentially no value to me; therefore I would not risk $99 for the chance of obtaining $1. Lindley (1985) offers the following more primitive definition of subjective probability. Suppose an individual is attempting to ascertain the probability of it raining tomorrow. Let an urn contain 100 balls, each of which is either black or white. The individual should determine the number of black balls such that he would be indifferent between receiving a small prize if the uncertain event occurred and receiving the same small prize if a black ball were drawn in a random draw from the urn. Since the more black balls the better the urn gamble, there must be some number b of black balls for which he is indifferent betwen the two gambles. The probability of the uncertain event is then $b/100$. For refinement it may be necessary to increase the number of balls to 1000, 10,000, etc. In the case of my neighbor's symptoms I would be indifferent if the number of black balls was 99 out of 100. With this definition, Lindley not only eliminates the need to wager; he also creates a cogent argument for associating real numbers with uncertain events. If we assume Lindley's definition of probability and further assume that (1) a person would prefer receiving a small prize for certain over the uncertain prospect of receiving that same small prize, and (2) he would prefer receiving the uncertain prospect of the small prize over definitely receiving nothing, then we can deduce coherency and therefore the axioms of probability theory.

Some object to probability being defined in terms of a gamble. They maintain that the introduction of a gamble is artificial. On the contrary, whenever we use probability it is to gamble. We simply do not call it gambling. For example, one may wish to ascertain the probability of it raining tomorrow in order to "gamble" on whether to plan a softball game.

A subjectivistic derivation of the axioms, which is not related to gambling, was developed by the physicist Cox. In 1946 Cox deduced the axioms by assuming that $P(E \cap F)$ is a real valued function of $P(E|F)$ and $P(F)$. He then used an elegant argument based on functional analysis. Some researchers (in particular, those with a formal background in physics) use Cox's argument as the justification for subjective probability theory. I find Cox's assumptions contrived and difficult to understand, much less accept. Furthermore, Cox's definition is not operational. That is, the definition does not supply a rule according to which one can assign a probability.

Probabilities therefore become nebulous entities. On the other hand, anyone can readily understand and find compelling the simple coherency argument, and both de Finetti's and Lindley's definitions are clearly operational. It seems perhaps that those who use Cox's assumptions may be trying to lend objectivity to subjective probability. For example, Cox's disciple Jaynes (1979) says that "the probabilities ... are an entirely correct description of our state of knowledge... ."

In 1954 Savage developed axioms concerning states of nature, decisions, and consequences. From his axioms he deduced not only the axioms of probability theory but also the *maximum expected utility principle* used in decision theory to prescribe the "best" decision in the face of uncertainty. (Ramsey (1926) was actually the first to do this. However, his work was not well understood at the time.) Many find Savage's postulates convincing; however, they have recently been brought into question by Shafer (1986a). Some decision theorists prefer to accept probability theory on other grounds and add the axioms concerning utility due to von Neumann and Morgenstern (1947) in order to conclude the maximum expected utility principle.

Note that subjective probabilities, like all probabilities, are relative to information. The Yankees either will or will not win a given game. If I conclude that the probability of them winning is .4, that probability might be relative to the two teams' respective records up to the time of this game. When I learn that the Yankees are starting their star pitcher, I may change the probability to .55.

Finally, the subjectivistic approach does not preclude the importance of relative frequencies. In repeatable experiments such as coin tossing, many people believe that the sequence that represents the outcome of a number of repetitions of the experiment is "infinitely exchangeable." For example, given a number of tosses n, they believe that the probability of k heads occurring is the same regardless of the trials at which the heads occur. Based on the assumption of exchangeability, in 1931 de Finetti proved the *de Finetti representation theorem*. This theorem implies that, except in the case of very unusual prior beliefs (for example as when a person claims that he knows for certain the value of the probability of heads), one must believe that, when n is large, the probability of heads on the $(n + 1)$st trial is about equal to k/n, where k is the number of heads in the first n trials. I discuss the method for updating the prior belief in light of the frequency data in Neapolitan (1990). For practical purposes an "infinitely exchangeable sequence" is the same as a "collective."

2.2.4. Probabilistic Inference in Expert Systems

Probabilistic inference can be accomplished in expert systems by using *Bayes' theorem* which is readily obtained from the definition of conditional probability. If, for example, D stands for the presence of a certain disease, M stands for the presence of certain symptoms, this theorem states that

$$P(D|M) = \frac{P(M|D)\ P(D)}{P(M)}$$

Thus, if one knows that a certain set of diseases are mutually exclusive and exhaustive, one knows the probability of the symptoms given each disease, and one knows the prior probability of each disease, one can infer the probability of each disease given the symptoms. This was the inference procedure used in the early systems that used a simple Bayes model in the 1960s. Modern expert systems represent complex chains of probabilistic dependencies in influence diagrams (belief networks) and use sophisticated algorithms to infer probabilities and maximize expected utility. Neapolitan (1990) describes these algorithms, while Clemens (1991) discusses maximum expected utility and the influence diagram.

At one time extreme frequentists did not accept Bayesian inference because the prior probability is often based on subjective judgment obtained from the prior experience brought to the problem. In their quest for objectivity, these frequentists would perform inference using only techniques such as significance testing, confidence intervals, and likelihood maximization. For example, if they randomly sampled the heights of 100 American males and the average height turned out to be 4 feet, they would obtain a small interval around 4 feet in which they would be highly confident the true average height lies. As noted by Good (1983), they are sweeping their prior experience under the carpet in order to reach this absurd conclusion. A more reasonable solution would be to form a prior probability distribution on the value of this average, and to update this distribution in light of the sample using Bayes' theorem. The prior distribution is based on one's prior beliefs concerning the average height. For example, my subjective prior distribution is peaked around 5'9". The method for updating this distribution in light of the frequency data is discussed in Howard (1970). Today most researchers realize the need for subjective judgments and do not take the extreme frequentist view. On the other hand, although Bayesian inference is the primary probabilistic inferential strategy used in expert systems, in many problems concerning uncertainty Bayesian inference should not be used. For example, Fisher (1973) shows that Bayesian inference is inappropriate for evaluating the proposition that stars of each magnitude are dispersed at random over the celestial sphere. This is due to the fact that we are unable to assign meaningful prior probabilities to all the events relevant to the problem. He shows further that significance testing should be used in this case. In the following subsection on the Dempster-Shafer theory of evidence, I give another example in which Bayesian inference is inappropriate because we are unable to assign a probability to every event that is relevant to the problem.

A non-Bayesian probability-based inferential technique, which has been used in expert systems, is the *maximum entropy formalism* (Jaynes, 1979). However, as is the case for any technique, one must carefully analyze the problem to see if this technique is appropriate. I show in Neapolitan (1990) how a mechanical application of maximum entropy can lead to quite unacceptable results.

2.3. Uncertainty and Expert Systems

The previous subsection shows that if (1) we represent our uncertainty by real numbers, and (2) we are able to assign a real number to every event that is relevant to the problem, then we are bound to the axioms of probability theory. All reasonable efforts to numerically represent uncertainty lead to these axioms. What, then, should we conclude about the alternative approaches mentioned in the introduction?

Nonmonotonic reasoning, including nonmonotonic logic and default logic, does not represent uncertainty by real numbers and therefore does not in any apparent way violate the axioms of probability theory. In default logic if a rule implies a conclusion and its premises are found to be true, the conclusion is accepted as true until the premises of a stronger rule, which implies the negation of the conclusion, are found to be true.

In expert systems the probabilities are usually relative to infinitely exchangeable sequences (collectives). Even those who question the subjectivistic arguments ordinarily find the use of probability theory compelling in these cases. For example, a medical application would use the probability of a symptom given a disease that is the limiting ratio of the number of all individuals who have both the symptom and the disease to the number of all individuals who have the disease. In such an application we are interested in inferring which diseases are present. However, we do not want only a most likely set of diseases (as would be obtained using default logic). We would also want to know if the probability of that set is .99 or .1 in order to decide whether to treat that set or gather additional information. Therefore the use of default logic in such problems would be far less effective than the use of probability theory.

The question remains whether there are some other problems involving uncertain inference in artificial intelligence for which the use of either nonmonotonic logic or default logic is most appropriate. Pearl (1988) has shown that his logical approach to probability, termed ε-semantics, can better handle many of the problems for which default logic and nonmonotonic logic were specifically designed. Indeed, in his response to Cheeseman (1988), he shows how his approach can represent the "Yale Shooting" problem (Hanks and McDermott, 1986). This problem has been used to expose the shortcomings in the logical approaches. Another useful logical approach to probability has been developed by Halpern and Bacchus (Bacchus, 1990) discusses the relative merits of his approach, Pearl's approach, and the logical approaches that are not based on probability theory.

I end this subsection with the following quote from the statistician Lindley (1990):

> It was good to realize that workers in expert systems are beginning to understand that uncertainty statements must be combined according to the rules of probability. What is surprising is that they took so long to see this. The explanation presumably is that workers in new fields seem to think that everything is new and sometimes fail to recognize connections with older work.

I've included this quote for two reasons. First, I tend to agree with Lindley's explanation as to why it took researchers in expert systems so long to realize that probability theory should be used to handle uncertainty. Second, the statement "The explanation presumably..." is an example of default reasoning. Both Lindley and myself are using default reasoning to arrive at that explanation. I am quite content to accept this explanation (which was formed directly using my human reasoning) as long as I am not going to base an important decision on the explanation. On the other hand, if I was going to base an important decision on that explanation, I would gather additional information, carefully model the problem, and perform a probabilistic analysis.

2.4. The Dempster-Shafer Theory of Evidence

I liken my efforts to find usefulness in both the Dempster-Shafer theory and fuzzy set theory to my efforts to find entertainment value in silent movies and the opera. In the past, when I had viewed silent movies, all I had ever seen was people running around fast and hitting each other. To me opera had always meant listening to a large, armor-clad lady scream. Yet many of my friends, whose opinions I valued, found great pleasure in attending both silent movies and operas. Recently, I have made an effort to appreciate these two types of entertainment, and I have met with moderate success. When I first saw the Dempster-Shafer theory and fuzzy set theory, my initial inclination was to dismiss them both as being cases of failed thinking. However, since many bright researchers professed the value of these two disciplines, I made efforts to see their usefulness. The fruits of my efforts are summarized in this subsection and the following section. The point here is that we should never offhandedly dismiss any new formalism. Such a dogmatic attitude can only lead to intellectual stagnation.

Diaconis and Zabell (1986), Pearl (1989), and Fagin and Halpern (1989) have all shown that mechanical applications of the Dempster-Shafer theory can lead to quite unacceptable results. Shafer (1990), however, cautions that "the use of belief functions in practical problems requires metaphors that can guide us in relating practical problems to the theory and in assessing the strength of evidence numerically." That is, we must establish the metaphor before applying the theory and not simply perform a mechanical application of it. I will focus on the metaphor of the witness, who may or may not be reliable, in order to demonstrate a useful application of belief functions. My example is an elaboration of an example that appeared in (Shafer, 1986b).

Suppose that my friend Joe is known to be careful about what he says 80 percent of the time; the remaining 20 percent of the time he is careless and therefore statements he makes are unreliable. A similar situation holds for my friend Sam; however he is careful only 10 percent of the time. Suppose further that Joe walks into my office and says that the streets are slippery. Five minutes later Sam walks in and announces that they are not slippery. Let:

$+L=$ "streets are slippery"
$+J =$ "Joe is being careful"
$+S =$ "Sam is being careful"
$+B =$ "Joe says streets are slippery"
$+C =$ "Sam says streets are not slippery"
$p =$ prior probability that the streets are slippery
$q_1 =$ probability of Joe making an accurate statement when he is being careless
$q_2 =$ probability of Sam making an accurate statement when he is being careless.

The relationships in this problem can be represented by the belief network in Figure 3.1. The arcs in the network represent the fact that the value assumed by a node is independent of the values assumed by all other nodes in the network, except the given node's children, given values of the parents of the given node. For example, L, J, and S are independent, while B is independent of C given L and J. It is straightforward to show that

$$O(+L| + B, + C) = \frac{8 + 2q_1}{2(1-q_1)} \times \frac{9(1-q_2)}{1 + 9q_2} \times \frac{p}{1-p}$$

where O stands for odds. Thus, if we assume total prior ignorance in the streets being slippery by taking p equal to .5, assume that q_1 and q_2 are equal, let P^* stand for upper probability, and P_* stand for lower probability, we have that

$$P^*(+L| +B,+C) = .973 \quad \text{and} \quad P_*(+ L|+B,+ C) = .818$$

Furthermore, if we have any prior belief concerning the slipperiness of the streets, that prior belief can be used as p, and we would still obtain meaningful upper and lower probabilities.

However, since q_1 and q_2 are such vague probabilities, an argument can be made that there is no reason to assume that they are equal. If we do not make this assumption, it is clear that

$$P^*(+ L| +B,+ C) = 1 \quad \text{and} \quad P_*(+ L| + B, + C) = 0$$

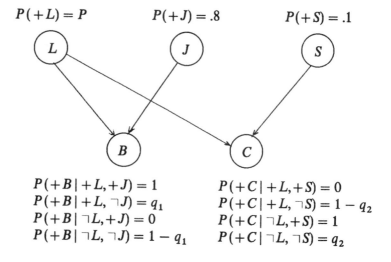

$$P(+L) = P \qquad\qquad P(+J) = .8 \qquad\qquad P(+S) = .1$$

$P(+B|+L,+J) = 1$

$P(+B|+L, \neg J) = q_1$

$P(+B| \neg L,+J) = 0$

$P(+B| \neg L, \neg J) = 1 - q_1$

$P(+C|+L,+S) = 0$

$P(+C|+L, \neg S) = 1 - q_2$

$P(+C| \neg L,+S) = 1$

$P(+C| \neg L, \neg S) = q_2$

Figure 3.1. A belief network representing the testimonies of Joe and Sam

These bounds are meaningless. Yet, since Joe is so much more reliable than Sam, we should tend to believe that the streets are slippery given the two testimonies. Even if one argues that q_1 and q_2 should be assumed to be equal, we can achieve a situation in which the upper and lower probabilities are meaningless by replacing Sam with a thermometer that is accurate 10% of the time, and by assuming that the reading on the thermometer indicates that it is too warm for the streets to be slippery. We would then have that $P(+ C| + L,+ S) = 0$ $P(+ C| + L, \neg S) = q_2$, $P(+C| \neg L, + S) = q_3$, and $P(+ C| \neg L, \neg S) = q_2$, where q_2 is now the probability of a warm reading on a broken thermometer, and q_3 is the probability of it being warm on a day when the streets are not slippery. In this case, no reasonable assumptions yield meaningful upper and lower probabilities.

There is not enough space to describe the mechanics of the Dempster-Shafer method in this paper. That description appears in many places, including Shafer's (1976) original monograph. When this method is applied to the above problem, we obtain $Bel(+L) = .783$ and $Plaus (+L) = .978$, where Bel stands for *belief* and $Plaus$ stand for *plausibility*. These informative values are obtained regardless of whether S stands for Sam's or the thermometer's reliability. Thus the Dempster-Shafer method is able to give meaningful results while the use of upper and lower probabilities using Bayesian analysis is not.

An alternative solution to the above problem would be to represent our uncertainty in the probabilities of the qs by probability distributions on the probabilities and to compute an expected value and variance for $P(+L| +B, +C)$. I've developed a method for doing this in Neapolitan and Kenevan (1990), Neapolitan (1991b), and Neapolitan and Kenevan (1991). The method, however, is most appropriate for the case where the probabilities are relative to infinitely exchangeable sequences, and we have beliefs concerning the probabilities that are based on experience with these sequences. It is difficult to conceive of distributions for the probabilities of the qs.

An often stated criticism of Dempster-Shafer theory is that Bel and Plaus are nebulous entities. That is, they are not probabilities of the event of interest or even lower and upper probabilities of that event. Therefore, what meaning can we attach to them? This criticism, however, does not pertain when the strength of evidence can be compared with the example of witnesses and testimonies. In the example above, $Bel(+L)$ is the conditional probability of $(+J, > S)$ (the event in the space (J,S) which is compatible with only $+L$) given $> (+J,+S)$. (We know that it is false that they are both being careful because their testimonies conflict.) Thus we become confident that the streets are slippery due to this high conditional probability that Joe is being careful and Sam is not. This is similar to the way we obtain confidence due to significance testing. Given the assumption that the stars of each magnitude are distributed at random over the celestial sphere, the probability of our actual observations is very small. Thus we become highly confident that they are not distributed at random. (See Fisher [1973] for a detailed analysis of this problem.) This confidence is not due to computing a low probability that they are distributed at random; rather, like the above application of Dempster-Shafer theory, it is due to a low probability in another space. Many statisticians have long accepted the usefulness of significance testing. In the same way we should accept the usefulness of Dempster-Shafer theory.

Notice, however, that in general $Bel(+L)$ is not the conditional probability of $(+J, > S)$ given all our information as would be most desirable. That is, our total information $(+B, +C)$ implies $> (+J,+S)$, but in general $> (+J, +S)$ does not imply $(+B, +C)$. It turns out that if all conditional probabilities of evidence are like the ones describing Joe and Sam (that is, they form a sequence $(1,q,0,1-q)$ or $(0,1-q,1,q)$ as in Figure 3.1), and if we represent prior ignorance in the probability of $+L$ by taking $p = .5$, then $Bel(+L)$ is equal to the conditional probability of $(+J, > S)$ given $(+B, +C)$. However, when we have conditional probabilities such as the ones involving the thermometer, this is no longer the case.

A practitioner can add the Dempster-Shafer theory to his or her bag of tools alongside Bayes' theorem, significance testing, and the others; however it should be used only when a careful analysis indicates that it is the correct tool. Just as the use of confidence intervals can lead to an unacceptable conclusion when used to analyze a sample of heights of 100 Americans, and Bayesian analysis can lead to an unacceptable conclusion when used to analyze the probability that the stars of each magnitude are distributed at random in the celestial sphere, Dempster-Shafer theory can lead to an unacceptable conclusion (as discussed in the references noted at the beginning of this subsection) when applied in the wrong situation. Unfortunately, as discussed by Pearl (1989), some Dempster-Shafer practitioners have done just that in applications to rule-based expert systems.

3. APPROXIMATE (FUZZY) INFERENCE

Fuzzy set theory and fuzzy logic address a fundamentally different class of problems from that addressed by probability theory. Probability theory deals with propositions that are either true or false. We are simply uncertain as to whether they are true. The real number we attach to the proposition is a measure of how much we believe it to be true. Fuzzy set theory, on the other hand, deals with propositions that have *vague meaning*. For example, if a physician says that there is a good chance the tumor is cancerous when the growth is quite large, the expression "good chance" is a statement of uncertainty and can be represented by a probability. However, although the term "quite large" is not precise, it is not an expression of uncertainty. We assume that we have measured the growth and know exactly how large it is. The question is how much the growth's particular size fits the physician's vague description of "quite large."

Zadeh (Yager et al., 1987) addresses such problems with his *fuzzy set theory*. Fuzzy set theory associates a real number between 0 and 1 with the membership of a particular element in a set. For example, let X be the set of all integers representing the concept "several." Are 3,

4 and 5 definitely in X and all other numbers definitely not in X? According to fuzzy set theory, the answer is no. Rather, the set memberships might be represented as follows:

$$.1\,|\,1 \quad .3\,|\,2 \quad .8\,|\,3 \quad .9\,|\,4 \quad .6\,|\,5 \quad .4\,|\,6 \quad .3\,|\,7 \quad .1\,|\,8$$

where the integer is on the right and its fuzzy set membership in X is on the left. This number is not a representation of uncertainty. We can never find out for certain whether 5 is in X. Rather, it is always partially in X.

Some argue that fuzzy set theory can be given a probabilistic interpretation. For example, if we asked 10,000 people if 5 represented "several," the membership of 5 in X would be the relative frequency with which they answered yes. The point in fuzzy set theory is that they could not answer definitely yes or no. The following example illustrates this concept more concretely.

Suppose we had a kennel in which there were 100 dogs, of which exactly 50 were full-blooded beagles. If we picked a dog at random from the kennel, the probability of that dog being a full-blooded beagle would be .5. Once we picked the dog and inspected it, we would know for certain whether it was a beagle. On the other hand, if one parent of a particular dog was a full-blooded collie and the other parent was a full-blooded beagle, then the dog's fuzzy set membership in the set of beagles would be .5. There is no uncertainty that we can eventually resolve. We know for certain that its fuzzy set membership is .5.

There is nothing contrived about the notion of fuzzy sets. Rather the notion has a long tradition of representing judgments. Olympic divers are judged on a scale of 1 to 10, where 10 is a perfect performance (a set membership of 1 in the set of perfect dives). In the movie *10* the number 10 was meant to represent the fact that the actress Bo Derek has a set membership of 1 in the set of beautiful women. If I maintain that Demi Moore is a 9, this means that I feel she is beautiful but not quite as beautiful as Bo Derek. The number has nothing to do with probability. That is, the 9 does not mean that, when I next view Demi Moore, there is a 1 in 10 chance that I will find out for certain she is really ugly. When I am asked to review articles, I am asked to judge their creativity on a scale of 1 to 5. Again, the number I assign represents partial set membership. When a physician says that there is a 95 percent chance that a back operation would improve one's condition at least 80 percent, the 95 percent represents a probability while the 80 percent represents fuzzy set membership.

The idea of being able to assign truth values other than true and false (as is done in fuzzy logic) has a long tradition in mathematics. It was after Kurt Gödel (1931) proved that it is impossible to establish the truth or falsity of every conceivable mathematical theorem by any route founded on traditional logic, that mathematicians first began inventing logical systems in which a statement can be something other than true or false. The simplest of these was a trivalent logical system in which a statement can be either true, false or in between.

Cheeseman (1986, 1988) has forcefully shown that fuzzy set theory is sometimes incorrectly applied to certain problems that really require uncertain inference. For example, suppose our goal is to determine Mary's age given that someone said "Mary is young." Since each age has a set membership in the set of "young ages," one may be tempted to apply fuzzy set theory to the problem. However, as noted by Cheeseman, we are conditioning on the proposition that it was said that Mary is young. Our goal is to determine the probability distribution of her age based on this information. This is a problem in uncertain inference. See Cheeseman (1986) for a solution to this problem.

Cheeseman et al. (1988), however, go too far when they imply that their Bayesian classification system subsumes fuzzy set theory. Cheeseman's (1990) thesis is that in a particular linguistic community a certain fraction of the poeple who are called tall are 73″ in height. This fraction is $P(73″\,|\,tall)$. If we are then able to obtain the prior probability of being called *tall* and the prior probability of a person being 73″ *tall*, we would have

$$P(tall\,|\,73″) = \frac{P(73″\,|\,tall)\;P(tall)}{P(73″)}$$

Cheeseman equates this computed value, $P(tall\,|\,73″)$, with $\mu_{tall}\,(73″)$, the fuzzy set membership of 73″ in the set of tall heights. He goes on to state (Cheeseman, 1990):

Note that if there is an existing class shared by a linguistic community (e.g., tall) then this class can be described to someone by giving them the following probability function: $pr\,(\text{tall}\,|\,\text{height} = x)$ — this says clearly what you mean by "tall" and can be interpreted as the probability that someone in the community would describe someone as *tall* if their height is x.

However, as I've already noted, $\mu_{tall}(73'')$ is *not* the percentage of people who would call a 73" person tall. This can be seen most clearly with the beagle example. No one would call a dog who is half beagle and half collie a full-blooded beagle. Everyone would call him a half-beagle.

Probabilities such as $P(tall \mid 73'')$ are useful in applications such as Auto Class (Cheeseman et al., 1988). However, they are not fuzzy set memberships. Cheeseman's justification for the axioms of probability theory is the argument due to Cox, and Cox (1946) states that "Probability is recognized also as providing a measure of the reasonable expectation of an event in a single trial." Thus, like all the approaches to probability theory, Cox recognizes probability is our measure of how certain we are that it will happen. Fuzzy set theory has nothing to do with this situation.

Equating probabilities such as $P(tall \mid 73'')$ with fuzzy set memberships such as $\mu_{tall}(73'')$ creates operational as well as theoretical problems. Suppose that we say that $\mu_{young}(21 \text{ years}) = .8$ and $\mu_{adult}(21 \text{ years}) = .3$. Then, taking fuzzy intersection, we have that

$$\mu_{young \cap adult}(21 \text{ years}) = \min(.8, .3) = .3$$

One the other hand, suppose $P(young \mid 21 \text{ years}) = .8$ and $P(adult \mid 21 \text{ years}) = .3$. Then, according to Cheeseman's interpretation of these probabilities, if a person is picked at random, the probability that he will describe a twenty-one-year-old as *young* is .8 and the probability that he would describe a twenty-one-year-old as an *adult* is .3. However, there is no reason to make the assumption that $P(young \text{ and } adult \mid 21 \text{ years}) = .3$. This assumption would mean that whenever a person described a twenty-one-year-old as an *adult* he would also describe him as *young*. Actually, I would expect quite the contrary. Thus we must keep the concepts of probability and fuzzy set membership separate. Taking the minimum makes sense when we are talking about set membership; however it does not hold when we are talking about probability.

Given that fuzzy set theory does address a fundamentally different class of problems from that of probability theory, the question remains whether there exists useful inference problems for which fuzzy set theory is applicable. I offer the following example taken from Bellman and Zadeh (1970). Suppose we have the constraints: $C_1 = $ "x should be close to 4" and $C_2 = $ "x should be close to 6," and the goals: $G_1 = $ "x should be close to 5" and $G_2 = $ "x should be close to 3." If we are restricted to the set of integers, these constraints and goals can be

Table 3.1. The fuzzy set memberships in G_1, G_2, C_1, and C_2

X	1	2	3	4	5	6	7	8	9	10
μ_{G_1}	0	0.1	0.4	0.8	1.0	0.7	0.4	0.2	0	0
μ_{G_2}	0.1	0.6	1.0	0.9	0.8	0.6	0.5	0.3	0	0
μ_{C_1}	0.3	0.6	0.9	1.0	0.8	0.7	0.5	0.3	0.2	0.1
μ_{C_2}	0.2	0.4	0.6	0.7	0.9	1.0	0.8	0.6	0.4	0.2

Table 3.2. The fuzzy set memberships in D

X	1	2	3	4	5	6	7	8	9	10
μ_D	0	0.1	0.4	0.7	0.8	0.6	0.4	0.2	0	0

represented by the fuzzy sets in Table 3.1. If we take $G_1 \cap G_2 \cap C_1 \cap C_2$, we obtain the fuzzy set D, which appears in Table 3.2. This fuzzy set is our decision. Since no x has full membership in D, we can define our optimal decision as being the x *that maximizes* μ_D. In this case the decision is to take x equal to 5. Notice that this problem has nothing to do with uncertainty; it is strictly a problem in approximate set membership. Thus I prefer to call the inference in this type of problem "approximate" and reserve the expression "uncertain inference" for applications of probability theory.

Finally, note that there are situations in which we manipulate real numbers in the face of uncertainty in which we do not use probability theory. For example, in my other paper in this volume (coauthored with James Kenevan), "A Model Theoretic Approach to Propositional Fuzzy Logic Using Beth Tableux," we assume the exact truth value of a proposition is somewhere in the interval [0,1]; however, due to our ignorance of the system under consideration, this truth value is known only to lie in some closed interval. We then develop a proof theory that deduces a closed interval containing the truth value of some proposition of interest from known closed intervals containing the truth value of other propositions. We are manipulating real numbers to narrow our uncertainty. This uncertainty, however, is the same kind of uncertainty one has when using an imprecise instrument; it is not the type of uncertainty addressed by probability theory. If I know that a ruler is accurate to .1 inches, and I measure one board to be 1 foot long and a second board to be 2 feet long, then I can conclude that the length of the two boards together is between 2 feet 10 inches and 3 feet 2 inches. Probability theory is compelling when we assign real numbers as measures of belief in propositions; probability theory is not relevant to manipulating bounds on unknown values.

Keywords: Bayesian approach, belief network, coherency, Dempster-Shafer theory, expert system, fuzzy logic, fuzzy set theory, influence diagram, probability, frequentistic interpretation, significance testing, subjectivist, collective

BIBLIOGRAPHY

Bacchus, F. (1990). *Representing and Reasoning with Probabilistic Knowledge.* Cambridge, MA: MIT Press.

Bellman, R.E. and L.A. Zadeh. (1970). Decision making in a fuzzy environment. *Management Science,* **17,** 141–164.

Buchanan, B. G. and E. H. Shortliffe. (1984). *Rule–Based Expert Systems.* Reading, MA: Addison-Wesley.

Carnap, R. (1950). *Logical Foundations of Probability.* Chicago: University of Chicago Press.

Cheeseman, P. (1986). Probabilistic vs. fuzzy reasoning. In L. N. Kanal and J. F. Lemmer (eds.): *Uncertainty in Artificial Intelligence.* Amsterdam: North-Holland.

Cheeseman, P. (1988). An Inquiry into Computer Understanding (with responses). *Computational Intelligence,* vol. 4.

Cheeseman, P. (1990). Private correspondence.

Cheeseman, P., J. Kelly, M. Self, J. Stutz, W. Taylor, and D. Freeman. (1988). Auto Class: A Bayesian classification system. *Proceedings of the Fifth International Conference on Machine Learning.* University of Michigan, Ann Arbor.

Clemens, R. T. (1991). *Making Hard Decisions.* Boston, MA: PWS-Kent.

Cohen, P. R. (1985). *Heuristic Reasoning about Uncertainty: An Artificial Intelligence Approach.* Boston: Pitman.

Cox, R. T. (1946). Probability, frequency, and reasonable expectation. *American Journal of Physics,* vol. 14, no. 1.

Cox, R. T. (1979). Of inference and inquiry. An essay in inductive logic. In R. D. Levine and M. Tribus (eds.): *The Maximum Entropy Formalism.* Cambridge: MIT Press.

Diaconis, P. and S. Zabell. (1986) Some alternatives to Bayes' rule. In B. Grofman and G. Owen (eds.): *Proceedings of Second University of California, Irvine, Conference on Political Economy.* Greenwich, CT: JAI Press.

Fagin, R. and J. Y. Halpern. (1989). A new approach to updating beliefs. IBM Res. Rep. RJ7222, IBM Almaden Research Center, San Jose, CA.

Fine, T. L. (1973). *Theories of Probability.* New York: Academic Press.

Finetti, B. de. (1931). La prévision: ses lois logiques, ses sources subjectives. *Annales de l'Institute Henri Poincaré,* vol. 7.

Finetti, B. de. (1964). Foresight: Its logical laws, its subjective sources. In H. E. Kyburg, Jr., and H. E. Smokler (eds.): *Studies in Subjective Probability.* New York: Wiley.

Finetti, B. de. (1972). *Probability, Induction, and Statistics.* New York: Wiley.

Fisher, R. A. (1973). *Statistical Methods and Scientific Inference.* New York: Hafner Press.

Geneva Conference. (1937). Colloque Consacré au Calcul des Probabilités. Proceedings of a conference at the Université de Genève in 1937. The papers concerning the foundations of probability were published in the series *Actualités Scientifiques et Industrielles,* vol. 735, Hermann (1938).

Gödel, K. (1931). Über Formal Unentscheidbar Sätze der Principia Mathematicae und Zerwandter Systeme I. *Monatshefte für Mathematik und Physik,* vol. 38.

Good, I. J. (1983). *Good Thinking.* Minneapolis: University of Minnesota.

Gorry, G. (197) Computer-assisted clinical decision making. *Methods of Information in Medicine,* vol. 12.

Hanks, S. and D. McDermott. (1986). Default reasoning, nonmonotonic logics, and the frame problem. *Proceedings of the National Conference on Artificial Intelligence,* Philadelphia.

Heckerman, D. E. (1990). *Probabilistic Similarity Networks.* Ph.D. dissertation, Department of Medical Information Sciences, Stanford University.

Howard, R. A. (1970). Decision analysis: Perspectives on inference, decision, and experimentation. *Proceedings of the IEEE,* vol. 58, no. 5.

Howard, R. A. and J. Matheson. (1981). Influence diagrams. In R. A. Howard, and J. Matheson (eds.): *Readings on the Principles and Applications of Decision Analysis,* vol. 2. Menlo Park, CA: Strategic Decisions Group.

Jaynes, E. T. (1979). Where do we stand on maximum entropy. In R. D. Levine and M. Tribus. (eds.): *The Maximum Entropy Formalism.* Cambridge: MIT Press.

Kanal, L. N. and J. F. Lemmer (eds.). (1986). *Uncertainty in Artificial Intelligence.* Amsterdam: North-Holland

Keynes, J. M. (1921). *A Treatise on Probability.* London: Macmillan.

Kerrich. J. E. (1946). *An Experimental Introduction to the Theory of Probability.* Copenhagen: Einer Munksgaard.

Kolmogorov, A. N. (1933). Grundbegriffe der Wahrscheinlichkeitsrechnung. *Ergebnisse der Wahrscheinlichkeitsrechnung.* Wien: Springer.

Lambalgan, M. van (1987). *Random Sequences.* Ph.D. dissertation, University of Amsterdam.

Laplace, P. S. de. (1820). *Théorie Analytique des Probabilités,* Paris. English translation: *A Philosophical Essay on Probabilities.* New York: Dover.

Lauritzen, S. L. and D. J. Spiegelhalter. (1988). Local computation with probabilities in graphical structures and their applications to expert systems. *Journal of the Royal Statistical Society B,* vol. 50, no. 2.

Lindley, D. V. (1965). *Introduction to Probability and Statistics From a Bayesian Viewpoint*. London: Cambridge University Press.

Lindley, D. V. (1985). *Making Decisions*. New York: Wiley.

Lindley, D. V. (1990). Private correspondence.

McDermott, J. (1982). R1: A Rule-Based Configurer of Computer Systems. *Artificial Intelligence*, vol. 19. no. 1.

McDermott, J. and J. Doyle. (1980). Non-monotonic logic. *Artificial Intelligence*, vol. 13, no. 1–2.

Mises, R. von (1919). Grundlagen der Wahrscheinlichkeitsrechnung. *Math. Z.*, vol. 5.

Neapolitan, R. E. (1990). *Probabilistic Reasoning in Expert Systems*. New York: Wiley.

Neapolitan, R. E. (1991a). A limiting frequency approach to probability based on the weak law of large numbers. Submitted to the *Philosophy of Science Journal*.

Neapolitan, R. E. (1991b). Propagation of Variances in Belief Networks. *Proceedings of SPIE Conference on Artificial Intelligence*, Orlando, FL.

Neapolitan, R. E. and J. R. Kenevan. (1990). Computation of Variances in Causal Networks. *Proceedings of the Sixth Conference on Uncertainty in Artificial Intelligence*. Cambridge: MIT.

Neapolitan, R. E. and J. R. Kenevan. (1991). Investigation of Variances in Belief Networks. *Proceedings of the Seventh Conference on Uncertainty in Artificial Intelligence*. University of California at Los Angeles.

Neumann, J. von and O. Morgenstern. (1947). *Theory of Games and Economic Behavior*. Princeton University Press.

Norusis, M. and J. Jacquez. (1975). Diagnosis 1: Symptom non-independence in mathematical models for diagnosis. *Computers and Biomedical Research*, vol. 8.

Pearl, J. (1986). Fusion, propagation, and structuring in belief networks. *Artificial Intelligence*, vol. 29.

Pearl, J. (1988). *Probabilistic Reasoning in Intelligent Systems*. San Mateo, CA: Morgan Kaufmann.

Pearl, J. (1989). Reasoning with belief functions: An analysis of compatibility. Los Angeles: UCLA Technical Report R-136.

Popper, K. R. (1935). *Logik der Forschung*. Vienna: Springer English translation: *Logic of Scientific Discovery*. Hutchinson, 1975.

Ramsey, F. P. (1926). Truth and probability. In F. P. Ramsey (1931), *The Foundations of Mathematics*. Guildford and Esher: Billing and Sons.

Reichenbach, H. (1949). *The Theory of Probability, and Inquiry into the Logical and Mathematical Foundations of Probability*. Berkeley: University of California Press.

Reiter, R. (1987). Nonmonotonic Reasoning. *Annual Review of Computer Science*, vol. 2.

Savage, L. J. (1954) *The Foundations of Statistics*. New York: Wiley.

Schachter, R. D. (1988). Probabilistic Inference and Influence Diagrams. *Operations Research*, vol. 36, no. 4.

Shafer, G. (1976). *A Mathematical Theory of Evidence*. Princeton University Press.

Shafer, G. (1986a). Savage Revisited. *Statisical Science*, vol. 1.

Shafer, G. (1986b). Probabilistic judgement in artificial intelligence. In L. N. Kanal, and J. F. Lemmer (eds.): *Uncertainty in Artificial Intelligence*. Amsterdam: North-Holland.

Shafer, G. (1990). Perspectives on the theory and practice of belief functions. School of Business Working Paper no. 218, University of Kansas, Lawrence.

Shortliffe, E. (1976). *Computer-based Medical Consultations: MYCIN*. New York: North-Holland.

Weatherford, R. (1982). *Philosophical Foundations of Probability*. London: Routledge & Kegan Paul.

Yager, R. R., S. Ovchinnikov, R. M. Tong, and H. T. Nguyen (eds.). (1987). *Fuzzy Sets and Applications: Selected Papers by L. A. Zadeh*. New York: Wiley.

4 Valuation-based systems: A framework for managing uncertainty in expert systems

Prakash P. SHENOY
School of Business
University of Kansas
Lawrence, KS 66045-2003, USA

Abstract. This paper describes valuation-based systems for managing uncertainty in expert systems. In valuation-based systems, we represent knowledge using functions called valuations. Making inferences involves using two operators called *combination* and *marginalization*. Combination tells us how to combine valuations to obtain the joint valuation. Marginalization tells us how to coarsen a valuation by eliminating some variables. Making inferences from a valuation-based system can be simply described as finding the marginal of the joint valuation for each variable in the system. We state some simple axioms that combination and marginalization need to satisfy to enable us to compute marginals using local computation. We describe a fusion algorithm for computing marginals using local computation. Finally, we describe how Bayesian probability theory, Dempster-Shafer's theory of belief functions, and Spohn's theory of epistemic beliefs fit in the framework of valuation-based systems.

1. INTRODUCTION

The main goal of this paper is to describe the framework of valuation-based systems (VBS) and its use for managing uncertainty in expert systems.

Valuation-based systems were first introduced in Shenoy (1989). In VBS, we represent knowledge by functions called valuations. We make inferences using two operators called combination and marginalization. Combination corresponds to aggregation of knowledge and marginalization corresponds to coarsening of knowledge. We make inferences in VBS by computing the marginal of the joint valuation for each variable in the system. The joint valuation is the valuation obtained by combining all valuations in the knowledge base.

The framework of VBS is general enough to include many problems. In this paper, we describe how Bayesian probability theory, Dempster-Shafer's theory of belief functions, and Spohn's theory of epistemic beliefs fit in the framework of VBS. Zadeh (1979) and Dubois and Prade (1990) describe how possibility theory fits in the framework of VBS.

Besides managing uncertainty in expert systems, VBS can also be used to represent optimization problems (Shenoy, 1991b), propositional logic (Shenoy, 1990a, 1900b), Bayesian decision theory (Shenoy, 1990c, 1990d), and constraint satisfaction problems (Shenoy and Shafer, 1988).

When there are many variables in a VBS, computing the joint valuation is computationally intractable. However, if combination and marginalization satisfy certain axioms, then it is possible to compute the marginals of the joint valuation using local computation, that is, without explicitly computing the joint valuation. In this paper, we describe three axioms that enable local computation. These axioms were first described in Shenoy and Shafer (1990).We also describe a fusion algorithm for computing the marginals using local computation. The fusion algorithm is algorithmically smilar to the Markov tree propagation described in Shenoy and Shafer (1990). The novelty of the fusion algorithm is that there are no references to either Markov trees or hypertrees.

An outline of this paper is as follows. Section 2 introduces the framework of valuation-based systems. Section 3 discusses three axioms that enable local computation. Section 4 examines fusion algorithm for computing marginals of the joint valuation. Section

5 describes how probability theory fits in the framework of VBS. Section 6 shows how Dempster-Shafer's theory of belief functions fits in the framework of VBS. Section 7 describes how Spohn's theory of epistemic beliefs fits in the framework of VBS. Section 8 contains concluding remarks. Finally, Section 9 contains a proof of the main theorem in the paper.

2. THE FRAMEWORK OF VALUATION-BASED SYSTEMS

In a VBS, we represent knowledge by functions called valuations. Valuations are functions that assign values to the elements of frames for sets of variables. We make inferences in a VBS using two operators called combination and marginalization. We use these operators on valuations.

Variables and Configurations. We use the symbol ω_x for the set of possible values of a variable X, and we call ω_x the *frame for* X. We are concerned with a finite set K of variables, and we assume that all the variables in K have finite frames.

Given a nonempty set h of variables, let ω_h denote the Cartesian product of ω_x for X in h; $\omega_h = \times \{\omega_x \mid X \in h\}$. We call ω_h the *frame for* h. We call the elements of ω_h *configurations of* h.

Valuations. Given a subset h of variables, there is a set v_h. We call the elements of v_h *valuations for* h. Let v denote the set of all valuations, that is, $v = \cup\{v_h \mid h \subseteq K\}$. If V is a valuation for h, and $X \in h$, then we say V *bears on* X.

Valuations are primitives in our abstract framework and as such require no definition. But as we shall see shortly, they are objects that can be combined and marginalized. Intuitively, a valuation for h represents some knowledge about the variables in h.

Proper Valuations. For each $h \subseteq K$, there is a subset γ_h of v_h whose elements are called *proper valuations for* h. Let γ denote $\cup\{\gamma_h \mid h \subseteq K\}$, the set of all proper valuations.

Intuitively, a proper valuation represents knowledge that is internally consistent. The notion of proper valuations is important as it enables us to define combinability of valuations, and it allows us to constrain the definitions of combination and marginalization to meaningful operators.

Examples of proper valuations are a *potential*, that is, a function P: $\omega_h \to [0,1]$ that is not identically zero for all configurations, a *basic probability assignment (bpa) potential*, that is, a function $M:2^{\omega_h} \to [0,1]$ (where 2^{ω_h} denotes the set of all nonempty subsets of ω_h) such that $M(\alpha)$ is not identically zero for all $\alpha \in 2^{\omega_h}$, and a *disbelief potential*, that is, a function $\delta:\omega_h \to N$ (where N denotes the set of natural numbers).

Combination. We assume there is a mapping $\otimes: v \times v \to v$, called *combination*, such that

(i) if G and H are valuations for g and h respectively, then $G \otimes H$ is a valuation for $g \cup h$;

(ii) if either G or H is not a proper valuation, then $G \otimes H$ is not a proper valuation; and

(iii) if G and H are both proper valuations, then $G \otimes H$ may or may not be a proper valuation.

If $G \otimes H$ is not a proper valuation, then we say that G and H are *not combinable*. If $G \otimes H$ is a proper valuation, then we say that G and H are *combinable* and that $G \otimes H$ is the *combination* of G and H.

Intuitively, combination corresponds to aggregation of knowledge. If G and H are proper valuations for g and h representing knowledge about variables in g and h, respectively, then $G \otimes H$ represents the aggregated knowledge about variables in $g \cup h$.

For potentials, combination is pointwise multiplication. For bpa potentials, combination is Dempster's rule (Dempster, 1966). For disbelief potentials, combination is pointwise addition (Shenoy, 1991a).

Marginalization. We assume that for each $h \subseteq K$, and for each $X \in h$, there is a mapping $\downarrow (h - \{X\}): v_h \to v_{h-\{x\}}$, called *marginalization* to $h - \{X\}$ such that:

(i) If H is a valuation for h, then $H^{\downarrow(h-\{X\})}$ is a valuation for $h - \{X\}$; and

(ii) $H^{\downarrow(h-\{X\})}$ is a proper valuation if and only if H is a proper valuation. We call $H^{\downarrow(h-\{X\})}$ the *marginal of H for* $h - \{X\}$.

Intuitively, marginalization corresponds to coarsening of knowledge. If H is a valuation for h representing some knowledge about variables in h, and $X \in h$, then $H^{\downarrow(h-\{X\})}$ represents the knowledge about variables in $h - \{X\}$ implied by H if we disregard variable H.

In the case of potentials, marginalization from h to $h - \{X\}$ is addition over the frame for X. In the belief-function case, marginalization from h to $h - \{X\}$ is minimization over the frame for X.

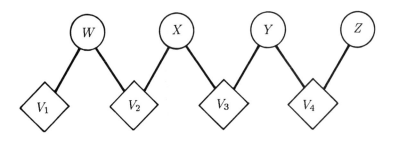

Figure 4.1. A valuation network for a VBS consisting of valuations V_1 for $\{W\}$, V_2 for $\{W, X\}$ V_3 for $\{X, Y\}$ and V_4 for $\{Y, Z\}$

In summary, a *valuation-based system* consists of a 3-tuple $\{\{V_1, ..., {}_m\}, \otimes, \downarrow\}$ where $\{V_1, ..., V_m\}$ is a collection of valuations such that valuation V_i is for h_i, $i = 1, ..., m$, $\otimes$ is the combination operator, and $\downarrow$ is the marginalization operator.

Valuation Networks. A graphical depiction of a valuation-based system is called a *valuation network*. In a valuation network, variables are represented by circular nodes, and valuations are represented by diamond-shaped nodes. Also each valuation node is connected by an undirected edge to each variable node that it bears on. Figure 4.1 shows a valuation network for a VBS that consists of valuations V_1 for $\{W\}$, V_2 for $\{W, X\}$, V_3 for $\{X, Y\}$, and V_4 for $\{Y, Z\}$.

Making Inference in VBS. In a VBS, the combination of all valuations, if proper, is called the joint valuation for each variable in the system.

If there are n variables in the system, and each variable has two configurations in its frame, then there are 2^n configurations of all variables. Hence, it is not computationally feasible to compute the joint valuation when there are a large number of variables. In Section 4, we describe an algorithm for computing marginals of the joint valuation without explicitly computing the joint valuation. So that this algorithm gives us the correct answers, we require combination and marginalization to satisfy theree axioms. The axioms and the algorithm are described in the next two sections, respectively.

3. AXIOMS FOR LOCAL COMPUTATION

In this section, we state three simple axioms that enable local computation of marginals of the joint valuation. These axioms were first formulated by Shenoy and Shafer (1990).

Axiom A1 (*Commutativity and associativity of combination*): Suppose G, H, K are valuations for g, h, and k, respectively. Then

$$G \otimes H = H \otimes G \text{ and } G \otimes (H \otimes K) = (G \otimes H) \otimes K$$

Axiom A2 (*Order of deletion does not matter*): Suppose G is a valuation for g, and suppose X_1, $X_2 \in g$. Then

$$(G^{\downarrow(g - \{X_1\})})^{\downarrow(g - \{X_1, X_2\})} = (G^{\downarrow(g - \{X_2\})})^{\downarrow(g - \{X_1, X_2\})}$$

Axiom A3 (*Distributivity of marginalization over combination*): Suppose G and H are valuations for g and h, respectively, suppose $X \in h$, and suppose $X \notin g$. Then

$$(G \otimes H)^{\downarrow(g \cup h) - \{X\}} = G \otimes (H^{\downarrow(h - \{X\})})$$

One implication of Axiom A1 is that when we have multiple combinations of valuations, we can write it without using parenthesis. For example, $(...((V_1 \otimes V_2) \otimes V_3) \otimes ... \otimes V_m)$ can be written simply as $\otimes \{V_i | i = 1, ..., m\}$ or as $V_1 \otimes ... \otimes V_m$, that is, we need not indicate the order in which the combinations are carried out.

If we regard marginalization as a coarsening of a valuation by deleting variables, then Axiom A2 says that the order in which the variables are deleted does not matter. One implication of this axiom is that $(G^{\downarrow(g - \{X_1\})})^{\downarrow(g - \{X_1, X_2\})}$ can be written simply as $G^{\downarrow(g - \{X_1, X_2\})}$, that is, we need not indicate the order in which the variables are deleted.

Axiom A3 is the crucial axiom that makes local computation possible. Axiom A3 states that computation of $(G \otimes H)^{\downarrow(g \cup h) - \{X\}}$ can be accomplished without having to compute $G \otimes H$. The combination operation in $G \otimes H$ is on the frame for $g \cup h$ whereas the combination operation in $G \otimes (H^{\downarrow(h - \{X\})})$ is on the frame for $(g \cup h) - \{X\}$.

4. A FUSION ALGORITHM FOR COMPUTING MARGINALS USING LOCAL COMPUTATION

In this section, we describe an algorithm for making inferences from a VBS using local computation. Suppose $\{\{V_1, ..., V_m\}, \otimes, \downarrow\}$ is a VBS with n variables and m valuations. Suppose that combination and marginalization satisfy the three axioms stated in Section 3. Suppose we have to compute the marginal of the joint valuation for variable X, $(V_1 \otimes ... \otimes V_m)^{\downarrow\{X\}}$. The basic idea of the fusion algorithm is to successively delete all variables but X from the VBS. The variables may be deleted in any sequence. Axiom 2 tells us that all deletion sequences lead to the same answers. But different deletion sequences may involve different computational costs. We will comment on good deletion sequences at the end of this section.

When we delete a variable, we have to do a "fusion" operation on the valuations. Consider a set of k valuations $A_1, ..., A_k$. Suppose A_i is a valuation for h_i. Let $\text{Fus}_x\{A_1, ..., A_k\}$ denote the collection of valuations after fusing the valuations in the set $\{A_1, ..., A_k\}$ with respect to variable X. Then

$$\text{Fus}_X\{A_1, ..., A_k\} = \{A^{\downarrow(h-\{X\})}\} \cup \{A_i | X \notin_i\}$$

where $A = \otimes\{A_i | X \in h_i\}$, and $h = \cup\{h_i | X \in h_i\}$. After fusion, the set of valuations is changed as follows. All valuations that bear on X are combined and the resulting valuation is marginalized such that X is eliminated from its domain. The valuations that do not bear on X remain unchanged.

We are ready to state the main theorem.

Theorem 1. Suppose $\{\{V_1, ..., V_m\}, \otimes, \downarrow\}$ is a VBS where V_i is a valuation for h_i, and suppose $\otimes$ and $\downarrow$ satisfy axioms A1–A3. Let $\mathcal{K}$ denote $h_1 \cup ... \cup h_m$. Suppose $X \in \mathcal{K}$, and suppose $X_1 X_2 ... X_{n-1}$ is a sequence of variables in $\mathcal{K} - \{X\}$. Then

$$(V_1 \otimes ... \otimes V_m)^{\downarrow\{X\}} = \otimes\left\{\text{Fus}_{X_{n-1}}\left\{...\text{Fus}_{X_2}\left\{\text{Fus}_{X_1}\{V_1, ..., V_m\}\right\}\right\}\right\}$$

To illustrate Theorem 1, consider a VBS with four variables: $W, X, Y,$ and Z, and four valuations: V_1 for $\{W\}$, V_2 for $\{W, X\}$, V_3 for $\{X, Y\}$, and V_4 for $\{Y, Z\}$. Suppose we need to compute the marginal of the joint for $Z, (V_1 \otimes ... \otimes V_4)^{\downarrow\{Z\}}$. Consider the deletion sequence WXY. After fusion with respect to W, we have $(V_1 \otimes V_2)^{\downarrow\{X\}}$ for $\{X\}$, V_3 for $\{X, Y\}$, and V_4 for $\{Y, Z\}$. After fusion with respect to X, we have

$((V_1 \otimes V_2)^{\downarrow\{X\}} \otimes V_3)^{\downarrow\{Y\}}$ for $\{Y\}$, and V_4 for $\{Y, Z\}$. Finally, after fusion with respect to Y, we have $(((V_1 \otimes V_2)^{\downarrow\{X\}} \otimes V_3)^{\downarrow\{Y\}} \otimes V_4)^{\downarrow\{Z\}}$ for $\{Z\}$. Theorem 4.1 tells us that $(((V_1 \otimes V_2)^{\downarrow\{X\}} \otimes V_3)^{\downarrow\{Y\}} \otimes V_4)^{\downarrow\{Z\}}$ $= (V \otimes \ldots \otimes V_4^{\downarrow\{Z\}}$. Thus, instead of doing combinations on the frame for $\{W, X, Y, Z\}$, we do combinations on the frame for $\{W, X\}$, $\{X, Y\}$, and $\{Y, Z\}$. The fusion algorithm is shown graphically in Figure 4.2.

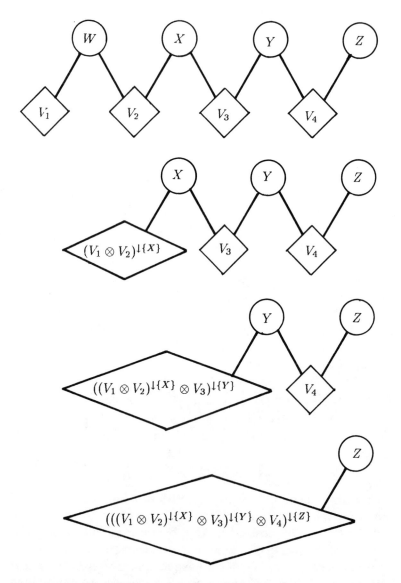

Figure 4.2. The first valuation network shows the initial VBS. The second network is the result after fusion with respect to W. The third network is the result after fusion with respect to X. The fourth network is the result after fusion with respect to Y.

If we can compute the marginal of the joint valuation for one variable, then we can compute the marginals for all variables. We simply compute them one after the other. It is obvious, however, that this will involve much duplication of effort. Shenoy and Shafer (1990) describe an efficient algorithm for simultaneous computation of all marginals without duplication of effort. Regardless of the number of variables in a VBS, we can compute marginals of the joint valuation for all variables for roughly three times the computational effort required to compute one marginal.

Deletion Sequences. Different deletion sequences may involve different computational efforts. Consider the VBS in the above example. Deletion sequence WXY involves less computational effort than for example XYW as the former involves combinations on the frame for two variables only whereas the latter involves combination on the frame for three variables. Finding an optimal deletion sequence is a secondary optimization problem that has shown to be NP-complete (Amborg et al., 1987). But, there are several heuristics for finding good deletion sequences (Kong, 1986; Mellouli, 1987; Zhang, 1988).

One such heuristic is called one-step-look-ahead (Kong, 1986). This heuristic tells us which variable to delete next. As per this heuristic, the variable that should be deleted next is one that leads to combination over the smallest frame. For example, in the VBS described above, if we assume that each variable has a frame consisting of two configurations, then this heuristic would pick W over X and Y for first deletion since deletion of W involves combination on the frame for $\{W, X\}$ whereas deletion of X involves combination on the frame for $\{W, X, Y\}$, and deletion of Y involves combination on the frame for $\{X, Y, Z\}$. After W is deleted, for second deletion, this heuristic would pick X over Y. Thus, this heuristic would choose deletion sequence WXY.

5. VALUATION-BASED SYSTEMS FOR PROBABILITY THEORY

In this section, we explain VBS for probability theory. More precisely, we define proper valuations, combination and marginalization. For probability theory, proper valuations are called potentials.

Potentials. A *potential H for h* is a function $H:\omega_h \to [0,1]$ such that $H(\mathbf{x})$ is not identically zero for all $\mathbf{x} \in \omega_h$. Potentials are unnormalized probability distribution functions.

Projection of Configurations. In order to develop a notation for the combination of potentials, we first need a notation for the projection of configurations of a set of variables to a smaller set of variables. Here projection simply means dropping extra coordinates; if (w, x, y, z) is a configuration of $\{W, X, Y, Z\}$, for example, then the projection of (w, x, y, z) to $\{W, X\}$ is simply (w, x), which is a configuration of $\{W, X\}$. If g and h are sets of variables, $h \subseteq g$, and x is a configuration of g, then $x^{\downarrow h}$ denotes the projection of x to h.

Combination. For potentials, combination is simply pointwise multiplication followed by normalization. If G is a potential for g, H is a potential for h, and there exists an $x \in \omega_{g \cup h}$ such that

$$G(x^{\downarrow g}) H(x^{\downarrow h}) > 0 \tag{1}$$

then their *combination*, denoted by $G \otimes H$, is the potential for $g \cup h$ given by

$$(G \otimes H)(x) = \alpha^{-1} G(x^{\downarrow g}) H(x^{\downarrow h}) \tag{2}$$

for all $x \in \omega_{g \cup h}$, where α is a normalization constant defined as follows:

$$\alpha = \Sigma \{G(x^{\downarrow g}) H(x^{\downarrow h}) \mid x \in \omega_{g \cup h}\} \tag{3}$$

If there exists no $x \in \omega_{g \cup h}$ such that $G(x^{\downarrow g}) H(x^{\downarrow h}) > 0$, then we say G and H are *not combinable*.

Intuitively, if the bodies of evidence on which G and H are based are independent, then $G \otimes H$ is supposed to represent the result of pooling these two bodies of evidence. Note that condition (1) ensures that α defined in (3) is a nonzero constant. If condition (1) does not hold, this means that the two bodies of evidence corresponding to G and H contradict each other completely and it is not possible to combine them.

It is clear from the definition of combination for potentials that it is commutative and associative. Thus Axiom A1 is satisfied.

Marginalization. Marginalization is familiar in probability theory; it means reducing a function for one set of variables to a function for a smaller set of variables by summing over the variables omitted.

Suppose H is a potential for h, and suppose $X \in h$. The *marginal of H for $h - \{X\}$*, denoted by $H^{\downarrow(h) - \{X\})}$, is the potential for $h - \{X\}$ defined as follows:

$$H^{\downarrow(h) - \{X\})}(y) = \Sigma \{H(y, x) \mid x \in \omega_X\}$$

for all $y \in \omega_{h - \{X\}}$.

It is obvious from the above definition that marginalization operator for potentials satisfies Axiom A2. Since multiplication distributes over addition, it is easy to show that combination and marginalization for potentials satisfy Axiom A3. Thus all axioms are satisfied, making local computation possible.

We would like to make an important observation for the case of probabilistic VBS. This observation relates to conditioning joint probability distributions. Suppose a joint probability distribution P for $\mathcal{K}$ represents our assessment of a given body of information, and we have a factorization of P into factors $A_1, ..., A_k$:

$$P = \otimes \{A_i \mid i = 1, ..., k\} \tag{4}$$

Suppose we now observe the values of some of the variables in $\mathcal{K}$; say we observe $Y_1 = y_1, Y_2 = y_2$, and so on up to $Y_q = v_q$. We change our assessment from P to $P^{|f = y}$ where $f = \{Y_1, ..., Y_q\}$, $y = \{y_1, ..., y_q\}$, and $P^{|f = y}$ denotes the joint probability distribution conditioned on the observations. Can we adapt (4) to a factorization of $P^{|f = y}$? Yes, we can. The adaptation is simple. It follows from the definition of conditional probability that

$$P^{|f = y} = \otimes \{A_i \mid i = 1, ..., k\} \otimes I^{Y_1 = y_1} \otimes ... \otimes I^{Y_q = y_q}$$

where $I^{Y_i = y_i}$ is the *indicator potential for* $Y_i = y_i$ for $\{Y_i\}$ defined by

$$I^{Y_i = y_i}(y) = \begin{cases} 0 & \text{if } x \neq y_i \\ 1 & \text{if } y = y_i \end{cases}$$

for all $y \in \omega_{Y_i}$. In words, each observation $Y_i = y_i$ is represented in a VBS as an indicator potential $I^{Y_i = y_i}$.

An Example: Diabetes. This example is adapted from Shachter and Heckerman (1987). Diabetes has two symptoms, blue toe and glucose in urine. Ten percent of the population suffers from diabetes. For persons known to suffer from diabetes, 1.4 percent exhibit blue toe, and 90 percent exhibit glucose in urine. On the other hand, for persons known to be free of diabetes, 0.6 percent exhibit blue toe, and 1 percent exhibit glucose in urine. Suppose that a person has blue toe but no glucose in urine. What is the probability that this person has diabetes?

Consider theree variables D, B, and G representing diabetes, blue toe, and glucose in urine, respectively. The frame for each variable has two configurations. $D = d$ represents the proposition *diabetes is present* and $D = \sim d$ represents the proposition *diabetes is not present*. Similarly for B and G. Let P denote the joint probability distribution for $\{D, B, G\}$. If we assume that B and G are conditionally independent (with respect to P) given D, then we can factor P as follows,

$$P = P^D \otimes P^{B|D} \otimes P^{G|D}$$

where P^D is the potential for $\{D\}$ representing the prior probability for D, $P^{B|D}$ is the potential for $\{D, B\}$ representing the conditional probability distributions of B given D, and $P^{G|D}$ is the potential for $\{D, G\}$ representing the conditional probability distributions of G given D. Table 4.1 displays these potentials. The observations that a person has blue toe but no glucose in urine are modeled by indicator potentials $I^{B=b}$ and $I^{G=\sim g}$, respectively. Figure 4.3 shows the valuation network for this VBS.

Table 4.1. The potentials P^D, $P^{B|D}$, and $P^{G|D}$ in the Diabetes example

W_D	p^D
d	.1
$\sim d$	.9

$W_{[D.B]}$		$p^{B|D}$
d	b	.014
d	$\sim b$	.986
$\sim d$	b	.006
$\sim d$	$\sim b$	.994

$W_{[D.G]}$		$p^{G|D}$
d	g	.90
d	$\sim g$	.10
$\sim d$	g	.01
$\sim d$	$\sim g$	.99

If we apply the fusion algorithm using deletion sequence BG, we get
$$(P^D \otimes P^{B|D} \otimes P^{G|D} \otimes I^{B=b} \otimes I^{G=\sim g})^{\downarrow \{D\}} = (I^{B=b} \otimes p^{B|D})^{\downarrow \{D\}} \otimes (I^{G=\sim g} \otimes P^{G|D})^{\downarrow \{D\}} \otimes P^D.$$

The details of the computations are shown in Table 4.2. The probability that diabetes is present is 0.0255.

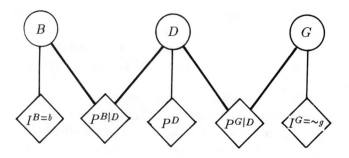

Figure 4.3. The valuation network for the Diabetes example

Table 4.2. The details of the computation of $(I^{B=b} \otimes P^{B|D})^{\downarrow \{D\}} \otimes$ $(I^{G=\sim g} \otimes P^{G|D})^{\downarrow \{D\}} \otimes P^D$

$W_{\{D,B\}}$	$I^{B=b}$	$P^{B|D}$	$(I^{B=b} \otimes P^{B|D})$	$(I^{B=b} \otimes P^{B|D})^{\downarrow \{D\}}$
d b	1	.014	.700	.700
d ~b	0	.986	.000	
~d b	1	.006	.300	.300
~d ~b	0	.994	.000	

$W_{\{D,G\}}$	$I^{G=\sim g}$	$P^{G|D}$	$(I^{G=\sim g} \otimes P^{G|D})$	$(I^{G=\sim g} \otimes P^{G|D})^{\downarrow \{D\}}$
d g	0	.90	.000	.092
d ~g	1	.10	.092	
~d g	0	.01	.000	.908
~d ~g	1	.99	.908	

W_D	$(I^{B=b} \otimes P^{B|D})^{\downarrow \{D\}}$	$(I^{G=\sim g} \otimes P^{G|D})^{\downarrow \{D\}}$	P_D	$(I^{B=b} \otimes P^{B|D})^{\downarrow \{D\}}$ $\otimes(I^{G=\sim g} \otimes P^{G|D})^{\downarrow \{D\}}$ $\otimes P^D$
d	.700	0.92	.1	.0255
~d	.300	.908	.9	.9745

The combination operation involves normalization. It is easy to see that in computing the marginal of the joint for a variable, the normalization operation can be left out of the combination operator and be done just once at the very end. This will result in some computational savings.

The use of probability theory in expert systems has been widely studied. Some of the influential works in this area are Pearl (1986), Lauritzen and Spiegelhalter (1988), Shafer and Shenoy (1990), and Jensen et al. (1990). The fusion algorithm applied to the case of probability theory is an abstraction of the methods described in these papers.

6. VALUATION-BASED SYSTEMS FOR BELIEF-FUNCTION THEORY

In this section, we describe proper valuations, combination and marginalization for the theory of belief-functions (Dempster, 1966;

Shafer, 1976). In belief-function VBS, proper valuations are called basic probability assignment potentials.

Basic Probability Assignment Functions. A *basic probability assignment (bpa) function M for h* is a function $M : 2^{W_h} \to [0, 1]$ such that $\Sigma\{M(a) \mid a \in 2^{W_h}\} = 1$. 2^{W_h} denotes the set of all nonempty subsets of W_h.

Intuitively, $M(a)$ represents the degree of belief assigned exactly to **a** (the proposition that the true configuration of h is in the set **a**) and to nothing smaller. A bpa function is the belief function equivalent of a probability mass function in probability theory. Whereas a probability mass function is restricted to assigning probability masses only to singleton configurations of variables, a bpa function is allowed to assign probability masses to sets of configurations without assigning any mass to the individual configurations contained in the sets.

Basic Probability Assignment Potentials. A *basic probability assignment (bpa) potential for h* is a function $M : 2^{W_h} \to [0, 1]$ such that $M(a)$ is not identically zero for all $a \in 2^{W_h}$. Bpa potentials are unnormalized bpa functions.

Projection and Extension of Subsets. Before we can define combination and marginalization for bpa potentials, we need the concepts of projection and extension of subsets of configurations.

If g and h are sets of variables, $h \subseteq g$, and **g** is a nonempty subset of W_g, then the *projection of* **g** *to* h, denoted by $g^{\downarrow h}$, is the subset of W_h given by $g^{\downarrow h} = \{x^{\downarrow h} \mid x \in g\}$. For example, If **a** is a subset of $W_{(W, X, Y, Z)}$, then the marginal of **a** to $\{X, Y\}$ consists of the elements of $W_{(X, Y)}$ that can be obtained by projecting elements of **a** to $W_{(X, Y)}$.

By extension of a subset of a frame to a subset of a larger frame, we mean a cylinder set extension. If **g** and **h** are sets of variables, **h** is a proper subset of **g**, and **h** is a nonempty subset of W_h, then the *extension of* **h** *to* g is $h \times W_{g-h}$. Let $h^{\uparrow g}$ denote the extension of **h** to g. For example, if **a** is a nonempty subset of $W_{(W, X)}$, then the extension of **a** to $\{W, X, Y, Z\}$ is $a \times W_{(Y, Z)}$.

Combination. For bpa potentials, combination is called *Dempster's rule* (Dempster, 1966). Consider two bpa potentials G and H for g and h, respectively. If

$$\Sigma\{G(a) H(b) \mid (a^{\uparrow(g \cup h)}) \cap (b^{\uparrow(g \cup h)}) \neq \phi\} \neq 0 \tag{5}$$

then their *combination*, denoted by $G \otimes H$, is the bpa potential for $g \cup h$ given by

$$(G \otimes H)(\mathbf{c}) = \alpha^{-1} \Sigma \{ G(\mathbf{a})H(\mathbf{b}) \,|\, (\mathbf{a}^{\uparrow(g \cup h)}) \cap (\mathbf{b}^{\uparrow(g \cup h)}) = \mathbf{c} \} \qquad (6)$$

for all nonempty $\mathbf{c} \subseteq W_{g \cup h}$, where α is a normalization constant given by

$$\alpha = \Sigma \{ G(\mathbf{a})H(\mathbf{b}) \,|\, (\mathbf{a}^{\uparrow(g \cup h)}) \cap (\mathbf{b}^{\uparrow(g \cup h)}) \neq \emptyset \} \qquad (7)$$

If $\Sigma \{ G(\mathbf{a})H(\mathbf{b}) \,|\, (\mathbf{a}^{\uparrow(g \cup h)}) \cap (\mathbf{b}^{\uparrow(g \cup h)}) \neq \emptyset \} = 0$, then we say that G and H are *not combinable*. Intuitively, if the bodies of evidence on which G and H are based are independent, then $G \otimes H$ is supposed to represent the result of pooling these two bodies of evidence. Note that condition (5) ensures that α defined in (7) is a nonzero constant. If condition (5) does not hold, this means that the two bodies of evidence corresponding to G and H contradict each other completely and it is not possible to combine such evidence.

It is easy to see that Dempster's rule of combination is commutative and associative (Shafer, 1976). Thus, combination for bpa potentials satisfies Axiom A1.

Marginalization. Like marginalization for potentials, marginalization for bpa potentials corresponds to addition. Suppose H is a bpa potential for h, and suppose $X \in h$. The *marginal of H for* $h - \{X\}$, denoted by $H^{\downarrow(h - \{X\})}$, is the potential for $h - \{X\}$ defined as follows:

$$H^{\downarrow(h - \{X\})}(\mathbf{a}) = \Sigma \{ H(\mathbf{b}) \,|\, \mathbf{b} \subseteq W_h \text{ such that } \mathbf{b}^{\downarrow(h - \{X\})} = \mathbf{a} \}$$

for all nonempty subsets $\mathbf{a}$ of $W_{h - \{X\}}$.

It is easy to see that marginalization for bpa potentials satisfies Axiom A2. Shafer and Shenoy (1988) show that the above definitions of marginalization and combination for bpa potentials satisfy Axiom A3. Thus all axioms are satisfied making local computation possible.

An Example: Is Dick a Pacifist? Consider the following items of evidence. Most (at least 90 percent) Republicans are not pacifists. Most Quakers (at least 99 percent) are pacifists. Dick is a Republican (and we are more than 99.9 percent certain of this). Dick is a Quaker (and we are more than 99.9 percent certain of this). What is the degree of belief that Dick is a pacifist?

We will model the four items of evidence as bpa respective frames. $R = r$ represents the proposition that Dick is a Republican and $R = \sim r$ represents the proposition that Dick is not a Republican. Similarly for Q and P. The four items of evidence are represented by bpa potentials M_1 for $\{R, P\}$, M_2 for $\{Q, P\}$, M_3 for $\{R\}$, and M_4 for $\{Q\}$, respectively, as displayed in Table 4.3. Figure 4.4 shows the valuation network for this example.

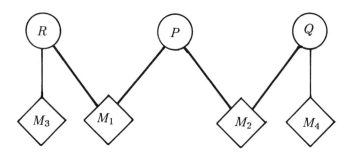

Figure 4.4. The valuation network for the Is Dick a Pacifist? example

Table 4.3. The bpa potentials M_1, M_2, M_3, and M_4 in the Is Dick a Pacifist? example

$2^{W_{\{R,P\}}}$	M_1
$\{(r,\sim p),(\sim r,p),(\sim r,\sim p)\}$	.90
$\{(r,p),(r,\sim p),(\sim r,p),(\sim r,\sim p)\}$	.10

$2^{W_{\{R,P\}}}$	M_3
$\{r\}$	.999
$\{r,\sim r\}$	.001

$2^{W_{\{Q,P\}}}$	M_2
$\{(q,p),(\sim q,p),(\sim q,\sim p)\}$	.99
$\{(q,p),(q,\sim p),(\sim q,p),(\sim q,\sim p)\}$	.01

$2^{W_{\{Q,P\}}}$	M_4
$\{q\}$	.999
$\{q,\sim q\}$	.001

If we apply the fusion algorithm using deletion sequence RQ, we get $(M_1 \otimes M_2 \otimes M_3 \otimes M_4)^{\downarrow\{P\}} = (M_1 \otimes M_3)^{\downarrow\{P\}} \otimes (M_2 \otimes M_4)^{\downarrow\{P\}}$. The details of the computations are shown in Table 4.4. The degree of belief that Dick is a pacifist is 0.9008. As in the case of probability theory, we can avoid the normalization operation in Dempster's rule and do it just once at the very end.

The use of belief functions in expert systems has been widely studied. Some of the influential works in this area are Shenoy and Shafer (1986), Kong (1986), Shafer, Shenoy and Mellouli (1987), and Dempster and Kong (1988). The fusion algorithm applied to the case of belief function theory is an abstraction of the methods described in these papers.

Table 4.4. The computation of $(M_1 \otimes M_3)^{\downarrow\{P\}} \otimes (M_2 \otimes M_4)^{\downarrow\{P\}}$

$2^{W_{\{R,P\}}}$	$M_1 \otimes M_3$	$2^{W_{\{Q,P\}}}$	$M_2 \otimes M_4$
$\{(r, \sim p)\}$	.8991	$\{(q,p)\}$	.98901
$\{(r,p),(r,\sim p)\}$	.0999	$\{(q,p),(q,\sim p)\}$	.00999
$\{(r,\sim p),(\sim r,p),$		$\{(q,p),(\sim q,p),$	
$(\sim r, \sim p)\}$	.0009	$(\sim q, \sim p)\}$	.00099
$\{(r,p),(r,\sim p),$		$\{(q,p),(q,\sim p),$	
$(\sim r,p),(\sim r,\sim p)\}$	.0001	$(\sim q,p),(\sim q,\sim p)\}$	.00001

2^{W_P}	$(M_1 \otimes M_3)^{\downarrow(P)}$	$(M_2 \otimes M_4)^{\downarrow(P)}$	$(M_1 \otimes M_3)^{\downarrow(P)}$ $\otimes (M_1 \otimes M_3)^{\downarrow(P)}$
$\{p\}$	.0000	.98901	.9008
$\{\sim p\}$	.8991	.00000	.0892
$\{p, \sim p\}$	.1009	.01099	.0100

7. VALUATION-BASED SYSTEMS FOR SPOHN'S THEORY OF EPISTEMIC BELIEFS

In this section, we describe proper valuations, combination and marginalization for Spohn's theory of epistemic beliefs (Spohn, 1988, 1990; Shenoy, 1991a). In Spohnian VBS, proper valuations are called disbelief potentials, combination is pointwise addition, and marginalization is minimization.

Disbelief Functions. A *disbelief function* for h is a function $\delta : 2^{W_h} \to N$ such that

(i)   there exists a configuration $x \in W_h$ for which $\delta(\{x\}) = 0$; and
(ii)   for any $a \in 2^{W_h}$, $\delta(a) = \text{MIN}\{\delta(\{x\}) \mid x \in a\}$

Intuitively, $\delta(a)$ represents the degree of disbelief in proposition a (the proposition that the true configuration of h is in a). The degree of belief in proposition a is given by $\delta(\sim a)$, where $\sim a = W_{h-\{x\}}a$. Thus δ represents an epistemic state in which a is believed iff $\delta(\sim a) > 0$, a is disbelieved iff $\delta(a) > 0$, and a is neither believed nor disbelieved if $\delta(a) = \delta(\sim a) = 0$. Also, in epistemic state δ, a is more believed than $\mathbf{b}$ if $\delta(\sim\mathbf{a}) > \delta(\sim\mathbf{b})$, and $\mathbf{a}$ is more disbelieved than $\mathbf{b}$ if $\delta(\mathbf{a}) > \delta(\mathbf{b}) > 0$. Note that from condition (ii) in the definition of a disbelief function, a disbelief function is completely determined by its values for singleton subsets. This motivates the following definition.

Disbelief Potentials. A *disbelief potential for h* is a function $\delta: W_h \rightarrow \mathbb{N}$. A disbelief potential is an unnormalized disbelief function defined only for singleton subsets of W_h.

Combination. For disbelief potentials, combination is simply pointwise addition followed by normalization (Shenoy, 1991a). If δ_1 is a disbelief potential for g, and δ_2 is a disbelief potential for h, then their *combination*, denoted by $\delta_1 \otimes \delta_2$, is the disbelief potential for $g \cup h$ given by

$$(\delta_1 \otimes \delta_2)(\mathbf{x}) = \delta_1(\mathbf{x}^{\downarrow g}) + \delta_2(\mathbf{x}^{\downarrow h}) - \kappa$$

for all $\mathbf{x} \in W_{g \cup h}$, where κ is a normalization constant defined as follows:

$$\kappa = \mathrm{MIN}\{\delta_1(\mathbf{x}^{\downarrow g}) + \delta_2(\mathbf{x}^{\downarrow h}) \,|\, x \in W_{g \cup h}\}$$

Intuitively, if the bodies of evidence on which δ_1 and δ_2 are based are independent, then $\delta_1 \otimes \delta_2$ is supposed to represent the epistemic state resulting from pooling these two bodies of evidence.

It is clear from the definition of combination for disbelief potentials that it is commutative and associative. Thus Axiom A1 is satisfied.

Marginalization. Suppose δ is a disbelief potential for h, and suppose $X \in h$. The *marginal of δ for $h - \{X\}$*, denoted by $\delta^{\downarrow(h - \{X\})}$, is the disbelief potential for $h - \{X\}$ defined as follows:

$$\delta^{\downarrow(h-\{X\})}(\mathbf{y}) = \mathrm{MIN}\{\delta(\mathbf{y}, \mathbf{x}) \,|\, \mathbf{x} \in W_{\{x\}}\}$$

for all $\mathbf{y} \in W_{h-\{x\}}$.

The above definition of marginalization follows from condition (ii) in the definition of a disbelief function since a proposition $\{\mathbf{y}\}$ about variables in $h - \{X\}$ is the same as proposition $\{\mathbf{y}\} \times W_x$ about variables in h.

It is easy to see that marginalization for disbelief potentials satisfies Axiom A2. Shenoy (1991a) shows that the above definitions of marginalization and combination for disbelief potentials satisfy Axiom A3. Thus all axioms are satisfied making local computation possible.

An Example: Is Dick a Pacifist? Consider the four items of evidence as described in Section 6. We will model the four items of evidence as disbelief potentials δ_1, δ_2, δ_3, and δ_4, respectively, as shown in Table 4.5. The valuation network for this VBS is similar to

Table 4.5. The disbelief potentials δ_1, δ_2, δ_3, and δ_4 in the Is Dick a Pacifist? example

$W_{\{R,P\}}$		δ_1
r	p	1
r	$\sim p$	0
$\sim r$	p	0
$\sim r$	$\sim p$	0

$W_{\{Q,P\}}$		δ_2
q	p	0
q	$\sim p$	2
$\sim q$	p	0
$\sim q$	$\sim p$	0

$W_{\{R\}}$	δ_3
r	0
$\sim r$	3

$W_{\{Q\}}$	δ_4
q	0
$\sim q$	3

that shown in Figure 4.4. If we apply the fusion algorithm using deletion sequence RQ, we get $(\delta_1 \otimes \delta_2 \otimes \delta_3 \otimes \delta_4)^{\downarrow\{P\}} = (\delta_1 \otimes \delta_3)^{\downarrow\{P\}} \otimes (\delta_2 \otimes \delta_4)^{\downarrow\{P\}}$. The details of the computations are shown in Table 4.6. We believe that Dick is a pacifist to degree 1. Note that we get roughly the same answer as in the belief function case if we interpret $\delta(x)$ as the negative of the logarithm (to base 10) of the probability of proposition x (Pearl, 1989; Spohn, 1990). As in the case of probability theory and belief-function theory, we can avoid the normalization in the combination operator and do it just once at the very end.

The use of Spohn's theory in expert systems has also been studied by Hunter (1990). The fusion algorithm applied to the case of Spohn's theory is an abstraction of the method described in Hunter (1990).

Table 4.6. The computation of $(\delta_1 \otimes \delta_3)^{\downarrow\{P\}} \otimes (\delta_2 \otimes \delta_4)^{\downarrow\{P\}}$

$W_{\{R,P\}}$		$(\delta_1 \otimes \delta_3)$
r	p	1
r	$\sim p$	0
$\sim r$	p	3
$\sim r$	$\sim p$	3

$W_{\{Q,P\}}$		$(\delta_2 \otimes \delta_4)$
q	p	0
q	$\sim p$	2
$\sim q$	p	3
$\sim q$	$\sim p$	3

W_P	$(\delta_1 \otimes \delta_3)^{\downarrow\{P\}}$	$(\delta_2 \otimes \delta_4)^{\downarrow\{P\}}$	$(\delta_1 \otimes \delta_3)^{\downarrow\{P\}} \otimes (\delta_1 \otimes \delta_3)^{\downarrow\{P\}}$
p	1	0	0
$\sim p$	0	2	1

8. CONCLUSION

In this paper, we have described the framework of valuation-based systems. We have stated three axioms that enable local computation. We have described a fusion algorithm that uses local computation to compute the marginals of the joint valuation for any variable. And we have described how Bayesian probability theory, Dempster-Shafer's theory of belief functions, and Spohn's theory of epistemic beliefs fit in the framework of VBS.

9. PROOFS

In this section, we give a proof for Theorem 1. First we state and prove a lemma needed to prove Theorem 1.

Lemma 1. Suppose $\{\{V_1, ..., V_m, \otimes, \downarrow\}$ is a VBS where V_i is a valuation for h_i, and suppose $\otimes$ and $\downarrow$ satisfy Axioms A1–A3. Let χ denote $h_1 \cup ... \cup h_m$. Suppose $X \in \chi$. Then

$$(V_1 \otimes ... \otimes V_m)^{\downarrow(\chi - \{X\})} = \otimes \operatorname{Fus}_X\{V_1, ..., V_m\}$$

Proof of Lemma 1. Suppose V_i is a valuation for h_i, $i = 1, ..., m$. Let $h = \cup \{h_i \mid X \in h_i\}$, and let $g = \cup \{h_i \mid X \notin h_i\}$. Let $G = \otimes \{V_i \mid X \notin h_i\}$. Note that $X \in h$, and $X \notin g$. Then

$$(V_1 \otimes ... \otimes V_m)^{\downarrow(\chi - \{X\})} = (G \otimes H)^{\downarrow(\{g \cup h\} - \{X\})} = G \otimes (H^{\downarrow(h - \{X\})} =$$
$$= (\otimes \{V_i \mid X \notin h_i\}) \otimes (\otimes \{V_i \mid X \in h_i\})^{\downarrow(h - \{X\})} = \otimes \operatorname{Fus}_x\{V_1, ..., V_m\}$$

Proof of Theorem 1. By Axiom A2, $(V_1 \otimes ... \otimes V_m)^{\downarrow(X)}$ is obtained by sequentially marginalizing all variables but X from the joint valuation. A proof of this theorem is obtained by repeatedly applying the result of Lemma 1. At each step, we delete a variable and fuse the set of all valuations with respect to this variable. Using Lemma 1, after fusion with respect to X_1, the combination of all valuations in the resulting VBS is equal to $(V_1 \otimes ... \otimes V_m)^{\downarrow(\chi - \{X_1\})}$. Again, using Lemma 1, after fusion with respect to X_2, the combination of all valuations in the resulting VBS is equal to $(V_1 \otimes ... \otimes V_m)^{\downarrow(\chi - \{X_1, X_2\})}$. And so on. When all variables but X have been deleted, we have the result.

Acknowledgments

This work was supported in part by the National Science Foundation under grant IRI-8902444. I would like to thank Ali Jenzarli and Leen-Kiat Soh for their comments and assistance.

BIBLIOGRAPHY

Amborg, S., D. G. Coreil, and A. Proskurowski. (1987). "Complexity of finding embeddings in a k-tree." *SIAM Journal of Algebraic and Discrete Metods*, **8**, 277–284.

Dempster, A. P. (1966). "New methods for reasoning toward posterior distributions based on sample data." *Annals of Mathematical Statistics*, **37**, 355–374.

Dempster, A. P. and A. Kong. (1988). "Uncertain evidence and artificial analysis." *Journal of Statistical Planning and Inference*, **20**, 355–368.

Dubois, D. and H. Prade. (1990). "Inference in possibilistic hypergraphs." *Proceedings of the Third International Conference on Information Processing and Management of Uncertainty in Knowledge-based Systems* (IPMU-90), Paris, France, 228–230.

Hunter, D. (1990). "Parallel belief revision." In Shachter, R. D., T. S. Levitt, J. F. Lemmer, and L. N. Kanal (eds.): *Uncertainty in Artificial Intelligence*, **4**, 241–252. Amsterdam: North-Holland.

Jensen, F. V., K. G. Olesen, and S. K. Andersen. (1990). "An algebra of Bayesian belief universes for knowledge-based systems. *Networks*, **20** (5), 637–659.

Kong, A. (1986). "Multivariate belief functions and graphical models." Ph.D. dissertation, Department of Statistics, Harvard University, Cambridge.

Lauritzen, S. L. and D. Spiegelhalter. (1988). Local computations with probabiities on graphical structures and their application to expert systems (with discussion)." *Journal of Royal Statistical Society, Series* **B**, **50** (2), 157–224.

Mellouli, K. (1987). "On the propagation of beliefs in networks using the Dempster-Shafer theory of evidence." Ph. D. dissertation, School of Business, University of Kansas, Lawrence.

Pearl, J. (1986). "Fusion, propagation and structuring in belief networks." *Artificial Intelligence*, **29**, 241–288.

Pearl, J. (1989). "Probabilistic semantics for nonmonotonic reasoning: A survey." *Proceedings of the First International Conference on Prnciples of Knowledge Representation and Reasoning*, Toronto, Canada, 505–516. Reprinted in Shafer, G. and J. Pearl (eds.): *Readings in Uncertain Reasoning*. San Mateo, CA: Morgan Kaufmann, 1990, 699–710.

Shachter, R. D. and D. Heckerman. (1987). "A backwards view for assessment." *AI Magazine*, **8** (3), 55–61.

Shafer, G. (1976). *A Mathematical Theory of Evidence*. Princeton University Press.

Shafer, G. and P. P. Shenoy. (1988). "Local computation in hypertrees." Working Paper no. 201, School of Business, University of Kansas, Lawrence.

Shafer, G. and P. P. Shenoy. (1990). "Probability propagation." *Annals of Mathematics and Artificial Intelligence*, **2**, 327–352.

Shafer, G. and P. P. Shenoy, and K. Mellouli. (1987). "Propagating belief functions in qualitative Markov trees." *International Journal of Approximate Reasoning*, **1** (4), 349–400.

Shenoy, P. P. (1989). "A valuation-based language for expert systems." *International Journal for Approximate Reasoning,* **3** (5), 384–411.

Shenoy, P. P. (1990a). "Valuation-based systems for propositional logic." In Ras, Z. W., M. Zemankova, and M. L. Emrich (eds.): *Methodologies for Intelligent Systems,* **5**, 305–312, Amsterdam: North-Holland.

Shenoy, P. P. (1990b). "Consistency in valuation-based systems." Working Paper no. 216, School of Business, University of Kansas, Lawrence.

Shenoy, P. P. (1990c). "Valuation-based systems for Bayesian decision analysis." Working Paper no. 220, School of Business, University of Kansas, Lawrence. To appear in 1992 in *Operations Research,* **40**, (3).

Shenoy, P. P. (1990d). "A new method for representing and solving Bayesian decision problems." Working Paper no. 223, School of Business, University of Kansas, Lawrence.

Shenoy, P. P. (1991a). "On Spohn's rule for revision of beliefs." *International Journal of Approximate Reasoning,* **5** (2), 149–181.

Shenoy, P. P. (1991b), in press. "Valuation-based systems for discrete optimization." In Bonissone, P. P. M. Henrion, L. N. Kanal, and J. Lemmer (eds.): *Uncertainty in Artificial Intelligence,* **6**, Amsterdam: North-Holland.

Shenoy, P. P. and G. Shafer. (1986). "Propagating belief functions using local computations." *IEEE Expert,* **1** (3), 43–52.

Shenoy, P. P. and G. Shafer. (1988). "Constraint propagation." Working Paper no. 208, School of Business, University of Kansas, Lawrence.

Shenoy, P. P. and G. Shafer. (1990). "Axioms for probability and belief-function propagation." In Shachter, R. D., T. S. Levitt, J. F. Lemmer, and L. N. Kanal (eds.): *Uncertainty in Artificial Intelligence,* **4**, 169–198. Amsterdam: North-Holland. Reprinted in Shafer, G. and J. Pearl (eds.): *Readings in Uncertain Reasoning,* San Mateo, CA: Morgan Kaufmann, 575–610.

Spohn, W. (1988). "Ordinal conditional functions: A dynamic theory of epistemic states." In Harper, W. L. and B. Skyrms (eds.): *Causation in Decision, Belief Change, and Statistics,* **2**, 105–134. Dordrecht: D. Reidel.

Spohn, W. (1990). "A general non-probabilistic theory of inductive reasoning." In Shachter, R. D., T. S. Levitt, J. F. Lemmer, and L. N. Kanal (eds.): *Uncertainty in Artificial Intelligence,* **4**, 149–158. Amsterdam: North-Holland.

Zadeh, L. A. (1979). "A theory of approximate reasoning." In Ayes, J. E., D. Mitchie, and L. I. Mikulich (eds.): *Machine Intelligence,* **9**, 149–194. Chichester, UK: Ellis Horwood.

Zhang, L. (1988). "Studies on finding hypertree covers of hypergraphs." Working Paper no. 198, School of Business, University of Kansas, Lawrence.

5 Rough sets: A new approach to vagueness

Zdzisław PAWLAK
Institute of Computer Science
Warsaw Technical University
ul. Nowowiejska 15/19
00-665 Warsaw, POLAND

Abstract. A brief exposition of the concept of a rough set is presented, with an extensive list of literature on its related theories and applications. A rough set is basically meant to represent a vague concept (a vaguely specified set) by two precisely specified sets, called lower and upper approximations, with their difference being a boundary region. Knowledge is basically defined in terms of rough classification whose main underlying concept is an indiscernibility relation. A measure of accuracy (vagueness) is presented. Numerous applications in a wide spectrum of fields are reviewed.

1. INTRODUCTION

The idea of a *rough set* (Pawlak, 1982) has been proposed as a new mathematical tool to deal with *vague concepts,* and seems to be of some importance to AI and cognitive sciences, in particular expert systems, decision support systems, machine learning, machine discovery, inductive reasoning, pattern recognition, and decision tables.

Vagueness is not a clearly understood idea and there are many approaches to it. The rough set approach to vagueness is closely related to the so-called "boundary-line" view, which is credited to Frege (1903) who writes:

The concept must have a sharp boundary. To the concept without a sharp boundary there would correspond an area that had not a sharp boundary-line all around.

Thus, according to Frege, a precise concept must have a sharp boundary, whereas a vague concept is characterized by its boundary-line cases. In other words, if a concept is precise, then for each object it can be decided whether it belongs to the concept or not; for vague concepts this is not the case.

For example, the concept of an odd (even) number is precise, because for each number it can be decided whether it is odd (even) or not. But the concept of a beautiful woman is vague, because for some women it cannot be decided whether they are beautiful or not (there are boundary-line cases).

Cantor's set theory can deal only with precise concepts. There are many approaches to "soften" classical set theory so that vague concepts could be also considered. One of the most successful approaches in this direction is the well-known *fuzzy set theory* of Zadeh.

The basic idea of *rough set theory* consists in replacing vague concepts with a pair of precise concepts (so that classical set theory can be applied). This is called *lower* and *upper approximation*. For example, the lower approximation of the concept of a beautiful woman contains all women that are beautiful with certainty (there is no doubt that they are beautiful), whereas the upper approximation of this concept contains all women that cannot be excluded from being considered beautiful. Clearly the upper and the lower approximations are precise concepts.

With each vague concept a *boundary region* is associated, which consists of all objects that cannot be placed clearly within the concept. For example, all women that cannot be said with certainty to be beautiful belong to the boundary region of the concept of a beautiful woman. The "size" of the boundary region can be used as a *measure of vagueness* of the vague concept. (The greater the boundary region, the more vague is the concept; precise concepts do not have boundary regions at all.) Obviously the boundary region is the difference between the upper and lower approximation of the concept.

Rough set theory is used mainly for data analysis. Among the types of problems that can be solved using rough set theory in data analysis are the following: data reduction (elimination of superfluous data), discovering of data dependencies, data significance, decision (control) algorithms generated from data, approximate classification of data, discovering similarities or differences in data, discovering patterns in data, and discovering cause–effect relationships.

The proposed approach has proved to be very useful in practice and many real-life applications of this concept have been implemented. Some of these are listed below:

Engineering design (Arciszewski et al. 1986, 1987)

Generation of cement kiln control algorithm from observation of kiln stoker actions (Mrozek, 1989)

Approximate (rough) classification of patients after highly selective vagotomy (HSV) for duodenal ulcer (Greenburg, 1987; Pawlak et al., 1986)

Analysis of peritoneal lavage in acute pancreatitis (Słowiński et al., 1989)

Analysis of hierarchy of factors of a surgical wound infection (Kandulski et al., 1990)

Aircraft pilot performance evaluation (Krasowski, 1988)

Analysis of relationship between structure and activity of drugs (Krysiński, 1990)

Study of water runoff from a river basin (Reinhard et al., 1989)

Control of water–air relation on a polder (Reinhard et al., 1989)

Vibration analysis (Nowak et al., 1990)

Switching function minimization (Rybnik, 1990)

Machine learning is one of the most important fields of artificial intelligence, and a growing number of researchers are involved in this area. There are a variety of approaches to machine learning; however, at present no commonly accepted theoretical foundations have been developed. It seems that the rough set approach can be used as a theoretical basis for some problems in machine learning. Some ideas concerning the application of rough sets in this area have been published by Grzymała-Busse (1988, 1989), Hadjimichael (1989), Orłowska (1986), Pawlak (1986a, b, 1987), Pawlak et al. (1988), Pettorossi et al. (1987), Raś and Zemankova (1986), Wasilewska (1990a, b), and Wong et al. (1986a, b).

The concept of a rough set has also inspired a variety of logical research: Jian-Ming and Nakamura (1990), Konikowska (1987), Krynicki (1989, 1990a, b), Krynicki and Tuschnick (1990), Nakamura and Jian-Ming (1988), Orłowska (1985a, b, 1989), Pawlak (1987b), Rasiowa (1985, 1986a, b), Rauszer (1985, 1986), Szczerba (1987), Vakarelov (1981, 1989) Wasilewska (1988, 1989), and others. Most of this research has been directed toward creating logical tools to deal with approximate reasoning.

Algebraic properties of rough sets have been studied by Comer (1991), Grzymała-Busse (1986), Iwiński (1987), Nieminen (1988), Novotny and Pawlak (1985–1991), Obtułowicz (1988) and Pomykała and Pomykała (1988).

The rough set concept overlaps in many areas with other mathematical ideas developed to deal with imprecision and vagueness, in particular with fuzzy sets. Fair comparison of rough sets and fuzzy sets can be found in Dubois and Prade (1988). Some remarks on comparison of fuzzy sets and rough sets can be also found in Chanas and Kuchta (1990), and Wygralak (1989). The relation of rough set theory to the Dempster-Shafer evidence theory has been discussed by Grzymała-Busse (1988) and Skowron (1989).

2. PRECISE AND VAGUE KNOWLEDGE

As we mentioned in the introduction, in the proposed approach we replace vague concepts with a pair of precise concepts. In other words, we would like to represent some concepts by means of other concepts. To this end we will need some operations on families of concepts. We must introduce here the idea of *knowledge*, which is simply a family of concepts (as a language in formal linguistics is defined as a set of sentences, or a theory in logic is understood as a set of theorems). Thus, any family of concepts will be called knowledge. If all concepts are precise the corresponding knowledge is precise; otherwise the knowlege is vague. More exactly, let U be a finite set called the *universe of discourse* (in short, the *universe*). Any subset X of U ($X \subseteq U$), will be called *a concept* in U and any family F of concepts in U ($F \subseteq P(u)$, $P(U)$ is the family of all subsets of U), will be referred to as *knowledge* about U. It seems natural to assume that the family F is closed under the set theoretic union, intersection and complement, that is if X and Y are concepts in F, so are $X, \cup Y, X \cap Y$, and $-X$.

Suppose we are given knowledge F about U and a concept $Y \subseteq U$. Now we may ask whether Y is precise or vague in F. Of course, if $Y \subseteq F$, then Y is precise in F, otherwise Y is vague in F. How we can approximate the vague concept Y in F? It seems to be justifiable to approximate the concept Y from below and from above as follows:

The *lower approximation* of Y in F, denoted $\underline{F}\,Y$, is the union of all exact concepts X in F that are included in Y.

The *upper approximation* of Y in F, denoted $\bar{F}Y$, is the intersection of all exact concepts X in F that include Y.

For practical and mathematical reasons, which will not be discussed here, we will assume a somewhat modified definition of approximation of vague concepts by means of precise concepts. The idea of approximation will be based not on arbitrary families of concepts, but on families of concepts that form classifications (partitions).

The reason we consider classification as a basis for definition of knowledge is that our belief is that knowledge is deep-seated in the classification abilities of human beings and other species. Hence, we assume here that knowledge consists of a family of various classification patterns, of a domain of interest, which provides explicit facts about the reality.

The basic idea underlying classification consists in the fact that objects being in the same equivalence class of the equivalence relation cannot be discerned; therefore we will call these the *indiscernibility classes*. Combining elements of U into indiscernibility classes can be done deliberately or can be due to our lack of knowledge. For example, in order to have the category of the color red we must ignore small differences between various shades of red, otherwise it would be impossible to form the category of the color red. On the other hand, the clustering of objects into categories can be caused by insufficient knowledge. Thus, knowledge about a certain set of objects can be identified with the ability to classify these objects into blocks of the partition induced by the indiscernibility relation. The more knowledge we have about some objects, the more exactly we can classify them. In the next section, we will explain these ideas more precisely.

3. KNOWLEDGE AND KNOWLEDGE BASE

Suppose we are given a finite set U (the universe) of objects we are interested in, and a family of classification patterns $C = \{C_1, C_2, ..., C_m\}$, where each C_i is a disjoint family of concepts in U (i.e., subsets of U).

A pair $K = (U, C)$ will be referred to as a *knowledge base*. Each classification C_i from C will be called an *attribute* in K and each element of C_i will be called a *basic category* of C_i (in U).

For example, if we classify elements of U according to colors, then the basic categories of the attribute color are *red, green, blue*, etc.

Thus, the knowledge base represents a variety of basic classification skills (e.g., according to colors, temperature, etc.) of an "intelligent" agent or group of agents (e.g., organisms or robots).

For mathematical reasons it is often better to use equivalence relations instead of classifications, since these two concepts are mutually exchangeable and relations are easier to deal with. Thus, the knowledge base can defined now as $K = (U, R)$, where $R = \{R_1, R_2, ..., R_1\}$ is the family of equivalence relations over U.

Of course, the set theoretical intersection of any family of equivalence relations is also an equivalence relation. Any subset of equivalence relations from our knowledge base also defines a family of categories, which will be called *elementary categories* in the knowledge base. It is obvious that any concept (subset of U) can be expressed in the knowledge base K only if it is the union of some elementary categories in K. Otherwise, the concept cannot be defined in the knowledge base. In other words, elementary categories are fundamental building blocks of our knowledge, or elementary properties of the universe that can be expressed employing the knowledge base.

Evidently, not every concept can be defined in the knowledge base using its elementary categories. This is where approximations come into the picture.

To express approximately an arbitrary concept in the knowledge base we define the lower and upper approximation of any concept in U (subset of U).

The *lower approximation* of $X \subseteq U$ by $\underline{R}$ (i.e., set of categories of R, where R is a relation defined by any subset of R) is the union of equivalence classes of R that are included in X, or formally,

$$\underline{R}X = \cup\{Y \in U/R : Y \subseteq X\}$$

where U/R denotes the family of all equivalence classes of R.

The *upper approximation* of $X \subseteq U$ by $\overline{R}$ is the union of all equivalence classes of R that do not have empty intersection with X:

$$\overline{R}X = \cup\{Y \in U/R: Y \cap X \neq \emptyset\}$$

It is easily seen that these are special cases of definitions given previously.

The boundary-line region is of course defined as $BN_R(X)$ $= \bar{R}X - \underline{R}X$ and will be called the *R-boundary* of X.

Set $\underline{R}X$ consists of all elements of U that can be *with certainty* classified as elements of X employing knowledge R; set $\bar{R}X$ is the set of all elements of U that can be *possibly* classified as elements of X using knowledge R; set $BN_R(X)$ is the set of all elements that cannot be classified either to X or to $-X$ having knowledge R.

Now we are able to give the definition of the rough set:

> Set $X \subseteq U$ is *rough with respect to R if* $\bar{R}X \neq \underline{R}Y$; otherwise set X is *exact with respect to R.*

Thus, a set is rough if it does not have a sharply defined boundary, that is, it cannot be uniquely defined employing available knowledge.

Let us note the difference between imprecision and vagueness that results from our considerations. Imprecision is due to the indiscernibility relation and vagueness is the effect of the borderline region. Thus, imprecision and vagueness are entirely different phenomena.

It is easy to show that approximations have the following properties:

(1) $\underline{R}X \subseteq \bar{R}X$

(2) $\underline{R}\emptyset = \bar{R}\emptyset = \emptyset;\ \underline{R}U = \bar{R}U = U$

(3) $\bar{R}(X \cup Y) = \bar{R}X \cup \bar{R}Y$

(4) $\underline{R}(X \cap Y) = \underline{R}X \cap \underline{R}Y$

(5) $X \subseteq Y$ implies $\underline{R}X \subseteq \underline{R}Y$

(6) $X \subseteq Y$ implies $\bar{R}X \subseteq \bar{R}Y$

(7) $\underline{R}(X \cup Y) \supseteq \underline{R}X \cup \underline{R}Y$

(8) $\bar{R}(X \cap Y) \subseteq \bar{R}X \cap \bar{R}Y$

(9) $\underline{R}(-X) = -\bar{R}X$

(10) $\bar{R}(-X) = -\underline{R}X$

(11) $\underline{R}\,\underline{R}X = \bar{R}\,\underline{R}X = \underline{R}X$

(12) $\bar{R}\,\bar{R}X = \underline{R}\bar{R}X = \bar{R}X$

I would like to stress properties (7), (8), (9) and (10), but the detailed discussion is left to the interested reader.

It is interesting to note that the lower and the upper approximations are respectively interior and closure operations in a topology generated by the equivalence relation R. In other words, vagueness is strictly related to granulation of knowledge, which induces topological structure in the knowledge base.

For practical applications we need a numerical characterization of vagueness, which will be defined as

$$\alpha_R(X) = \text{card } \underline{R}X / \text{card } \overline{R}X$$

where $X \neq \emptyset$; this is called the *accuracy measure*.

The accuracy measure $\alpha_R(X)$ is intended to capture the degree of completeness of our knowledge about the set X.

Obviously, $0 \leqslant \alpha_R(X) \leqslant 1$, for every R and $X \subseteq U$; if $\alpha_R(X) = 1$ the R-boundary region of X is empty and the set X is definable in knowledge R; if $\alpha_R(X) < 1$ the set X has some nonempty R-boundary region and consequently is undefinable in knowledge R.

4. KNOWLEDGE REPRESENTATION

The assumed model of knowledge, as a family of equivalence relations, is very well suited to prove some mathematical properties of the concepts introduced. However, the definition has some disadvantages when considering algorithmic properties of knowledge and the method of processing knowledge. To avoid this drawback we need a special representation of the set of equivalence relations so that all necessary algorithms can be easily derived. Therefore, for algorithmic reasoning knowledge bases will be represented in tabular form, sometimes called *information system,* or *attribute-value system.* We will refer to it as *knowledge representation system.*

Knowledge representation system is a finite table with rows labeled with elements from U, and columns labeled with elements from a set A, called the set of attributes. With each attribute α from A a finite set of values V_a is associated, and is referred to as *domain of α.*

To each object x and attribute α there corresponds an entry in the table, which is a value of attribute α associated with object X. For example, if the object were an *apple* and the attribute *color*, then the corresponding entry in the table could be *red.*

In Table 5.1, set $\{1, 2, 3, 4, 5, 6, 7\}$ is the set of objects, $\{a, b, c, d, e\}$ is the set of attributes, and the domain of each attribute is the set $\{0, 1, 2\}$.

Table 5.1.

U	a	b	c	d	e
1	1	0	0	1	1
2	1	0	0	0	1
3	0	0	0	0	0
4	1	1	0	1	0
5	1	1	0	2	2
6	2	2	0	2	2
7	2	2	2	2	2

It is easily seen that each attribute in the table defines an equivalence relation, such that two objects x, y belong to the same equivalence class if they have the same attribute values. Thus, such a table can be considered as representation of a knowledge base with the family of equivalence relations defined by the set of attributes. Each subset of objects (concept) can be now described in terms of attributes and their values. If the concept is exact it can be described uniquely; otherwise, the concept can be described approximately, by its lower and upper approximations.

Moreover, we can now easily define a variety of other concepts needed to analyze knowledge represented by the table. We are mostly interested in discovering various relations between attributes, for instance, exact or approximate dependency of attributes (cause–effect relations), redundancy of attributes, significance of attributes, etc. The proposed approach has also given rise to new efficient methods of decision rule generation from data.

The rough set theory has proved to be a very effective tool for data analysis. Several systems based on the ideas discussed in this paper were implemented on personal computers (IBM PC) and work stations (SUN) in Poland and elsewhere, and have found many real-life, nontrivial applications.

It is worthwhile to observe that the rough sets philosophy is close to statistical data analysis and perhaps can be viewed as "deterministic statistics." Comparison of statistical and rough set methods can be found in Krusińska et al. (1990).

Keywords: rough set, indiscernibility, approximation, vagueness knowledge representation, learning, classification

BIBLIOGRAPHY

Arciszewski, T., and W. Ziarko. (1986). Adaptive expert system for preliminary engineering design. *Proceedings of the Sixth International Workshop on Expert Systems and Their Applications, Paris,* pp. 695-712.

Arciszewski, T., W. Ziarko, and M. Mustafa. (1987). A methodology of design knowledge acquisition for use in learning expert systems. *International Journal of Man-Machine Studies,* **27,** 23-32.

Chanas, S. and D. Kuchta. (1991). Further remarks on the relation between rough and fuzzy sets. *Fuzzy Sets and Systems.* In press.

Comer, S. D. (1991). An algebraic approach to the approximation of information. *Fundamenta Informaticae.* In press.

Dubois, D. and H. Prade. (1988). Rough fuzzy sets and fuzzy rough sets. *International Journal of General Systems.* In press.

Fibak, J., K. Słowiński, and R. Słowiński. (1986). The Application of rough set theory to the verification of indications for treatment of duodenal ulcer by HSV. *Proceedings of the Sixth International Workshop on Expert Systems and Their Applications. Avignon, April 28–30,* pp. 587–599.

Frege, G. (1903). Grundgesetze der Arithmetik, Vol. 2. In Geach and Black: (eds.): *Selections from the Philosophical Writings of Gotlob Frege.* Blackwell (Oxford), 1970.

Greenburg, A. G. (1987). Commentary on the paper by Pawlak. *Computing Reviews,* **27,** 413–433.

Grzymała-Busse, J. (1986). On reduction of knowledge representation systems. *International Workshop on Expert Systems and Their Applications, Avignon, April 28–30,* pp. 453–478.

Grzymała-Busse, J. (1986). Algebraic properties of knowledge representation systems. *Proceedings of the First ACM SIGART International Symposium on Methodologies for Intelligent Systems, Knoxville, TN,* pp. 432–440.

Grzymała-Busse, J. (1987). Learning from examples based on rough multisets. *Proceedings of the Second International Symposium on Methodologies for Intelligent Systems, Charlotte, ORNL,* pp. 325–332.

Grzymała-Busse, J. (1988). Knowledge acquisition under uncertainty—A rough set approach. *Journal of Intelligent and Robotic Systems,* **1,** 3–36.

Grzymała-Busse, J. (1988). Dempster-Shafer Theory Interpretation of Rough Set Approach to Knowledge Acquisition under Uncertainty. *University of Kansas, Department of Computer Science (Report).*

Gupta, D. (1988). Rough sets and information systems. *In Proceedings of the Eleventh International Conference on Research and Development in Information Retrieval.* Baltimore, MD.

Hadjimichael, M. (1989). Conditions suggestion algorithm for knowledge representation systems. *Proceedings of the Fourth International Symposium on Methodologies for Intelligent Systems. Charlotte, NC, ORNL/DSRD-24.*

Hadjimichael, M. and A. Wasilewska. (1990). Rule reduction for knowledge representation systems. *Bull. Polish. Acad. Sci. Math.* In press.

Iwiński, T. (1987). Algebraic approach to rough sets. *Bull. Polish Acad. Sci. Math.,* **35,** 673–683.

Jian-Ming, Gao and A. Nakamura. (1990). A semantic decision method for the logic of indiscernibility relation. *Fundamenta Informaticae.* In press.

Kandulski, T., B. Litewka, A. Mrózek, and K. Tukałło. (1990). An attempt to establish the hierarchy of factors of a surgical wound infection by means of the rough set theory. *Bull. Acad. Sci. Biol.* In press.

Konikowska, B. (1987). A formal language for reasoning about indiscernibility. *Bull. Polish Acad. Sci. Math.*, **35**, 239–250.

Krasowski. H. (1988). Aircraft pilot performance evaluation using rough sets. Ph.D. dissertation, Technical University of Rzeszów (Poland). In Polish.

Krusińska, E., R. Słowiński, and J. Stefanowski. (1990). Discriminant versus rough sets approach to vague data analysis. *Journal of Applied Statistics and Data Analysis.* In press.

Krynicki, M. (1989). Linearly ordered quantifiers. *Bull. Polish Acad. Sci. Math.*, **37** (6), 295–303.

Krynicki, M. (1990a). Quantifiers determined by partial order. *Zeitschrift feur Grundlagen der Mathematik und Logic*, **36**, 79–86.

Krynicki, M. (1990b). A note on rough concept logic. *Fundamenta Informaticae*, **13**, 227–235.

Krynicki, M. and H. P. Tuschnik. (1990). An axiomatisation of the logic with rough quantifiers. *Journal of Symbolic Logic.* In press.

Krysiński, J. (1990). Rough set approach to analysis of relationship between structure and activity of quaternary imidazolium compounds. *Arzneimittel-Forschung Drug Research*, **40** (II), 7, 795–799.

Mrózek, A. (1989). Rough set dependency analysis among attributes in computer implementation of expert inference models. *International Journal of Man-Machine Studies*, **30**, 457–473.

Nakamura, A. and Gao Jian-Ming. (1988). Modal logic for similarity-based data analysis. *Hiroshima University Technical Report*, C-26.

Nieminen, J. (1988). Rough tolerance and tolerance black boxes. *Fundamenta Informaticae.* In press.

Novotny, M. and Z. Pawlak. (1985a). Characterization of rough top equalities and rough bottom equalities. *Bull. Pol. Acad. Sci. Math.*, **33**, (1–2), 91–97.

Novotny, M. and Z. Pawlak. (1985b). On rough equalities. *Ibid.*, **33** (1–2), 99–104.

Novotny, M. and Z. Pawlak. (1985c). Black box analysis and rough top equalities. *Ibid.*, **33** (1–2), 105–113.

Novotny, M. and Z. Pawlak. (1987). Concept forming and black boxes. *Ibid.*, *Math.*, **35** (1–2), 134–141.

Novotny, M. and Z. Pawlak. (1988a). Partial dependency of attributes. *Bull. Polish Acad. Sci. Math.*, **36** (7–8), 453–458.

Novotny, M. and Z. Pawlak. (1988b). Independence of attributes. *Ibid.*, **36** (7–8), 459–465.

Novotny, M. and Z. Pawlak. (1991). On superreducts. *Ibid.* In press.

Nowak, R., R. Słowiński, and J. Stefanowski. (1990). Rough sets based diagnostic classifier of reducers. *Maintenance Management International* (Submitted).

Obtułowicz, A. (1988). Rough sets and Heyting algebra valued sets. *Bull. Polish Acad. Sci. Math.*, **35**, 667–673.

Orłowska, E. (1985a). Logic of indiscernibility relation. *Bull. Polish Acad. Sci. Math.*, 475–485.

Orłowska, E. (1985b). Logic approach to information systems. *Fundamenta Informaticae*, **8**, 359–378.

Orłowska, E. (1986). Semantic analysis of inductive reasoning. *Theoretical Computer Science*, **43**, 81–86.

Orłowska, E. (1989). Logic for reasoning about knowledge. *Zeitschr. f. Math. Logik und Grundlagen d. Math.*, **35**, 559-572.

Orłowska, E. and Z. Pawlak. (1984). Logical foundations of knowledge representation. *Institute of Computer Science, Polish Academy of Sciences Reports*, **537**, 1–106.

Pawlak, Z. (1982). Rough sets. *International Journal of Computer and Information Sciences*, **11**, 341–356.

Pawlak, Z. (1986a). Learning from examples. *Bull. Pol. Acad. Sci. Tech.*, **34**, 573–586.

Pawlak, Z. (1986b). On learning – A rough set approach. *Lecture Notes in Computer Sciences*, Springer-Verlag, **208**, 197–227.

Pawlak, Z. (1987a). Rough logic. *Bull. Pol. Acad. Sci. Tech.*, **35**, 253–258.

Pawlak, Z. (1987b). Learning from examples—The case of an imperfect teacher. *Bull. Pol. Acad. Sci. Tech.*, **35**, 259–264.

Pawlak, Z., K. Słowiński, and R. Słowiński. (1986). Rough classification of patients after highly selective vagotomy for duodenal ulcer. *Int. Journal of Man-Machine Studies*, **24**, 413–433.

Pawlak, Z., S. K. M. Wong, and W. Ziarko. (1988). Rough sets: Probabilistic versus deterministic approach. *International Journal of Man-Machine Studies*, **29**, 81–85.

Pettorossi, A., Z. Ras, and M. Zemankova. (1987). On learning with imperfect teachers. *Proceedings of the Second ACM SIGART International Symposium on Methodologies for Intelligent Systems*, pp. 256–263. New York: North-Holland.

Pomykała, J. and J. A. Pomykała. (1988). The stone algebra of rough sets. *Bull. Pol. Acad. Sci. Math.*, **36**, 495–508.

Ras, Z. and M. Zemankova. (1986). Learning in knowledge based systems, a probabilistic approach. *Proceedings of the 1986 CISS, Princeton, NJ*, pp. 844–847.

Rasiowa, H. (1986). Rough concepts and multiple valued logic. *Proc. of 16th. Intl. Symp. on Multiple Valued Logic, Washington DC, IIIE Computer Society Press*, pp. 228–288.

Rasiowa, H., and G. Epstein. (1986). Approximation reasoning and Scott's information systems. In *Proceedings of the Second International Symposium on Methodologies for Intelligent Systems*, pp. 33–42. New York: North-Holland.

Rasiowa, H. and A. Skowron. (1985). Rough concept logic. *Proc. of the 5th Symp. on Computer Theory, Zaborów*, December 3–8, 1984. *Lecture Notes in Computer Science*, Springer-Verlag, **208**, 288–297.

Rasiowa, H. and A. Skowron (1986a). The first step towards an approximation logic. *Meeting of the Association for Symbolic Logic, (Chicago 1985), Journal of Symbolic Logic*, **51**, 509.

Rasiowa, H. and A. Skowron. (1986b). Approximation logic. *Proc. of*

Mathematical Methods of Specification and Synthesis of Software Systems Conf. 1985, **31**, 123–139. Berlin: Akademie-Verlag.

Rauszer, C. M. (1984). An equivalence between indiscernibility relations in information systems and a fragment of intuitionistic logic. In *Lecture Notes in Computer Science.* Berlin: Springer-Verlag, pp. 298–317.

Rauszer, C. M. (1985a). Dependency of attributes in information systems. *Bull. Pol. Acad. Sci. Math.,* **33**, 551–559.

Rauszer, C. M. (1985b). An equivalence between theory of functional dependencies and fragment of intuitionistic logic. *Bull. Pol. Acad. Sci. Math.,* **33**, 571–679.

Rauszer, C. M. (1985c). An algebraic and logical approach to indiscernibility relations. *ICS PAS Reports* (1985), no. 559.

Rauszer, C. M. (1986). Remarks on logic for dependencies. *Bull. Pol. Acad. Sci. Math.,* **34**, 249–252.

Rauszer, C. M. (1987). Algebraic and logical description of functional and multivalued dependencies. *Proc. of the Second Int. Symp. on Methodologies for Intelligent Systems, Charlotte,* 1987, pp. 145–155. New York: North-Holland.

Rauszer, C. M. (1988). Algebraic properties of functional dependencies. *Bull. Pol. Acad. Sci. Math.,* **33**, 561–569.

Rauszer, C. M. (1990). Reducts in information systems. *Fundamenta Informaticae.* In press.

Reinhard, A., B. Stawski, and T. Weber. (1989a). Application of rough sets to study the water outflow from the river basin. *Bull. Pol. Acad. Sci. Tech.,* **37**, 97–104.

Reinhard, A., B. Stawski, W. Szwast, and T. Weber. (1989b). An attempt to use the rough sets theory for the control of water-air relation on a given polder. *Bull. Pol. Acad. Sci. Tech.,* **37**, 339–349.

Rybnik, J. (1990). Minimization of partially defined switching functions using rough sets. *Manuscript.*

Skowron, A. (1989). The relationship between rough set theory and evidence theory. *Bull. Pol. Acad. Sci. Math.,* **37**, 87–90.

Słowiński, K., R. Słowiński, and J. Stefanowski. (1989). Rough sets approach to analysis of data from peritoneal lavage in acute pancreatitis. *Medical Informatics,* **13**, 143–159.

Słowiński, K. and R. Słowiński. (1990). Sensitivity analysis of rough classification. *International Journal of Man-Machine Studies,* **32**, 693–705.

Szczerba, L. W. (1987). Rough quantifiers. *Bull. Pol. Acad. Sci. Math.,* **35**, 251–254.

Vakarelov, D. (1981). Abstract characterization of some modal knowledge representation systems and the logic NIM of nondeterministic information. In Jorraud, Ph. and V. Sgurev (eds.): *Artificial Intelligence, Methodology, Systems, Applications.* Amsterdam: North-Holland.

Vakarelov, D. (1989). Modal logic of knowledge representation systems. In *Lecture Notes on Computer Science.* Berlin: Springer-Verlag, **363**, 257–277.

Wasilewska, A. (1988). On correctness of decision algorithms in information systems. *Fundamenta Informaticae,* **11**, 219–239.

Wasilewska, A. (1989). Syntactic decision procedures in information systems. *International Journal of Man-Machine Studies,* **50**, 273–285.

Wasilewska, A. (1990a). Conditional knowledge representation systems – Model for an implementation. *Bull. Pol. Acad. Sci. Math.* In press.

Wasilewska, A. (1990b). An inductive learning system. *Bull. Pol. Acad. Sci. Math.* In press.

Wong, S.K.M. and J. H. Wong. (1987). An inductive learning system-ILS. *Proceedings of the Second ACM SIGART International Symposium on Methodologies for Intelligent Systems,* pp. 370–378. Amsterdam: North Holland.

Wong, S.K.M. and W. Ziarko. (1987). INFER—An adaptive decision support system based on the probabilistic approximate classification. *The Sixth International Workshop on Expert Systems and their Applications, Avignon,* 1, 713–726.

Wong, S.K.M., W. Ziarko, and R. L. Ye, (1986a). Comparison of rough set and statistical methods in inductive learning. *International Journal of Man-Machine Studies,* **24,** 53–72.

Wong, S.K.M., W. Ziarko, and R. L. Ye. (1986b). On learning and evaluation of decision rules in context of rough sets. *Proceedings of the First ACM SIGART International Symposium on Methodologies for Intelligent Systems, Knoxville, TN,* pp. 308–324.

Wygralak, M. (1989). Rough sets and fuzzy sets—some remarks on interrelations. *Fuzzy Sets and Systems,* **29,** 241–243.

Ziarko, W. (1987). On reduction of knowledge representation. *Proceedings of the Second International Symposium on Methodologies for Intelligent Systems (Colloquia Programm),* pp. 99–113. Charlotte, ORNL.

Ziarko, W. (1991). The discovery, analysis and representation of data dependencies in databases. In *Knowledge Discovery in Databases,* AAAI Press.

2

ASPECTS
OF FUZZY LOGIC:

THEORY
AND
IMPLEMENTATIONS

6 *LT*-fuzzy logic

Helena RASIOWA
Institute of Mathematics
University of Warsaw
ul. Banacha 2
02-097 Warsaw, POLAND

Nguyen CAT HO
National Center for Scientific
Research of Vietnam
Center for System and
Management Research
Lieugiai–Badinh–Hanoi
P.O. Box 626 Bo Ho
VIETNAM

Abstract. The purpose of this paper is to propose a class of first-order *LT*-fuzzy logics of any poset type $(T, \leqslant)$, intended to serve as a tool for approximation reasoning. They are obtained from approximation logics of any poset type $(T, \leqslant)$ (Rasiowa, 1987, 1988); see also Rasiowa (1990, 1991a) for the case without modal connectives, by assuming another—but equivalent – semantics based on *LT*-fuzzy sets (Rasiowa and Cat Ho, 1991). The concept of *LT*-fuzzy sets permitted the development in (Rasiowa and Cat Ho, 1991) of a uniform axiomatic approach to *LT*-fuzzy algebra on the basis of the theory of plain semi-Post algebras of any poset type $(T, \leqslant)$ (Cat Ho and Rasiowa, 1989). This approach concerns particularly *L*-fuzzy sets introduced by Goguen (1969), and a slight modification of fuzzy sets (Zadeh, 1965). *LT*-fuzzy sets in a nonempty universe U are functions assigning to objects in U certain subsets of a fixed poset $(T, \leqslant)$, interpreted as sets of membership values. *LT*-fuzzy logics differ from fuzzy logic (see, e.g., Zadeh, 1974; Bellman and Zadeh, 1977) among others by another implication, characterized by the algebraic relative pseudocomplementation — as in intuitionistic logic — and, above all, by an approach leading to a class of formalized axiomatic deductive systems and to completeness results. Proofs can be found in Rasiowa (1988, 1991b). In spite of the fact that *LT*-fuzzy logics are conventional ones, they were built according to the spirit of fuzziness reflected in their name. The authors believe that they may be useful in applications.

1. INTRODUCTION

The aim of the present paper is to announce a class of first-order *LT*-fuzzy logics. These are intended to serve as a tool for approximation reasoning.

Any *LT*-fuzzy predicate logic is not a fuzzy logic in the sense of Zadeh (1974, 1975) or Bellman and Zadeh (1977, cf. Dubois and Prade, 1980). A fuzzy logic, as formulated by Bellman and Zadeh (1977), is characterized following Haack (1981; see also Turner, 1984) by these features: (i) truth-values are fuzzy, (ii) the set of linguistic truth-values is not closed under logical connectives, (iii) truth-values are subjective and local, (iv) the validity can be characterized only semantically, that is, not in terms of axioms and rules of inference, and (v) the completeness, consistency and axiomatization are "peripheral" (Zadeh and Bellman, 1976).

LT-fuzzy predicate logics resulted from partially ordered set (poset) – based approximation logics (Rasiowa, 1987, 1988), and vary from these logics by a different — but equivalent — semantics. They are intended to deal with vague predicates. The essential idea was to assume *LT*-fuzzy sets introduced by Rasiowa and Cat Ho (1991) as a tool. This concept seems to provide great elasticity in applications, and is formulated in the spirit of fuzziness. On the other hand, a semantics based on *LT*-fuzzy sets permits us to consider completeness and consistency for *LT*-fuzzy logics, and to characterize a semantic consequence within the framework of axiomatic deductive systems.

The following example presents a motivation for introducing *LT*-fuzzy sets. In order to approximate a vague predicate such as "beautiful x" in a set U of girls, we use in practice certain parameters that are in general not linearly but partially ordered with respect to their importance. These parameters and their values reflect features of the concept "beautiful" in the set U and can be chosen very subjectively. A partial ordering induced on U according to our understanding of a "beautiful girl" should be compatible with the choice of parameters and their possible values. These parameters and their partially ordered values would be assumed as a poset $(T, \leqslant)$. Sets of the parameters' values form *LT*-fuzzy membership values for objects in U.

Given a poset $(T, \leqslant)$, considered as a poset of membership values, by a *T*-fuzzy membership value (*T-f.m.v.*), or a *T*-ideal (see Cat Ho and Rasiowa, 1989), we will mean any nonempty subset I of T such that for any *s*, *t* in *T* if $s \leqslant t$ and $t \in I$, then $s \in I$. Let *LT* be the family of subsets of *T* consisting of the empty set ø and all *T*-*f.m.v.*'s.

An *LT*-fuzzy set in a nonempty universe *U* is any function $f: U \rightarrow LT$, and an *n*-ary *LT*-fuzzy relation in *U* is any function $f: U^n \rightarrow LT$. By this definition, any *LT*-fuzzy set in $U \neq$ ø associates with each object *u* in *U* a *T*-fuzzy membership value, being a set of membership values, according to the spirit of fuzziness.

Any vague predicate $p(x)$ in *LT*-fuzzy logic is interpreted in a set $U \neq$ ø as an *LT*-fuzzy set $p_R(x): U \rightarrow LT$, and by such an interpretation adopts as logical values sets in *LT*, interpreted as *T*-fuzzy truth-values, playing the role of linguistic truth-values in fuzzy logic. In constrast to fuzzy logic, *LT* is closed under all operations representing logical connectives and quantifiers.

For any poset $(T, \leqslant)$, the family *LT* is a complete set lattice and hence a pseudo-Boolean algebra. In the case of a symmetric (self-dual) poset *T* a quasi-complementation operation (see Białynicki-Birula and Rasiowa, 1957), being a substitute of complementation, is also definable in *LT*. Moreover, under additional unary operations d_t, for $t \in T$, and zero-argument operations e_I, $I \in LT$, the algebra *LT* is a basic plain semi-Post algebra of type *T* (shortly a basic *psP*-algebra of type *T*). Plain semi-Post algebras, which are a simplification of semi-Post algebras (Cat Ho and Rasiowa, 1987), were introduced and investigated in Cat Ho and Rasiowa (1989). The theory of these algebras is a tool to an axiomatic algebraic approach to *LT*-fuzzy sets including *L*-fuzzy sets and in some sense fuzzy sets, if the operation charaterizing the Łukasiewicz implication in the interval [0, 1] (cf., e.g., Rescher, 1969) is replaced by the operation of the relative pseudocomplementation in [0, 1].

Deductive systems of *LT*-fuzzy logics are formulated with the completeness results in the case of a denumerable, well-founded poset $(T, \leqslant)$ or a denumerable *LT*. The case when there is a monomorphism from the interval [0, 1] into *LT*, namely of the poset $(Q(0, 1), \leqslant)$, where $Q(0, 1)$ is the set of all rational numbers from the open interval (0, 1), is announced in the present paper and discussed in Rasiowa (1991b).

Since the semantics for *LT*-fuzzy logics is equivalent to the semantics for approximation logics of type *T*, all results concerning approximation logics of type *T* are valid for *LT*-fuzzy logics.

It is worth it to emphasize that in the case of any finite poset $(T, \leqslant)$ there are mechanical proof systems for *LT*-fuzzy logics, of the Gentzen style and of the resolution style (Rasiowa, 1991a).

In order to keep the present paper self-contained, an introduction to LT-fuzzy sets theory will be given in Section 2. Section 3 is devoted to LT-fuzzy logics.

To simplify the notation, we often identify any poset $(T, \leqslant)$ with the set of its elements, and write poset T instead of poset $(T, \leqslant)$. Similarly, we often identify any abstract algebra $(P, o_1,...,o_n)$ with the set of its elements and just write algebra P. For brevity, we will also use "iff" instead of "if and only if."

2. LT-FUZZY SETS

A fuzzy set (Zadeh, 1965) in a nonempty universe U is a set of ordered pairs $\{(f(u), u)\}$ for $u \in U$, where

$$f: U \to [0, 1] \tag{1}$$

is a membership function of this fuzzy set, and $[0, 1]$ is the closed interval of the real line. The values $f(u)$ for u in U are called membership degrees or membership values of u. A fuzzy set is said to be empty if $f(u) = \emptyset$ for each $u \notin U$. We will identify here any fuzzy set with its membership function. Moreover, by a universe U we always mean a nonempty set.

An L-fuzzy set (Goguen, 1967) in a universe U is any function

$$f: U \to L \tag{2}$$

where L is a poset, in particular a lattice, a complete lattice, an interval $[0, 1]$.

In Rasiowa and Cat Ho (1991) the concept of an LT-fuzzy set was introduced and investigated, being a modification of that of an L-fuzzy set, and also a generalization of the concept of a fuzzy set. According to our intention, any LT-fuzzy set over a universe U — in contrast to an L-fuzzy set and a fuzzy set — associates to each object in U a set of membership values.

Let $(T, \leqslant)$ be an arbitrary poset, particularly as a partial ordering can be taken the identity relation on T. By a T-ideal (see Cat Ho and Rasiowa, 1989) or a T-fuzzy membership value (T-$f.m.v.$) we mean any nonempty subset I of T, such that for any $s, t \in T$, if $s \leqslant t$ and $t \in I$, then $s \in I$. Note that for all $t \in T$, the set $I(t) = \{s \in T: s \leqslant t\}$ is a T-ideal (T-$f.m.v.$) generated by t. By an expansion of $(T, \leqslant)$ we understand the family LT of subsets of T, consisting of the empty set $\emptyset$ and of all

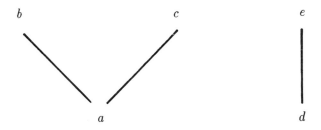

Figure 6.1.

T-f.m.v.'s. Of course, $(LT, \leqslant)$ is a poset under the inclusion relation denoted here by $\leqslant$. In the following we will identify each $t \in T$ with $I(t)$ and treat poset T as a subposet of LT. Under this assumption $t \leqslant I$ can be meant as $I(t) \leqslant I$ or as $t \in I$.

We will use the following notation. A least (greatest) element in poset T, provided it exists, will be denoted by $\perp$ ($\top$). The least element in LT is $\varnothing$ and will often be denoted by $\wedge$. The greatest element in LT is the set T and will often be denoted by $\vee$.

Clearly, the union and intersection of any family of sets in LT is also in LT, hence the following statement holds:

2.1. The expansion LT of any poset T is a complete set lattice under the inclusion relation denoted by $\leqslant$. Moreover, for each $I \in LT$:

$$I = \bigcup_{t \in T} \{I(t) : I(t) \leqslant I\} \tag{3}$$

Example 1. Let $(T, \leqslant)$ be a poset (shown in Figure 6.1), where $T = \{a, b, c, d, e\}$ and $a \leqslant b, a \leqslant c, d \leqslant e$, and $t \leqslant t$ for each $t \in T$. Then $LT = \{\varnothing, \{a\}, \{b, a\}, \{c, a\} \{a, b, c\}, \{d\}, \{e, d\}, \{a, d\}, \{b, a, d\}, \{c, a, d\}, \{a, b, c, d\}, \{a, e, d\}, \{b, a, e, d\}, \{c, a, e, d\}, T\}$.

Example 2. Let $Q(0, 1)$ denote (in this paper) the set of all rational numbers x from the open interval $(0, 1)$. It will be treated as a poset with the natural ordering relation $\leqslant$. Then $LQ(0, 1)$ consists of all sets $I(q) = \{x \in Q(0, 1) : x \leqslant q\}$ for q from $Q(0, 1)$, of all sets $I_q = \{x \in Q(0, 1) : x < q\}$ for q from $Q(0, 1)$, of all sets $I_{ir} = \{x \in Q(0, 1) : q < ir\}$ for each irrational number ir from $[0, 1]$, and of the empty set $\varnothing$ as well as of $Q(0,1)$. Identifying the integer 0 with the empty set ø, the integer 1 with the set $Q(0,1)$, every rational number q from $Q(0,1)$ with $I(q)$, and every irrational number ir from $[0,1]$ with I_{ir}, we can after such an identification treat the interval $[0,1]$ as a subposet of $LQ(0,1)$. More exactly, there is a monomorphism h from the poset $([0,1], \leqslant)$ into the poset $(LQ(0,1), \leqslant)$, defined as follows: $h(0) = ø$, $h(q) = I(q)$ for $q \in Q(0,1)$, $h(ir) = I_{ir}$ for each irrational number $ir \in [0,1]$. Identifying any $x \in [0,1]$ with $h(x)$ we can treat the poset $([0,1], \leqslant)$ as a subposet of $(LQ(0,1), \leqslant)$.

It is worth mentioning that

$$I = \bigcup_{q \in Q(0,1)} \{I(q): I(q) \leqslant I\} \tag{4}$$

results from (3). Note also the following statement:

2.2. There is no subset T of $Q(0,1)$ such that LT is isomorphic with $[0,1]$ as a complete lattice.

Proof. Suppose that $h:[0,1] \to LT$ is an isomorphism from $[0,1]$ onto LT for some $T \subset Q[0,1]$. Let $t \in T$ and $I = \bigcup_{s \in T} \{I(s): s < t\}$. Then $I \leqslant I(t)$ and $I \neq I(t)$. Since h maps $[0,1]$ onto LT, there are two numbers r, r' in $[0,1]$ such that $I = h(r)$ and $I(t) = h(r')$. Clearly, $r < r'$. Hence, there is an $r'' \in [0,1]$ such that $r < r'' < r'$. This yields $I \leqslant h(r'') \leqslant I(t)$. By (3) $h(r'') = \bigcup_{s \in T} \{I(s): I(s) \leqslant h(r'')\} = \bigcup_{s \in T} \{I(s): s < t\} = I$, because the condition $I(s) \leqslant h(r'') \leqslant I(t)$ implies $s < t$. This contradicts $I \neq h(r'')$.

By an LT-fuzzy set in a universe U we mean any function

$$f: U \to LT \tag{5}$$

The intended meaning of poset T for any LT-fuzzy set in U is similar to that of $(L, \leqslant)$ for L-fuzzy sets in U, and of $([0,1], \leqslant)$ in the case of fuzzy sets in U, i.e., of a scale of membership degrees of objects $u \in U$ in LT-fuzzy sets. According to this definition, any LT-fuzzy set (5) assigns to each $u \in U$ a T-f.m.v. (T-ideal), i.e., a subset of T. The T-f.m.v.'s play for poset T the role of the initial segments in the interval $(0,1)$.

An LT-fuzzy set (5) is said to be *empty* if $f(u) = ø$ for every $u \in U$, and is said to be *full* if $f(u) = T$ for every $u \in U$.

Observe that for any poset $(L, \leqslant)$ an L-fuzzy set $f: U \to L$ in Goguen's (1967) sense is an LT-fuzzy set. In fact, consider poset $T = L$. Then LT is the expansion of $(L, \leqslant)$, and $(L, \leqslant)$ can be considered as a subposet of $(LT, \leqslant)$. Hence, $f: U \to L$ can be considered as a function from U into LT and, therefore, as an LT-fuzzy set. Equally true, every LT-fuzzy set is an L-fuzzy set if we take $(LT, \leqslant)$ as a poset $(L, \leqslant)$.

Example 3. Consider a poset T defined as in Example 1. It is illustrated in Figure 6.2. Let $U = \{u_1, u_2, u_3, u_4, u_5, u_6\}$ be a set of people. Define "healthy x" in U as an *LT*-fuzzy set $f: U \to LT$ thus: $f(u_1) = \emptyset, f(u_2) = \{b, c, a\}, f(u_3) = \{e, d, a\}, f(u_4) = \{e, d\}, f(u_5) = T$, and $f(u_6) = \{d\}$. Then, *LT*-fuzzy set f induces the following partial ordering $\leqslant_f$ in U: $u_2 \leqslant_f u_5$, and $u_6 \leqslant_f u_4 \leqslant_f u_3 \leqslant_f u_5$. Thus u_5 is definitely healthy, u_1 is definitely not healthy, and the degrees of membership to f, belonging to *T-f.m.v.*'s assigned to particular $u \in U$, may be interpreted as values of certain parameters concerning the condition of health.

Another important motivation for introducing *LT*-fuzzy sets is a rich algebraic structure of the expansion *LT* for any poset $(T, \leqslant)$. We observed earlier (in Statement 2.1) that *LT* is a complete set lattice. This implies that for any *T-f.m.v.*'s I_1 and I_2 from *LT* there exists in *LT* the relative pseudocomplement $I_1 \Rightarrow I_2$ that is defined as

$$I_1 \Rightarrow I_2 = \cup \{I \in LT : I_1 \cap I \leqslant I_2\} \tag{6}$$

i.e., it is the union of all I from *LT* such that the intersection $I_1 \cap I$ is contained in I_2. Moreover, for any I_1 in *LT* there exists its pseudocomplement $\neg I_1$ defined by assuming

$$\neg I_1 = I_1 \Rightarrow \emptyset = \cup \{I \in LT : I_1 \cap I = \emptyset\} \tag{7}$$

The operation $\Rightarrow$ is characterized by the following equivalence:

$$I \leqslant I_1 \Rightarrow I_2 \text{ iff } I_1 \cap I \leqslant I_2 \tag{8}$$

Note that the condition $I_1 \leqslant I_2$ implies that $I_1 \Rightarrow I_2 = T = \vee$.

2.3. The algebra $(LT, \cup, \cap, \Rightarrow, \neg)$ is a pseudo-Boolean algebra (see, e.g., Rasiowa, 1974) also called a Heyting algebra.

Introduce in *LT* unary operations d_t for $t \in T$ — called *approximation operators* — determined as follows:

$$d_t I = \begin{cases} T = \vee \text{ if } t \in I \\ \emptyset = \wedge \text{otherwise} \end{cases} \tag{9}$$

Then, the algebra

$$(LT, \cup, \cap, \Rightarrow, \neg, (d_t)_{t \in T}, (e_I)_{I \in LT}) \tag{10}$$

where $e_I = I$ for every $I \in LT$, and every algebra isomorphic with this algebra, is said to be a basic plain semi-Post algebra of type T (briefly, a basic *psP*-algebra of type T) (see Rasiowa, 1987; Cat Ho and Rasiowa, 1989). It is worth mentioning that:

2.4. For every finite poset $(T, \leqslant)$ the basic psP-algebra of type T is functionally complete, i.e., every n-argument operation $o: LT^n \to LT, n = 1, 2, ...,$ is definable in LT by means of operations in algebra (10).

Proof. Define for every $I \in LT$ an operation c_I, assuming $c_I a = \bigcap_{t \in I} d_t a \cap \bigcap_{t \notin I} \neg d_t a$, where $a \in LT$. In particular, $c_{\vee} a = \bigcap_{t \in T} d_t a$ and $c_{\wedge} a = \bigcap_{t \in T} \neg d_t a$. It can be shown by a calculation that for all i, j in LT, $c_I e_J = e_{\vee}$ if $I = J$, and $c_I e_J = e_{\wedge}$ if $I \neq J$. Applying these operations and their properties mentioned above, it can be proved in a way similar to that in Rosser and Turquette (1952) for m-valued Łukasiewicz's logics that Statement 2.4 holds.

Example 4. Consider poset T defined in Example 1 and illustrated by the diagram in Figure 6.1. Then, for instance, $\{b, a\} \cup \{e, d\} = \{b, a, e, d\}$, $\{b, a\} \cap \{c, a\} = \{a\}$, $\{b, a, d\} \Rightarrow \{c, a, d\} = \{c, a, e, d\}$, $\{c, a, d\} \Rightarrow \{b, a, d\} = \{b, a, e, d\}$, $\neg\{a\} = \{e, d\}$, $\neg\{e, d\} = \{a, b, c\}$, $d_a\{a, b, c\} = T = \vee$, and $d_e\{a, b, c\} = \emptyset = \wedge$.

Example 5. Consider poset $(Q(0, 1), \leqslant)$, discussed in Example 2. For any I, I_1, I_2 in $LQ(0, 1)$ the following holds:

$$I_1 \Rightarrow I_2 = \begin{cases} \vee & \text{if } I_1 \leqslant I_2 \\ I_2 & \text{otherwise} \end{cases} \tag{11}$$

$$\neg I = I \Rightarrow \emptyset = \begin{cases} \vee & \text{if } I = \emptyset \\ \wedge & \text{otherwise} \end{cases} \tag{12}$$

The pseudocomplement operation does not have the property of the double complementation, nor does it satisfy de Morgan's laws. However, for some posets T it is possible to introduce in LT an operation $\sim$ of the quasi-complementation (Białynicki-Birula, 1957; Rasiowa, 1974) that has the properties mentioned above, and moreover, $\sim \vee = \wedge$ and $\sim \wedge = \vee$.

A poset $(T, \leqslant)$ is said to be symmetric or self-dual if there exists an involution $-: T \to T$ (i.e., a mapping satisfying $--t = t$ for each $t \in T$), such that for all s, t in T, $s \leqslant t$ iff $-t \leqslant -s$. Any such mapping will be said to be a symmetry mapping. Applying a symmetry mapping we can define a quasi-complementation operation $\sim$ on LT by assuming for every $I \in LT$

$$\sim I = \{t \in T : -t \notin I\} \tag{13}$$

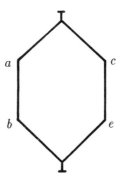

Figure 6.2.

It can be shown (Rasiowa and Cat Ho, 1991) that $\sim I \in LT$ and

$$\sim\vee = \wedge, \ \sim\wedge = \vee, \ \sim\sim I = I, \ \sim(I_1 \cup I_2) = \ \sim I_1 \cap \sim I_2,$$
$$\sim(I_1 \cap I_2) = \ \sim I_1 \cup \sim I_2 \tag{14}$$

$$d_t \sim I = \neg d_{-t} I, \text{ for every } t \in T \tag{15}$$

Example 6. Consider a poset $(T, \leqslant)$ where $T = \{\perp, a, b, c, e, \top\}$ and $\perp \leqslant t$ for each $t \in T$, $t \leqslant \top$ for each $t \in T$, $b \leqslant a, e \leqslant c, t \leqslant t$ for each $t \in T$. This poset is illustrated by the diagram in Figure 6.2. Observe that $LT = \{\varnothing, \{\perp\}, \{b, \perp\}, \{a, b, \perp\}, \{e, \perp\}, \{c, e, \perp\}, \{b, e, \perp\}, \{a, b, e, \perp\}, \{c, e, b, \perp\}, \{a, b, c, e, \perp\}, T\}$. Define a symmetry mapping $-: T \to T$ as follows: $-a = b, -b = a, -c = e, -e = c, -\perp = \top, -\top = \perp$. According to (13), $\sim\wedge = \ \sim\varnothing = T = \vee, \ \sim\vee = \ \sim T = \varnothing = \wedge, \ \sim\{\perp\} = \{\perp, a, b, c, e\}, \ \sim\{\perp, a, b, c, e\} = \{\perp\}, \ \sim\{b, \perp\} = \{\perp, b, c, e\}, \ \sim\{\perp, b, c, e\} = \{b, \perp\}, \ \sim\{a, b, \perp\} = \{c, e, \perp\}, \ \sim\{c, e, \perp\} = \{a, b, \perp\}, \ \sim\{e, \perp\} = \{e, a, b, \perp\}, \ \sim\{e, a, b, \perp\} = \{e, \perp\}, \ \sim\{b, e, \perp\} = \{b, e, \perp\}$.

Example 7. Let us consider poset $(Q(0, 1), \leqslant)$ (see Example 2). Then the symmetry mapping $-$ is defined by assuming for each $q \in Q(0, 1)$, $-q = 1 - q$. It is extended on the interval $(0, 1)$ by the formula $-ir = 1 - ir$ for every irrational number ir from $(0, 1)$. It is easy to verify that (13) yields the following equalities: $\sim I(q) = I_{-q}, \ \sim I_q = I(-q)$ for all $q \in Q(0, 1)$, and $\sim I_{ir} = I_{-ir}$ for each irrational number $ir \in [0, 1]$.

If we consider the interval $[0, 1]$ as the set of truth-values in the Łukasiewicz $\mathcal{L}_{aleph_1}$ logic (cf. Rescher, 1969), then $-x = 1 - x$ characterizes the negation. Thus, there is a strong connection between the operation $\sim$ in LT and the negation in the Łukasiewicz logic $\mathcal{L}_{aleph_1}$.

For every symmetric poset $(T, \leqslant)$ with a symmetry mapping $\neg$, we shall consider its expansion LT as a basic psP-algebra of type T with the quasi-complementation $\sim$ defined by (13).

With every poset $(T, \leqslant)$ (symmetric poset $(T, \leqslant)$ with a symmetry mapping $\neg$) there will be associated a class of plain–semi Post algebras of type T (with the quasi-complementation $\sim$ determined by $\neg$), i.e., of algebras $(P, \cup, \cap, \Rightarrow, \neg, (\sim), (d_t)_{t \in T}, (e_I)_{I \in LT})$, satisfying the following axioms (Cat Ho and Rasiowa, 1989; Rasiowa and Cat Ho, 1991): (p_0) $(P, \cup, \cap, \Rightarrow, \neg)$ is a pseudo-Boolean algebra with the unit element $e_{\vee}$ and the zero element $e_{\wedge} = \neg e_{\vee}$, (p_1) $d_t (a \cup b) = d_t a \cup d_t b$, (p_2) $d_t(a \cap b) = d_t a \cap d_t b$, $(p_3) d_s d_t a = d_t a$, $(p_4) d_t e_I = \begin{cases} e_{\vee} & \text{if } t \in I \\ e_{\wedge} & \text{otherwise} \end{cases}$, $(p_5) d_t a \cup \neg d_t a = e_{\vee}$, $(p_6) a = \bigcup_{t \in T} (d_t a \cap e_t)$, $(p_7) d_t \sim a = \neg d_{-t} a$ in the case of a symmetric poset (Rasiowa and Cat Ho, 1991), where a and b are any elements in P, s and t belong to T, and $I \in LT$.

In (p_6) $\cup$ denotes the least upper bound in P. If T is finite, then $\cup$ in (p_6) reduces to a finite join. Since pseudo-Boolean algebras are equationally definable (see, e.g., Rasiowa and Sikorski, 1963; Rasiowa, 1974), we infer that:

2.5. For any finite poset T the class of all psP-algebras of type T is equationally definable.

The plain semi-Post algebras have been introduced and examined in Rasiowa and Cat Ho (1989). They are a simplification of semi-Post algebras (Cat Ho and Rasiowa, 1987).

The simplest example of a psP-algebra of type T is offered by the basic psP-algebra LT (with a quasi-complementation).

The algebraic structure of the expansion LT of any poset T induces an analogous algebraic structure on the collection $FLT(U)$ of all LT-fuzzy sets in any universe U. Clearly, for any LT-fuzzy sets $f : U \to LT, g : U \to LT$, we define $f \cup g, f \cap g, f \Rightarrow g, \neg f, \sim f, d_t f$ for $t \in T$, and e_I for $I \in LT$ as usually, assuming:

$$(f \cup g)(u) = f(u) \cup g(u) \tag{16}$$
$$(f \cap g)(u) = f(u) \cap g(u) \tag{17}$$
$$(f \Rightarrow g)(u) = f(u) \Rightarrow g(u) \tag{18}$$
$$(\neg f)(u) = \neg(f(u)) \tag{19}$$
$$(\sim f)(u) = \sim(f(u)) \tag{20}$$
$$(d_t f)(u) = d_t(f(u)) \tag{21}$$
$$e_I(u) = e_I \tag{22}$$

where the operations $\cup$, $\cap$, $\Rightarrow$, $\neg$, $\sim$, d_t for $t \in T$, e_I for $I \in LT$, on the right-hand sides of (16) – (22) are operations in *LT*. Let us note that (Rasiowa and Cat Ho, 1991):

2.6. For every poset $(T, \leqslant)$ and universe U, the algebra of *LT*-fuzzy sets in U, i.e.,

$$(FLT(U), \cup, \cap, \Rightarrow, \neg, (\sim), (d_t)_{t\in T}, (e_I)_{I\in LT}) \tag{23}$$

is a *psP*-algebra of type T and a complete lattice. For any set $(f_j)_{j\in J}$ of *LT*-fuzzy sets in U:

l.u.b.$_{j\in J}f_j = f$, where for every $u \in U$, $f(u) = \cup_{j\in J}f_j(u)$ $\qquad$ (24)

g.l.b.$_{j\in J}f_j = g$, where for every $u \in U$, $g(u) = \cap_{j\in J}f_j(u)$ $\qquad$ (25)

where l.u.b. and g.l.b. denote the least upper bound and greatest lower bound in $FLT(U)$, respectively, and $\cup$ and $\cap$ denote the set-theoretic union and intersection.

Among fundamental properties of *psP*-algebras of any type T, note the following ones:

$a \leqslant c$ iff $d_t a \leqslant d_t c$ for every $t \in T$ $\qquad\qquad$ (26)

$a = c$ iff $d_t a = d_t c$ for every $t \in T$ $\qquad\qquad$ (27)

if $s \leqslant t$, then $d_t a \leqslant d_s a$, if $a \leqslant b$, then $d_t a \leqslant d_t b$ $\qquad$ (28)

the set $B_p = \{d_t a : \in P, t \in T\}$ is a set of complemented elements in P and algebra $(B_p, \cup, \cap, \Rightarrow, \neg)$ is a Boolean algebra $\qquad\qquad$ (29)

For every poset T (maybe symmetric) we associate with each *LT*-fuzzy set $f : U \to LT$ and $t \in T$, similarly to the case of fuzzy sets, a set t-cut of f, denoted by $Cut_t f$ and defined as follows:

$$Cut_t f = \{u \in U : I(t) \leqslant f(u)\} = \{u \in U : t \varepsilon f(u)\} \tag{30}$$

It follows that if $s \leqslant t$, then $Cut_t f \subseteq Cut_s f$. Thus a T-sequence $(Cut_t f)_{t\in T}$ associated with each *LT*-fuzzy set f in U is a descending one.

Observe that (9), (21), and (29) yield

$$\begin{cases} u \in Cut_t f \text{ iff } d_t f(u) = \vee \\ u \notin Cut_t f \text{ iff } d_t f(u) = \wedge \end{cases} \tag{31}$$

This yields the following statement, worth mentioning:

2.7. (i) For every *LT*-fuzzy set $f : U \to LT$, $d_t f : U \to \{\vee, \wedge\}$ is a characteristic function of the set t-cut of f, i.e., of $Cut_t f$.

(ii) $(Cut_t f)_{t \in T}$ is a descending T-sequence of subsets of U, i.e., if $s \leqslant t$, then $Cut_t f \subseteq Cut_s f$.

Let us set for any LT-fuzzy sets $f \colon U \to LT$, $g \colon U \to LT$

$$(Cut_t f)_{t \in T} \leqslant (Cut_t g)_{t \in T} \text{ iff } Cut_t f \subseteq Cut_t g \text{ for each } t \in T \quad (31)$$

Let $CFLT(U)$ be the collection of all $(Cut_t f)_{t \in T}$ for $f \in FLT(U)$. It can be proved that $CFLT(U)$ under partial ordering defined by (31) is a complete lattice. Moreover, it is possible to introduce on $CFLT(U)$ the operations $\Rightarrow$, $\neg$, d_t for $t \in T$, e_I for $I \in LT$ (and $\sim$ in the case of a symmetric poset T) in such a way that $(CFLT(U), \cup, \cap, \Rightarrow, \neg, (\sim),$ $(d_t)_{t \in T}, (e_I)_{I \in LT})$ is a psP-algebra of type T (with quasi-complementation). Let us quote without proof the following theorem proved in Rasiowa and Cat Ho (1991) (for a weaker form, see Negoita and Ralescu, 1975):

2.8. $FLT(U)$ and $CFLT(U)$ for every poset T and universe U as psP-algebras of type T (with quasi-complementation) are isomorphic. Moreover, the mapping $h \colon FLT(U) \to CFLT(U)$ defined by $h(f)$ $= (Cut_t f)_{t \in T}$ is the required isomorphism.

It was also proved in Rasiowa and Cat Ho (1991) that the following theorem holds:

2.9. If a poset T (a symmetric poset T) is denumerable and well-founded (in particular finite) or LT is denumerable, then every denumerable psP-algebra of type T (with quasi-complementation) is isomorphic with the algebra of all LT-fuzzy sets over a universe U, i.e., it can be treated as an algebra of LT-fuzzy objects.

Clearly, all considerations in this section can also be treated as concerning n-ary LT-fuzzy relations because they are LT-fuzzy sets in U^n.

3. *LT*-FUZZY PREDICATE LOGICS

The purpose of this section is to propose a class of first-order LT-fuzzy logics that have a close relation with fuzzy logic in the sense of reasoning about vague concept in an approximation manner.

In classical predicate calculi n-ary predicates are traditionally interpreted as n-ary relations in a universe U, or equivalently as their characteristic functions $f \colon U \to \{\wedge, \vee\}$, where $\wedge$ and $\vee$ denote the unit element and the zero element of the two-element Boolean algebra, or the logical truth-values of the truth and falsehood, respectively.

In contrast, *LT*-fuzzy predicate calculi are intended to deal with vague predicates corresponding to concepts such as "tall," "young," "beautiful," "healthy," etc., and to formalize a model for approximation reasoning, i.e., leading to vague conclusions. Predicates and formulas in these logics will be interpreted as *LT*-fuzzy sets or *LT*-fuzzy relations in any universe *U*.

Let $(T, \leq)$ be a fixed arbitrary denumerable poset (maybe symmetric) assumed to be a type of logic, and *LT* its expansion (see Section 2) considered as a basic *psP*-algebra of type *T* (see (10) in Section 2) (with a quasi-complementation). The sets $I \in LT$ are *T*-fuzzy truth-values. The algebra

$$(LT, \cup, \cap, \Rightarrow, (\sim), (d_t)_{t \in T}, (e_I)_{I \in LT}) \tag{32}$$

will play the role of a *T*-fuzzy truth-table.

Type $(T, \leq)$ of a logic can be subjectively chosen according to vague predicates that are intended to be considered. The partial ordering in *LT* induced by the partial ordering in *T* should reflect partial orderings of the objects in a universe of discourse *U*, induced by the vague predicates associated with *LT*-fuzzy relations representing these predicates. For instance, the use of a linearly ordered *T* is proper for concepts like "tall," "young," but is not suitable for more complex concepts as "beautiful," "healthy," etc.

With a poset $(T, \leq)$ chosen as a type of logic and its expansion *LT* we will associate first-order predicate languages L_T of type *T*. Assume that an alphabet of any language L_T consists of a countable set *Var* of free individual variables, of finite sets *Pred*$_n$ (maybe empty) of *n*-ary predicates $n = 1, 2, \dots$, where at least one *Pred*$_n$ is nonempty, of propositional constants e_I for $I \in LT$, disjunction sign $\cup$, conjunction sign $\cap$, implication sign $\Rightarrow$, negation sign $\neg$ (quasi-negation sign $\sim$ if *T* is symmetric), approximation connectives d_t for $t \in T$. Moreover, the existential and universal quantifiers, $\cup_x$ and $\cap_x$, respectively, for $x \in Var$, occur in any alphabet of L_T. Atomic formulas are e_I for $I \in LT$ and $p(x_1, \dots, x_n)$ for any predicate $p \in Pred_n$, and $x_1, \dots, x_n \in Var$. The set *F* of all formulas is the least set containing the atomic formulas, and such that if *A* and *B* are in *F*, then $A \cup B, A \cap B, A \Rightarrow B, \neg A, \sim A$ (if *T* is symmetric), $d_t A$ for $t \in T$, $\cup_x A \cap_x A$ belong to *F*, too. For each formula *A* we will denote by *Var*(*A*) the set of all free individual variables appearing in *A*, i.e., not being in the scope of any quantifier that occurs in *A*.

Now we will introduce an *LT*-semantics in language L_T.

An LT-realization of a language L_T in a universe U is any mapping R assigning to each propositional constant e_I for $I \in LT$ the T-f.m.v. (T-fuzzy truth-value) $e_{IR} = I$, and to each predicate $p \in Pred_n$ an n-ary LT-fuzzy relation $p_R : U^n \to LT$. It associates with each n-tuple $(u_1, ..., u_n)$ of elements in U a T-f.m.v. (interpreted also as a T-fuzzy truth-value) $p_R(u_1, ..., u_n)$.

Let $Val(R)$ denote the set of all valuations of individual variables in the universe U of realization R, i.e., of all mappings $v : Var \to U$.

Extend realization R on the set F of all formulas treating the basic psP-algebra LT (with a quasi-complementation) as a T-fuzzy truth-table. For every formula A let A_R be its realization as an LT-fuzzy set or LT-fuzzy relation in U and $A_R(v)$, the value of A_R by values of free individual variables determined by a valuation v.

Accordingly, we define: (r_0) $e_{IR}(v) = I$ for each $I \in LT$, (r_1) $p(x_1, ..., x_n)_R(v) = p_R(v(x_1), ..., v(x_n))$, (r_2) $(A \cup B)_R(v) = A_R(v) \cup B_R(v)$, (r_3) $(A \cap B)_R(v) = A_R(v) \cap B_R(v)$, (r_4) $(A \Rightarrow B)_R(v) = A_R(v) \Rightarrow B_R(v)$, (r_5) $(\neg A)_R(v) = \neg(A_R(v))$, (r_6) $(\sim A)_R(v) = \sim A_R(v))$, (r_7) $(d_t A)_R(v) = d_t(A_R(v))$, (r_8) $(\bigcup_x A_R(v) = \bigcup_{u \in U} A_R(v_u)$, (r_9) $(\bigcap_x A)_R(v) = \bigcap_{u \in U} A_R(v_u)$, where $v_u(x) = u$ and $v_u(y) = y$ for each $y \neq x$, $y \in Var$.

The symbols $\cup, \cap, \Rightarrow, \neg, (\sim), d_t$ for $t \in T, \cup$, and $\cap$ on the right–hand sides of $(r_0) - (r_9)$ denote algebraic operations in the basic psP-algebra LT (with a quasi-complementation).

It follows from this definition that for each formula $A(x_1, ... x_n)$ with $Var(A) = \{x_1, ..., x_n\}$, realization $A_R : U^{Var} \to LT$ is in fact an n-ary LT-fuzzy relation, because the values of A_R depend on $v(x_1), ..., v(x_n)$. It is also interpreted as a function assigning to any n-tuple $(v(x_1), ..., v(x_n))$ for $v \in Val(R)$ a T-fuzzy truth-value $A_R(v)$ concerning the satisfiability of a formula $A(x_1, ..., x_n)$ by $(v(x_1), ..., v(x_n))$.

For LT-fuzzy relation $A_R(x_1, ..., x_n)$ and every $t \in T$ consider a t-cut of $A_R(x_1, ..., x_n)$ as defined in Section 2, i.e.,

$$Cut_t A_R(x_1, ..., x_n) = \{(u_1, ..., u_n) \in U^n : t \in A_R(u_1, ..., u_n)\} \qquad (33)$$

where $A_R(u_1, ..., u_n) = A_R(v)$ for each valuation $v \in Val(R)$ such that $v(x_i) = u_i$ for $i = 1, ..., n$. Thus $Cut_t A_R(x_1, ..., x_n)$ consists of all n-tuples $(u_1, ..., u_n) \in U^n$ such that T-f.m.v. (T-fuzzy truth-value represented by $A_R(u_1, ..., u_n)$ includes T-membership value t (T-truth value t). It follows from 2.7 (Section 2) that:

3.1. For every formula $A(x_1, ..., x_n)$ such that $Var(A) = \{x_1, ..., x_n\}$ and each $t \in T$, $d_t A_R(x_1, ..., x_n)$ is the characteristic function of $Cut_t A_R(x_1, ..., x_n)$. Moreover, the family of sets $(Cut_t A_R(x_1, ..., x_n))_{t \in T}$ is a descending T-sequence.

Example 8. Let $(T, \leqslant)$ be the poset considered in Example 6, Section 2. Assume that poset T is a type of *LT*-fuzzy logic and there are exactly two unary predicates p and q in L_T. Interpret p and q in a set $U = \{u_1, ..., u_6\}$ of pianists as "perfect Chopin player" and "young," respectively. With the first one we may associate two parameters: the one corresponding to a technical level and represented by T-truth values $\perp \leqslant b \leqslant a \leqslant \top$, and the one corresponding to a Chopin interpretation and represented by T-truth values $\perp \leqslant e \leqslant c \leqslant \top$. Predicate "young" can be linearly represented by T-fuzzy truth values $\emptyset$, $\{\perp\}$, $\{b, e, \perp\}$, $\{a, b, c, e, \perp\}$, and T. An *LT*-realization of L_T can be defined as, say: $p_R(u_1) = T, p_R(u_2) = \{a, b, c, e, \perp\}$, $p_R(u_3) = \{b, \perp, e\}$, $p_R(u_4) = \{a, b, \perp\}$, $p_R(u_5) = \{c, e, \perp\}$, $p_R(u_6) = \{\perp\}$, $q_R(u_1) = q_R(u_3) = \{\perp\}$, $q_R(u_2) = T$, $q_R(u_4) = \{b, e, \perp\}$, $q_R(u_5) = \{a, b, c, e, \perp\}$, $q_R(u_6) = \emptyset$. Clearly, p_R induces a partial order on the set U and q_R induces a linear order on U. If $v(x) = u_1$ and $v(y) = u_3$, then, for instance, $(p(x) \cap q(y))_R(v) = p_R(u_1) \cap q_R(u_3)$ $= T \cap \{\perp\} = \{\perp\}$, $\sim q(y)_R(v) = \sim q_R(u_3) = \sim\{\perp\} = \{\perp, a, b, c, e\}$, $\neg q(y)_R(v), \neg q_R(u_3) = \emptyset, \cup_x p(x)_R(v) = T, \cap_x p(x)_R(v) = \{\perp\}$.

A formula A in a language L_T is said to be t-satisfied in an *LT*-realization R by a valuation v if $d_t A_R(v) = \vee$, i.e., if $t \in A_R(v)$. A formula A is said to be t-valid in R if $d_t A_R = \vee$ for every valuation $v \in Val(R)$. A formula A is said to be satisfied in R by a valuation v if $A_R(v) = \vee$, i.e., if it is t-satisfied for every $t \in T$. A formula is said to be a tautology in *LT*-fuzzy logic if it is valid in every *LT*-realization R. An *LT*-realization R of a language L_T is said to be an *LT*-model for a set Σ of formulas if every formula from Σ is valid in R. A formula A is said to be a semantic consequence of a set Σ of formulas provided it is valid in every *LT*-model R for the set Σ. This is written as $\Sigma \models A$. A set Σ of formulas is said to be consistent if there is a formula A in L_T such that not $\Sigma \models A$.

Given a formalized language L_T, we will construct an axiomatic deductive system of *LT*-predicate logic by distinguishing a set of *LT*-tautologies as a set of logical axioms and establishing rules of inference. A formula A is said to be deducible from a set Σ of formulas if there is a formal proof of A from these formulas and logical axioms by means of rules of inference. This is written $\Sigma \vdash A$. In particular, if Σ is empty, we write $\vdash A$, which means that A is deducible from logical axioms by means of rules of inference.

For any formulas A, B, C in any language L_T the following formulas are *LT*-tautologies and are assumed to be logical axioms: (i_1) $A \Rightarrow (B \Rightarrow A)$, (i_2) $(A \Rightarrow (B \Rightarrow C)) \Rightarrow ((A \Rightarrow B) \Rightarrow (A \Rightarrow C))$, (i_3) $A \Rightarrow (A \cup B)$, (i_4) $B \Rightarrow (A \cup B)$, (i_5) $(A \Rightarrow C) \Rightarrow ((B \Rightarrow C) \Rightarrow ((A \cup B) \Rightarrow$

C)), (i_6) $(A \cap B) \Rightarrow A$, (i_7) $(A \cap B) \Rightarrow B$, (i_8) $(A \Rightarrow B) \Rightarrow ((A \Rightarrow C) \Rightarrow (A \Rightarrow (B \cap C)))$, (i_9) $(A \Rightarrow \neg B) \Rightarrow (B \Rightarrow \neg A)$, (i_{10}) $\sim(A \Rightarrow A) \Rightarrow B$, (p_1^*) $d_t(A \cup B) \Leftrightarrow (d_t A \cup d_t B)$, (p_2^*) $d_t(A \cap B) \Leftrightarrow (d_t A \cap d_t B)$, (p_3^*) $d_t e_I$ for $t \in I$, $\neg d_t e_I$ for $t \notin I$, (p_4^*) $d_s d_t A \Leftrightarrow d_t A$, (p_5^*) $d_t A \cup \neg d_t A$, (p_6^*) $(d_t A \cap e_t) \Rightarrow A$, $(p_7^*) d_t \sim A \Leftrightarrow \neg d_{-t} A$ if poset T is symmetric, where s, $t \in T$ and $I \in LT$.

The well-known rules of inference in classical predicate calculi (see, e.g., Rasiowa and Sikorski, 1963), namely modus ponens, rule of substitution for free individual variable, rules of introduction and of elimination of existential quantifiers, rules of introduction and of elimination of universal quantifiers, and the two additional rules:

$$\text{(rin)} \quad \frac{A \Rightarrow B}{d_t A \Rightarrow d_t B} \text{ for } t \in T \qquad \text{(rel)} \quad \frac{\{d_t A \Rightarrow d_t B\}_{t \in T}}{A \Rightarrow B}$$

are allowed in the deductive system under consideration. In the case of any denumerable poset T the (rel) rule is the infinitistic rule.

The following completeness theorem holds for deductive systems of LT-fuzzy logics.

3.2. If poset $(T, \leqslant)$ is denumerable and well-founded or its expansion LT is denumerable, then for any consistent set Σ of formulas in language L_T and any formula A in this language the following conditions are equivalent:

(i) $\Sigma \vdash A$, i.e. A is deducible in LT-fuzzy logic from Σ

(ii) $\Sigma \models A$, i.e., A is valid in every LT-model for Σ

(iii) $\Sigma \models d_t A$ for every $t \in T$, i.e., A is t-valid in every LT-model for Σ

(iv) $\Sigma \models d_t A$ for every maximal $t \in T$

The proof is analogous to that for approximation logics of any poset type T satisfying the hypotheses of 3.2 (Rasiowa, 1988). As a corollary we obtain the following theorem:

3.3. If poset T is denumerable and well-founded or LT is denumerable, then the following conditions for any formula A in L_T are equivalent:

(i) A is deducible in LT-fuzzy logic

(ii) A is an LT-tautology

Theorem 3.2 does not concern *LT*-fuzzy predicate logic for $T = Q(0, 1)$, where $Q(0, 1)$ is the set of all rational numbers q such that $0 < q < 1$. This case is comprehensively discussed in Rasiowa (1991b). In this paper we will present only a weaker completeness result. The expansion *LT* of $T = Q(0, 1)$ is an uncountable set (see Example 2 in Section 2), therefore any formalized language L_T in that case contains the uncountable set e_I for $I \in LT$ of propositional constants.

A deductive system for *LT*-fuzzy predicate logic in the case of $T = Q(0, 1)$ is obtained from that formulated above by adjoining to the axiom scheme $(i_1) - (i_{10})$, $(p_1^*) - (p_7^*)$ a new axiom scheme: (i_{11}) $(A \Rightarrow B) \cup (B \Rightarrow A)$ for any formulas A and B.

Then the following theorem (Rasiowa, 1991b) holds:

3.3. For any denumerable set Σ of formulas in a language $L_{Q(0, 1)}$ and any formula A in this language the following conditions are equivalent:

(i) $\Sigma \vdash A$, i.e., A is deducible from the set Σ in $LQ(0, 1)$-logic

(ii) $\Sigma \models A$, i.e., A is valid in every $LQ(0, 1)$-model for Σ

(iii) $\Sigma \models d_t A$ for each $t \in Q(0, 1)$, i.e., every $d_t A$ is valid in every $LQ(0, 1)$-model for Σ

As a corollary from Theorem 3.3 we obtain the following completeness theorem

3.4. For any formula A in a language $L_{Q(0, 1)}$ the following conditions are equivalent:

(i) A is deducible in $LQ(0, 1)$-fuzzy logic
(ii) A is an $LQ(0, 1)$-tautology

It is worth mentioning that in case of any finite poset $(T, \leqslant)$ there are automata proving systems of the Gentzen style and of the resolution style for *LT*-fuzzy logic (Rasiowa, 1991a). The first ones consist of decomposition schemes for formulas and are analogous to that for classical predicate calculi (Rasiowa and Sikorski, 1963), and also to systems for *m*-valued predicate calculi (Orłowska, 1985). The introduction of resolution theorem proving systems analogous to Robinson's (1965) for classical logic and to systems for *m*-valued predicate calculi (Orłowska, 1985) was preceeded by theorems on a prenex form of formulas having an approximation connective d_t in front, theorem on a normal form, theorem on the elimination of quantifiers using Skolem's method, as well as by introducing Herbrand models and proving Herbrand's resolution style theorem.

Keywords: fuzzy set, L-fuzzy set, LT-fuzzy set, poset, complete lattice, pseudo-Boolean algebra, quasi-complement, basic plain semi-Post algebra, deductive system

BIBLIOGRAPHY

Białynicki-Birula, A. and H. Rasiowa. (1957). On the representation of quasi-Boolean algebras. *Bull. Pol. Acad. Sci.* Cl.III, **5**, 615–619.

Bellman, R. E. and L. A. Zadeh. (1977). Local and fuzzy logics. In J. M. Dunn, and G. Epstein (eds.): *Modern Uses of Multiple-Valued Logics*. Dordrecht: Reidel, pp. 103–165.

Cat Ho, Ng. and H. Rasiowa. (1987). Semi-Post algebras. *Studia Logica*, **46**, 147–158.

Cat Ho, Ng. and H. Rasiowa. (1989). Plain semi-Post algebras as a poset-based generalization of Post algebras and their representability. *Studia Logica*, **48**, 509–530.

Dubois, D. and H. Prade. (1980). *Fuzzy Sets and Systems*. New York: Academic Press.

Goguen, J. A. (1967). L-fuzzy sets. *J. Math. Anal. Appls.*, **18**, 145–174.

Haack, S. (1981). *The Philosophy of Logics*. Cambridge University Press.

Negoita, C. V. and D. A. Ralescu. (1975). *Applications of Fuzzy Sets to System Analysis*. Basel and Stuttgart: Birkhäuser.

Orłowska, E. (1985). Mechanical proof methods for Post logics. *Logique et Analyse*, Nouvelle Serie, 28e Année, 110–121, 173–192.

Rasiowa, H. (1974). *An Algebraic Approach to Non-Classical Logics*. Amsterdam: North-Holland.

Rasiowa, H. (1987). An algebraic approach to some approximate reasoning. *Proc. ISMVL'87*. Boston: Computer Society Press, pp. 342–347.

Rasiowa, H. (1988). Logic of approximation reasoning. *Proc. First Workshop on Computer Science Logic (Karlsruhe, 1987)*. LNCS 329, Berlin: Springer-Verlag, pp. 188–210.

Rasiowa, H. (1990). On approximation logics: a survey. *Jahrbuch 1990*, Vienna: Kurt Gödel Society, 63–87.

Rasiowa, H. (1991a). Mechanical proof systems for logic of reaching consensus by groups of intelligent agents. *Int. Journ. of Approximate Reasoning*, **5**, 415–432.

Rasiowa, H. (1991b). Axiomatization and completeness of uncountably valued approximation logic. Manuscript.

Rasiowa, H. (1992). Toward fuzzy logic. In the present volume.

Rasiowa, H. and Ng. Cat Ho. (1991). LT-fuzzy sets. *Fuzzy Sets and Systems*. In press.

Rasiowa, H. and R. Sikorski. (1963). *The Mathematics of Metamathematics*. Warsaw: PWN Publ. (3rd ed., 1970).

Rescher, N. (1969). *Many Valued Logic*. New York: McGraw-Hill.

Robinson, G. A. (1965). Machine oriented logic based on the resolution principle. *Journ. of ACM*, **12**, 23–41.

Rosser, J. B. and A. R. Turquette. (1952). Many-valued logics. *Studies in Logic and the Foundations of Mathematics*. Amsterdam: North-Holland.

Turner, R. (1984). *Logics for Artificial Intelligence*. Chichester: Ellis Horwood.

Zadeh, L. A. (1965). Fuzzy sets. *Information and Control*, **8**, 338–353.

Zadeh, L. A. (1974). Fuzzy logic and approximate reasoning. Memo. no. ERL-M479, Electronics Res. Lab., University of California, Berkeley.

Zadeh, L. A. (1975). Fuzzy logic and approximate reasoning. *Synthese*, **30**, 407–428.

Zadeh, L. A. and R. E. Bellman. (1976). Local and fuzzy logics. Memo. no. ERL-M584, Electronics Res. Lab., University of California, Berkeley.

7 A model theoretic approach to propositional fuzzy logic using Beth Tableaux

James R. KENEVAN
Department of Computer
Science
Illinois Institute
of Technology
Chicago, IL 60616, USA

Richard E. NEAPOLITAN
Department of Computer
Science
Northeastern University
Chicago, IL 60625, USA

Abstract. This paper begins a model theoretic study of propositional fuzzy logic. Fuzzy logic was first described by Zadeh almost a quarter of a century ago. Though fuzzy logic has a large literature, its applications have been somewhat limited by its inability to provide a proof system. By introducing model theory and allowing the truth values to exist within closed intervals, a proof theory can be established and correctness of the theory shown.

1. INTRODUCTION

Fuzzy logic is one family of the larger class of multivalued logics, named as such because they allow more than the values of true and false of the older classical logics. The form of fuzzy logic used in this paper is single valued, with the value lying in the closed unit interval $[0,1] = \{x \mid 0 \leqslant x \leqslant 1\}$. Zero in our logic corresponds to absolute false in the classical logics, while one corresponds to absolute truth. We focus on the operators *and* ($\wedge$), *or* ($\vee$), *not* ($\neg$), *implies* ($\Rightarrow$), and *equivalent* ($\Leftrightarrow$).

In the theory that we propose in this paper the exact truth value of any proposition or well-formed formula is assumed to exist. But, because of our ignorance of the system under consideration, this truth value is known only as the closed interval that contains it. The motivation and justification for this point of view will be presented in the following sections.

Given, at least for now, this need to distinguish between fuzzy truth values and what we might be able to infer about these values, a model theoretic approach to the subject seems warranted. Briefly, a model is the collection, over some alphabet and some reasonable grammar, of all well-formed formulas or propositions that can be stated in the logic, together with a fuzzy truth assignment to these propositions. The truth assignments are preserved under the ordinary compositional rules of fuzzy logic as specified by Zadeh and others. These models are always infinite, and their full specification would require, in general, infinite time and infinite space. As usual we have the rules of the system (called compositional rules), together with truth assignments to a certain finite set of the propositions (called the *axiom set* for our system). In classical systems of two-valued logic, we are also often provided with a proof theory, or rules of inference, which allows the determination of truth values of certain propositions, by methods other than direct composition. It is this latter form of knowledge extension, or proof, that this paper attempts to apply to fuzzy logic. There are certain "rules" of reasoning that, if taken as axioms, should be taken by all systems specified in the given logic. An example from classic two-valued logic is the statement that $a \vee \neg a$ is always true. Another way of introducing this type of construct is with the aid of inference rules that allow us to prove that $a \vee \neg a$ is in fact true. We find it convenient to introduce these rules as von Neumann did as axiom schemata.

For general inference, or proof theory, we have chosen Beth Tableaux, perhaps not so much for its elegance as for its general popularity and the aid that this gives us in exposition. We will give and extremely abbreviated description of Beth Tableaux to refresh the reader's memory and to define our notation. It should not be accepted as a definitive description of the technique. Readers unfamiliar with Beth Tableaux and model theory can find descriptions of them in many texts on logic.

We will be using the max and min functions extensively in what follows. We propose, and use, the following notation for these operators. Let

$$\overline{ab...z} = \max(a, b, ..., z)$$

$$\underline{ab...z} = \min(a, b, ..., z)$$

In classical two-valued logic normally only the "true" propositions are stated. There are exceptions to this, however, as in Smullyan's signed formula extension of Beth Tableaux. In our case, the truth value is a bit more complex and must be stated differently. As a provisional (but not to be entirely abandoned) notation, we will separate the proposition (written on the left) from its truth value (written on the right) by a colon, as in $a : 0.732$, when a has truth value 0.732. This notation will be generalized in a couple of ways in the following discussion.

2. ZADEH'S RULES FOR FUZZY LOGIC

In his classic work, Zadeh proposed the following compositional rules for fuzzy logic:

$$a \wedge b : \underline{AB} \tag{F_1}$$

$$a \vee b : \overline{AB} \tag{F_2}$$

$$\neg a : 1 - A \tag{F_3}$$

where A is the truth value of proposition a, and $0 \leqslant A \leqslant 1$. The connectives for *implies* and *equivalence* have not been included here. They are easily obtained from the above definitions and the reductions of these operators to those of *and*, *or*, and *not*.

Note that these rules are purely compositional in nature. That is, if we know the value of propositions a and b, the rules tell us how to combine these values to find the value of a compound proposition, such as $a \vee b$. These rules do not, however, help with inference. For example, if the truth value of $a \vee b$ is known, these rules do not tell what values to assign to proposition a or to proposition b. Compositional rules such as these cannot tell us how to perform even such standard inferences as Modus Ponens.

3. COMPOSITION RULES FOR PROPOSITIONAL FUZZY INTERVAL LOGIC

Discrete-valued fuzzy logic is insufficient to handle the problems imposed by inference. In the construction of a proof a lack of precise knowledge of truth values can force the use of subintervals to describe the truth values of propositions. This does not lead to any inherent loss of generality, since a proposition with a truth value of x in the unit interval can be represented as having a truth value in the range of $[x, x]$.

The concept of fuzzy logic is easily extended to encompass these intervals of truth. Such an extension has the advantage of allowing a proof method, as is shown in the following sections. This can even be done without the model theoretic approach that we shall take, but this approach results in a lack of precision or "tightness" in the values that can be assigned in our theory. Although we will not pursue this non–model-theoretic theory, it is at least informative to show how the logical operators would act in such a theory. In fact, the compositional rules governing these intervals of truth are valid in our theory. We present them without proof here, since they will be shown to follow from the inference rules of our logic, at least when restricted to our logic.

AND Composition Rule. *Given* $a : [a_0, a_1]$ *and* $b : [b_0, b_1]$ *we can infer*

$$a \wedge b : [\underline{a_0 b_0},\ \underline{a_1 b_1}] \tag{I_1}$$

OR Composition Rule. *Given* $a : [a_0, a_1]$ *and* $b : [b_0, b_1]$ *we can infer*

$$a \vee b : [\overline{a_0 b_0},\ \overline{a_1 b_1}] \tag{I_2}$$

NOT Composition Rule. *Given* $a : [a_0, b_0]$, *we can infer*

$$\neg a : [1 - a_1,\ 1 - a_0] \tag{I_3}$$

There is one other useful inference rule, that of intersection. This rule would be trivial and useless in either two-valued logic or the standard real-valued fuzzy logics.

INTERSECTION Inference Rule. *Given* $a : [x_0, x_1]$ *and also* $a : [y_0, y_1]$, *we can infer*

$$a : [\overline{x_0 y_0},\ \underline{x_1 y_1}] \tag{I_4}$$

This last rule is really an inference rule, and not a rule of composition. It is generally applicable, however, and needs no special machinery for its definition, and hence would likely be included in a definition of interval-valued fuzzy logic.

4. MODEL THEORY

We introduce a model theory for fuzzy logics in this section. This theory will allow us to define the inference rules and proof methods in the following sections.

The model theory that we introduce is for propositional logic with the operators $\wedge$, $\vee$, $\neg$, $\Rightarrow$, $\Leftrightarrow$ and no others. We allow parentheses to be used in the logic in the standard way, and we imagine some fixed alphabet for representing meaningful logical expressions called sentences or well-formed formulas. The letters a, b, . . . represent logical constants or variables. Now let S be the set of all well-formed formulas, using the given operators, variables, and parentheses. A model for two-valued logic is, from our point of view, a function that maps S into the set of values {true, false}, i.e.,

$$M : S \rightarrow \{\top, \bot\}$$

This is done in such a way as to preserve the truth values under the logical operators. For fuzzy logics, a model is a function that maps S into the unit interval $[0, 1]$ with the restriction that the map M must be faithful to the compositional rules of fuzzy logic. This is formalized by insisting that the function or model M must satisfy the following three rules:

Composition Rule for $\vee$. *Given* $M(a) \rightarrow A$ *and* $M(b) \rightarrow B$, *the function M must map* $a \vee b$ *as:*

$$M(a \vee b) \rightarrow \overline{AB} \qquad\qquad (C_1)$$

Composition Rule for $\wedge$. *Given* $M(a) \rightarrow A$ *and* $M(b) \rightarrow B$, *the function M must map* $a \wedge b$ *as:*

$$M(a \wedge b) \rightarrow \underline{AB} \qquad\qquad (C_2)$$

Composition Rule for $\neg$. *Given* $M(a) \rightarrow A$, *then the function M must map* $\neg a$ *as:*

$$yM(\neg a) \rightarrow 1 - A \qquad\qquad (C_3)$$

Given such a model M, we can speak of truth in the model, and in an alternate sense, provable truth. Truth in the model, whose values may or may not be known, is called *forcing* and is written as:

$$M \models a:A$$

and is read "Model M *forces* (or *models*) proposition a with truth value A." Often, when the model is understood, this is simplified to $\models a:A$. The value A is a single value lying in the interval $[0, 1]$.

When we prove or otherwise know the interval containing the truth value of a proposition, perhaps from axioms or axiom schemata, or through composition from smaller known propositions or via the application of inference in proof, the truth value will in general be denoted as:

$$\vdash a:[a_0, a_1]$$

and is read "It has been shown that the model M entails proposition a with truth value in the interval $[a_0, a_1]$." The exact value of this interval depends not just on the axioms but also on the proof used to create it. We do not bother to index this by either the model or the proof since these will always be obvious from the context.

5. INFERENCE RULES FOR PROPOSITIONAL FUZZY LOGIC

This section presents the inference rules. More rules, of a slightly different nature, are presented in the section on axiom schemata. Our model for inference and proof theory in this paper is that of Beth Tableaux.

Syntactic Substitution Rule. *This rule states that occurrences of propositions that are syntactically equivalent can be substituted for one another without change of truth value. This also applies to parenthesized subpropositions.*

For example, once de Morgan's laws have been given as syntactical substitution rules, we can write

$$\vdash a \wedge (\neg(b \vee \neg c)) : [p_0, p_1]$$

as:

$$\vdash a \wedge (\neg(b \wedge \neg c)) : [p_0, p_1]$$

The following rules will give a tree structure for a Beth Tableaux–style proof system. The meaning of the rules is roughly as follows: If the condition above the horizontal line is known to hold, then the condition below the line must hold. In the case of *not*, this is a simple condition. For the other logical operators separation occurs, which means that below the line we have two possible worlds, either one of which (we don't immediately know which) must occur. These rules are strung together into a tree to form the next section.

Inference Rule for $\vee$.

$$a:[a_0, a_1]$$
$$b:[b_0, b_1]$$
$$a \vee b:[p_0, p_1]$$

$a:[a_0, p_1 a_1]$	$a:[\overline{p_0\, a_0}, p_1 a_1]$
$b:[\overline{p_0 b_0}, p_1 b_1]$	$b:[b_0, p_1 b_1]$
$a \vee b:[\overline{p_0 a_0 b_0}, \overline{p_1 a_1 b_1}]$	$a \vee b:[\overline{p_0 a_0 b_0}, \overline{p_1 a_1 b_1}]$

Inference Rule for $\wedge$.

$$a:[a_0, a_1]$$
$$b:[b_0, b_1]$$
$$a \wedge b:[p_0, p_1]$$

$a:[\overline{p_0 a_0}, a_1]$	$a:[\overline{p_0\, a_0}, p_1 a_1]$
$b:[\overline{p_0 b_0}, p_1 b_1]$	$b:[\overline{p_0 b_0}, b_1]$
$a \wedge b:[\overline{p_0 a_0 b_0}, \overline{p_1 a_1 b_1}]$	$a \wedge b:[\overline{p_0 a_0 b_0}, \overline{p_1 a_1 b_1}]$

Inference Rule for $\neg$.

$$a:[a_0, a_1]$$
$$\neg a:[1 - a_1, 1 - a_0]$$

The next inference rule states that if a proposition is known to be true via two different intervals, then it can be inferred to be true to the interval that is the intersection of the two given closed intervals. This can be generalized to the intersection of any finite number of closed subsets of the unit interval. The resulting set must also be a closed subset of the unit interval (from the definition of the standard topology on the unit interval).

Intersection Inference Rule. *Given a proposition a, and the following knowledge of its logical value within the model being considered as:* $\vdash a : [x_0, x_1]$ *and* $\vdash a : [y_0, y_1]$, *then we can infer*

$$\vdash a : [\overline{x_0 y_0}, \underline{x_1 y_1}]$$

Written in the style of Beth Tableaux, this becomes:

$$a : [x_0, x_1]$$
$$a : [y_0, y_1]$$

$$\overline{\qquad\qquad\qquad\qquad}$$
$$a : [\overline{x_0 y_0}, \underline{x_1 y_1}]$$

Meta-Proof of the $\vee$ **Inference Rule.** This proof is given as six claims. Each claim is needed to determine the endpoints of the truth value intervals shown below the horizontal line in the referenced tableau. We assume that there does exist a model, and that the model has single-valued fuzzy truths.

$$M \models a : A$$
$$M \models b : B$$
$$M \models a \vee b : P$$

Using this, and some knowledge of intervals,

$$\vdash a : [a_0, a_1]$$
$$\vdash b : [b_0, b_1]$$
$$\vdash a \vee b : [p_0, p_1]$$

we have

$$a_0 \leqslant A \leqslant a_1 \tag{1}$$
$$b_0 \leqslant B \leqslant b_1 \tag{2}$$
$$p_0 \leqslant P \leqslant p_1 \tag{3}$$
$$P = \max(A, B) \tag{4}$$

The proof now proceeds by showing that the intervals below the line in the tableaux are correct.

Claim 1: $A \leqslant \min(a_1, p_1)$.

Proof:

$$A \leqslant a_1 \quad \text{from (1)}$$
$$A \leqslant \max(A, B) = P \quad \text{from (4)}$$
$$A \leqslant p_1 \quad \text{from (3)}$$

Since $A \leqslant a_1$ and $A \leqslant p_1$ we have

$$A \leqslant \min(a_1, p_1)$$

as claimed, showing that $\vdash a : [0, \underline{p_1 a_1}]$.

Claim 2: $B \leqslant \min(b_1, p_1)$.

Proof: By symmetry in a and b, from Claim 1. This shows that $\vdash b : [0, \underline{p_1 b_1}]$.

Claim 3: $\max(p_0, a_0, b_0) \leqslant P$.

Proof:

$\quad a_0 \leqslant A \quad$ from (1)
$\quad b_0 \leqslant B \quad$ from (2)

hence

$$\max(a_0, b_0) \leqslant \max(A, B) = P$$

Further,

$$p_0 \leqslant P \quad \text{from (3)}$$

We therefore get

$$\max(p_0, \max(a_0, b_0)) = \max(p_0, a_0, b_0) \leqslant P$$

as claimed. This means that $\vdash a \wedge b : [\overline{p_0 a_0 b_0}, 1]$.

Claim 4: $P \leqslant \min(p_1, \max(a_1, b_1))$.

Proof:

$\quad A \leqslant a_1 \quad$ from (1)
$\quad B \leqslant b_1 \quad$ from (2)

together with (4) imply

$$P \leqslant \max(A, B) \leqslant \max(a_1, b_1)$$

This together with $P \leqslant p_1$, from (3), implies that

$$P \leqslant \min(p_1, \max(a_1, b_1))$$

as claimed. Hence $\vdash a \wedge b : [0, p_1\overline{a_1 b_1}]$. Combining Claims 3 and 4 with the Intersection Inference Rule shows that $\vdash a \wedge b : [\overline{p_0 a_0 b_0}, \underline{p_1 \overline{a_1 b_1}}]$.

Claim 5: One of the following two cases must occur. Either:

Case 1:

$$a_0 \leqslant A \quad \text{and} \quad \max(p_0, b_0) \leqslant B$$

or

Case 2:

$$\max(p_0, a_0) \leqslant A \quad \text{and} \quad b_0 \leqslant B$$

Proof: Note that either $A \leqslant B$ or else $B \leqslant A$, but we may not know which of these two cases occurs.

Case 1: Assume that $A \leqslant B$. It then follows that $P = \max(A, B) = B$ from (4).

$$p_0 \leqslant P \Rightarrow p_0 \leqslant B \quad \text{from (3)}$$
$$b_0 \leqslant B \quad \text{from (2)}$$

and hence

$$\max(p_0, b_0) \leqslant B$$

Since nothing can be said about A now, $a_0 \leqslant A$, and Case 1 has been shown. Case 2 is similarly proved, by assuming that $B \leqslant A$.

This concludes the proof of the meta-theorem. The other inference rules are proved in the same way.

It is interesting to note that the rules and proofs for *and* and for *or* are dual. They both demonstrate separation, or the splitting of knowledge into two potentially different universes. This is in contrast to the standard two-valued logical approach in which only the *or* operator demonstrates such splitting. There is a stronger sense of duality demonstrated in the inference rules, however. The rules map to one another, in both statement and in proof, if the intervals are reversed and if max is everywhere replaced by min and vice versa. This duality is hidden in the two-valued case.

One might wonder how strong the inference rules really are. In one sense, they are as strong as possible; the inferred intervals, given the original values of the propositions, cannot be strengthened.

Meta-Theorem. *The fuzzy inference rules are as strong as possible; the intervals cannot be decreased.*

We offer this statement without proof, rather leaving it as an exercise for the reader. An obvious method of showing it is to give cases that force each of the bounds in each of the inference rules.

6. PROOF THEORY

To prove a statement using Beth Tableaux in the two-valued unsigned formula case, all the axioms are written at the first node of the tree, above the first line. The proposition to be proved is negated and written with these propositions. Each time an inference is made, the modified propositions are written below the line, along with all other propositions that occurred above that line. The inference rules show only those propositions that are being used in the inference. If a path in the tree, or its terminal node, results in assigning a value of true to both a proposition and its negation, that node is declared closed, or dead, and is ignored for the rest of the proof. If all the paths close, the theorem is proved since there can exist no model that encompasses the axioms and the negated statement of the proposition to be proved. Hence the proposition must in fact be true in all models that contain the axioms.

As an example of the use of Beth Tableaux in two-valued logic, we offer a proof of Modus Ponens. Assuming that $\vdash a : \top$ and $\vdash a \Rightarrow b : \top$, we will show that $\vdash b : \top$. Since this version of Beth Tableaux proof uses proof by contradiction, we will assume that $\vdash b : \bot$, or equivalently, $\vdash \neg b : \top$.

$$
\begin{array}{c}
a : \top \\
\neg b : \top \\
a \Rightarrow b : \top \\
\hline
a : \top \\
\neg b : \top \\
a \vee b : \top \\
\end{array}
$$

$a : \top$	$a : \top$
$\neg b : \top$	$\neg b : \top$
$\neg a : \top$	$b : \top$

The left branch of this tree is closed because both a and $\neg a$ are shown to be true. The right branch is closed since it shows that both b and $\neg b$ must be true. Since all branches of the tableaux are closed, there is no model for the first path of the tree. The assumption that b is false is itself shown to be false, and hence the theorem is true. Therefore b must in fact be true in all models that admit the axioms $a : \top$ and $a \Rightarrow b : \top$.

The situation is somewhat different for fuzzy Beth Tableaux. Contradiction is not the primary method of proof. The tableaux ends either because no further improvement can be done to any of the propositions or because we have tired of the proof and and quit. For each proposition (or at least each proposition that we are interested in), we take the union of the truth sets along every nonclosed terminal node of the tableaux, and we call this union (which must be a closed subinterval of the unit interval or else a finite union of such intervals) the truth set of the proposition.

When the interval containing the truth value of a proposition is shown to be null, the associated path in the fuzzy Beth Tableaux is said to be closed. As soon as a path in the Beth Tableaux closes, as in the two-valued case, we do no further expansion on that path. As stated above, this node contributes nothing to the truth values of the propositions it contains. If all the branches of the tree close, we have reached a contradiction and no model exists that includes the original axioms and proposition.

7. INFERENCE AND COMPOSITION

As an application of the inference rules of the last section, we show that they are powerful enough to define the appropriate compositional rules in both our logic (in the sense of entails) and also in the model itself (forces). This should not surprise the reader since the Beth rules of two-valued logic are also strong enough to derive the compositional rules of that logic.

Meta-Theorem. *If* $\vdash a : [a_0, a_1]$ *and* $\vdash b : [b_0, b_1]$, *then it follows that*

$\vdash a \wedge b : [a_0 b_0, a_1 b_1]$.

Proof: Using the Inference Rule for $\wedge$, replacing $[p_0, p_1]$ by $[0, 1]$, consistent with our complete lack of knowledge of the logic value of proposition p, we have:

$$a : [a_0, a_1]$$
$$b : [b_0, b_1]$$
$$a \wedge b : [0, 1]$$

$a : [\overline{0 a_0}, a_1] \equiv [a_0, a_1]$	$a : [\overline{0 a_0}, 1 a_1] \equiv [a_0, a_1]$
$b : [\overline{0 b_0}, 1 b_1] \equiv [b_0, b_1]$	$b : [\overline{0 b_0}, b_1] \equiv [b_0, b_1]$
$a \wedge b : [\overline{0 a_0 b_0}, 1 a_1 b_1] \equiv$	$a \wedge b : [\overline{0 a_0 b_0}, 1 a_1 b_1] \equiv$
$\equiv [\underline{a_0 b_0}, a_1 b_1]$	$\equiv [\underline{a_0 b_0}, \underline{a_1 b_1}]$

Note that both leaves of this tree end in exactly the same set of proposition, truth value pairs, and that these pairs are exactly the appropriate compositional rules for intervals. Hence the meta-theorem is proved.

If we replace the intervals $[a_0, a_1]$ and $[b_0, b_1]$ in the above meta-theorem and its proof by the intervals $[A, A]$ and $[B, B]$, respectively, we have a meta-proof of the real-valued compositional rule for *and* according to Zadeh. The other compositional rules for both standard fuzzy logic and for intervalized fuzzy logic follow from the appropriate inference rules as given above. The proofs are similar to the one above and are omitted. Note that the computational rules within the model itself are now forced into existence, assuming that a model exists.

8. AXIOM SCHEMATA

Unfortunately not everything from two-valued propositional logic is immediately extensible to fuzzy logic. An example is the proposition $a \vee \neg a$. This is directly provable, with no axioms, using the inference rules for Beth Tableaux. Such a proposition, which must be true in any possible (in this case two-valued) propositional logic is called a tautology. Such truths are also sometimes referred to as "syntactic truths." The situation is not quite so comfortable in fuzzy logic, however. We assume that nothing is known about the truth value of proposition a. One can always assume that $\vdash a : [0, 1]$, since this statement gives no restriction to the actual value of a. Similarly, prior to proof, the only value that can be assumed for $a \vee \neg a$ is the interval $[0, 1]$. If we apply the fuzzy inference rule to this, we obtain no sharpening of the intervals; nothing is learned. This is different from the two-valued case, where a Beth proof of $a \vee \neg a$ is given as follows:

$$\frac{\neg(a \vee \neg a) : \top}{\neg a \vee a : \top}$$

$$\begin{array}{l} a : \top \\ \neg a : \top \end{array}$$

We can prove that $\vdash a \wedge \neg a : [0.5, 1]$, independent of the value of a, but not by using the inference rules.

Meta-Theorem. *For any a, where a can be some variable or proposition,*

$$\vdash a \vee \neg a : [0.5, 1]$$

Proof: Though we don't know the exact values, write $\models a : A$ and $\models a \vee \neg A : X$. We have two cases, first where $A \leqslant 0.5$ and second where $A \geqslant 0.5$. It is clear that, from the model theoretic definition of $\vee$ we must have $X \geqslant 0.5$ in each of these cases.

9. CONCLUSION

This paper has presented a proof theory for fuzzy logic. Classical two-valued logic is imbedded in this logic even though one should exercise caution with the axiom schemata. There is also a projection from the multivalued fuzzy logic onto two-valued logic. These issues will be addressed in another paper.

One might ask how time consuming the proof method demonstrated here actually is. The embedding referred to above gives us the answer.

Meta-Theorem. *Proof in our fuzzy logic is NP-hard.*

It can take an exponential amount of time to refine the interval of truth of the proposition to its best, or smallest, possible value.

Proof: The embedding of two-valued logic into fuzzy logic can be done in polynomial time. This reduction, combined with the well-known fact that proof in ordinary two-valued propositional logic is NP-hard, suffices to show that proof in this system is also NP-hard.

As discussed in the section on proof, the function of a proof in this theory is to assign the smallest possible closed subset of the unit interval to the proposition as its "truth containing set." This is done by taking the union of the truth values of each proposition at each nonclosed branch of the Beth Tableaux. Since we admit only finite proof trees, it is clear that for a given proposition the union of the closed truth intervals produces a closed subset of the unit interval. There is no a priori reason, however, that this closed subset need be an interval.

Exercise: Suppose it is known that $\vdash a \vee \neg a : [.7,.9]$, $\vdash b \vee \neg b :$ $[.6,.98]$, and $\vdash a \vee b : [.65,.95]$. Find and prove the best possible values for a and for b.

The inference rules and proof system have been stated only for closed intervals. The obvious question is: how should we extend the concepts presented here to include the finite, disconnected union of closed intervals? It seems only such an extension would do justice to the original goal of the paper, that of providing a proof theory for fuzzy logic. We now propose three alternate extensions to the theory.

As a first approach, let us assume that we restrict our axioms and our axiom schemata to allow only closed, connected intervals of truth. Now let us suppose a proof is provided. A particular proposition can exist, with different values, at several nonclosed terminal branches of the Beth proof tree. Since this proposition is on different branches of the tree, the Intersection Inference Rule does not apply, and, if we choose to declare the proof finished, we must take the union of all the closed truth intervals on all these branches as the truth value of the proposition, which may of course not be connected. Now what happens if we wish to use this result in the proof of another theorem? Our answer (at least for this extension of the proof method) is that we cannot do this. Rather, we continue the first proof, adding in those axioms needed to continue through the first proof and into the second proof, all at one go, as it were. This will give closed sets of truth for both (or all) propositions that we were originally interested in, but does not require us to deal with anything but intervals at any level of the proof tree, clearly an advantage. It is as though we produce exactly one theorem and one proof encompassing all the results we were looking for originally.

The next extension is to allow the axioms and, if absolutely necessary, even the axiom schemata, to have truth values that are the union of a finite number of pairwise disjoint subintervals of the unit interval. Doing so will allow the proof of one or more propositions to be treated as axioms in a later proof. Now instead of producing a single proof tree, we produce one for each of the (finite number) combinations of subintervals from the axioms. For example, suppose we know $\vdash a : I_{a_1} \cup I_{a_2}$ and also $\vdash b : I_{b_1} \cup I_{b_2} \cup I_{b_3}$, where the I_a are disjoint closed intervals and where the I_b are also pairwise disjoint closed intervals. If these are the only axioms, or known facts, at the beginning of our proof that have truth sets that are not intervals, we produce six different Beth Tableaux, one for each combination of one interval per axiom. In the above example, we would have six different tableaux. The results of the truth values for each proposition are formed by taking the union of the truth values of the proposition as obtained from each tableau. This method has the advantage (compared to the previous method) of allowing axioms to have disconnected truth sets. It has the apparent disadvantage of having an exponential number of trees in terms of the number of propositions with disconnected truth domains. This last point, although depressing at first glance, should be considered in the light of the fact that the proof technique was known to be NP-hard to begin with. We just made it slightly harder.

Possibly the best method of handling disjoint truth values is to modify the inference rules to deal directly with the disjoint union of intervals. This would allow the axioms to be disjoint, an advantage if more than one theorem is to be provided, and also reduces the work needed to provide a proof back down to a single tableau. As an example, imagine a modified rule for *and* or *or*. Suppose that we are combining proposition a, whose known truth is composed of the disjoint union of k different closed intervals, with another proposition, say b, whose truth set is composed of l disconnected intervals. If, to simplify, we know $\mid -a \wedge b : [0, 1]$ before the application of the modified inference rule, after its application we would know $a \wedge b$ in kl subnodes of the given node in the proof tree, not necessarily all of which are distinct. We would then represent this as a collection of at most kl subnodes by replacing identical nodes with just one representative node. This gives an alternate set of inference rules.

Keywords: fuzzy logic, fuzzy set theory, Beth Tableaux, inference, theorem proving

BIBLIOGRAPHY

Baldwin, J. F. (1981). Fuzzy logic and fuzzy reasoning. In E. Mamdani and B. Gaines (eds.): *Fuzzy Reasoning and Applications*. New York: Academic Press.

Barwise, J. (ed). (1977). *Handbook of Mathematical Logic*. Amsterdam: North-Holland.

Barwise, J. and S. Feferman (eds.), (1985). *Model-Theoretic Logics*. Berlin: Springer-Verlag.

Beth, E. W. (1965). *The Foundations of Mathematics*. Amsterdam: North-Holland.

Bowen, K. A. (1979). *Model Theory for Modal Logic. Kripke Models for Modal Predicate Calculi.* Dordrecht: Reidel.

Chang, C. and R. C. Lee. (1973). *Symbolic Logic and Mechanical Theorem Proving.* New York: Academic Press.

Giles, R. (1981). Lukasiewicz logic and fuzzy set theory. In E. Mamdani and B. Gaines (eds.): *Fuzzy Reasoning and its Applications.* New York: Academic Press.

Giles, R. (1982). Semantics for fuzzy reasoning. *Int. J. Man-Machine Studies,* 17, 401–415.

Goguen, J. A. (1969). The logic of inexact concepts. *Synthesis,* 19, 325–373.

Goguen, J. A. (1979). *Fuzzy sets and the social nature of truth.* In M. Gupta, R. Ragade, and R. Yager (eds.): *Advances in Fuzzy Set Theory and Applications.* Amsterdam: North-Holland.

Kaufmann, A. and M. M. Gupta. (1985). *Introduction to Fuzzy Arithmetic, Theory and Applications.* New York: Van Nostrand Reinhold.

MacLane, S. (1971). *Categories for the Working Mathematician.* Berlin: Springer Verlag.

Mamdani, E. H. and B. R. Gaines. (eds.) (1981). *Fuzzy Reasoning and its Applications.* New York: Academic Press.

Manin, Y. I. (1977). *A Course in Mathematical Logic.* Berlin: Springer-Verlag.

McCawley, J. D. (1981). *Everything that Linguists Have Always Wanted to Know about Logic,* But Were Ashamed to Ask. University of Chicago Press.

Montague, R. (1974). The proper treatment of quantification in ordinary English. In J. Hintikka, J. Moravcsik, and P. Suppes (eds.): *Approaches to Natural Language,* pp. 247–270. Dordrecht: Reidel.

Negoita, C. V. (1985). *Expert Systems and Fuzzy Systems.* Menlo Park, CA: Benjamin/Cummings.

Schütte, K. (1977). *Proof Theory.* Berlin: Springer-Verlag.

Smullyan, R. M. (1967). *First-Order Logic.* Berlin: Springer-Verlag.

Thistlewaite, P. B., M. A. McRobbie, and R. K. Meyer. (1988). *Automated Theorem-Proving in Non-Classical Logics.* New York: Pitman, Wiley.

Wos, L., R. Overbeek, E. Lusk, and J. Boyle. (1984). *Automated Reasoning, Introduction and Applications.* Englewood Cliffs, NJ: Prentice Hall.

Zadeh, L. A. (1965). Fuzzy sets. *Inform. Control,* 8, 338–353.

Zadeh, L. A. (1968). Fuzzy algorithms. *Inform. Control,* 12, 94–102.

Zadeh, L. A. (1972). A fuzzy set theoretic interpretation of linguistic hedges. *J. of Cyb.,* 2, 4–34.

Zadeh, L. A. (1975). Fuzzy logic and approximate reasoning. *Synthesis,* 30, 407–428.

Zadeh, L. A. (1979). A theory of approximate reasoning. In J. Hayes, D. Michie, and L. Mikulich (eds.): *Machine Intelligence,* vol. 9. New York: Elsevier.

8 On fuzzy intuitionistic logic

Esko TURUNEN
Lappeenranta University of Technology
SF-53851 Lappeenranta, FINLAND

Abstract. A fuzzy logic inference system is introduced. Being a generalization of that of intuitionistic logic, this system has finitely many values for truth, but only one value for falsehood. Semantic and syntax are constructed, and a complete fuzzy logic is obtained.

1. INTRODUCTION

The appearance of fuzzy sets and fuzzy theories has provoked the questioning of the logical foundations of these new theories. A complete fuzzy logic has both theoretical and practical importance. Pavelka (1979) was the first who studied the completeness of fuzzy logic. Later Novák (1989) generalized the results.

In mathematical logic the subject of research is a given set of formulae that is studied from two points of view, syntactically and semantically.

In *semantics* one is interested in *valid formulae,* i.e., formulae that are, roughly speaking, true independently of the truth values of their elements. Semantics is a task that can be left to a computer, while finding a proof for some special formula can be much more complicated.

In *syntax* (or proof theory) one starts from *axioms* (assumed to be true formulae) from which one obtains by means of *rules of inference* new true formulae called *theorems*. When one fixes the axioms and the rules of inference one obtains a *mathematical theory*. Syntax without semantics is evidently meaningless.

A mathematical theory is *complete* if the set of valid formulae coincide with the set of theorems. A complete theory of zero-order has the advantage that the question of provability of any formula can be solved semantically, i.e., by a *truth-value table*. A complete mathematical theory also avoids some paradoxes (see Rasiowa and Sikorski, 1963).

Practically all mathematical theories can be reduced to the modern set theory and that set theory is a complete mathematical theory composed of 6 rules of inference and 18 axioms (12 of them are logical axioms and 6 of them are mathematical axioms).

In this study we introduce a first-order fuzzy logic, called *fuzzy intuitionistic logic*. It is a generalization of the classical intuitionistic logic developed by Brouwer (1908).

2. THE FOUNDATIONS OF FUZZY INTUITION-ISTIC LOGIC

The starting point in fuzzy intuitionistic logic is to fuzzify truth. We accept formulae as having different truth values. This corresponds to the use of sentences in everyday life; they may be true "in different ways." By accepting different truth values, we also break the true-false dualism of classical logic. If we know the degree of truth of a sentence, we do not necessarily know the degree of falsehood of the sentence. In fuzzy intuitionistic logic a half-true expression is not always half false.

Since we are not interested in the false sentences of a theory, we let the falsehood be crisp. There is only one falsehood in fuzzy intuitionistic logic. The negation of any formula being true to any degree is a false formula, and the negation of any false formula is an absolutely true formula.

In everyday life we often experience sentences as being true "to some degree" but we are not able to decide which of them is more true than the other. These kinds of incomparable truth values are accepted in fuzzy intuitionistic logic. We also accept the principle that for any set of truth values there exists a truth value that is at least as true as any of the truth values in the set under consideration, and another truth value that is less than or equally true to any of the truth values in the set under consideration. This leads to a state of affairs in which the set of degrees of truth consists of the largest element (the absolute truth, often marked by 1) and the smallest element (which differs from the truth value false or 0).

The set of truth values, composed of different degrees of truths and falsity, is always a finite set.

Similarly, as in classical first-order logic, a set of well-formed formulae Σ is composed of atomic formulae, containing the formula "contradiction," and additional formulae obtained from the atomic formulae by means of logical connectives **and, or, implies, not** and the quantifiers "there exists" and "for each" in the following way:

if **a** and **b** are formulae, then **a and b, a or b, a implies b** and **not a** are formulae, and

if $a(x)$ is a formula, where x is a free variable (see Rasiowa and Sikorski, 1963), then there exists x **a** (x) and for each x **a** (x) are formulae

Let L be some partially ordered set of truth values. Assume the binary operations $\wedge$ (meet), $\vee$ (join) and $\rightarrow$ (residuum with respect to $\wedge$) are defined in L. The *model theory* can be defined similarly as in classical logic; an *interpretation T*, which is roughly speaking the map

$$T : \Sigma \rightarrow L$$

and has the following properties (see Rasiowa and Sikorski, 1963): $T(contradiction) = 0$ (the zero element of L), $T(\textbf{a and b}) = T(\textbf{a}) \wedge T(\textbf{b})$, $T(\textbf{a or b}) = T(\textbf{a}) \vee T(\textbf{b})$, $T(\textbf{a implies b}) = T(\textbf{a}) \rightarrow T(\textbf{b})$, $T(\textbf{not a}) = T(\textbf{a}) \rightarrow 0$, $T(\text{there exists } x \ \textbf{a}(x)) = \wedge T(\textbf{a}(x))$, $T(\text{for each } x \ \textbf{a}(x)) = \vee T(\textbf{a}(x))$.

The value $T(\textbf{a}) \in L$ s the *degree of truth* of **a** in interpretation T. If $T(\textbf{a}) \neq 0$, we say that T is a *model* of **a**. If $T(\textbf{a}) = 0$, then **a** is *false* in interpretation T. By *semantics* S_X with respect to some set of formulae X, we understand the set of all models of X.

As in classical logic, it is reasonable to assume that formulae (**a and b**) **or c** and (**a or c**) **and** (**b or c**) have the same degree of truth. Also formulae (**a or b**) **and c** and (**a and c**) **or** (**b and c**) should have the same truth values. This implies that the truth value set L must be distributive, i.e.,

$$(a \wedge b) \vee c = (a \vee c) \wedge (b \vee c), \quad (a \vee b) \wedge c = (a \wedge c) \vee (b \wedge c)$$
for each $a, b, c \in L$

This is actually the case for operations $\wedge$ and $\vee$ in L. Also, the symmetry of these operations is a valuable property since it is natural to assume that formulae **a or b (a and b)** and **b or a (b and a)** have the same degree of truth.

There exists in classical logic the *paradox of bald*, which can be expressed as follows.

As our everyday experience tells us, we call a person bald even if he is not totally without hair, i.e., he has *some* hair. The property of baldness does not depend on one hair, i.e., it is quite natural to label the sentence "If a person having m hair is bald, then a person having $(m + 1)$ hair is bald" with the mark TRUE (if we have to choose between TRUE and FALSE, as is the case in classical logic).

A well-known rule of inference, modus ponens,

$$\frac{\textbf{a, a implies b}}{\textbf{b}}$$

expresses that whenever the premises **a** and **a implies b** are true, then conclusion **b** is also true.

Now set **a** = "A man with 0 hair is bald" (which is TRUE for sure!) and **a implies b** = "If a man with 0 hair is bald, then a man with 1 hair is bald" (which we decided to be TRUE). By using modus ponens, we conclude that sentence **b** = "A man with 1 hair is bald" is TRUE.

Next, set **a** = "A man with 1 hair is bald" (TRUE as we just proved!) and **a implies b** = "If a man with 1 hair is bald the a man with 2 hairs is also bald" (TRUE by the general principle we have accepted above). By using modus ponens we conclude that sentence **b** = "A man with 2 hairs is bald" is TRUE.

Each of us have a finite number, k, of hair so that repeating this procedure k times one proves that everybody is bald!

In fuzzy intuitionistic logic the paradox of bald does not occur since we have more truth values than one and since we set the following condition:

> The form of formula **a implies b** is absolutely true
> if and only if the degree of truth of **a** is less than or   (1)
> equal to the degree of truth of **b**

In fuzzy intuitionistic logic the sentence "If a person with m hair is bald, then a person with $(m + 1)$ hair is bald" is not absolutely true and the degree of truth of the sentence "A person with m hair is bald" is less and less true as m increases.

Between the connectives **and** and **implies** we set the following condition:

$T(\mathbf{a}$ and $\mathbf{b}) \leqslant T(\mathbf{c})$ if and only if $T(\mathbf{a}) \leqslant T(\mathbf{b}$ implies $\mathbf{c})$ for any interpretation T \hfill (2)

This can be done if in value set L there exists the Galois connection

$$\mathbf{a} \wedge \mathbf{b} \leqslant \mathbf{c} \text{ if and only if } \mathbf{a} \leqslant \mathbf{b} \to \mathbf{c} \text{ for any } \mathbf{a}, \mathbf{b}, \mathbf{c} \in L \qquad (3)$$

By (2) we generalize (1).

Since for any interpretation T

$$\begin{aligned} T(\text{not } \mathbf{a}) &= T(\mathbf{a}) \to 0 \\ &= T(\mathbf{a}) \to T(\text{contradiction}) \\ &= T(\mathbf{a} \text{ implies contradiction}) \end{aligned}$$

we may combine the operations **not** and **implies** by

not a is equal to **a implies contradiction** \hfill (4)

Rules of inference have a central role in proof theory. In classical logic a conclusion is connected with the premises in such a way that whenever the premises are true then the conclusion is also true. This is also the case in fuzzy intuitionistic logic. We define a rule of inference **R** in the following way:

$$\mathbf{R} = \left(\frac{\mathbf{a}_1, \ldots, \mathbf{a}_n}{\mathbf{b}}, \quad \frac{a_1, \ldots, a_n}{b} \right)$$

where $\mathbf{a}_1, \ldots, \mathbf{a}_n$ are the premises and $\mathbf{b}$ is the conclusion. The values $a_1, \ldots, a_n$, $b \in K \subseteq L - \{0\}$ are the corresponding truth values.

In everyday life we sometimes hear reasoning like "If you're not wih me, then you're against me." This is not accepted in fuzzy intuitionistic logic. We assume that there exists formulae **a** such that **a or (not a)** is not absolutely true. Also, such reasoning as "The enemy of my enemy is my friend" is not generally valid in our logical system. This means that the formulae **a** and **not (not) a** are not necessarily true to the same degree.

These two conditions imply that in set of truth values L (cf. Rasiowa and Sikorski, 1963; Turunen, 1989):

$$a \vee (a \to 0) \neq 1 \text{ for some } a \text{ in } L \qquad (5)$$

and

$$a \neq (a \to 0) \to 0 \text{ for some } a \text{ in } L \qquad (6)$$

It often happens that we associate truth value a (different from the absolute true 1 and false 0) to some phenomenon **a**. Then, we receive new independent information about **a** and associate another truth value $b \notin \{0, a, 1\}$ to the phenomenon **a**. Finally we conclude that the truth value c of **a** must be more than or equal to both a and b. This also characterizes fuzzy intuitionistic logic. It is reasonable to assume that classical logic is a special case of fuzzy intuitionistic logic.

3. FINITE BROUWERIAN LATTICES WITH EXACTLY ONE ATOM

As we saw in the previous section, logic is reducible to the structure of the set of truth values. We are looking for a finite residuated lattice L probably containing incomparable elements. The definition of a rule of inference implies that the set of nonfalse truth values should be closed with respect to the operations $\vee$, $\wedge$ and $\Rightarrow$, i.e., whenever a, $b \in L - \{0\}$, then $a \wedge b$, $a \vee b$, $a \Rightarrow b \in L - \{0\}$ also.

Any finite Brouwerian lattice with exactly one atom (i.e., an element $c \in L$, $c \neq 0$, such that if $a \in L$, $a \neq 0$, then $a \geqslant c$) (see Rasiowa and Sikorski, 1963) has these properties. The residuum operation $\Rightarrow$ is defined by

$$a \Rightarrow b = \sup \{x \mid a \wedge x \leqslant b\} \tag{7}$$

Example 1. Let $0 = a_1 < a_2 < ... < a_n = 1$ be real numbers. Set

$$a_m \Rightarrow a_k = \begin{cases} 1 & \text{if } m \leqslant k \\ a_k & \text{if } m > k \end{cases}$$

Let $\wedge$, $\vee$ be the min and max operations, respectively. We obtain a Brouwerian chain L_n. The values $a_2, a_3, ..., a_n$ could represent different values of truth, and a_1 the falsehood.

Example 2. Let $a_{i_1} < a_{i_1} < ... < a_{i_n}$ $(i = 1, ..., m)$ be m Brouwerian chains as defined in Example 1. Put

$$L = L_{1_n} \times ... \times L_{m_n} = \{ <a_{1_k}, ..., a_{m_k}> = \hat{a}_k \mid a_{i_k} \in L_{i_k} \}$$

and define the operations $\wedge$, $\vee$ and $\Rightarrow$ in L componentwise. Define $0 < \hat{a}_k$ for any $\hat{a}_k \in L$ and add 0 to L. We then obtain a finite Brouwerian lattice with exactly one atom that is not a chain.

Example 3. The following set (in Figure 8.1) is a Brouwerian lattice with exactly one atom, where the operations $\wedge$, $\vee$ and $\Rightarrow$ are defined as follows:

Figure 8.1

∧	a	b	c	d	e	f	g	0
a	a	b	c	d	f	e	g	0
b	b	b	d	d	f	e	g	0
c	c	c	c	d	f	e	g	0
d	d	d	d	d	e	f	g	0
e	e	e	e	e	e	g	g	0
f	f	f	f	f	g	f	g	0
g	g	g	g	g	g	g	g	0
0	0	0	0	0	0	0	0	0

∨	a	b	c	d	e	f	g	0
a	a	a	a	a	a	a	a	a
b	a	b	b	b	b	b	b	b
c	a	b	c	c	c	c	c	c
d	a	b	c	d	d	d	d	d
e	a	b	c	d	e	d	e	e
f	a	b	c	d	d	f	f	f
g	a	b	c	d	e	f	g	g
0	a	b	c	d	e	f	f	0

⇒	a	b	c	d	e	f	g	0
a	a	b	c	d	f	e	g	0
b	a	a	c	c	e	f	g	0
c	a	b	a	b	e	f	g	0
d	a	a	a	a	e	f	g	0
e	a	a	a	a	a	f	f	0
f	a	a	a	a	e	a	e	0
g	a	a	a	a	a	a	a	0
0	0	0	0	0	0	0	0	f

The truth values could be called e.g.:

a = absolutely true
b = quite probably true
c = quite possibly true
d = probably and possibly true
e = probably true
f = possibly true
g = not out of question
0 = false

Note that the truth values b and c as well as e and f do not compare with each other, as shown in Figure 8.1.

4. SOME MORE DEFINITIONS

Let the truth-value lattice L be fixed. A *fuzzy theory* X is composed of the set of the well-formed formulae Σ, containing a proper subset X_A of the *axioms* (formulae assumed to be true to some degree), a set R of the rules of inference, and the set L of the truth values, i.e., X is a four-tuple

$$X = <\Sigma, X_A, R, L>$$

The degree of L-*validity* of formula $a \in \Sigma$ in fuzzy theory X is defined by

$$C_S X(a) = \wedge \{T(a) \mid T \text{ is a model of } X_A\} \qquad (8)$$

If $C_S X(a) \neq 0$, then a is L-valid in X.

An L-*deduction* ω of formula **a** is a system

$$
\begin{array}{lll}
\omega_1 & \omega_1 X & (B_1) \\
\cdot & \cdot & \cdot \\
\cdot & \cdot & \cdot \\
\cdot & \cdot & \cdot \\
\omega_{n-1} & \omega_{n-1} X & (B_{n-1}) \\
\omega_n & \omega X & (B_n)
\end{array}
$$

where $\omega_j\text{'}s\,(j = 1, \ldots, n)$ are formulae and $\omega_j X\text{'}s$ the corresponding truth values so that $\omega_n = $ **a** and each ω_j is an axiom or obtained by a rule of inference from some previous $\omega_j\text{'}s$ $(j < i)$. $B_j\text{'}s(j = 1, \ldots, n)$ are elucidating comments.

If formula **a** has an L-deduction, we say that it is L-*deducible* in **X**. The set of all L-deducible formulae in theory **X** will be marked by Σ^{ded}. Since L-deducible formula **a** may have different L-deductions, we define the *degree of L-deduction* of **a** by

$$
C_R X(\mathbf{a}) = \vee\{\omega X \,|\, \omega \text{ is an L-deduction of } \mathbf{a}\} \tag{9}
$$

The *subtheory* $\mathbf{X}^{sub}$ of fuzzy theory **X** is the four-tuple

$$
\mathbf{X}^{sub} = \langle \Sigma^{ded}, \mathbf{X}_A, \mathbf{R}, \mathbf{L} - \{\mathbf{0}\} \rangle
$$

Fuzzy theory **X** is L-*consistent* if for any $\mathbf{a} \in \mathbf{L}$ there exists $\mathbf{a} \in \Sigma$ such that $C_R X(\mathbf{a}) = a$. Finally, fuzzy theory **X** is L-*complete*, if for any $\mathbf{a} \in \Sigma$

$$
\mathbf{a} \text{ is L-valid if and only if } \mathbf{a} \text{ is L-deducible} \tag{10}
$$

and for any $\mathbf{a} \in \Sigma^{ded}$

$$
C_R \mathbf{X}^{sub}(\mathbf{a}) = C_S \mathbf{X}^{sub}(\mathbf{a}) \tag{11}
$$

5. THE L-COMPLETENESS OF FUZZY INTUITIONISTIC LOGIC

Let **L** be a finite Brouwerian lattice with exactly one atom. Let $\mathbf{X}_A$ contain the following forms of formulae:

(Ax.1)   (a implies a)

(Ax.2)   {(a implies b) implies [(b implies c) implies (a implies c)]}

(Ax.3)   {a implies (a or b)}

(Ax.4) {b implies (a or b)}
(Ax.5) {(a implies c) implies [(b implies c) implies ((a or b) implies c))]}
(Ax.6) {(a and b) implies a)}
(Ax.7) {(a and b) implies b)}
(Ax.8) {(c implies a) implies [(c implies b) implies (c implies (a and b)]}
(Ax.9) {[a implies (b implies c)] implies [(a and b) implies c]}
(Ax.10) {[(a and b) implies c) implies [a implies (b implies c)]}
(Ax.11) {[a and (not a)] implies b}
(Ax.12) {[a implies (a and (not a))] implies (not a)}
(Ax.13) {(a or a) implies a}
(Ax.14) (contradiction implies a)
(Ax.15) {[(a implies b) and a] implies b}

Using the properties of T one verifies that $T(\mathbf{d}) = 1$ for any interpretation T and any formula $\mathbf{d}$ of the form (Ax.1) – (Ax.15). We may therefore assume, without any restriction, that all formulae of the form (Ax.1) – (Ax.15) are absolutely true.

Let the set **R** of rules of inference contain the following rules:

$$R_1 = \left(\frac{\mathbf{a}, \mathbf{a} \text{ implies } \mathbf{b}}{\mathbf{b}}, \ \frac{a, b}{a \wedge b} \right) \qquad (a, b \neq 0)$$

$$R_2 = \left(\frac{\mathbf{a}(x)}{\mathbf{a}(y)}, \ \frac{1}{1} \right) \qquad (x, y \text{ are free individual variables in } \mathbf{a})$$

$$R_3 = \left(\frac{\mathbf{a}(x) \text{ implies } \mathbf{b}}{\text{there exists } x, \mathbf{a}(x) \text{ implies } \mathbf{b}}, \ \frac{1}{1} \right) \quad \begin{array}{l} (x \text{ is a free} \\ \text{individual variable} \\ \text{in } \mathbf{a} \text{ and } x \text{ does not} \\ \text{occur freely in } \mathbf{b}) \end{array}$$

$$R_4 = \left(\frac{\mathbf{a} \text{ implies } \mathbf{b}(x)}{\mathbf{a} \text{ implies for each } x, \mathbf{b}(x)}, \ \frac{1}{1} \right) \quad \begin{array}{l} (x \text{ is a free} \\ \text{individual variable} \\ \text{in } \mathbf{b} \text{ and } x \text{ does not} \\ \text{occur freely in } \mathbf{a}) \end{array}$$

$$R_5 = \left(\frac{\text{there exists } x, \mathbf{a}(x) \text{ implies } \mathbf{b}}{\mathbf{a}(x) \text{ implies } \mathbf{b}}, \ \frac{1}{1} \right) \quad \begin{array}{l} (x \text{ is a free} \\ \text{individual varia-} \\ \text{ble in } \mathbf{a} \text{ and } x \text{ does} \\ \text{occur freely in } \mathbf{b}) \end{array}$$

$$R_6 = \left(\frac{\mathbf{a} \text{ implies for each } x, \mathbf{b}(x)}{\mathbf{a} \text{ implies } \mathbf{b}(x)}, \ \frac{1}{1} \right) \quad \begin{array}{l} (x \text{ is a free individual} \\ \text{variable in } \mathbf{b} \text{ and } x \\ \text{does not occur freely} \\ \text{in } \mathbf{a}) \end{array}$$

$$R_7 = \left(\frac{\textbf{a, b}}{\textbf{a and b}}, \ \frac{a, \, b}{a \wedge b} \right) \quad (a, \, b \neq 0)$$

$$R_8 = \left(\frac{\textbf{a, b}}{\textbf{a or b}}, \ \frac{a, \, b}{a \vee b} \right) \quad (a, \, b \neq 0)$$

$$R_9 = \left(\frac{\textbf{a, b}}{\textbf{a implies b}}, \ \frac{a, \, b}{a \Rightarrow b} \right) \quad (a, \, b \neq 0)$$

We then have:

Completeness Theorem. Every L-consistent fuzzy theory **X** (containing $\textbf{X}_A$ and **R** as defined above) is L-complete.

The proof of the theorem is rather long and can be found in Turunen (in press; 1989). Let us fix an L-consistent fuzzy theory **X**. Now replace the value lattice L by the two-valued Brouwerian lattice $\{0, 1\}$ and mark the crisp theory obtained in this way by the symbol **X'**. Then, one can prove the following (see Turunen, in press).

Proposition. Formula **a** is L-deducible in the fuzzy theory **X** if and only if **a** is a theorem in crisp theory **X'**.

This proposition is useful in some applications.

Example. Assume we have five sentences **a, b, c, d** and **e**. We know that

    b is absolutely true
    b implies d is very probably true
    b implies e is not out of question
    a and b is very probably true
    (a and b) imply c is quite sure

Let the truth values absolutely true (1), very probably true (a), quite sure (b), not out of question (c), and false (0) form set **L** (Figure 8.2). To what degree, if any, is formula **c** true?

Define fuzzy theory **X** with the rules of inference R_1-R_q, logical axioms (Ax.1) – (Ax.15), and special axioms:

Figure 8.2

(Ax.16) **b**	(with truth value 1)
(Ax.17) **b implies d**	(with truth value a)
(Ax.18) **b implies e**	(with truth value c)
(Ax.19) **a and b**	(with truth value a)
(Ax.20) **(a and b) imply c**	(with truth value b)

We obtain an L-complete fuzzy theory. Using (Ax.19), (Ax.20), and R_1 we may construct the following L-deduction ω of **c**:

$\omega_1 = $ **a and b**	$\omega_1 X = a$	((Ax.19), assumption)
$\omega_2 = $ (**a and b**) imply **c**	$\omega_2 X = b$	((Ax.20), assumption)
$\omega = $ **c**	$\omega = a \wedge b = c$	(apply R_1 to ω_1 and ω_2)

This means that

$$c \leqslant C_R X(\mathbf{c}) \tag{12}$$

Could there exist another L-deduction ω' of **c** so that $\omega' X > c$? Since **X** is L-complete, this question can be solved semantically: Let T_1 be such an interpretation that $T_1(b) = 1$, $T_1(a) = a$, $T_1(d) = a$, $T_1(e) = c$, $T_1(c) = a$. One easily verifies that $T_1 \in S_X$. We conclude that $C_S X(\mathbf{c}) \leqslant a$. Let T_2 be another interpretation so that $T_2(b) = 1$, $T_2(a) = 1$, $T_2(d) = 1$, $T_2(e) = c$, $T_2(c) = b$. Then $T_2 \in S_X$ also. We conclude that $C_S X(\mathbf{c}) \leqslant b$, but then we have

$$C_S X(\mathbf{c}) \leqslant c \tag{13}$$

Because of the L-completeness of **X** and the equations (12) and (13), we conclude that

$$C_S X(\mathbf{c}) = c$$

i.e., **c** is not out of question.

Exercise. Using the assumptions as above, define the degree of L-deduction of formulae **d** and **e**.

Keywords: fuzzy logic, intuitionistic logic, Brouwerian logic

BIBLIOGRAPHY

Brouwer, L.E.J. (1908). De onbetrouwhaarheid der logische principes. *Tijdschrift voor wijsbegrerte*, **2**, 152–158.
Novák, V. (1989). First order fuzzy logic. *Studia Logica*, **XLVI**, 87–108.
Pavelka, J. (1979). On fuzzy logic I, II, III. *Zeitsch f. Math. Logik u. Grund. d. Math.*, **25**, 45–52, 119–134, 447–464.
Rasiowa, H., and R. Sikorski. (1963). *The Mathematics of Metamathematics*. Warszawa: PWN.
Turunen, E. (1989). On Brouwerian valued fuzzy logic. Università di Pisa. Dipartimento di Matematica, **2**, 14 (461).
Turunen, E. (In press). The completeness of first order fuzzy intuitionistic logic. Lappeenranta University of Technology.

9 A nonmonotonic fuzzy logic

Dimiter DRIANKOV and Patrick DOHERTY
Department of Computer
and Information Science
Linköping University
S-58183 Linköping, SWEDEN

Abstract. The use of fuzzy sets to represent extension of predicates has as a consequence that the truth of a predicate belongs to the interval [0, 1]. In this case the underlying logic is a many-valued one in which the law of excluded middle does not hold. This is due to the presence of a truth-value that expresses ignorance about whether an object has a property or not without rejecting the possibility that it might have this property. This is exactly the type of knowledge used in nonmonotonic reasoning systems, which allow a fact to be asserted as true by default. We capitalize on the natural existence of such a truth value when interpreting fuzzy predicates and propose a formalization of a fuzzy nonmonotonic logic. We start by extending fuzzy logic with two connectives M and L where $M\alpha$ reads as "it may be the case that α is true" and $L\alpha$ reads as "it is the case that α is true". In addition, a default operator D is added where $D\alpha$ is interpreted as "α is true by default." The logic has an intuitive model theoretic semantics without any appeal to the use of a fixpoint semantics for the default operator. The semantics is based on the notion of *preferential entailment,* where a set of sentences Γ preferentially entails a sentence α, if and only if a preferred set of the models of Γ are models of α. We also show that the logic belongs to the class of cumulative nonmonotonic formalisms which are a subject of current interest.

1. BACKGROUND

The fundamental thesis of fuzzy sets theory is that set-membership may be partial or gradual, that is, it need not be either-or as in ordinary set theory. A fuzzy set F has no sharp boundaries and the degree of membership of an element u in it is given by a membership function $\mu_F : U \to L$, where U is the universe of discourse and L is a partially ordered set. In practice, L is usually chosen as the real interval $[0, 1]$ with $\mu_F(.) = 1$ being the ordinary membership, $\mu_F(.) = 0$ being the ordinary nonmembership, and $\mu_F(.) = 0.5$ expressing ignorance about whether u belongs to F or not.

In this context, it is easily seen that if one decides to represent the extension of a first-order predicate F with a fuzzy set (or an n-ary fuzzy relation if F is an n-place predicate), then the truth of F, when interpreted, will be in the interval $[0, 1]$. In this case one talks about F being a fuzzy (vague) predicate and the underlying logic as a many-valued one in which the excluded middle law does not hold. This is due to the presence of a truth-value, 0.5, which expresses ignorance about whether an object has the property F or not without rejecting the possibility that it might have this property. Thus, $\mu_F(u) = 0.5$ can be interpreted as

- not conclusive evidence for the truth of "u has the property F"
- not conclusive evidence against the truth of "u has the property F"
- evidence that suggests the possibility of "u has the property F" being true

This is similar to the type of knowledge used in nonmonotonic reasoning systems that allow some fact, i.e., "u has the property F," to be asserted as true if there exists a possibility of it being true and nothing contradicts it. Thus, the natural existence of this special truth value of 0.5 in fuzzy logic lays the groundwork for what is often called defeasible reasoning: we want the option of withdrawing "u has the property F" if later on we decide to decrease the degree of membership of u in F (i.e., to make $\mu_F(u) < 0.5$, which then becomes evidence against the truth of "u has the property F").

Surprisingly enough, in all of the existing fuzzy logics, the presence of this special truth value has always been hushed up by either making it a member of the set of designated truth-values or by modifying the notion of satisfiability of a formula so that a formula in fuzzy logic is valid if and only if it is valid in standard first-order logic. The subsequent result is that standard first-order logic is a special case of fuzzy logic: if all fuzzy truth-values are in the set $\{0, 1\}$, then fuzzy logic is reduced to standard first-order logic and thus is a monotonic logic.

In the present paper, we depart drastically from the existing treatments of fuzzy logic and capitalize on the natural existence of a degree of membership of 0.5 in the extension of a fuzzy predicate. We then treat the proposition $F(u)$, where F is a fuzzy predicate, u a particular object from U, and $\mu_F(u) = 0.5$ as a piece of knowledge without conclusive evidence for its truth and with the possibility of it being true. Now, one can treat $F(u)$ as an assumption rather than a fact and assert it is true by default. Technically, this can be represented by the following formula:

$$MP(u) \rightarrow DP(u)$$

where we read $MP(u)$ as "it may be the case that u has the property F," and $DP(u)$ as "$P(u)$ is true by default." Here, M is a truth-functional connective that asserts the possibility of $P(u)$ being true when we are ignorant as to whether u has the property F, and D is a modal-like operator that asserts the truth of $P(u)$ by default.

It is along these lines that we propose a formalization of a fuzzy nonmonotonic logic that integrates the concept of incomplete information states due to the presence of degrees of membership of 0.5, with the notion of default defined in terms of a preferential ordering on these incomplete information states. As an extra feature, the logic belongs to the class of cumulative logics, which are a subject of current interest.

The paper is structured as follows. In Section 2, we consider general issues regarding nonmonotonic formalisms. In Section 3, we introduce the basic ideas of our approach to nonmonotonic reasoning. In Section 4 we introduce the basic ideas of our approach toward integrating fuzzy logic and nonmonotonic logic. In Section 5, the propositional version of a fuzzy nonmonotonic formalism FNM3 is described. In Section 6, we consider some properties of FNM3, in particular the property of *cumulativity*. In Section 7, we comment on future and related work.

2. INTRODUCTION

Traditionally, formal logical systems have been characterized as containing the following components:

1. A formal language L defining the set of well-formed formulas (wff's).
2. A set of wff's called the axioms.
3. A set of "inference rules" for deriving theorems from the axioms.

Different logics can then be distinguished by the minimal set of theorems (including the axioms) closed under the rules of inference. Furthermore, extending the set of axioms can never prevent the derivation of theorems already derived from the original set of axioms. This approach has proved to be quite adequate for modeling the domain of mathematics, as was the intention. Unfortunately, it has proved to be less than adequate for modeling the domain of commonsense reasoning for two important reasons.

First, reasoning agents are forced to draw conclusions based on an *incomplete specification* of the relevant information. *Assumptions* are made about the missing information and *conjectures,* based upon the assumptions, are derived instead of the more static notion of theorems. New evidence may prove the assumptions invalid and the conjectures may no longer be derivable, thus the *nonmonotonic* nature of commonsense formalisms.

Second, the characterization of a logic as a minimal set of theorems generated by axioms and inference rules is too narrow a characterization for the types of logic needed to adequately model the tentative nature of human reasoning. An approach better serving the purpose is to concentrate on "what follows from what," or more formally the semantic notion of *entailment,* an idea popularized by Shoham (1988). In FNM3, both the *axioms* and *default rules* are represented as wff's in the logical language. This set, which will be called the *premise set,* may be considered as an initial set of hypotheses that constrain the set of models considered when using the entailment relation.

The assumptions about missing information and the ensuing conjectures are often classified as *defaults.* Some of the more important distinguishing characteristics of *default reasoning* are:

- Defaults or conjectures are made in the context of incomplete information.
- Before "jumping" to a conclusion some form of *consistency* or *possibility* check is made, assuring that the default is coherent relative to the current reasoning context.
- Default conclusions are weaker than those derived in the normal way. They are subject to retraction. Surprisingly, most of the

standard default formalisms fail to mark this difference syntactically. The default machinery is "hidden" in some sense in the meta-level.

The distinguishing characteristics of our approach parallel the points mentioned above:

- Fuzzy logic is used with an information ordering on partial interpretations of fuzzy predicates. A partial interpretation is interpreted as representing a situation with incomplete information. Such situations are natural when interpreting fuzzy predicates due to the presence of membership degrees of 0.5.
- A normative statement of the type "birds normally fly" is represented as the wff $LBird(x) \wedge MFlies(x) \to DFlies$. $M\alpha$ may be read as "it *may be* the case that α is true (to a degree)." $L\alpha$ may be read as "it is the case that α is true (to a degree)." Technically, fuzzy logic is extended with two additional truth-functional connectives M and L where $M\alpha$ is true when α is true or undecided and $L\alpha$ is true only when α is true.
- The default connective D is a modal operator and will be defined in another section. $D\alpha$ may be read as "α is true by default." A distinction is made between the default $D\alpha$ and the assertion α. This distinction resolves some difficulties associated with consistency-based nonmonotonic formalisms.

3. BASIC IDEAS

Consider the following scenario:

1. Birds typically don't suffer from high anxiety.
2. Ostriches typically do suffer from high anxiety.
3. Fred is an ostrich and Tweety is a bird.

The obvious interpretation is that Fred has high anxiety and Tweety doesn't. We represent the scenario in FNM3 as follows:

1. $L(Bird(x) \wedge M(\neg Ostrich(x) \wedge \neg \text{High-Anxiety}(x)) \to D \neg \text{High-Anxiety}(x)$
2. $LOstrich(x) \wedge M\text{High-Anxiety}(x) \to D\text{High-Anxiety}(x)$
3. $L(Ostrich(fred) \wedge Bird(fred) \wedge Bird(tweety))$

The premise set *preferentially* entails the defaults

1. DHigh-Anxiety(*fred*)
2. D$\neg$High-Anxiety(*tweety*)

The nonmonotonic character of the logic becomes apparent when additional premises are added to those above. If the following premises are added to the premise set,

1. LNo-Wings(x) → $\neg$**M**$\neg$High-Anxiety(x)
2. No-Wings(*tweety*)

then D$\neg$High-Anxiety(*tweety*) is no longer preferentially entailed, but $\neg$D$\neg$High-Anxiety(*tweety*) is.

The approach we advocate is dependent on generating the preferred models, which are then used to check whether a sentence is preferentially entailed.

4. FUZZINESS

Let $P(x)$, where P is a predicate symbol and x is an individual variable, be a first-order predicate. Let I be an interpretation over a nonempty domain U that assigns to P a unary fuzzy relation in the form of a membership function $\mu_P: U \to [0,1]$. If P is an n-ary predicate then I would assign to it an n-ary fuzzy relation characterized by an n-place membership function.

Furthermore, given I and a valuation V that assigns to x an element of U, the truth-value of the proposition $P(u)$ is the degree of membership of u in μ_P. Thus, the truth of a fuzzy predicate is graded in contrast to a classical crisp predicate whose truth-value is in the set $\{0,1\}$.

Here, one should make a strong distinction between the notion of graded truth, due to the existence of fuzzy predicates in the presence of complete information, and degrees of uncertainty due to incomplete and/or uncertain information as to exactly which truth-value a fuzzy or a crisp predicate should take. In Dubois and Prade (1988), the following three cases are identified:

- The case of uncertain propositions that are either true or false (thus involving crisp predicates only) but due to the lack of complete information one can in general only estimate to what extent it is possible or necessary that a proposition is true. Possibilistic logic (Prade, 1988), and probabilistic logic (Genesereth and Nilsson, 1987; Pearl, 1988), deal with this type of proposition.

- The case of fuzzy propositions that leads to intermediary degrees of truth that can be specified with absolute certainty. The class of fuzzy logics developed in Orci (1989), Ishizuka and Kanai (1985), and Mukaidono, Shen, and Ding (1989) and based on an extended resolution principle deal with this sort of proposition.
- The general case of uncertain fuzzy propositions which, due to the presence of fuzzy predicates, have intermediary degrees of truth, but the lack of complete information does not allow these degrees of truth to be specified with absolute certainty. Prade (1985) and Yager (1984) have come up with certain preliminary ideas for reasoning with this sort of proposition in terms of their underlying possibility distributions.

FNM3 deals with the second case of fuzzy propositions. Several approaches to automate reasoning with such propositions have been proposed. These are more or less based on Lee's resolution method for fuzzy predicates (see Lee, 1972). In all these approaches the fuzzy logics employed are defined as an algebraic system $([0, 1], \vee, \wedge, \neg, \rightarrow)$ where the unit interval is the set of truth-values and the most popular choice of operations is

1. $/p \vee q/ = \max(/p/, /q/)$
2. $/p \wedge q/ = \min(/p/, /q/)$
3. $/\neg p/ = 1 - /p/$
4. $/p \rightarrow q/ = /\neg p \vee q/$

where $/p/$ is the truth-value of p and $/p/$ belongs to the unit interval.

Using these connectives, the properties of Boolean algebra are preserved except for the laws of contradiction and excluded middle. In other words, one obtains a complete distributive lattice with a pseudocomplementation. However, despite the absence of the law of excluded middle, the fuzzy logics used in the different approaches are reduced in one way or another to classical logic. The result, in a proof-theoretical perspective is that fuzzy binary resolution is a conservative version of ordinary binary resolution. This also entails that the different systems of fuzzy logic are monotone logical systems. In the present paper we keep the basic algebraic structure of fuzzy logic and extend it with two additional truth-functional operators

L and **M**: Lα reads as "it is the case that α is true to a degree" and Mα reads as "it may be the case that α is true to a degree."

Furthermore, using the so-called information ordering on fuzzy models to be defined later we define a non–truth-functional operator Dα, which reads as "α is true by default." The fuzzy models considered are partial because of the existence of the truth-value 0.5 or also *undecided:* if $\mu_P(u) = 0.5$ this means that the object u may or may not have the fuzzy property P, but one is undecided as to which is exactly the case.

5. A FUZZY NONMONOTONIC LOGIC

In this section we introduce a simple language for propositional logic and a truth definition based on fuzzy logic. We also introduce an information ordering on fuzzy models.

5.1. The Language

The language Σ consists of a finite set of sentence symbols S. It also contains the following primitive connectives: $\neg$, $\vee$, $\wedge$. The set of Σ sentences is built up from S using $\neg$, $\wedge$, and $\vee$ in the usual way.

In addition to the primitive connectives, the following non-primitive connective is introduced:

$$(\varphi \rightarrow \psi) =_{def} \neg \varphi \vee \psi$$

5.2. Definitions

We begin with some definitions for both a truth and information ordering on truth values, where the information ordering is extended to partial interpretations.

Definition 5.1 (Partial Interpretation). *A (partial) interpretation v is a function $v : S \rightarrow Tr$ where S is the domain of sentence symbols and Tr, the set of truth-values, is defined as follows:*

$$Tr = TrT \cup TrF \cup TrU$$

where:

$$TrT = \{[x,y]: x, y \in (0.5,1] \text{ and } x \leqslant y\} \cup \{(0.5,y): y \in (0.5,1]\}$$
$$TrF = \{[x,y]: x, y \in [0,0.5) \text{ and } x \leqslant y\} \cup \{(x,0.5): x \in (0,0.5)\}$$
$$TrU = \{[0.5,0.5]\}$$

The values given to the sentence symbols could reflect either a *degree-of-information* ordering or a *degree-of-truth* ordering which can then be extended to partial interpretations. The degree-of-information ordering will be used to compare partial interpretations, while the degree-of-truth ordering will be used to evaluate formulas in a partial interpretation.

Definition 5.2 (Degree-of-Information Ordering – $\leqslant_i$). *Let Il and Iu be the lower and upper bound respectively of an interval truth-value I.*

$TrU <_i I$, for each $I \in TrT$ or for each $I \in TrF$
$I \leqslant_i J$, *iff* $I, J \in TrT$ and $Iu \leqslant Jl$
$I \leqslant_i J$, *iff* $I, J \in TrF$ and $Il \geqslant Ju$

Definition 5.3 (Degree-of-Information Ordering on Partial Interpretations). *Let v_1 and v_2 be two partial interpretations, that is, $v_1 : S \rightarrow Tr$ and $v_2 : S \rightarrow Tr$.*

$v_1(S) \leqslant_i v_2(S)$ *iff* for each $s \in S, v_1(s) \leqslant_i v_2(s)$
$v_1(S) < v_2(S)$ *iff* there exists $s \in S, v_1(s) <_i v_2(s)$ and
  for each $s' \neq s, v_1(s') \leqslant_i v_2(s')$

Definition 5.4 ($<_i$ – minimal Interpretation). *Let Δ be a set of interpretations. An interpretation $u \in \Delta$ is a $\leqslant_i$-minimal interpretation if for all $v \in \Delta$, if $v \leqslant_i u$ then $v = u$. The set of $\leqslant_i$-minimal interpretations of Δ is denoted by min $\leqslant_i (\Delta)$.*

Definition 5.5 (Degree-of-Truth Ordering – $<_t$). *Let I and J belong to the set of truth-values Tr.*

$I \leqslant_t J$ *iff* $Iu \leqslant Jl$

5.3. Default Formulas

One of the simplest formalizations of nonmonotonic reasoning is to define a default theory as a pair (T, D), where T is a base theory consisting of a set of facts and D is a set of defaults. A preferred default theory would be one where the maximal set of defaults are accepted. In the default logic of Reiter (1980), there appear to be two weaknesses: (1) the distinction made between a base theory and the set of defaults and (2) the fact that no distinction is made between asserting a fact γ and asserting γ by default. The former case makes it difficult to resolve problems that arise when defaults interact with each other and the latter case results in certain default theories having no extensions. Our solution is to make the defaults "first class citizens" placing them on equal footing with the formulas in the base theory and to use a default operator to syntactically distinguish between asserting facts and defaulting to facts. Thus, a normative statement such as "normally birds fly" is represented as the formula

$$\textbf{L}Bird \wedge \textbf{M}Flies \rightarrow \textbf{D}Flies$$

which can be read as "if it is true that something is a bird, and it may be the case that it flies, then it flies by default."

5.4. The Notion of Entailment

Suppose Γ is a set of wff's in Σ. We are interested in those sentences *preferentially entailed* by the premise set. Classically, a sentence α is entailed by Γ if

for each $m \in \text{Mod}(\Gamma): m \models \alpha$

where $\text{Mod}(\Gamma)$ denotes the class of all models for Γ. Preferential entailment strengthens the notion of entailment by characterizing a preferred subclass of $\text{Mod}(\Gamma)$, denoted by $\text{Pmod}(\Gamma)$. A sentence α is said to be preferentially entailed by Γ if it is satisfied by all models in $\text{Pmod}(\Gamma)$. The set $\text{Pmod}(\Gamma)$ can be defined equivalently, by placing an ordering on $\text{Mod}(\Gamma)$. The subclass of preferred models will then be those that are minimal relative to the defined ordering. In our formalism, models are replaced by *model frames* (defined below) and the preference on model frames is induced by the nature of the wffs in the premise set.

Definition 5.6 (Model Frame). *A* model frame *is a pair* $\langle \Delta, u \rangle$, *where* Δ *is a (nonempty) set of interpretations and* $u \in \Delta$ *is viewed as the* actual situation *(interpretation). It is always assumed that* $u \leqslant_i v$, *for any* $v \in \Delta$. *If* $u \in \Delta$, *then we write* Δ_u *to denote the set* $\{v \in \Delta : u \leqslant_i v\}$.

5.4.1. The Rules of Satisfaction

The rules of satisfaction are defined relative to a model frame $M = \langle \Delta, u \rangle$ and an interpretation in Δ. The following notation is used.

Let $v \models_M \varphi \odot$ mean that v assigns the interval truth-value I, $I \in TrT (I \in TrF)$ to φ when $\odot$ is $+(-)$, respectively. $v \models_M \varphi^+$ and $v \models_M \varphi^-$ are abbreviated to val$(\varphi, v, M) = I, I \in TrT$ and val$(\varphi, v, M) = I, I \in TrF$, respectively.

The binary operators min and max are defined on Tr relative to the truth ordering $\leqslant_t$. The function val is defined recursively as follows:

val$(\varphi, v, M) = v(\varphi)$ for sentence symbols S.
val$(\varphi \wedge \psi, v, M) = \min(\text{val}(\varphi, v, M), \text{val}(\psi, v, M))$.
val$(\varphi \vee \psi, v, M) = \max(\text{val}(\varphi, v, M), \text{val}(\psi, v, M))$.

$$\text{val}(\neg \varphi, v, M) = \begin{cases} [1 - Iu, 1 - Il] \in TrT \text{ if val}(\varphi, v, M) = [Il, Iu] \in TrF \\ [1 - Iu, 1 - Il] \in TrT \text{ if val}(\varphi, v, M) = [Il, Iu] \in TrT \\ [0.5, 0.5] \qquad\qquad\qquad\qquad \text{otherwise} \end{cases}$$

Furthermore, min is defined as: Let val(φ, v, M) be equal to either one of the interval truth-values $[x, y]$, $[x, 0.5]$, or $(0.5, y]$ and val(φ, v, M) be equal to either one of $[z, w]$, $[z, 0.5)$, or $(0.5, w]$.

$\min([x, y], [z, w]) = [\min(x, z), \min(y, w)]$
$\min([x, y], (0.5, w]) = [x, \min(y, w)]$, if $x \leqslant 0.5$
$\min([x, y], (0.5, w]) = (0.5, \min(y, w)]$ if $x > 0.5$
$\min([x, y], [z, 0.5)) = [\min(x, z), 0.5)$ if $y \geqslant 0.5$
$\min([x, y], [z, 0.5)) = [\min(x, z), y]$ if $y < 0.5$
$\min([x, 0.5), [z, 0.5)) = [\min(x, z), 0.5)$
$\min([x, 0.5), (0.5, w]) = [x, 0.5)$
$\min((0.5, y], (0.5, w]) = (0.5, \min(y, w)]$

Finally, max is defined as

$\max([x, y], [z, w]) = [\max(x, z), \max(y, w)]$
$\max([x, y], (0.5, w]) = (0.5, \max(x, w)]$ if $x \leqslant 0.5$
$\max([x, y], (0.5, w]) = (x, \max(y, w)]$ if $x > 0.5$
$\max([x, y], [z, 0.5)) = (\max(x, z), 0.5)$ if $y < 0.5$
$\max([x, y], [z, 0.5)) = (\max(x, z), y]$ if $y \geqslant 0.5$
$\max([x, 0.5), [z, 0.5)) = (\max(x, z), 0.5)$
$\max([x, 0.5), (0.5, w]) = (0.5, w]$
$\max((0.5, y], (0.5, w]) = (0.5, \max(y, w)]$

The Assertion Connective. The connective L is often referred to as the *external assertion* connective. $L\varphi$ is true to the degree to which φ is true, otherwise it is false to the degree to which φ is false. When φ is undecided then $L\varphi$ is false but since the exact degree to which it is false cannot be determined its truth-value is the whole interval $[0, 0.5)$. The satisfaction rule is:

$$\text{val}(L\varphi, v, M) = \begin{cases} I & \text{if val}(\varphi, v, M) = I, I \in TrT \text{ or } I \in TrF \\ [0, 0.5) & \text{if val}(\varphi, v, M) = TrU \end{cases}$$

The Maybe Connective. $M\varphi$ is true to the degree to which φ is true, otherwise it is false to the degree to which φ is false. When φ is undecided then $M\varphi$ is true but since the exact degree to which it is true cannot be determined its truth-value is the whole interval $(0.5, 1]$. Furthermore, $M\varphi$ is equivalent to $\neg L \neg \varphi$. The satisfaction rule is:

$$\text{val}(M\varphi, v, M) = \begin{cases} I & \text{if val}(\varphi, v, M) = I, I \in TrT \text{ or } I \in TrF \\ (0.5, 1] & \text{if val}(\varphi, v, M) = TrU \end{cases}$$

The D Operator. In addition, the satisfaction rules are extended for the D operator as follows:

$$\text{val}(D\varphi, v, M) = \begin{cases} [1, 1] & \text{if for each } v' \in \Delta_v : \text{val}(M\varphi, v', M) = I, I \in TrT \\ & \text{and there exists } v' \in \Delta_v : \text{val}(\varphi, v', M) = I, \\ & I \in TrT \\ 0 & \text{otherwise} \end{cases}$$

We believe that FNM3 captures the natural interpretation of defaults in a clear and intuitive way. α is accepted as a default in a situation v iff

1. α is possibly true to a degree in all situations informationally above v.
2. α is true to a degree in at least one potentially reachable situation.
3. $D\alpha$ is forced by the *context*. By "context," we mean a premise set Γ that includes default sentences.

Points 1 and 2 clearly follow from the satisfaction condition for the default operator. Point 3 will become clearer when preference ordering on model frames and the notion of preferential entailment is defined below.

5.4.2. Satisfaction and Entailment

We now proceed to define the notions of satisfaction in a model frame and entailment.

Definition 5.7 (Satisfaction). *An interpretation $u \in \Delta$ in the model frame $M = \langle \Delta, v \rangle$ satisfies a sentence φ in $\Sigma(\rho)$ iff $u \models_M \varphi^+$.*

The definition is extended for model frames where $M \models \varphi^+$ iff $u \models$
$_M \varphi^+$ for all $u \in \Delta$ according to the satisfaction conditions defined above.
For a set Γ of sentences in $\Sigma(\rho)$, $M \models \Gamma$ iff $M \models \varphi^+$ for all $\varphi \in \Gamma$.
Γ is said to be satisfiable iff it has a model frame.

Definition 5.8 (Preferred Model Frames). *Suppose $M = \langle \Delta, u \rangle$ and*
$M' = \langle \Delta', u' \rangle$ are two model frames satisfying a set of premises Γ. M is
said to be preferred to M', written $M <_P M'$, iff

$$u <_i u' \vee [u = u' \wedge \Delta_u \supset \Delta_{u'}]$$

Remark 5.1. *The definition above prefers the model frame(s) that*
satisfy the sentences in the context Γ using the minimal amount of
information. If $u = u'$, prefer the frame(s) with the maximal number of
interpretations in Δ. This is only one of a number of alternatives. Another
interesting alternative would be to minimize only those propositional
constants in the scope of the M connective, thus providing a finer-
grained minimization criterion.

Remark 5.2. *Notice that there is no guarantee of a unique preferred*
model frame for a premise set Γ. Suppose Γ contains $L\alpha \vee L\beta$. There are
two preferred model frames for Γ; one where the actual situation makes
α true and β unknown and another that makes β true and α unknown. It is
interesting to note that while $L\alpha \vee L\beta$ is preferentially entailed by Γ,
neither $L\alpha$ nor $L\beta$ is.

We now define the notion of preferential entailment:

Definition 5.9 (Preferential Entailment). *Let Γ, Π be sets of*
sentences in $\Sigma(\rho)$. Γ preferentially entails Π, written $\Gamma \mid\approx \Pi$, iff for all
$M \in \mathrm{Pmod}(\Gamma) : M \models \Pi$, where $\mathrm{Pmod}(\Gamma)$ is the set of preferred model
frames for Γ as defined by $<_P$ above.

We write $PE(\Gamma)$ to denote the set of all formulas preferentially
entailed by Γ. Γ is *preferentially satisfiable (p-satisfiable* for short) iff it
has a preferred model frame.

6. SOME PROPERTIES OF FNM3

One recent approach to the study of nonmonotonic formalisms has
been to characterize different classes of nonmonotonic logics by

studying their consequence operations and the degree to which they lack the condition of monotonicity. The approach was used by Gabbay (1985) in a seminal paper and the investigation has been continued independently, by Makinson (1988) and Kraus, Lehman, and Magidor (1988). The latter two have studied a particularly interesting class of nonmonotonic formalisms that have been given the name *cumulative logics*. In Gabbay's case, the basic idea was to replace the monotonicity condition on a deductive consequence relation $\vdash$, with the condition of *weak monotonicity*. The resulting plausibility relation, $\Gamma|\sim\alpha$, is to be read: as "from Γ, plausibly infer α." The weak monotonicity condition is stated as:

$$\frac{\Gamma|\sim\alpha \text{ and } \Gamma|\sim\beta}{\Gamma\cup\{\alpha\}|\sim\beta}$$

The condition in effect says that if both α and β are plausibly inferred by Γ, then if α is later observed to be true, this doesn't affect other plausible inferences.

Makinson (1988) generalized Gabbay's finitary conditions on a consequence relation to the following infinitary conditions on a consequence operation C:

$$\Delta \subseteq C(\Delta) \tag{1}$$
$$\Delta \subseteq \Gamma \subseteq C(\Delta) \text{ implies } C(\Gamma) \subseteq C(\Delta) \tag{2}$$
$$\Delta \subseteq \Gamma \subseteq C(\Delta) \text{ implies } C(\Delta) \subseteq C(\Gamma) \tag{3}$$

The last two conditions, cumulative transitivity and cumulative monotony, can be expressed as a conditional equivalence:

$$\Delta \subseteq \Gamma \subseteq C(\Delta) \text{ implies } C(\Delta) \subseteq C(\Gamma) \tag{4}$$

While Makinson develops an infinitistic view of nonmonotonic consequence relations, Kraus, Lehmann, and Magidor (1988) develop a finitistic approach in the style of Gentzen. The main point of their work is to characterize the consequence relations that can be defined by models similar to Shoham's in terms of proof-theoretic properties.

They consider five logical systems and families of models, providing soundness and completeness results for each system. Two systems of interest are System C and System P. The former corresponds to Gabbay's proposal, while the latter turns out to be the flat fragment of a conditional logic studied by Burgess (1981), Adams (1975), Veltman (1986) and more recently, Pearl (1988).

Whereas Lehmann et al. start with a classical propositional logic and augment it with a plausible consequence relation represented as a meta-notion and whose properties are characterized by Gentzen type rules, we must use a different approach. Our motivation is to characterize the properties of the preferential entailment relation $|\approx$, of FNM3, in the spirit of their approach. We do this by providing semantic equivalents of the Gentzen type rules described by Kraus, Lehmann, and Magidor (1988), starting with the fuzzy logic augmented with $|\approx$ and the D-operator.

6.1. Cumulative Entailment

In this section, we first state an inference rule from Kraus, Lehmann, and Magidor (1988), followed by a semantic translation of the rule characterizing a property of $|\approx$. Proofs for the semantic versions of the rules are in Doherty (1990).

Definition 6.1 (Cumulative Entailment). *An entailment relation $|\approx$ is said to be* cumulative *iff it contains all instances of the reflexivity axiom and is closed under the inference rules of left logical equivalence, right weakening, cut, and cautious monotony (described below).*

The condition of *left logical equivalence* is stated as:

$$\frac{\models \alpha \leftrightarrow \beta, \ \alpha |\sim \gamma}{\beta |\sim \gamma}$$

The conditional assertion expresses the requirement that logically equivalent formulas have exactly the same consequences. Consequences of formulas depend on meaning, not form.

Theorem 6.1 (Left Logical Equivalence). *If $\alpha \leftrightarrow \beta \in P\,E(\alpha)$ and $\alpha \leftrightarrow \beta \in P\,E(\beta)$ and $\gamma \in P\,E(\alpha)$, then $\gamma \in P\,E(\beta)$.*

The condition of *right weakening* is stated as:

$$\frac{\models \alpha \rightarrow \beta, \ \gamma |\sim \alpha}{\gamma |\sim \beta}$$

The conditional assertion expresses the requirement that one should accept as plausible consequences all that is logically implied by what one thinks are plausible consequences.

Theorem 6.2 (Right Weakening). *If $\alpha \rightarrow \beta \in P\,E(\gamma)$ and $\alpha \in PE(\gamma)$, then $\beta \in P\,E(\gamma)$.*

The next rule, *cut*, is similar to Gentzen's *Schnitt*, and is stated as:

$$\frac{\alpha \wedge \beta \,|\!\sim \gamma, \; \alpha \,|\!\sim \beta}{\alpha \,|\!\sim \gamma}$$

The conditional assertion expresses the fact that it is permitted when trying to show a plausible conclusion (γ) to first add a hypothesis (β) to the facts already known to be true (α), prove the plausible conclusion from the enlarged set of facts ($\alpha \wedge \beta$), and then plausibly conclude the added hypothesis from the facts.

Theorem 6.3 (Cut). *Let $\{\alpha\}$ be a p-satisfiable set of premises. If $\gamma \in P E(\alpha \wedge \beta)$ and $\beta \in P E(\alpha)$, then $\gamma \in P E(\alpha)$.*

The next rule, *cautious monotony*, is due to Gabbay (1985) and is stated as:

$$\frac{\alpha \,|\!\sim \gamma, \; \alpha \,|\!\sim \beta}{\alpha \wedge \beta \,|\!\sim \gamma}$$

The conditional assertion expresses the fact that learning a new fact (β), the truth of which could have been plausibly concluded, should not invalidate previous conclusions (γ).

Theorem 6.4 (Cautious Monotony). *Let $\{\alpha\}$ be a p-satisfiable set of premises. If $\gamma \in P E(\alpha)$ and $\beta \in P E(\alpha)$, then $\gamma \in P E(\alpha \wedge \beta)$.*

The conditions of cautious monotony and cut together tell us that if plausible consequences are later acquired as facts, then the original set of plausible consequences remains unchanged. Such a property is useful, as it can make the belief revision process normally associated with nonmonotonic formalisms more efficient.

Lemma 6.1. *The rules of cut and cautious monotony may be expressed together by the following principle: if $\beta \in P E(\alpha)$, then $P E(\alpha) \equiv P E(\alpha \wedge \beta)$.*

The inference relation defined by the rules above corresponds to System C. The entailment relation $|\!\approx$, has similar properties.

6.2. Cumulative Preferential Entailment

If, in addition to the rules in System C described above, an inference relation is further constrained by the *or* rule below, then it corresponds to System P. Kraus, Lehmann, and Magidor (1988) strongly suggest that any reasonably plausible inference relation should meet the criteria of System P.

The next rule, *or*, is stated as:

$$\frac{\alpha|\sim\gamma,\ \beta|\sim\gamma}{\alpha\vee\beta|\sim\gamma}$$

The conditional assertion expresses the fact that any formula that is, separately, a plausible consequence of two different formulas, is a plausible consequence of their disjunction.

Theorem 6.5 (Or). *If* $\gamma\in P\,E(\alpha)$ *and* $\gamma\in P\,E(\beta)$, *then* $\gamma\in PE\,(\alpha\vee\beta)$.

We strongly suspect that the **Or** rule holds in our system, but we have no proof. However, the following weaker result is easily obtainable.

We say that a formula $\alpha\in\Sigma$ is *positively persistent* iff for any partial interpretations u and v for Σ, $u\leqslant_i v$ and $u(\alpha)=T$ imply $v(\alpha)=T$.

Theorem 6.6. *For any* $\Gamma\subseteq\Sigma(S)$, *any positively persistent formulas* $\alpha,\beta\in\Sigma(S)$, *(6.5) holds*.

FNM3 appears to have reasonable properties if the judgment criteria used is that of Kraus, Lehmann, and Magidor (1988). It can be described as a fuzzy approximation of System P. Of course the comparison is not altogether satisfying, since they emphasize the proof theoretic aspect, whereas we emphasize the semantic aspect.

6.3. Consistency and Uniqueness of Extensions

We would like to emphasize two important properties of FNM3 not shared by many of the current nonmonotonic formalisms.

First, the set of formulas preferentially entailed from a preferentially satisfiable set of formulas is preferentially satisfiable:

Corollary 6.1. *If* Γ *is p-satisfiable and* $\Gamma\approx\alpha$, *then* $\Gamma\cup\{\alpha\}$ *is p-satisfiable*.

The second important property of FNM3 is that for each set of premises Γ, there exists a unique set of formulas preferentially entailed by Γ. In default logic and auto-epistemic logic, this is simply not the case, although one may choose to extralogically define entailment relative to the intersection of all extensions or stable expansions, respectively.

7. SUMMARY

In this paper, we've introduced a fuzzy nonmonotonic logic that permits a great deal of expressivity in the language. It has a sound and intuitive semantics that we believe directly models the characteristics normally associated with default reasoning. The semantics follows naturally from the notion of partial interpretations that are inherently connected with the use of fuzzy predicates.

FNM3 has some nice formal properties and belongs to the class of cumulative logics. At the present moment we are developing a decision procedure for a subset of the language, based on semantic tableaux.

More practically, FNM3 should be applied to a number of different domains and the resulting entailments compared with our intuitions. We've capitalized very little on the feature that default rules are part of the object language and can be manipulated. This property should be useful for studying strategies for adjudicating among conflicting default rules and representing priority among defaults. In this connection, the study of appropriate types of implication operators, which can reflect the strength of association between the degree of truth of the premise and a default conclusion $D\alpha$, is of special interest. In the immediate future, we hope to pursue these ideas.

BIBLIOGRAPHY

Adams, Ernest W. (1975). *The Logic of Conditionals*. Dordrecht: Reidel.

Belnap, Nuel D. (1977). A useful four-valued logic. In J. M. Dunn and G. Epstein (eds.): *Modern Uses of Multiple-valued Logic*. Dordrecht: Reidel, pp. 8–37.

Burgess, J. P. (1981). Quick completeness proofs for some logics of conditionals. *Notre Dame J. Formal Logic*, 22, 76–84.

Doherty, P. (1989). A correspondence between inheritance hierarchies and a logic of preferential entailment. In *Methodologies for Intelligent Systems*, 4 (ISMIS'89).

Doherty, P. (1990). A three-valued approach to non-monotonic reasoning. Master's thesis, Linköping University.

Doherty, P. and W. Łukaszewicz. (1990). Distinguishing between facts and default assumptions. Forthcoming technical report.

Dubois D. and H. Prade. (1988). An introduction to possibilistic and fuzzy logic. In P. Smets, A. Mamdani, D. Dubois, and H. Prade (eds.): *Nonstandard Logics for Automated Reasoning*. New York: Academic Press, pp. 287–327.

Etherington, D. (1988). *Reasoning with Incomplete Information*. Los Altos, CA: Morgan Kaufmann.

Gabbay, D. M. (1985). Theoretical foundations for non-monotonic reasoning in expert systems. In K. R. Apt (ed.): *Proc. of the NATO Advanced Study Institute on Logics and Models of Concurrent Systems*. Berlin: Springer-Verlag, pp. 439–457.

Ginsburg, M. (1988). Multivalued logics: A uniform approach to reasoning in artificial intelligence. *Comput. Intell.*, 4, 265–316.

Genesereth, M. and N. Nilsson. (1987). *Logical Foundations of AI*. Los Altos, CA: Morgan Kaufman 4, 265–316.

Ishizuka, M. and N. Kanai. (1985). Prolog-elf incorporating fuzzy logic. In *Proc. of the 9th IJCAI*, pp. 701–703.

Kraus S., D. Lehmann, and M. Magidor. (1988). Preferential models and cumulative logic. Technical Report TR-88-15, Department of Computer Science, Hebrew University, Jerusalem.

Lee, R.C.T. (1972). Fuzzy logic and the resolution principle. *J. Assoc. for Computing Machinery*, 19, 109–119.

Makinson. D. (1988). General theory of cumulative inference. In M. Ginsburg, M. Reinfrank, and E. Sandewall (eds.): *Non-Monotonic Reasoning, Second International Workshop*. Berlin: Springer-Verlag.

Mukaidono, M., Z. L. Shen, and L. Y. Ding (1989). Fundamentals of fuzzy prolog. *Int'l Journal of Approximate Reasoning*, 3, 179–193.

Orci, I. (1980). Programming in possibilistic logic. *Int'l Journal of Expert Systems*, 2 (1), 79–96.

Pearl, J. (1988). *Probabilistic Reasoning in Intelligent Systems: Networks of Plausible Inference*. Los Altos, CA: Morgan Kaufmann.

Prade, H. (1985). A computational approach to approximate and plausible reasoning with applications to expert systems. *IEEE Trans. on Pattern Analysis and Machine Intelligence*, 7, 260–283.

Przymusinski, T. (1989). Three-valued formalizations of non-monotonic reasoning and logic programming. In *First Int. Conf. on Principles of Knowledge Representation and Reasoning*, pp. 341–348.

Reiter, R. (1980). A logic for default reasoning. *Artificial Intelligence*, 13, 81–132.

Reinfrank, M. (1988). Defaults as preferences among partial worlds. In *European Workshop on Logical Methods in Artificial Intelligence*. JE-LIA88.

Sandewall, E. (1985). A functional approach to non-monotonic logic. In *Int. Joint Conf. on Artificial Intelligence*. IJCAI85.

Sandewall, E. (1988a). Non-monotonic entailment for reasoning about time and action: Part iii: Decision procedure. Technical Report LITHI-DA-R-88-29, Department of Computer and Information Science, Linköping University.

Sandewall, E. (1988b). The semantics of non-monotonic entailment defined using partial interpretations. In M. Ginsburg, M. Reinfrank, and E. Sandewall, (eds.): *Non-Monotonic Reasoning, Second International Workshop*. Berlin: Springer-Verlag.

Shoham, Y. (1988). *Reasoning about Change*. Cambridge: MIT Press.

Veltman, F. (1986). *Logics for Conditionals*. Ph.D. dissertation, Filosofisch Instituut, Universiteit van Amsterdam.

Yager, R. R. (1984). Approximate reasoning as a basis for rule-based expert systems. *IEEE Trans. Syst. Man Cyber.*, 14, 636–643.

10 On modifier logic

Jorma K. MATTILA
Department of Information Technology
Lappeenranta University of Technology
SF-53851 Lappeenranta, FINLAND

Abstract. A syntactical theory of modifier operators is created by adding to lower predicate calculus a set of axiom schemata and inference rules. This formation of a logical theory is based on the general principle of calculus. Some examples for the application of the system to the logic of hedges are given, and some preliminary comments considering possibility theory are made.

1. INTRODUCTION

We consider the *logic of modifier operators* applied to *inferences with hedges*. This logic has also many other application possibilities, such as multimodality and dynamic logics, and such fields of logics of operators where the deduction theorem (familiar from classical logic) can be used. So this modifier logic cannot be applicable, for instance, to temporal logics, where the deduction theorem is not valid in classical form. We call this logic a system $LPC + Ch$ (LPC comes from Lower Predicate Calculus and **Ch** is an abbreviation from the word **Characteristic**).

Consider some general intuitive ideas for this logical system. Lakoff (1973, p. 464) introduces a general principle of *semantic entailment* in many-valued *fuzzy propostional logic* (*FPL*) as follows: For any well-defined wffs (well-formed formulae) P and Q in *FPL*

$$P \models Q \text{ iff } \mathbf{V}(P) \leqslant \mathbf{V}(Q) \tag{1}$$

(**V** is a valuation), which means that

$$P \models Q \text{ iff } \models P \to Q$$

We suppose this holds for all possible valuations **V**. He gives the following example.

Example 1. Let $P =$ "John is very tall" and $Q =$ "John is tall." Clearly P semantically entails Q, i.e., $\models P \to Q$.

In our article this idea is carried out by introducing operators for hedges like "very," etc. Thus it is possible to restrict the logical system to two-valued one, which is easier to implement for computers than a many-valued system because of the properties of the resolution principle. According to this idea, in the above example we need only one proposition: $Q =$ "John is tall," and an operator F for "very." We then get $\mathbf{F}(Q) =$ "John is very tall," and thus we get

$$\models \mathbf{F}(Q) \to Q \tag{2}$$

because (1) holds, of course, in a two-valued system. Here we call F a *substantiating operator*. We can present an additional illustration.

Example 2. Let $P =$ "Dogs bark much," and **H** stands for "more or less." Then we have $\mathbf{H}(P) =$ "Dogs bark much," and **H** stands for "more or less." Then we have $\mathbf{H}(P) =$ "Dogs bark more or less much." **H** is here a *weakening operator*. By means of the entailment we have

$$\models P \to \mathbf{H}(P) \tag{3}$$

Let then P be any wff of some logical system, say, our two-valued system $LPC + Ch$. Because we have by means of the entailment $\models \mathbf{F}(P) \to P$ and $\models P \to \mathbf{H}(P)$, we get

$$\models \mathbf{F}(P) \to \mathbf{H}(P) \tag{4}$$

by *PC* (Propositional Calculus). In general, by means of the entailment the assertion (4) is correct if **F** is at least as strong as **H**. Another important thing is that **F** is at least as strong as **H** iff for any wff *P*, $V(\mathbf{F}(P)) \leqslant V(\mathbf{H}(P))$ holds for all valuations **V**. Thus, again, by means of the entailment the condition

for any *P*, **F** is at least as strong as **H** iff $\models \mathbf{F}(P) \to \mathbf{H}(P)$

holds. This is the idea for the main axiom schema of *LPC + Ch* (given below).

In our formation of the theory we use the so-called *idea of calculus* (due to Leibniz). It is as follows. For a formal theory:

(a) the alphabet is given
(b) the formation of wffs is given
(c) the axioms are chosen
(d) the rules of inference are chosen

By these means we can get all the correct expressions of the theory.

2. DESCRIPTION OF THE SYSTEM *LPC + Ch*

We start by introducing the general concept of a *system*. There is an excellent description of systems in Lemmon (1977). For example, a propositional system *PC* is a set of propositions (propositional sentences), say Γ, with the property that if $\alpha \in \Gamma, \alpha \to \beta \in \Gamma$, then $\beta \in \Gamma$, i.e., Γ is *closed with respect to modus ponens*. If *S* is any system, we refer to the members of *S* (wffs in *S*) as *theorems of S*, and usually write $\vdash_s \alpha$ in place of $\alpha \in S$ (We shall regularly use the term "system" in the sense that a system is understood to *include the classical propositional calculus PC*.)

If *S* is a system, by an *S-system* we mean a system *S'* including *S*, i.e., such that $S \subset S'$. *S*-systems are sometimes called *extensions* of *S*. Clearly, if $\Gamma \vdash_s \alpha$, then α belongs to all *S*-extensions of Γ. The set $\{\alpha \mid \Gamma \vdash_s \alpha\}$ is an *S*-extension of Γ, and contained in all *S*-extensions of Γ.

From now on, a system is a set of wffs Γ consisting of the theorems of *LPC*, and if $\alpha, \alpha \to \beta \in \Gamma$, then $\beta \in \Gamma$. The fact $PC \subset LPC \subset S$ for any system *S* follows from the above.

A system *S* is *consistent* iff not all wffs belong to *S;* equivalently in the light of *PC*, iff $\perp \notin S$ ($\perp$ is any wff of the form $\alpha \wedge -\alpha$). Otherwise *S* is *inconsistent*. A system *S* is *complete* iff for all wffs α either $\alpha \in S$ or $-\alpha \in S$ ($\alpha \rightarrow \perp \in S$). More generally, a set of wffs Γ is *s-consistent* (consistent with respect to the system *S*) iff it is not the case that $\Gamma \vdash_s \alpha$ for all wffs α. Also a set Γ of wffs is *S-complete* (complete with respect to *S*) iff for all wffs α either $\Gamma \vdash_s \alpha$ or $\Gamma \vdash_s \neg\alpha$. A system that is both consistent and complete is called a *maximal consistent* system.

We note simple facts about system *S* and sets of wffs Γ:

(i)   for any system *S* if $\alpha \in S$ then $\neg\alpha \notin S$ and if $\neg\alpha \in S$ then $\alpha \notin S$

(ii)   for any complete *S*, $\alpha \rightarrow \beta \in S$ iff if $\alpha \in S$ then $\beta \in S$

(iii) for any maximal consistent *S*, $\alpha \in S$ iff $\neg\alpha \notin S$ and $\neg\alpha \in S$ iff $\alpha \notin S$

(iv) if Γ is *S*-consistent, *S* is consistent

(v)   if Γ is *S*-consistent and S' is an *S*-system, then Γ is *S-consistent*

For *LPC + Ch* we adopt the *logical alphabet* from *LPC*, which is natural because *LPC + Ch* is an *LPC*-system. The *symbolic alphabet* is that of *LPC* augmented by a set of *operator symbols* $\mathbb{O} = \{J, F_1, F_2, ...\}$. We denote these *modifier operators* by metasymbols H, F, V, ... (with or without numerical subscripts). The set $\mathbb{O}$ is linearly ordered by the strength relation "$<$" which means that if $F_1 < F_2$, then the strength of F_1 is not more than that of F_2. If F_2 is (strictly) stronger than F_1, we write $F_1 < F_2$. In addition to this, the relation "$<$" is strongly connected in $\mathbb{O}$. Thus "$<$" is a strongly connected simple ordering in $\mathbb{O}$. The operator J is an *identity operator* included in $\mathbb{O}$, such that for all other operators $F \in \mathbb{O}$ either $J < F$ or $F < J$, and especially $J \leqslant J$. An operator F is called *weakening (substantiating)*, if $F < J (J < F)$. Thus we have the symbolic alphabet in the form of an ordered triple $S = (F, P, \mathbb{O})$, where F is the set of function symbols, and P is the set of predicate symbols.

We give the definition of the set W of wffs of *LPC + Ch* as follows:

Definition 2.1. If $S = (F, P, \mathbb{O})$ is the symbolic alphabet, then the set of *S-formulae* or *wffs* W_s is the smallest set W for which it holds:

(1°) the set *W* of wffs of *LPC* is subset of W

(2°) if $\alpha \in W$ and $F \in \mathbb{O}$, then $F(\alpha) \in W$

(3°) if $\alpha \in W$, then $\neg\alpha \in W$

(4°) if $\alpha, \beta \in W$, then $(\alpha \rightarrow \beta) \in W$

(5°) if $\alpha \in W$ and x is a variable, then for each x $\alpha \in W$

(6°) All the wffs are generated by the steps (1°)-(5°)

We can call these wffs belonging to W *Ch-formulae*. We now give the axiom schemata for the system *LPC + Ch*.

Definition 2.2.

    (i)   All the *Ch*-formulae belonging to the system *LPC* are axioms.

    (ii)   If $H, F \in \mathbb{O}$, and $H \leqslant F$, then for all $\alpha \in W$

$$F(\alpha) \to H(\alpha) \tag{5}$$

is an axiom.

    (iii) For all wffs $\alpha \in W$ and for the identity operator $J \in \mathbb{O}$

$$J(\alpha) \leftrightarrow \alpha \tag{6}$$

is an axiom.

Actually (6) is a shorter formula following logically from the formulae $J(\alpha) \to \alpha$ and $\alpha \to J(\alpha)$, which originally are the axioms considering the operator **J**. We need the following inference rules:

    (iv) *Modus ponens:* if $\alpha, \beta \in W$, then

$$\alpha \to \beta, \alpha \vdash \beta \tag{7}$$

holds.

    (v)   *Modified modus ponens:* If $\alpha, \beta \in W$ and $F \in \mathbb{O}$ is an arbitrary operator, then

$$\alpha \to \beta, F(\alpha) \vdash F(\beta) \tag{8}$$

holds.

    (vi) *Rule of Substantiation:* For wffs $\alpha \in W$ and all substantiating operators $F \in \mathbb{O}$,

$$\vdash \alpha \Rightarrow \vdash F(\alpha) \tag{9}$$

holds.

Rule (9) can be illustrated intuitively by saying that a true fact remains true even if we try to substantiate it. Thus a system $LPC + Ch$ is a set of wffs Γ such that the wffs (i)–(iii) belong to Γ, and Γ is closed with respect to (7)–(9).

Definition 2.3. We say that a system S is *classical* if for any $\alpha, \beta \in W$ and any $F \in \mathbb{O}$, whenever $\vdash_s \alpha \leftrightarrow \beta$, then $\vdash_s F(\alpha) \leftrightarrow F(\beta)$.

The system $LPC + Ch$ is classical. In fact, a stronger result

$$\alpha \leftrightarrow \beta \vdash F(\alpha) \leftrightarrow F(\beta) \tag{10}$$

holds in $LPC + Ch$. It is also consistent, but not maximal consistent, because PC is not maximal consistent and $LPC + Ch$ is a PC-extension. These things are proved in Mattila (1990d). We examine some properties of $LPC + Ch$ by presenting some results that are proved in Mattila (1986, 1988, 1989).

Duality of Identifier. For all $\alpha \in W$, and for the identity operator $J \in \mathbb{O}$ the condition

$$\vdash J(\alpha) \leftrightarrow -J(\neg\alpha) \tag{11}$$

holds. Especially in (11), we say that the wffs $J(\alpha)$ and $\neg J(\neg\alpha)$ are logically equivalent, and we denote this by $J(\alpha) \equiv \neg J(\neg\alpha)$. In cases like this we also say that the operators J and $\neg J\neg$ are equal $(J = \neg J\neg)$.

Reflexivity Laws. For all $\alpha \in W$, and for any operator $F \in \mathbb{O}$

$$\vdash F(\alpha) \rightarrow \alpha \quad (J \leqslant F) \tag{12}$$

$$\vdash \alpha \rightarrow F(\alpha) \quad (F \leqslant J) \tag{13}$$

The following result deals also with two important properties of operators.

Let $F \in O$ be any operator. Then

(a)   If $J \leqslant F$, then for all $\alpha \in W$, $\vdash J(\alpha) \rightarrow \neg F(\neg\alpha)$, and

(b)   if $F \leqslant J$, then for all $\alpha \in W$, $\vdash \neg F(\neg\alpha) \rightarrow J(\alpha)$.

By means of the last result, for any operator $F \in \mathbb{O}$ we may introduce an operator F^* such that

$$F^* =_{df} \neg F\neg \tag{14}$$

We say that such operators F, F^*, according to (14), for which either the condition (a) or (b) of the above result holds, are *duals* of each other, or a *dual pair* of operators. Clearly by means of (14) $F^{**} = F$.

We have to extend the set $\mathbb{O}$ such that also all dual operators belong to $\mathbb{O}$ if $F \in \mathbb{O}$. We also need the following extension of the relation "$\leqslant$" consisting also of dual operators.

Definition 2.4. If $F \in \mathbb{O}$ (thus $F^* \in \mathbb{O}$ by means of the extension of $\mathbb{O}$) then

(a)   if $J \leqslant F$ then $F^* \leqslant J$

(b)   if $F \leqslant J$ then $J \leqslant F^*$

The immediate consequence of Definition 2.4 is: If $F \in \mathbb{O}$ then

(c)   if $J \leqslant F$ then $F^* \leqslant F$

(d)   if $F \leqslant J$ then $F \leqslant F^*$

The following result is closely related to (c) and (d).

Duality Laws. If $\mathbf{F}$ is weakening, then for all $\alpha \in \mathbf{W}$

$$\vdash \mathbf{F}^*(\alpha) \to \mathbf{F}(\alpha) \tag{15}$$

If $\mathbf{F}$ is substantiating, then for all $\alpha \in \mathbf{W}$

$$\vdash \mathbf{F}(\alpha) \to \mathbf{F}^*(\alpha) \tag{16}$$

Law of the Strength of Duals. Suppose $\mathbf{H}_1$, $\mathbf{H}_2 \in \mathbb{O}$ are two operators such that $\mathbf{H}_2 \leqslant \mathbf{H}_1$. Then for all $\alpha \in \mathbf{W}$

$$\vdash \mathbf{H}^*_1(\alpha) \to \mathbf{H}^*_1(\alpha) \tag{17}$$

If $\mathbf{F}$, $\mathbf{H} \in \mathbb{O}$ are two operators such that $\mathbf{J} \leqslant \mathbf{F}$, and $\mathbf{H}$ and $\mathbf{F}$ are duals, then for all α, $\beta \in \mathbf{W}$ holds the following results.

Weak Distributivity Law of Implication

$$\vdash \mathbf{F}(\alpha \to \beta) \to (\mathbf{F}(\alpha) \to \mathbf{F}(\beta)) \tag{18}$$

Negation Transition Law

$$\vdash \mathbf{F}(\neg\alpha) \to \neg\mathbf{H}(\alpha) \text{ and } \vdash \neg\mathbf{F}(\alpha) \to \mathbf{H}(\neg\alpha) \tag{19}$$

Distributivity Laws of Conjunction. If $\mathbf{F}$ is a substantiating operator, then for α, $\beta \in \mathbf{W}$

$$\vdash \mathbf{F}(\alpha \wedge \beta) \leftrightarrow \mathbf{F}(\alpha) \wedge \mathbf{F}(\beta) \tag{20}$$

If $\mathbf{H}$ is a weakening operator, then for any α, $\beta \in \mathbf{W}$

$$\vdash \mathbf{H}(\alpha \wedge \beta) \to \mathbf{H}(\alpha) \wedge \mathbf{H}(\beta) \tag{21}$$

Distributivity Laws of Disjunction. If $\mathbf{H}$ is weakening operator, then

$$\vdash \mathbf{H}(\alpha \vee \beta) \leftrightarrow (\mathbf{H}(\alpha) \vee \mathbf{H}(\beta)) \tag{22}$$

If $\mathbf{F}$ is a substantiating operator, then for all α, $\beta \in \mathbf{W}$

$$\vdash \mathbf{F}(\alpha) \vee \mathbf{F}(\beta) \to \mathbf{F}(\alpha \vee \beta) \tag{23}$$

Quantifier Transition Laws. If $\mathbf{F} \in \mathbb{O}$ is any modifier operator and $\alpha \in \mathbf{W}$, then it holds

$$\vdash \mathbf{F}(\text{for each } x, \alpha) \to \text{for each } x \, \mathbf{F}(\alpha)) \tag{24}$$

If $\mathbf{F}$ is any operator, then for any $\alpha \in \mathbf{W}$

$$\vdash \text{there exists } x, \mathbf{F}(\alpha) \to \mathbf{F}(\text{there exists } x, \alpha) \tag{25}$$

The formula

$$\mathbf{H}(\alpha) \to \mathbf{F}(\alpha) \tag{26}$$

where $\mathbf{H} \leqslant \mathbf{F}$, is a theorem if $\vdash \alpha$, or if α is a contradiction.

Definition 2.5. Let $F_1, F_2, ..., F_n \in O$ be any modifier operators and $\alpha \in W$. An expression $F_1, F_2 ... F_n$ is a *modifier chain*, which can be associated with a wff α as follows:

$$F_1(F_2 (...F_n (\alpha))...) \tag{27}$$

Especially, if in a modifier chain $F_i = F_j$ for all i and j, then we have the following special case of (27):

$$F (F(...F(\alpha)...)) =_{df} F^n(\alpha), n \in N \tag{28}$$

for all $\alpha \in W$. If $n = 0$, then $F^n = F^0 = J$. Let $n, k \in N$, $n \geqslant k$, and $\alpha \in W$. If F is substantiating, then

$$\vdash F^n (\alpha) \rightarrow F^k (\alpha) \tag{29}$$

If F is weakening, then

$$\vdash F^k (\alpha) \rightarrow F^n(\alpha) \tag{30}$$

Let $F, H, V \in \mathbb{O}$ be such that F is substantiating, $V \leqslant F$, and H is arbitrary. Then for any $\alpha \in W$

$$\vdash H (F)(\alpha)) \rightarrow H(V(\alpha)) \tag{31}$$

Let $F, H, \in O$ such that F is substantiating. Then for any $\alpha \in W$

$$\vdash H (F(\alpha)) \rightarrow H (\alpha) \tag{32}$$

We can generalize the result of (31) by saying that in wffs where an operator chain $F_1, F_2, ...,F_n$ is associated with a wff α, if any operator F_i is replaced by a weaker one, say H_i, we get

$$\vdash F_1 (F_2 (...F_i (...F_n (\alpha))...)) \rightarrow F_1(F_2(...F_{i-1}(H_i(F_{i+1} (...F_n(\alpha))...))))$$

This follows from (30) by replacing α with $F_{i+1}(...F_n(\alpha)...)$ and operating on both sides of the implication by $F_1 F_2...F_{i-1}$.

The modal version of the modified modus ponens (8)

$$\alpha \rightarrow \beta, M (\alpha) \vdash M (\beta) \tag{33}$$

where M is either $\square$ (necessity) or $\lozenge$ (possibility), holds in all standard modal systems. This result is proved in Mattila (1988, 1989).

3. APPLICATION OF *LPC* + *Ch* TO THE LOGIC OF HEDGES

We throw some light on the application of *LPC* + *Ch* to the logic of hedges by means of some "textbook" examples, the first one due to Kickert.[1]

Example 1. We consider the following inference:

> Socrates is *very healthy.*
> Healthy people *live long.*
> ─────────────────────
> Socrates *lives very long.*

We need the inference rule (8) in the proof of our inference above. First we have to formalize the premises and the conclusion. Let s = "Socrates," Hx = "x is a healthy person," Lx = "x lives long," and "very" = **V**. Thus we get the inference into the formalized form

> $\mathbf{V}(Hs)$
> for each $x\ (Hx \rightarrow Lx)$
> ─────────────────────
> $\mathbf{V}(Ls)$

The proof of this inference is as follows:

1. $\mathbf{V}\,(Hs)$
2. for each $x(Hx \rightarrow Lx)$
3. for each $(Hx \rightarrow Lx) \rightarrow (Hs \rightarrow Ls)$
4. $Hs \rightarrow Ls$
5. $\mathbf{V}\,(Ls)$

Thus, if we accept the rule (8) and are of the opinion that it is sufficiently closely, logically true, then the conclusion follows logically (sufficiently closely) from the premises. Zimmermann[2] presents an example of the same form as Example 1. His inference example runs as follows: *"This tomato is very red. If a tomato is red then the tomato is ripe. Thus this tomato is very ripe."* In *LPC* + *Ch* this is provable as in Example 1.

---

[1] W.J.M. Kickert, *Fuzzy Theories on Decision-Making* (Dordrecht: Nijhoff, 1978), p. 122.

[2] H.-J. Zimmermann, *Fuzzy Sets Decision Making, and Expert Systems* (Dordrecht: Kluwer, 1987), p. 246.

Example 2. This example is mentioned by Negoita and Ralescu.[3] Turner[4] has also given the same example. The inference is as follows:

> *a* is *small.*
> *a* and *b* are *approximately equal.*
> _____
> *b* is *more or less small.*

To formalize this inference, let Sa denote "*a* is *small,*" H "*approximately,*" and V "*more or less.*" Besides we suppose that $V \leqslant H$. The formalization of the inference is

$$Sa$$
$$H(a = b)$$
$$\overline{V(Sb)}$$

We get the following deduction:

1. Sa	given
2. $H(a = b)$	given
3. $(a = b \wedge Sa) \rightarrow Sb$	theorem of LPC (concerning the equality)
4. $a = b \rightarrow (Sa \rightarrow Sb)$	PC, step 3
5. $H(Sa \rightarrow Sb)$	(8) steps 2,4
6. $H(\neg Sa \vee Sb)$	$(\alpha \rightarrow \beta) \leftrightarrow (\neg \alpha \vee \beta)$
7. $H(\neg Sa \vee Sb) \rightarrow H(\neg Sa) \vee H(Sb)$	Distributivity law of disjunction
8. $H(\neg Sa) \vee H(Sb)$	(7), steps 6, 7
9. $\neg H^*(Sa) \vee H(Sb)$	Negation transition law & PC, step 8
10. $H^*(Sa) \rightarrow H(Sb)$	$(\alpha \rightarrow \beta) \leftrightarrow (\neg \alpha \vee \beta)$
11. $H^*(H(Sb))$	(8), steps 1, 10
12. $H^*(H(Sb)) \rightarrow H(Sb)$	Reflexivity law (12) $(J \leqslant H^*)$
13. $H(Sb)$	(7), steps 11, 12
14. $H(Sb) \rightarrow V(Sb)$	(5) $(V \leqslant H)$
15. $V(Sb)$	(7), steps 13, 14

It has to be noted that $LPC + Ch$ may not be a complete basis for the logic of hedges. It is well-defined from the syntactical point of view, but changing the approach is not in this case quite clear. Especially some peculiarities can appear in the logic of hedges. For example, consider the following inference:

---

[3] C.V. Negoita and D. Ralescu, Applications of Fuzzy Sets to Systems Analysis (Stuttgart: Birkhäuser, 1975), p. 82.

[4] R. Turner, Logics for Artificial Intelligence (Chichester: Ellis Horwood, 1984), p. 107.

> *Much* barking animals are dogs.
> This animal barks *very much.*
> _____
> This animal is *very* a dog.

This inference is formally provable by means of $LPC + Ch$ (its form is in principle the same as in Example 2) but this inference is amusing. This system is able to create formally correct inferences, but they may be irrelevant at the level of everyday language. In this situation we might experimentally try to find that part of $LPC + Ch$ corresponding as well as possible to the logic of hedges, and vice versa. For example, in the above-mentioned inference there can be deduced from the conclusion "This animal is very a dog" a new one, "This animal is a dog" by the reflexivity law (12). It is quite easy to see that $LPC + Ch$ is not a good formalism for the logic of hedges.

4. ON THE GENERAL CONCEPT OF IMPLICA-TION

By means of the well-known *Axiom of Separation (or Axiom of Specification)* of set theory there exists for any statement $p(x)$ and any nonempty set X a set

$$A = \{a \mid a \in X, P(a) \text{ is true}\} \tag{34}$$

which leads in the known way to the following logical equivalences

$$A \subset B \Leftrightarrow \text{for each } x \ (x \in A \to x \in B) \Leftrightarrow$$
$$\Leftrightarrow \text{for each } x \ (P(x) \to Q(x)) \tag{35}$$

So we have the consequence that "$x \in A \to x \in B$" and hence $P(x) \to Q(x)$ are true for all $x \in A$. If $A \subset B$, then both of the statements $P(x)$ and $Q(x)$ are true for all $x \in A$, i.e.,

for each $x \ (P(x) \to Q(x))$

is always true. The implication of this case is analogous to the *logical implication.* On this fact we base the following examination.

Suppose that $A, B \subset X$ are *fuzzy sets* with respective α-level sets A_α and β_α, and $A \subset B$. Then also $A_\alpha \subset B_\alpha$ for any $\alpha \in [0,1]$. Let $\alpha_0 \in [0,1]$ be an arbitrarily fixed value of the level α. By means of (35) we have

$$A_{\alpha_0} \subset B_{\alpha_0} \Leftrightarrow \text{for each } x(x \in A_{\alpha_0} \rightarrow x \in B_{\alpha_0}) \Leftrightarrow$$

$$A^{\alpha_0} \leqslant \mu_A(x) \leqslant \mu_B(x), \text{ for each } x \in A_{\alpha_0} \tag{36}$$

where μ_A and μ_B are the membership functions of A and B, respectively. Because the fixing of α_0 is arbitrary, (36) holds for any $\alpha \in [0,1]$. The consequence is, that for any sets A and B, being crisp or fuzzy, the condition

$$A \subset B \Leftrightarrow \text{for each } x \ (P(x) \rightarrow Q(x) \Leftrightarrow \mu_A(x) \leqslant \mu_B(x),$$
$$\text{for each } x \in X \tag{37}$$

holds. Thus $P(x) \rightarrow Q(x)$ is generally true exactly for those elements $x \in X$ for which the condition $\mu_A(x) \leqslant \mu_B(x)$ holds. Thus we can use the values of membership functions as truth-values.

In the following considerations wffs $\alpha \in \mathbf{W}$ can get values from the interval $[0, 1]$. We use a definition for implicative algebras given by Rasiowa (1974, p. 16). She says:

> The propositional and predicate calculi of the logic we consider have algebraic interpretations in abstract algebras which, with respect to certain operations, are implicative algebras. Moreover, implicative algebras play, for the weakest logic in the class discussed here, a role analogous to that played by Boolean algebras for classical logic.

This is our motive for trying to use implicative algebras together with modifier operators. We assign a wff with the truth-value TRUE if and only if that wff is true. According to the definition of implicative algebra the system (or actually an abstract algebra) $(\mathbf{T}, \text{TRUE}, \rightarrow)$ is an implicative algebra, where $\mathbf{T}$ is a nonempty partially ordered set of truth-values. According to the definition of implicative algebra, suppose $P, Q, R \in \mathbf{T}$. The truth-value TRUE is a 0-argument function fixing the constant TRUE, and the implication operation is a two-argument operation. By assigning the truth-value TRUE as follows

(IA1) $P \rightarrow P = \text{TRUE}$
(IA2) if $P \rightarrow Q = \text{TRUE}$ and $Q \rightarrow R = \text{TRUE}$,
       then $P \rightarrow R = \text{TRUE}$
(IA3) if $P \rightarrow Q = \text{TRUE}$ and $Q \rightarrow P = \text{TRUE}$ then $P = Q$
(IA4) $P \rightarrow \text{TRUE} = \text{TRUE}$

we get an implicative algebra $(\mathbf{T}, \text{TRUE}, \rightarrow)$. Thus wffs represent truth-functional variables and their combinations. According to the definitions of a *positive implication algebra* and an *implication algebra* we have: for all $P, Q \in \mathbf{W}$

(i)   for any implicative algebra, $(T, \text{TRUE}, \rightarrow)$ in which the conditions

(p_1) $P \rightarrow (Q = \text{TRUE}) = \text{TRUE}$

and

(p_2) $(P \rightarrow (Q \rightarrow R)) \rightarrow ((P \rightarrow Q) \rightarrow (P \rightarrow R)) = \text{TRUE}$

hold is a positive implication algebra (Rasiowa, 1974, p. 23).

(ii) for any implicative algebra, $(T, \text{TRUE}, \rightarrow)$ is an *implication algebra* provided it is a positive implication algebra and in addition the following equation holds (Rasiowa, 1974, p. 30):

(P) $(P \rightarrow Q) \rightarrow P = P$

These additional properties of Definition 4.2 and Definition 4.3 give more sharpness to implication operations. According to Rasiowa, from the conditions (IA1)–(IA4) it follows that an implicative algebra gives in T a partial ordering which relates to implication in the following way

$$P \leqslant Q \text{ iff } P \rightarrow Q = \text{TRUE} \tag{38}$$

This is in accordance with (1). The ordered pair $(T, \leqslant)$ is a partially ordered set, where TRUE is the maximal element of T. (Instead of $(T, \leqslant)$ we can also say that $(T, \rightarrow)$ is a partially ordered set.) So it follows from the facts that one of the properties of implicative algebras is that in any partially ordered set $(X, \leqslant)$, with a greatest element v we can define a two-argument operation "$\rightarrow$" in such a way that $(X, v, \rightarrow)$ is an implicative algebra. For instance, the operation "$\rightarrow$" defined as

$$a \rightarrow b = \begin{cases} v & \text{iff } a \leqslant b \\ a_0 & \text{otherwise} \end{cases} \tag{39}$$

for all $a, b \in X$, where $a_0 \neq v$ is a fixed element in X, fulfills the conditions of the definition of implicative algebras (Rasiowa, 1974, p. 17). The implication operation of our system $LPC + Ch$ is a special case of (39). Actually our system is a two-valued, and because wffs cannot get many-valued truth-values in $LPC + Ch$, we use hedges to associate nonfalse wffs into the system such that they can be equipped with modifiers so that we get expressions with truth-value TRUE. Implicative algebras are one way to provide frames for that. Thus an ordered set of truth-values is associated with a logical system forming an implicative algebra. We will use (39) later on. When we assign values to atomic wffs and combine them by means of logical connectives, we get connected wffs that are functions of those atomic wffs. This concerns quantitative values such as, for instance, truth-values and such qualitative values from which there can be formed partially ordered sets. For instance, in the set of truth-values a connected wff is a truth-function of its atomic parts. On the other hand, an interpretation function assigns to wffs informative qualitative values, which are called interpretations. Generally, these values cannot be ordered partially. Suppose $P \rightarrow Q = \text{TRUE}$. According to the order properties of implicative algebras, if the wffs P and Q get values from a set X of quantitative values, say $P = a$ and $Q = b$, then it has to be $a \leqslant b$. Thus, by means of (1), we have

$$a \rightarrow b \text{ iff } a \leqslant b \tag{40}$$

Especially in the set of "actual" truth-values $T_2 = \{\text{TRUE}, \text{FALSE}\}$, if $P \rightarrow Q = \text{TRUE}$ and $Q = \text{FALSE}$, it must be $p = \text{FALSE}$, because the order in T_2 is $\text{FALSE} \leqslant \text{TRUE}$. This is the situation, e.g., in classical logic and our actual system $LPC + Ch$.

The partial ordering in implicative algebras gives the basis for assigning membership values to logical concepts which, e.g., are fuzzy. For example, let P and Q be any predicates not equipped with any operators and t_1 and t_2 be terms such that the assertions Pt_1 and Qt_2 are fuzzy. If $Pt_1 \rightarrow Qt_2$, then the membership value assigned to Pt_1 must be equal to or less than that assigned to Qt_2, i.e., $\mu_A \leqslant \mu_B$, where $A = \{x \in X \mid Px\}$ and $B = \{x \in X \mid Qx\}$ are fuzzy sets and μ_A and μ_B are the membership functions of these fuzzy sets A and B, respectively, and X is the universe of discourse.

According to the logic of hedges, let $T = [0,1]$. An element $\mu \in T$ may be, e.g., a value of a membership function equipped with P for some value of a variable x in P. According to (37), μ can be represented as a truth-value in many-valued fuzzy logic. For any weakening hedge V associated with P, the truth-value of $V(P)$ is equal to or greater than μ. Correspondingly, for any substantiating hedge F the truth-value of $F(P)$ is equal to or less than μ. This can be seen, e.g., by means of those properties of hedges, which have some similarities with modal operators. Thus the property (39) holds in the logic of hedges.

We can use any ordered sets of truth-values, especially truth-values of many-valued logics, if we insist that the implication operation must satisfy (39), because the ordering property of the implication operation implied by the axiom (5) is in harmony with that given by implicative algebras, even when the set of truth-values would be other than the usual classical one or belonging to the set [0,1]. Thus the characteristic axiom (5) can be applied, e.g., to many-valued logical systems. For instance, these axioms can be used with Łukasiewicz' system $\mathbf{L}_{aleph_1}$ (or with some other Ls) for manipulating hedges. Suppose the set of truth-values is $\mathbf{T}_{aleph_1} = [0,1]$. If we define TRUE $= 1$ we can connect the set $\mathbf{T}_{aleph_1}$ with the actual truth-value TRUE by means of (5) as follows. Suppose $a, b \in [0,1]$ such that $a \leqslant b$, and let wffs P and Q get truth-values $P = a$ and $Q = b$. Thus by means of (39) we have $P \to Q =$ TRUE. On the other hand, if a wff $P = a$ such that $0 < a < 1$, we can operate on it by some suitable fuzzifier $\mathbf{H}$ such that $\mathbf{H}(P) =$ TRUE. In this case the hedge $\mathbf{H}$ enlarges the scope of P or makes P rougher in such a way that we can accept $\mathbf{H}(P) =$ TRUE. For instance, suppose Ba is interpreted as "a is big" and we can accept a truth-value, say, 0.75 for it. Now we can operate on Ba with a fuzzifier $\mathbf{R}$ such that we can accept the truth-value TRUE for $\mathbf{R}(Ba) =$ "a is rather big." Thus by means of (5) or the reflexivity laws (13) and (39) we can assign the truth-value TRUE to the wff $Ba \to \mathbf{R}(Ba)$. Clearly $\mathbf{R}$ is a weakening hedge. This is in accordance with the reflexivity law (13), as it must be. Using modifiers in this way a modifier $\mathbf{F} \in \mathbb{O}$ is a mapping $\mathbf{F}:[0, 1] \to \{$FALSE, TRUE$\}$, where $\mathbf{F}(1) =$ TRUE and $\mathbf{F}(0) =$ FALSE for any $\mathbf{F} \in \mathbb{O}$. Especially, $\mathbf{J}(\alpha) = \alpha$ for all $\alpha \in [0, 1]$. Suppose we have a fuzzy inference scheme, say,

$$\frac{\alpha_1, \ \alpha_2, \ ..., \ \alpha_n}{\beta}$$

where the truth-values of the premises are not all equal to TRUE. When we apply modifiers to the premises in order to get the fully true new premises $\mathbf{V}_i(\alpha_i), i = 1, ..., n$, we get in this new inference the conclusion $\mathbf{H}(\beta)$. Then the inverse mapping

$$\mathbf{H}^{-1}: \{$$FALSE, TRUE$$\} \to [0,1]$$

gives an approximation of the many-valued truth-value of β in the original inference. The result depends on the degree of the strength of $\mathbf{H}$.

Example. Consider an inference of the form

$$\begin{array}{c|c} 0.7 & \alpha \\ 0.8 & \alpha \to \beta \\ \hline ? & \beta \end{array}$$

In the first premise we apply modifiers as hedges so that we operate the wff α by such a weakening modifier $\mathbf{H}$ that the truth-value of $\mathbf{H}(\alpha)$ becomes 1, i.e., the modifier $\mathbf{H}$ is a mapping $\mathbf{H}: [0, 1] \to \{0, 1\}$, which maps 0.7 into 1. In the second premise the truth-value of β is less than that of α, because the truth-value of the implication is less than 1. We now operate the wff β by such a weakening modifier $\mathbf{V}$ that the truth-value of $\mathbf{V}(\beta)$ becomes greater than that of α. Then by means of (1) the implication $\alpha \rightarrow \mathbf{V}(\beta)$ has the truth-value 1. Now we get the inference

$$
\begin{array}{c|l}
1 & \mathbf{H}(\alpha) \\
1 & \alpha \rightarrow \mathbf{V}(\beta) \\
\hline
1 & \mathbf{HV}(\beta)
\end{array}
$$

by (8). Because in the conclusion β is operated by a chain of two weakening modifiers, the truth-value of β must be less than that of any premise in the original inference, i.e., less than 0.7, say, 0.5 or 0.6 This is still merely an idea about how to use linguistic approximations in fuzzy inferences to create fuzzy truth-values for conclusions when we know those values for the premises.

5. THE CONNECTION OF $L PC + Ch$ TO POSSIBILITY THEORY

We begin with the definition of possibility measure and necessity measure (see Zadeh, 1978 and Dubois and Prade, 1980).

If $U = \{u_i \mid i \in I\}$ is a set of elementary events, when any $A \in P(U)$ is an event combined by some elementary events, then a *possibility measure* on U is a set function

$$\Pi : P(U) \rightarrow [0, 1] \tag{41}$$

such that:

$$\Pi(\varnothing) = 1 \tag{42}$$
$$\Pi(U) = 1 \tag{43}$$
$$\Pi(A \cup B) = \sup(\Pi(A), \Pi(B)), \text{ for each } A, B \subset U \tag{44}$$

If $\pi : U \rightarrow [0, 1]$ is a function such that for each $A \subset U$

$$\Pi(A) = \sup_{u \in A} \pi(u) \tag{45}$$

then $\pi(u)$ is a *possibility distribution* on U.

A necessity measure on U is set function

$$N : P(U) \rightarrow [0, 1] \tag{46}$$

such that:

$$N(\emptyset) = 0 \tag{47}$$
$$N(U) = 1 \tag{48}$$
$$N(A \cup B) = \min(N(A), N(B)) \text{ for each } A, B \subset U \tag{49}$$

Generally, there are some known connections between possibility theory and modal logic, and thus through that fact, connections to the system $LPC + Ch$. Zadeh (1978) says especially that the interpretation of the concept of possibility in his possibility theory is quite different from the concepts of possibility and necessity in modal logic but, after Dubois and Prade (1980) created the necessity measure, the counterparts *are* there, and the logical base of possibility theory seems to be the same as that of modal logic when we substitute atomic propositions for elementary events such that for any event there is a wff that indicates the state of affairs of that event. We have the well-known facts

$$N(A) = 1 - \Pi(\bar{A}) \text{ corresponding to } \Box A = \neg \Diamond \neg A$$
$$\Pi(A) = 1 - N(\bar{A}) \text{ corresponding to } \Diamond A = \neg \Box \neg A$$

These conditions of possibility theory hold also in the system $LPC + Ch$, if N is considered as a substantiating operator and π as a weakening operator corresponding to N, i.e., $N = \neg \Pi \neg$. The condition

$$N(A) \leqslant \Pi(A) \tag{50}$$

corresponds to that partial ordering relation which is analogous to the general condition of implication that holds also in the system $LPC + Ch$. The equivalence parts of the conditions

$$\text{if } N(A) > 0 \text{ then } N(\bar{A}) = 0 \Leftrightarrow \Pi(A) = 1 \tag{51}$$

and

$$\text{if } \Pi(A) < 1 \text{ then } \pi(\bar{A}) = 1 \Leftrightarrow N(A) = 0 \tag{52}$$

are also provable in modal logic, and their counterparts hold in the system $LPC + Ch$. These connections to $LPC + Ch$ and modal logic are only just a starting point for the logical base of possibility theory. Also in Kacprzyk's (1991) application of possibility theory his *compatibility relation of type 0* is a special case of the *accessibility relation* **R**, and the sets of states associated with compatibility relations are special cases of universes of worlds in the semantics of $LPC + Ch$ (see Mattila, 1990a).

Let $x \in A = \{\alpha_i \mid i \in I\}$, $A \subset \mathbf{W}$, where any wff α_i can get values from the interval $[0,1]$, and let $\mathbf{V}_j \in \mathbb{O}$ $(\mathbf{V}_j \leqslant \mathbf{J})$ for all $j \in J$ such that for all $x \in A$ it can be found an expression

$$\mathbf{V}_j(\alpha_i) \equiv \mathbf{H}_j(\Diamond\, \alpha_i) \tag{53}$$

which gives the linguistic expression for the possibility of the event $v_i \in X$ expressed by the wff $\alpha_i \in \mathbf{W}$. Thus we have the one-to-one correspondence between π (x_i) and $\mathbf{V}_j(\alpha_i)$ created by weakening modifiers, which are mappings

$$\mathbf{V}_j : [0,\ 1] \to \{0,1\} \text{ or } \mathbf{H}_j : [0,\ 1] \to \{0,1\} \tag{54}$$

for all $j \in \mathbf{J}$. We can translate Zadeh's possibility distribution $\pi(x)$ into a discrete sequence of the expressions (53), and using the inverse modifiers we can translate a sequence of linguistic expressions (53) into a possibility distribution $\pi(x)$. Accordingly it seems that the system $LPC + Ch$ is one plank in the logical base of possibility theory.

Keywords: modifier, hedge, lower predicate calculus, modal logic, possibility

BIBLIOGRAPHY

Dubois, D. and H. Prade. (1980). *Fuzzy Sets and Systems: Theory and Application*. New York, London, Toronto, Sydney, San Francisco: Academic Press.

Hughes, G. E and M. J. Cresswell. (1985). *An Introduction to Modal Logic*. London and New York: Methuen, reprinted.

Kacprzyk, J. (1991). Compatibility relations for the representation of associations between variables on knowledge–based systems, and their use in approximate reasoning. *Fuzzy Sets and Systems*, **42**, 273–291.

Lakoff, G. (1973). Hedges: A study in meaning criteria and the logic of fuzzy concepts *Journal of Philosophical Logic*, **2**.

Lemmon, E. J. (1977). An Introduction to Modal Logic. *Amer. Phil. Quarterly*, Monograph no. 11 (ed., K. Segerberg), Oxford.

Margaris, A. (1967). *First Order Mathematical Logic*. Blaisdell.

Mattila, J. K. (1986). *Proof-theoretical aspects of fuzzy logic*. In W. Bandler and A. Kandel (eds.): Recent Developments in the Theory and Applications of Fuzzy Sets. *Proceedings of North American Fuzzy Information Processing Society, NF AFIPS'86 Conference, New* Orleans, LA, pp. 386–398.

Mattila J. K. (1988). On similarities between modal logic and the logic of hedges. *Proc. Workshop on Knowledge-Based Systems and Models of Logical Reasoning* (Cairo, Egypt).

Mattila J. K. (1989). *Calculus of modifier operators in fuzzy logic.* Publications of the Institute for Applied Mathematics, no. 14, University of Turku, Finland.

Mattila, J. K. (1990a). *The construction of a propositional modifier logic.* Research Report no. 21, Lappeenranta University of Technology, Department of Information Technology, Lappeenranta.

Mattila, J. K. (1990b). *Modified modus ponens and modal logic.* Paper presented at International Symposium on Fuzzy Approach to Reasoning and Decision-Making, Bechyne, Czechoslovakia.

Mattila, J. K. (1990c). *A "resolution friendly" approach to inference systems including inexact concepts.* Paper presented at the Fourth Finnish-Polish Conference on Computer Support, Problem Solving and Decision Making, Lappeenranta, Finland.

Mattila J. K. (1990d). *The construction of fuzzy logic system LPC + Ch.* Submitted for publication.

Rasiowa, H. (1974). *An Algebraic Approach to Non-classical Logics.* Amsterdam: North-Holland.

Zadeh L. A. (1978). Fuzzy sets as a basis for a theory of possibility. *Fuzzy Sets and Systems,* 1, 3–28.

11 VLSI fuzzy chip and inference accelerator board systems

Hiroyuki WATANABE
and James R. SYMON
Department of Computer
Science
University of North Carolina
Chapel Hill, NC 27514, USA

Wayne D. DETLOFF
and Kathy E. YOUNT
MCNC
Research Triangle Park, NC
27514, USA

Abstract. Fuzzy logic-based control uses a rule-based expert system paradigm in the area of real-time process control. The VLSI implementation of a fuzzy logic inference mechanism allows the use of rule-based control and decision making in demanding real-time applications. The second generation of full custom CMOS VLSI has been designed. The chip consists of 688,131 transistors of which 476,160 are used for RAM memory. A Fuzzy chip has been successfully fabricated and tested. This paper presents VLSI architecture in detail. We have built VMEbus single board systems based on the chip for Oak Ridge National Laboratory (ORNL) and for NASA Ames Research Center. The board is installed in a robot at ORNL. Researchers at ORNL use this board for experiment in autonomous robot navigation. The fuzzy logic system board places the fuzzy chip into a VMEbus environment to provide application process control through a VMEbus host.

1. INTRODUCTION

Fuzzy logic-based control uses a rule-based expert system paradigm in the area of real-time process control (King and Mamdani, 1977). It has been used successfully in numerous areas including train control (Yasunobu and Miyamoto, 1985), cement kiln control (Holmblad and Østergaard, 1982), robot navigation (Maeda, 1990), and auto-focus cameras (Shingu and Nishimori, 1989). In order to use this paradigm of a fuzzy rule-based controller in demanding real-time applications, the VLSI implementation of the inference mechanism has been an active research topic (Corder, 1989; Togai and Watanabe, 1986; Watanabe et al., 1990; Yamakawa and Miki, 1986). Potential applications of such a VLSI inference processor include real-time decision making in the area of command and control (Kawano et al., 1984), and control of precision machinery.

An original prototype experimental chip designed at AT&T Bell Laboratories (Togai and Watanabe, 1986) was the precursor to the fuzzy logic inference engine IC that is the heart of our hardware system. The current chip was designed cooperatively at the University of North Carolina and the MCNC (Microelectronics Center of North Carolina) (Watanabe et al., 1990). The MCNC fabricated and tested fully functional chips.

The new architecture of the inference processor has the following important improvements compared with previous work:

1. Programmable rule set memory
2. On-chip *fuzzification* operation by table lookup
3. On-chip *defuzzification* operation by centroid algorithm
4. Reconfigurable architecture
5. RAM redundancy for higher yield

The fuzzy chips are incorporated in VMEbus circuit boards. One of the single-chip boards was designed for Oak Ridge National Laboratory (ORNL) and another board was designed for NASA Ames Research Center. The former board has been installed and is currently performing navigational tasks on experimental autonomous robots (Weisbin, de Saussure, Einstein, and Pin, 1989; Pin, Cachiero, Symon, and Watanabe, in press).

ORNL received the second version of the board system featuring seven fuzzy chips in a software reconfigurable interconnection network. The network provides host and interchip I/O in any logical configuration of the seven chips.

The fuzzy logic system board places the fuzzy chip into a VMEbus environment to provide application process control through a VME-bus host. High level C language functions hide the operational details of the board from the applications programmer. The programmer treats rule memories and fuzzification function memories as local structures passed as parameters to the C functions. The high degrees of parallelism and integration of the fuzzy chip allow sophisticated reasoning to be performed within the limited time frame of real world decision making.

2. FUZZY LOGIC

Some aspects of fuzzy logic challenge a basic scientific dogma on pursuit of precision. The fuzzy logic, at least in some applications, claims that precision is costly and should not be pursued more than necessary. Such pursuit is not only costly but many times it is harmful. It also challenges another more philosophical dogma. The fuzzy logic proposes the multiple and varying degree of truths as opposed to the single and unique truth. Consequently, there has been a strong opposition and hostility toward fuzzy logic in the scientific community (Zadeh, 1990).

However, fuzzy logic has been very successfully applied in many areas, especially in control engineering field (Sugeno and Murakami, 1984; Lee, 1990). In fuzzy logic based control, an if-then type rule is used for mapping from a current state observation to a control action. Conditions in if-part and actions in then-part are expressed using fuzzy logic.

Here, we review the basic concept of fuzzy logic and its application in the inference process. For the further details, refer to the original works by Zadeh (1965, 1971, 1973), and by Fukami et al. (1980) or to the textbooks by Kandel (1986) or Klir and Folger (1988).

2.1. Fuzzy Set

A *fuzzy set* is based on a generalization of the concept of the ordinary set. In an ordinary set, we associate a characteristic function with each set. For example, we can define a set S with its characteristic function $f_s : U \to \{0,1\}$. Then, for all e in the universal set U,

$e \in S$ if $f_s(e) = 1$
$e \notin S$ if $f_s(e) = 0$

Each element of the universe either belongs to or does not belong to the set S. In a fuzzy set, an element can be a member of the set with

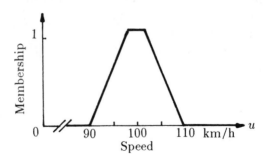

Figure 11.1. Approximately 100 km/h

a varying *degree of membership.* The associated characteristic function, therefore, returns any real number between 0 and 1, and it is termed as a *membership function.* For a fuzzy set **f**, we have an associated membership function $\mu_f: U \rightarrow [0,1]$. For example, if element e is a member of fuzzy set **f** with degree 0.34, the membership function returns this value, $\mu_f(e) = 0.34$. If $\mu_f(e) = 0$, e is entirely outside of fuzzy sef **f** and if $\mu_f = 1$, e is entirely inside of fuzzy set **f**. Fuzzy set is represented by a set of ordered pairs of an element u_i and its grade of membership $\mu_f(u_i)$:

$$\mathbf{f} = \{(u_i, \mu_f(u_i))\}, \, u_i \in U$$

where U is the universe of discourse. In practice, however, a fuzzy set is represented by a vector **f** of membership values:

$$\mathbf{f} = (\mu_f(u_i)), \, i = 1,...,n$$

where element u_i is implicitly represented by *ith* position and n is the cardinality of U.

Using a fuzzy set, we can represent and manipulate imprecise and vague concepts and data. For example, the concept of *approximately 100 km/h* is represented by the fuzzy set whose membership function is shown in Figure 11.1. *"Approximately 100 km/h"* is called a linguistic label of this fuzzy set.

In fuzzy logic applications, especially in control application, a group of fuzzy sets over a possible range is used. These fuzzy sets overlap each other. This feature is very important for implicit interpolation capability of the fuzzy inference mechanism. The example of a group of fuzzy sets is shown in Figure 11.2.

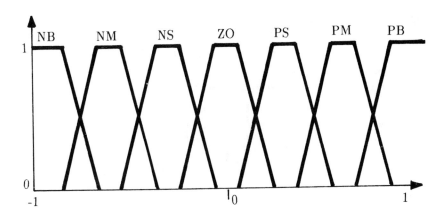

Figure 11.2. A group of fuzzy sets

2.2. Set-theoretic Operators

Given the above definition of fuzzy set as an extension of the classical set, one can extend set-theoretic operators accordingly. Originally, the following three operators were proposed by Zadeh (1965) for intersection, union, and complement:

$$\mu_{a \cap b}(e) = \min(\mu_a(e), \mu_b(e)), \quad e \in U$$
$$\mu_{a \cup b}(e) = \max(\mu_a(e), \mu_b(e)), \quad e \in U$$
$$\mu_{\neg a}(e) = 1 - \mu_a(e), \quad e \in U$$

They are most widely accepted as basic fuzzy logic operations. However, there are alternative operators that are proposed as intersection and union operators. The following lists some of the operators proposed for intersection (T-norm):

logical product $\quad a \wedge b = \min(a, b)$

algebraic product $a \cdot b = ab$

bounded product $a \odot b = 0 \ (a + b - 1)$

drastic sum $\qquad a \wedge b = \begin{cases} a \text{ if } b = 1 \\ b \text{ if } a = 1 \\ 0 \text{ otherwise} \end{cases}$

The above intersection operators have the corresponding union operators (*S*-norm):

logical sum	$a \vee b = \max(a, b)$
algebraic sum	$a + b = a + b - ab$
bounded sum	$a \oplus b = 1 \wedge (a \dot{+} b)$
drastic sum	$a \dot{\vee} b = \begin{cases} a \text{ if } b = 0 \\ b \text{ if } a = 0 \\ 1 \text{ otherwise} \end{cases}$

2.3. Fuzzy Inference

In the traditional logic, one of the most important inference rules is *modus ponens,* that is

Premise	**A** is true
Implication	If **A** then **B**
Conclusion	**B** is true

Here, **A** and **B** are crisply defined propositions. We can construct a *fuzzy proposition* using a fuzzy set such as:

Current speed is *approximately 100 km/h*

By introducing fuzzy propositions into modus ponens, we can generalize modus ponens. Let **c**, **c′**, **d**, **d′** be fuzzy sets. Then the *generalized modus ponens* states:

Premise	x is **c′**
Implication	If x is **c** then y is **d**
Conclusion	y is **d′**

We can use different premises to arrive at different conclusions using the same implication. For example,

Premise	Visibility is *slightly low*
Implication	If visibility is *low* then condition is *poor*
Conclusion	Condition is *slightly poor*

or

Premise	Visibility is *very low*
Implication	If visibility is *low* then condition is *poor*
Conclusion	Condition is *very poor*

In order to perform the above generalized modus ponens, inference methods are proposed based on fuzzy logic (Zadeh, 1973; Fukami et al., 1980). The fuzzy inference is based on two concepts: fuzzy implication and a compositional rule of inference. *Fuzzy implication* is represented as

a → **b**

where **a** and **b** are fuzzy sets. Fuzzy implication is defined by a fuzzy relation. A *fuzzy relation,* in turn, is represented by a matrix. Fuzzy relation R associated with the implication **a** → **b** is a fuzzy set of the Cartesian product $U \times V$ where $\mathbf{a} \in U$ and $\mathbf{b} \in U$. One of the most commonly used fuzzy implications is based on the min operator. In this implication, R is defined as

$$\mu_R(u, v) = \min(\mu_a(u), \mu_b(v)) \quad u \in U, v \in V$$

Relation $R = (\mu_R(u, v))$ is, therefore, a matrix. Note that we can define many other fuzzy relations using other operators such as the bounded product ($\odot$).

If R is a fuzzy relation from U to V, and x is a fuzzy subset of U, then the fuzzy subset **y** of V that is induced by **x** is given by the composition of R and x. That is

$$\mathbf{y} = \mathbf{x} \circ R$$

In order to interpret the above espression, we use the *compositional rule of inference*. The most commonly used method is the *max-min composition*. In this method, **y** is computed by the max-min product of **x** and **R**. The operation is similar to that of a vector and a matrix multiplication. The multiplication is replaced by the min operation and addition is replaced by the max operation

$$\mu_b(v) = \max_{u \in U} \min(\mu_a(u), \mu_R(u, v))$$

Note that when $R = (a \to b)$ and $x = a$ we obtain

$$\mathbf{y} = \mathbf{x} \circ (\mathbf{a} \to \mathbf{b}) = \mathbf{b}$$

as an exact identity. Therefore, the above method can be viewed as an extension of modus ponens.

2.4. Fuzzy Rules

A fuzzy rule is defined by the relation between observation (or antecedent) and action (or conclusion). The fuzzy rule is equivalent to the fuzzy implication. From each rule of the form "If **a** then **b**," we need to generate a matrix. If there are many if-then rules, we need to have multiple matrices. To generate and store so many matrices is expensive in both time and space. Also, computation associated with inference becomes very expensive as the number of rules increases.

In a special case, we can perform the inference by using two vectors **a** and **b** without generating a matrix. In order to do so, an impiication operator and a product (i.e., the second) operator of the inference method must be the same. In our example, we use min for both operations. Suppose we have a fuzzy observation **a'** and an overall relation R. Then the conclusion **b'** is computed by

$$\mathbf{b'} = \mathbf{a'} \circ R$$

The above expression is expanded as follows:

$$
\begin{aligned}
\mu_{b'}(v) &= \max_u \left[\mu_{a'}(u) \wedge \mu_R(u, v) \right] \\
&= \max_u \left[\mu_{a'}(u) \wedge (\mu_a(u) \wedge \mu_b(v)) \right] \\
&= \max_u \left[(\mu_{a'}(u) \wedge \mu_a(u)) \wedge \mu_b(v) \right] \\
&= \left[\max_u (\mu_{a'}(u) \wedge (\mu_a(u))) \right] \wedge \mu_b(v) \\
&= \alpha \wedge \mu_b(v)
\end{aligned}
$$

where $\alpha = \max_u (\mu_{a'}(u) \wedge \mu_a(u))$.

In the above computation, we do not need to generate a matrix for the relation R from the rule "If **a** then **b**." We need to apply the min operation over the two vectors **a'** and **a**, then find the maximum element over the results. This single maximum, α, is used as one of the arguments for the min operation along with vector **b**. Note that not only storage space but also computation is reduced by the above method.

We can extend the above computation for a rule whose if-part has multiple conditions. For example, we consider the rule with two clauses in conditional part

If **a** and **b** then **c**

Here, **a, b** and **c** are fuzzy sets defined over universe of discourse **U, V,** and **W**, respectively. The if-part of the rule is now two-dimensional. The relation R is now represented as

$$R = (\mathbf{a} \times \mathbf{b}) \rightarrow \mathbf{c}$$

where $\times$ represents the Cartesian product. The and connective is interpreted as the intersection; therefore the Cartesian product is realized by the min operation. Using the min operator for implication $\rightarrow$, we have

$$\mu_R(u, v, w) = \mu_a(u) \wedge \mu_b(v) \wedge \mu_c(w) \quad u \in U, v \in V, w \in W$$

Relation R is now ternary rather than binary. R is, therefore, represented by a three-dimensional array.

Suppose we have fuzzy observations **a'** and **b'**; then the fuzzy conclusion **c'** is computed by

$$\mathbf{c}' = (\mathbf{a}' \times \mathbf{b}') \circ R$$

which is expanded as

$$\mu_{c'}(w) = \max_u \max_v \left[(\mu_{a'}(u) \wedge \mu_{b'}(v)) \wedge (\mu_a(u) \wedge \mu_b(v) \wedge \mu_c(w)) \right]$$
$$= \max_u \max_v \left[\mu_{a'}(u) \wedge \mu_{b'}(v) \wedge (\mu_a(u) \wedge \mu_b(v) \wedge \mu_c(w)) \right]$$
$$= \max_u \left[\mu_{a'}(u) \wedge \mu_a(u) \right] \wedge \max_v \left[\mu_{b'}(v) \wedge \mu_b(v) \right] \wedge \mu_c(w)$$
$$= \alpha \wedge \mu_c(w)$$

where $\alpha = \max_u \left[\mu_{a'}(u) \wedge \mu_a(u) \right] \wedge \max_v \left[\mu_{b'}(v) \wedge \mu_b(v) \right]$.

This is a direct extension of the previous result where a rule has only one condition in the conditional part. A generalization for rules with more than two conditions is obvious.

Two or more rules are combined using the else connective.

If $\mathbf{a}_1$ and $\mathbf{b}_1$ Then $\mathbf{c}_1$, else
If $\mathbf{a}_2$ and $\mathbf{b}_2$ Then $\mathbf{c}_2$, else
If $\mathbf{a}_3$ and $\mathbf{b}_3$ Then $\mathbf{c}_3$, etc.

The connective *else* is interpreted as the *or* condition. The most common operator used for the fuzzy set *or* operation is the max

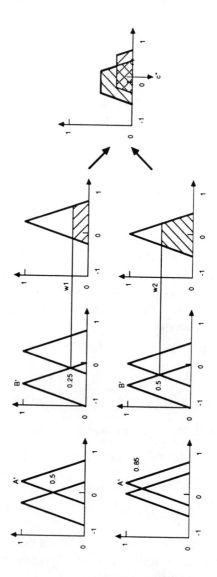

Figure 11.3. Inference process

operator. Hence, the overall result is computed by combining individual results from each rule by the max operator. This process by the max operator is equivalent to superimposing all the results. The overall inference process is shown in Figure 11.3. When we have to control a physical device, we need to produce a single crisp number rather than a fuzzy set as a conclusion. The most common method is to compute the centroid under the fuzzy membership function as shown in Figure 11.3. This process is called *defuzzification* of a conclusion.

In the above example, we used the min operator for computing a fuzzy implication relation and the max-min compositional rule. These two choices define one method of inference. It is one of the most widely used methods. There are, however, other operators for implication and compositional rules of inference that we can use. For example, Holmblad used an algebraic product ($\cdot$) as a fuzzy implication operator and the max-product as the compositional rule of inference (Holmblad and Østergaard, 1982). The multiplication operation is used instead of the min operation. The inference is now performed as

$$\mu_{c'}(w) = \alpha \cdot \mu_c(w)$$

where $\alpha = \max_u \left[\mu_{a'}(u) \cdot \mu_a(u) \right] \cdot \max_v \left[\mu_{b'}(v) \cdot \mu_b(v) \right]$. Since the value of α and the final centroid change more smoothly depending on inputs (observations), the inference based on this method is more sensitive to small changes. However, its computation is much more expensive due to the use of multiplication instead of the min operation.

Also, a bounded product may be a good operator for replacing the min operator in the implication and in the compositional rule of inference. With a bounded product, the sensitivity of inference is as high as the algebraic product but computational cost of the bounded product is similar to that of the logical product (min).

3. RULE-BASED CONTROLLER

The usual approach for automatic process control is to establish a mathematical model of the process. This is not always feasible. In some cases, there is no proper mathematical model because the process is too complex or ill-understood. In other cases, experimenting with physical plants for construction of mathematical models is too expensive. In other cases, the mathematical models are too complicated or computationally expensive and are not suitable for real-time use. For such processes, however, skilled human controllers may be able to operate the plant satisfactorily. The operators are quite often able to express their operating practice in the form of rules that may be used in a rule-based controller. The rule-based controllers model the behavior of the expert human operator instead of the process itself. The following is a rule from an aircraft flight controller (Larkin, 1985). This rule takes three inputs and has two outputs:

IF   (1) The rate of descent is *Positively Medium*,

           (2) The airspeed is *Negatively Big* (compared to the desired airspeed),

           (3) The glideslope is *Positively Big* (compared to the desired glideslope).

THEN (1) change engine speed by *Positively Big*, and

           (2) change elevator angle by *Insignificant Change*.

The expressions *Positively Medium, Positively Big, Insignificant Change*, etc. represent imprecise amounts. They represent the intuitive feel of the expert human controller. These expressions correspond to the imprecise expessions used by the expert in communicating a rule of thumb. In a rule-based controller they are represented using fuzzy sets with associated membership functions. In the following section, we discuss how to process vague information and make inferences.

A fuzzy set, such as *Positively Medium* is represented by a membership function over an appropriate universe of discourse such as revolutions per minute (rpm). Possible definitions of fuzzy sets are shown in Figure 11.2. The control rules are encoded typically using 10 to 70 rules. The control is performed based on the fuzzy inference mechanism described in Section 2.3 and Figure 11.3. In controlling a process, all of the rules are compared to the current inputs (observations) and fired. The action (THEN-part) of each rule is weighted by how close its IF-part matches the current observation. In the example of Figure 11.3, a rule has two inputs and a single output. The weights are represented by w_1 and w_2. The results of firing the rules are then combined by superimposing them. The final result, which is supplied to a controller, should be a crisp number rather than a fuzzy set; therefore we need to perform a defuzzification operation. This is computed by taking the center of area under the fuzzy membership function of the final result. Even though each individual rule is an incomplete rule of thumb, the results of firing the rules are properly weighted and combined, and the final result represents a reasonable compromise.

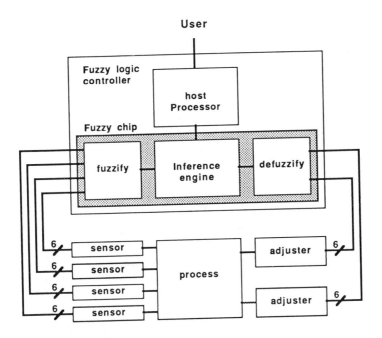

Figure 11.4. Fuzzy logic controller

4. CHIP ARCHITECTURE AND IMPLEMEN-TATION

In this VLSI implementation, we chose the logical sum (min) and logical product (max) as the intersection and union operations. We also chose the max-min compositional rule for inference. It is one of the most commonly used fuzzy inference methods in control application. Another common method is based on the max-product compositional rule of inference. The max-product method requires substantially larger circuits (i.e., multiplier) than the max-min method.

Figure 11.4 shows the fuzzy chip in a typical real-time, closed-loop controller configuration with 4 inputs and 2 outputs. Primary considerations for the VLSI implementation of a fuzzy logic controller include system speed and interface size (x-axis in Figure 11.3); and grade (y-axis) of fuzzy sets; number of inputs and outputs; and design of the min, max, fuzzification, and defuzzification functions. Host interaction is accomplished via a TTL-compatible, infinite wait state, interrupt-driven, memory-mapped interface. Rules are downloaded into the fuzzy memory at boot-time and can be updated dynamically with minimal disruption. Two words are reserved for the status registers that control the mode (load, process, or test) and the configuration.

4.1. Fuzzy Set Representation

Previous work (Larkin, 1985; Sugeno and Murakami, 1984) used three to sixteen fuzzy elements with grades of fuzziness from three to twelve levels. The former determines the number of elements in the universe of discourse and has ramifications affecting memory size, I/O requirements, and system speed. The latter influences the accuracy, logic complexity, and actual device operation frequency. Setting the chip speed to match the maximum allowed by the technology and the TTL interface optimizes the performance. The number of transistors will be limited by the package type, which is ultimately driven by the number of pins and the die size. Maximum utility for the general purpose user is obtained with an 84-pin device with 64 (2^6) elements and 16 (2^4) discrete levels.

For the representation of membership, 0 represents no membership, 15 represents full membership, and other numbers represent points in the unit interval $[0, 1]$. A fuzzy membership function is, therefore, discretized using 64 numbers of 4 bit; that is 256 bits of memory storage. The representation of a fuzzy set is as follows:

u_0	u_1		u_i		u_{63}
0000	0011	...	$\mu_F(u_i)$	...	1111

Each fuzzy membership function requires 64 × 4 bits of memory storage. Performance and size considerations prohibit broadcasting 256 signals to all rules simultaneously. Complete serialization (Kandel, 1986) would complicate the state machine and limit the system sample rate to once every 256 device clock cycles. Processing 4 bits (one membership value) in parallel defines a system speed to within that of commercially available A/Ds and D/As. The previous work (Togai and Watanabe, 1986) depended on the host processor to create the necessary input streams and interpret the output streams.

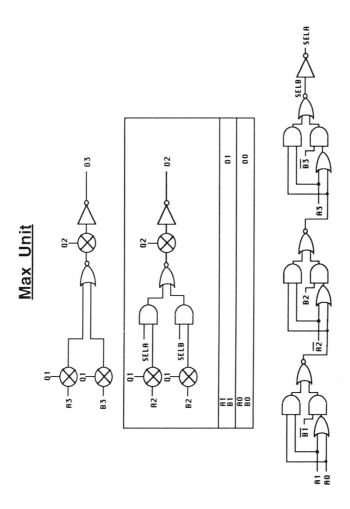

Figure 11.5. Max unit

Integrating the fuzzification and defuzzification functions alleviates the severe I/O bandwidth problems and completely frees the host from the run-time operation. Thus, the simplest configuration is a sensor and a 6-bit A/D driving the fuzzy device directly, and an adjuster receiving the output of a 6-bit D/A, also directly connected to the fuzzy device.

4.2. Pipelining

THEN processing cannot commence until all premises have been compared to the inputs and defuzzification cannot begin until the entire output function is defined. Hence, a three-stage pipeline naturally emerges. Fuzzification, the process of converting crisp values to fuzzy sets, can occur simultaneously with IF processing. A qualified clocking scheme guarantees the separation of calculations yet allows all of the logical blocks to operate simultaneously.

4.3. Max Unit

Figure 11.5 depicts the logic required to implement the intersection or max function of two 4-bit membership expressions. Each 98-transistor block operates in 25 ns and can be isolated.

4.4. Architectural Flexibility

The number of system inputs and outputs consequently determines pin count, rule logic complexity and the number of fuzzifiers and defuzzifiers. Choosing fixed numbers, however, potentially limits flexibility so two architectural features were implemented to maxi-

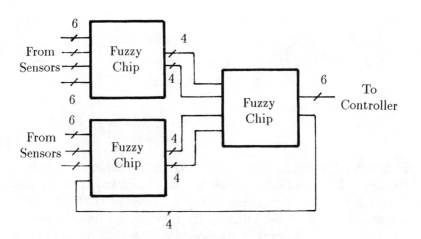

Figure 11.6. Multiple-chip configuration

mize applicability. First, the chip can be software-configured for two input/output combinations, whereupon the latter provides for twice as many total rules. An original configuration with 51 rules:

IF   A and B and C and D
THEN   Do E, and
            Do F.

An alternative configuration with 102 rules is:

IF A and B THEN Do E,
IF C and D THEN Do F.

Secondly, devices can be cascaded (Figure 11.6) for a multiple-layered rule set under software control. Feedback may also be implemented but research into the potential of such a generalized formulation has yet to be reported.

4.5. Fuzzifier

Fuzzification is done using a table look-up. For each observation (i.e., input stream), we store a table of the membership function normalized at the center of the horizontal axis. That is, the center of membership function has height of one (i.e., full membership). The operation of fuzzification is shown in Figure 11.7. According to an input value, the membership function is shifted. The chip can produce 64 different shifted membership functions from a single stored pattern. The shape of the membership function can be associated with a predicted measurement error of a sensor. Uncertainty or inaccuracy of the

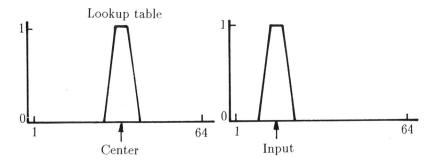

Figure 11.7. Rule logic

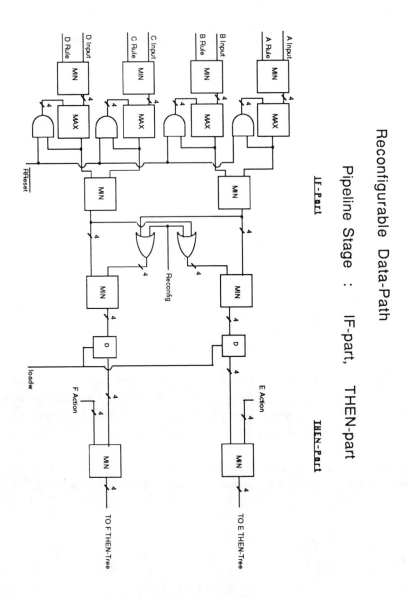

Figure 11.8. Fuzzification

sampled values from the sensors is related to the "width" of the stored fuzzification function. If we do not need fuzziness in an observed value (i.e., input value is "crisp"), we can store a pulse function, that is, only a central entry has membership of 1 and all the other entries have 0's. The result of the fuzzification is broadcasted to all of the rules.

In the actual chip implementation, the fuzzifiers are independent counteraddressed RAMs and the stored membership function is not shifted. Rather, a starting address for table look-up is shifted based on an observed input which is sampled every 64 clock cycles. Accessing and broadcasting the 4-bit membership functions every clock cycle is one of the primary speed limiting paths of the device.

4.6. Rule Datapath

Figure 11.8 shows a block diagram of the IF logic for every rule. Fuzzified inputs are compared to the rule memory by the first column of min units. Max units then determine the peak (α subi) of the premise camparison. A small binary tree of min units computes the limiting proposition for the entire rule (ω_i). Finally, the output goes to the THEN-part which calculates that rule's contribution (C_i) to the final result. Not shown is test logic designed to allow controllability and observability for each min and max unit. Reconfigure logic steers the data streams to be combined or delayed appropriately. The output proceeds to a tree of max units, which combines the results of all the rules and feeds the defuzzifier.

4.7. Defuzzifier

Defuzzification is done by computing the *center of gravity* (COG) under the final membership function. Denoting the final fuzzy subset as A, the COG algorithm computes the following:

$$C^* = \sum_{n=1}^{64} n\,\mu_A(n) \left/ \sum_{n=1}^{64} \mu_A(n) \right.$$

Since each element of the universe is processed serially, we can substitute multiple addition for multiplication in the above computation. The data sequence from the THEN-part is produced starting from the most significant data point as follows:

$$\mu_A(64),\ \mu_A(63),\ ...,\ \mu_A(2),\ \mu_A(1)$$

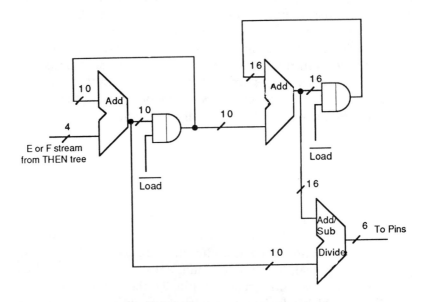

Figure 11.9. Defuzzifier circuit

Two adders and two registers are used as shown in Figure 11.9. The numerator is computed by the first adder and the denominator is produced by the second adder. The denominator is computed as by repeated addition of the result of the first adder by the second adder, which computes the following formula:

$$\sum_{n=1}^{64} n\,\mu_A(n) = \mu_A(64) +$$

$$\mu_A(64) + \mu_A(63) +$$
$$\mu_A(64) + \mu_A(63) + \mu_A(62) +$$
$$\vdots$$
$$\mu_A(64) + \mu_A(63) + \mu_A(62) + \dots + \mu_A(1)$$

For this purpose, the second adder is designed as a 16-bit adder. Finally, a 16×10 divider circuit, implemented as a repeated adder/subtracter, computes the value that appears on the pins. Another critical path in the device is the 16-bit adder, consuming 27ns of the device cycle (Figure 11.9). Hence, the three-stage pipeline is complete. An input is sampled during every major cycle but the result does not appear at the pins until two and a half additional cycles have passed.

4.8. Streaming Mode

Both the fuzzification and defuzzification circuits can be bypassed. Bypassing is controlled independently for each input and output by appropriate bits in the status register. This feature allows outputs of one fuzzy chip to be connected directly to inputs of another fuzzy chip. The bypassing feature is used in the multiple-chip board.

4.9. Rule Capacity

The system's utility and global design considerations determined the total number of rules to incorporate onto the chip. Clock generation, data bus loading, and control signal routing become system-limiting speed issues above one hundred rules but multiple chips can be utilized if an application requires more capability than a single device can provide. Since 102 rules fit into a standard 84-pin pad frame and the system speed was not compromised by accessing $102 \times 12 = 1224$ bits of static RAM in parallel every clock cycle, the issue of rule capacity was resolved.

4.10. Redundancy

Redundancy is essential for yield enhancement purposes. A processing defect in the datapath is remedied with a single laser cut to the appropriate fuse (Figure 11.10), effectively disconnecting the entire

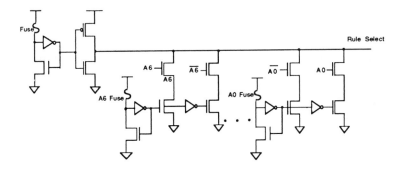

Figure 11.10. Redundancy

rule. Other fuses allow memory congruency to be maintained since any address can be reprogrammed to replace any removed block. Systems requiring only 90 rules can use any device with up to 12 defective memory cells, min/max units, sense amps, etc.

Table 11.1. Summary of fuzzy chip

Die Size	7750 μm $\times$ 9050 μm
#Transistors	688,131 (476,160 in RAM)
#Pins	84 (16 Powers/GND)
Package Type	PGA (Standard Pad Frame)
Power Supply	3.0–3.3V
Power	1.2 W at 0°C
Interface	TTL compatible
Modes	4 in / 2 out / 51 rules
	2 in / 1 out / 102 rules
	I/O individally programmable
	Test
Redundancy	Laser programmable
Testability	Overall 99.8% stuck-at fault coverage
Process	1.1μm N-well CMOS
Gate Length / t_{ox}	1.1μm / 22.5nm
Poly / Metal / Metal2	2.8 / 2.8 / 4.0 μm pitch

4.11. Test Mode

To facilitate the testing of the 688 K transistor device, a test mode was implemented. RAMs can be fully accessed at device speed. Inputs to the rules can be driven as primary inputs, and outputs of the THEN trees go directly to the pins, isolating these blocks of random logic representing 117K transistors. Furthermore, the rules themselves are transposed to allow immediate access to their internal state and with automatic vector generation software (Calhoun et al., 1987), 99.8 overall stuck-at fault coverage was achieved.

4.12. Summary

Table 11.1 summarizes the process (Sharma et al., 1987), device specifications, and primary architectural features. The device was

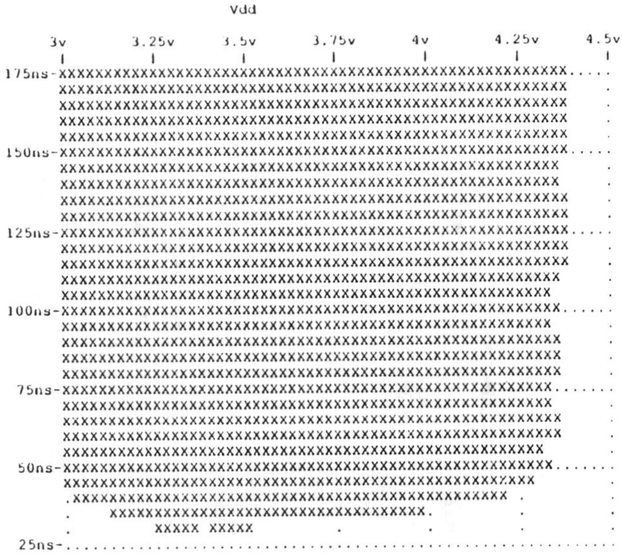

```
                              Vdd

           3v       3.25v      3.5v     3.75v     4v      4.25v     4.5v
           |         |         |         |        |         |        |
    175ns-XXXXXXXXXXXXXXXXXXXXXXXXXXXXXXXXXXXXXXXXXXXXXXXXXXXXXXXX.....
          XXXXXXXXXXXXXXXXXXXXXXXXXXXXXXXXXXXXXXXXXXXXXXXXXXXXXXXX    .
          XXXXXXXXXXXXXXXXXXXXXXXXXXXXXXXXXXXXXXXXXXXXXXXXXXXXXXXX    .
          XXXXXXXXXXXXXXXXXXXXXXXXXXXXXXXXXXXXXXXXXXXXXXXXXXXXXXXX    .
          XXXXXXXXXXXXXXXXXXXXXXXXXXXXXXXXXXXXXXXXXXXXXXXXXXXXXXXX    .
    150ns-XXXXXXXXXXXXXXXXXXXXXXXXXXXXXXXXXXXXXXXXXXXXXXXXXXXXXXXX.....
          XXXXXXXXXXXXXXXXXXXXXXXXXXXXXXXXXXXXXXXXXXXXXXXXXXXXXXXX    .
          XXXXXXXXXXXXXXXXXXXXXXXXXXXXXXXXXXXXXXXXXXXXXXXXXXXXXXXX    .
          XXXXXXXXXXXXXXXXXXXXXXXXXXXXXXXXXXXXXXXXXXXXXXXXXXXXXXXX    .
          XXXXXXXXXXXXXXXXXXXXXXXXXXXXXXXXXXXXXXXXXXXXXXXXXXXXXXXX    .
    125ns-XXXXXXXXXXXXXXXXXXXXXXXXXXXXXXXXXXXXXXXXXXXXXXXXXXXXXXXX.....
          XXXXXXXXXXXXXXXXXXXXXXXXXXXXXXXXXXXXXXXXXXXXXXXXXXXXXXXX    .
          XXXXXXXXXXXXXXXXXXXXXXXXXXXXXXXXXXXXXXXXXXXXXXXXXXXXXXXX    .
          XXXXXXXXXXXXXXXXXXXXXXXXXXXXXXXXXXXXXXXXXXXXXXXXXXXXXXXX    .
          XXXXXXXXXXXXXXXXXXXXXXXXXXXXXXXXXXXXXXXXXXXXXXXXXXXXXX      .
    100ns-XXXXXXXXXXXXXXXXXXXXXXXXXXXXXXXXXXXXXXXXXXXXXXXXXXXXXXXX.....
          XXXXXXXXXXXXXXXXXXXXXXXXXXXXXXXXXXXXXXXXXXXXXXXXXXXXXXXX    .
          XXXXXXXXXXXXXXXXXXXXXXXXXXXXXXXXXXXXXXXXXXXXXXXXXXXXXXXX    .
          XXXXXXXXXXXXXXXXXXXXXXXXXXXXXXXXXXXXXXXXXXXXXXXXXXXXXXXX    .
          XXXXXXXXXXXXXXXXXXXXXXXXXXXXXXXXXXXXXXXXXXXXXXXXXXXXXXXX    .
    75ns-XXXXXXXXXXXXXXXXXXXXXXXXXXXXXXXXXXXXXXXXXXXXXXXXXXXXXXXX......
          XXXXXXXXXXXXXXXXXXXXXXXXXXXXXXXXXXXXXXXXXXXXXXXXXXXXXXXX    .
          XXXXXXXXXXXXXXXXXXXXXXXXXXXXXXXXXXXXXXXXXXXXXXXXXXXXXXXX    .
          XXXXXXXXXXXXXXXXXXXXXXXXXXXXXXXXXXXXXXXXXXXXXXXXXXXXXXXX    .
          XXXXXXXXXXXXXXXXXXXXXXXXXXXXXXXXXXXXXXXXXXXXXXXXXXXXXXXXX   .
    50ns-XXXXXXXXXXXXXXXXXXXXXXXXXXXXXXXXXXXXXXXXXXXXXXXXXXXXXXXX......
          XXXXXXXXXXXXXXXXXXXXXXXXXXXXXXXXXXXXXXXXXXXXXXXXXXXXXXXXXX   .
          .XXXXXXXXXXXXXXXXXXXXXXXXXXXXXXXXXXXXXXXXXXXXXXX   .
          .    XXXXXXXXXXXXXXXXXXXXXXXXXXXXXXXXXXXXX.          .
          .         XXXXX XXXXX            .                .
    25ns-...........................................................
```

Figure 11.11. Performance

designed to operate at 36MHz, which translates to 580K fuzzy logical inferences per second with up to 102 rules per inference. Current performance (Figure 11.11) indicates a yet unsolved speed-limiting design problem. The chip photomicrograph and corresponding layout map are shown in Figures 11.12 and 11.13 respectively.

5. INFERENCE ACCELERATOR BOARD SYSTEMS

5.1. Single-Chip Systems

The fuzzy logic system boards place the fuzzy chip into a VMEbus environment to provide application process control through a VMEbus host. The single-chip system designed for NASA Ames Research Center uses an off-the-shelf VMEbus prototyping board (XYCOM,

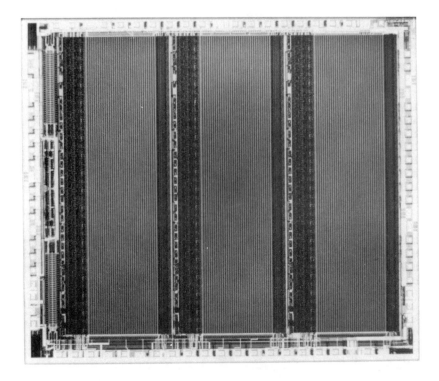

Figure 11.12. Photomicrograph

1987). The overall configuration of the design is shown in Figure 11.14. In this design, the VMEbus interface is provided by the prototyping board system and needed a minimum of design for integration of the fuzzy chip. The fuzzy chip interface to the board is realized using discrete TTL parts and wire-wrapping. In the board system for ORNL, the VMEbus interface was designed by Watanabe and realized using a programmable logic device (PLD) and TTL parts. More robust printed circuit board (PCB) technology was used. The PCB architectural concept is shown in Figure 11.15. The UNIX device driver interfaces of these two boards are quite similar.

The ORNL board is designed to standard VMEbus specifications for a 24-bit address, 16-bit data, slave module as found in *The VMEbus Specification*, Revision C.1 (1985). It provides digital communication between the host and the fuzzy chip. A large, UV erasable PLD generates the board control signals. VMEbus interface is through

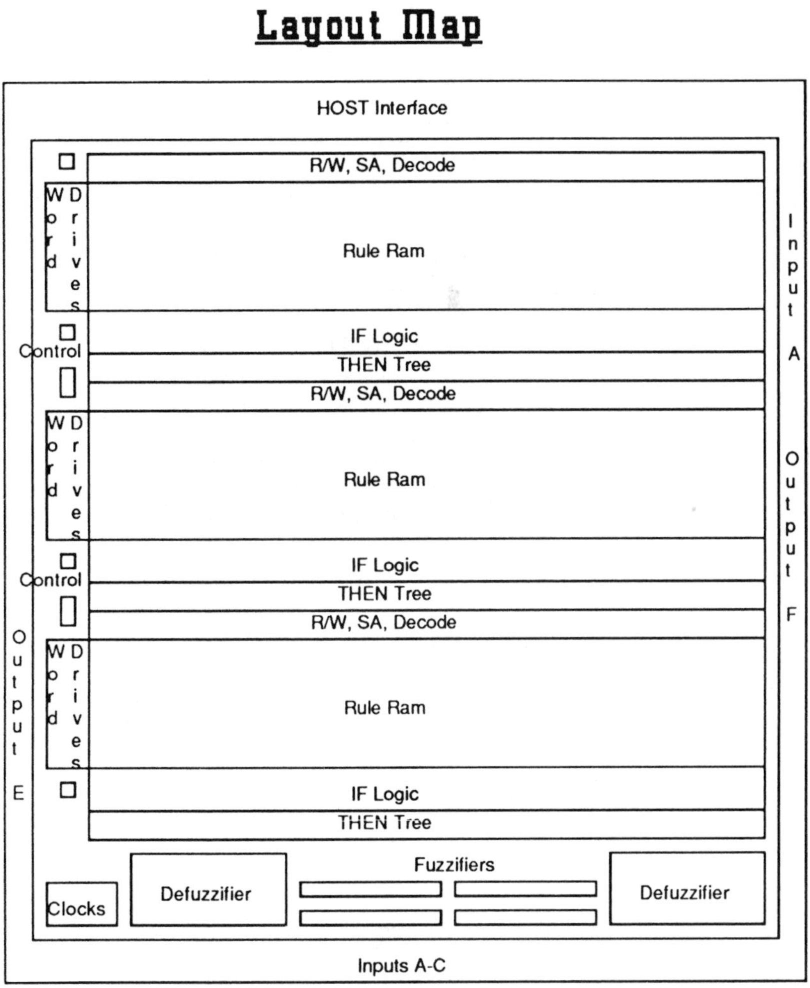

Layout Map

Figure 11.13. Layout map

TTL parts. One fuzzy inference IC processes four 6-bit inputs to generate two 6-bit outputs. The interface with the host computer uses memory mapping to include the fuzzy chip's I/O addresses in the application process storage space. All of the chip's memory as well as its inputs and outputs are accessed through addresses on the VMEbus so that the entire fuzzy logic board system responds like a section of memory.

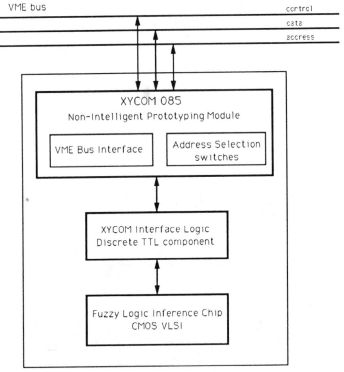

Figure 11.14. Single-chip system based on prototyping board

The board's address space is 1024 bytes or 512 16-bit words in length. Most of the addresses in that space are not used by the board. The lower 128 word addresses of the board are mapped into the fuzzy chip. One hundred addresses are for rule memory. Another six addresses are mapped to four *fuzzification* tables and two status registers. The board has six addresses for I/O for the fuzzy chip, and addresses for hardware reset and board ID. On-board dip switches and signal jumpers allow the user to select the board base address comprised of the upper 14 bits of the 24-bit address, and the board's user privilege response characteristic determined by the VMEbus *address modifier* bits. Further design details are shown in Figure 11.16.

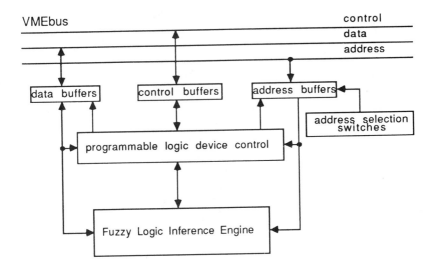

Figure 11.15. Single-chip system based on custom PCB

5.2. Multiple Fuzzy Chip System

The multiple-chip system board keeps the standard VMEbus interface of the first version but adds significant new capabilities. The
system consists of two printed circuit board components connected
by ribbon cables designed to plug into two slots of a full-height
VMEbus backplane.

Seven fuzzy chips communicate with each other and the host
through a software reconfigurable interconnection network. Two
Texas Instruments digital crossbar switch IC's implement the network. Any logical configuration of the seven chips may be specified in
software, e.g., seven in parallel, 4-2-1 binary tree, etc. Any fuzzy output
may be routed to any input. With the new board more inputs may be
processed and hierarchies of rule sets may be explored. We can
simulate rules with up to 16 conditions in the IF-part by using three
layers of fuzzy chips. Another application is to load multiple-rule sets
for different tasks in a single board. This is done by configuring

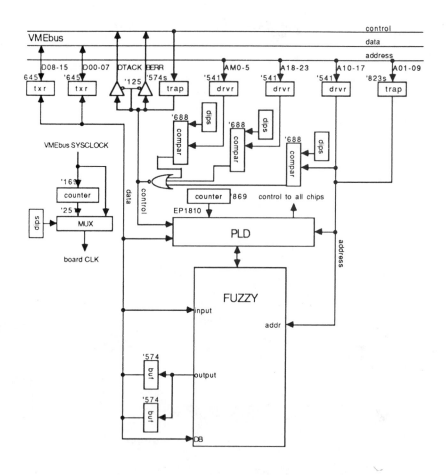

Figure 11.16. Details of PCB architecture

multiple chips in parallel. The printed circuit board architectural concept is shown in Figure 11.17.

This arrangement exploits an important feature of the fuzzy chip. A normal input to the chip is by 6-bit integers that the chip *fuzzifies* into 64-value membership functions to be fed into the processing pipeline. The final output membership function is *defuzzified* into a 6-bit output integer. However, the chip has another mode of operation. Any input or output can bypass the [de]fuzzification process so that I/O occurs in *streaming* mode. The full 64-value input or output membership function is placed on the pins, one value per

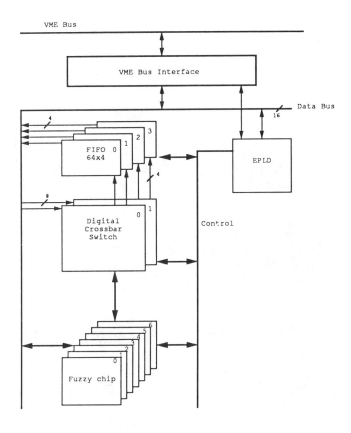

Figure 11.17. Seven-chip system architecture

clock cycle. When an output of one chip is connected to an input of
another chip (or itself), communication can be done in streaming
mode without the loss of information inherent in the [de]fuzzification
operations. On this system board, all interchip communication is
done in streaming mode.

The board also has four 64-value FIFO queues that allow final
output to the host to be done in streaming mode. The application
process is then free to perform its own custom operations on the full
output membership functions. The final defuzzification is no longer
limited to the centroid method. One can also generate the result in
higher precision than 6 bits, if necessary.

The multiple-chip board was installed at ORNL in November 1990. In addition to navigational tasks the system will be used to explore fuzzy logic control of manipulator arm functions. Figure 11.18 is a picture of the multiple-chip board system.

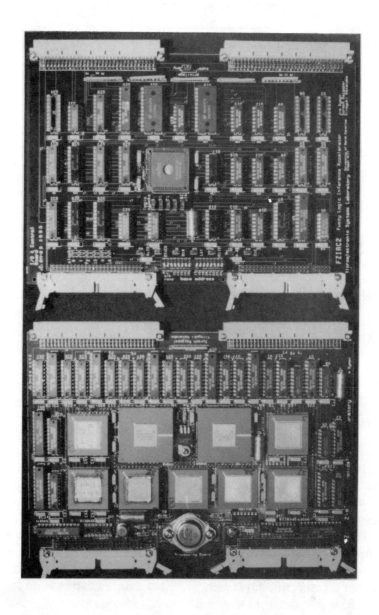

Figure 11.18. Seven-chip inference board

6. SOFTWARE INTERFACE

High-level C language functions can hide the operational details of the board from the applications programmer. The programmer treats rule memories and fuzzification function memories as local program structures passed as parameters to the C functions. Similarly, local input variables pass values to the system and outputs return in local variable function parameters. Programmers are required to know only the library procedures. Some procedures provided for the single-chip board are listed here:

1. *Write Rule (rulenum, ruledata)* –The rule data structure pointed to by *ruledata* is written to the board.
2. *Read Rule (rulenum, ruledata)* – Reads back into *ruledata* the rule identified by *rulenum* currently stored in the chip.
3. *Write Fuzz (fuzznum, fuzzdata)* – The fuzzification table is written to the board.
4. *Start FZIAC (inpA, inpB, inpD)* – Four inputs are sent to the fuzzy board and inference processing will be started.
5. *Read Out (outE, outF)* – Both outputs are read from the board. Inference processing will be continued.
6. *Stop FZIAC (outE, outF)* – Both outputs are read from the board. Inference processing will be halted.

A multiple-chip board version of the above routines includes an additional parameter to specify one of seven fuzzy chips. There are also routines to configure networks to interconnect fuzzy chips, and routines to read data from FIFO chips.

7. CONCLUSION

An integrated fuzzy inference acceleration board system consists of a custom VLSI fuzzy inference chip, VMEbus-compatible board system, and C function library. They allow use of a fuzzy logic inference mechanism in demanding real-time application. The board system is integrated in a standard VMEbus and UNIX environment. C programming language library functions are used to drive the accelaration board, and the detail knowledge of the board is hidden.

We have built two versions of a single-chip system and a version of a multiple-chip system. They are installed in an autonomous robot at ORNL and VMEbus worksations at NASA Ames Research Center and the University of North Carolina.

Acknowledgments

The research reported here is supported in part by Oak Ridge National Laboratory, by MCNC Design Initiative Program, and by NASA Ames Research Center. Watanabe's research activity is in part supported by a corporate gift from Omron Corporation.

BIBLIOGRAPHY

Calhoun, J., D. Bryan, and F. Brglez. (1987). Automatic test pattern generation for scan-based digital logic. *MCNC Technical Report TR87-16*, MCNC, RTP, NC, August.

Corder, R. J. (1989). A high-speed fuzzy processor. *Proc. of Third IFSA Congress*, pp. 379–381, August.

Fukami, S., M. Mizumoto, and K. Tanaka. (1980). Some considerations on fuzzy conditional inference. *Fuzzy Sets and Systems*, **4**, 243–273.

Holmblad, L. P. and J. J. Østergaard. (1982). Control of a cement kiln by fuzzy logic. In M. M. Gupta and E. Sanchez (eds.): *Fuzzy Information and Decision Processes*. Amsterdam: North-Holland.

Kandel, A. (1986). *Fuzzy Mathematical Techniques with Applications*. Reading, MA: Addison-Wesley.

Kawano, K., M. Kosaka, and S. Miyamoto. (1987). An algorithm selection method using fuzzy decision-making approach. *Trans. Society of Instrument and Control Engineers*, **20**, 42–49 (in Japanese).

King, P. J. and E. H. Mandani. (1977). The application of fuzzy control systems to industrial processes. *Automatica*, **13**, 235–242.

Klir, G. J. and T. A. Folger. (1988). *Fuzzy Sets, Uncertainty, and Information*. Englewood Cliffs, NJ: Prentice-Hall.

Larkin, L. I. (1985). A fuzzy logic controller for aircraft flight control. In M. Sugeno (ed.): *Industrial Applications of Fuzzy Control*. Amsterdam: North-Holland, pp. 87–103.

Lee, C. C. (1990). Fuzzy logic in control systems. *IEEE Trans. on Systems, Man and Cybernetics*, **20** (2).

Maeda, Y. (1990). Fuzzy obstacle avoidance method for a mobile robot based on the degree of danger. *Proc. of NAFIPS'90*, pp. 169–172, June.

Pin, F. G., R. A. Cachiero, J. R. Symon, and H. Watanabe. Navigation of an autonomous robot in unstructured environment using a custom design VLSI fuzzy logic chip. In press.

Sharma, D., S. Goodwin-Johansson, D. S. Wen, C. K. Kim, and C. M. Osburn. (1987). A 1μm CMOS technology with low temperature processing. *Extended Abstracts of 171 Meetings of the Electrochemical Society,* vol. 87–1, pp. 213–214, May.

Shingu, T. and E. Nishimori. (1989). Fuzzy-based automatic focusing system for compact camera. *Proc. of Third IFSA Congress,* pp. 436–439, August.

Sugeno, M. and Murakami, K. (1984). Fuzzy parking control of model car. *Proc. the Twenty–third IEEE Conf. Decision and Control,* December.

Togai, M. and H. Watanabe. (1986). An inference engine for real-time approximate reasoning: Toward an expert on a chip. *IEEE EXPERT,* 1 (3), 55–62 (August).

Watanabe, H., W. Dettloff, and E. Yount. (1990). A VLSI fuzzy logic inference engine for real-time process control. *IEEE Journal of Solid-State Circuits,* **25** (2), 376–382 (April).

Weisbin, C. R., G. de Saussure, J. R. Einstein, and F. G. Pin. (1989). Autonomous mobile robot navigation and learning. *Computer,* **22** (6), (June).

Yamakawa, T. and T. Miki. (1986). The current mode fuzzy logic integrated circuits fabricated by the standard CMOS process. *IEEE Transactions on Computers,* **C-35** (2), 161–167.

Yasunobu, S. and S. Miyamoto. (1985). Automatic train operation system by predictive fuzzy control. In M. Sugeno (ed.): *Industrial Applications of Fuzzy Control.* Amsterdam: North-Holland, pp. 1–18

Zadeh, L. A. (1965). Fuzzy set. *Information and Control,* **8,** 338–353.

Zadeh, L. A. (1971). Similarity relations and fuzzy orderings. *Information Sciences,* **3,** 177–200.

Zadeh, L. A. (1973). Outline of a new approach to the analysis of complex systems and decision-making approach. *IEEE Transactions on Systems, Man and Cybernetics,* **SME-3** (1), 28–45 (January).

Zadeh, L. A. (1990). The birth and evolution of fuzzy logic. *Proceedings of North American Fuzzy Information Processing Society '90,* pp. xiii–xxi, June.

XYCOM. (1984). *XVME-85 Prototyping Module Preliminary Manual.*

3

FUZZY LOGIC FOR APPROXIMATE REASONING

12 Fuzzy logic as a basis of approximate reasoning

Vilém NOVÁK
Czechoslovak Academy of Sciences
Mining Institute
708 000 Ostrava-Poruba
CZECHOSLOVAKIA

Abstract. This paper is a brief overview of first-order fuzzy logic and its role in approximate reasoning. This logic is a nontrivial generalization of the classical one. First, the structure of truth values is chosen to be a residuated lattice, being a chain. Then, syntax and semantics of first-order fuzzy logic are introduced, including the definitions of rules of inference, the concept of a proof, and that of a fuzzy theory. The paper presents some theorems about properties of this logical system, including theorems of deduction and completeness.

In the last section, a general theory of approximate reasoning based on first-order fuzzy logic is outlined. We exactly define and justify the concepts of a translation rule and a rule of inference. We also demonstrate that approximate reasoning can be understood to be a derivation of a special kind of fuzzy sets of formulae using sets of proofs from a fuzzy set of special axioms.

1. WHY FUZZY LOGIC?

A typical feature of classical logic and classical mathematics is a "black-and-white" reasoning: Either a fact holds true, or it does not, and nothing more. We cannot avoid this way of thinking in science. On the other hand, it brings us nearer to God than to common, everyday life. The latter is not so simple. There are no purely good or purely bad people; if a few drops are falling, it is hard to say whether it rains; and even the color white is sometimes a little black. We confront similar problems when using natural language—even seemingly simple and clear things can be very vague. For example, the sentence "Take a few steps" is vague, since we may be doubtful about the kind of movement that is a step (is it a jump?), and what does *few* mean? This type of reasoning leads us to what is now called *fuzzy logic*. Unlike classical logic with only two truth values, *true* and *false*, fuzzy logic is many-valued. Two cases can be distinguished:

(a) Truth values are elements of a given set, usually the interval [0, 1].
(b) Truth values are expressed in natural language, e.g., *true, rather false*, etc.

In case (b), we sometimes speak about *linguistic logic*. This logic is based on linguistic applications of fuzzy set theory and is quite complicated. In any case, its basis is many-valued fuzzy logic of type (a).

A special case is *approximate reasoning*. Its aim is to comprehend how the human mind copes with situations such as those mentioned above and to imitate (at least some aspects of) its functioning on the computer. Approximate reasoning leads to treatment with fuzzy relations and it has already proved successful in many applications. Despite this, there is still much work left to do. For instance, we lack the analysis of approximate reasoning with respect to many-valued fuzzy logic.

This paper presents an overview of the main results of fuzzy logic and demonstrates its connection with approximate reasoning.

2. FIRST-ORDER FUZZY LOGIC

2.1. The Structure of Truth Values

There are good reasons to assume the structure of truth values to be the *residuated lattice*, i.e., a complete, infinitely distributive lattice

$$L = (L, \lor, \land, \otimes, \rightarrow, 0, 1) \tag{1}$$

where $0, 1$ are the smallest and the greatest elements, respectively, $\lor$ and $\land$ are the operations of *supremum* and *infimum* respectively, $\otimes$ is the operation of *bold multiplication* (product) which is isotone in both variables and $(L, \otimes, 1)$ is a commutative monoid, and $\rightarrow$ the operation of *residuation*, which is antitone in the first variable and isotone in the second. Moreover, the adjunction property

$$a \otimes b < c \text{ iff } a < b \to c$$

holds for every $a, b, c \in L$.

The reasons for accepting such a structure are analyzed in Pavelka (1979), Novák and Pedrycz (1988) and Novák (1989). As a special case, most often used in applications, the degrees of truth are assumed to be based on the unit interval of real numbers $L = [0, 1]$. Then we put $V := \max$, $\Lambda := \min$,

$$a \otimes b = 0 \text{ V} (a + b - 1) \tag{2}$$

and

$$a \to b = 1 \Lambda (1 - a + b) \tag{3}$$

for all the $a, b \in [0, 1]$. The use of this interval is very natural but sometimes causes confusion of truth values with probabilities. Let us stress that this is only a formal similarity as the same sets of measures have been used for the two, and in essence different, phenomena.

Another special case is $L = \{0 := a_0 < ... < a_m := 1\}$. Then (2) and (3) become

$$a_k \otimes a_l = a_{\max\{0, k+l-m\}} \tag{4}$$

and

$$a_k \to a_l = a_{\min\{m, m-k+l\}} \tag{5}$$

In modeling natural language semantics it is necessary to introduce new, additional operations. Put

$$a \leftrightarrow b = (a \to b) \Lambda (b \to a)$$

(biresiduation) and

$$a^p = a \otimes ... \otimes a$$
$$\quad p\text{--times}$$

(power) for all the $a, b \in [0, 1]$.

When introducing a new n-ary operation o on L, the following *fitting condition* must be fulfilled: there are $p_1,..., p_n$ such that

$$(a_1 \leftrightarrow b_1)^{p_1} \otimes ... \otimes (a_n \leftrightarrow b_n)^{p_n} \leqslant o(a_1, ..., a_n) \leftrightarrow o(b_1, ..., b_n) \tag{6}$$

holds for every $a_i, b_i \in L$, $i = 1, ..., n$. The justification of the fitting condition can be found in Pavelka (1979) and Novák and Pedrycz (1988).

2.2. Syntax

The basic language of first-order fuzzy logic consists of:

- (i)   variables x, y,...
- (ii)   constants **c, d, r**,...
- (iii) n–ary functional symbols f, g,...
- (iv)   a set of symbols for truth values $\{\mathbf{a}: \mathbf{a} \in L\}$
- (v) n–ary predicate symbols p, q,...
- (vi)   a binary connective $\Rightarrow$ and a set of additional m–ary connectives $\{o_i: i \in J\}$
- (vii) a symbol for the general quantifier "for each"

Terms are defined as usual.

Formulae.

- (a)   A symbol a for a truth value $a \in L$ is an atomic formula.
- (b)   If t_1,..., t_n are terms and p an n–ary predicate symbol, then $p(t_1,... t_n)$ is an atomic formula.
- (c)   If A, B, A_1,...,A_m are formulae and o an m-ary connective, then $A \Rightarrow B$, o $(A_1,..., A_m)$, and (for each x) A are formulae.

The formula $\neg A$ (negation) is an abbreviation of $A \Rightarrow 0$. Similarly, we can define $A \lor B$ (disjunction), $A \land B$ (conjunction), $A \& B$ (bold conjunction), $B \Leftrightarrow A$ (equivalence), (there exists x) A (existential quantifier) and

$$A^k: = A \& A \& ... \& A \text{ (power)}$$
$$\underset{k-\text{times}}{}$$

Given a language J of first-order fuzzy logic, a set of all the terms is denoted by M_j and a set of all the formulae by F_j.

As in classical logic, we introduce the concepts of free and bound variables and a substitutible term. If t is a term and A a formula, then $A_x[t]$ is a formula resulting from A when substituting the term t instead of each free occurence of x in A.

2.3. Semantics

A *structure* for the language J of first-order fuzzy logic is

$$\mathbf{D} = (D, p_D ,..., f_D ,..., u,v,...)$$

where D is a set, $p_D \subseteq D^n$,... are n-ary relations assigned to each n- ary predicate symbol p, ..., and f_D, ... are ordinary n-ary functions on D assigned to each n-ary functional symbol f. Finally, the u, v, ... $\in$ D are elements assigned to each constant $\mathbf{u}$, $\mathbf{v}$, ... of the language J.

Truth Valuation of Formulae. Let D be a structure for the basic language J. A truth valuation of formulae in $\mathbf{D}$ is a function $\mathbf{D}$: $F_j \to L$, which assigns a truth value to every formula from F_j as follows:

(i) $\mathbf{D}(\mathbf{a}) = a, a \in L$

(ii)   Let $t_1,...,t_n$ be terms without variables and p and n-ary predicate symbol. Then $\mathbf{D}\ (p(t_1,...,t_n)) = p^D(\mathbf{D}(t_1),...,\mathbf{D}(t_n))$ where $\mathbf{D}(t_i) \in D$ is an interpretation of the term $t_i \in M_j$, $i = 1,...,n$.

(iii) $\mathbf{D}(A \Rightarrow B) = \mathbf{D}(A) \to \mathbf{D}(B)$, provided that A and B are closed formulae.

(iv) $\mathbf{D}(o(A_1,...,A_n)) = o(\mathbf{D}(A_1),...,\mathbf{D}(A_n))$, provided that $A_1,...,A_n$ are closed formulae.

(v) $\mathbf{D}((\text{for each } x)A(x)) = \bigwedge\limits_{d \in D} \mathbf{D}(A_x[\mathbf{d}]$ where $\mathbf{d}$ is a name of the element $d \in \mathbf{D}$.

(vi) $\mathbf{D}(A(x_1,...,x_n)) = \bigwedge\limits_{d_1,...,d_n} \mathbf{D}(A_{x_1...x_n}[\mathbf{d}_1,...,\mathbf{d}_n])$

The definition of the truth valuation gives us

$$\mathbf{D}(A \wedge B) = \mathbf{D}(A) \wedge \mathbf{D}(B)$$
$$\mathbf{D}(A \vee B) = \mathbf{D}(A) \vee \mathbf{D}(B)$$
$$\mathbf{D}(A \mathbin{\&} B) = \mathbf{D}(A) \times \mathbf{D}(B)$$
$$\mathbf{D}(A^n) = (\mathbf{D}(A))^n$$
$$\mathbf{D}(\neg A) = \neg \mathbf{D}(A) = \mathbf{D}(A) \to 0$$
$$\mathbf{D}(A \Leftrightarrow B) = \mathbf{D}(A) \leftrightarrow \mathbf{D}(B)$$
$$\mathbf{D}((\text{there exists } x)A(x)) = \bigvee\limits_{d \in D} \mathbf{D}(A_x[\mathbf{d}])$$

Let $X \subseteq F_j$ be a fuzzy set of formulae. Then a *fuzzy set of semantic consequences* of the fuzzy set X is

$$(\mathbf{C}^{sem} X)A = \bigwedge \{\mathbf{D}(A): \mathbf{D} \text{ is a } structure \text{ for } J \text{ and (for each } A \in F_j)(X(B) \leqslant \mathbf{D}(B))\}$$

where $X(B) \in L$ is the grade of membership of B in X. It can be proved that $\mathbf{C}^{sem}$ is a closure operation on L(see Pavelka, 1979).

If $(\mathbf{C}^{sem} X)A = 1$ for every fuzzy set of formulae X, then we will write $\models A$ and call A a tautology.

Lemma 1.

(a) $\models A \Rightarrow B$ *iff* $\mathbf{D}(A) \leqslant \mathbf{D}(B)$
(b) $\models A \Leftrightarrow B$ *iff* $\mathbf{D}(A) = \mathbf{D}(B)$ *holds in every structure* $\mathbf{D}$.

This theorem serves us as a basis for the derivation of the tautologies. A list is given in Novák (1990a, b).

2.4. Deduction

It is characteristic of fuzzy logic that we work with many truth values. Therefore, it is also permissible to introduce fuzzy sets of axioms. However, this leads us to evaluated syntax, where each step in deriving new formulae is evaluated by a truth value. Thus, we must extend the notion of a rule of inference as follows. An *n*-ary *rule of inference r* is a couple

$$r = (r^{syn}, r^{sem})$$

where r^{syn} is its syntactic part, which is a partial *n*-ary operation on F_j and r^{sem} is a semantic part, which is an *n*-ary operation on L preserving arbitrary nonempty joins in each argument (semicontinuity). The syntactic part has the same role as in classical logic. The semantic part evaluates each step in the process of the derivation of new formulae.

A fuzzy set X of formulae is *closed* with respect to r if

$$X(r^{syn}(A_1,...,A_n)) > r^{sem}(X(A_1),...,X(A_n)) \tag{7}$$

holds for all $A_1,...,A_n \in F_j$ for which r^{syn} is defined. A rule of inference is *sound* if (7) holds for every function $G{:}f_j \rightarrow L$ being a homomorphism with respect to the connectives.

The rules of inference are usually written in the form

$$r{:}\ \frac{A_1,...,A_n}{r^{syn}\ (A_1,...,A_n)} \left(\frac{a_1,...,a_n}{r^{sem}\ (a_1,...,a_n)}\right) \tag{8}$$

where $a_i \in L$ are truth valuations of the respective formulae A_i, $i = 1,...,n$.

We introduce the following rules of inference:

(a) Modus ponens

$$r^{MP}{:}\frac{A, A \Rightarrow B}{B}\left(\frac{a,b}{a \otimes b}\right)$$

(b) a-lifting rule

$$r^{Ra}: \frac{B}{a \Rightarrow B}\left(\frac{b}{a \to b}\right)$$

(c) Generalization

$$r_G: \frac{A}{(\text{for each } x) A}\left(\frac{a}{a}\right)$$

Let X be a fuzzy set of formulae. Then

$(C^{syn}X)A = \Lambda\{U(A): U \subseteq F_j, U \text{ is closed with respect to all } \textit{rules of inference and } A, X \subseteq U\}$

defines a fuzzy set of *syntactic consequences* of the fuzzy set X. A *proof* of a formula A from a fuzzy set X is a sequence

$$w: = A_1[a_1; P_1], A_2[a_2; P_2],..., A_n[a_n; P_n] \tag{9}$$

such that A_n is A and $P_i, i < n$ is **LA** or **SA** if A is a logical or a special axiom respectively, or P_i is r if A is a formula

$$r^{syn}(A_{i_1},..., A_{i_n}), i_1,..., i_n < i$$

and r is an n-ary sound rule of inference. Furthermore, $a_i = \text{Val}_x(w_{(i)})$ is a *value* of the proof $w_{(i)}: = A_1[a_1; P_1],..., A_i[a_i; P_i]$ defined as follows:

$$\text{Val}_x(w_{(i)}) = \begin{cases} A_L(A_i) & \text{if } P_i = \text{LA (i.e., } A \text{ is a logical axiom)} \\ X(A_i) & \text{if } P_i = \text{SA (i.e., } A \text{ is a special axiom)} \\ r^{sem}(\text{Val}_x(w_{(i_1)}),..., \text{Val}_x(w_{(i_n)})) & \text{if } A_i = r^{syn}(A_{i_1},...,A_{i_n}) \end{cases}$$

Theorem 1. $(C^{syn}X)A = V\{\text{Val}_x(w): w \text{ is a proof of } A \text{ from } X \subseteq F_j\}.$

Hence, finding a proof, say w, of a formula A assures us only that the degree in which A is a theorem is greater than or equal to $\text{Val}_{x(w)}$. If $\text{Val}_{x(w)} < 1$, then it is difficult to assure ourselves that we cannot find a proof with a greater value.

2.5. Theories of First-Order Fuzzy Logic

A *theory* T in the language J of first-order fuzzy logic (a *fuzzy theory*) is a triple

$$T = (A_L, A_S, \mathbf{R})$$

where $A_L \subseteq F_J$ is the fuzzy set of logical axioms, $A_S \subseteq F_J$ is a fuzzy set of special axioms and $\mathbf{R}$ is a set of rules of inference that must contain at least the rules r_{MP}, $\{r_{Ra}; a \in L\}$ and r_G. By $J(T)$ we denote language of the fuzzy theory T. Fuzzy predicate calculus is the fuzzy theory with $A_S = \emptyset$.

Let $\mathbf{D}$ be a structure for $J(T)$. Then $\mathbf{D}$ is a *model* of the theory T, $D \models T$, if

$$A_S(A) \leqslant \mathbf{D}(A)$$

holds for every $A \in F_J$. We have $A_L(A) \leqslant \mathbf{D}(A)$ in any model $\mathbf{D} \models T$ for every formula $A \in F_J$ (cf. Novák, 1990a, b). If $(\mathbf{C}^{sem}X)A = a$, then the formula A is *true* to degree a in the theory T and we write

$$T \models aA$$

If $(\mathbf{C}^{sem}X)A = a$, then A is a *theorem* to degree a of the theory T and we write

$$T \vdash aA$$

We write $T \vdash A$, $T \models A$ instead of $T \vdash_1 A$, $T \models_1 A$, respectively, and say that A is a theorem (true) of the theory T.

If w is a proof in theory T, then we write $\mathrm{Val}_T(w)$ for its value.

A theory T is *contradictory* if there is a formula A and proofs w and w' of A and $\neg A$, respectively, such that

$$\mathrm{Val}_T(w) \otimes \mathrm{Val}_T(w') > 0$$

It is *consistent* in the opposite case.

Theorem 2 (closure theorem). Let $A \in F_J$ and A' be its closure. Then

$$T \vdash aA \text{ iff } T \vdash a A'$$

A language J' *is an extension* of J if $J \subseteq J'$. Then, obviously, $F_{J(T)} \subseteq F_{J'(T)}$. Let $T = (A_L, A_S, \mathbf{R})$, $T' = (A'_L, A'_S, \mathbf{R})$ be theories in the respective language. Put $\overline{A}'_S(A) = A_S(A)$ if $A \in F_J$ and $\overline{A}_S(A) = 0$ otherwise. If

$$\overline{A}_S \subseteq A'_S$$

then T' is an extension of T. To simplify the notation, we will write A_S instead of $\overline{A}_S$ and understand that $A_S(A) = 0$ for all $A \in F_{J'} - F_J$.

The extension T' is a *conservative extension* of T if $T' \vdash b A$ and $T \vdash a A$ implies $a = b$ for every formula $A \in F_J$.

Theorem 3 (deduction theorem). Let A be a closed formula and $T' = T \cup \{1/A\}$.

(a) If $T \vdash_a A^n \Rightarrow B$ and $T' \vdash_b B$ for some n, then $a \leqslant b$

(b) To every proof w' of B in T' there are an n and a proof w of $A^n \Rightarrow B$ in T such that

$$\mathrm{Val}_{T'}(w') = \mathrm{Val}_T(w)$$

Theorem 4. *Let T be a consistent theory, $T \vdash (\exists x)(A(x))^n$ for every n, and $t \in J(T)$ be a new constant. Then the theory*

$$T' = T \cup \{1/A_x[t]\}$$

in the language $J(T) \cup \{t\}$ is a conservative extension of the theory T.

The following theorem, analogous to the classical one, can also be proved.

Theorem 5. *Let A be a formula of T, p a new n-ary predicate symbol, and let*

$$T' = T \cup \{1/(p(x_1,...,x_n) \Leftrightarrow A)\}$$

Then T' is a conservative extension of T, and to every formula B of T' there is a formula B^* of T such that

$$T' \vdash B \Leftrightarrow B^*$$

Let A_0 be a chosen closed formula and $T \vdash_a A_0$. Put

$$b = \begin{cases} a & \text{if L is a finite chain} \\ c, c > a & \text{if } L = [0, 1] \text{ and } a < 1 \\ 1 & \text{if } a = 1 \end{cases} \tag{10}$$

The following theorems are generalizations of classical Gödel's completeness theorems.

Theorem 6 (completeness theorem II). *A fuzzy theory T is consistent iff it has a model. If T is consistent, then to every $A \in F_J$ and b defined in (10) there is a model $\mathbf{D}$ such that $\mathbf{D}(A) \leqslant b$.*

Theorem 7 (completeness theorem I). *Let T' be a consistent theory. Then*

$$T \vdash_a A \quad \text{iff} \quad T \models_a A$$

holds true for every formula $A \in F$.

The proofs of all these theorems are quite complicated and they are based on deep algebraic properties of the structure of closed formulae. For the proofs see Novák (1990a, b).

It can be demonstrated (see Pavelka, 1979) that fuzzy logic cannot be complete, if the set of truth values is an infinitely countable chain. If it is a finite or uncountable chain, then the structure (1) with operations (2), (3) or (4), (5) is the only plausible one provided that we demand fuzzy logic to be syntactico-semantically complete. If L is not a chain and not a Boolean lattice, then the answer is not yet known. Let us stress that first-order fuzzy logic is isomorphic with classical logic if $L = \{0, 1\}$.

3. OUTLINE OF A GENERAL THEORY OF APPROXIMATE REASONING

Approximate reasoning is a mathematical tool the aim of which is to model the way humans reason when vague notions are present. The theory proposed by L. A. Zadeh and the others (see all references) is based on the rules derived rather on intuition, and they lead to operations with fuzzy relations. However, successful applications have convinced us that this approach works quite well. Thus, it is very important to develop a concise formal theory that will help us comprehend the problem in depth.

In this section, we demonstrate that the first-order fuzzy logic we have presented can serve us as a mathematical basis for the theory of approximate reasoning.

3.1. Introduction

The formulation of a concept (notion) leads to formation of a grouping of elements having a certain property φ. In other words, there is a property φ of objects such that a given construed by means of a grouping

$$X = \{x : \varphi(x)\} \tag{11}$$

of all the elements x that have a property φ.

Let us now consider an element x_0 and ask whether it has a property φ. The answer can take the form of a proposition "$\varphi(x)$ is true to degree a." We thus naturally come to (first-order) fuzzy logic presented in the preceding section and, by this means, to fuzzy sets.

Furthermore, most words of natural language can be construed to be names of the above-mentioned properties φ. Hence, fuzzy sets can be in principle used in modeling natural language semantics.

A special feature of human thinking is the effective use of natural language even in the process of logical reasoning. We may thus conclude that the mathematical model of human reasoning could be based on fuzzy sets and fuzzy logic.

In the sequel, we will consider a set **J** of syntagms[1] of natural language and a language of first-order fuzzy logic **J**, which will be used to model the meaning of the syntagms from **J**. We denote the elements of **J** by **A**, **B**,.... For example, **A**: $=$ *the temperature is high*, **B**: $=$ *if the vehicle goes to the left then turn the wheel to the right*, **C**: $=$ *John is very old*, etc. Let M_J and F_J be sets of terms and formulae of a language J, respectively.

The theory of approximate reasoning consists especially in the formation of two kinds of rules:

(a) *Translation rules*, i.e., the rules for obtaining fuzzy sets from the syntagms taken from **J**.

(b) *Rules of inference*, i.e., the rules for obtaining conclusions from some premises stated in the form of elements from **J**.

3.2. Translation Rules of Approximate Reasoning

A *translation rule* is a triple

$$s = \; <s^{form}, s^{fuzz}, s^{ext}>$$

where $s^{form}: \mathbf{J} \to J \cup F_J \cup M_J$ is a partial function assigning formulae $A(x) \in F_J$ (in general, open ones) to some syntagms $\mathbf{A} \in \mathbf{J}$; s^{fuzz} is a function assigning a fuzzy set

$$s^{fuzz}(A(x)) = \{a_t / A_x[t] : t \in M_J\} \subseteq F_J \tag{12}$$

of closed formulae to $A(x)$, and s^{ext} is a function assigning an extension

$$s^{ext}(s^{fuzz}(A(x))) = \{a_t / t; t \in M_J\} \subseteq M_J \tag{13}$$

to the fuzzy set $s^{fuzz}(A(x))$. We will write $A(x)$ instead of $s^{form}(\mathbf{A})$, $Z(A(x))$ instead of $s^{fuzz}A(x)$, and $E(A(x))$ instead of $s^{ext}(s^{fuzz}(A(x)))$.

---

[1] A syntagm is a part of a sentence (even a word or the whole sentence) that is constructed according to the grammatical rules.

To be independent of the concrete model, we consider the set M_J of all the terms. They stand for the elements of any model. Our further deliberation thus proceeds within the syntax rather than within the semantics. Note that the same $Z(A(x))$ may have different interpretations in various models **D**.

Thus, a syntagm **A** is interpreted as a formula $A(x)$, which represents the property expressed by **A** (cf. the deliberation above). As the property is, in general, vague, we represent it by a fuzzy set of closed formulae $Z(A(x))$. The formula $A(x)$ together with $Z(A(x))$ can also be understood as a formal expression of an intension of the property under consideration. Its extension is then a fuzzy set of elements $E(A(x))$.

For example, let **A**: $=$ *the temperature is high*. Then $A(x)$ is a formula representing the property of "being high," which is the property of elements ($=$ degrees) through which the variable x ($=$ temperature) ranges. Next is a translation of $A(x)$ into a fuzzy set of closed formulae $\{a_t / A_x[t]; t \in M_J\}$. Each $A_x[t]$ is a formal expression of the proposition *the temperature t is high* and is assigned a truth value a_t. The last step, $E(A(x))$, leads to an abstract fuzzy set of temperatures $t \in M_J$ with no special meaning. Its meaning, i.e., to be the fuzzy set of *high temperatures*, emerges only when moving higher to $Z(A(x))$.

The function s^{form} can tentatively be defined as follows: Let **N** be a noun. Then

$$s^{form}(\mathbf{N}) = x$$

where x is some variable.[2] Let **A** be an adjective. Then

$$s^{form}(\mathbf{AN}) = s^{form}(\mathbf{N} \text{ is } \mathbf{A}) = A(x) \tag{14}$$

where $A(x)$ is a formula representing the property named by the adjective **A**. Let m be a linguistic modifier (e.g., *very, highly, more or less*, etc.). Then

$$s^{form}(m) = o_m$$

where o_m is a unary connective and

$$s^{form}(m\mathbf{AN}) = s^{form}(\mathbf{N} \text{ is } m\mathbf{A}) = o_m(A(x)) \tag{15}$$

Let $\mathbf{B}_\infty$, $\mathbf{B}_\in$ be syntagms such that $s^{form}(\mathbf{B}_1) = B_1(y)$ and $s^{form}(\mathbf{B}_2) = B_2(z)$. If $'\mathbf{B}_\infty$ and $\mathbf{B}'_\in \in J$, $'\mathbf{B}_\infty$ or $\mathbf{B}'_\in \in J$ and $'$If $\mathbf{B}'_\infty$ then $\mathbf{B}'_\in \in J$ then

$$s^{form}(\mathbf{B}_1 \text{ and } \mathbf{B}_2) = B_1 \Diamond B_2 \tag{16}$$

$$s^{form}(\mathbf{B}_1 \text{ or } \mathbf{B}_2) = B_1 \square B_2 \qquad (17)$$
$$s^{form}(\text{If } \mathbf{B}_1 \text{ then } \mathbf{B}_2) = B_1 \Rightarrow B_2 \qquad (18)$$

where $\diamond$ denotes a conjunction-type connective (not necessarily & or $\wedge$, and $\square$ denotes a disjunction-type connective (cf. Novák and Pedrycz, 1988). Similarly, we may consider also an implication-type connective in (18) instead of the basic one $\Rightarrow$.

The more detailed definition of s^{form} can be done on the basis of further linguistic research. So far, we usually put $\diamond := \wedge$ and $\square := \vee$. However, this may not always work well.

A crucial point is the determination of function s^{fuzz}. From the point of fuzzy logic, we may consider the following kinds of $Z(A(x))$.

$$Z_s(A(x)) = \{a_t / A_x[t] : t \in M_J \text{ and } a_t = A_s(A_x[t])\} \qquad (19)$$

i.e., each a_t, $t \in M_J$, is a degree of truth that $A_x[t]$ is a special axiom.

$$Z_\vdash(A(x)) = \{a_t / A_x[t] : t \in M_J \text{ and } T \vdash_{a_t} A_x[t]\} \qquad (20)$$

i.e., each a_t, $t \in M_J$, is a degree of provability of $A_x[t]$ in the given theory T.

$$Z_\mathbf{D}(A(x)) = \{a_t / A_x[t] : t \in M_J \text{ and } a_t = \mathbf{D}(A_x[t])\} \qquad (21)$$

i.e., each a_t, $t \in M_J$, is a degree of truth of $A_x[t]$ in the given model $\mathbf{D}$.

$$Z_\models(A(x)) = \{a_t / A_x[t] ; t \in M_J \text{ and } T \models_{a_t} A_x[t]\} \qquad (22)$$

i.e., each a_t, $t \in M_J$, is a degree of truth of $A_x[t]$ in the given theory T.

Due to the completeness theorem, $Z_\vdash(A(x)) = Z_\models(A(x))$ holds for every formula A.

The fuzzy sets Z_s and Z_D are rather supplementary, since in approximate reasoning we want to obtain intensions of derived, not originally known syntagms. As very complex relations among formulae may exist, $Z_\vdash$ is the most valuable to us (this immediately gives $Z_\models$).

Lemma 2. *Let $C: \to L$ be a homomorphism and $E \subseteq F_J$. Put $A_s(B) = C(B)$ for every $B \in E$ and $A_s = 0$ otherwise. Then*
$$(C^{syn} A_s) B = A_s(B)$$

for every $B \in E$.

---

[2] Here and in the sequel, we understand that various $\mathbf{N}$ are assigned various variables x. For the sake of simplicity, however, we will not especially stress this in the notation. The same principle is considered also for the other symbols.

Proof. Consider a canonical structure $\mathbf{D}_0$ with $\mathbf{D}_0(B) = C(B)$ for every $B \in E$. Then $\mathbf{D}_0$ is, obviously, a model and

$$A_s(B) \leqslant (C^{syn} A_s) B \leqslant \mathbf{D}_0(B) = A_s(B)$$

holds for every for every $B \in E$.

In approximate reasoning, we must define fuzzy sets of closed formulae $s^{fuzz}(s^{form}(\mathbf{A}))$ for some primary words $\mathbf{A}$ (e.g., *small, big,* etc.). These fuzzy sets are, in fact, fuzzy subsets of a fuzzy set of special axioms. Thus, approximate reasoning can be understood to be a derivation of new formulae in fuzzy theory defined by the fuzzy set of special axioms.

3.3. Rules of Inference in Approximate Reasoning

It follows from the preceding section that the situation in approximate reasoning is a follows. We are given a set $\mathbf{I}$ of syntagms and a language $\mathbf{J}$. Our aim is to know the intensions of all the syntagms $\mathbf{A} \in \mathbf{I}$, i.e., all the corresponding formulae

$$A(x) \in F_J \tag{23}$$

and fuzzy sets of formulae

$$Z_\vdash(A(x)) \subsetneqq F_J \tag{24}$$

The fuzzy sets (24) are obtained in the frame of a fuzzy theory determined by a fuzzy set of axioms, $A_s \subsetneqq F_J$, which consists of:

(a) Fuzzy subsets $Z_s(A(x))$ for some primary words $\mathbf{A} \in \mathbf{I}$
(b) Fuzzy subsets $Z_s(B(y))$ for some additional syntagms (statements) $\mathbf{B} \in \mathbf{I}$, which we use to describe the process

Due to Lemma 2 we suppose Z_s in (a) and (b) to be equal to $Z_\vdash$. In most cases, the syntagms (b) represent conditional statements (e.g., in fuzzy controller) but they are not, in general, restricted to them.

Thus, the task of approximate reasoning is to find $A(x)$ and $Z_\vdash(A(x))$ for some $\mathbf{A}$, or vice versa. This task, however, is quite difficult due to Theorem 1, since we have to find all the proofs with the targets $A_x[t]$ for all $t \in M_J$. The solution can be more or less approximate using rules of inference defined as follows.

Given a rule of inference r of first-order fuzzy logic, a *rule of inference* $\mathbf{R}$ in approximate reasoning based on a rule r is a quadruple of functions

$$\mathbf{R} = (\mathbf{R}^{ling}, r^{syn}, \mathbf{R}^{fuzz}, \mathbf{R}^{ext})$$

Corresponding to the above-mentioned four levels of translation and they are defined as follows. On the level of language, $\mathbf{R}^{ling} : \mathbf{I}^n \to \mathbf{I}$ is a partial function that can be written in a more transparent form as

$$\mathbf{R}^{ling} : \frac{\mathbf{A}_1, \ldots, \mathbf{A}_n}{\mathbf{B}}$$

where $\mathbf{A}_1, \ldots, \mathbf{A}_n, \mathbf{B} \in \mathbf{I}$. The syntagm $\mathbf{B}$ is such that the diagram

$$
\begin{array}{ccc}
\mathbf{I}^n & \xrightarrow{\mathbf{R}^{ling}} & \mathbf{I} \\
\downarrow{\scriptstyle (s^{form})^n} & & \downarrow{\scriptstyle s^{form}} \\
(F_j)^n & \xrightarrow{r^{syn}} & F_J
\end{array}
$$

commutes where r^{syn} is a syntactic part of r.

Let $s^{form}(\mathbf{A}_i) = A_i(x_i, y)$, $i = 1, \ldots, n$, and $s^{form}(\mathbf{B}) = B(y)$. Then the function $\mathbf{R}^{ling}$ is a linguistic representation of the proof

$$w := A_1(x_1, y), \ldots, A_n(x_n, y), r^{syn}(A_1(x_1, y), \ldots, A_n(x_n, y)) := B(y) \quad (25)$$

The next step leads to fuzzy sets of closed formulae $Z(A_i(x_i, y))$, $Z(B(y))$. As we may consider any stage of inference, $Z(A_i(x_i, y)) = Z_{\vdash}(A_i(x_i, y))$ need not hold. Thus, if

$$Z(A_i(x_i, y)) = \{a_{t_i s} / A_{x_i y}[t_i, s] : t_i, s \in M_J\}$$

then $a_{t_i s} \geqslant A_s(A_{x_i y}[t_i, s])$, but it need not be a maximal one. Given terms $t_1, \ldots, t_n, s \in M_J$, we may consider the proof

$$w_{t_1 \cdots t_n, s} := A_{1, x_1 y}[t_1, s][a_{t_1 s}], \ldots, A_{n, x_n y}[t_n, s][a_{t_n s}], B_y[s]$$
$$[r^{sem}(a_{t_1 s}, \ldots a_{t_n s}) : r]$$

obtained in an obvious way on the basis of proof (25). Therefore, to each $s \in M_J$ there is a set of proofs

$$W_s = \{w_{t_1 \cdots t_n, s} : t_1, \ldots, \in M_J\}$$

being a subset of all the proofs of $B_y[s]$. Theorem 1 then justifies the following definition: $\mathbf{R}^{fuzz} : (L^{F_J})^n \to L^{F_J}$ is n-ary partial function assigning a fuzzy set

$$Z(B(y)) = \{b_s / B_y[s] : s \in M_J\} \quad (26)$$

to the fuzzy sets $Z(A_i(x, y)) = \{a_{i, t_i s} / A_{i, x_i y}[t_i, s] : t_i, s \in M_J\}$ such that

$$b_s = \bigvee\{r^{sem}(a_{t_1 s}, \ldots, a_{t_n s}) : t_1, \ldots, t_n \in M_J\} \quad (27)$$

for every b_s, $s \in M_J$. The equation (27) is exactly the formula for computation of membership degrees of the consequent in the rules of approximate reasoning presented in the literature (having rather been derived on the basis of intuition). Here, it is justified also on the basis of first-order fuzzy logic. However, the degrees b_s are only a lower estimation of the degrees of provability of $B_y[s]$, $s \in M_J$, since there may be many other proofs of these formulae with potentially higher value, i.e., we have only

$$Z(B(y)) \subseteq Z_{\vdash}(B(y)) \tag{28}$$

However, there may be some special conditions under which the inclusion may be changed into equality.

Proposition 1. *Let $s \in M_J$. If there is a model* **D** *such that*

$$\mathbf{D}(B_y[s]) = c = \mathbf{V}\{r^{sem}(a_{t_1 s}, \dots, a_{t_n s}) : t_1, \dots, t_n \in M_J\}$$

for some $a_{t_1 s}, \dots, a_{t_n s}$, $t_n \in M_J$, then $T \vdash_{b_s} B_x[s]$, $s \in M_J$.

Proof. Immediately from the completeness theorem.

This simple proposition makes sense especially when considering $A_1, \dots, A_n$ to be the only known linguistic statements leading to the fuzzy set of special axioms. Let us demonstrate this on the rule of *modus ponens*.
Let

$$\mathbf{R}_{MP}^{ling} : \frac{\mathbf{A}, \text{ If } \mathbf{A} \text{ then } \mathbf{B}}{\mathbf{B}}$$

$s^{form}(\mathbf{A}) = A(x)$, $s^{form}(\text{If } \mathbf{A} \text{ then } \mathbf{B}) = A(x) \Rightarrow B(y)$
and

$$A_s(A_x[t]) = a_t, \ t \in M_J$$
$$A_s(A_x[t]) \Rightarrow B_y[s]) = b_{ts}, \ t, s \in M_J$$
$$A_s(C) = 0 \text{ for the other, } C \in F_J$$

Let $\mathbf{D}_0$ be a canonical structure where

$$\mathbf{D}_0(A_x[t] = a_t, \ t \in M_J$$
$$\mathbf{D}_0(B_y[s]) = \mathbf{V}\{a_t \otimes b_{ts} ; t \in M_J\} = c_s, \ s \in M_J$$

Then

$$\mathbf{D}_0(A_x[t] \Rightarrow B_y[s]) = a_t \to c_s \geqslant b_{ts}$$

since

$$a_t \otimes b_{ts} \leqslant c_s^3$$

---

[3] Use the adjunction.

and, therefore, D_0 is a model. Hence, the rules of generalized modus ponens used in approximate reasoning so far can be considered as giving the best result when we assume we are working in a restricted theory with **A** and If **A** then **B** as the only special axioms.

The last step concerns the function $R^{ext}:(L^{M_J})^n \to L^{M_J}$. We define it analogously as R^{fuzz} when replacing all the occurences of $A_{x_{iy}}[t_i, s]$ or $B_y[s]$ simply with (t_i, s) or s, respectively. The extensions $E(A_i(x_i, y))$, $E(B(y))$ are abstract fuzzy sets (fuzzy relations) and formula (27) then becomes the formula for the composition of fuzzy relations. Hence, we obtain the theory of approximate reasoning as presented so far in the literature.

The level of extensions is very important as we do not always know the resulting syntagm **B**, and even the formula $B(y) = s^{ling}(\mathbf{B})$. Thus, we may start from fuzzy set $C \subset M_J$ obtained from $E(A_1(x_1, y))$, ..., $E(A_n(x_n, y))$ using the formula (27) and try to find $\mathbf{B} \in I$ and $B(y) \in F_J$ such that $E(B(y)) \approx C$. This reversed process is called a *linguistic approximation* in fuzzy set theory (cf. Novák, 1989; Esragh and Mamdani, 1979; and others).

4. CONCLUSION

In this paper, we have presented some results of first-order fuzzy logic and outlined the general theory of approximate reasoning. It follows from this theory that approximate reasoning presented in the literature may be explicated within first-order fuzzy logic. This result has two consequences, at least. First, it justifies the theory of approximate reasoning from the formal point of view and demonstrates the limits that must be kept when we want the theory to be well founded and to be a nontrivial generalization of classical logic preserving many important formal properties of the latter. Second, it opens an extensive space for further research and shows us the way to derive new rules, using which we may obtain the intensions of syntagms taken from J (i.e., the formulae a(x) and fuzzy sets $Z_{|-}(A(x))$). Let us stress that the basic rules of inference r_{MP}, r_{Ra} and r_G are necessary to keep the completeness of first-order fuzzy logic but their repertoire can be extended without limit depending on the demands of practical tasks. Of special interest are rules of the kind

$$\frac{o_1(A), \ A \Rightarrow^* B}{o_2(B)}$$

where $\Rightarrow^*$ is some implication-type connective (not necessarily the basic one $\Rightarrow$) and o_1, o_2 are additional unary connectives serving as natural interpretations of linguistic modifiers. These problems will be elaborated on elsewhere.

Keywords: fuzzy logic, approximate reasoning

BIBLIOGRAPHY

Bezdek, J. (ed.). (1987a). *Analysis of Fuzzy Information, vol. 1: Mathematics and Logic.* Boca Raton, FL: CRC Press.

Bezdek, J. (ed.). (1987b). *Analysis of Fuzzy Information, vol. 2: Artificial Intelligence and Decision Systems.* Boca Raton, FL: CRC Press.

Bezdek, J. (ed.). (1987c). *Analysis of Fuzzy Information, vol. 3: Applications in Engineering and Science.* Boca Raton, FL: CRC Press.

Dubois, D. and H. Prade. (1980). *Fuzzy Sets and Systems: Theory and Applications.* New York: Academic Press.

Esragh, F. and E.H. Mamdani. (1979). A general approach to linguistic approximation. *Int. J. Man-Mach. Stud.,* 11, 101–519.

Gupta, M. M. and T. Yamakawa (eds.). (1988a). *Fuzzy Computing: Theory, Hardware and Applications.* Amsterdam: North-Holland.

Gupta, M. M. and T. Yamakawa. (1988b). *Fuzzy Logic in Knowledge-Based Systems, Decision and Control.* Amsterdam: North-Holland.

Lee, C. C. (1990). Fuzzy logic in control systems: Fuzzy logic controller. Part I, II. *IEEE Trans. Syst. Man and Cybern.,* 20, 404–418; 419–433.

Negoita C. V. and D. A. Ralescu. (1975). *Application of Fuzzy Sets to System Analysis.* Stuttgart: Birkhäuser.

Novák, V. (1989). *Fuzzy Sets and Their Applications.* Bristol: Adam Hilger,

Novák, V. (1990a). On the syntactico-semantical completeness of first-order fuzzy logic. Part I – Syntactical aspects. *Kybernetika,* 26.

Novák, V. (1990b). On the syntactico-semantical completeness of first-order fuzzy logic. Part II – Main results. *Kybernetika,* 26, 134–154.

Novák, V. and W. Pedrycz. (1988). Fuzzy sets and t-norms in the light of fuzzy logic. *Int. J. Man-Machine Stud.,* 29, 113–127.

Pavelka, J. (1979). On fuzzy logic I, II, III. *Zeit. Math. Logik Gurndl. Math.,* 25, 45–52, 119–134, 447–464.

Sanchez, A. and L.A. Zadeh. (eds.). (1987). *Approximate Reasoning in Intelligent Systems, Decision and Control.* Oxford: Pergamon Press.

Zadeh, L. A. (1965). Fuzzy sets. *Inf. Control,* 8, 338–353.

Zadeh, L. A. (1973). Quantitative fuzzy semantics. *Inf. Sci.,* 3, 159–176.

Zadeh, L. A. (1975). The concept of a linguistic variable and its application to approximate reasoning I, II, III. *Inf. Sci.,* 8, 199–257, 301–357; 9, 43–80.

Zadeh, L. A. (1978b). PRUF – A meaning representation language for natural languages. *Int. J. Man-Machine Stud.,* 10, 395–460.

Zadeh, L. A. (1983). A computational approach to fuzzy quantifiers in natural languages. *Comp. Math. with Appl.,* 9, 149–184.

13 Presumption, prejudice, and regularity in fuzzy material implication

Thomas WHALEN and Brian SCHOTT
Department of Decision Sciences
Georgia State University
Atlanta, GA 30303, USA

Abstract. A fuzzy if-then rule is often represented by an implication relation based on a multivalent truth function that generalizes material implication. Major families of such functions are the R-implications, S-implications, and Q-implications. If the membership in the implication relation of an element of the Cartesian product of the antecedent and consequent universes is interpreted as the truth of a multivalent material implication, undesirable properties such as presumption and prejudice arise. An alternative interpretation for R-implications based on set inclusion and degree of regularity preserves several widely used forms of approximate reasoning without leading to logical paradoxes.

1. INTRODUCTION

One of the principal approaches to approximate reasoning involves the use of fuzzy material implication relations. In order to allow inferences about one variable Y to be drawn from information about another variable X, rules of the form "if X is A then Y is C" are created. A and C are fuzzy subsets of the domains of X and of Y, respectively, usually elicited from expert knowledge about the relationship between the two variables. The rule itself is represented by a fuzzy implication relation: that is, a fuzzy subset of the Cartesian product of the domains of X and Y. If x is a point in the domain of X that belongs to A to the degree $\mu_A(x)$ and y is a point in the domain of Y that belongs to C to the degree $\mu_C(y)$, then $\mu_{A \to C}(x, y)$ belongs to the implication relation $A \to C$ to the degree $\mu_{A \to C}(x, y) = I(\mu_A(x), \mu_C(y))$, where I (.,.) is one of a variety of generalized material implication functions drawn from the literature of multiple-valued logic or created especially for fuzzy approximate reasoning. Finally, the implication relation is composed with crisp or fuzzy information about the actual value of X according to some "detachment" or "generalized modus ponens" operator in order to infer a fuzy set of possible Y values that is either reported in fuzzy form or "defuzzified" into a point value for the Y variable.

In this paper we examine the interpretation of the membership grade $\mu_{A \to C}(x, y)$ and the generalized material implication function I which generates it. It is shown that viewing membership grades as truth values in multiple-valued logic entails several paradoxical inference modes, including presumption and prejudice, which impose a priori restrictions on X and Y that are detrimental to most practical applications.

A straightforward interpretation of the rule "If X and A then Y is C" affirms that the set of objects whose X attribute satisfies fuzzy set A is included within the set of objects whose Y attribute satisfies fuzzy set C. This interpretation eliminates the paradoxes, but at the cost of limiting the fuzzy implication operator to a single choice, the standard strict operator (1 if $\mu_A(x) \leq \mu_C(y)$, 0 otherwise). This restriction can be relaxed by adding an implicit "regularity" qualifier to all fuzzy rules, so that the rule becomes "If p's X attribute is in A and p is regular, then p's Y attribute is in C." The choice of various T-norms for the "and" in the rule generates the set of R implications, which includes the Łukasiewicz, Quotient, and Brouwer/Gödel implication functions.

2. MATERIAL IMPLICATION IN PROPOSITIONAL LOGIC

2.1. Standard Logic

In standard propositional logic, knowing whether an implication $A \rightarrow C$ is true or false provides some information about the truth of the antecedent A and the consequent C, even without the use of modus ponens or modus tollens. To assert $A \rightarrow C$ is true is equivalent to asserting that either A is false or C is true (or both). Contrariwise, to assert that $(A \rightarrow C)$ is false is to assert unambiguously that proposition A is true and that proposition C is false. The following subsections examine similar conclusions that can be drawn from the truth value of an implication when the truth values of A and C can vary between 0 and 1. This is important because, while applications of classical logic rarely hinge on implications asserted to be false, many treatments of approximate reasoning use implications that are only partly true (and hence partly false).

2.2. Truth $(A \rightarrow C) = 1.0$ When A and C May Be Fuzzy

Suppose that an implication is given a crisp truth value in the context of a fuzzy logical system. A very large number of different functions have been proposed to calculate the truth value of an implication from the truth values of the antecedent and the consequent. (See Cao and Kandel [1989] for a quasi-empirical evaluation of 36 of these in the context of an automatic control system.) In this chapter we will restrict our attention to three families of functions: S-implications, R-implications (Trillas and Valverde, 1985), and Q-implications. The various members of each family are distinguished by the choice of a T-norm, $T(.)$, and/or complementary T-conorm, S (.) (Schweizer and Sklar, 1961, 1963). The three families are all true generalizations of material implication in the sense that they return a truth value of 1.0 when the antecedent is crisply false or the consequent is crisply true, and they return a truth value of 0.0 when the antecedent is crisply true and the consequent is crisply false. Another widely used logical system, the Mamdani conjunctive logic, is not considered because it is not a material implication.

A truth value equal to 1.0 for the proposition $A \rightarrow C$ when A and C are fuzzy has different consequences in different systems of predicate logic.

2.2.1. S-implications

The S-implication function $I(a, c)$ has a truth value equal to $S(1-a, c)$ where a is the truth value of proposition A, c is the truth value of proposition C, and $S(.)$ is a T-conorm. To assert that the Łukasiewicz S-implication $I_1 = \min(1.1 - a + b)$ is equal to 1.0 is equivalent to asserting that the consequent is at least as true as the antecedent. To assert that either the Kleene-Dienes-Łukasiewicz implication $I_2 = 1 - a + ac$ or the Kleene-Dienes implication $I_3 = \max(1 - a, c)$ is equal to 1.0 is equivalent to asserting that either the antecedent is crisply false or else the consequent is crisply true (or both).

2.2.2. Q-implications

Quantum logics may be defined by a family of implication $Q = S(1 - a, T(a, c))$ where $S(.)$ is a T-conorm and $T(.)$ is the corresponding T-norm. Using the Łukasiewicz norm, conorm pair yields $Q_1 = \min(1, \max(0, a + c - 1) + 1 - a)$, which reduces to $\max(1 - a, c)$; hence Q_1 is equivalent to S_3, and requires no further discussion. Using the Kleene-Dienes-Łukasiewicz norm-conorm pair yields $Q_2 = 1 - a + a^2 c$, while using the min-max norm-conorm pair yields the early Zadeh implication function $Q_3 = \max(1 - a, \min(a, c))$. Q_2 and Q_3, like I_2 and I_3, are crisply true if and only if either the antecedent is crisply false or the consequent is crisply true (or both).

2.2.3. R-implications

Among R-implications, the Łukasiewicz propositional implication function $R_1 = \max(1 - a + c, 1)$, the quotient propositional implication function $R_2 = \min(1, c/a)$, and the Brouwer/Gödel function $R_3 = (1 \text{ if } a \leqslant c, c \text{ otherwise})$ are each equal to 1.0 if and only if $a \leqslant c$;

hence to assert that any of these R-implications is crisply true is equivalent to asserting that the consequent is at least as true as the antecedent.

2.3. Truth $(A \rightarrow C) = 0.0$ When A and C May Be Fuzzy

The value of a conorm equals zero if and only if both its arguments are zero $(S(0, x) = S(x, 0) = x$; see (Schweizer and Sklar, 1961, 1963). As a result, asserting that an S-implication is crisply false is equivalent to asserting that its antecedent is crisply true and its consequent is crisply false. It is easily shown that the same is true of the Q-implications.

The Łukasiewicz R-implication equals zero if and only if $a = 1$ and $c = 0$ since this implication is unique in being both an S-implication and an R-implication. The quotient propositional implication function R_2 and the Brouwer/Gödel function R_3 are exactly zero if and only if the consequent is crisply false and the antecedent is not crisply false.

In every example of generalized material implication, a truth value of zero for the implication guarantees a truth value of zero for the consequent. In S-implications and Q-implications the antecedent is guaranteed to be crisply true, while in R-implications the antecedent is guaranteed to be at least partly true.

2.4. Fuzzy Assertion

Suppose the truth value of the implication $A \rightarrow C$ is asserted to be equal to i, $0 < i < 1$. The fact that i is less than 1 imposes restrictions on the truth values of the antecedent and consequent similar to, but not in general as strong as, the restrictions imposed by asserting that the truth of the implication is zero.

If $\rightarrow$ is defined by an S-implication, asserting that the truth value of the implication is equal to i is equivalent to asserting that the consequent is no truer than i and the antecedent is at least as true as $1-i$, since the value of a conorm is always less than or equal to both of its arguments: $i \geqslant c$ and $i \geqslant 1 - a$. This equivalence is the same for I_1, I_2, and I_3.

If a Q-implication is used to define $\rightarrow$, Q_1 is identical to S_3, and behaves as an S-implication. To assert that $Q_2 = 1 - a + a^2 c = i$ requires that $c < i$; this also guarantees that the solution for a when $c > 0$, $a = (1 \pm \sqrt{(1 - 4c(1 - i))})/2c$, is real. $Q_2 = 1 - a + a^2 c = i$ is also equivalent to asserting $c = (i + a - 1)/a^2$, which requires that the antecedent is at least as true as 1-i, since otherwise c would be negative. To assert that $Q_3 = \max(1 - a, \min(a, c)) = i$ requires that the antecedent is at least as true as 1-i; if $i > 0.5$ there is no restriction on c until a is further specified, but if $i \leqslant 0.5$ the consequent cannot be any truer than i. For example, if $i = 0.4$ then $a \geqslant 0.6$ but since $\min(a, c) \leqslant 0.4$, c must be $\leqslant 0.4$; on the other hand, if $i = 0.6$ then $a \geqslant 0.4$, which permits $\min(a, c)$ to be $\leqslant 0.6$ regardless of c.

To summarize, we have shown that simply specifying any truth value other than complete truth (1.0) for an implication in propositional logic imposes restrictions on the possible truth values of the antecedent and the consequent even without resorting to modus ponens or modus tollens. In general, these take the form of lower bounds on the truth value of the antecedent and upper bounds on the truth value of the consequent; elsewhere (Whalen and Schott, 1988) we have labeled these phenomena presumption and prejudice respectively. These restrictions are summarized in Table 13.1.

3. MATERIAL IMPLICATION IN PREDICATE LOGIC

The basic form of an implication rule under predicate logic is "If X is A then Y is C," or "If A (XY) then C (Y)," for short. X and Y are variables with their respective universes of discourse and A and C are predicates that constrain the values of X and Y. The meaning is that if the predicate A is true of the quantity X, then the predicate C is also true of the quantity Y. Our focus will be on implication rules for approximate reasoning in which A and C are fuzzy predicates which impose elastic constraints on X and Y by restricting them to fuzzy subsets of their respective universes of discourse. If the variable X takes on a particular crisp value x_i, then the truth of the predicate A, $\mathrm{Tr}\{A(x_i)\}$, is equal to the membership grade of the x_i in the fuzzy set corresponding to A, $\mu_A(x_1)$, and similarly for Y. Thus, for some values of X and Y the respective predicates A and C will have truth values intermediate between 1 ("true") and 0 ("false").

Table 13.1. Restrictions on consequent and antecedent

Conorm $S(x, y)$	S-implications $I(a,c) = S = (1 - a,c)$	case	Prejudice	Presumption
$S_1 = \text{Min}(1, x + y)$	Łukasiewicz $I_1 = \text{Min}(1, 1 - a + c)$	$i = 0$ $0 < i < 1$ $i = 1$	$c = 0$ $c \leqslant i$ $c \leqslant 1$	$1 = a$ $1 - i \leqslant a$ $0 \leqslant a$
$S_2 = x + y - xy$	Probabilistic $I_2 = 1 - a + ac$	$i = 0$ $0 < i < 1$ $i = 1$	$c = 0$ $c < 1$ $c \leqslant 1$	$1 = a$ $0 < a$ $0 \leqslant a$
$S_3 = \text{Max}(x,y)$	Kleene-Dienes $I_3 = \text{Max}(1 - a,c)$	$i = 0$ $0 < i < 1$ $i = 1$	$c = 0$ $c \leqslant i$ $c \leqslant 1$	$1 = a$ $1 - i \leqslant a$ $0 \leqslant a$

Norm $T(x,y)$	R-Implications $R(a,c)$	case	Prejudice	Presumption
$T_1 = \text{Max}(0, x + y - 1)$	Łukasiewicz $R_1 = 1$ if $a \leqslant c$ else $1 - a + c$	$i = 0$ $0 < i < 1$ $i = 1$	$c = 0$ $c \leqslant i$ $c \leqslant 1$	$1 = a$ $1 - i \leqslant a$ $0 \leqslant a$
$T_2 = x, y$	Quotient $R_2 = 1$ if $a \leqslant c$ else c/a	$i = 0$ $0 < i < 1$ $i = 1$	$c = 0$ $0 < c \leqslant i$ $c \leqslant 1$	$0 < a$ $0 < a$ $0 \leqslant a$
$T_3 = \text{Min}(x, y)$	Brouwer/Gödel $R_3 = 1$ if $a \leqslant c$ else c	$i = 0$ $0 < i < 1$ $i = 1$	$c = 0$ $c = i$ $c \leqslant 1$	$0 < a$ $i < a$ $0 \leqslant a$

Norm/Conorm Pair	Q-implications $R(a, c)$	case	Prejudice	Presumption
T_1, S_1	Kleene-Dienes $Q_1 = \text{Max}(1 - a,c)$	$i = 0$ $0 < i < 1$ $i = 1$	$c = 0$ $c \leqslant i$ $c \leqslant 1$	$1 = a$ $1 - i \leqslant a$ $1 - i \leqslant a$
T_2, S_2	Quadratic $Q_2 = 1 - a + a^2 c$	$i = 0$ $0 < i < 1$ $i = 1$	$c = 0$ $c \leqslant i$ $c \leqslant 1$	$1 = a$ $1 - i \leqslant a$ $1 - i \leqslant a$
T_3, S_3	Early Zadeh $Q_3 = \max\{1 - a, \min(a, c)\}$	$i = 0$ $0 < i \leqslant \frac{1}{2}$ $i = \frac{1}{2}$	$c = 0$ $c \leqslant i$ $c \leqslant 1$	$1 = a$ $1 - i \leqslant a$ $1 - i \leqslant a$

Note: $a = \text{Tr}(A)$, $c = \text{Tr}(C)$, $i = \text{Tr}(A \rightarrow C)$

Given any truth-function $I\{\mathrm{Tr}(A(X)), \mathrm{Tr}\ (C(Y))\}$ representing implication, such as the R-, S-, and Q- implications discussed above, it is easy to compute a fuzzy subset of the Cartesian product of the universes of discourse of X and Y, $\mu_{A \to C}(x_i, y_j)$, based on the membership grades of each element x_i in A and y_j in C, $\mu_A(x_i)$ and $\mu_C(y_j)$:

$$\mu_{A \to C}(x_i, y_j) = I\{\mu_A(x_i), \mu_C(y_j)\}$$

Regardless of which implication operator is used, some of the restrictions inherent in approximate reasoning with propositional logic recur in predicate logic when we try to interpret the meaning of the individual membership grade $\mu_{A \to C}(x_i, y_j)$ of an (x_i, y_j) pair in the implication relation. Most fundamentally this membership grade is the truth value of the implication "If x_i belongs to the hypothetical value A then y_j belongs to the hypothetical value C." Interpreted as such, all of the modes of inference discussed for propositional logic are perfectly valid: $\mu_{A \to C}(x_i, y_j)$ by itself gives a correct lower bound on $\mu_A(x_i)$ through presumption and a correct upper bound on $\mu_C(y_j)$ through prejudice. In addition, $\mu_{A \to C}(x_i, y_j)$, and $\mu_A(x_i)$ together give correct bounds for $\mu_C(y_j)$ through modus ponens, and $\mu_{A \to C}(x_i, y_j)$ and $\mu_C(y_j)$ together give correct bounds for $\mu_A(x_i)$ through modus tollens. (By "correct bounds" we simply mean that the actual truth value of the fuzzy predicate in question for any specific x_i or y_j is within the range specified by the inference.) Although this interpretation allows sound inferences with respect to the hypothetical values A and C, such inferences are of little or no practical benefit. Applied approximate reasoning requires that the knowledge contained in the implication rules be applicable to data arising outside the system. To do this, we take $\mu_{A \to C}(x_i, y_j)$ to be the truth value of the implication "If X is x_i then Y is y_j."

In the typical application, generalized modus ponens is then performed using external data about the perceived value of X to make inferences about the unknown value of Y. The inferred possibility of each y_j is found in two stages. The first stage is to use the membership grade of each x_i in the external datum "X is A'" as a truth value for the crisp proposition "X is x_i" in order to perform generalized modus ponens, yielding one lower bound, mp $\{.,.\}$, for the truth of "Y is y_j" per base value in the X universe of discourse:

$$\mathrm{Tr}\{"Y = y_j" \,|\, A \to C, \mathrm{Tr}\ ("X = x_i") = \mu_{A'}(x_i)\} \geq$$
$$\geq \mathrm{mp}\{\mu_{A'}(x_i), \mu_{A \to C}(x_i, y_j)\}$$

The second stage is to combine these lower bounds into an overall truth value for "Y is y_j." This is generally done using the max operator S_3, although it may be more appropriate to use the conorm proper to the logical system in use (when this system is not R_3 or I_3). Taken together, the truth values for each individual base value y_j, reinterpreted as membership grades, determine C', the inferred predicate on the Y universe of discourse.

However, this procedure leads to a paradox, because if $\mu_{A \to C}(x_i, y_j)$ is less than 1, presumption imposes a priori restrictions on what truth values for "X is x_i" may be asserted, while prejudice imposes a priori restrictions on what truth values for "Y is y_j" may be inferred. And these restrictions on truth values carry over into a priori restrictions on membership grades in A' and C', respectively. In a multirule system, the presumptions and prejudices imposed by the various rules may aggregate to form a "knowledge-base psychosis" in which no X value may be denied without violating the presumption of some rule, and no Y value may be affirmed without violating some rule's prejudice! (see Whalen and Schott, 1988).

For a multivalent logical system to be simultaneously useful and rigorous, it is necessary to preserve modus ponens with respect to external data without simultaneously subjecting that data to presumption and prejudice. One promising approach, which we now take up, is a return to the foundations of approximate reasoning, the theory of fuzzy subsets (Zadeh, 1965).

4. MATERIAL IMPLICATION IN SET LOGIC

In set logic, the concept of implication is replaced with the more fundamental concept of set inclusion; the set logic relation corresponding to "If A then C" is "All A's are C's," or "If p is an A then p is a C." The latter representation is formally similar to the propositional implication "If X is A then Y is C" except that both the antecedent and the consequent in the set logic form refer to a common universe of discourse. The elements of this universe may be referred to as objects, cases, possible worlds, or some term more specific to the application.

The correspondence between set logic and propositional logic can be further enhanced by using the object-attribute-value formalism. If we define the set A in "If p is an A then p is a C" as the set of objects whose X attribute is in the set of X-values A and define the set C as the set of objects whose Y attribute is in the set of Y-values C, then the antecedent and consequent of the set logic version express exactly the same information, respectively, as the antecedent and consequent of the propositional logic version discussed above. In this case, the rule takes the form "If X_p is in A then Y_p is in C" where X_p and Y_p are the values of the two attributes X and Y for a single object p; for example, the height and weight of a particular person.

Despite the equivalence in expressive power between the two logical systems, the natural rules of inference differ strongly when the sets or equivalent propositions involved are fuzzy ones. The most straightforward interpretation of "If p is an A then p is a C" is that the membership grade of any object p in C is at least as great as its membership grade in A:

$$\mu_A(p) \leqslant \mu_C(p), \text{ for all } p$$

Expressed in terms of the attributes X and Y, this becomes

$$\mu_A(Xp) \leqslant \mu_C(Yp), \text{ for all } p$$

If we know the precise value of Xp, we can use modus ponens to make an inference about the value of Yp for the same object. The first step is to find the degree to which Xp belongs to A: denote that membership grade as α. Note that α is also the membership grade of object p in A, and by the implication relation we can infer that the membership grade of p in C is greater than or equal to α: in other words, p is an element of the α-cut C_α, defined as the set of objects whose membership in C is $\geqslant \alpha$. This in turn is equivalent to saying that the value of p on attribute Y, Yp, belongs to the α-cut $\mathbf{C}_\alpha$, the set of Y-values belonging to C at least to degree α. Since α is here a crisp value, $\mathbf{C}_\alpha$ is a crisp subset of the Y universe of discourse. In many applications A and C will be convex fuzzy sets, so a crisp value for Xp causes us to infer a crisp interval of values for Yp.

If the value of Xp is given as a fuzzy subset A' of the universe of X values, the principle is the same although the procedure is more complicated. $\mu_A(Xp)$ becomes $\mu_A(A')$, the degree to which the fuzzy set A' belongs to the fuzzy set A. This membership grade is a fuzzy subset of the universe of ordinary membership grades, given by the following formula:

$$\mu_A(A') = \sum_x \mu_A(x)/\mu_A(x)$$

Since $\mu_A(A') = \mu_A(p)$, $\mu_A(p) \leqslant \mu_C(p)$, and $\mu_C(p) = \mu_C(Yp)$, we have

$$\mu_C(Yp) \geqslant \sum_x \mu_{A'}(x)/\mu_A(x)$$

Taking into account the fact that two or more x values in the X universe of discourse may have equal membership grade in A, we can rewrite this as

$$\mu_C(Yp) \geqslant \sum_{\alpha} \sup_{x:\mu_A(x) = \alpha} \{\mu_A,(x)\}/\alpha$$

Each element α of this fuzzy set of membership grades corresponds to an α-cut, $C_\alpha = \{y:\mu_C(y) \geqslant \alpha\}$, derived from the fuzzy set C given in the rule. Using the resolution identity of fuzzy mathematics (Zadeh, 1971, 1975), we can combine these α-cuts according to the membership grades of their corresponding α values to form the fuzzy set C', which is our best inference of the value of Yp:

$$C' = \sum_{\alpha} \sup_{x:\mu_A(x) = \alpha} \{\mu_A,(x)\} C_\alpha$$

C' is thus the fuzzy set defined by a fuzzy set of α-cuts of C: in other words, by an α-cut of C for which α is itself a fuzzy set of membership grades.

In the case of a crisp data value for Xp, $Xp = x_i$, it is easy to show that this version of modus ponens in fuzzy set logic is equivalent to the use of the standard strict implication operator in fuzzy propositional modus ponens: in both cases the grade of membership of a particular y_j in C' is 1 if $\mu_A(x_i) \leqslant \mu_C(y_j)$ and zero otherwise. The two versions of modus ponens are also equivalent in the case of fuzzy data; the proof, which is omitted here, centers on expressing the inferred C' of propositional modus ponens in terms of its α-cuts using the resolution principle.

Despite this equivalence, the problems posed by presumption and prejudice do not arise. If a particular (x_i, y_j) pair has a membership grade of zero in the fuzzy set implication (inclusion) relation, this asserts only that there exists no p such that $Xp = x_i$ and $Yp = y_j$. Without more information about Yp, this leaves Xp unconstrained, and without information about Xp, Yp is similarly unconstrained.

Fuzzy set logic obeys the law of contrapositive symmetry ($A \to C$ is equivalent to Not $C \to$ Not A) since $\mu_A(p) \leqslant \mu_C(p)$ implies that $\mu_{Not\ C}(p) \leqslant \mu_{Not\ A}(p)$. Because of this, all of the results given above for modus ponens and for prejudice are also true, mutatis mutandis, for modus tollens and for presumption.

To summarize, fuzzy set logic succeeds in preserving generalizations of the classically valid forms of modus ponens and modus tollens, while eliminating the restrictions imposed by presumption and prejudice. But by mandating the standard strict implication operator, it incurs the cost of requiring a degree of crispness in fuzzy implication that, while convenient for some applications, is quite inappropriate in others.

5. REGULARITY-QUALIFIED FUZZY SET LOGIC

Zadeh's main discussions of usuality center on the relative sigma count. However, in the same context he also introduces another concept that can form the basis for a more flexible fuzzy set logic while avoiding the difficulties that have surfaced in fuzzy propositional and predicate logics. This is the concept of conditioned usuality (Zadeh, 1985, p. 756):

> *Usuality* connotes a dependence on the assumption of normality. More generally, let Z denote what might be called a conditioning variable whose normal (or regular) value is R, where R in general is a fuzzy set which is the complement of a set of exceptions. In terms of the conditioning variable, the dispositional valuation (usually X is F) may be expressed as

> (usually) $(X$ is $F) \leftrightarrow$ if $(Z$ is $R)$ then (most X's are F)

The essential first step is to interpret the linguistic rule "If A then C" as a regularity qualified set inclusion relation in object-attribute -value form: "If Xp is in A then Yp is usually in C," where Xp and Yp are two attributes of one entity p. We take this to mean that if p has an X value in A but a Y value that is not in C, then there must be some unusual characteristic about p that explains this. Thus, the rule can be restated as "If Xp is in A and Zp is in R then Yp is in C."

The power of this formalism for representing fuzzy knowledge stems from the fact that Z and R do not need to be specified in the linguistic rule. Although in practice an expert's rule may have many clauses in the antecedent ("If $A1$ and $A2$ and $A3$ and ... then C"), there are almost always many other conditions left out; these are the proverbial "other things" in the time-honored hedge "other things being equal" (ceteris paribus). Only when the rule fails seriously do the details of Z and R come under close examination, whether for improving the rule base through knowledge refinement, or merely for special pleading and excuse making.

Expressed in terms of membership functions, the linguistic rule "If X is A then Y is (usually) C" asserts that every object p belongs to the set C at least as much as it belongs to the intersection of the set A and the set R of "usual" or "regular" objects:

$$\mu_{AR}(p) \leq \mu_C(p)$$

where A is the set of p's whose X values are in A, and similarly for C and R.

We can readily define $\mu_C(p)$ by $\mu_C(Yp)$ as before; in the same way, $\mu_A(p)$ is equal to $\mu_A(Xp)$. By analogy, let $\mu_R(p)$ equal $\mu_R(Zp)$, the degree to which "other things" about p (Zp) are "as usual" (R). Given an appropriate choice of T-norm to represent "and,"

$$\mu_{AR}(p) = T(\mu_A(Xp), \mu_R(Zp))$$

we can express the rule in terms of the attributes Xp, Zp and Yp:

$$T(\mu_A(Xp), \mu_R(Zp)) \leq \mu_C(Yp), \text{ for all } p$$

The simplest case of modus ponens using this rule arises when we know the precise value of Xp and (less realistically) we also know that p belongs to R to the degree β: in other words, we know precisely how "usual" p is. In this case, we can find the membership grade of p in A by the membership grade of Xp in A, $\mu_A(Xp)$. Now if we define α to be the membership grade of p in the intersection set AR, we have

$$\mu_{AR}(p) = \alpha = T(\mu_A(Xp), \beta)$$

and therefore $\mu_C(p) > \alpha$. p is thus inferred to belong to the level set C_α of objects, which means that Yp must belong to the corresponding level set C_α of Y values.

Next, consider the case where we know the precise value Xp of X, and thus can find $\mu_A(p) = \mu_A(p)$, but we have no knowledge about how usual or unusual an object p is. In such a case, the principles of default reasoning imply that we should tentatively replace the variable Zp by its usual value. But, by definition, the usual value of Zp is R, the fuzzy set "usual" itself! Applying the extension principle (Zadeh, 1971), to the membership function shows that the grade of membership of any fuzzy set in itself is the fuzzy set of membership grades called "unitor," defined by

$$\mu_U(\beta) = \beta \quad (\text{Unitor} = \Sigma\, \beta\,/\,\beta.)$$

Thus from the default assumption $Zp = R$ we obtain a fuzzy membership grade of individual p in the fuzzy set $\mathbf{R}$ of usual individuals:

$$\mu_R(p) = \Sigma \, \beta / \beta$$

where β varies over the lattice of membership grades (commonly the unit interval). The interpretation of this is that, lacking any specific information about the regularity of any object p, our best estimate of the fuzzy set $\mathbf{R}$ of usual objects is a second-order fuzzy set in which p's membership grade is the fuzzy set unitor. (This is also the membership of Zp, p's value of the conditioning variable Z, in the second-order fuzzy set of Z values R).

If the mapping from β to $T(\mu_A(Xp), \beta)$ is 1-to-1 for fixed $\mu_A(Xp)$, then p's fuzzy grade of membership in the intersection set $\mathbf{AR}$ is:

$$\mu_{AR}(p) = \Sigma T(\mu_A(pX), \beta)) / \beta$$

but since in general there may be many different values of β that combine with $\mu_A(Xp)$ according to $T(.)$ to yield the same value α, the correct formula is

$$\mu_{AR}(p) = \Sigma \sup \{\beta' : T(\mu_A(Xp), \beta') = \alpha\} / \alpha$$

Since any T-norm is monotonically increasing in both its arguments, it is permissible to replace the equality constraint by an inequality within the supremum:

$$\mu_{AR}(p) = \Sigma \sup \{\beta' : T(\mu_A(Xp), \beta') \leqslant \alpha\} / \alpha$$

The advantage of this is that $\sup \{\beta' : T(\mu_A(Xp), \beta') \leqslant \alpha\}$ is algebraically equivalent to the R-implication function corresponding to the T-norm, which enables us to simplify the membership formula to:

$$\mu_{AR}(p) = \Sigma R(\mu_A(Xp), \alpha) = \alpha\} / \alpha$$

Applying the inference rule $\mu_C(p) > \mu_{AR}(p)$ we obtain the following fuzzy set of lower bounds for p's membership grade in the fuzzy set of objects $\mathbf{C}$:

$$\mu_C(p) = \Sigma R(\mu_A(Xp), \alpha) / \alpha$$

The fuzzy set of lower bounds also applies to the membership grade of Yp in the fuzzy set of Y-values C:

$$\mu_C(Yp) \geqslant \Sigma R(\mu_A(Xp), \alpha) / \alpha$$

The element α of this fuzzy set of membership grades corresponds to a level set $C_\alpha = \{y : \mu_C(y) \geqslant \alpha\}$. Using the resolution identity of fuzzy mathematics (Zadeh, 1971), we can combine these level sets according to the membership grades of their corresponding α's to form the fuzzy set C', Which is our best inference of the value of Yp:

$$C' = \Sigma R(\mu_A(Xp), \alpha) C_\alpha$$

A similar result, detailed in Whalen and Schott (submitted), holds for the case of fuzzy rules and fuzzy data. The principal difference is that the membership grade $\mu_A(Xp)$ is replaced by the fuzzy set of membership grades $\mu_A(A')$.

C', the inferred fuzzy set of Y values obtained by regularity-conditioned fuzzy set logic, is algebraically equal to the result that would be obtained by modus ponens under fuzzy predicate logic with the same A, A', and C and the same T-norm, R-implication pair. When Xp is crisply known, modus ponens in effect selects a row of the implication matrix, while when Xp is fuzzy both methods yield the same fuzzy composition of rows, each weighted via the T-norm according to the possibility of the corresponding singleton Xp.

Despite this equivalence under modus ponens, there is an important difference. In fuzzy predicate logic, $R(\mu_A(x), \mu_C(y))$ is the truth value of the implication "If x is compatible with our knowledge of X then y is compatible with our knowledge of Y"; as we have seen, any truth value other than 1 causes presumption to impose an a priori constraint on our knowledge of X by placing a lower bound on the truth of the antecedent, and prejudice's upper bound on the truth of the consequent likewise imposes an a priori constraint on our knowledge of Y. In regularity-conditioned fuzzy set logic, on the other hand, $R(\mu_A(x), \mu_C(y))$ is the upper bound on the regularity of an object whose X attribute has the value x and whose Y attribute has the value y; in other words, $1 - R(\mu_A(x), \mu_C(y))$ measures how unusual an object would have to be to have this combination of attributes.

In summary, the regularity-conditioned fuzzy set logic formulation allows us to derive modus ponens (and, by a parallel argument, modus tollens) characteristics identical with those of fuzzy predicate logic for any R-implication, while avoiding the undesirable implications of presumption and prejudice.

Keywords: material implication, fuzzy logic, propositional logic, predicate logic, set logic, regularity

BIBLIOGRAPHY

Cap, Z. and A. Kandel. (1989). Applicability of some fuzzy implication operators. *Fuzzy Sets and Systems*, **24**, 65–78.

Schweizer, B. and A. Sklar. (1961). Associative functions and statistical triangle inequalities. *Publ. Math. Debrecen* **8**, 169–186.

Schweizer, B. and A. Sklar. (1963). Associative functions and abstract semigroups. *Publ. Math. Debrecen*, **10**, 69–81.

Trillas, E. and L. Valverde. (1985). On mode and implication in approximate reasoning. In M. M. Gupta et al. (eds.): *Approximate Reasoning in Expert Systems*. North-Holland: Elsevier.

Whalen, T. and B. Schott. (1988). Prejudice, denial, and modus ponens in forward inference. *Proceedings of NAFIPS '88*, pp. 263–266.

Whalen, T. and B. Schott. Usuality, regularity, and fuzzy set logic. (Submitted to *International Journal of Approximate Reasoning*.)

Zadeh, L. A. (1965). Fuzzy sets. *Information and Control*, **8**, 338–353.

Zadeh, L. A. (1971). Similarity relations and fuzzy orderings. *Information Sciences*, **3**, 177–200.

Zadeh, L. A. (1975). The concept of a linguistic variable and its application to approximate reasoning I. *Information Sciences*, **8**, 199–249.

Zadeh, L. A. (1985). Syllogistic reasoning in fuzzy logic and its application to usuality and reasoning with dispositions. *IEEE Trans. on Systems, Man and Cybernetics*, **6**, 754–763.

14 A comparative study of the behavior of some popular fuzzy implication operators on the generalized modus ponens

Etienne E. KERRE
Seminar for Mathematical Analysis
State University of Gent
Galglaan 2
B-9000 Gent, BELGIUM

Abstract. Since Zadeh's introduction of the compositional rule of inference a lot of research has been performed on the suitability of a fuzzy implication operator to represent the relation between two variables linked together by means of an if-then rule and on the choice of the confluence operator used to combine this relation with a given fact or an a priori possibility distribution about the first variable, in order to obtain a value for the second variable involved.

In this paper we give a detailed study of the compositional rule of inference for three popular choices of the fuzzy implication operator, Łukasiewicz, Gödel-Brouwer, and Kleene-Dienes, as well as for two popular choices of the triangular norm, minimum and W. The compositional rule of inference is discussed for different situations with regard to the overlap between the given fact and the antecedent of the rule. The results are presented by means of summarizing tables.

1. INTRODUCTION

An expert system consists of a knowledge base and an inference engine. The knowledge base can be decomposed into a database and a rulebase. The power of the so-called fuzzy expert systems lies in their ability to model and to reason with the imprecision that is inherent to the knowledge of experts. Let us briefly describe how this is realized in the different parts of an expert system.

First, a general fact in the database specifies the value of some attribute for some object and has the form X is A, where X denotes a variable taking values in some universe U and A represents a fuzzy set in U. If the given information is precise, then A reduces to a singleton, and if it is imprecise, nonfuzzy, then A reduces to a crisp subset of U with cardinality at least equal to two. In the framework of the calculus of fuzzy restrictions (Zadeh, 1974) a general fact X is A is transformed into a relational assignment equation $R(X) = A$, which means that the fuzzy set A is considered as a fuzzy restriction on the values that the variable X may take. In the framework of possibility theory (Zadeh, 1978) a fact of the form X is A is translated into a possibility assignment equation $\pi_X = A$, where $\pi_X(u)$ is interpreted as the possibility that X takes the value u given the information X is A. These two representations provide the user with adequate rules to represent composite facts obtained from simple ones by applying logical conjunction and disjunction modeled by triangular norms and conorms. For an extensive treatment of the operations of bounded sum and bold intersection as alternatives for the most frequently used operators maximum and minimum, we refer to Guinan, Streicher, and Kerre (1990).

Second, a general rule of the rulebase takes the form: if X is A then Y is B, where X is a variable taking values in U, Y a variable taking values in V, A a fuzzy set in U, and B a fuzzy set in V. In terms of fuzzy relations this causal link between the two variables X and Y is represented as a fuzzy relation from U to V defined by

$$R(X, Y): U \times V \to [0,1]$$

$$(u,v) \to I(A(u), B(v)), \text{ for each } (u,v) \in U \times V$$

where I stands for an extended implication operator.

The quantity $I(A(u), B(v))$ may be interpreted as the strength of the link between the values u and v for X and Y. In terms of possibility theory a general rule is represented by means of a conditional possibility distribution $\pi_{Y/X}$ defined as

$$\pi_{Y/X}(v,u) = I\,(A(u), B(v)), \quad \text{for each } (v, u) \in V \times U$$

where $\pi_{Y/X}(v, u)$ is the possibility that Y takes the value v given that X has taken the value u. As mentioned in Dubois and Prade (1984) $\pi_{Y/X}$ extends the concept of a multivalued mapping. Now let's have a short look at the inference engine in a fuzzy expert system. From a rule only we cannot infer any knowledge. For this we need some information about at least one of the variables involved in the given rule "if X is A then Y is B." One of the major advantages of fuzzy expert systems is that there is no need for a perfect matching between the antecedent of the rule and the given information about one of the variables, i.e., the given fact may be of the form X is A' where A' is a fuzzy set in U. Now the two pieces of information "X is A'" and "if X is A then Y is B" may be merged by means of a suitable connective in order to obtain information about X and Y. Starting from intuitive acceptable conditions it has been shown that triangular norms are suitable candidates for this confluence operator. From this joint information, restrictions on the second variable Y may be inferred by projection on V. This leads to the generalized modus ponens:

X is A'
if X is A then Y is B
$\overline{}$
$\qquad\qquad Y$ is B'

where $B'(v) = \sup_{u \in U} T\,(A'(u), I(A(u), B(v)))$.

In this paper we will focus on three popular choices for the generalized implication operator I, namely Łukasiewicz, Kleene-Dienes, Gödel-Brouwer, and two important traingular norms T, namely minimum and bold intersection. The last two operators have one important feature in common: if the evaluation set $[0,1]$ is restricted to a finite set such as the set $\left\{0, \dfrac{1}{15}, \dfrac{2}{15}, ..., \dfrac{14}{15}, 1\right\}$ used in fuzzy hardware, then these operations remain internal as opposed to the triangular norm product.

2. A DETAILED STUDY OF SOME POPULAR GENERALIZED IMPLICATION OPERATORS

There exists and overwhelming list of operators extending the classical implication defined by $I(1,0) = 0$, $I(0,0) = I(0,1) = I(1,1) = 1$. Dubois and Prade (1984) have given an excellent classification of these extended operators. Here we will only consider three very popular ones and list their most important properties or failures.

2.1. Łukasiewicz Implication Operator

The Łukasiewicz implication operator from many-valued logic I_L is defined as:

$$I_L : [0,1] \times [0,1] \to [0,1]$$
$$(x, y) \to \min(1, 1 - x + y), \text{ for each } (x, y) \in [0,1]^2$$

i.e., truth-value of $P \Rightarrow Q$ is equal to $\min(1, 1 - \text{truth-value of } P + \text{truth-value of } Q)$.

The main properties of I_L are listed in Table 14.1. In this table x and y represent arbitrary elements $[0,1]$. All the proofs being quite straightforward we will give only some explanatory comments on the different properties:

1. I_L extends classical two-valued implication.
2. If the antecedent is completely true, then the Łukasiewicz implication is as true as its consequent.
3. If the antecedent is completely false, then the Łukasiewicz implication is completely true independent of the truth-value of its consequent.
4. If the consequent is completely false, then I_L is as true as the antecedent is false.
5. The Łukasiewicz implication with completely true consequent is completely true.
6. Applying negation, formula 6 of Table 14.1 can be rewritten $x < 1$ or $y > 0 \Leftrightarrow I_L(x,y) > 0$, i.e., as soon as the antecedent is not completely false, the implication cannot be completely false.

Table 14.1. Main properties of Łukasiewicz implication

1. $I_L(1,0) = 0$
   $I_L(1,1) = I_L(0,1) = I_L(0,0) = 1$
2. $I_L(1,y) = y$
3. $I_L(0,y) = 1$
4. $I_L(x,0) = 1 - x$
5. $I_L(x,1) = 1$
6. $I_L(x,y) = 0 \Leftrightarrow x = 1$ and $y = 0$
7. $x = 0$ or $y = 1 \Rightarrow I_L(x,y) = 1$
8. $x \leqslant y \Leftrightarrow I_L(x,y) = 1$
9. $I_L(.,y)$ is decreasing
10. $I_L(x,.)$ is increasing
11. I_L is continuous
12. $I_L(1 - y, 1 - x) = I_L(x,y)$
13. $I_L(x,x) = 1$
14. $I_L(x,I_L(y,z)) = I_L(y,I_L(x,z))$
15. $I_L(x,I_L(y,z)) = I_L(\max(0,x + y - 1), z)$
16. $I_L(x,I_L(y,x)) = 1$
17. $I_L(x,y) \geqslant \min(x,y)$

7. Formula 7 is a combination of 3 and 5: a completely false antecedent or a completely true consequent implies a completely true implication.
8. As soon as the consequent is at least as true as the antecedent, the implication is completely true.
9. Increasing the truth of the antecedent cannot lead to an increase of the truth of the implication.
10. Increasing the truth of the consequent leads to an increase of the truth of the implication.
11. A small variation in the truth-values of antecedent and consequent cannot lead to a large change in the truth-value of the implication.
12. I_L satisfies the law of contraposition.
13. I_L generalizes the classical tautology $P \Rightarrow P$.
14. I_L satisfies the exchange principle

$$(P \Rightarrow (Q \Rightarrow R) \Leftrightarrow (Q \Rightarrow (P \Rightarrow R))$$

15. I_L satisfies the reducibility property

$$(P \Rightarrow (Q \Rightarrow R)) \Leftrightarrow (P \wedge Q \Rightarrow R)$$

provided the conjunction $\wedge$ is modeled by the bold intersection.

16. This property is a generalization of the classical tautology $P \Rightarrow (Q \Rightarrow P)$.
17. The truth-value of the Łukasiewicz implication cannot be smaller than the minimum of the truth-value of its antecedent and consequent.

2.2. Kleene-Dienes Implication Operator

The Kleene-Dienes operator is defined as:

$$I_{KD} : [0,1] \times [0,1] \rightarrow [0,1]$$

$$(x,y) \rightarrow \max(1 - x, y), \text{ for each } (x,y) \in [0,1]^2$$

The main properties of I_{KD} are listed in Table 14.2.

Here we will give some comments only on deviations of I_{KD} with respect to I_L.

Table 14.2. Main properties of Kleene-Dienes implication

1. $I_{KD}(1,0) = 0$
   $I_{KD}(1,1) = I_{KD}(0,1) = I_{KD}(0,0) = 1$
2. $I_{KD}(1,y) = y$
3. $I_{KD}(0,y) = 1$
4. $I_{KD}(x,0) = 1 - x$
5. $I_{KD}(x,1) = 1$
6. $I_{KD}(x,y) = 0 \Leftrightarrow x = 1$ and $y = 0$
7. $I_{KD}(x,y) = 1 \Leftrightarrow x = 0$ or $y = 1$
8. $x \leqslant y \nRightarrow I_{KD}(x,y) = 1$
9. $I_{KD}(.,y)$ is decreasing
10. $I_{KD}(x,.)$ is increasing
11. I_{KD} is continuous
12. $I_{KD}(1 - y, 1 - x) = I_{KD}(x,y)$
13. $I_{KD}(x,x) \geqslant 0.5$
14. $I_{KD}(x,I_{KD}(y,z)) = I_{KD}(y,I_{KD}(x,z))$
15. $I_{KD}(x,I_{KD}(y,z)) = I_{KD}(\min(x,y), z)$
16. $I_{KD}(x,I_{KD}(y,x)) \neq 1$
17. $I_{KD}(x,y) \geqslant \min(x,y)$

7. In contrast with I_L, the Kleene-Dienes operator also satisfies
   $$x \neq 0 \text{ and } y \neq 1 \Rightarrow I_{KD}(x,y) < 1$$
   i.e., the Kleene-Dienes implication cannot be absolutely true as soon as its antecedent is not completely false and its consequent is not completely true.
8. From $x \leqslant y$ we cannot infer any special value for $I_{KD}(x,y)$.
13. I_{KD} does not keep the classical tautology $P \Rightarrow P$. This is related to the fact that the law of the excluded middle $\neg P \vee P$ is violated with the choice of maximum for the disjunction $\vee$.
16. I_{KD} does not keep the classical tautology $P \Rightarrow (Q \Rightarrow P)$.

2.3. Gödel-Brouwer Implication Operator

The Gödel-Brouwer operator is defined as:

$$I_{GB} : [0,1] \times [0,1] \to [0,1]$$
$$(x,y) \to 1 \text{ if } x \leqslant y$$
$$(x,y) \to y \text{ if } x > y$$

Table 14.3 lists the main properties of this operator.

Table 14.3. Main properties of Gödel-Brouwer implication

1. $I_{GB}(1,0) = 0$
   $I_{GB}(1,1) = I_{GB}(0,1) = I_{GB}(0,0) = 1$
2. $I_{GB}(1,y) = y$
3. $I_{GB}(0,y) = 1$
4. $I_{GB}(x,0) = 0$ if $x \in [0,1]$
5. $I_{GB}(x,1) = 1$
6. $x = 1$ and $y = 0 \Rightarrow I_{GB}(x,y) = 0$
7. $x = 0$ or $y = 1 \Rightarrow I_{GB}(x,y) = 1$
8. $x \leqslant y \Rightarrow I_{GB}(x,y) = 1$
9. $I_{GB}(.,y)$ is decreasing
10. $I_{GB}(x,.)$ is increasing
11. I_{GB} is not continuous
12. $I_{GB}(1 - y, 1 - x) \neq I_{GB}(x,y)$
13. $I_{GB}(x,x) = 1$
14. $I_{GB}(x,I_{GB}(y,z)) = I_{GB}(y,I_{GB}(x,z))$
15. $I_{GB}(x,I_{GB}(y,z)) = I_{GB}(\min(x,y),z)$
16. $I_{GB}(x,I_{GB}(y,x)) = 1$
17. $I_{GB}(x,y) \geqslant \min(x,y)$

Remarkable deviations from the Łukasiewicz operator are:

4. The Gödel-Brouwer operator is completely false as soon as the consequent is completely false and the antecedent is not completely false.
6. The Gödel-Brouwer implication can be completely false without being the antecedent completely true and the consequent completely false.
11. The Gödel-Brouwer implication is not continuous in every element of the set $\{(x,y)\,|\,x \in [0,1]\}$. For example, the sequence $\left(\dfrac{1}{n},0\right)$, $n \in N^*$, converges to $(0,0)$ while the sequence $\left(I_{GB}\left(\dfrac{1}{n},0\right)\right)$, $n \in N^*$, converges to 0, which is different from $I_{GB}(0,0)$.
12. Gödel-Brouwer implication does not satisfy the law of contraposition.

3. GENERALIZED MODUS PONENS

In this section we will discuss the generalized modus ponens scheme as outlined in Section 1. For practical computational considerations in terms of trapezoidal fuzzy quantities we refer to Martin-Clouaire (1987). Here we will first give some generalizations of properties given for the Gödel implication in Dubois and Prade (1985). Afterwards we will give a detailed analysis of the generalized modus ponens for the possible T-I combinations.

3.1. Some General Features of the Generalized Modus Ponens

3.1.1. Conclusion versus Consequent of the Rule

The conclusion B' obtained by applying the generalized modus ponens cannot be more specific or more restrictive than the consequent B of the rule, i.e., $B \subseteq B'$ as soon as the given fact A' is normalized.

Proof. Suppose $A'(u_0) = 1$ for some $u_0 \in U$, i.e., u_0 is considered as a completely possible value for the variable X. Then we have for every $v \in V$:

$$B'(v) = \sup_{u \in U} T(A'(u), I(A(u), B(v)))$$

$$\geqslant T(A'(u_0), I(A(u_0), B(v)))$$
$$= I(A(u_0), B(v))$$
$$\geqslant \min(A(u_0), B(v)) \text{ if } I \in \{I_L, I_{KD}, I_{GB}\}$$
$$\geqslant B(v)$$

3.1.2. Conclusion versus Nested Antecedents of the Rule

The conclusion B' obtained by applying the generalized modus ponens is all the more restrictive the given data A' is more restrictive, i.e., from $A'' \subseteq A'$ we infer $B'' \subseteq B'$.

Proof. From $A''(u) \leqslant A'(u)$ and the monotonicity of a triangular norm T we obtain:

$$T(A''(u), I(A(u), B(v))) \leqslant T(A'(u), I(A(u), B(v)))$$

and hence by taking supremum over $u \in U$, $B''(v) \leqslant B'(v)$.

3.1.3. Uniform Level of Indetermination

As soon as there is no perfect matching between the fact A' given and the antecedent A of the rule, there may be a level of indetermination. This level is a measure for the possibility that the variable X is outside the support of A given X is A' or equivalently as the possibility that X is not A given X is A'. More concretely, we have (for each $v \in V$) $(B'(v) \geqslant \lambda)$ where

$$\lambda = \text{height}(A' \cap_T coA) \text{ if } I = I_L \text{ or } I = I_{KD}$$
$$\lambda = \sup_{u \notin \text{supp } A} A'(u) \qquad \text{if } I = I_{GB}$$

Proof. Since for every $I \in \{I_L, I_{KD}, I_{GB}\}, I(x, .)$ is increasing, we may write $I(A(u), 0) \leqslant I(A(u), B(v))$ and hence

$$T(A'(u), I(A(u), 0)) \leqslant T(A'(u), I(A(u), B(v)))$$

from which: (for each $v \in V)(B'(v) \geqslant \lambda)$ where $\lambda = \sup_{u \in U} T(A'(u), I(A(u), 0))$. According to property 4 in Tables 14.1, 14.2, and 14.3, we have to differentiate between I_L and I_{KD} on one hand, and I_{GB} on the other. It is easily verified that λ reduces to the given values.

Corollaries:

(1) If $T = \min$ and $I \in \{I_L, I_{KD}\}$ we may write:

$$\lambda > 0 \Leftrightarrow A' \cap coA \neq 0$$
$$\Leftrightarrow (\text{there exists } u \in U)(\min(A'(u), 1 - A(u)) > 0)$$
$$\Leftrightarrow (\text{there exists } u \in U)(A'(u) > 0 \text{ and } 1 - A(u) > 0)$$
$$\Leftrightarrow (\text{there exists } u \in U)(u \in \operatorname{supp} A' \text{ and } u \notin \operatorname{core} A)$$
$$\Leftrightarrow \neg(\text{for each } u \in U)(u \notin \operatorname{supp} A' \text{ or } u \in \operatorname{core} A)$$
$$\Leftrightarrow \neg(\text{for each } u \in U)(u \in \operatorname{supp} A' \Rightarrow u \in \operatorname{core} A)$$
$$\Leftrightarrow \neg(\operatorname{supp} A' \subseteq \operatorname{core} A)$$

i.e., $\lambda > 0$ as soon as there is one value $u \in U$ such that $A'(u) > 0$ and $A(u) < 1$. In other words, the level of indetermination is all the greater that a significant part of A' is not included in A.

(2) If $T = W$ and $I \in \{I_L, I_{KD}\}$ we obtain:

$$\lambda > 0 \Leftrightarrow A' \cap_W coA \neq 0$$
$$\Leftrightarrow (\text{there exists } u \in U)(\max(0, A'(u) + 1 - A(u) - 1) > 0)$$
$$\Leftrightarrow (\text{there exists } u \in U)(A'(u) > A(u))$$
$$\Leftrightarrow \neg(\text{for each } u \in U)(A'(u) \leqslant A(u))$$
$$\Leftrightarrow \neg(A' \subseteq A)$$

(3) Combining properties 1 and 3 we obtain for the conclusion B' in case the given fact A' is normalized:

$$B'(v) = \text{ if } B(v) = 1$$
$$B'(v) \in [\max(\lambda, B(v)), 1] \text{ if } 0 < B(v) < 1$$
$$B'(v) = \lambda \text{ if } B(v) = 0$$

3.2. Generalized Modus Ponens under Perfect Matching

More explicitly, we consider the following inference scheme:

X is A
if X is A then Y is B
_____

Y is B'

where $B'(v) = \sup_{u \in U} T(A(u), I(A(u), B(v)))$, for each $v \in V$.

The resulting information for the conclusion B' is summarized in Table 14.4 for two possible choices for T and three possible choices

Table 14.4. Generalized modus ponens under perfect matching

I	T	$B'(v)$	CONDITION
I_L	min	$\leqslant \dfrac{1 + B(v)}{2}$	
I_L	W	$B(v)$	A is normalized
I_{KD}	min	$\leqslant \max(0.5, B(v))$	A is normalized
I_{KD}	W	$B(v)$	A is normalized
I_{GB}	min	$B(v)$	A is normalized
I_{GB}	W	$B(v)$	A is normalized

for I. From this table we may conclude that the pairs (I_L, W), (I_{KD}, W), and (I_{GB}, W) are suitable choices for the extension of classical modus ponens to imprecise information items that are normalized, i.e., at least one value of the universe is completely possible.

As an example we prove the result for $I = I_{GB}$ and $T = \min$. We obtain successively:

$$B'(v) = \sup_{u \in U} \min(A(u), I_{GB}(A(u), B(v)))$$

$$= \max(\sup_{A(u) \leqslant B(v)} \min(A(u), 1), \sup_{A(u) > B(v)} \min(A(u), B(v)))$$

$$= \max(\sup_{A(u) \leqslant B(v)} A(u), \min(\sup_{A(u) > B(v)} A(u), B(v)))$$

$$= \min(\max(\sup_{A(u) \leqslant B(v)} A(u), \sup_{A(u) > B(v)} A(u)), \max(\sup_{A(u) \leqslant B(v)} A(u), B(v)))$$

$$= \min(\text{height } A, B(v))$$

$$= B(v) \text{ if } A \text{ is normalized}$$

3.3. Generalized Modus Ponens under More Precise Information

Suppose the given fact A' is more precise or more specific than the antecedent A of the rule, i.e., $A' \subseteq A$. A concrete example of this situation is $A' = \text{VERY } A$, where the hedge VERY is represented by means of a concentration operator such as the square mapping. It only makes sense to consider the good combinations of the previous section. The results are shown in Table 14.5.

Table 14.5. Generalized modus ponens under more precise information

I	T	$B'(v)$	CONDITION
I_L	W	$B(v)$	A' is normalized
I_{KD}	W	$B(v)$	A' is normalized
I_{GB}	min	$B(v)$	A' is normalized
I_{GB}	W	$B(v)$	A' is normalized

From Section 3.1.1 it follows that the most specific information we can obtain for Y is Y is B. It may be seen from the results of Table 14.5 that this best boundary is obtained for the four combinations (I_L, W), (I_{KD}, W), (I_{GB}, min), and (I_{GB}, W). These results are in agreement with the fact that from X is VERY A and if X is A then Y is B we cannot infer Y is VERY B (Dubois and Prade, 1985). In order to obtain the latter conclusion we have to presuppose some intensity link. For an extensive treatment of such a link we refer to Prade (1988). As an example we prove the second case $I = I_{KD}$ and $T = W$. We obtain successively:

$$B'(v) = \sup_{u \in U} \max(0, A'(u) + \max(1 - A(u), B(v)) - 1)$$

$$= \sup_{u \in U} \max(0, \max(A'(u) - A(u), A'(u) + B(v) - 1))$$

$$= \sup_{u \in U} \max(0, A'(u) + B(v) - 1)$$

$$= \max(0, \sup_{u \in U} A'(u) + B(v) - 1)$$

$$= \max(0, \text{height } A' + B(v) - 1)$$

$$= B(v) \text{ if height } A' = 1$$

3.4. Generalized Modus Ponens under the Denial of the Antecedent

Consider the following inference scheme:

X is coA
if X is A then Y is B
———————————————
Y is B'

The results for six possible combinations are summarized in Table 14.6. As soon as coA is normalized, i.e., as soon as there exists at least one value outside the support of A that is completely possible, we obtain that the value of the variable Y is completely undetermined. In the other case we obtain more complex expressions for $B'(v)$. As an example we prove the first case $I = I_L$ and $T = \min$. We may write:

$$B'(v) = \sup_{u \in U} \min(1 - A(u), \min(1, 1 - A(u) + B(v)))$$

$$= \sup_{u \in U} \min(1 - A(u), 1, 1 - A(u) + B(v))$$

$$= \sup_{u \in U} \min(1 - A(u), 1 - A(u + B(v))$$

$$= \sup_{u \in U} 1 - A(u) = \text{height}(coA) = 1 - \text{plinth } A$$

$$= 1 \text{ if } coA \text{ is normalized}$$

This result is in agreement with the uniform level of indetermination obtained in Section 3.1.3; indeed, from $B'(v) \geqslant \text{height}(coA \cap_T coA)$ we obtain $B'(v) = 1$ as soon as $\text{height}(coA) = 1$.

Table 14.6. Generalized modus ponens under the denial of the antecedent

I	T	$B'(v)$	CONDITION
I_L	min	$1 - \text{plinth } A$ 1	/ coA is normalized
I_L	W	$1 - \inf_{A(u) \leqslant B(v)} A(u)$ 1	(there exists $u \in U)(A(u) \leqslant B(v))$ coA is normalized
I_{KD}	min	$1 - \text{plinth } A$ 1	/ coA is normalized
I_{KD}	W	$\max(0, 1 - 2\inf_{A(u) < 1 - B(v)} A(u))$ 1	(there exists $u \in U)(A(u) < 1 - B(v))$ coA is normalized
I_{GB}	min	$1 - \inf_{A(u) \leqslant B(v)} A(u)$ 1	(there exists $u \in U)(A(u) \leqslant B(v))$ coA is normalized
I_{GB}	W	$1 - \inf_{A(u) \leqslant B(v)} A(u)$ 1	/ coA is normalized

3.5. Generalized Modus Ponens under Precise Data

More concretely we consider the following scheme:

X is u_0
if X is A then Y is B
_____
Y is B'

i.e., $A' = \{u_0\}$ where $u_0 \in U$. Applying the generalized modus ponens for $T \in \{\min, W\}$ and $I \in \{I_L, I_{KD}, I_{GB}\}$ we obtain:

$$B'(v) = \sup_{u \in U} T(A'(u), I(A(u), B(v)))$$

$$= \max(T(1, I(A(u_0), B(v))), \sup_{u \in U \setminus \{u_0\}} T(0, I(A(u), B(v))))$$

$$= I(A(u_0), B(v)) \text{ since } T(1, x) = x \text{ and } T(0, x) = 0$$

If $A(u_0) = 1$, then $B' = B$, i.e., if the given precise fact is completely compatible with the antecedent of the rule, then the conclusion of the rule can be inferred.

If $A(u_0) = 0$, then (for each $v \in V)(B'(v) = 1)$, i.e., if the given precise fact is completely incompatible with the antecedent of the rule, then nothing can be inferred with respect to Y, i.e., every value of V remains completely possible for Y.

If $0 < A(u_0) < 1$, then (for each $v \in V)(B'(v) = I(A(u_0), B(v)) \geqslant B(v))$, i.e., in this case the conclusion inferred will be less precise than the conclusion of the rule ($B \subset B'$); the smaller $A(u_0)$ (i.e., the greater the distance between $A'(u_0)$ and $A(u_0)$) the greater the uncertainty that is produced with respect to the value of Y.

4. CONCLUSION

In this paper we have shown that under very simple normalization conditions the generalized modus ponens gives very good results for the four combinations: Łukasiewicz-bold intersection, Kleene-Dienes-minimum, Kleene-Dienes-bold intersection, Gödel-Brouwer-minimum and Gödel-Brouwer-bold intersection. Moreover, all these implications and conjunction operators are internal if the evaluation set $[0, 1]$ is restricted to a finite set such as the set $\left\{ 0, \dfrac{1}{15}, \dfrac{2}{15}, \ldots, \dfrac{14}{15}, 1 \right\}$, as used in fuzzy hardware.

Keywords: fuzzy implication, compositional rule of inference, triangular norm

BIBLIOGRAPHY

Dubois, D. and H. Prade. (1984). Fuzzy logics and the generalized modus ponens revisited. *Cybernetics and Systems,* 15, 293–331.

Dubois, D. and H. Prade. (1985). The generalized modus ponens under sup-min composition. In M. M. Gupta, A. Kandel, W. Bandler, and J. B. Kiszka (eds.): *Approximate Reasoning in Expert Systems.* Amsterdam: North-Holland, pp. 217–232.

Guinan, D., K. Streicher, and E. E. Kerre. (1990). Set-theoretic properties of the class of fuzzy sets endowed with the bounded sum and the bold intersection. University of Nebraska–Lincoln, Department of Computer Science and Engineering, Report Series no. 114.

Martin-Clouaire, R. (1987). Semantics and computation of the generalized modus ponens. Rapport L.S.I, no. 270

Prade, H. (1988). A quantitative approach to approximate reasoning in rule-based expert systems. In L. Bolc and M. Coombs (eds.): *Expert System Applications.* Berlin: Springer-Verlag, pp. 199–256.

Zadeh, L. A. (1974). Calculus of fuzzy restrictions. In L. A. Zadeh, K. S. Fu, K. Tanaka, and M. Shimura (eds.): *Fuzzy Sets and Their Applications to Cognitive and Decision Processes.* New York: Academic Press, pp. 1–39.

Zadeh, L. A. (1978). Fuzzy sets as a basis for a theory of possibility. *Fuzzy Sets and Systems,* 1, 3–28.

15 A fast algorithm for fuzzy inference by compact rules

László T. KÓCZY
Communication Electronics
Technical University of
Budapest
Sztoczek u. 2, Budapest,
H-1111
HUNGARY

Kaoru HIROTA
Instrument and Control
Engineering
College of Engineering
Hosei University, Kajino-cho
Koganei-shi, Tokyo 184
JAPAN

Abstract. One of the important applications of fuzzy systems is in the field of fuzzy control and fuzzy expert systems based on approximate (linguistic) reasoning by using fuzzy inference rules. In this paper a method to define and combine rules will be treated. The method is especially suitable for obtaining fuzzy conclusions and performing multistage inference; we call it inference by compact rules. A great disadvantage of compact rules is a high computational complexity of the algorithm. The clue of the new method described here is the introduction of restrictions and the modification of the algorithm so that its complexity is reduced and kept well in hand.

1. INTRODUCTION

What is the reason for the "fuzzy explosion," unexpected by many scientists and industrial engineers, which burst into industrial applications in the 1980s? It is a fact that even modern control theory has failed to cope with some classes of control problems in industrial processes, robotics, vehicles, household equipment, video cameras, etc. The essence of the problem is that classical control theory properly describes and models only a limited class of not very complex systems.

While there is no exact method to control optimally many of the above mentioned systems, a human operator often solves the problem succesfully when using some heuristic and intuitive control algorithm, and even very complex systems can be treated in a satisfactory degree. Let us take a very common example: driving a car can be managed by most adults quite succesfully (at least after a period of appropriate training) and yet the fully automatic control of driving a car in a real traffic environment is still an open problem. The system consisting of the car, street conditions, traffic environment, etc. seems to be too complicated to be modeled satisfactorily by any known mathematical method.

If we tried to model roughly the "algorithm" used by the driver, probably the best estimation is the description of a pool of knowledge in the form of experience rules. These rules are accumulated first of all during the learning period when a driving teacher intentionally hands over a set of most important behavioral patterns, but the collection is continuously enlarged by new experience obtained in "sharp" driving. Such rules can be "Drive slower if the street is wet." "Step on the brake firmly if you are coming to a red light" or "Drive very slowly if you see children playing on the sidewalk."

The challenge for AI engineers is the possible implementation of this kind of pool of knowledge in some formal way.

2. APPROXIMATE REASONING AND FUZZY RULE-BASED INFERENCE

How do we treat formally rules like "Step on the brake firmly if you are coming to a red light"? This instruction is a typical sentence in a natural language containing linguistic terms like *firmly* and *coming to* (*near*). Algorithms using instructions of this type were first proposed in Zadeh (1968). The concept of linguistic variables used in approximate reasoning were discussed later in detail, e.g., in Zadeh (1974, 1975).

Parallel with the detailed elaboration of approximate reasoning methods based on fuzzy linguistic terms, the first applicational results utilizing the idea of a fuzzy algorithm were produced in a laboratory environment by Mamdani and colleagues (Mamdani, 1974; King and Mamdani, 1977; Mamdani, 1977). Aside from purely linguistic approaches, some other ways to implement fuzzy algorithms were also proposed quite early, e.g., in Kacprzyk (1978), where the system of rules is represented by a decision tree.

Returning to the linguistic approach and recent years, clearly the center of gravity of applications has shifted unambiguously to Japan. Beginnings of interesting foundational works in the direction of real industrial aplications can be represented by the results of research done by Sugeno and Nishida (1985), and Hirota, Arai and Hachisu (1987), among others.

The essential idea in these applications is some treatable implementation of the approximate reasoning algorithm represented by fuzzy "if-then" rules. A model of such a reasoning method is the following: given two spaces, the observation space X and the conclusion space Y, a single rule always has the form

"If X is C_1 then Y is S_j"

In the above C_i and S_j are fuzzy sets over X and Y, respectively, both of them representing a fuzzy term or a combination of terms. In a general case both X and Y are constructed as the direct product of k_1 and k_2 component spaces, respectively, i.e.,

$$X = X_1 \times X_2 \times \dots \times X_{k_1} \text{ and } Y = Y_1 \times Y_2 \times \dots \times Y_{k_2}$$

Of course, terms C_i and S_j are composed similarly of k_1 and k_2 simple terms over $X_1, \dots, X_{k_1}$ and $Y_1, \dots, Y_{k_2}$, respectively. An example for such a rule is

$R_1 =$ "If the street is **quite wet** and there is **little light** and a pedestrian is crossing **quite near**, then drive **very slowly** and watch out **very carefully**."

Here $F(X) = \{$terms of wetness for a street$\} \times \{$terms of degree of light$\} \times \{$terms for distance$\}$ and $F(Y) = \{$degrees of driving speed$\} \times \{$degrees of carefulness$\}$ are the sets of fuzzy linguistic terms over the observation and the conclusion spaces, respectively. Chosing one of the components of X, e.g., X_2, we have a set as $\{$**very slowly, slowly, quite slowly, with medium speed, quite fast, fast, very fast**$\}$, of which all the elements represent a simple linguistic term.

A composed linguistic term can be described formally as, e.g., (**quite wet, little** [referring to light], **quite near**) or another composed term (however, over Y) is (**very slowly, very carefully**). Every linguistic term is a fuzzy set over the universe of discourse X_i or Y_j. An example is the fuzzy term **very slowly** over Y_1 shown in Figure 15.1.

Suppose we are given a set of rules (like R_1) and an observation A is taken over X which is, similarly to C_i, $A \in F(X)$. An example for A could be "The street is **little wet** and there is **much** light and the pedestrian is crossing **rather far away**." It is clear that any rule referring to a "**rather wet**" street refers only to a certain degree (<1) to an observation containing "**little wet**," although there is certainly an overlapping with the condition part of the rule. If the number and type of rules is sufficient to conclude to a fuzzy set, and maybe to a crisp value in Y, the reasoning was successful.

There are various methods known from the literature and from the industrial applications that make a conclusion possible in the form:

$$(R_1, R_2, ..., R_r; A) \Rightarrow B$$

We are summarizing now two of them, probably those two which are applied most frequently. In both algorithms the simplifying restrictions are applied that every membership function has triangular shape and is symmetrical.

Algorithm 1 is the following:

For $i = 1$ to r
    let $m_i = \max_x \{C_i(x) \wedge A(x)\}$
    let $S_i^A(y) = \min\{m_i, S_i(y)\}$
Let $B(y) = 0$
For $i = 1$ to r
    let $B(y) = B(y) \vee S_i^A(y)$

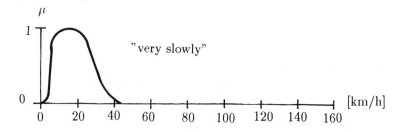

Figure 15.1.

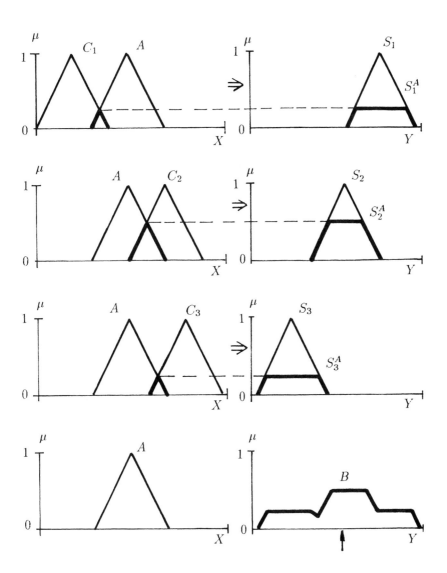

Figure 15.2.

For $i = 1$ to k_2

$$\text{let } b_1 = \sum_{y_i \in Y - Y_i} y_i \, B(y_i) \Bigg/ \sum_{y_i \in Y_i} y_i$$

where $\wedge$ stands for min and $\vee$ for max. S_i^A are the fuzzy sets obtained by "truncating" S_i with the maximum of the intersection of the observation (A) and C_i. B is the fuzzy set obtained as the union of all truncated conclusions of the rules. The crisp conclusion is b, the center of gravity of the area below $B(y)$.

Figure 15.2 shows an example for the bove algorithm where both X and Y are one dimensional and the membership functions of C_i and S_i are symmetrical and triangular (which properties are in no way an essential part of the algorithm).

Algorithm 2 is as follows:

> For every (x, y)
>   let $R(x, y) = 0$
> For $i = 1$ to r
>   let $R_i(x, y) = \min\{C_i(x), S_i(y)\}$
>   let $R(x, y) = R(x, y) \vee R_i(x, y)$
> For every (x, y)
>   let $B(x, y) = A(x) \wedge R(x, y)$
> For $i = 1$ to k_2
>
> $$\text{Let } b_i = \sum_{x \in X} \sum_{y \in Y - Y_i} yB(x, y) \left/ \sum_{y_i \in Y_i} y_i \right.$$

R_i are the compact rules that are represented as fuzzy relations in $X \times Y$. R is the compact rule system including all information in $\{R_1, R_2, ..., R_r\}$. $B(x, y)$ is the fuzzy conclusion, this time in the form of a fuzzy relation, and b is the crisp conclusion as a "spatial" center of gravity. Figure 15.3 is a simple case with only two rules in the system (and X, Y being both one dimensional). $B(x, y)$ is a complicated broken surface (the minimum of $R(x, y)$ and $A(x, y)$) so it was not drawn by hand, however calculation of the values of $B(x, y)$ is very easy.

Another example is shown in Figure 15.4, where we applied computer graphics to show the membership function surfaces. Part 4a illustrates the two rules in the rule system with the axonometric view of $R(x, y)$. Part 4b is the same but also shows the hidden edges. In part 4c also the observation is marked, with hidden edges and the interpenetration lines of the cut of the cylindrical extension with the rule system. Finally, part 4d shows only the conclusion relation including the hidden edges.

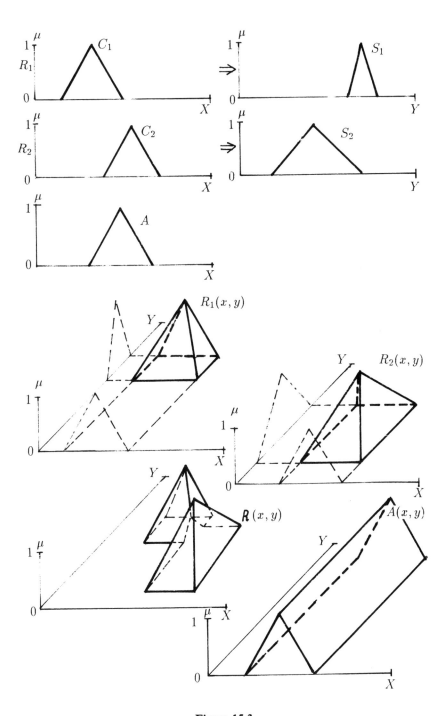

Figure 15.3.

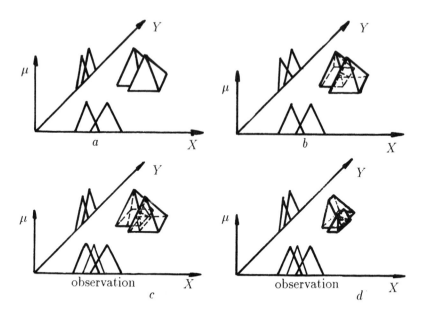

Figure 15.4.

3. ADVANTAGES AND DISADVANTAGES

The two methods for approximate reasoning described in Section 2 have both advantages and disadvantages. As the two main aspects of evaluating these methods we have chosen *functionality* and *applicability*.

Many successful applications have proven the basic functionality of both algorithms. However, our investigations have shown a clear difference in the sensitivity of the methods in respect of changes in the rule system and/or observation. Let us suppose there is given a rule system $R = \{R_1, R_2, ..., R_r\}$. Taking now an arbitrary observation A, the conclusion can be calculated by using both of the algorithms, so we obtain b_1 and b_2 by method 1 and 2, respectively. In a general case $b_1 \neq b_2$. Suppose now that we take observation A' where $A \neq A'$ and e.g., A' is "more" X' than A. Then, obtaining the new conclusions b_1' and b_2' it can be expected that b' is also "more x" (greater in X, according to some ordering in X, in harmony with the expression "more") than b (for both indices).

Intuitively, it can be expected that conclusion B (with both methods) will be in some sense near to S_i if the observation (A) was near to C_i in R_i. If the observation then moves from C_i near to C_j $(i \neq j)$, it can be also expected that the new conclusion is nearer to S_j now. The same way of thinking is applicable for any change in the rule system. If in R' there is a rule R_1 near to A (in X), B' will be also near to R_1 (in Y), while B obtained from R was near to R_j as in R the near rule to A was R_j.

Sensitivity of the reasoning algorithm can be intuitively defined as the property of changing B in the above sense if A is changing. We have implemented both methods by a computer program and compared the sensitivity in Kóczy and Hirota (1990). We will summarize the results of this comparison.

Our computational examples have proven that applying the compact rule method the fuzzy conclusion changes more sensitively than with applying the truncation method.

In order to show the above fact some technicalities of the program must be explained. In the rules and the observation we always applied symmetrical triangular membership functions. In that case if X and Y are both one-dimensional and they are represented by the interval $[1, ..., n]$ of integer numbers, every membership function can be described by a simple pair of parameters. So if, for example, the maximum of the membership function is at $x = 9$ and the width of the triangle is 4, we can describe $\mu(x)$ by the pair (9, 4). Any rule is described in the form $(m_c, w_c) \Rightarrow (m_s, w_s)$. (This simplification cannot be used, of course, with the truncated membership functions or with their union.) In the illustrative examples $n = 20$ was always chosen. It is difficult to represent the "spatial" membership function surfaces in print, so we applied a top-view of the pyramids obtained by compacting the rules. The top-view is represented by level sets expressed by changing levels of darkness on the pictures.

Figure 15.5 shows a simple three-rules system representing approximately

"If X is **little**, then Y is **not so much**"
"If X is **not so much**, then Y is **slightly over the medium**"
"If X is **rather**, then Y is **rather not**" (part 5a)

The observation is

"X is **slightly under the medium**" (part 5c, left side).

Using Algorithm 1, overlappings of the observation with the "if parts" of the rules, further on the truncated conclusions from the "then

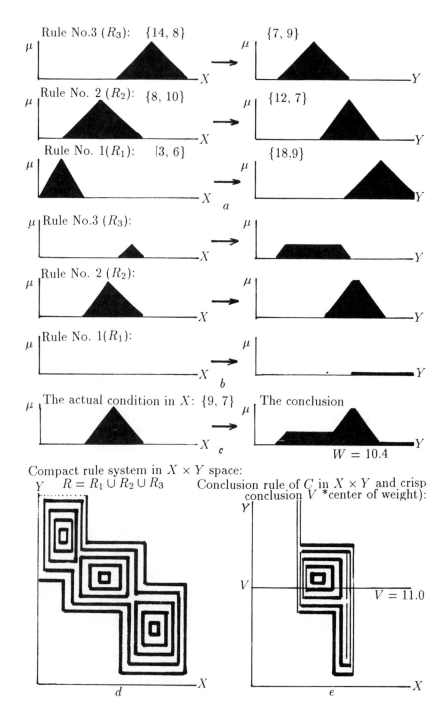

Figure 15.5.

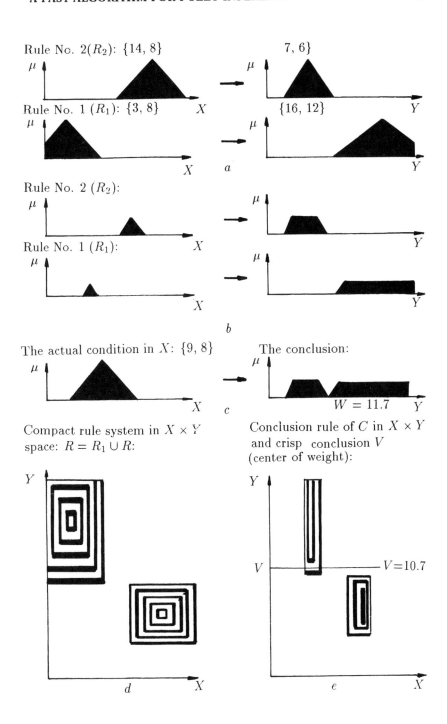

Figure 15.6.

parts" of the rules are shown in part 5b, fuzzy and crisp conclusion (the latter being the center of gravity of the former, marked by $w = 10.4$) are in part 5c, right side. The rule system according to Algorithm 2 is depicted in part 5d (top view, level sets), and the fuzzy conclusion (also in top view) is in part 5e. When comparing d with e, clearly seen are the borderlines of the cylindrical extension of the observation and also the change in the steepness of the sides of the pyramids (level sets come nearer to each other in part 5e. The crisp conclusion is marked by $v = 11.0$ (w and v on the picture correspond to b_1, and b_2 in the previous notation of the text). As expected, w and v are not equal, but their difference is not very large.

Figure 15.6 compares the sensitivity of the two algorithms. As a very simple start a two-rules system is taken

$$(3, 8) \Rightarrow (16, 12); \ (14, 8) \Rightarrow (7, 6)$$

with the observation (actual condition) $(9, 8)$. Results by using Algorithm 1 and 2 are 11.7 and 10.7, respectively. In Figure 15.7 the rules are slightly changed in the "if parts." Width of the triangle in Rule 1 is increased: $(3, 8)$ to $(3, 12)$, while the width of Rule 2 is decreased: $(14, 8)$ to $(14, 6)$. So the same observation has a greater overlapping with Rule 1 now: we expect that the conclusion is shifted in the direction of the maximum of Rule 1. Indeed, w is 12.7 here (shifted by 1.0), but v is 13.5 (shifted by 2.8). This is fully in accordance with the approximate fact that R_1 has become dominating in this conclusion. Algorithm 2 proved to be more sensitive to the change here.

In Figure 15.8 the change is in the opposite direction: The "if part" of R_2 has been increased: $(14, 8)$ to $(14, 12)$ and of R_1 decreased: $(3, 8)$ to $(3, 6)$. Now R_2 dominates completely and indeed: $w = 10.5$ (1.2 nearer to the maximum of the "then part" of R_2) and $v = 8.0$ (2.7 nearer to R_2). Again Algorithm 2 has reacted more sensitively.

In the next example (Figure 15.9), the triangles in the "then parts" of the rules have been changed: $(176, 12)$ to $(16, 6)$ and $(7, 6)$ to $(7, 12)$. In the original reasoning R_2 had more overlapping with the observation, so both w and v were nearer to R_2 than to R_1. Now the degree of overlapping ("similarity" with the "if parts") has not changed, but Rule 2 became more vague in the conclusion part, i.e., independently from the observation it now dominated the conclusion space. Now w changed to 9.4 (2.3 less), v to 8.7 (2.0 less). The sensitivity of the reaction is higher now in the case of Algorithm 1.

Finally, in Figure 15.10 the observation is changed (shifted from (9, 8) to (7, 8), i.e., nearer to the condition part of R_1). In effect, this is

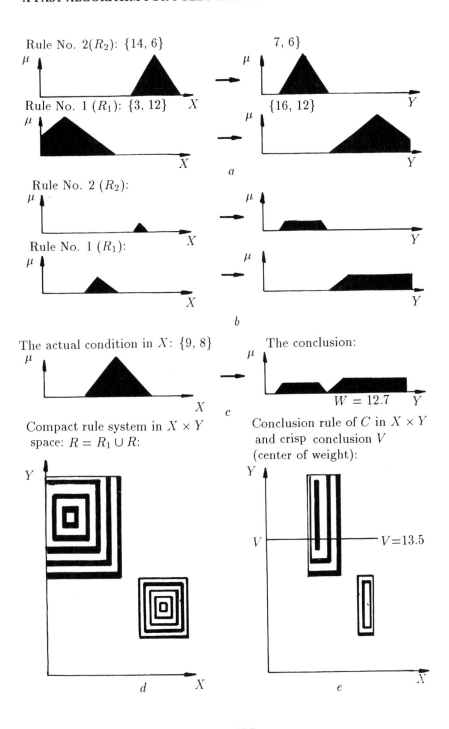

Rule No. 2(R_2): {14, 6}

7, 6}

Rule No. 1 (R_1): {3, 12}

{16, 12}

Rule No. 2 (R_2):

Rule No. 1 (R_1):

The actual condition in X: {9, 8}

The conclusion:

$W = 12.7$

Compact rule system in $X \times Y$ space: $R = R_1 \cup R$:

Conclusion rule of C in $X \times Y$ and crisp conclusion V (center of weight):

$V = 13.5$

Figure 15.7.

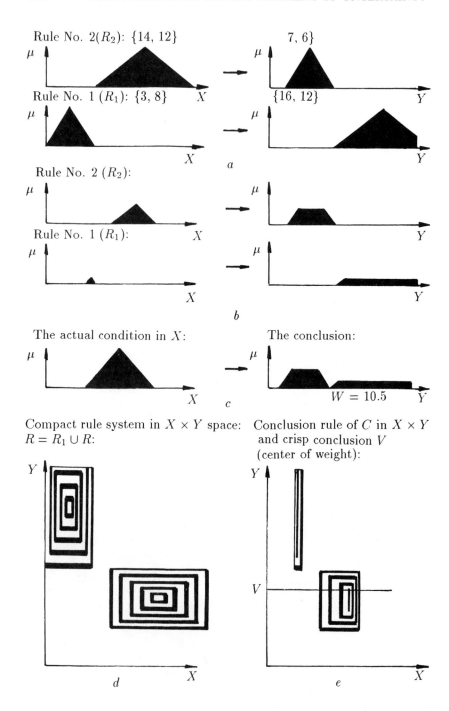

Rule No. 2(R_2): {14, 12}

7, 6}

Rule No. 1 (R_1): {3, 8}

{16, 12}

Rule No. 2 (R_2):

Rule No. 1 (R_1):

a

b

The actual condition in X:

The conclusion:

$W = 10.5$

c

Compact rule system in $X \times Y$ space: $R = R_1 \cup R$:

Conclusion rule of C in $X \times Y$ and crisp conclusion V (center of weight):

d

e

Figure 15.8.

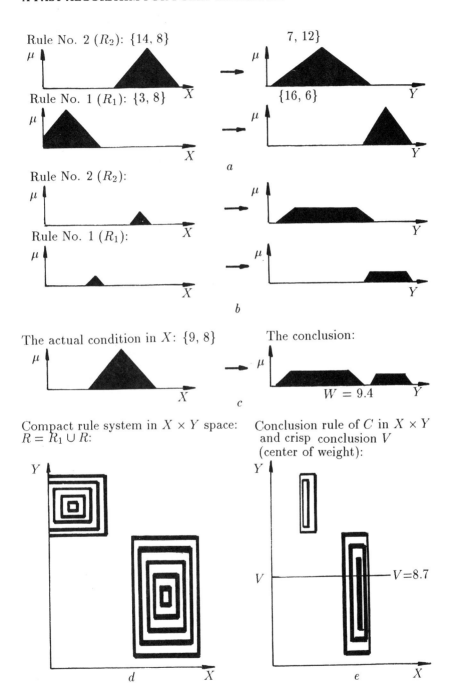

Figure 15.9.

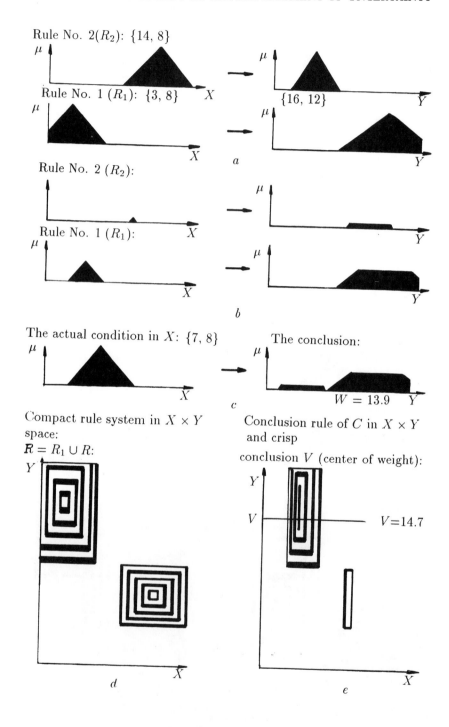

Figure 15.10.

similar to the case when R_1 is brought nearer to A, and, indeed, w is increased remarkably (to 13.8, by 2.2), and v even more (to 14.7, by 4.0). Here, again Algorithm 2 shows more definite changes.

In conclusion, we may state that in all but one case of the examples Algorithm 2 showed a clearer reaction, but also in the single exception the absolute value of v was definitely nearer to the dominant rule than to the other. Because of this we recommend Algorithm 2 for the applications, at least from the point of view of reasoning.

The second aspect of comparison is the applicability of the methods, where the possibility of a real-time implementation is in question. The cardinal problem is computational speed, which can be described by the algebraic complexity, as in Aho, Hopcroft and Ullman (1974). So the subject of comparing the two algorithms was their algebraic (computational) complexity.

Suppose we have r rules in the form

"If X is C_i then Y is S_j"

Suppose that

$$X = X_1 \times ... \times X_{k_1} \text{ and } Y = Y_1 \times ... \times Y_{k_2}$$

where the cardinalities of the universes of discourse are

$$\# X_1 = m_i \leqslant m, \quad \# Y_j = n_j \leqslant n; \text{ so}$$
$$\# X = \Pi \leqslant m^{k_1}, \quad \# Y = \Pi n_j \leqslant n^{k_2}$$

Input size (uniform complexity) is $r(k_1 m + k_2 n)$ for the rule system and $k_1 m$ for an observation.

In the case of Algorithm 1 calculation of the crisp conclusion takes $C_1 = r(2k_1 m + 2k_2 n) + 3k_2 n + k_2$ steps (which is the size in uniform complexity). In Algorithm 2, however, the same calculation takes $C_2 = (r + 1)m^{k_1}n^{k_2} + k_2(2m^{k_1}n^{k_2-1} + n + k_2)$ steps.

If we introduce $k = \max\{k_1, k_2\}$ and $N = \max\{m, n\}$, we have $C_1 = O(rkN)$, $C_2 = O(rN^{2k})$ which is a clear indication that the computational speed of Algorithm 2 is very low and exponentiality in the expression makes an application very difficult if k is not very small (or even small constant). For details on the calculations in connection with the above algorithms, see Kóczy (1990; 1991a, b).

The balance of this section is as follows:

	Sensitivity in reasoning	Computational complexity
Algorithm 1	weak	low
Algorithm 2	good	high

4. THE FAST AND SENSITIVE ALGORITHM

Clearly, it would be optimal to find Algorithm 3, which unifies the advantages of both algorithms treated in Sections 2 and 3: a sensitive, yet fast algorithm. As we see it, this problem cannot be solved satisfactorily from every aspect. In this section we shall show an algorithm that resembles Algorithm 2 very closely, however, by a series of restrictions its computational time is reduced considerably. These restrictions are applicable only for a certain class of problems, so our algorithm will certainly not be an all-purpose one.

The crucial problem is the exponentiality in terms of m and n (or, in general, N) which is caused by the fact that, theoretically, all membership functions representing the condition or conclusion parts, the rules or observations, are considered to have a support equal to the component universes of discourse. In practice, usually such linguistic terms as **little, very, rather** etc. cover only a very limited subset of the universe. More formally, $\# \operatorname{supp}(\operatorname{proj}_{z_j}(\mu(\zeta))) \leqslant L \ll N$, where $\zeta = x$ or y, $\mu = C_i, S_j$ or A, $\operatorname{proj}_{z_j}$ stands for the projection of a membership function to $Z = X_i$ or Y_j, i.e., $\mu(x_i)$ or $\mu(y_j)$ and supp is the support. (We suppose that all universes in question have a finite cardinality that is in all applications automatically fulfilled.)

Another restriction must be that k_1 and k_2 are kept constant, i.e., the number of linguistic variables in the rules is limited as well.

L is a small constant, k_i as well, so is L^{k_i} ($i = 1, 2$). Under these restrictions we have constructed a new algorithm.

Algorithm 3 is as follows:

> Let $R(\text{nil}) = 0$
> For $j = 1$ to k_1 let $d_j = u_j = \text{nil}$
> For $j = 1$ to k_2 let $D_j = U_j = \text{nil}$
> For $i = 1$ to r
> For $j = 1$ to k_1
>   Mark $m_{i,j} = \min \{\operatorname{supp}(\operatorname{proj}_{X_j}(C_i))\}$
>   Mark $M_{i,j} = \max \{\operatorname{supp}(\operatorname{proj}_{X_j}(C_i))\}$
> For $j = k_1 + 1$ to $k_1 + k_2$
>   Mark $m_{i,j} = \min \{\operatorname{supp}(\operatorname{proj}_{X_j}(S_i))\}$
>   Mark $M_{i,j} = \max \{\operatorname{supp}(\operatorname{proj}_{X_j}(S_i))\}$
> For $(x, y) \in [m_i, M_i]$
>   Let $R(x, y) = R(x, y) \vee \min \{C_i(x), S_i(y)\}$

Comment: $[m_i, M_i]$ stands for $[m_{i,1}, M_{i,1}] \times \dots \times [m_{i,k_1}, M_{i,k_1}] \times [m_{i,k_1+1}, M_{i,k_1+1}] \times \dots \times [m_{i,k_1+k_2}, M_{i,k_1+k_2}]$ so there are $k_1 k_2$ limited cycles nested into each other here; min $\{C_i(x), S_i(y)\}$ equals $R_i(x, y)$

For $j = 1$ to k_1
    if $d_j = $ nil, then let $d_j = m_{i,j}$ else if $m_{i,j} < d_j < M_{i,j}$
    then let $d_j = m_{i,j}$ else if $d_j < m_{i,j} < u_j$ then
    nop else if $D_j < m_{i,j}$ then let $d_j = (d_j \rightarrow m_{i,j})$
    if $u_j = $ nil then let $u_j = M_{i,j}$ else if $M_{i,j} > u_j > m_{i,j}$
    then let $u_j = M_{i,j}$ else if $u_j = M_{i,j} > d_j$ then
    nop else if $d_j > M_{i,j}$ then let $u_j = (u_j \rightarrow M_{i,j})$

Comment: $<$ and $>$ are understood as referring to any element in the chains d_j and u_j, respectively
For $j = k_1 + 1$ to $k_1 + k_2$
    if $D_j = $ nil then let $D_j = m_{i,j}$ else if $m_{i,j} < D_j < M_{i,j}$
    then let $D_j = m_{i,j}$ else if $D_j < m_{i,j} < U_j$ then
    nop else if $D_j = m_{i,j}$ then let $D_j = (D_j \rightarrow m_{i,j})$
    if $U_j = $ nil then let $U_j = M_{i,j}$ else if $M_{i,j} > U_j < m_{i,j}$
    then let $U_j = M_{i,j}$ else if $U_j > M_{i,j} > D_j$ then
    nop else if $D_j = M_{i,j}$ then let $U_j = (U_j \rightarrow M_{i,j})$

Comment: $<$ and $>$ are understood as referring to any element in the chains D_j and U_j, respectively
For $(x, y) \in [\min \{\mathrm{supp}(\mathrm{proj}_{x_j}(A))\}, \max \{\mathrm{supp}(\mathrm{proj}_{x_j}(A))\} \times [D_j, U_j]$ let $B(x, y) = R(x, y) \wedge A(x)$
For $i = 1$ to k_2

$$\text{let } b_i = \sum_{x \in X} \sum_{y \in Y - Y_i} y_i B(x, y) \Big/ \sum_{y \in Y_i} y_i$$

This algorithm seems to be very complicated. Indeed, the program realizing it is much longer than the one for Algorithm 2. However, running time is much shorter! The size of the spaces where the rules are different from 0 are small in comparison to the universe sizes. The accumulation of an arbitrary rule needs only a number of computational steps bounded by a not very large constant, and so the whole subspace of $X \times Y$ where $R(x, y)$ is different from 0 is small in comparison to the total space size. Also the number of steps in connection with $A(x, y)$ will be only proportional with r. The total number of steps in the algorithm will grow proportionally with the number of rules in the system. An essential property of the algorithm is that it does not care about clearing the representational matrix for the rule space, so there is absolutely no need for going along the points of the space. Instead of clearing we apply a system of administering the hyperintervals representing any rule with the help of intervals or interval chains while all other parts in the space are marked as empty (but not empty physically).

The computational complexity is

$$C_3 = rL^{k_1+k_2} + L^{k_1}(rL)^{k_2} + k_2(2L^{k_1}(rL)^{k_2-1} + n + k_2)$$

As L and k_i are constants, $C_3 = O(r^{k_2})$ i.e., it is polynomial.

Applying Algorithm 3 for an unlimited number of rules with an unlimited number of fuzzy terms is still allowed and as restriction only the boundedness of terms and the constantness of the number of fuzzy variables (stability of the structure of the "If... then ..." statements) is required.

A serious disadvantage of Algorithm 3 is that although it allows fast and "good" reasoning, the boundedness of fuzzy terms results in a universe of discourse thinly covered by rules. How to overcome this difficulty is the topic of some further investigations in the direction of rule interpolation, which has been done in Kóczy (1991b).

We would like to express our gratitude to A. Juhász, who wrote the programs demonstrating Algorithms 1, 2 and 3, and prepared the computer graphics illustrations.

Keywords: rule-based fuzzy inference, approximate reasoning, rule compaction, polynomial complexity

BIBLIOGRAPHY

Aho, A. V., J. E. Hopcroft, and J. D. Ullmann. (1974). The design and analysis of computer algorithms. Reading, MA: Addison-Wesley.

Hirota, K., Y. Arai, and Sh. Hachisu. (1987). Real time fuzzy pattern recognition and fuzzy controlled robot-arm. *Prepr. Second IFSA Congr.,* Tokyo, 274–277.

Kacprzyk, J. (1978). A branch-and-bound algorithm for the multistage control of a nonfuzzy system in a fuzzy environment. *Control and Cyb.,* 7, 51–64.

King, P. J. and E. H. Mamdani. (1977). The application of fuzzy control systems to industrial processes. *Automatica,* 13, 235–242.

Kóczy, L. T. (1990). Complexity of bounded compact rule based fuzzy inference. *Proc. Third Joint IFSA-EC & EURO-WG Workshop on Fuzzy Sets,* Visegrád, 59–60.

Kóczy, L. T. (1991a). On the computational complexity of rule based fuzzy inference. *NAFIPS-91* Columbia, MO.

Kóczy, L. T. (1991b). Complexity of fuzzy rule based reasoning. *EURO XI,* Aachen.

Kóczy, L. T. and K. Hirota. (1990). Fuzzy inference by compact rules. *Proc. of Inf. Conf. Fuzzy Logic & Neural. Network, IIZUKA '90,* Iizuka, pp. 307–310.

Kóczy, L. T. and K. Hirota. (1991). Rule interpolation in approximate reasoning based fuzzy control. *4th IFSA World Congr.* Brussels.

Mamdani, E. H. (1974). Application of fuzzy algorithms for the control of a dynamic plant. *Proc. IEE 121,* **12,** 1585–1588.

Mamdani, E. H. (1977). Application of fuzzy logic to approximate reasoning using linguistic synthesis. *IEEE Tr. Comp. C-26,* **12,** 1182–1191.

Sugeno, M. and M. Nishida. (1985). Fuzzy control of model car. *Fuzzy Sets and Systems,* **16,** 103–113.

Zadeh, L. A. (1968). Fuzzy algorithms. *Info. Control,* **12,** 94–102.

Zadeh, L. A. (1974). Fuzzy logic and approximate reasoning. *Memo. ERL-M479.* Electronics Res. Lab., University of California, Berkeley.

Zadeh, L. A. (1975). The concept of a linguistic variable and its application to approximate reasoning. *Info. Sci.,* **8,** 199–249.

16 Positive and negative explanations of uncertain reasoning in the framework of possibility theory

Henri FARRENY and Henri PRADE
Institut de Recherche en Informatique de Toulouse
Université Paul Sabatier, 118 route de Narbonne
31062 Toulouse Cédex, FRANCE

Abstract. This paper presents an approach for developing the explanation capabilities of rule-based expert systems managing imprecise and uncertain knowledge. The treatment of uncertainty takes place in the framework of possibility theory where the available information concerning the value of a logical or numerical variable is represented by a possibility distribution, which restricts its more or less possible values. We first discuss different kinds of queries asking for explanations before focusing on the following two types: (1) how a particular possibility distribution is obtained (emphasizing the *main* reasons only); (2) why, in a computed possibility distribution, a particular value has received a possibility degree which is so high, so low, or so contrary to the expectation. The approach is based on the exploitation of equations in max-min algebra. This formalism includes the limit case of certain and precise information.

1. INTRODUCTION

If we take apart pioneering works like MYCIN and TEIRESIAS (Shortliffe, 1976; Davis and Lenat, 1982; Buchanan and Shortliffe,

1984) or PROSPECTOR (Reboh, 1983), most of the works for developing the explanation capabilities of expert systems do not take into account uncertainty. What is proposed in MYCIN is limited to the treatment of two types of questions: "how has this conclusion been established?" and "why has the system tried to establish this fact?" In both cases, answers are directly built by exhibiting an appropriate part of the evaluation tree of the fact to which the question refers. However, there exist various attempts to explain conclusions obtained by probabilistic inference, e.g., in the PATHFINDER system (Horvitz et al., 1986); see Horvitz et al., (1988, pp. 283–286) for a survey. Moreover, a new approach has been recently proposed by Strat (1987), and Strat and Lowrance (1988) for the explanation of results obtained in the framework of a Shafer evidence theory-based inference system. Indeed, taking into account uncertainty somewhat enriches the variety of questions worth considering and creates further problems. This is explored in the following, using possibility theory (Zadeh, 1978; Dubois and Prade, 1988) for the modeling of imprecision and uncertainty.

Section 2 gives the necessary background on the possibilistic inference method, which is used in expert system shells such as TAIGER (Farreny et al., 1986) or TOULMED (Buisson et al., 1987). In Section 3, various kinds of queries asking for explanations are introduced and discussed. Section 4 proposes a unified approach, based on the exploitation of equations in max-min algebra, to the management of (1) questions asking for the main facts which lead to a(n) (uncertain) conclusion, (2) explanations of the way of improving the certainty of a conclusion, and (3) explanations giving conditions that should be satisfied in order to have a particular conclusion, different from the real one. This extends the distinction between *positive* and *negative* explanations (Rousset and Safar, 1987). In the concluding remarks, the approach is briefly compared with one developed by Strat and Lowrance.

2. POSSIBILISTIC INFERENCE

2.1. Basic Steps of the Inference Process

In possibility theory, the available information about the value of a single-valued attribute **a** for a given item x is represented by a possibility distribution $\pi_{a(x)}$, i.e., a mapping from the attribute domain U to $[0,1]$, which restricts the more or less possible values of $a(x)$, $\pi_{a(x)}(u)$ estimates to what extent it is possible that $a(x) = u$; $\pi_{a(x)}$ is supposed to be normalized, i.e., $\sup_{u \in U} \pi_{a(x)}(u) = 1$; this is satisfied as soon as at least one value in U is considered as completely possible (i.e., possible to degree 1) for $a(x)$. The state of total ignorance about the value of $a(x)$ is represented by $\pi_{a(x)}(u) = 1$, for each $u \in U$. The uncertainty attached to a rule "if p then q" is represented by the possibility distribution $(\pi(q|p), \pi(\neg q|p)) \in [0,1]^2$ on the two element set $\{q, \neg q\}$ in the context p. The normalization condition writes here $\max(\pi(q|p), \pi(\neg q|p)) = 1$. We may also have similar information in the context $\neg p$. Note that $\pi(q|p) = 1$ and $\pi(\neg q|p) = 0$ means that q is certainly true in the context p, while the larger $\pi(\neg q|p)$ the more uncertain q (when $\pi(q|p) = 1$). We consider rules of the form "if p_l and... and p_n then q" with $p \triangleq p_1 \wedge ... \wedge p_n$. Then the inference proceeds along five distinct steps (Dubois and Prade, 1988):

(i) The inference engine estimates to what extent it is possible that the elementary condition p_i is satisfied (let $\pi(p_i)$ denote this possibility) and to what extent it is possible that the condition is not satisfied $(\pi(-p_i))$, taking into account the available information in the factual basis; $\pi(p_i)$ and $\pi(\neg p_i)$ are obtained through a fuzzy pattern-matching technique

$$\pi(p_i) = \sup_{u \in U} \min(\mu_{p_i}(u), \pi^{p_i}(u));$$
$$\pi(\neg p_i) = \sup_{u \in U} \min(1 - \mu_{p_i}(u), \pi^{p_i}(u)) \quad (1)$$

where μ_{p_i} and π^{p_i} are the normalized membership functions of the subsets (maybe fuzzy) of U, which respectively represent the condition p_i and the corresponding available information (i.e., π^{p_i} is the possibility distribution restricting the more or less possible values of the attribute concerned by p_i for the considered item). When p_i is a nonvague property, thus represented by a nonfuzzy subset p_i, we have $\max(\pi(p_i), \pi(\neg p_i)) = 1$.

(ii) These possibility degrees are aggregated (in accordance to possibility theory) in order to estimate to what extent it is possible that the whole condition p holds $(\pi(p))$, or does not hold $(\pi(\neg p))$. It is assumed that the elementary conditions are logically independent. Then we have

$$\pi(p) = \min_{i=1,n} \pi(p_i)$$
$$\pi(\neg p) = \max_{i=1,n} \pi(\neg p_i) \quad (2)$$

In case the elementary conditions are not equally important, in order to detach the conclusion, formulas (2) are generalized by

$$\pi(p) = \min_{i=1,n} \max \ (\pi(p_i), \ 1 - w_i)$$
$$\pi(\neg p) = \max_{i=1,n} \min \ (\pi(p_i), \ w_i)$$

(3)

where the weights of importance w_i satisfy the normalization condition $\max_{i=1,n} w_i = 1$. In case of the disjunction (rather than the conjunction) of elementary conditions, we have to change min into max, max into min, and w_i into $1 - w_i$ in (2) and (3).

(iii) The possibility degrees $\pi(\neg q)$ and $\pi(\neg q)$ that the conclusion is true, respectively false is obtained via the matrix product

$$\begin{bmatrix} \pi(q) \\ \pi(\neg q) \end{bmatrix} = \begin{bmatrix} \pi(q|p) & \pi(q|q \ \neg p) \\ \pi(\neg q|p) & \pi(\neg q|\neg p) \end{bmatrix} \begin{bmatrix} \pi(p) \\ \pi(\neg p) \end{bmatrix}$$

(4)

where the maximum operation plays the role of the sum and the minimum operation the role of the product (i.e., for instance $\pi(q) = \max \ (\min(\pi(q|p), \ \pi(p)), \min(\pi q|\neg p), \ \pi(\neg p)))$). This matrix product preserves the normalization condition.

(iv) Let μ_Q be the membership function that represents the restriction expressed by q, i.e., $q \overset{\Delta}{=} "b(y)$ is $Q"$ where b denotes the attribute underlying q and y is the considered item (we have $\pi_{b(y)} = \mu_Q$). Then the uncertainty, modeled by $(\pi(q), \pi(\neg q))$, which pervades the conclusion, induces the new possibility distribution $\pi^*_{b(y)}$

$$\pi^*_{b(y)} = \min \ (\max \ (\mu_Q, \ \pi(\neg q)), \ \max \ (\mu_{\neg Q}, \pi(q)))$$

(5)

with $\mu_{\neg Q} = 1 - \mu_Q$; $\pi^*_{b(y)}$ expresses that if q is uncertain $(\pi(\neg q) > 0$ and $\pi(q) = 1)$, then the values outside Q are possible to degree $\pi(\neg q)$. When μ_Q is the membership function of an ordinary (i.e., nonfuzzy) subset, (5) can be equivalently written

$$\pi^*_{b(y)} = \max \ (\min \ (\mu_Q, \pi(q)), \ \min(u_{\neg Q}, \pi(\neg q)))$$

(6)

This latter expression is more convenient for performing the conjunctive combination in step (v).

(v) Several rules may conclude on the value of the same attribute b, then the different possibility distributions $\pi^*_{b(y)}$ obtained at step (iv) have to be combined; for instance, in case of two possibility distributions $\pi^*_{b(y)1}$ and $\pi^*_{b(y)2}$, using (6) and the distributivity, we get

$$\min \ (\pi^*_{b(y)1}, \ \pi^*_{b(y)2} = \max \ (\min \ (\mu_{Q1}, \mu_{Q2}, \pi(q_1), \pi(q_2)),$$

$$\min(\mu_{Q1}, \mu_{\neg Q2}, \pi(q_1), \pi(\neg q_2)), \min(\mu_{\neg Q1}, \mu_{Q2},$$
$$\pi(\neg q_1), \pi(q_2)), \min(\mu_{\neg Q1}, \mu_{\neg Q2}, \pi(\neg q_1), \pi(\neg q_2))) \qquad (7)$$

This combination is clearly associative and symmetrical, and thus can be iterated. The expression (7) is easy to interpret since it is a weighted union of mutually disjoint subsets $Q_1 \cap Q_2, Q_1 \cap \neg Q_2, \neg Q_1 \cap Q_2$ and $\neg Q_1 \cap \neg Q_2$, which cover the attribute domain.

Note: The max-min form (6) is permitted only if Q is an ordinary subset. However, this is not a severe limitation. Indeed, consider the case of two rules "if p then q," and, "if p then q'''" where $Q \subseteq Q'$ and $\pi(\neg q|p) \geqslant \pi(\neg q'|p)$ since a rule should be all the more certain as its conclusion is imprecise. Then, we obtained as the result of the combination step a possibility distribution equal to (when $\pi(p) = 1$)

$$\max(\mu_Q, \min(\mu_{Q'}, \pi(\neg q)), \pi(\neg q')) =$$
$$= \max[\max(\mu_Q, \min(\mu_{Q'}, \pi(\neg q|p)), \pi(\neg q'|p)), \pi(\neg p)]$$

It indicates that several rules with the same condition part and more or less precise and uncertain (but not vague) conclusions bearing on the same attribute (the more precise the conclusion, the more uncertain), are equivalent to one rule with a vague conclusion represented by a fuzzy set (with a stairlike membership function). Thus a rule with a fuzzy conclusion can be always approximated by a collection of rules with uncertain (but nonfuzzy) conclusions.

2.2. Example

Let us illustrate this approach on the following simple example where we have four rules, which, in a very sketchy and incomplete way, conclude on professions that can be recommended to people:

R1: if a person likes meeting people, then recommended professions are professor, businessperson, lawyer, or doctor.

R2: if a person is fond of creation/invention, then recommended professions are engineer, researcher, or architect.

R'2: if a person is not fond of creation/invention, then he or she cannot be an engineer, a researcher, or an architect.

R3: if a person looks for job security and is fond of intellectual speculation, then recommended professions are professor or researcher.

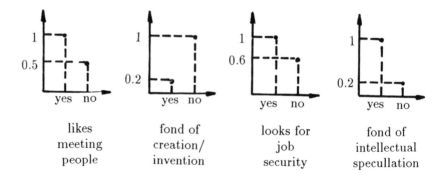

Figure 16.1.

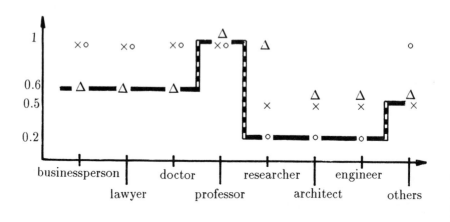

× × ×:	results given by $R1$
○ ○ ○:	results given by $R'2, R''2$
△△△:	results given by $R3$
▬▬▬:	final result

Figure 16.2.

All these rules are pervaded with uncertainty; they are respectively represented by the matrices

$$\begin{bmatrix} 1 & 1 \\ 0.3 & 1 \end{bmatrix} \text{for R1,} \begin{bmatrix} 1 & 0.2 \\ 0.4 & 1 \end{bmatrix} \text{for R2 and R'2, and} \begin{bmatrix} 1 & 1 \\ 0.3 & 1 \end{bmatrix} \text{for R3}$$

The numbers mirror our beliefs in the possibility of exceptions for the various rules. Let us consider a person, say Peter, whose profile is indicated in Figure 16.1. For instance, the first possibility distribution in Figure 16.1 indicates that it is not sure at all that Peter truly likes meeting people even if he has some propensity for that, i.e., π(Peter does not like meeting people) $= 0.5$. Applying the five steps of the inference procedure to this example yields the possibility distribution given in Figure 16.2. Note the introduction of "others" in the profession domain. It corresponds to the following understanding of the rules: professions not explicitly recommended (including "others") will be possible only to the extent to which the rule does not apply or has exceptions. The resulting possibility distribution may then be unnormalized for some preference profiles. A way to guarantee its normalization is to consider that "others" is implicitly among the recommended professions in any case (i.e., only professions explicitly considered by the expert can be [somewhat] excluded).

3. VARIOUS KINDS OF QUERIES ASKING FOR EXPLANATIONS

We have seen that a conclusion obtained by the inference system is represented under the form of a possibility distribution. Then the following questions can be considered:

a. How is the possibility distribution obtained? This is the direct counterpart of the MYCIN question "how." The answer is elaborated from the complete sequence of operations from which the possibility distribution results.

b. How, *mainly*, is the possibility distribution obtained? This may be understood at least in two different ways:

. What are the main facts (and/or rules) that determine the resulting possibility distribution? This means, for instance, that partial conclusions that are too imprecise or too uncertain to influence the final conclusion need not be explained;

. What are the intermediary results that may be the most surprising ones for the person who questions the system? This requires maintaining a model of the user's beliefs. The extent to which a conclusion appears surprising can be computed as a degree of incompatibility between the obtained conclusion and the user's belief, i.e., by the quantity

$$1 - \sup_u \min (\mu_{Co}(u), \mu_{Be}(u))$$

where Co and Be are the fuzzy sets of possible values representing the conclusion and the user's belief, respectively. This quantity estimates to what extent the intersection between the fuzzy sets Co and Be is empty.

c. Why do particular values of the conclusion domain have a possibility degree which is zero (or which is so low)? Then the problem is to point out the key facts determining the considered possibility degrees. More generally, one may ask why a particular possibility distribution has not been derived in place of the obtained one. We shall see in Section 4 that this leads to the resolution of relational equations in max-min algebra.

d. Why is the obtained conclusion so uncertain and imprecise (i.e., all the values in the domain have a possibility degree equal or close)? This may be due to (1) the uncertainty and imprecision pervading the available information; (2) the existence of a conflict between partial conclusions, which makes impossible the emergence of some values(s); (3) the limitations of the inference system (e.g., many rule-based inference systems are not able to conclude "s or t" from "if p then s," "if q then t" and "p or q"; for avoiding this limitation, the system has to be able to combine the rules themselves rather than the obtained conclusions). Note also that the research of ways to improve a too-uncertain or imprecise conclusion may oblige the system to not limit the investigation to the evaluation tree of the conclusion. For instance, if we have two rules, one "if p then r" which is quite uncertain and another one "if q then e," which is not pervaded with uncertainty, but which was not fired due to the lack of information about q, the way to improve the conclusion is to obtain information about q.

e. How would the possibility distribution of the conclusion be modified if the possibility distribution(s) attached to (a) particular fact(s) is (are) modified? This requires a sensitivity analysis based on analytical expressions.

f. Why did the system try to evaluate a particular fact? This is the counterpart of the MYCIN question "why," which can be dealt with in a similar way.

4. PRESENTATION OF THE PROPOSED APPROACH

In this section we focus our attention on the relationship between facts and obtained conclusions. We are more particularly interested in the treatment of questions of type b, c, d, e, considered in the preceding section. One sequence of steps, i, ii, iii, iv, v (presented in Section 2), constitutes an inference layer. In the course of a reasoning this process is iterated. In the following we consider the production of explanations for a given inference layer. Clearly more complex explanations can be built by iteration.

For performing explanations at the level of an inference layer, it is pÑossible to take advantage of a system of equations (linear in max-min algebra) that relates the degrees of compatibility between facts and conditions of rules to the possibility distribution representing the conclusion. Indeed for each (uncertain) rule R_i of the form "if p_i then $x \in E_i$", the propagation law can be written

$$\begin{bmatrix} \pi(E_i) \\ \pi(\neg E_i) \end{bmatrix} \begin{bmatrix} \alpha_i \\ \beta_i \end{bmatrix} = \begin{bmatrix} \pi(E_i|p_i) & \pi(E_i|\neg p_i) \\ \pi(\neg E_i|p_i) & \pi(\neg E_i|\neg p_i) \end{bmatrix} \begin{bmatrix} \pi(p_i) \\ \pi(\neg p_i) \end{bmatrix} \triangleq \begin{bmatrix} 1 & s_i \\ r_i & 1 \end{bmatrix} \begin{bmatrix} \lambda_i \\ \rho_i \end{bmatrix}$$

that is,

$\alpha_i = \max(\lambda_i, \min(s_i, p_i)) = \max(\lambda_i, s_i)$ since $\max(\lambda_i, \rho_i) = 1$
$\beta_i = \max(\min(r_i, \lambda_i), \rho_i) = \max(r_i, \rho_i)$

The possibility distribution π resulting from the combination of the obtained results from each rule R_i is given by (in the case of 3 partial conclusions as in our example)

$$\begin{aligned} \pi &= \min_{i=1,3} \max[\min(\mu_{Ei}, \alpha_i), \min(\mu_{-Ei}, \beta_i)] \\ &= \max_{\substack{j=1,2; k=1,2 \\ l=1,2}} \min(\mu_{Fj}, \mu_{Fk}, \mu_{Fl}, \gamma_j, \gamma_k, \gamma_l) \\ &= \max_{\substack{j=1,2; k=1,2 \\ l=1,2}} \min(\mu_{Fj \cap Fk \cap Fl}, \gamma_j, \gamma_k, \gamma_l) \end{aligned}$$

with: $F_j = E_1$ and $\gamma_j = \alpha_1$ if $j = 1$; $F_j = \neg E_1$ and $\gamma_j = \beta_1$ if $j = 2$; $F_k = E_2$ and $\gamma_k = \alpha_2$ if $k = 1$; $F_k = \neg E_2$ and $\gamma_k = \beta_2$ if $k = 2$; $F_l = E_3$ and $\gamma_l = \alpha_3$ if $l = 1$; $F_l = -E_3$ and $\gamma_1 = \beta_3$ if $l = 2$.

In our example, $E_1 \cap E_2 = \emptyset$ and $E_3 \subseteq E_1 \cup E_2$. This induces the partition $E_1 \cap \neg E_3 = \{$businessperson, lawyer, doctor$\}$, $E_1 \cap E_3 = \{$professor$\}$, $E_2 \cap E_3 = \{$researcher$\}$, $E_2 \cap \neg E_3 = \{$engineer, architect$\}$, $\neg E_1 \cap \neg E_2 = \{$others$\}$. It yields

$$
\begin{array}{ll}
\text{if } u \in E_1 \cap \neg E_3 & \pi(u) = \min(\alpha_1, \beta_2, \beta_3) \\
\text{if } u \in E_1 \cap E_3 & \pi(u) = \min(\alpha_1, \beta_2, \alpha_3) \\
\text{if } u \in E_2 \cap E_3 & \pi(u) = \min(\beta_1, \alpha_2, \alpha_3) \\
\text{if } u \in E_2 \cap \neg E_3 & \pi(u) = \min(\beta_1, \alpha_2, \beta_3) \\
\text{if } u \in \neg E_1 \cap \neg E_2 & \pi(u) = \min(\beta_1, \beta_2, \beta_3)
\end{array}
$$

and finally replacing the α_1 and β_j by their values, it gives, in a matrix form

$$
\begin{bmatrix}
x_{E_1 \cap \neg E_3} \\
x_{E_1 \cap E_3} \\
x_{E_2 \cap E_3} \\
x_{E_2 \cap \neg E_3} \\
x_{\neg E_1 \cap \neg E_2}
\end{bmatrix}
=
\begin{bmatrix}
s_1 & 1 & 1 & r_2 & 1 & r_3 \\
s_1 & 1 & 1 & r_2 & s_3 & 1 \\
1 & r_1 & s_2 & 1 & s_3 & 1 \\
1 & r_1 & s_2 & 1 & 1 & r_3 \\
1 & r_1 & 1 & r_2 & 1 & r_3
\end{bmatrix}
\blacksquare
\begin{bmatrix}
\lambda_1 \\
\rho_1 \\
\lambda_2 \\
\rho_2 \\
\lambda_3 \\
\rho_3
\end{bmatrix}
$$

where $\blacksquare$ denotes the *min-max product*. In the example we have for the rules $r_1 = 0.3$; $s_1 = 1$; $r_2 = 0.4$; $s_2 = 0.2$; $r_3 = 0.3$; $s_3 = 1$, which gives

$$x_{E_1 \cap \neg E_3} = x \text{ professor or doctor} = \min(\max(p_2, 0.4), \max(\rho_3, 0.3)) \qquad (\alpha)$$
$$x_{E_1 \cap E_3} = x \text{ professor} = \max(\rho_2, 0.4) \qquad (\beta)$$
$$x_{E_2 \cap E_3} = x \text{ researcher} = \min(\max(\rho_1, 0.3), \max(\lambda_2, 0.2)) \qquad (\gamma)$$
$$x_{E_2 \cap \neg E_3} = x \text{ engineer or architect} = \min(\max(\rho_1, 0.3), \max(\lambda_2, 0.2),$$
$$\max(\rho_3, 0.3)) \qquad (\delta)$$
$$x_{\neg E_1 \cap \neg E_2} = x \text{ others} = \min(\max(\rho_1, 0.3), \max(\rho_2, 0.4), \max(\rho_3, 0.3)) \qquad (\varepsilon)$$

where λ_1 (resp. ρ_1) is the possibility that the person likes (resp. does not like) meeting people, λ_2 (resp. ρ_2) is the possibility that the person is fond of (resp. is not fond of) creation/invention, λ_3 (resp. ρ_3) is the possibility that the person looks for job security *and* is fond of intellectual speculation (resp. does not look for job security *or* is not fond of intellectual speculation).

Generally speaking, an equation system, such as S, relates an input vector IV representing the compatibility between facts and conditions of rules, an output vector OV describing the resulting possibility distribution, and a matrix MR that characterizes the set of rules. It can be formally written $OV = MR \blacksquare IV$. There are two main ways for using this equation for explanation purposes according to what is the unknown, IV or OV.

Considering the equations of system S, we can directly read the components of IV that contribute to the expression of a particular component of OV. It should be clear that any value in the domain is a priori completely possible and that partial conclusions may only contribute to make a particular value (more or less) impossible. For instance, equation (α) in the example expresses that businessperson, lawyer, or doctor are somewhat impossible (however the possibility cannot go below 0.3 in any case) among the recommended professions if it is (quite) certain that the person is fond of creation/invention (ρ_2 is zero or low), or he or she looks for job security and is fond of intellectual speculation (ρ_3 is zero or low); in fact these two situations lead to other recommended professions. Obviously the expressions (α) through (ε) enable the system to perform a straightforward sensitivity analysis of OV in terms of IV.

Let us suppose that IV is known. For instance, in Peter's case $\rho_2 = 1$ and $\rho_3 = 0.6$. Then equation (α) makes clear (since $\min(\max(1,0.4), \max(0.6,0.3)) = \rho_3 = 0.6$) that the conclusion that businessperson, lawyer, or doctor is possible only to degree 0.6 is mainly due to the fact that it is somewhat certain (to degree $1 - \rho_3 = 0.4$) that the person looks for job security and is fond of intellectual speculation. Thus, it is possible to point out the state of facts that determines any particular possibility degree.

Let us suppose now that OV is fixed (and IV unknown). For instance, looking at Peter's case, we are astonished that his degree of possibility for having the profession of researcher recommended is so low (0.2), and we ask for what would make it possible (at least) to degree 0.8. The equation (γ), which makes obvious that the possibility degree may take any value between 0.2 and 1, leads to the condition $\rho_1 \geqslant 0.8$ and $\lambda_2 \geqslant 0.8$; i.e., it should be possible at least to degree 0.8 that the person does not like meeting people (otherwise other professions would be recommended according to rule R1) and it should be possible at least to degree 0.8 that the person is fond of creation/invention (since it is a somewhat *necessary condition* for being a researcher according to R'2). Note that any pair (ρ_1, $\lambda_2) \in [0.8,1]^2$ guarantees the required degree of possibility. We see that the information conveyed by the equations of system (S), here the equation (γ), is not trivial in the sense that it encompasses the effect of several rules.

More generally, the possibility that a particular OV is obtainable can be discussed by solving the equation OV = MR ■ IV. This can be easily done using results on fuzzy relation equations (see Sanchez, 1977 in particular). These results give (1) the conditions of existence of a solution, (2) the expression of the smallest solution (in the sense of fuzzy set inclusion: $F \subseteq G \rightleftharpoons \mu_F \leqslant \mu_G$) if there exists a solution, and (3) the largest solutions (there may be several), if there exists a solution.

We have discussed only the system of equations relating the compatibility of facts with conditions of rules and the possibility distribution representing the conclusion, for the sake of brevity. Two other families of max-min or min-max equations can be exploited in an explanation process, namely the expressions of the compatibility of an elementary condition of a rule with available information (given by equations (1), and the expressions of the global compatibilities in terms of elementary ones (taking into account the level of importance of elementary conditions if they are unequal) in case of compound conditions (see equation (3)). We have presented the explanation process for one layer of inference only, for the sake of brevity. We believe that we have often to remain at this level in order to produce explanations understandable by the user. Obviously, we can work across several layers of inference, by iterating the explanation process in cascade. See Farreny and Prade (1989) for details. Alternatively, it would be possible to take advantage of the properties of the max-min algebra for producing the equations relating an input vector and an output vector through several layers of rules.

Note: In our approach, what is computed by the system is a possibility distribution, which can be explained and justified to the user as shown above. However, the user may also ask his or her questions in terms of *certainty* (rather than possibility). For instance, in our example, why it is not more certain that Peter should be professor? This is equivalent to explaining why it is still somewhat possible that he considers other professions, i.e., to explaining the other relatively high degrees of possibility.

5. CONCLUSION

In this paper we use the framework of possibility theory for representing uncertainty and imprecision. It turns out that this framework seems convenient to produce rather sophisticated explanations in a rather manageable way. The approach takes advantage of the properties of max-min algebra. It enables us also to identify easily in a min (or max) combination what are the components determining the value of the result (it contrasts with operations used in other calculus, such as probabilities: in a product, for instance, all the factors "contribute" to the result except one of them is the neutral element "1". In our approach we have chosen to build the explanation in terms of facts, considering that the levels of uncertainty of the rules could not be discussed and also that the expert rules were more or less known by the user. If it is not the case, the equations on which our approach is based can also be exploited for pointing out the role played by the uncertainty of rules.

As we noted earlier, Strat and Lowrance (1987, 1988) have recently developed an approach in the framework of Shafer's (1976) evidence theory. However, in their system, GISTER, the uncertainty pervades only the facts (since the so-called compatibility relations they allow between universes of discourse are equivalent to imprecise but certain rules). Their system is able to explain the degree of belief of a fact and what are the facts that make not too imprecise or uncertain a conclusion. Their sensitivity analysis is based on the way a conclusion is modified when facts are discounted and makes use of entropylike measures, which respectively estimate the dissonance and the specificity (i.e., precision) of a basic probability assignment representing a fact. Mathematically speaking, possibility measures are particular cases of Shafer's plausibility functions. So, it would be possible to apply Strat and Lowrance's approach in the possibilistic case and to take advantage of specificity measures for characterizing the quality of conclusions in a *global way* (dissonance measures are always zero in possibility theory; see Dubois and Prade [1987] for a survey of entropy-like measures in possibility and evidence theories). The simplest measure of imprecision (or nonspecificity) of a finite fuzzy set F is its scalar cardinality $|F| = \Sigma u \; \mu_F(u)$. Clearly the smaller the cardinality of a possibility distribution the more precise the result that this distribution represents. However, it is perhaps more useful to analyse the *local* influence of facts on the possibility of a particular output value, rather than their global influence on the whole possibility distribution.

Keywords: expert system, inference, uncertainty, explanation, possibility theory

BIBLIOGRAPHY

Buchanan, B. and E. Shortliffe. (1948). *Rule-Based Expert Systems – The MYCIN Experiments of the Stanford Heuristic Programming Project.* Reading, MA: Addison-Wesley.

Buisson, J. C., H. Farreny, H. Prade, M. C. Turnin, J. P. Tauber, and F. Bayard. (1987). TOULMED, an inference engine which deals with imprecise and uncertain aspects of medical knowledge. *Proc. Europ. Conf. on Artificial Intelligence in Medicine* (AIME-87), Marseille, 1987, J. Fox, M. Fieschi, R. Engelbrecht (eds.), vol. 33, Lecture Notes in Medical Informatics, Springer-Verlag, pp. 123–140.

Davis, R. and D. B. Lenat. (1982). *Knowledge-Based Systems in Artificial Intelligence.* New York: McGraw-Hill.

Dubois, D. and H. Prade. (1987). Properties of measures of information in evidence and possibility theories. *Fuzzy Sets and Systems,* 24, 161–182.

Dubois, D. and H. Prade. (1988) (with the collaboration of H. Farreny, and R. Martin-Clouaire, C. Testamale). *Possibility Theory: An Approach to Computerized Processing of Uncertainty.* New York: Plenum Press. (French version: 1st ed. 1985 and 2d ed. 1987).

Farreny, H. and H. Prade. (1989). Explications de raisonnements dans l'incertain. Tech. Rep. LSI-IRIT, Univ. P. Sabatier, Toulouse (29 p.).

Farreny, H., H. Prade, and E. Wyss. (1986). Approximate reasoning in a rule-based expert system using possibility theory; a case study. *Proc. Tenth World IFIP Congress,* Dublin, 1986; Information Processing '86, H.J. Kugler (ed.), Amsterdam: North-Holland, pp. 407–413.

Horvitz E. J., J. S. Breese, and M. Henrion. (1988). Decision theory in expert systems and artificial intelligence. *Int. J. of Approximate Reasoning* 2, 247–302.

Horvitz, E. J., D. E. Heckerman, B. N. Nathwani, and L. M. Fagen. (1986). The use of a heuristic problem solving hierarchy to facilitate the explanation of hypothesis directed reasoning. *Proc. Medinfo 86,* Washington, D.C., R. Salomon, B. Blum, M. Jorgensen (eds.). Amsterdam: North-Holland, pp. 27–31.

Reboh, R. (1983). Extracting useful advice from conflicting expertise. *Proc. Sixth Inter. Joint Conf. on Artificial Intelligence (IJCAI 83),* Karlsruhe, West Germany, August, pp. 145–150.

Rousset, M. C. and B. Safar. (1987). Negative and positive explanations in expert systems. *Applied Artificial Intelligence,* 1, 25–38.

Sanchez, E. (1977). Solutions in composite fuzzy relation equations: Application to medical diagnosis in Brouwerian logic. In M. M. Gupta, G. N. Saridis, and B. R. Gaines (eds.): *Fuzzy Automata and Decision Processes.* New York: North-Holland, pp. 221–234.

Shafer, G. A. (1976). *A. Mathematical Theory of Evidence.* Princeton University Press.

Shortliffe, E. H. (1976). *Computer-Based Medical Consultations: MYCIN.* New York: American Elsevier.

Strat, T. M. (1987). The generation of explanations within evidential reasoning systems. *Proc. Tenth Inter. Joint Conf. on Artificial Intelligence (IJCAI-87),* Milano, August, pp. 1097–1104.

Strat, T. M. and J. D. Lowrance. (1988). Explaining evidential analyses. Tech. Rep. SRI Inter., Menlo Park, CA. (To appear in *Int. J. of Approximate Reasoning.*)

Zadeh, L. A. (1978). Fuzzy sets as a basis for a theory of possibility. *Fuzzy Sets and Systems,* **1,** 3–28.

17 Inconsistency in possibilistic knowledge bases: To live with it or not live with it

Didier DUBOIS, Jérôme LANG
and Henri PRADE
Institut de Recherche en Informatique de Toulouse
Université Paul Sabatier, 118 route de Narbonne
31062 Toulouse Cédex, FRANCE

Abstract. This short paper sketches a new approach for reasoning from an inconsistent knowledge base containing pieces of information whose certainty may be graded. The approach considers the different maximal consistent sub-bases with their graded propositions instead of restoring consistency. The uncertainty of the conclusions that can be obtained from an inconsistent knowledge base, using the approach, is graded according to four indices that synthesize the global behavior of the sub-bases with respect to specific conclusions. A level of acceptability of maximal consistent sub-bases may be also estimated, which induces a natural way of ranking them. All numerical estimates are calculated in the framework of possibility theory. The approach can be viewed as a generalization of ideas already proposed for data fusion problems in case of conflicting information. Analogy with nonmonotonic reasoning is described. The problem of the revision of an inconsistent knowledge base by selecting the "best" maximal sub-base(s) is also discussed.

1. INTRODUCTION

The available knowledge may have two kinds of defects. It may be incomplete or it may be inconsistent. In the first case there is a lack of information, while in the second case, the inconsistency can be considered as created by a (local) excess of information. In case of incomplete or partial information, the truth of some propositions may remain unknown. Default knowledge may sometimes be used to establish their plausibility in a provisional way. With the addition of a new piece of information, a knowledge base that was consistent may become inconsistent and a revision process is necessary for restoring consistency. Reasoning from incomplete knowledge as well as belief revision and updating have recently been the topics of active research in artificial intelligence. See Léa Sombé (1990) and Gärdenfors (1988), respectively, for surveys on these two related issues. However, in some cases we *start* with a knowledge base that is inconsistent, and we would still like to try to reason from it. In classical logic, anything can be deduced from an inconsistent database. Some authors have proposed approaches to this problem using various nonclassical logics or systems such as relevance logics, truth-maintenance systems, or modal logics (e.g., Mitchell and O'Donnell, 1986; Martins and Shapiro, 1986; Cholvy, 1989). In the following, we deal with inconsistent knowledge bases in the framework of possibilistic logic (Dubois and Prade, 1987), taking advantage of the ordering existing between the pieces of information whose certainty is graded. The uncertainty about the truth of a given piece of knowledge may reflect the lack of complete information, the reliability of the source providing it or the fact that it is considered as an old (obsolete) item. The approach presented in Section 3 can be viewed as a generalization of ideas already proposed for data fusion problems in case of conflicting sources (Dubois and Prade, 1988a) and can be related to current concerns in nonmonotonic logic. In Section 4 we address the problem of the revision of an inconsistent knowledge base viewed as the selection of a maximal consistent sub-base. First, Section 2 restates the necessary background on possibilistic logic.

2. BACKGROUND

Let us consider a knowledge base K made of a collection of pairs of the form (c, α) where c is a ground clause in the sense of classical logic and α is a number belonging to [0,1], expressing our certainty about the truth of c. More precisely α is understood as a lower bound of the value of a necessity measure N for c, i.e., $N(c) \geqslant \alpha > 0$. The number is an estimate of the extent to which we consider c as certainly true. A clause regarded as definitely true has a weight $\alpha = 1$. A necessity measure (Dubois and Prade, 1988b) is a function N from a Boolean algebra of propositions to $[0,1]$ such that for any pair of propositions p and q we have

$$N(p \wedge q) = \min(N(p), N(q)) \tag{1}$$

and $N(p) = 1$ whenever p is a tautology, $N(p) = 0$ whenever p is a contradiction. A necessity measure N is the dual of a possibility measure Π in the sense of Zadeh (1978), i.e., we have

$$\Pi(p) = 1 - N(-p), \text{ for each } p \tag{2}$$

Interestingly enough, it can be shown (Dubois and Prade, 1990b) that the ordering induced by a necessity measure is equivalent to the ordering defined by an epistemic entrenchment relation in the sense of Gärdenfors (1988), and that only necessity measures produce this kind of ordering. The significance of this fact can be explained as follows. Epistemic entrenchment relations are at work in any rational revision process acting on a closed set of formulas, as shown by Gärdenfors. Revision is achieved by deleting the least entrenched formulas involved in the inconsistency created by the arrival of some new piece of information.

Let c_1, ..., c_n be the clauses whose conjunction is equivalent to a propositional formula f, then (f, α) is clearly equivalent to $\{(c_1, \alpha), ... (c_n, \alpha)\}$ due to the basic axiom (1) of necessity measures. Hence we can restrict ourselves to necessity-valued clauses.

Let $\mathbf{K}^*$ be classical knowledge base obtained from $\mathbf{K}$ when we forget the weights of uncertainty. Then, as proved in Dubois and Prade (1987), there is an equivalence between the inconsistency of $\mathbf{K}^*$ in the usual sense and the fact that the assignment of weights in $\mathbf{K}$ is in contradiction with axiom (1). Indeed (1) forbids simultaneous partial certainty that p is true and that p is false, since (1) entails that for each p, $\min(N(p), N(\neg p)) = N(\bot)$ where $\bot$ stands for the ever-false proposition, and $N(\bot) = 0$ by definition.

An extended resolution principle (Dubois and Prade, 1987)

$$\frac{(c,\alpha) \ (c',\beta)}{(\text{Res}(c,c'), \ \min(\alpha,\beta))} \tag{3}$$

where Res (c,c') denotes the resolvent of c and c', has been established and the refutation method can still be used, since the weight γ attached to an empty clause $\bot$ obtained by applying (3) repeatedly on pairs of clauses belonging to the union of K and the set of clauses equivalent to $(-p,1)$ is a lower bound of the necessity of the refuted proposition p, *provided that K^* is consistent.*

The soundness and completeness of the resolution principle with the refutation method has been established (Dubois, Lâng, and Prade, 1989) with respect to a semantics expressed in terms of a fuzzy set of models of the knowledge base. If f is a formula, let $M(f)$ be the set of models of f. Then the models of (f,α) will be represented by a fuzzy set $M(f,\alpha)$ with a membership function:

$$\mu_{M(f,\alpha)}(I) = \begin{cases} 1 & \text{if } I \in M(f) \\ 1 - \alpha & \text{if } I \in M(\neg f), \end{cases} \text{ where } I \text{ is a (classical)}$$
$$\text{interpretation}$$

Then the fuzzy set of models of a set of weighted formulas $K = \{(f_1,\alpha_1), ..., (f_n,\alpha_n)\}$ is defined by means of the usual fuzzy set intersection, that is:

$$\mu_{M(K)}(I) = \min_{i = 1,...,n} \mu_{M(f_i,\alpha_i)}(I)$$

The consistency degree of K will be defined by Const $(K) = \max_I \mu_{M(K)}(I)$: it estimates the degree to which the set of models of K is not empty. The quantity $\text{Inc}(K) = 1 - \text{Const}(K)$ will be called degree of inconsistency of K. A consistent possibilistic knowledge base is one such that $\text{Inc}(K) = 0$. Otherwise it is said to be inconsistent.

In the following, when K is consistent, we shall write $K \vdash (p,\gamma)$ only if $\gamma > 0$ and γ is the *greatest lower bound* of $N(p)$ that can be produced by refutation from K', where K' is the union of K with the set of clauses equivalent to $(-p,1)$. It can be shown (see Dubois, Lang, and Prade, 1989) that $\gamma = \text{Inc}(K')$, which establishes the completeness and the soundness of the refutation method. Moreover, we have: there exists $\gamma > 0$, $K \vdash (p,\gamma)] \Rightarrow K^* \vdash p$, which means that it is impossible to have $K \vdash (p,\gamma)$ and $K \vdash (-p,\gamma')$ simultaneously, if K is consistent.

3. REASONING FROM INCONSISTENT KNOWLEDGE

3.1. Four Indices for Assessing the Potential Truth of a Proposition

Now let us consider an inconsistent knowledge base B where the pieces of information are of the form (c,α) with the interpretation given in the previous section. Let $K_1^*, ..., K_m^*$ be all the maximal consistent sub-bases of B^* and $K_1, ..., K_m$ the possibilistic knowledge bases obtained by restoring the weights. By definition a sub-base K_i is such that if we add any clause in $B-K_i$ to it, the result is an inconsistent knowledge base. Each K_i can be regarded as a potential consistent "realization" of the inconsistent knowledge base B.

Then two different approaches can be considered. We may think of selecting a particular K_i and then of substituting the chosen consistent sub-base K_i to the inconsistent knowledge base B in order to evaluate propositions of interest. For choosing K_i, we may consider that K_i is all the better as the (weighted) clause(s) that have been erased from B in order to obtain K_i are less certain or less entrenched, i.e., have a smaller weight. More precisely, we may think of estimating the level of acceptability a_i of K_i by

$$a_i = 1-\max \{\alpha \,|\, (c,\alpha) \notin K_i, (c,\alpha) \in B\} \qquad (4)$$

Then it is natural to select a K_i which maximizes a_i. This is in agreement with the idea of considering the less entrenched pieces of information first, as possible candidates to be erased in order to restore the consistency of a knowledge base in a revision process; see Gärdenfors (1988). This view is discussed in further details in Section 4.

The second approach, which is the topic of Section 3, considers the whole collection of the different K_i's and, when evaluating a proposition p, tries to synthesize the relationships between p and the various K_i's from the point of view of deduction. Given a proposition p, the set of maximal consistent sub-bases $\{K_i, i = 1,m\}$, the set of indices $I = \{1,...,m\}$ can be partitioned into three parts:

(i)   Let $I^+ \subseteq I$ such that for each $i \in I^+$, K_i is such that there exists $\alpha > 0$, $K_i \vdash (p,\alpha)$
(ii) Let $I^- \subseteq I$ such that for each $i \in I^-$, K_i is such that there exists $\alpha > 0$, $K_i \vdash (-p,\alpha)$
(iii) Let $I^0 = I-(I^+ \cup I^-)$ such that if $i \in I^0$, then K_i entails neither p nor $-p$ with a positive weight

The fact that this is a partition is due to the consistency of the K_i's. Then we can distinguish between four levels of propensity to be true for a proposition p with respect to the inconsistent knowledge base B:

- p is *certainly true* to some extent if for each $i = 1,m$, $K_i^* \vdash p$, where K_i^* is the classical knowledge base obtained from K_i by omitting the positive uncertainty weights. Then $I^+ = I$. The extent to which p is certain with respect to B is then computed as

$$\text{Cert}(p) = \begin{cases} \min_i \{\alpha_i \,|\, \mathbf{K}_i \vdash (p,\alpha_i)\} \\ 0 \end{cases} \quad \text{if } I^+ \neq I \tag{5}$$

Note that $\min(\text{Cert}(p), \text{Cert}(\neg p)) = 0$.

- The truth of p will be said to be *supported* to some extent if there exists i, $\mathbf{K}_i^* \vdash p$. Then, $I^+ = \emptyset$. Then extent to which p is supported with respect to **B** is then computed as

$$\text{Supp}(p) = \begin{cases} \max_i \{\alpha_i \,|\, \mathbf{K}_i \vdash (p,\alpha_i)\} \\ 0 \end{cases} \quad \text{if } I^+ = \emptyset \tag{6}$$

Note that nothing forbids having both $\text{Supp}(p) > 0$ and $\text{Supp}(\neg p) > 0$. Even $\text{Supp}(p) = \text{Supp}(\neg p) = 1$ can be obtained.

- The truth of p is *consistent* with **B** if there exists no i, $\mathbf{K}_i^* \vdash \neg p$, i.e., $I^- = \emptyset$ or if we prefer $I = I^+ \cup I^0$. The extent to which p is consistent with respect to **B** is then given by

$$\text{Cons}(p) = \begin{cases} 1 - \max_i \{\alpha_i \,|\, \mathbf{K} \vdash (\neg p, \alpha_i)\} \\ 1 - \text{Supp}(\neg p) \end{cases} \tag{7}$$

Note that $\text{Cons}(p) = 1$ as soon as $I^- = \emptyset$.

- The truth of p is *not-excluded* with respect to **B** if it is wrong that each $\mathbf{K}_i^*$ entails $\neg p$, i.e., if $I^- \neq I$. The extent to which p is not-excluded with respect to **B** is then given by

$$\text{No-Ex}(p) = \begin{cases} 1 - \min_i \{\alpha_i \,|\, \mathbf{K}_i \vdash (p, \alpha_i)\} \\ 1 - \text{Cert}(\neg p) \end{cases} \tag{8}$$

Clearly $\text{No-Ex}(p) = 1$ if $I^- \neq I$. The following inequalities are easy to check

$$\text{Cert}(p) \leqslant \min(\text{Supp}(p), \text{Cons}(p) \leqslant \max(\text{Supp}(p), \\ \text{Cons}(p)) \leqslant \text{No-Ex}(p) \tag{9}$$

which extends, at the numerical level, the implications $I^+ = I \Rightarrow (I^+ \neq \emptyset$ and $I^- = \emptyset)$, and $(I^+ \neq \emptyset$ or $I^- = \emptyset) \Rightarrow I^- \neq I$. Note also that Cert, Supp, Cons and No-Ex are monotonically increasing with respect to the semantic entailment (for instance, $\text{Cert}(q) \geqslant \text{Cert}(p)$ as soon as $p \rightarrow q$ is a tautology in the usual sense).

Thus, four indices are meaningful when discussing the truth of a proposition with respect to an inconsistent knowledge base **B**. In case of a consistent knowledge base **B**, **B** coincides with its (unique) maximal consistent sub-base. Then $\text{Cert}(p) = \text{Supp}(p)$ and $\text{Cons}(p) = \text{No-Ex}(p)$; moreover, they coincide with standard necessity and possibility measures respectively, in that case. They are the numerical counterparts of the two modalities, usually called the "necessary" and the "possible," which may be used for discussing the truth of a proposition with respect to an incomplete knowledge base.

We might think of taking into account the weights a_i defined by (4) for refining the four indices proposed above, by using weighted min and max operations (Dubois and Prade, 1986). Indeed the conclusions that can be deduced from a sub-base should be regarded as less important than the ones obtained from other sub-bases with larger levels of acceptability, when synthesizing the behaviors of the various K_i's with respect to a proposition p. However, this is already implicitly taken into account in the indices defined by (5)–(8). As a matter of fact, when a clause of **B** with a high degree of certainty is needed to prove p and is not in K_i, we have to use clauses with smaller degrees of certainty, if any, for establishing p, and then the resolution principle will lead to a smaller α_i such that $K_i \vdash (p, \alpha_i)$. Thus it is unnecessary to introduce the a_i's explicitly in the indices if we do not want to take into account the same information twice.

In the above approach we may consider that we have to restrict ourselves to the K_i's where no completely certain clause $(c, 1)$ of **B** is missing (i.e., the K_i's are such that $a_i > 0$), as far as there exists at least one K_i of this kind. Indeed, it may seem reasonable to admit that a completely certain piece of information cannot be questioned. Some authors (e.g., Gärdenfors, 1988) consider that only tautologies are allowed to be entrenched at the degree 1. With such a convention we are sure that all the K_i's are such that $a_i > 0$. However, in the following we allow nontautological clauses to have a degree of certainty equal to 1, if we consider that they express an undebatable matter of fact that cannot be forgotten in order to restore consistency. It is also clear that if we only consider the K_i's which are such that $a_i > 0$, it has obvious computational advantages.

Some researchers are currently trying to relate the problem of belief updating to the setting of nonmonotonic logics, which are traditionally devoted to coping with incomplete information (Gärdenfors and Makinson, 1990). In the same spirit Froidevaux and Grossetête (1990) try to put together possibilistic logic and default logic (Reiter, 1980). There is some analogy between extensions in a default theory and maximally consistent sub-bases of an inconsistent set of classical formulas. Both notions even coincide if we consider the default theory obtained by translating each formula p into the free default "true: p/p" (see Léa Sombé, 1990 for this concept). This analogy is carried further if we note that McDermott and Doyle (1980) have proposed several notions of entailment, in their nonmonotonic logic, that are similar to our treatment of inconsistent knowledge base. Their notions of "provable," "arguable," "doubtless" and "conceivable" respectively correspond to "certain," "supported," "consistent" and "not-excluded" in our terminology, provided we replace maximally consistent sub-bases by fixed points theories.

These similarities point to some sort of duality between incompleteness and inconsistency that deserves further study.

3.2. Data Fusion Issues

Let us consider an example with the following knowledge base $\mathbf{B} = \{(a,\alpha), (b,\beta), (c,\gamma), (\neg a \lor \neg b, 1), (\neg b \lor \neg c, 1)\}$. This example corresponds to the situation where three sources, with different levels of reliability, are claiming that the value of some variable of interest is respectively in A, B and C and that we observe that $A \cap B = \emptyset$ and $B \cap C = \emptyset$ (we use capital letters for denoting the subsets corresponding to the literals in the clauses). Then there are only two maximal consistent sub-bases with a nonzero level of acceptability. Indeed, in this data fusion problem, it is natural to question the clauses $(a,\alpha), (b,\beta)$ or $(c\gamma)$, while $(\neg a \lor \neg b\ 1)$ and $(\neg b \lor \neg c, 1)$ are matters of fact:

$$\mathbf{K}_1 = \{(a,\alpha), (c,\gamma), (\neg a \lor \neg b, 1), (\neg b \lor \neg c, 1)\}$$
$$\mathbf{K}_2 = \{(b,\beta), (\neg a \lor \neg b, 1), (\neg b \lor \neg c, 1)\}$$

Let p be the proposition $(a \land c) \lor b$, then using the resolution principle and the refutation method, we obtain

$$\mathbf{K}_1 \vdash (p, \min(\alpha,\gamma)), \text{ and}$$
$$\mathbf{K}_2 \vdash (p,\beta)$$

In that case $I^+ = I$. Then

$$\text{Cert}(p) = \min(\alpha, \gamma, \beta), \text{ and}$$
$$\text{Supp}(p) = \max(\min(\alpha, \gamma), \beta)$$

while $\text{Cons}(p) = 1 = \text{No-Ex}(p)$. If we now consider $p' = a \land c$, we have

$$\mathbf{K}_1 \vdash (p', \min(\alpha,\gamma))$$
$$\mathbf{K}_2 \vdash (\neg p', \beta)$$

Then $I \neq I^+ \neq \emptyset$ and $I^- \neq \emptyset$, $\text{Cert}(p') = 0$ and $\text{Cert}(\neg p') = 0$; $\text{Suppy}(p') = \min(\alpha, \gamma)$ and $\text{Supp}(\neg p') = \beta$.

This example shows how the approach distinguishes between propositions that are considered as somewhat certain because they are logical consequences of **B**, once consistency is restored, whatever way it is done, and more specific propositions that are implicants of the former propositions and are only partially supported (because they are not logical consequenes of *all* the maximal consistent sub-bases of **B**).

This approach is in agreement with the combination by means of a disjunction operation in data fusion problems when the sources are conflicting, as advocated by the authors (e.g., Dubois and Prade, 1988a). Indeed, if source 1 says that the value of the variable of interest is in a subset A and source 2 says that it is in **B**, where $A \cap B = \emptyset$, then it is absolutely certain that at least one of the sources is wrong. However, rather than to conclude nothing from the two pieces of information we may like to keep the plausible (nontrivial) conclusion that the variable is in $A \cup B$. This result is obtained with the approach presented here. From $\mathbf{B} = \{(a,\alpha), (\neg a \vee \neg b, 1)\}$ we get $\mathbf{K}_1 = \{(a,\alpha), (\neg a \vee \neg b, 1)\}$ and $\mathbf{K}_2 = \{(b,\beta), (\neg a \vee \neg b, 1)\}$. Then it can be checked that $\mathbf{K}_1 \vdash (a \vee b, \alpha)$, $\mathbf{K}_2 \vdash (a \vee b, \beta)$, and finally $\text{Cert}(a \vee b) = \min(\alpha,\beta)$ and $\text{Supp}(a \vee b) = \max(\alpha,\beta)$.

Rather than using maximal consistent sub-bases, we might think of deleting the minimal inconsistent sub-bases from **B**. The small example above shows that this procedure is more drastic since $\{(a,\alpha), (b,\beta) (\neg a \vee \neg b, 1)\}$ coincides with its minimal inconsistent sub-base and then we would be unable to conclude anything if we delete it.

4. REVISING INCONSISTENT KNOWLEDGE BASES BY SELECTING THE BEST MAXIMAL CONSISTENT SUB-BASES

The approach presented in Section 3 takes into account *all* the maximal consistent sub-bases when evaluating the nature and the value of the degree of confidence in the truth of a proposition with respect to an inconsistent knowledge base. In this section we discuss a revision-based approach, which consists in restoring the consistency by selecting the sub-bases satisfying a given optimality criterion, among the maximally consistent one(s). If this criterion leads to a unique optimal sub-base, then the certainty degree of any proposition to evaluate is taken as the certainty degree with which it is entailed from the optimal sub-base; this makes things easy since then we only compute the degree of certainty of the proposition of interest with respect to one sub-base. On the contrary, in case the criterion leads to several incomparable optimal sub-bases, then we have to compute the degree of certainty according to each optimal sub-base again and synthesize them into several degrees, as in Section 3. This indicates the importance of reducing the number of optimal maximal consistent sub-bases by defining a very selective criterion.

In the following we define three criteria for selecting the optimal sub-bases. The first one is directly based on the acceptability level defined in the previous section, and leads to select the sub-bases maximizing it. In the case that there is only one maximal consistent sub-base with the maximal acceptability degree, the process is achieved. The point is that in the general case, there are several (and sometimes many) such maximal consistent sub-bases; this is the reason why we now propose two successive refinements of the acceptability-based criterion. Note that the maximal value of a_i is $1 - \text{Inc}(\mathbf{B})$ since the inconsistency in $\mathbf{B}$ is created at least by a formula with weight Inc $(\mathbf{B})$ and possibly formulas of lower weight only (see proposition 1 in the Appendix).

The second criterion is based on the idea that given a subset of formulas involved in a contradiction, we should delete one of the formulas with the lowest weight when restoring consistency. This is also the basic idea underlying the epistemic entrenchment ordering (Gärdenfors, 1988) whose numerical counterpart has been proved to be necessity measures (Dubois and Prade, 1990b), as already noted. This leads to the following defintion:

A sub-base $\mathbf{B}_i$ of a possibilistic knowledge base $\mathbf{B}$ is said to be *strongly maximal consistent* iff it is consistent and

$$\text{Inc}(\mathbf{B}_i \cup \{(f, \alpha)\}) = \alpha, \text{ for each } (f, \alpha) \in \mathbf{B} - \mathbf{B}_i$$

In the Appendix (proposition 2), we prove that all strongly maximal consistent sub-bases have a maximal acceptability degree; hence we define here a refinement of the acceptability-based selection criterion. The claim that it is a strict refinement is verified by considering an illustrative example.

Let $\mathbf{B}$ be the following possibilistic knowledge base: $\mathbf{B} = \{(p,0.9),$

$(\neg p \lor q, 0.8), (\neg q, 0.7), (\neg p \lor r, 0.6), (\neg p \lor \neg r, 0.6), (\neg r \lor s, 0.5),$ $(r \lor (t \land u), 0.4), (\neg s, 0.3), (\neg t, 0.2)\}$. It is inconsistent, and $\text{Inc}(B) = 0.7$ since the three clauses $p, \neg p \lor q, \neg p$ leads to an inconsistency of level 0.7.

B has many maximal consistent sub-bases in the classical sense; let us consider the following ones (we point out that the list is not exhaustive):

$$B_1 = B - \{(p, 0.9)\}$$
$$B_2 = B - \{(\neg q, 0.7), (\neg p \lor r, 0.6), (r \lor (t \land u), 0.4)\}$$
$$B_3 = B - \{(\neg q, 0.7), (\neg p \lor r, 0.6), (\neg s, 0.3)\}$$
$$B_4 = B - \{(\neg q, 0.7), (\neg p \lor r, 0.6), (\neg t, 0.2)\}$$

B_1 has an acceptability degree of 0.1 and that B_2, B_3 and B_4 have an acceptability degree of 0.3 (it can be checked that this degree is the greatest one).

We can check that B_3 and B_4 are strongly maximal consistent sub-bases of B, and that they are the only ones whose acceptability is 0.3.

B_2 is not strongly maximal consistent because $\text{Inc}(B_2 \cup \{((r \lor (t \land u), 0.4)\}) = 0.2 < 0.4$.

An even more selective criterion enables the ranking of strongly maximal consistent sub-bases to be refined. The basic idea is to attach to a strongly maximal consistent sub-base B_1 of B the multiset consisting of the weights of the formulas of B, which do not belong anymore to B_1, and to consider then the lexicographical ordering among these multisets: a sub-base B_1 is preferred to a sub-base B_2 iff the most certain among the formulas of $B - B_1$ is less certain than the most certain among the formulas of $B - B_2$, or, in case of equality, if the second most certain among the formulas of $B - B_1$ is less certain than the second most certain among the formulas of $B - B_2$, or, in case of equality, the third most certain formulas are considered, etc. More formally, if B_i is a strongly maximal consistent sub-base of B, let List $(B - B_i)$ be the multiset of the valuations of the formulas of $B - B_i$; then B_1 is said to be lexicographically preferred to B_2, or $B_1 \leqslant_L B_2$ iff List $(B_1) \leqslant_L$ List(B_2), where $\leqslant_L$ is the usual lexicographic ordering, defined resursively by

$$\text{List}(B - B_1) \leqslant_L \text{List}(B - B_2)$$

$\Leftrightarrow$

(i)   List$(B - B_1) = \emptyset$ or
(ii) $\max(\text{List}(B - B_1)) < \max(\text{List}(B - B_2))$ or
(iii) $\max(\text{List}(B - B_1)) = \max(\text{List}(B - B_2))$
      and List$(B - B_1) - \{\max(\text{List}(B - B_1))\} \leqslant_L \text{List}(B - B_2) -$
      $- \{\max(\text{List}(B - B_2))\}$

(In this definition we have to remember that we deal with *multisets* and that in case there are several formulas with a weight equal to max List($\mathbf{B} - \mathbf{B}_i$), only one occurrence of the weight is deleted by the '$\neg$' operation).

The minimal elements of the set of strongly maximal consistent sub-bases relatively to $\leqslant_L$ are called lexicographically maximal consistent sub-bases. There is generally not a unique lexicographically maximal consistent sub-base. In our example, we have List($\mathbf{B} - \mathbf{B}_3$) = (0.7, 0.6, 0.3) and List($\mathbf{B} - \mathbf{B}_4$) = (0.7, 0.6, 0.2); thus, the only lexicographically maximal consistent sub-base is $\mathbf{B}_4$.

The definition we give here can be more generally applied to consistent sub-bases of $\mathbf{B}$; then it can be proved that the set of lexicographically optimal consistent sub-bases (i.e., the $\leqslant_L$ minimal elements among the set of consistent sub-bases of $\mathbf{B}$) is included in the set of strongly maximal consistent sub-bases. (See proposition 3 in the Appendix.)

Let us consider the special case when two distinct formulas of the possibilistic knowledge base $\mathbf{B}$ have distinct weight; it entails that the ordering < on the formulas induced by the weights is strict, i.e., for any distinct formulas f, f' of the knowledge base, either $f < f'$ or $f' < f$. Then it is easy to prove that there is a unique lexicographically maximal consistent sub-base of $\mathbf{B}$; this sub-base is also the preferred one according to the axioms of the epistemic entrenchment (Gärdenfors, 1988).

In this section we have not discussed a practical way for obtaining strongly or lexicographically maximal consistent sub-bases. This work can be done using the functionalities of a possibilistic assumption truth-maintenance system (Dubois, Lang, and Prade, 1990), which is an extension of a classical ATMS (De Kleer, 1986a,b) capable of handling clauses weighted by lower bounds of necessity measures. Roughly speaking, a possibilistic ATMS computes, incrementally, the minimal sets of formulas involved in every partial inconsistency (these sets are called minimal nogoods); then, in order to compute all strongly maximal consistent sub-bases, we have to consider all minimal nogoods in the decreasing order of their inconsistency degree (we consider first the strongest contradictions), and we "break" each nogood by deleting (one of) the least entrenched formula(s) involved in it, and the resulting sets of deleted formulas are the complements of the strongly maximal consistent sub-bases. This algorithm can be slightly modified in order to obtain lexicographically maximal consistent sub-bases. A complete description of the algorithm roughly described here is in Dubois, Lang, and Prade (1990).

Let us point out that the revision process for possibilistic knowledge bases described here is more effective than with classical knowledge bases, because the weights induce a selection of the "best" maximal knowledge bases; this can be all the more useful as one of the problems of working with maximally consistent sub-bases in classical logic is the prohibitive complexity caused by a too-large number of maximal consistent sub-bases in general.

Restoring consistency by selecting a lexicographically maximal consistent sub-base is somewhat complementary to the approach presented in Section 3: when the number of maximal consistent sub-bases is too large and one cannot take into account all of them, then the complexity of the query-answering process of Section 3 becomes prohibitive and a lot of answers may be weakly informative (since a large number of sub-bases may lead to degrees of certainty and consistency close to 1); in this case, the revision approach reduces the complexity by taking into account the most entrenched sub-bases only and gives generally more informative results; its drawback is that it may be considered as somewhat arbitrary to neglect all other sub-bases, and the query answering process may then tend to present some results as more reliable than they really are.

5. CONCLUSION

This short paper is an attempt to show how it is possible to deal with an inconsistent knowledge base and to produce reasonable conclusions with a numerical estimation of their uncertainty. The proposed approach is cast in the framework of possibility theory, where the level of confidence in each piece of information in the knowledge base is graded in terms of a necessity measure that is the numerical counterpart of an epistemic entrenchment relation.

The approach outlined in Section 3 here is nonstatistical since the estimations of uncertainty evaluate to what extent *all* maximally consistent sub-bases of an inconsistent knowledge base imply some proposition, and to what extent *there exists* such a sub-base. A further step would consist in evaluating the (weighted) *proportion* of maximally consistent sub-bases that imply a proposition. Then we would get closer to probabilistic notions of uncertainty that reflect conflicting (rather than incomplete) evidence.

APPENDIX

Proposition 1: The maximal acceptability degree of consistent sub-bases of a possibilistic kowledge base **B** is $1 - \text{Inc}(\mathbf{B})$, i.e.,

$$\min \mathbf{B}_i \ \max\{\alpha \mid (f\alpha) \notin \mathbf{B}_i, \ \mathbf{B}_i \text{ consistent}, \ \mathbf{B}_i \subseteq \mathbf{B}\} = \text{Inc}(\mathbf{B})$$

Proof: Let a_i be the degree of acceptability of $\mathbf{B}_i$ as defined by (4). The sub-base $\mathbf{B}_> = \{(f, \ \alpha) \in \mathbf{B}, \ \alpha > \text{Inc}(\mathbf{B})\}$ is consistent and its acceptability is $a_> = 1 - \text{Inc}(\mathbf{B})$ by constructon. Besides, if $\mathbf{B}_i \subseteq \mathbf{B}_j$ then $a_i \leqslant a_j$. Hence, we can restrict ourselves to maximal consistent sub-bases of $\mathbf{B}$. Let $\mathbf{B}_i$ be such a maximal consistent sub-base. Let $B_\geqslant = \{(f, \ \alpha) \ \in \mathbf{B}, \ \alpha \geqslant \text{Inc}(\mathbf{B})\}$, $\mathbf{B}_\geqslant$ is still inconsistent and $\text{Inc}(\mathbf{B}_\geqslant) = \text{Inc}(\mathbf{B})$. Hence, $\mathbf{B}_i$ cannot contain all formulas in $\mathbf{B}_\geqslant$ and so there exists (f,α), $\alpha \geqslant \text{Inc}(\mathbf{B})$, $(f, \ \alpha) \notin \mathbf{B}_i$, hence $a_i \leqslant 1 - \text{Inc}(\mathbf{B})$. Let $\mathbf{B}_i$ be a maximal consistent sub-base containing $B_>$; then $a_i \geqslant a_> = 1 - \text{Inc}(\mathbf{B})$. Hence, there exists i, $a_i = 1 - \text{Inc}(\mathbf{B})$.

Proposition 2: The acceptability degree of a strongly maximally consistent sub-base of a possibilistic knowledge base is maximal.

Proof: Let $\mathbf{B}_i$ be a strongly maximal consistent sub-base of $\mathbf{B}$, i.e. for each $(f,\beta) \in \mathbf{B} - \mathbf{B}_i$, $\text{Inc}(\mathbf{B}_i \cup \{(f,\beta)\}) = \beta$. Obviously we have for each $(f,\mathbf{B}) \in \mathbf{B} - \mathbf{B}_i$, $\text{inc}(\mathbf{B}_i \cup \{(f,\beta)\}) \leqslant \text{Inc}(\mathbf{B})$, which entails that for each $(f,\beta) \in \mathbf{B} - \mathbf{B}_i$, $\beta \leqslant \text{Inc}(\mathbf{B})$, then for each i, $a_i \geqslant 1 - \text{Inc}(\mathbf{B})$. Proposition 1 enables us to conclude that $a_i = 1 - \text{Inc}(\mathbf{B})$. Hence a strongly maximal consistent sub-base has a maximal acceptability degree. Besides, a strongly maximal consistent sub-base is maximal consistent since it is consistent, and adding any formula to it creates inconsistency.

Proposition 3: Any lexicographically optimal consistent sub-base of **B** is strongly maximal consistent.

Proof: First note that the lexicographical ordering is consistent with set-inclusion, that is: if $\mathbf{B}_i \subseteq \mathbf{B}_j$ then $\mathbf{B}_j \leqslant_L \mathbf{B}_i$ since $\text{List}(\mathbf{B} - \mathbf{B}_j) \subseteq \text{List}(\mathbf{B} - \mathbf{B}_i)$. Hence, any lexicographically optimal consistent sub-base of **B** is maximal consistent. Moreover, if $\mathbf{B}_i$ and $\mathbf{B}_j$ have different admissibilities, then $a_i < a_j$ is enough to conclude that $\mathbf{B}_j <_L \mathbf{B}_i$ since $\max(\text{List}(\mathbf{B} - \mathbf{B}_j)) < \max(\text{List}(\mathbf{B} - \mathbf{B}_i))$. Hence, any lexicographically optimal consistent sub-base of **B** is maximal consistent with maximal admissibility. Let us consider such a sub-base $\mathbf{B}_i \subseteq \mathbf{B}$, supposedly not strongly maximal consistent. That is, there is some $(f, \alpha) \in \mathbf{B} - \mathbf{B}_i$ such that $\text{Inc}(\mathbf{B}_i \cup \{(f,\alpha)\}) = \beta < \alpha$. Then there is also some $(f',\beta) \in \mathbf{B}_i$ such that (f,α) and (f',β) belong to the same minimal inconsistent subset of $\mathbf{B}_i \cup \{(f, \alpha)\}$. It is possible to break this inconsistency by deleting (f',β). Let $\mathbf{B}'_i = \mathbf{B}_i \cup \{(f, \alpha)\} - \{(f',\beta)\}$. Clearly, $\text{Inc}(\beta'_i \cup \{(f',\beta)\}) = \beta$ and $\mathbf{B}'_i <_L \mathbf{B}_i$ because they are the same except the exchanged formulas (f,α) and (f',β) and $\beta < \alpha$. Unfortunately $\mathbf{B}'_i$ may be inconsistent since (f,α) may belong to more than one minimal inconsistent subset of $\mathbf{B}'_i$. So we need to break all these inconsistencies by deleting one formula per minimal inconsistent subset. Clearly $\text{Inc}(\mathbf{B}'_i) \leqslant \beta$ so that these deleted formulas may all have weight at most β, and (f,α) can be kept. By doing so, we obtain a subset $\mathbf{B}''_i$ of $\mathbf{B}$ that is consistent and such that $\mathbf{B}_i - \mathbf{B}''_i$ is a set of formulas with weights at most $\beta < \alpha$ while $\mathbf{B}''_i - \mathbf{B}_i = \{(f,\alpha)\}$. So, we still preserve the strict ordering $\mathbf{B}''_i <_L \mathbf{B}_i$. Hence, no maximal consistent sub-base of $\mathbf{B}$ with maximal admissibility that is not strongly maximal consistent can be lexicographically optimal.

Acknowledgments

This paper is a thoroughly revised and extended version of a short note (Dubois and Prade, 1990a) presented at the Ninth European Conference on Artificial Intelligence. Sections 2, 3 and 5 have been expanded. Section 4 and the Appendix are new. The authors are indebted to the anonymous referee who pointed out to them the analogy to McDermott and Doyle's work when reviewing the previous version of this paper. They are also indebted to Claudette Cayrol-Testemale for valuable comments on Section 4. This work has been supported by the ESPRIT Basic Research Action project no. 3085: "DRUMS."

Keywords: inconsistency, propositional logic, belief revision, possibility theory

BIBLIOGRAPHY

Cholvy, L. (1989). Querying an inconsistent database. Report Final no. 1/13318, DERI/ONERA-CERT, Toulouse, France.

De Kleer, J. (1986a). An assumption-based truth maintenance system. *Artificial Intelligence*, **28** (1)127–162.

De Kleer, J. (1986b). Extending the ATMS. *Artificial Intelligence*, **28** (1), 163–196.

Dubois D.,H. Prade. (1986). Weighted minimum and maximum operations in fuzzy set theory. *Information Sciences*, **39**, 205–210.

Dubois, D.,H. Prade. (1987). Necessity measures and the resolution principle. *IEEE Trans. on Systems, Man and Cybernetics*, **17**, 474–478.

Dubois, D. and H. Prade. (1988a). Representation and combination of uncertainty with belief functions and possibility measures. *Computational Intelligence*, **4**, 244–264.

Dubois, D. and H. Prade (with the collaboration of H. Farreny, R. Martin-Clouaire, and C. Cayrol-Testemale). (1988b). *Possibility Theory: An Approach to Computerized Processing of Uncertainty*. New York: Plenum Press.

Dubois, D. and H. Prade. (1990a). Reasoning with inconsistent information in a possibilistic setting. *Proc. of the Europ. Conf. on Artificial Intelligence (ECAI-90)*, Stockholm, Sweden, August 8–10, pp. 259–261.

Dubois, D. and H. Prade. (1990b). Epistemic entrenchment and possibilistic logic. (A preliminary version of this paper is published in the Bulletin BUSEFAL, IRIT, Univ. P. Sabatier, Toulouse, France, no. 39, 66–74, July 1989). In Tech. Report IRIT/90-2/R, IRIT, Univ. P. Sabatier, Toulouse, France. *Artificial Intelligence*, in press.

Dubois, D., J. Lang, and H. Prade. (1989). Automated reasoning using possibilistic logic: Semantics belief revision–Variables certainty weights. *Preprints of the Fifth Workshop on Uncertainty in Artificial Intelligence*, Windsor, Canada, October, pp. 81–87.

Dubois, D., J. Lang, and H. Prade. (1990). *Proc. of the ECAI-90 Workshop on Truth Maintenance Systems*, Stockholm, Sweden, August 6, 1990, J. Martins (ed.), Springer-Verlag, in press.

Froidevaux, C., and C. Grosstête. (1990). Graded default theories for uncertainty. *Proc. of Europ. Conf. on Artificial Intelligence* (ECAI-90), Stockholm, August 6–10, pp. 283–288.

Gärdenfors, P. (1988). *Knowledge in Flux — Modeling the Dynamics of Epistemic States*. Cambridge: MIT Press.

Léa Sombée, P. Besnard, M.O. Cordier, D. Dubois, L. Fariñas del Cerro, C. Froidevaux, Y. Moinard, H. Prade, C. Schwind, and P. Siegel. (1990). Reasoning under incomplete information in artificial intelligence: A comparison of formalisms using a single example. *Special Issue of the Int. J. of Intelligent Systems*, **5**(4), 323–471, available in monograph. New York: Wiley. French edition, Teknea, Toulouse, France, 1989.

P. Gärdenfors, and D. Makinson. (1990). Relations between the logic of theory change and nonmonotonic logic. *Proc. of the Konstanz Workshop on Belief Revision*, A. Furhmann, M. Moreau (eds.), Berlin: Springer-Verlag, in press.

Martins, J. P. and S. C. Shapiro. (1986). Theoretical foundations for belief revision. *Proc. of the 1986 Conf. on Theoretical Aspects of Reasoning about Knowledge,* pp. 383–398.

McDermott, D. and J. Doyle. (1980). Non-monotonic logic I. *Artificial Intelligence,* **13,** 41–72.

Mitchell, J. C. and M. J. O'Donnell. (1986). Realizability semantics for error-tolerant logics (preliminary version). *Proc. of the 1986 Conf. on Theoretical Aspects of Reasoning about Knowledge,* pp. 363–381.

Reiter, R. (1980). A logic for default reasoning. *Artificial Intelligence,* **13,** 81–132.

Zadeh, L. A. (1978). Fuzzy sets as a basis of a theory of possibility. *Fuzzy Sets and Systems,* 1(1), 3–28.

18 Inference for information systems containing probabilistic and fuzzy uncertainties

J. F. BALDWIN
Engineering Mathematics Department
University of Bristol
Bristol BS8 1TR, ENGLAND

Abstract. Information systems are defined in terms of mass assignments over a set of system labels and allow for both probabilistic and fuzzy uncertainties. General information in the form of a priori mass assignments is distinguished from specific information and the latter is used to update the general information to provide an inference in the specific case. This updating is achieved by an iterative assignment method. Information systems can be combined using a general assignment method, which is also described. A simple diagnostic example is used to illustrate the methods. How these methods perform the process of "filling in" for incomplete information is also discussed. Space restrictions force the treatment of fuzzy uncertainties in this paper to be restricted to fuzzy observations, although they play a much fuller part in the general theory. The theory can be used for nonmonotonic reasoning and forms the basis for a new form of parallel computation, but these are only briefly dealt with here.

1. INTRODUCTION

Inference under probabilistic and/or fuzzy uncertainty in knowledge engineering has received considerable attention by researchers in recent years. Probability and fuzzy logics play central roles in handling these uncertainties (Zadeh, 1965, 1978). If the formulation of the application is in terms of binary predicates and crisp variable instantiations, then probability logic is applicable. If, in addition, fuzzy predicates and fuzzy set variable instantiations are used, then fuzzy logic is also required. Incompleteness of information in an application requires probability logic for handling lack of data and fuzzy logic for lack of definition. If the object in the photograph cannot be seen clearly, any conclusion for its recognition must be probabilistic. If the definition of any object thought to be in the photograph is imprecise, then doubt regarding the classification of a given object can occur even if the whole object can be seen clearly. The conclusion in this case will be uncertain because of the fuzziness of the classification rules.

The difficulties do not end here. Information that would allow, for example, probability logic to deduce a probability for a given possible conclusion can be incomplete. We can then give only an interval containing the probability of a conclusion. More generally, we may be able to infer only a family of distributions, rather than a unique probability distribution. In order to infer a point value probability, or more generally, a unique distribution, we require some other criterion to choose one from the set of possibilities. The analogue in the fuzzy case is to derive a possibility distribution from a family of possibility distributions. Maximum entropy considerations can resolve the ambiguity.

Another difficulty we encounter is how to combine statistical information concerning a population of objects with probabilistic information concerning a specific object. For example, what is the analogue of Bayes' conditioning or updating when the given information is probabilistic rather than precise? We will consider the iterative assgnment method for this purpose, which again relates to relative entropy minimization. The problems of nonmonotonic logic can be resolved in this way.

The above considerations are part of the general field of plausible or common sense reasoning. Computational complexity and parallel computational architectures are also important aspects for the practicability of possible common sense reasoning methods. Humans are particularly good at some forms of common sense reasoning, such as vision recognition and other forms of perception. Connectionism, even present-day artificial neural nets, play a central role in this respect. Humans have limitations in common sense reasoning. We should not restrict the approaches for common sense reasoning using computers to human methods even if we understood these more fully. It is important to understand more of how humans reason in the face of incomplete information and why the differences, if there are differences, from other inference methods occur.

In this paper we provide a general framework for common sense reasoning. The inference process will be formulated in terms of combining and conditioning information systems. An information system is an uncertainty measure over a set of labels where a label is an instantiation of the concatenation of all the variables in the system and an instantiation of a variable is a crisp or fuzzy set belonging to a frame of discernment associated with that variable.

2. INFORMATION SYSTEMS

2.1. Mass Assignments

A *mass assignment* over a finite *frame of discernment* X, where X is a set of labels, is a function

$$m : P(X) \rightarrow [0, 1]$$

where $P(X)$ is the power set of X such that

$$m(\emptyset) = 0$$

and

$$\sum_{A \in P(X)} m(A) = 1$$

and corresponds to the basic probability assignment function of the Shafer/Dempster theory of evidence (Shafer, 1976; Klir and Folger, 1988). $m(A)$ represents a probability mass assigned exactly to A. It does not include any masses assigned to subsets of A.

2.2. Support Pairs

We use the concept of belief and plausibility measures of Shafer (1976) to define necessary support and possible support measures. Names are changed to be consistent with the notation used in support logic programming (Baldwin, 1986, 1987) and the FRIL language (Baldwin et al., 1987), and to avoid confusion with conclusions and derived results based on the use of the Dempster rule of combining evidences. The methods given here do not use the Dempster rule, which requires independence assumptions, and the necessary and possible supports are more in keeping with upper and lower probabilities (Dubois and Prade, 1986).

A **necessary support measure** is a function

$$\text{Sn}: P(X) \to [0, 1]$$

defined below, where X is a set of labels and $P(X)$ is the power set of X. A **possible support measure,** denoted by Sp, is associated with the necessary support measure and is defined below.

Given a basic mass assignment m, a necessary support measure and possible support measure are uniquely determined by the formulae

$$\text{Sn}(A) = \sum_{B \subseteq A} m(B)$$

and

$$\text{Sp}(A) = \sum_{A \cap B \neq \emptyset} m(B)$$

which are applicable for all $A \in P(X)$. $\text{Sn}(\emptyset) = 0$ and $\text{Sn}(X) = 1$ where $\emptyset$ is the empty set.

For each $A \in P(X)$, $\text{Sn}(A)$ is interpreted as the necessary support based on available evidence, that a given label of X belongs to the set A of labels. It is easy to show that

$$\text{Sp}(A) = 1 - \text{Sn}(\overline{A}), \text{ for all } A \in P(X)$$

Similarly,

$$\text{Sn}(A) = 1 - \text{Sp}(\overline{A})$$

For every $A, B \in P(X)$, if $A \subseteq B$, then $\text{Sn}(A) \leqslant \text{Sn}(B)$ and also that

$$\text{Sn}(A) + \text{Sn}(\overline{A}) \leqslant 1$$

Necessary support measures and possible support measures are therefore mutually dual and it is easy to show that

$$\text{Sp}(A) + \text{Sp}(\overline{A}) \geqslant 1$$

$\text{Sn}(A)$ will not, in general, correspond to Shafer's belief function since we do not use Dempster's rule for combining evidences.

2.2.1. Focal Elements

Every set $A \in P(X)$ for which $m(A) > 0$ is called a focal element of m. We can represent the mass assignment as (m, F) where F is the set of focal elements.

Total ignorance is expressed in terms of the mass assignment by

$m(X) = 1$ and $m(A) = 0$, for all $A \neq X$

Using the formula above for Sn in terms of m, we can therefore also express total ignorance as

$Sn(X) = 1$ and $Sn(A) = 0$, for all $A \neq X$

The total ignorance in terms of the possible support measure is

$Sp(\emptyset) = 0$ and $Sp(A) = 1$, for all $A \neq \emptyset$

A **support pair** for $A \in P(X)$ is given by $[\text{MIN } Sn(A), \text{MAX } Sp(A)]$ and this defines an interval containing the $Pr(A)$ where the MIN and MAX are over the set of values of any possible parameters that $Sn(A)$ and $Sp(A)$ may depend on.

3. GENERAL ASSIGNMENT METHOD

3.1. Combining Mass Assignments

Let $m1$ and $m2$ be two mass assignments over the power set $P(X)$ where X is a set of labels. Evidence 1 and evidence 2 are denoted by $(m1, F1)$ and $(m2, F2)$, respectively, where $F1$ and $F2$ are the sets of focal elements of $P(X)$ for $m1$ and $m2$, respectively. Suppose $F1 = \{L1k\}$ for $k = 1, ..., n1$, and $F2 = \{L2k\}$, for $k = 1, ..., n2$, then Lij is a subset of $P(X)$ for which $mi(\text{Lij}) \neq 0$. Let (mF) be the evidence resulting from combining evidence 1 with evidence 2 using the general assignment method with respect to the conjunction of statements corresponding to the mass assignments $m1$ and $m2$. This is denoted as

$(m, F) = (m1, F1) \oplus (m2, F2)$

where

$F = \{L1i \cap L2j \mid m(L1i \cap L2j) \neq 0\}$

$m(Y) = \displaystyle\sum_{i,j: L1i \cap L2j = Y} m'(L1i \cap L2j)$

for any $Y \in F$,

$m'(L1i \cap L2j)$ for $i = 1, ..., n1; j = 1, ..., n2$ satisfies

$$\sum_j m'(L1i \cap L2j) = m1(L1i)$$

for $i = 1, ..., n1$,

$$\sum_i m'(L1i \cap L2j) = m(L2i)$$

for $j = 1, ..., n2, m'(L1i \cap L2j) = 0$ if $L1i \cap L2j = \emptyset$ (the empty set); for $i = 1, ..., n1; \ j = 1, ..., n2$. There is no simple rule for combining evidences without making additional assumptions such as independence of the mass assignments.

If there are more than two evidences to combine then they are combined two at a time. For example, to combine $(m1, F1), (m2, F2)$, $(m3, F3)$ and $(m4, F4)$ use

$$(m, F) = (((m1, F1) \oplus (m2, F2)) \oplus (m3, F3)) \oplus (m4, F4)$$

In general, the solution (m, F) will not be unique and a parametrized family of solutions will be obtained. These possible parameter values must be taken into account when determining support pairs from the necessary and possible support measures. In the case when each member of the family of solutions corresponds to a probability distribution over a partition of X, we can obtain a unique solution by choosing that member of the family of distributions which maximizes the entropy of the system. A more detailed discussion of the general assignment method can be found in Baldwin (1990b, c, d, e).

3.2. A Diagnostic Test Example

In order to relate the development here with Dalkey's logic of information systems (Dalkey, 1988), we will discuss the general assignment method with respect to a similar example considered by him and further modified examples.

Two tests, $\{T1, T2\}$, are available to test for a person suffering from a given disease d. Each test can return a positive or negative result, $\{+, -\}$. The likelihoods of the tests are

$T1$: $\Pr(+|d) = 0.5, \Pr(-|d) = 0.5, \Pr(+|\neg d) = 0.1, \Pr(-|\neg d) = 0.9$

T2: $\Pr(+|d) = 0.9, \Pr(-|d) = 0.1, \Pr(+|\neg d) = 0.5, \Pr(-|\neg d) = 0.5$

The prior probability for d, $\Pr(d) = 0.5$.

How can we combine the two test results when we know nothing about the dependencies of one on the other? Information systems, E1, E2, corresponding to test 1 and test 2 respectively are:

E1:
$\{d + \_\}:0.25$
$\{d - \_\}:0.25$
$\{\neg d + \_\}:0.05$
$\{\neg d - \_\}:0.45$

E2:
$\{d \_ +\}:0.45$
$\{d \_ -\}:0.05$
$\{\neg d \_ +\}:0.25$
$\{\neg d \_ +\}:0.25$

since $\Pr(d, + \text{ for test } 1) = \Pr(+ \text{ for test } 1 \mid d) \Pr(d) = 0.5 \times 0.5 = 0.25 = \{d + \_\}:0.25$, etc.

Thus, using the general assignment method

$$E1 \oplus E2 = E$$

where E is the parametrized information system

E:
$d + +:0.25 - x;\ d + -:x;\ d - +:0.2 + x;\ d - -:0.05 - x$
$\neg d + +:y;\ \neg d + -:0.05 - y;\ \neg d - +:0.25 - y;\ \neg d - -:0.2 + y$

where $0 \le x \le 0.05$ and $0 \le y \le 0.05$, since the assignment method gives

	0.45 $\{d \_ +\}$	0.05 $\{d \_ -\}$	0.25 $\{\neg d \_ +\}$	0.25 $\{\neg d \_ -\}$
0.25 $\{d + \_\}$	$d + +$ $0.25 - x$	$d + -$ x	$\emptyset$ 0	$\emptyset$ 0
0.25 $\{d - \_\}$	$d - +$ $0.2 + x$	$d - -$ $0.05 - x$	$\emptyset$ 0	$\emptyset$ 0
0.05 $\{\neg d + \_\}$	$\emptyset$ 0	$\emptyset$ 0	$\neg d + +$ y	$\neg d + +$ $0.05 - y$
0.45 $\{\neg d - \_\}$	$\emptyset$ 0	$\emptyset$ 0	$\neg d - +$ $0.25 - y$	$\neg d - -$ $0.2 + y$

$0 \le x \le 0.05$
$0 \le y \le 0.05$

where the x and y parameters are introduced since the tableau contains two loops, using alternative horizontal and vertical jumps as in the operations research assignment algorithm, and for each loop assignments can be added and subtracted around the loop without violating the column and row constraints.

From this we can deduce that

$$\Pr(d \,|\!+ +) = (0.25 - x)/(0.25 - x + y)$$
$$\Pr(d \,|\!+ -) = x/(0.05 - y + x)$$
$$\Pr(d \,|\!- +) = (0.2 + x)/(0.45 + x - y)$$
$$\Pr(d \,|\!- -) = (0.05 - x)/(0.25 + y - x)$$

3.2.1. Maximum Entropy Solution

The entropy of this combined system is

$$\text{Ent } \{E(x, y)\} = (0.25 - x) \ln (0.25 - x) + x \ln (x) + (0.2 + x) \ln$$
$$(0.2 + x) + (0.05 - x) \ln (0.05 - x) + y \ln (y) + (0.05 - y) \ln$$
$$(0.05 - y) + (0.25 - y) \ln (0.25 - y) + (0.2 + y) \ln (0.2 + y)$$

and the values $x = 0.025$ and $y = 0.025$ maximize this entropy. Hence the unique solution corresponding to maximum entropy of E is given by

E:
$d + + : 0.225; \; d + - : 0.025; \; d - + : 0.225; \; d - - : 0.025$
$\neg d + + : 0.025; \; \neg d + - : 0.025; \; \neg d - + : 0.225; \; \neg d - - : 0.225$

and correspondingly

$$\Pr(d \,|\!+ +) = 0.9 \qquad \Pr(d \,|\!- +) = 0.5$$
$$\Pr(d \,|\!+ -) = 0.5 \qquad \Pr(d \,|\!- -) = 0.1$$

In this case, this is also the solution if we combined $E1$ and $E2$ using Dempster's rule of combination (Shafer, 1976), but this correspondence is not generally true.

An alternative to maximizing the entropy of E is to maximize the expected value of the entropy of $(D \,|\!{\_\_})$ where D stands for d or $\neg d$ and $\_\_$ for $+ +, + -, - +$ or $- -$. This expected value is given by

$$H(x, y) = \Pr(+ +) \text{En} (\Pr(d \,|\!+ +) + \Pr(+ -) \text{En} (\Pr(d \,|\!+ -) +$$
$$\Pr(- +) \text{En} (\Pr(d \,|\!- +) + \Pr(- -) \text{En} (\Pr(d \,|\!- -)$$

where $\text{En}(x) = x \ln (x) + (1 - x) \ln (1 - x)$. The maximization of $H(x, y)$ with respect to x and y is obtained with $x = 0$ and $y = 0.05$. This gives:

$$\Pr(d \,|\!+ +) = 0.83 \qquad\qquad \Pr(d \,|\!- +) = 0.5$$

$$\Pr(d \,|\, + -) = ? \text{ i.e., undetermined} \qquad \Pr(d \,|\, - -) = 0.17$$

and the above rules could be written in terms of these point values.

This corresponds to Dalkey's least upper bound solution (Dalkey, 1988) in his logic of information systems, and max $H(x, y)$ represents a guaranteed score, whatever admissible score function is assumed. Let $S(\Pr(D \,|\, \_\, \_))$ be the expected score for using the distribution $\Pr(D \,|\, \_\, \_)$ where the score function is $\Pr(\_\, \_) s(\Pr(D \,|\, \_\, \_)$, $\_\, \_)$ summed over all values of $\_\, \_$ and $s(P, e)$ is an admissible scoring function satisfying

$$\Sigma_{\text{all } e} \Pr(e) s(P, e) \geqslant \Sigma_{\text{all } e} \Pr(e) s(Q, e)$$

for any distribution Q. The function $-H(x, y)$ is an example of $s(\Pr(D \,|\, \_\, \_))$ where $s(P, e) = \ln(P)$.

An information system $P1$ is said to dominate an information system $P2$, denoted by $P1 \geqslant P2$, if $S(P1) \geqslant S(P2)$ for all admissible scoring rules. The set of information systems with binary D with $\geqslant$ forms a lattice. Let $K(x, y)$ represent the set of distributions given by the general assignment method above and let P_{E1}, P_{E2} represent the distributions for $E1$ and $E2$ respectively. Dalkey shows that the score if we accept the least upper bound, $P_{E1} \vee P_{E2}$, of P_{E1} and P_{E2} as the distribution resulting from combining these distributions is better than the score of either P_{E1} or P_{E2} whatever the admissible scoring function chosen. Furthermore, any $R \in K$ dominates $P_{E1} \vee P_{E2}$.

If the object is to find rules, of the form head IF body, which are to be used when the truths of the body of the rules can be determined, then Dalkey's solution provides a form of inductive logic from which to draw conclusions about the head of the rules.

If only probabilistic information concerning the bodies of the rules is available, then we still have the problem of how to make an inference.

3.3. A Modified Diagnostic Test Example

Consider the following incomplete information for the likelihoods

$$\text{Test 1: } \begin{array}{l} \Pr(+ \,|\, \neg d) = 0.1 \\ \Pr(- \,|\, \neg d) = 0.9 \end{array} \qquad \text{Test 2: } \begin{array}{l} \Pr + \,|\, d) = 0.9 \\ \Pr(- \,|\, d) = 0.1 \end{array}$$

and $\Pr(d) = 0.5$ as before. This gives the following mass assignments

$$\{\neg d + \,-\}:0.05 \qquad\qquad \{d\,-\,+\}:0.45$$
$$\text{Test 1: } \{\neg d - \,\_\}:0.45 \qquad \text{Test 2: } \{d\,-\,-\}:0.45$$
$$\{\{d\,\_\,\_\}:0.5 \qquad\qquad \{\neg d\,\_\,\_\}:0.5$$

These can be combined using the general assignment method to give

$$\{\neg d + \,-\}:0.05 \qquad\qquad \{d\,-\,+\}:0.45$$
$$\{\neg d - \,\_\}:0.45 \qquad\qquad \{d\,-\,-\}:0.05$$

since

	0.45 $\{d\,-\,+\}$	0.05 $\{d\,-\,-\}$	0.5 $\{\neg d\,\_\,\_\}$
0.05 $\{\neg d+\,\_\}$	Ø 0	Ø 0	$\{\neg d+\,\_\}$ 0.05
0.45 $\{\neg d-\,\_\}$	Ø 0	Ø 0	$\{\neg d-\,\_\}$ 0.45
0.5 $\{d\,\_\,\_\}$	$\{d\,\_\,+\}$ 0.45	$\{d\,\_\,-\}$ 0.05	Ø 0

giving the solution. This corresponds to the following family of distributions:

$d++:0.45 - x;\quad d+-:0.05 - y;\quad d-+:x;\quad d--:y;\quad \neg d++:$ $0.05 - u;\quad \neg d+-:u;\quad \neg d-+:0.45 - v;\quad \neg d--:v;\quad$ where $0 \leqslant x \leqslant 0.45,\ 0 \leqslant y \leqslant 0.05,\ 0 \leqslant u \leqslant 0.05,\ 0 \leqslant v \leqslant 0.45$, from which we can determine

$$\Pr(d\,|++) = (0.45 - x)/(0.5 - x - u)$$
$$\Pr(d\,|+-) = (0.05 - y)/(0.05 - y + u)$$
$$\Pr(d\,|-+) = x/(0.45 - v + x)$$
$$\Pr(d\,|--) = y/(y + v)$$

The support pair for each of these conditional probabilities is $[0, 1]$. The maximum entropy solution, i.e., MAX Ent $\{E(x, y, u, v)\}$, is obtained when $x = v = 0.225;\ y = u = 0.025$, giving:

$$d\,|++:0.9 \qquad\qquad d\,|-+:0.5$$
$$d\,|+-:0.5 \qquad\qquad d\,|--:0.1$$

If Dempster's rule is used to combine $E1$ and $E2$, then we will obtain the same solution in this case.

This solution is not surprising. It is the same as that given above for problem 1. This problem is equivalent to problem 1 if we distribute the 0.5 mass assigned to $\{d \_ \_\}$ for test 1 equally between $\{d + \_\}$ and $\{d - \_\}$, and the 0.5 mass assigned to $\{\neg d \_ \_\}$ for test 2 equally between $\{\neg d \_ +\}$ and $\{\neg d \_ -\}$. This is what we would do if we applied a maximum entropy argument to the data for each test separately before combining the information systems.

4. ITERATIVE ASSIGNMENT METHOD

4.1. Updating Problem

This is discussed in Baldwin (1990b, c, d, e). We summarize the method here and discuss further how the method handles incomplete information.

Suppose an a priori mass assignment m_a is given over the focal set A whose elements are subsets of the power set $P(X)$ where X is a set of labels. This assignment represents general tendencies and is derived from statistical considerations of some sample space or general rules applicable to such a space.

Suppose we also have a set of specific evidences $\{E1, E2, ..., En\}$ where for each i, Ei is (mi, Fi) where Fi is the set of focal elements of $P(X)$ for Ei and mi is the mass assignment for these focal elements. These evidences are assumed to be relevant to some object and derived by consideration of this object alone and not influenced by the sample space of objects from which the object came.

We wish to update the a priori assignment m_a with $\{E1,...,En\}$ to give the updated mass assignment m. If m_a and the evidences are probability distributions the update should minimize the relative information of m with respect to m_a.

The iterative assignment method updates m_a first with $E1$ to give $m^{(1)}$. This is updated with $E2$ to give $m^{(2)}$ and so on until $m^{(n)}$ is reached. $m^{(i)}$ satisfies Ei but not necessarily $E1,..., E(i\text{-}1)$. m_a is then replaced with $m^{(n)}$ and the whole process repeated. This is repeated until the process converges in which case $m^{(1)} = m^{(2)} = ... = m^{(n)} = m'$, say. This process can be depicted as

$$m_a \xrightarrow{\quad E1 \quad} m^{(1)} \xrightarrow{\quad E2 \quad} m^{(2)} \quad - \quad - \quad - \xrightarrow{\quad En \quad} m^{(n)}$$

The one-step algorithm is as follows.

Consider that we wish to update the mass assignment m with E to give the mass assignment m' where

$m = (t, T)$
where $t = \{t1, ..., tm\}$ and $T = \{T^1, ..., Tm\}$ where Ti is a subset of $P(X)$. i.e.,
m:
$T1: t1$
$\vdots \quad \vdots$
$Tm: tm$
and $E = (t^E, T^E)$
where $t^E = \{t^E 1, ..., t^E s\}$ and $T^E = \{T^E 1, ..., T^E s\}$, where $T^E i$ is a subset of $P(X)$, i.e.,
E:
$T^E 1 : t^E 1$
$\vdots \quad \vdots$
$T^E s : t^E s$
$m' = (t', T')$
where $t' = \{t'1, ..., t'r\}$ and $T' = \{T'1, ..., T'r\}$,
$T' = \{Ti \cap T^E j \mid Ti \cap T^E j \neq \emptyset\}$;

$$t'k = \sum_{i,j: Ti \cap T^E j = T'k} K_j \, ti \, t'j \text{ for, } k = 1, ..., r$$

$$\text{where } K_j = 1/1 - \sum_{q: Tq \cap T^E j = \emptyset} t_q, \text{ for } j = 1, ..., s$$

It should be noted that the label set can change from stage to stage of the complete process.

If the a priori mass assignment is a probability distribution, say p, defined over the set of labels X, and the specific evidences $E1, ..., En$ are also probability distributions over a partition of X, then the iterative assignment method determines an updated probability distribution over X, say p', such that

$$\sum_{x \in X} p'(x) \ln (p'(x)/p(x))$$

is minimized subject to the constraints E1, ..., En, and is equivalent to using Jeffrey's rule.

p' is said to satisfy the minimum information principle (Kullback, 1959), for updating the distribution p over X with specific evidences E1, ..., En where each Ei is expressed as a distribution over a partition of X. Convergence of such an iteration is discussed by Csiszár (1975).

If the evidences are expressed as mass assignments over X with the a priori assignment still being a probability distribution over the set of labels X, then a more complicated case must be considered. In this case the update solution p' satisfies the following relative information optimization problem.

$$\sum_{x \in X} p'(x) \ln (p'(x) / p(x))$$

is minimized subject to the constraints $\mathrm{Sn}(Y) \leqslant p'(Y) \leqslant \mathrm{Sp}(Y)$, for all subsets Y of P(X) and m = 1, ..., n, where $\mathrm{Sn}(Y)$ and $\mathrm{Sp}(Y)$ are determined from the mass assignment (mr, Fr).

For the more general case with an a priori mass assignment and the evidences being mass assignments, the interpretation of the iterative assignment method is much more complicated. This is discussed in more detail in Baldwin (1990f) and here we give only a brief interpretation. In the one-stage process the update chosen is that one which is obtained using Jeffrey's rule in which the conditional probabilities are determined from a probability distribution, p, selected from the family of a priori distributions defined by m_a such that one has the maximum consistency between p and the specific evidence of the one-stage update. The update corresponding to the maximum entropy update can be constructed from the tableau by subtracting from any cell whose label is a true subset of the a priori row label a mass and adding this to the other column cells. For problems in which there are more than one specific evidence the maximum entropy update is normally obtained without having to resort to this modification.

A family of updates can be recovered by considering loops in the final update tableau and treating these as in the general assignment method. This is illustrated below.

4.2. Conjunction Example

Consider the rather artificially posed problem of determining the probability of the conjunction of two statements, $A \wedge B$, when given the probability of each of the conjuncts. We will determine this by first selecting an a priori over the set

$$\{ab, a \neg b, \neg ab, \neg a \neg b\}$$

and then updating this with $E1$ and $E2$, where

$$E1: \{a\_\}:0.9; \{\neg a\_\}:0.1$$

corresponding to $\Pr(a) = 0.9$,

$$E2: \{\_b\}:0.75; \{\_\neg b\}:0.25$$

corresponding to $\Pr(b) = 0.75$. Starting with a priori

$$ab:0.25; \ a \neg b:0.25; \ \neg ab:0.25; \ \neg a \neg b:0.25$$

the iterative assignment method gives the final update

$$ab:0.675; \ a \neg b:0.225; \ \neg ab:0.075; \ \neg a \neg b:0.025$$

Starting with a priori

$$ab:0.1; \ a \neg b:0.4; \ \neg ab:0.4; \ \neg a \neg b:0.1$$

the iterative assignment method gives the final update

$$ab:0.6524; \ a \neg b:0.2476; \ \neg ab:0.0976; \ \neg a \neg b:0.0024$$

after several iterations.

Suppose that nothing is known about the a priori, which would be the case if this is a one off example. The a priori can then be represented as the mass assignment $\{\_\_\}:1$ and we update this with $E1$ and $E2$. We obtain

	0.9 $\{a\_\}$	0.1 $\{\neg a\_\}$			0.75 $\{\_b\}$	0.25 $\{\_\neg b\}$
1 $\{\_\_\}$	$\{a\_\}$ 0.9	$\{\neg a\_\}$ 0.1		0.9 $\{a\_\}$	ab 0.675	$a \neg b$ 0.225
				0.1 $\{\neg a\_\}$	$\neg ab$ 0.075	$\neg a \neg b$ 0.025

This is in fact the final update since the second tableau satisfies the constraints of the first. The solution obtained is the values of the various conjunctions corresponding to choosing the a priori to be equally likely, i.e., maximum entropy a priori.

In this example, the final tableau gives the maximum entropy result. If we wish to recover all possible solutions without making any assumptions, i.e., not allowing any filling of missing information, then we can add and subtract around the loop in the final tableau as shown:

	0.75 $\{\_b\}$	0.25 $\{\_\neg b\}$
0.9 $\{a\_\}$	ab $0.675+$ x	$a\neg b$ 0.225 $-x$
0.1 $\{\neg a\_\}$	$\neg ab$ 0.075 $-x$	$\neg a\neg b$ 0.025 $+x$

Therefore, we have:

$$ab: 0.675 + x \qquad \neg ab: 0.075 - x$$
$$a\neg b: 0.225 - x \qquad \neg a\neg b: 0.025 + x$$

so that in terms of support pairs

$$ab: [0.65, 0.75]; \; a\neg b: [0.15, 0.25]; \; \neg ab: [0, 0.1]; \; \neg a\neg b: [0, 0.1]$$

which, of course, is the most general solution for this example:

$$\text{MAX} \{\Pr(a) + \Pr(b) - 1, 0\} \leqslant \Pr(ab) \leqslant \text{MIN} \{\Pr(a), \Pr(b)\}$$

4.3. The Diagnostic Test Example Revisited

The same solutions as for both examples discussed above are obtained for the following updating schemes.

M. ass. a priori $\xrightarrow{\quad T1(+):1 \quad}$ 1st update $\xrightarrow{\quad T2(+):1 \quad}$ 2nd update

M. ass. a priori $\xrightarrow{\quad ++:1 \quad}$ Update

Similar conclusions can be made when the results of the tests are known only in probabilistic terms. For example, suppose the observer of test 1 estimates that the result indicates a + with a degree of certainty at least equal to 0.8. Then we have the specific mass assignment:

Test 1: $\begin{array}{l} + : 0.8 \\ \{+,-\} : 0.2 \end{array}$

Suppose a similar result for test 2 is

$+ : 0.7$
$\{+,-\} : 0.3$

Scheme

$$T1 : -+ : a; \{+,-\} : 1-a \qquad T2 : -+ : b; \{+,-\} : 1-b$$

M. ass. a priori $\longrightarrow$ 1st update $\longrightarrow$ Update

with iteration gives $d : 0.9$ for $a, b > 0$. If $a, b = 0$, then $d : 0.5$. This says that if the only support is for $+$ in the first test and $+$ in the second test, i.e., there is no support for $-$ on the first test or $-$ on the second test, then d is supported to the degree 0.9.

This specific information can be combined using the general assignment method to give

$$+ + : 0.7 - x; \ \{+ \_\} : 0.1 + x; \ \{\_ +\} : x; \ \{\_ \_\} : 0.2 - x, \text{ for } 0 \leqslant x \leqslant 0.2$$

so that we can also use the scheme

$$\begin{array}{c} ++ : 0.7 - x; \{+\_\} : 0.1 + x \\ \{\_+\} : \{\_\_\} : 0.2 - x \\ 0 \leq x \leq 0.2 \end{array}$$

M. ass. a priori $\longrightarrow$ Update

which will give the same solution if the maximum entropy distribution, corresponding to $x = 0.1$, of the family of distributions for the combined specific informations is used. This solution will also be obtained if the mass assignment a priori is replaced with the maximum entropy distribution of the family of distributions given by the mass assignment a priori.

Let us now consider

Test 1: $\begin{array}{l} + : a \\ - : a' \\ \{+,-\} : 1 - a - a' \end{array}$

Suppose a similar result for test 2 is

$+:b$
$-:b'$
$\{+,-\}:1-b-b'$

We use the scheme

$$T1$$
$$+\,:\,a;-\,:\,a\prime;\{+,-\}\,:\,1-a-a\prime \qquad\qquad +\,:\,b;-\,:\,b\prime;\{+,-\}\,:\,1-b-b\prime$$

M.a.ap ──────────────────➤ 1stupdate ┈┈┈┈┈┈┈➤ Update

This gives the same results as using a form of Jeffrey's (1965) rule:

$$P'r(d) = Pr(d\,|++)P'r(++) + Pr(d\,|+-)P'(+-) +$$
$$Pr(d\,|-+)P'(-+) + Pr(d\,|--)P'r(--)$$

where the primed probabilities are those obtained from the maximum entropy distribution of the combined specific informations while the nonprimed probabilities are equal to those derived from the maximum entropy a priori distribution. Examples of updates are:

a	a'	b	b'	d
0.8	0.1	0.7	0.2	0.7667
0.9	0.1	0.1	0.9	0.5
0.9	0.1	0.3	0.7	0.58
0.9	0.1	0.4	0.6	0.62
0.9	0.1	0.5	0.5	0.66
0.9	0.1	0.6	0.4	0.7
0.9	0.1	0.7	0.3	0.74

4.4. Iterative Assignment versus Dalkey's Method

Consider now the first tests problem:

$$E\,1: \begin{array}{l} \{d+\_\}:0.25 \\ \{d-\_\}:0.25 \\ \{\neg d+\_\}:0.05 \\ \{\neg d-\_\}:0.45 \end{array} \qquad E\,2: \begin{array}{l} \{d\_+\}:0.45 \\ \{d\_-\}:0.05 \\ \{\neg d\_+\}:0.25 \\ \{\neg d\_-\}:0.25 \end{array}$$

If a specific person is given both tests and the result of each test is used to infer the probability of him suffering from d, obtained using the updating method, and these results are then combined, we have

For **Test 1:**
Result $+$ implies d: 0.8333; Result $-$ implies d: 0.3571
For **Test 2:**
Result $+$ implies d: 0.6429; Result $-$ implies d: 0.1667

We can combine these results using Dempster's rule of combination to give:

If $+ +$ then d: 0.9   If $+ -$ then d: 0.5
If $- -$ then d: 0.1   If $- +$ then d: 0.5

which is the result given by the iterative assignment method.

It does not agree with Dalkey's result. If the tests are thought to be independent then intuitively the result given here is more reasonable. For example, in the case of $+ +$ then both tests imply a greater chance of d than *not d*. Therefore, the result of combining these should give a chance greater than the maximum given by each of the tests alone since we expect the one to increase the chance given by the other. Dalkey's result gives the maximum of the two separate results. In the case of $- -$ we would expect the result of each test to lower the result of the other since they both give a chance for d of less than 0.5. Dalkey's result gives the lower of the two separate results. In the other two cases the results are contradictory in that one gives better than even chance and the other worse than even chance for d. We would expect the $+$ result to raise the probability associated with the $-$ result and the $-$ result to lower the probability of the $+$ result. The iterative assignment method gives the same result as Dempster since the maximum entropy a priori distribution, in the s case, corresponds to independence of tests.

How we combine inconsistent mass assignments from different sources depends on what can be assumed about the independence of the sources. If a pure averaging is required, then one can use a relative information method of combining. For the case discussed here, in which we wish to combine

$$m1: - d: p1, \neg d: 1 - p1$$

with

$$m2: - d: p2, \neg d: 1 - p2$$

this amounts to choosing the combined mass assignment

$$n: - d:p, \neg d:1 - p$$

such that

$$p\ln(p/p1) + (1 - p)\ln((1 - p)/(1 - p1)) = p\ln(p/p2) + (1 - p)$$
$$\ln((1 - p)/(1 - p2))$$

This finds an assignment nearest to both m1 and m2 in the relative entropy sense. For the example here, this method gives

For + + then d:0.746   For + − then d:0.5
For − + then d:0.5   For − − then d:0.254

It should be emphasized that this method of treating the inference as combining inferences from the separate tests can only be approximate.

5. RULES REPRESENTATION

We can represent the test problem discussed above in the following rule form:

For any $X:X$ suffers from d IF *test 1* for X gives + : 0.8333
For any $X:X$ suffers from d IF *test 1* for X gives − : 0.3571
For any X: *test 1* for X gives + : 0.3
For any X: *test 1* for X gives − : 0.7
For any $X:X$ suffers from d IF *test 2* for X gives + : 0.6429
For any $X:X$ suffers from d IF *test 2* for X gives − : 0.1667
For any X: *test 2* for X gives + : 0.7
For any X: *test 2* for X gives − : 0.8

This is the form of knowledge representation used by the AI language FRIL (Baldwin et al., 1987). Any query concerning an individual suffering from d with results such as

test 1 for Tommy gives + : [0.8, 0.9]
test 2 for Tommy gives − : [0.7, 0.8]

can be determined by the iterative assignment method with the specific mass assignments about Tommy, to update the a priori mass assignment formed using the general assignment method and the general rules about any individual.

Alternatively, the information systems form of knowledge representation can be used:

$\{X$ has D, Test 1 for X gives $t1\}$:	**D**	**t1**	
	d	$+$	: 0.25
	d	$-$	: 0.25
	$\neg d$	$+$	: 0.05
	$\neg d$	$-$	: 0.45

$\{X$ has D, Test 2 for X gives $t2\}$:	**D**	**t2**	
	d	$+$	: 0.45
	d	$-$	: 0.05
	$\neg d$	$+$	: 0.25
	$\neg d$	$-$	: 0.25

$\{$Test 1 for Tommy gives $t1\}$	**t1**	
	$+$	: 0.8
	$-$	: 0.1

$\{$Test 2 for Tommy gives $t2\}$	**t2**	
	$-$	: 0.7
	$+$	: 0.2

Other forms of knowledge representation such as those in Shenoy (1989), Pearl (1988), and Lauritzen and Spiegelhalter (1988) are also relevant in this context.

6. FUZZY OBSERVATION

We can associate a mass assignment with any normalized fuzzy set (Klir and Folger, 1988; Baldwin, 1990a). For example, the fuzzy set $\mathbf{f} = a/1 + b/0.8 + c/0.5 + d/0.1$ is associated with the mass assignment

$$m_f: -a:0.2; \{a,b\}:0.3; \{a,b,c\}:0.4; \{a,b,c,d\}:0.1$$

This has a voting model semantics as discussed by Baldwin (1990a).

We can treat nonnormalized fuzzy sets as an intersection of normalized fuzzy sets. For example, the nonnormalized fuzzy set

$$\mathbf{g} = a/0.9 + b/0.7 + c/0.3$$

is the intersection of

$$\mathbf{g1} = 1/a + 0.7/b + c/0.3$$

with mass assignment m_{g1}: $- a:0.3; \{a,b\}:0.4; \{a,b,c\}:0.3$, and

$$g2 = 0.9/a + b/1 + c/1$$

with mass assignment m_{g2}: $- \{c,b\}:0.1; \{a,b,c\}:0.9$. We choose the least restricted form of fuzzy sets for this decomposition.

We can combine m_{g1} and m_{g2} using the general assignment method to give

$$m_{g1} \oplus m_{g1}: - a:0.3; b:0.1; \{a,b\}:0.3; \{a,b,c\}:0.3$$

It is necessary that the sum of the membership values in g is at least 1 for this method to be valid.

Consider the diagnostic test problem discussed above. Imagine that the result classification of the test, $\{+, -\}$, corresponds to fuzzy concepts. For example, $+$ may correspond to "severe bruising." Experts may not agree in an individual case if the results correspond to $+$ or $-$. Suppose 90% think that the result cold be $+$ and 40% think it could be $-$. This includes those who think it could be either. This can be represented by the observation fuzzy set $t = +/0.9 + -/0.4$ which has the associated mass assignment $m_t:\{+\}:0.6; \{-\}:0.1; \{+, -\}:0.3$.

Instead of thinking of a group of experts giving this result we can think in terms of an individual expert who gives a 0.9 possibility of the result being $+$ and 0.4 possibility of it being $-$. This would correspond to the expert thinking 60% of the time it is a $+$, 10% of the time it is a $-$, and 30% of the time it is either.

Thus, the above method of inference can accommodate fuzzy observation. The method can be extended to the case in which the a priori is represented over a set of labels where any label can include imstantiations of variables with fuzzy sets. The interplay between fuzzy sets and mass assignments is important and allows efficient computational schemes by sometimes using the techniques associated with mass assignments and sometimes using the calculus of fuzzy sets.

7. CONCLUSION

Forms of inference and knowledge representation for knowledge engineering that allow for both incompletely specified probabilistic and fuzzy uncertainties have been described.

The inference method associated with the iterative assignment method can be used for common sense reasoning and more particularly for nonmonotonic reasoning, induction, and abduction. Decomposition principles for decomposing the computational tasks have been discussed in Baldwin (1990c, e), which decomposes an inference into a set of subinference problems.

Parallel computational machines for computing the iterative assignment updates have been described in Baldwin (1990e).

Keywords: evidential reasoning, fuzzy reasoning, expert systems, nonmonotonic reasoning, inductive logic, Bayesian conditioning, common sense reasoning

BIBLIOGRAPHY

Baldwin, J. F. (1986). Support logic programing. In A. I. Jones et al. (eds.): *Fuzzy Sets Theory and Applications.* Dordrecht-Boston: Reidel.

Baldwin, J. F. (1987). Evidential support logic programming. *Fuzzy Sets and Systems,* **24,** 1–26.

Baldwin, J. F. et al. (1987). *FRIL manual.* FRIL Systems Ltd., St. Anne's House, St. Anne's Rd., Bristl BS4 4A, UK.

Baldwin, J. F. (1990a). Computational models of uncertainty reasoning in expert systems. *Computers Math. Applic.,* **19,** 105–119.

Baldwin, J. F. (1990b). Combining evidences for evidential reasoning. *Int. J. of Intelligent Systems.* In press.

Baldwin, J. F. (1990c). Towards a general theory of intelligent reasoning. *Third Int. Conf IPMU, Paris,* July 1990.

Baldwin, J. F. (1990d). Evidential reasoning under probabilistic and fuzzy uncertainties. ITRC Univ. of Bristol Report 151, pp. 1–32. In press.

Baldwin, J. F. (1990e). Inference under uncertainty for expert system rules. ITRC Univ. of Bristol Report 152, pp. 1–31. In press.

Baldwin, J. F. (1990f). Approximate reasoning using fuzzy sets and mass assignments. In press.

Csiszår, I. (1975). I-divergence geometry of probability distributions and minimisation problems. *Annals of Probability,* 3 (1), 146–158.

Dalkey, N.C. (1988). A logic of information systems. In G. Evickson and C. Smith (eds.): *Maximum-Entropy and Bayesian Methods in Science and engineering.* Vol. 1. Dordrecht: Kluwer.

Dubois, D. and H. Prade. (1986). On the unicity of Dempster rule of combination. *Int. J. of Intelligent Systems,* 1, 133–142.

Jeffrey, R. (1965). *The Logic of Decision.* New York: McGraw-Hill.

Klir, G. J. and T. A. Folger. (1988). *Fuzzy Sets, Uncertainty, and Information.* Englewood Cliffs, NJ: Prentice-Hall.

Kulback, S. (1959). *Information Theory and Statistics.* New York: Wiley.

Lauritzen, S. I. and D. J. Spiegelhalter. (1988). Local computations with probabilities on graphical structures and their application to expert systems. *J. Roy. Stat. Soc. Ser. B,* **50** (2), 157–224.

Pearl, J. (1988). *Probabilistic Reasoning in Intelligent Systems.* Los Altos: Morgan Kaufmann.

Shafer, G. (1976). *A Mathematical Theory of Evidence.* Princeton University Press.

Shenoy, P. P. (1989). A valuation-based language for expert systems. *Int. J. of Approx. Reasoning,* **3** (5).

Zadeh, L. (1965). Fuzzy sets. *Information and Control,* **8,** 338–353.

Zadeh, L. (1978). Fuzzy sets as a basis for a theory of possibility. *Fuzzy Sets and Systems,* **1,** 3–28.

19 Approximate reasoning in a system combining prototypical knowledge with case-based reasoning

Pietro TORASSO,
Luigi PORTINALE
and Marco CASASSA MONT
Dipartimento di Informatica
Università di Torino
Corso Svizzera, 185
10149 Torino, ITALY

Luca CONSOLE
Dipartimento di Matematica
e Informatica
Università di Udine
Via Zanon, 6
43100 Udine, ITALY

Abstract. In this paper we describe a system that combines prototypical knowledge with case-based reasoning. In particular, prototypical knowledge is used to solve typical cases while case-based reasoning is mainly used for dealing with cases that correspond to "exceptions" with respect to prototypical knowledge. The presence of a case-based component allows us also to deal with problems at the boundary of the knowledge represented in the prototypical part. The need for approximate reasoning mechanisms is apparent in both the prototypical and the case-based components. In fact, some forms of fuzzy matching are needed both for retrieving cases and for discovering the similarities between them. Particular attention has been paid to the design of a uniform approach for dealing with uncertain knowledge in the two components of the system.

1. INTRODUCTION

The interest in *Case-Based Reasoning* (CBR) has grown significantly in recent years and the number of systems adopting such an spproach is growing (Kolodner, 1991; Slade, 1991). Since CBR is aimed at solving problems by exploiting past experience of a human (or artificial) agent, the representation of experience plays a major role: the experience is represented by cases containing both the description of the case in terms of relevant features and the solution (a diagnostic class if the problem concerns diagnostic reasoning, a partial plan if the problem concerns planning, etc.).

The core of a case-based system is formed by a *case memory* from which a *retrieving process*, by means of some *similarity rules*, gets the cases most similar to a particular *input problem* to be solved. It is possible to distinguish between two types of CBR: *Case-Based Problem Solving* and *Precedent Case-Based Reasoning*. In the former, once the most similar cases are retrieved, the solutions attached to them are adapted to the case under examination by means of *adaptation rules* (common in Case-Based Planning; see Hammond, 1989). In the latter, no adaptation is required and the retrieved case is used as a justification of a solution (for example, in legal reasoning; see Ashley and Rissland, 1987). Some different approaches have been proposed as regard memory organization and the adaptation process. In particular, the first aspect has been investigated quite deeply: the simplest organization is based on a *flat memory,* in which the cases are stored sequentially using very simple structures such as lists or vectors; obviously, in such a situation the process of retrieving a case is very expensive (but it can be improved with parallel search techniques). Other approaches propose a *structured memory* organization based on shared feature nets, discrimination nets, etc.; particularly significant to such a purpose is the approach of "conceptual memory" adopted by Kolodner (1984) in her seminal work on CBR which makes use of the E-MOP structures (Episodic Memory Organization Packet) investigated by Schank and his group (1975).

The basic idea is that similar cases which refer to the same "concept" should be grouped together and should be discriminated by their differences. In particular, an E-MOP represents an abstraction of a set of cases (that is, a conceptual category), clustering data concerning the same concept and indexing cases or other abstractions by means of their relevant differences. In fact, we have two major-components in an EMOP: the *norms* representing characteristic information of the abstraction (i.e., features shared by the majority of cases described by the E-MOP) and the *indices* representing discriminant information (features different from one case to another).

It is worth noting that the use of CBR is mainly concerned with the intuition that in many fields, as for example in human diagnostic problem solving, such a form of reasoning seems to play a fundamental role and in many cases human experts are able to solve a new case by retrieving a similar case solved in the past. Some diagnostic systems tried to mimic such a capability (see, for example, some of the systems presented in Kolodner [1988] and Lenhert [1990]); however, the adoption of case-based reasoning as the unique problem solving mechanism seems to be problematic mainly for time and space complexity. In particular, the amount of memory needed in order to store new cases grows very quickly. If we consider the E-MOP model, for example, when a *reminding* occurs (i.e., when an old case is retrieved on the basis of the current data), then a new E-MOP, representing the generalization of the two cases, is created; this can lead to an explosion of the number of E-MOP structures. The recent results by Aghassi (1990) show how the growth of memory can be very high even when the number of cases is moderate (in evaluating the CASEY [Koton, 1989] system it is shown that almost 9000 nodes are needed to index 200 cases). The consequence of such a space complexity is an increase of the complexity of the retrieval process (in the analysis by Aghassi the system searched over 1200 nodes in a memory of only 200 cases). Furthermore, CBR is relevant and useful only for particular types of problems when the use of past experience can be very helpful. The possibility of generalizations from previous cases makes CBR suitable in domains with weak theory or where the computation of a solution is very complex. In many real-world domains CBR is only a component of the whole reasoning process.

Another important aspect (neglected in the early works on CBR) is concerned with the importance and the utility of approximate reasoning mechanisms. Some forms of fuzzy matching are needed both for retrieving cases and for discovering the similarities among cases. Fuzzy matching can greatly increase the performance of CBR systems, since it can be used for matching cases in a flexible way. In particular, the analysis of the similarity between two cases involves the partial match between data characterizing them (moreover, also the relevance of data should be taken into account).

The analysis of the difficulties arising in systems using CBR as the only problem solving mechanism has recently stimulated some research on the possibility of integrating CBR and "more traditional" problem solving approaches. In the CASEY system an integration between a causal model and a case-based system is realized in the field of medical diagnosis. When presented with a new case, CASEY recalls similar problems solved in the past and tries to modify them in order to fit the current situation; this modification is guided by the causal model and by a set of principles for reasoning about evidence in the causal explanations. The use of a causal model can provide more strength to the system while the "evidence principles" allow it to evaluate the differences between the current problem and the retrieved one; if these differences are found to be irrelevant, then adaptation criteria, based on causal explanations, are used in order to obtain the solution for the current problem.

Another integrated approach is the one developed within the MARS system (Bonissone and Dutta, 1990), in which rule-based and case-based reasoning are viewed as complementary methodologies and used for dealing with different aspects of a problem. The most important issue addressed by MARS is relative to the problem of matching cases; it is argued that the uncertainty calculi used in the rule-based part can also be used within the case-based component. CBR is viewed as just one possible way to obtain a result when the expert feels that it is important; for this reason all the cases are stored as rule templates and used in the same way as other rules.

The work reported in the present paper is similar in spirit to the two projects mentioned above, since it advocates the integration of CBR with other forms of knowledge representation and reasoning. In particular, the paper describes an integrated system devoted to diagnostic problem solving that combines prototypical knowledge with CBR. Two major components can be identified in our system: the first is a frame-based component (a variation of the surface level of the CHECK system described in Torasso and Console [1989b]) allowing the representation of prototypical knowledge and used to solve typical problems; the second is a case-based component (modeled after the conceptual memory adopted by Kolodner) used for dealing with "atypical" cases (that is, with cases that do not fit very well in any prototypical description). The focus of the paper is about the mechanisms for approximate reasoning in the case-based component; in particular, we concentrate on the problem of evaluating a degree of match between current input data and a retrieved case (i.e., on a defintion of a measure of similarity between cases). The approach is based on the design of a uniform method for dealing with uncertain knowledge in both components of the system, in such a way extending the work in Torasso and Console (1989a).

The rest of the paper is organized as follows. In Section 2 we give a brief description of the architecture of our system with particular attention to the roles of the two components and the cooperation between them. In Section 3 we describe how the basic mechanism for approximate reasoning used for dealing with prototypical knowledge, can be adapted to fit in the case-based component.

2. ARCHITECTURE OF THE SYSTEM

The architecture of the system is sketched in Figure 19.1, where the main modules composing the system are represented together with their connections. In particular it is worth noting that the INTE-GRATION MODULE is responsible for the activation of the case-based system and the frame-based one, and that the WORKING MEMORY is shared between the two systems and contains the description of the particular problem under examination as well as the intermediate results obtained during the reasoning process.

2.1. Basic Motivations

In the introduction we noticed that various reasons suggest the integration of CBR with other problem solving paradigms; in

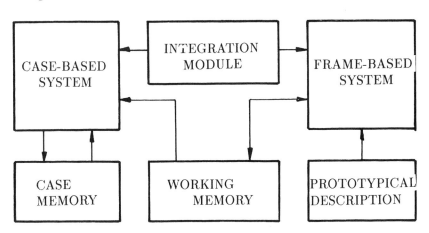

Figure 19.1. Architecture of the integrated system

particular space and time complexity increase in a considerable way when using a system merely based on previous cases; moreover, in many real-world domains a priori knowledge can be available often in form of prototypes. This suggests that a potentially useful integration could involve a prototypical (frame-based) and a case-based system.

It is in general useless and redundant to use a case-based system only for storing the past cases already solved by the frame-based system; in fact, if the system is able to give a correct answer to such cases, then the conclusion is obtained in a relatively simple way using heuristic knowledge. Also, storing these cases into the *conceptual memory* (i.e., the case memory) implies a considerable waste of resources, because we already have a correct description of the represented problems and an efficient way to use it. The integration becomes useful when the case-based component is used for storing cases that correspond to exceptions with respect to prototypical knowledge.

There are various reasons for the existence of such exceptions. First of all, since in the frame system we model prototypical knowledge, it is quite obvious that a typical property does not necessarily hold for all the individuals. Moreover, in many diagnostic systems the proto-typical description refers to situations in which the malfunctioning fully manifests. However, it could be useful to identify the malfunc-tioning at an early stage when not all the typical findings are present in the case under examination (see Console et al. [1989] for a discussion of the role of temporal aspects in the diagnostic process).

The architecture that we are describing is devoted to diagnostic problem solving in which the frame-based part is composed of prototypical descriptions of diagnostic categories viewed as collec-tions of findings (observable parameters in the modeled system). Each frame provides a stereotyped description of a disorder, but it may be the case that there are some exceptions to such descriptions (i.e., situations where some nontypical findings are present or some typical ones are not present). Traditional diagnostic systems based on frame structures are usually able to deal only with typical cases and fail when they try to analyze exceptional cases.

Exceptions are usually not modeled for several reasons. First of all, it is very often difficult to make a priori predictions about exceptional cases. Moreover, even in those situations when it is possible to identify all the possible exceptions, inserting them into the proto-typical knowledge could reduce the system's performance in a con-siderable way. In other words, making the prototype "too weak," in order to handle exceptions, weakens the conclusions obtained by the system (making them very imprecise).

Adding a case-based component in order to deal with such "boundary conditions" allows the frame-based system to analyze only "typical" situations, switching to the case-based component in the presence of "atypical" situations. Only the exceptional cases are inserted and indexed in the conceptual memory and retrieved when similar cases are presented to the system. Moreover, the conceptual memory is naturally dynamic and it is able to modify itself in a more efficient way than the modification of the prototypical knowledge base.

2.2. Frame-Based Component

In this section we shall briefly describe the structure of the frame--based subsystem, which has been derived from the surface level of the CHECK system (Torasso and Console, 1989b).

To keep the discussion as simple as possible, in the following we will assume to have just a set of diagnostic hypotheses without any taxonomic link among them; in this way we do not have to deal with classifications of cases at different levels of detail.[1]

In our system, prototypical knowledge is modeled by two different types of slots: NECESSAR FINDINGS and SUPPLEMENTARY FINDINGS.

The slot NECESSARY FINDINGS contains a description of the findings that must be necessarily observed in order to establish the diagnostic hypothesis associated with the frame. In particular, the slot is formed by a list (conjunction) of finding descriptions, each one of which has the form:

$$<finding, \ <value_1, \ com\_degree_1>,$$
$$<value_2, \ comp\_degree_2>,$$
$$............$$
$$<value_n, \ comp\_degree_n>>$$
$$relevance: \ m$$

---

[1] Obviously, taxonomies of disorders or faults play a major role in many diagnostic systems (among many others, the CHECK system) as well as in diagnostic reasoning performed by humans.

where each value is a linguistic value. A *compatibility degree* is associated with each value to indicate the compatibility of such a value with respect to the diagnostic category; moreover, a *relevance measure m* is associated with each finding and models the "strength of necessity" of the finding itself (this will be described more clearly in the section devoted to approximate reasoning; see also Torasso and Console, 1989a). The findings occurring in the NECESSARY FINDINGS are implicitly AND-ed.

SUPPLEMENTARY FINDINGS allow us to complete NECESSARY FINDINGS by describing more specific findings that are not strictly necessary. SUPPLEMENTARY FINDINGS are implicitly OR-ed since we can consider that the instantiation of even one of them can contribute to a better characterization of a hypothesis; however, they cannot confirm a hypothesis by themselves (they are not sufficient conditions). Their structure is the same as that of NECESSARY FINDINGS.

Besides prototypical knowledge, other forms of knowledge must be represented in a diagnostic system. In particular, different forms of control knowledge play a fundamental role in the diagnostic process. In our system, two types of control knowledge are modeled in each frame, namely TRIGGERS and VALIDATION RULES. TRIGGERS are activation rules; a frame is considered and its instantiation is attempted only if these rules are satisfied by actual data. A TRIGGER is represented as a conjunction of conditions *<finding, value>*. Different types of triggering rules can be defined at different levels of specificity; this is obtained through the use of a relevance measure indicating the importance of the corresponding condition. VALIDATION RULES are used to confirm or disregard the current hypothesis by augmenting or reducing its evidence degree; also their importance is weighed by a relevance measure.

In the following we will concentrate on prototypical knowledge, but it is worth noting that all the considerations about approximate reasoning mechanisms are valid also for control knowledge (see the discussion in Torasso and Console, 1989b).

2.3. Case-Based Component

As stated in the introduction, this component of the system is modeled after the conceptual memory introduced by Kolodner (1984). In our particular application each E-MOP corresponds to a diagnostic hypothesis or a syndromic situation resulting from an abstraction of the case descriptions in terms of findings.

One of the main advantages of the conceptual memory is its ability of reorganization when a new case is inserted. At the beginning, the conceptual memory contains an empty E-MOP for each one of the diagnostic hypotheses; such E-MOPs are then initialized during a *training phase* by considering a set of atypical and a priori classified cases.

When a new case is presented to the case-based system, the retrieval process starts. There are two possibilities: if the results of the reasoning in the prototypical system can be used as focusing information, then some particular initial E-MOPs can be selected in order to start the search; in the other case, we must start from each initial E-MOP present in the memory. The retrieval process fundamentally consists in two types of operations; given an E-MOP and a current case we must first delete from the current case all the findings that match the norms and then we must follow all the possible indices. Following an index can lead either to another E-MOP or to a specific case. If we reach another E-MOP the operations previously described are repeated, while if we reach a specific case a *reminding* occurs and we can evaluate the similarity between the retrieved and the actual case.

If this process stops without retrieving a case (i.e., it stops in an E-MOP from which no index can be followed), there are two possibilities:

- If in the current case there is no finding that can be used as an index[2] (we say that the case is *exhausted* in the E-MOP), we try to retrieve the other cases "exhausted" in the E-MOP.
- If in the current case there are findings that can be used as indices, then the fact that no index can be followed means that the current case is different from all the cases stored in the memory and thus the retrieval process must stop with a failure.

Another important process is the insertion of a case in the conceptual memory. This is a decision taken from the external world: in our case by the user when he or she believes that the actual case is a *relevant atypical case* for a particular diagnostic hypothesis. This means that the case to be inserted is already classified by the system or by the user itself.

The insertion is analogous to the retrieval process with the

---

[2] We will see in the following when a finding can be used as an index.

following differences. When a reminding occurs, a new E-MOP representing a generalization of the involved cases is created; its norms will be the common findings between the cases and the indices (pointing to these cases) will be chosen among the relevant discriminating findings. When the search stops on an E-MOP, if in the actual case there are some findings available as indices, then new indices are created into the E-MOP pointing to the actual case; otherwise we mark the actual case as "exhausted" in the E-MOP. The navigation in the conceptual memory allows us, by matching the norms and following the indices, to retrieve cases that are similar to the one under examination as well as to insert the current case, if needed. It is worth noting that the information associated with the norms can become meaningless when the system evolves; in fact, it is possible to have an *undergeneralized norm* when this norm is present in an E-MOP E_1 where it is shared among many cases indexed also in an E-MOP E_2 such that E_2 indexes E_1. In this case, the right position of the norm should be into E_2. On the contrary, we have an *overgeneralized norm* when it is present in an E-MOP where it is shared among few indexed cases; such a norm is no longer meaningful. The mechanisms developed in order to handle these problems are discussed in a detailed way in Portinale (1991).

2.4. Integration Module

After the brief sketch of the two basic components of the system, let us summarize how they cooperate. When a new case is presented to the system, the frame-based component is invoked first in order to perform a diagnosis on the basis of prototypical knowledge.

If the diagnostic conclusions obtained using prototypical knowledge are not well-supported, because their global evidence degree is low (that is, there is no diagnostic hypothesis that has a good match with current data), then the case-based component is invoked in order to verify whether cases similar to the one under examination were already encountered in the past.

If case-based reasoning provides a solution and the current case is considered by the user as a *relevant atypical case,* then it can be stored into the conceptual memory and made available for future retrievals. If CBR fails, it is possible to provide a classification of the case from the external and store it in the conceptual memory. Notice that this is a global way of using CBR when the low global evidence of a hypothesis is caused by low evidence in each part of the corresponding frame (TRIGGERS, NECESSARY FINDINGS, etc.); this means also that no information about the starting point of the case-based process (the intial E-MOP) is available. In this case, the system searches from each possible initial E-MOP.

There is another possibility of interaction between CBR and prototypical knowledge. If a hypothesis has been triggered with a high evidence degree, but it has not been confirmed in a next phase, then the case-based module can try to get a solution. The fact that the hypothesis has been strongly evoked by TRIGGERS suggests that the failure in matching the prototypical description with the actual case can be due to the presence of some exceptions (so that the case can be better dealt with by the case-based component). This is a local way of using the case-based component, because the failure of a hypothesis can be ascribed to some specific part of the associated frame. In this case, we can start the search in the case memory from the E-MOP associated with that particular hypothesis.

The interface between the two parts of the system is represented by the *working memory*, which contains factual knowledge as a collection of <*finding, value*> pairs.

In conclusion, it is important to point out that we do not mean that the adoption of a case-based component can solve all the problems that affect heuristic (associational) diagnostic systems. In particular,we do not mean that CBR can be an alternative to the adoption of deep models (and of systems integrating heuristic and deep knowledge), which is still needed. The integration that we propose can only enlarge the spectrum of solvable problems making the system more flexible in the presence of cases at the extremes of this spectrum.

Actually, an integrated system offers another facility that will not be discussed here for lack of space: a CBR system can in fact be used for testing and monitoring the prototypical structures. In order to test the adequacy of a prototypical knowledge base in a different setting, it is useful to evaluate how many cases of a large training set are correctly dealt with just by using prototypical knowledge. Moreover, it is quite useful to compare prototypical knowledge with the structures emerging from the case memory when the cases contained in the training set have been fed up to the CBR. For example, we can monitor the construction of the norms in the E-MOPs that are not considered as NECESSARY or SUPPLEMENTARY FINDINGS in the prototypical knowledge. However, this is outside the scope of this paper and in the following we shall assume that only atypical cases are stored in the case memory.

3. APPROXIMATE REASONING IN THE INTE-GRATED SYSTEM

3.1. Representing Uncertain Prototypical Knowledge

In the discussion about the organization of the frame-based component of the system, we have not detailed the aspects concerning the representation of uncertain knowledge. The need for a partial match between frames and data leads to the design of more flexible prototypical descriptions. In this section, we shall briefly recall the problem (analyzed in previous works) of defining fuzzy prototypical representations and the mechanisms for combining evidences values (the reader interested in a more detailed discussion is referred to Torasso and Console [1989a, b]).

As we noticed in Section 2.2, a first way to make a prototypical description less rigid is to associate with each linguistic value v of each finding F a *compatibility degree* with the hypothesis. For the moment, we will assume that the values of a finding can be defined in a crisp way (i.e., without defining the linguistic values by means of fuzzy sets). This assumption might result in a limitation since in some cases the value would be more correctly represented by means of fuzzy linguistic terms[3] (Zadeh, 1983).

In each slot, associated with the finding F_i, there will be a list of pairs of the form:

$$<\text{ling\_value } V_{ij}, \text{comp\_degree } \mu_{ij}>$$

The interpretation follows Zadeh's (1978) possibility theory: the fact that the finding F_i takes the value V_{ij} is compatible with the hypothesis H with degree μ_{ij} ($\mu_{ij}\in[0,1]$).

We have previously observed that the introduction of a *relevance measure* could be interesting in order to weight the importance of a datum (a similar concept is used also in the expert system CENTAUR; see Aikins, 1983): we associate with each atomic datum a relevance measure in the interval [0,1] (a value close to 1 implies high relevance and a value close to 0 implies a low relevance).

---

[3] Notice that the extension of our system to the fuzzy case would require only the definition of an operator for combining the possibility value of the linguistic terms with the compatibility degree of the pair *<finding, value>*.

A relevance measure is associated with each finding in the NECES-SARY FINDINGS and in the SUPPLEMENTARY ones (and with each TRIGGER and VALIDATION RULE). Notice that the relevance measure allows us to model, for NECESSARY FINDINGS (which are AND-ed), different strengths of necessity (only those with relevance equal to 1 have to be considered as strictly necessary). The interpretation that we assign to SUPPLEMENTARY FINDINGS (which are OR-ed) allows us to consider the relevance as a strength of sufficiency with a fundamental difference from sufficient condition: SUPPLEMENTARY FINDINGS cannot establish by themselves the associated hypothesis.

Compatibility degrees and relevance measures are combined in the evaluation of the degree of match between prototypical structures and data. In particular, the way in which they are combined depends on the logical connectives used to form complex conditions; moreover, if an atom is relevant, its contribution has to be high (i.e., has to depend directly from its compatibility degree) and vice versa. In Torrasso and Console (1989a) we showed that a good way to combine compatibility degree (e) and relevance (m) of a datum to provide a *revised evidence* for the datum is the following:

$$f_{and}(e, m) = me + (1-m)$$
$$f_{or}(e, m) = me$$

The function f_{and} is used with NECESSARY FINDINGS and the function f_{or} with SUPPLEMENTARY FINDINGS.

Once the revised evidence has been computed for each finding, we have to get the evidence degree of complex descriptions (for example, the evidence of NECESSARY or SUPPLEMENTARY FINDINGS). Since NECESSARY (SUPPLEMENTARY) FINDINGS are implicitly AND-ed (OR-ed), we need to define a conjunction (disjunction) operator AND (OR).

For this task we adopt the following formulas discussed in Lesmo et al. (1985):

$$e(AND(T_1,...T_n)) = \alpha + \beta(\beta - \alpha)$$

where $\alpha = \prod_{j=1}^{n} e(T_j)$ and $\beta = \min_{j=1}^{n} e(T_j)$;

$$e(OR(T_1,...T_n)) = e(NOT(AND((NOT\ T_1),...,(NOT\ T_n))))$$

where $e(NOT\ T) = 1 - e(T)$. The term $e(T_i)$ represents the revised evidence of the finding F_i.

Finally, evidence values from different chunks of knowledge have to be combined in order to obtain the global degree of evidence of prototypical description. Since NECESSARY and SUPPLEMEN-TARY FINDINGS play very different roles in the instantiation of a frame, they cannot be treated in the same way when combining their evidence values. In particular, SUPPLEMENTARY FINDINGS cannot by themselves confirm a hypothesis. For this reason a particular operation, called *unfair addition*, has been proposed in which the first operand is privileged:

$$e_1 +_u e_2 = e_1 + (1 - e_1)e_1e_2$$

where we assume that e_1 and e_2 are respectively the evidence of NECESSARY and SUPPLEMENTARY FINDINGS. The final degree of the hypothesis represented by the frame is computed in a similar way by taking into account also the evidence values obtained from control knowledge (see Torasso and Console [1989b] for more details).

3.2. Dealing with Uncertainty in the Case-Based Component

In CBR systems some form of approximate reasoning is needed in order to deal with diffrent types of problems. In particular, it plays a fundamental role in the problem of the *relevancy* of the cases and of the *similarity* between cases. In the previous sections we have conjectured that the integration of CBR and more traditional problem solving approaches can be very useful in addressing these tasks and some works have shown that useful results can be obtained when integrating CBR with causal models (Koton, 1989) or with rule-based systems (Bonissone and Blau, 1990; Bonissone and Dutta, 1990).

In our system, we have designed a uniform approach, based on the approximate calculi developed for the prototypical-based part, for dealing with uncertainty in both components; in particular, the problems of the choice of indices and of the evaluation of similarity can be solved in our framework partially by exploiting the pieces of information present in prototypical knowledge and the same notions of evidence combination proposed for this type of knowledge.

Let us consider a specific case C (for which the prototypical system oncludes the hypothesis H with a low global evidence degree) and suppose that the use of the case-based component allows the system to retrieve a case C' similar to C.

There are many similarities between the notion of prototypical description as stereotypical case and the E-MOP generalization in which the norms represent "common findings" of the indexed cases. In fact, the generalization mechanisms single out structures and regularities among data. This means that, when the reminding of C' occurs, we can use the prototypical description of the hypothesis H' associated with C' in order to guide the match between C and C'.

A first type of information useful for our purposes is the distinction between NECESSARY and SUPPLEMENTARY FINDINGS; moreover the concept of relevance of a datum is very important in the choice of indices and in defining similarity measures; for this reason the case-based component can access the information about the *relevance measure* of the findings and use them for evaluating the similarity between cases.

In the following we discuss how the mechanisms for approximate reasoning, introduced in the previous section, can be used in the case-based component. In particular, we first discuss the problem of selecting the indices in the case memory and then the problem of evaluating the similarity between two cases.

Let us now examine how the prototypical information can help in the choice of indices. This task is very important in CBR because, in general, in order to avoid a combinatorial explosion, it is not possible to use all the findings as indices. An index has to be a finding with a high predictive power and high importance; a high predictive power means that the finding should be present in many similar cases. An index must also be able to distinguish two cases that share many relevant findings, but have a different value for the finding used as an index. It should be clear that this discrimination process becomes inadequate when using findings with low importance.

On the basis of the previous considerations, we propose to choose indices looking at the different roles played by the findings in the prototype and using some thresholds. In fact, a particular finding can be used as an index if and only if it belongs to one of the following categories:

- TRIGGERS with *relevance* $> \tau$
- NECESSARY FINDINGS with *relevance* $> \sigma$
- SUPPLEMENTARY FINDINGS with *relevance* $> \sigma'$

where τ, σ ($\sigma > \tau$) and σ' ($\sigma' \gg \sigma$) are appropriate thresholds.

Since TRIGGERS are activation rules (they allow the system to evoke a diagnostic hypothesis), it seems reasonable to assume that many similar cases, even if atypical, share the same triggering findings; for this reason, TRIGGERS can have potential predictive power and can be selected as candidate indices. Similar considerations can be done for NECESSARY and SUPPLEMENTARY FINDINGS by recalling their role in the description of a malfunctioning. Notice that we are interested in considering as potential indices only findings with a significant degree of relevance. For this reason, we have defined some thresholds, on the relevance measures of the findings, that constrain the choice of indices. It is worth noting that the threshold σ, settled for SUPPLEMENTARY FINDINGS, must be higher than that of NECESSARY ones, because only "very important" SUPPLEMENTARY conditions had to be considered for discrimination.

A second problem to be discussed concerns the evaluation of the similarity between two cases. In the previous sections we assumed that linguistic values are defined in a crisp way, so that in the following we shall limit ourselves to such a case (notice that quite often the training set contains cases characterized by this type of feature and, in general, we must be able to evaluate a match even in presence of binary features). The availability of fuzzy descriptions for the linguistic values would greatly increase the flexibility and the accuracy of the evaluation of similarity. Since we assumed that such distributions are not available, we must make some assumptions on the linguistic values. In particular, we assume that the values v_i of the finding F are ordered according to a given criterion (this is much less demanding than knowing the definition of the linguistic term via membership function).

The hardest problem in such a case is to quantify the difference between two linguistic values of the same findings. First of all, it is important to introduce the notion of *antinomy* or *incompatibility* between two values. Very often, in the set of admissible values of a given finding, some of the values are completely incompatible (e.g., the values *absent* and *very high* of the finding *fever* in a medical domain); the system must know which values are antithetical and has to take into account this piece of information during the evaluation of the degree of match among cases. For this reason, when the antinomy of values can be assumed, this type of knowledge has to be made explicit in the system.

In all the other cases we can determine a *distance* between two values; such a distance represents a measure of their difference.

Let us consider a finding f such that V_f is the set of admissible linguistic values of f; each value is indexed by an index i such that $1 \leqslant i \leqslant$ card (V_f). Moreover, we impose a total order among these values such that for each v_i, $v_j \in V_f$ we have that $v_i < v_j \leftrightarrow i < j$. The distance is then defined as follows:

$$d(v_i, v_j) = \frac{|i - j|}{\text{card}(V_f) - 1}$$

while the *similarity* or *degree of match* is simply

$$s(v_i, V_j) = 1 - d(v_i, v_j)$$

Given these definitions, a value of the similarity close to 0 implies a low degree of match and a value close to 1 a high degree of match. It should be clear that, if two values are identical, then their distance is equal to 0 and we get a perfect match ($s(v_u, v_j) = 1$).

Notice that the above formulas make antithetical two values at the extremes of the ordering. In case there are values that are defined to be antithetical, one must extend the definition of distance given above by considering that if v_i and v_j ($v_i < v_j$) are antithetical, then each value v_h, such that $v_h < v_i$, and each value v_k, such that $v_j < v_k$, must in turn be antithetical. In other words, let $V_f = <v_1, v_2,..., v_n>$ be the ordered set of admissible values for a finding f; if the user defines v_i and v_j ($v_i < v_j$) as antithetical, then we have

$$d(v_h, v_k) = 1 \text{ for each } h \leqslant i \text{ and for each } k \geqslant j$$

The criteria allow us to evaluate the similarity between each corresponding pair $<finding, value>$ in the input and in the retrieved case.

Given that notion of similarity betwen two values of the same finding, we need some mechanisms to determine the similarity between a new case C and a classified case C' (with associated hypothesis H'). As we noticed in the previous section the prototypical description of H' is used to guide such a match. In particular, we take into account the "relevance" of each finding with respect to H so that we weigh in a different way the contribution of each finding. Let us consider a finding f and two values v_i and v_j of f; let m be the relevance measure of f with respect to the hypothesis H'. We need a method able to combine the similarity value s between v_i and v_j with the relevance of the finding f. The idea is that the similarity measure plays the same role as the compatibility degree of a value with respect to a hypothesis when matching current data with a prototypical description. Moreover, considering the distinction between NECESSARY and SUPPLEMENTARY FINDINGS allows us to use the same functions used in the frame-based component.

In fact, the *revised similarity* can be evaluated for extension of the NECESSARY FINDINGS using the function

$$f_{and}(s, m) = ms + (1 - m)$$

and for extension of the SUPPLEMENTARY FINDINGS using the function

$$f_{or}(s, m) = ms$$

A further possibility could be the presence of a supplementary value in only one of the cases (the input or the past case).[4] When the value is present only in the retrieved case, it is reasonable to assume no match (degree of match = 0). Otherwise, the information present in the prototype of the diagnosis associated with the retrieved case can be helpful; following the above considerations we take as the degree of match of such a value the compatibility degree relative to the hypothesis associated to the prototype. This value is then corrected with the relevance of the feature.

Given the revised similarity of each finding, we can determine the similarity (N) between the NECESSARY FINDINGS of the retrieved case and the NECESSARY FINDINGS of the current case as well as the similarity (S) concerning the SUPPLEMENTARY FINDINGS as follows:

$$N = e(\text{AND } (T_1, \dots T_n)) = \alpha + \beta(\beta - \alpha)$$
$$S = e(\text{OR } (T_1, \dots T_n)) = e(\text{NOT}(\text{AND}((\text{NOT } T_1), \dots, (\text{NOT } T_n))))$$

where $\alpha = \prod_{j=1}^{n} e(T_j)$, $\beta = \min_{j=1}^{n} e(T_j)$, $e(\text{NOT } T) = 1 - e(T)$, and each $e(T_j)$ represents the revised similarity of each finding.

The total similarity M (i.e., the final degree of match between input data and the retrieved case) is computed using the *unfair addition* operation:

$$M = N + (1 - N)\,\text{NS}$$

---

[4] It is not a limitation to assume that necessary features are always present (if they are not volunteered by the user, the frame-based component asks the user for the value of these findings).

Obviously, if the retrieval process has pointed out many cases that are potentially similar to the input one, the mechanisms for evaluating the similarity between the input case and the retrieved ones allow one to single out the *most similar*.

4. CONCLUSION

In this paper we have presented a system combining prototypical knowledge with case-based reasoning. While the former is used to solve typical problems, the latter deals with cases that are difficult (or impossible) to solve merely by using prototypical knowledge because they deviate from the stereotype (in other words, they present exceptions in one or more relevant findings).

We have also presented a uniform formalism able to handle uncertainty and approximate reasoning in both components of the system. This formalism extends previous work of the authors devoted to developing a mechanism for dealing with uncertain prototypical knowledge.

By exploiting the conceptual relationship between prototypical descriptions and atypical cases, we have shown that, by taking into account the distinction between NECESSARY and SUPPLEMEN-TARY FINDINGS, all the functions used to evaluate the final evidence of a hypothesis on the basis of current data can be used to compute a similarity measure between the input and the retrieved case(s).

Apart from experimental work for evaluating the limits of the approach and in particular the possibility of scaling up to large real-world problems, some work has still to be done, mainly in the direction of dealing with fuzzy linguistic terms and in improving, in this way, the notions of distance and similarity among cases.

Keywords: prototypical knowledge, case-based reasoning, similarity measure, degree of match

BIBLIOGRAPHY

Aghassi, D. S. (1990). *Evaluating case-based reasoning for heart failure diagnosis.* Master's Thesis, Dept. of EECS, MIT, Cambridge, MA.

Aikins, J. S. (1983). Prototypical knowledge for expert systems. *Artificial Intelligence,* **20** 163–210.

Ashley, K. and E. Rissland. (1987). Compare and contrast, a test for expertise. *Proc. AAAI 87,* Seattle, pp. 273–278.

Bonissone, P. P. and S. Dutta. (1990). Integrating case based and rule based reasoning: The possibilistic connection. *Proc. Sixth Conf. on Uncertainty in Artificial Intelligence,* Cambridge, M.A.

Bonissone, P. P., L. Blau, and S. Ayub. (1990). Leveraging the integration of approximate reasoning systems. *Working Notes AAAI Spring Case-Based Reasoning Symposium,* Stanford, CA.

Console, L., A. Janin Rivolin, D. Theseider Dupre, and P. Torasso. (1989). Integration of causal and temporal reasoning in diagnostic problem solving. *Proc. Ninth Int. Work. on Expert Systems and Their Applications (Conf. on Second Generation Expert Systems),* Avignon, pp. 309–323.

Hammond, K. J. (1989). *Case-Based Planning: Viewing Planning as a Memory Task.* New York: Academic Press.

Kolodner, J. L. (1984). *Retrieval and Organization Strategies in Conceptual Memory: A Computer Model.* Lawrence Erlbaum.

Kolodner, J. L. (ed.). (1988). *Proceedings of the DARPA Case-Based Reasoning Workshop.* Clearwater Beach, FL: Morgan Kaufmann.

Kolodner, J. L. (1991). Improving human decision making through case-based decision aiding. *AI Magazine,* **12**(2), 52–68.

Koton, P.A. (1989). Using experience in learning and problem solving. MIT/LCS/TR-441, MIT, Cambridge, MA.

Lenhert, W. (Chair). (1990). *AAAI spring symp. on case-based reasoning.* Stanford, CA.

Lesmo, L., L. Saitta, and P. Torasso. (1985). Evidence combination in expert systems. *Int J. of Man-Machine Studies,* **22**, 307–326.

Portinale, L. (1991). Generalization handling in a dynamic case memory. *Proc. Sixth ISMIS 91,* Lecture Notes in Artificial Intelligence. Berlin: Springer-Verlag.

Schank, R. C. (1975). *Conceptual Information Processing.* Amsterdam: North-Holland.

Slade, S. (1991). Case-based reasoning: A research paradigm. *AI Magazine,* **12** (1), 42–55.

Torasso, P. and L. Console. (1989a). Approximate Reasoning and Prototypical knowledge. *International Journal of Approximate Reasoning,* **3,** 157–178.

Torasso, P. and L. Console. (1989b). *Diagnostic Problem Solving: Combining Heuristic, Approximate and Causal Reasoning.* New York: Van Nostrand Reinhold.

Zadeh, L. A. (1978). Fuzzy sets as a basis for a theory of possibility. *Fuzzy Sets and Systems,* **1,** 3–28.

Zadeh, L. A. (1989). The role of fuzzy logic in the management of uncertainty in expert systems. *Fuzzy Sets and Systems,* **11,** 199–227.

4

FUZZY LOGIC FOR KNOWLEDGE REPRESENTATION AND ELICITATION

20 Fuzzy logic and knowledge representation using linguistic modifiers

Bernadette BOUCHON-MEUNIER
LAFORIA, Université Paris VI, Tour 46
4 place Jussieu, 75252 Paris Cédex 05
FRANCE

Abstract. We study knowledge-based systems using fuzzy logic and we focus on the representation of knowledge through linguistic variables characterized by means of fuzzy qualifications. Linguistic modifers enable us to slightly change the qualifications and they are important tools for approximate reasoning for several reasons: they lead to simple rules given in a symbolic way, avoiding computations and compatible with the fuzzy logic; they take place in the comparison of various available fuzzy implications; they enable gradual rules to be used in the context of deduction rules.

1. INTRODUCTION

Several kinds of imperfection can be observed in pieces of knowledge. In the case where the imperfections are concerned only with uncertainty (probabilistic uncertainty, subjective uncertainty, doubt, lack of credibility), there exist several ways to manage the given knowledge, using for instance probability theory or evidence theory. When there exists some inaccuracy in descriptions of the available evidence, interval analysis could be useful in specific cases. If the situation is more complex, for instance, if vague concepts must be handled, possibility theory and fuzzy logic provide a useful tool that permits the management of both uncertainty and imprecision.

As pointed out by several authors (Zadeh, 1981; Wenstøp, 1981; Eshragh and Mamdani, 1981; Baldwin, 1981; Baldwin and Pilsworth, 1980), linguistic modifiers are important issues in the treatment of data by means of a fuzzy logic and we will study some of them, presenting their interesting properties. One thing of particular interest is their ability to be used symbolically in the framework of a numerical approach based on fuzzy logic, which emphasizes the fact that possibility theory provides an interface between numerical and symbolic descriptions of evidences. Fuzzy logic is sometimes reproached as involving heavy computations and yielding conclusions that are not easily expressible, even though the original pieces of information are expressible; when modifiers are used, these criticisms are not apparent any more, at least for the pieces of knowledge concerned with the modifers.

Modifiers are interesting for two other reasons. First, their study provides ways of *comparison for fuzzy implications,* and yields a kind of classification of the various aspects of fuzzy logics. Second, they enable *gradual knowledge* to be used in the context of deduction rules.

2. THE FUZZY LOGIC FRAMEWORK

Fuzzy logic, introduced by Zadeh and Bellman, has inspired various developments and applications. Its aim is to provide a model for approximate reasoning. Following the possibilistic framework introduced by Zadeh (1979) for fuzzy logics, we consider *linguistic variables* X_i taking values in ordered universes U_i. If C_i is fuzzy characterization of X_i associated with a possibility distribution $\mu_i \colon U_i \to [0, 1]$, a fuzzy proposition is expressed as "X_i is C_i," or as conjunctions or disjunctions of predicates of this form. A *deduction rule* describes a relationship between such propositions in the following way:

$$\text{"if } X_1 \text{ is } C_1 \text{ then } X_2 \text{ is } C_2 \text{"} \tag{DR}$$

The foundations of fuzzy logic have been established in several frameworks and they yield multiple systems. All of them can be presented in some way as generalizations of classical logic and they sometimes stem from works in multivalued logics. This multiplicity can be regarded as an advantage since the set of available tools is large and every problem can be solved with a fuzzy logic suitable for its own characteristics. Nevertheless, this property raises several questions, mainly concerning the preservation of obtained results when changing the underlying fuzzy logic, and also concerning the criteria dictating the choice of one fuzzy logic over another.

A peculiarity of fuzzy logics is to allow inferences even though the predicates that are supposed to be satisfied are only approximately satisfied. The rule of inference used in fuzzy logic is a generalization of modus ponens. Then the choice of a fuzzy logic is based on the determination of modus ponens. Then the choice of a fuzzy logics is based on the determination of a fuzzy implication. This one gives the weight of the relationship between the possible values of X_1 and the possible values of X_2 entailed by rule (DR). It is defined in the following way:

$$r(x, y) = F(\mu_1(x), \mu_2(y), \text{ for each } x \in U_1, \text{ for each } y \in U_2 \qquad (1)$$

for a given function $F: [0, 1] \times [0, 1] \rightarrow [0,1]$.

The list of the most important ones is given in the appendix, but several others are possible and the justification of this list is based on the applications of these implications in knowledge-based systems.

The generalized modus ponens allows us to deduce a conclusion from rule (DR) and from an observed particular situation described as "X_1 is C'_1", where C'_1 is associated with a possibility distribution μ'_1. This conclusion is associated with a possibility distribution μ'_2 defined on U_2 and lying in [0, 1]. In the general case, there is no directly expressible characterization of X_2 corresponding to μ'_2. We shall see in Section 4 that some expressions of C'_1 lead to a clear description C'_2 of X_2. The distribution μ'_2 is computed as follows:

$$\mu'_2(y) = \sup_{x \in U_1} G(\mu'_1(x), r(x, y)), \text{ for each } y \in U_2 \qquad (2)$$

for a given function $G: [0, 1] \times [0, 1] \rightarrow [0, 1]$, which is chosen to enable the generalized modus ponens to be compatible with the classical modus ponens ($\mu'_2 = \mu_2$ if $\mu'_1 = \mu_1$).

3. LINGUISTIC MODIFIERS

The aim of fuzzy logic is to enable conclusions to be stated even though the facts characterizing a studied situation are only ap-

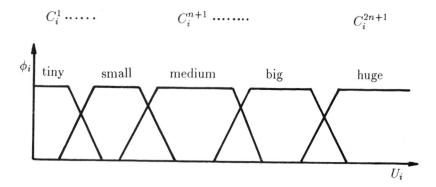

Figure 20.1. Example of an ordered list of characterizations of the variable X_1 = "size" by means of L_1 = {tiny, small, medium, big, huge}

proximately those expected and standardized by the expert who expressed the deduction rules. This idea of approximation of a standard evidence is at the root of the concept of a linguistic modifier, or a hedge.

Several works on fuzzy logic stress the interest of modifiers (such as "very," "more or less," acting on the fuzzy qualifications C_i to give new characterizations mC_i), for a modifier m, associated with possibility distributions $t_m(\mu_i)$ obtained from μ_i by means of some transformation t_m (Bouchon, 1987). This definition is very general and "not" can be viewed as a modifier corresponding to the tranformation $t_m(u) = 1 - u$. But, generally, the purpose of modifiers is to produce slightly different characterizations that are not too far from the original ones in their neighborhood, so to speak.

Two main families of modifiers can be studied according to their effect on the qualifications they modify.

3.1. Reinforcing Modifiers

The first family regroups the *reinforcing modifiers;* they provide a characterization that is stronger than the original one. Zadeh (1975) proposed the modifier "very" associated with the transformation $t_m(u) = u^2$. We can think of other so-called *restrictive modifiers* defined by transformations such that $t_m(u) \leqslant u$ for any $u \in [0, 1]$.

Nevertheless, it should be remarked that there is a relationship between the reinforcement of a characterization C_i (very C_i, strongly

C_i, really C_i,...) and the fact that the modifier is restrictive, mainly in the case where the possibility distribution μ_i is a "half-bell" (which means that there exists $x_0 \in U_i$ such that $\mu_i(x) = 1$ for every x smaller or greater than x_0). In other cases, it is sometimes not equivalent to reinforce C_i and to use a restrictive modifier; for instance, in Figure 20.1, "very tiny" should be included in "tiny," but "very small" should not be included in "small," it would rather be intermediate between "tiny" and "small."

3.2. Weakening Modifiers

The second family of modifiers regroups the *weakening modifiers,* providing new characterizations that are less strong than the original one. Zadeh (1975) introduced the modifier "more or less," associated with the transformation $t_m(u) = u^{1/2}$. Other so-called *expansive modifiers* can be defined by choosing a transformation such that $t_m(u) \geqslant u$ for any $u \in [0, 1]$. A remark analogous to the previous one can be made with regard to the relationship between the weakening of a characterization and its representation through an expansive modifier; this relationship does not exist for all characterizations (for instance, in Figure 20.1, "relatively small" should be intermediate between "small" and "medium" and it does not include "small").

There exist several ways of weakening a characterization and we focus on the three following ones: "approximately," which yields $m(C_1)$ less specific and less imprecise than C_1; "rather," which preserves the specificity of C_1 but increases its imprecision; "about," which gives $m(C_1)$ less specific and at least as imprecise as C_1 (see Figure 20.2).

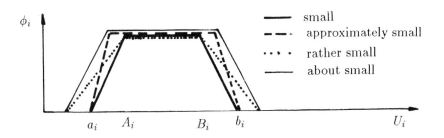

Figure 20.2. Effect of the modifiers m_1, m_2, m_3, on the characterization "small"

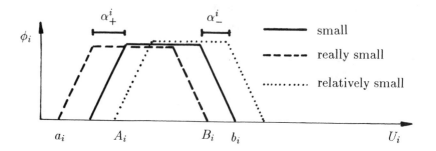

Figure 20.3. Effect of the modifier m^* on the characterization "small"

3.3. Ambivalent Modifiers

We answer the questions raised previously by introducing modifiers that reinforce or weaken the characterizations without being either restrictive or expansive. Further, the effect of these modifiers depends on the context of the qualifications used.

Let us suppose a given linguistic variable X_i lying in a universe U_i defined as the interval $[U_i^-, U_i^+]$ of real or integer numbers, with U_i^- and U_i^+ finite or infinite. This variable can be characterized by any element of a finite ordered list of primary terms $L_i = \{C_i^1, ..., C_i^{n+1}, ..., C_i^{2n+1}\}$ (see Figure 20.1).

We define a modifier m^* by means of a translation of the original possibility distribution. This modifier reinforces the qualification C_i^j if $1 \leqslant j \leqslant n$ (respective $n + 2 \leqslant j \leqslant 2n + 1$) and the distribution is translated to the left respective to the right); the modifier is called "really" and denoted by m^*_4. Conversely, the modifier m^* weakens the qualification C_i^j if $1 \leqslant j \leqslant n$ (respective $n + 2 \leqslant j \leqslant 2n + 1$) and the distribution is translated to the right (respective to the left); it is then called "relatively" and denoted by m^*_5. See Figure 20.3 for an example.

3.4. Transformations Defining the Modifiers $m_1, m_2, m_3, m^*_4, m^*_5$

We suppose that the possibility distributions are trapezoidal, which means that $\mu_i(x) = 0$ for every $x \in [U_i^-, a_i] \cup [b_i, U_i^+]$, with $a_i \geqslant U_i^-$

and $b_i \leqslant U_i^+$; $\mu_i(x) = \varphi'_i(x)$ for every $x \in [a_i, A_i]$, with $a_i < A_i$; $\mu_i(x) = 1$ for every $x \in [A_i, B_i]$, with $A_i \leqslant B_i$; $\mu_i(x) = \varphi_i''(x)$ for every $x \in [B_i, b_i]$, with $B_i < b_i$. The functions φ'_i and φ''_i are linear and such that $\varphi'_i(a) = \varphi''_i(b) = 0$, $\varphi'_i(A_i) = \varphi''_i(B_i) = 1$, most of the results would be preserved if φ'_i and φ''_i were not linear. We denote by φ_i the function identical with φ'_i on $[U_i^-, A_i]$ and identical with φ''_i on $[B_i, U_i^+]$.

We give real-valued parameters $\lambda, v, \beta, \alpha$, describing the range of the alteration associated with the modifier. The formal definitions of the modifier give the following possibility distributions of $m(C_i)$, for every $x \in U_i$:

with $m_1 : g_i(x) = \min(1, \lambda\varphi_1(x)$, for $\lambda \in [1, 2]$ (3)

with $m_2 : g_i(x) = \max(0, v\varphi_1(x) + 1 - v)$, for $v \in [1/2, 1]$ (4)

with $m_3 : g_i(x) = \min(1, \max(0, \varphi_i)x) + \beta))$, for $\beta \in [0,1/2]$ (5)

with m^* : $g_i(x) = \varphi_i(x + \alpha)$ if $x + \alpha \in U_i$

$g_i(x) = \varphi_i(U_i^-)$ if $x + \alpha \leqslant U_i^-$, $g_i(x) = \varphi_i(U_i^+)$ (6)

                   if $x + \alpha \geqslant U_i^+$

for $\alpha > 0$ if $m^* = m^*_4$ and $1 \leqslant j \leqslant n$, or $m^* = m^*_5$ and $n + 2 \leqslant j \leqslant 2n + 1$, and $\alpha < 0$ otherwise. Further, we ensure the compatibility of C_i and $m^*(C_i)$ by requiring that

$$|\alpha| \leqslant \min(B_i - A_i, (b_i - B_i)/2, (A_i - a_i)/2) \tag{7}$$

4. SYMBOLIC MANAGEMENT OF FUZZY CHARACTERIZATIONS COMPATIBLE WITH A FUZZY LOGIC

When a characterization $C_1 = m(C_1)$ of X_1 is observed for a modifier $m \in \{m_1, m_2, m_3, m^*\}$ and rule (DR) is used, the generalized modus ponens (2) provides a possibility distribution μ'_2 such that the qualification C'_2 of X_2 can be regarded as C_2 itself or an approximation of C_2, generally with an uncertainty (Bouchon, 1988).

It is possible to express simple nonfuzzy rules equivalent to the use of a fuzzy logic, if we choose the fuzzy implication in the appropriate way (Bouchon, 1990). These simple rules are

Rule 1: If observation X_1 is $m(C_1)$, then conclusion X_2 is $m(C_2)$ with an uncertainty γ,

Rule 2: If observation X_1 is $m(C_1)$, then conclusion X_2 is C_2 with an uncertainty γ,

Rule 3 (for $1 \leqslant j \leqslant 5$): If observation X_1 is $m(C_1)$, then conclusion X_2 is $m_j(C_2)$ with an uncertainty γ, for $m_j \neq m$ and $1 \leqslant j \leqslant 5$.

The uncertainty γ accompanying the rules depends on the parameter defining m and also on the imprecision of C_1 in case of m^*. The rule 1, 2 or 3 is independent of the function G chosen for the generalized modus ponens. The main results are summarized in Table 20.1.

5. COMPARISONS OF FUZZY IMPLICATIONS

From the previous results, we may deduce elements of comparison for the fuzzy implications given in the appendix (Desprès, 1988; Bouchon, 1989).

Almost all of them have the same kind of behavior with regard to the above-mentioned modifiers, and this behavior is generally cautious. When restrictive modifiers are used to describe an observation, they represent a particular case of the situation expected in the premise of rule (DR); as far as we do not have special information about the effect of this particularization on the variable involved in the consequent of (DR), it is prudent to preserve the conclusion of (DR); this is not the case for r_{Re}. Conversely, if an expansive modifier is used to modify C_1, the information contained in the observation is less specific and/or precise than the description given in the premise of (DR), and a prudent behavior consists in thinking that the consequent of the rule will not be a convenient conclusion; this is not the case if we use the fuzzy implication r_M.

The value of the uncertainty weighting the conclusions depends on the chosen fuzzy implication. It is possible to obtain no uncertainty if we use r_{Re}, r_{BG} or r_G and modifier m_1; or if we use r_R or r_L and any restrictive modifier; or if we use r_M and any modifier, which is interesting since the chaining of deduction rules is easy and does not entail a rapid increase of the uncertainty.

Table 20.1. Conformity of a simple rule 1, 2, or 3 (j = 1,...,5) with the use of a pair (modifier for the observation, fuzzy implication)

		Modifier					
		m_1	m_2	m_3	m^*_4	m^*_5	restrictive
F u z z y i m p l i c a t i o n	r_R	rule 3.2.	rule 2	rule 3.2	rule 3.2	rule 3.2	rule 2
	r_W	rule 2	rule 2	rule 2	rule 2	rule 2	rule 2
	r_{Re}	rule 1 $\gamma = 0$	rule 1	rule 1	rule 3.3	rule 3.3	
	r_{KD}	rule 2	rule 2	rule 2	rule 2	rule 2	rule 2
	r_{BG}	rule 1 $\gamma = 0$	rule 1	rule 1	rule 3.3	rule 3.3	rule 2
	r_G	rule 1 $\gamma = 0$	rule 1	rule 1	rule 3.3	rule 3.3	rule 2
	r_L	rule 3.3	rule 1	rule 1	rule 3.3	rule 3.3	rule 2
	r_M	rule 2 $\gamma = 0$	rule 2 $\gamma = 0$	rule 2 $\gamma = 0$	rule 2 $\gamma = 0$	rule 2 $\gamma = 0$	rule 2
Uncertainty		$1 - 1/\lambda$	$1 - v$	β	$\alpha/\kappa 1$	$\alpha/\kappa 2$	0

with

	$1 \leqslant j \leqslant n$	$n+1 \leqslant j \leqslant 2n+1$
$\kappa 1$	A-a	B-b
$\kappa 2$	B-b	A-a

6. MODIFIERS AND GRADUAL RULES

6.1. Different Types of Graduality

Gradual knowledge has often to be managed, since graduality is natural in various domains where there exist relations between the evolution of several variables. Thus, rules such as:

"the more (less) X_1 is D_1, the more (less) X_2 is D_2"   (GR)

have to be dealt with (for example "the less cumbersome, the more costly"). Their treatment is not obvious in the framework of classical deduction rule systems.

Let us suppose we are given the two lists of primary terms L_1 and L_2 indicated in Section 3.3 and a collection of rules of the form "if X_1

is C_1^j, then X_2 is C_2^k" for every j between 1 and $2n + 1$. A *gradual variation* concerns the variable X_i if we study successive characterizations, following some order. We may think of the following gradual variations.

- **Gradual variation of type 1:** X_i is successively characterized by C_i^j, C_i^{j+1}, C_i^{j+2}, ..., taken in the list L_i.
- **Gradual variation of type 2:** X_i is qualified by means of successive variations around a primary term, obtained by using modifiers that are more and more weakening (or reinforcing), for instance, "really C_i^j", C_i^j, "relatively C_i^j."
- **Gradual variation of type 3:** X_i is qualified by means of a given primary term C_i^j, but the certainty about the piece of knowledge "X_i is C_i^j" is either increasing or decreasing; for example "X_i is C_i^j" is uncertain, "X_i is C_i^j" is more or less certain, "X_i is C_i^j" is certain.

A gradual relationship between gradual variations concerning two variables is expressed in a *gradual rule*. Rule (GR) expresses the fact that a gradual variation of type 1, 2 or 3 in the description of X_1 entails a simultaneous gradual variation of type 1, 2 or 3 in the description of X_2.

We remark that D_1 and D_2 are not always elements of the lists L_1 and L_2 (think of $L_1 = $ {tiny, small, medium, big, huge}, $L_2 = $ {expensive, reasonable, cheap}, $D_1 = $ cumbersome, $D_2 = $ costly). In fact, two *kinds of graduality* can be distinguished:

- The first one is *global* and it consists in the fact that a progressive change of the label describing X_1 (a characterization of X_1 from C_1^1 to C_1^2, ..., to C_1^n for instance), corresponding to a gradual variation of type 1, entails a gradual variation of the qualification concerning X_2.
- The second one is *local* and it appears as a binding between a progressive change of the characterization of X_i *around* a given label (C_i^j for instance), corresponding to a gradual variation of type 2 or 3, and a gradual variation of the qualification concerning X_2.

Gradual rules can be dealt with in the framework of a fuzzy-logic-based system, by means of the choice of a reference rule such as:

"if X_1 is C_1^j then X_2 is C_2^k" (RR)

for elements C_1^j of L_1 and C_2^k of L_2.

A so-called *bundle* of other deduction rules is constructed with the help of modifiers either weakening (to model "the less ...") or reinforcing (to model "the more ...") the qualifications.

The fuzzy implication that is used determines the possible types of gradual variations we are able to work with. If we choose carefully, it is equivalent to have a gradual rule or to have a bundle of deduction rules based on a reference rule (Bouchon and Desprès, 1990; Bouchon and Yao, 1990, 1991). In the following we give the properties we obtain for classes of fuzzy implications.

6.2. Local Graduality

6.2.1. Modifiers m_1, m_2, m_3

We construct the bundle of rules by iterating the use of modifier m_1, m_2 or m_3, which more and more weakens the qualifications considered in the premise of (RR).

- With fuzzy implications r_{Re} r_{BG}, r_G and modifier m_1: the qualification considered in its consequent will be also more and more weakened by series of the same modifier. We model relations between gradual variations of type 2 corresponding to a gradual rule of the form:

"the less X_1 is C_1, the less X_2 is C_2"

for C_1 in L_1 and C_2 in L_2.

- With fuzzy implications r_R, r_W, r_{KD} or r_L and modifier m_1 or with fuzzy implications r_R, r_W, r_{Re}, r_{KD}, r_{BG}, r_G, or r_L associated with modifier m_2 or m_3: we obtain the same kind of behavior as in the previous case, but an uncertainty weights the validity of the rule, giving for instance:

"it is rather certain that the less X_1 is C_1, the less X_2 is C_2"

6.2.2. Restrictive Modifier

We construct the bundle of rules by iterating the use of a restrictive modifier, such as "very," to qualify the variable X_1. With fuzzy implication r_R, the characterization of X_2 becomes also more restrictive. This fact concerns gradual variations of type 2 corresponding to:

"the more X_1 is C_1, the more X_2 is C_2"

We observe that this kind of gradual rule is not easy to manage since almost no fuzzy implication operates a reinforcement of the consequent. It is therefore more interesting to replace it with converse:

"the less X_1 is C'_1, the less X_2 is C'_2"

with C_1 and C_2 the antynomous of C_1 and C_2.

6.2.3. Graduality Concerning the Certainty

We construct the bundle of rules by modifying the certainty concerning the observed characterizations of X_1. With fuzzy implications r_R, r_W, r_{Re}, r_{KD}, r_{BG}, r_G, the certainty concerning the qualification of X_2 varies in the same way. We model relations between gradual variations of type 3 corresponding to a gradual rule of the form:

"the more certain X_1 is c_1, the more certain X_2 is C_2"

6.3. Global Graduality

We construct the bundle of rules by iterating the use of a modifier m^*, chosen as m^*_4 or m^*_5 to change the qualification of X_1 in an adequate way. We restrict ourselves to the case of primary terms C_1^j such that $1 \leqslant i \leqslant n$, an analogous treatment would be possible for the terms corresponding to $n+2 \leqslant i \leqslant 2n+1$.

- With fuzzy implications r_W, r_{KD}, we obtain a variation of the certainty in the qualification of X_2. We model relations between gradual variations of type 2 and gradual variations of type 3, such as:

"the more (less) X_1 is C_1, the more (less) X_2 is C_2"

For every C_1^j L_1, let us denote by α^i_+ (resp. α^j_-) the extreme value of the parameter $\alpha > 0$ (respectively $\alpha < 0$) given in (7). We suppose that the primary terms C_1^i of L_1 are such that $A_{i+1} - \alpha_+^{i+1} \leqslant B_i - \alpha^i_-$, for every i such that $1 \leqslant i \leqslant n-1$, and

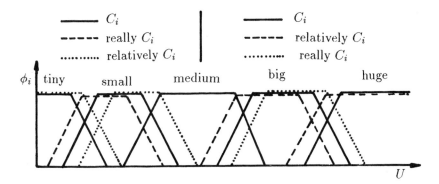

Figure 20.4. Sequence of characterizations and their modified forms by means of modifier m^*

$A_{n+1} \leqslant B_{n-} \quad \alpha^n_-$ (see Figure 20.4). This means that any value x of the universe U_1 less than B_{n+1} has a possibility equal to 1 to correspond either to one characterization C^i_1 $(\mu(x) = 1)$, for $1 \leqslant i \leqslant n+1$, or to a modified characterization $m_-(C^i_1)$, $(\mu_i(x - \alpha^i_-) = 1)$ or $m_+(C^i_1)$, $(\mu_i(x + \alpha^i_+) = 1)$, for $1 \leqslant i \leqslant n$.

Then, the modifier m^* allows to pass gradually from a qualification C^i_1 to $m^*(C^i_1)$, then to C^{i+1}_1 or C^{i-1}_1, according to the direction of the translation defining m^*. We are thus able to model relations between gradual variations of type 1 and gradual variations of type 3, such as:

"the more (less) X_1 is D_1, the more (less) certain X_2 is D_2"

- With fuzzy implications r_R, r_{Re}, r_{BG}, r_G, r_L, we obtain a variation of the qualification of X_2 represented by a weakening of the certainty in this description. We model a gradual rule of the form:

"it is rather certain that the less X_1 is A_1, the more approximate the fact that X_2 is A_2"

7. CONCLUSION

Linguistic modifiers provide useful tools to standardize variations of qualifications of linguistic variables, they avoid computations necessary in approximate reasoning processes while being compatible with fuzzy logic and they are involved in the problem of categorization of concepts when boundaries of categories are difficult to determine.

APPENDIX

List of fuzzy implications, defined for each $x \in U_1$, for each $y \in U_2$, by $r(x,y) = F(f_1(x), f_2(y))$:

$r_R(x, y) = 1 - f_1(x) + f_1(x) f_2(y)$	(Reichenbach's implication)
$r_W(x, y) = \max(1 - f_1(x), \min(f_1(x), f_2(y)))$	(Willmott's implication)
$r_{Re}(x, y) = 1$ if $f_1(x) \leqslant f_2(y)$ and 0 otherwise	(Rescher's implication)
$r_{KD}(x, y) = \max(1 - f_1(x), f_2(y))$	(Kleene-Dienes' implication)
$r_{BG}(x, y) = 1$ if $f_1(x) \leqslant f_2(y)$ and $f_2(y)$ otherwise	(Brouwer-Gödel's implication) (Goguen's implication)
$r_G(x, y) = \min(f_2(y)/f_1(x), 1)$ if $f_1(x) \neq 0$ and 1 otherwise	(Łukasiewicz' implication)
$r_L(x, y) = \min(1 - f_1(x) + f_2(y), 1)$	(Mamdani's implication)
$r_R(x, y) = \min(f_1(x), f_2(y))$	

(Note that r_M does not have the same status as the other fuzzy implications since it does not generalize the material implication).

Generalized modus ponens operators:

$$g_2(y) = \sup_{x \in U_1} G(g_1(x), r_i(x,y))$$

where G is an operator on [0, 1], generally a triangular norm, and the following example provides results compatible with the classical modus ponens when the observation C'_1 is identical with the premise C_1 of the rule $G(a, b) = \max(a + b - 1, 0)$.

Keywords: fuzzy logic, approximate reasoning, linguistic variables, linguistic modifiers, fuzzy implications, gradual knowledge

BIBLIOGRAPHY

Baldwin, J. F. (1981). Fuzzy logic and fuzzy reasoning. In E. H. Mamdani and B.R. Gaines (eds.): *Fuzzy reasoning and its applications.* New York: Academic Press.

Baldwin, J. F. and B.W. Pilsworth. (1980). Axiomatic approach to implication for approximate reasoning with fuzzy logic. *Fuzzy Sets and Systems,* 3, 193–219.

Bouchon, B. (1987). Linguistic variables in the knowledge base of an expert system. In J. Rose (ed.): *Cybernetics and Systems: Present and Future.* Thales, pp. 745–752.

Bouchon, B. (1988). Stability of linguistic modifiers compatible with a fuzzy logic. In *Uncertainty in Intelligent Systems,* Lecture Notes in Computer Science, vol. 313, Springer-Verlag.

Bouchon, B. (1989). On the management of uncertainty in knowledge-based systems. In A. G. Holzman, A. Kent, and J.G. Williams (eds.): *Encyclopedia of Computer Science and Technology.* New York: Marcel Dekker.

Bouchon, B. (1989). Coherence of linguistic qualifications. *Proc. Third IFSA Congress (Seattle).* 1989.

Bouchon, B. (1990). How to replace computations by simple rules in the framework of fuzzy logic. *Proc. Congrès Cognitiva, Madrid: AFCET.*

Bouchon, B. and S. Desprès. (1990). Acquisition numérique /symbolique de connaissances graduelles. *Actes des 3èmes Journées du PRC-GDR Intelligence Artificielle,* Paris: Hermès.

Bouchon, B. and Jia Yao. (1990). Gradual change of linguistic category by means of modifiers. *Proc. Third International Conference IPMU,* Paris, pp. 242–244.

Bouchon, B. and Jia Yao. (1991). Linguistic modifiers and gradual membership to a category. *International Journal on Intelligent Systems.* In press.

Desprès, S. (1988). *Un apport à la conception de systèmes à base de connaissances: les opérations de déduction floues.* Thèse de l'Université Paris VI.

Dubois, D. and H. Prade. (1990). Gradual inference rules in approximate reasoning. *Information Sciences.* In press.

Eshragh, F. and E.H. Mamdani. (1981). A general approach to linguistic approximation. In E. H. Mamdani and B. R. Gaines (eds.): *Fuzzy Reasoning and its Applications.* New York: Academic Press.

Hersh, M. M. and A. Caramazza. (1976). A fuzzy set approach to modifiers and vagueness in natural language. *J. Experimental Psychology,* General, **105,** 254–276.

Macvicar-Whelan, P.J. (1978). Fuzzy sets, the concept of height and the edge very. *IEEE Trans. Systems, Man and Cybernetics,* **8,** 507–512.

Prade, H. (1988). Raisonner avec des règles d'inférence graduelle. Une approche basée sur les sous-ensembles flous. *Revue d'Intelligence Artificielle,* **2,** 29–44.

Schwartz, D. G. (1985). The case for an interval-based representation of linguistic truth. *Fuzzy Sets and Systems,* **17,** 153–165.

Schwartz, D.G. (1988). An alternative semantics for linguistic variables. In *Uncertainty in Intelligent Systems,* Lecture Notes in Computer Science vol. 313, 87–92.

Schwartz, D.G. (1990). A system for reasoning with imprecise linguistic information. *Intern. J. Approximate Reasoning.* In press.

Wenstøp, F. (1981). Deductive verbal models of organization. In E. H. Mamdani and B. R. Gaines (eds.): Deductive verbal models of organization. In E. H. Mamdani and B. R. Gaines (eds.): *Fuzzy reasoning and its Applications.* New York: Academic Press.

Yager, R. R. (1984). General multiple objective decision functions and linguistically quantified statements. *Int. J. Man Machine Studies,* **21,** 389–400.

Zadeh, L. A. (1975). The concept of linguistic variable and its application to approximate reasoning. *Information Sciences,* **8,** 199–249, 301–357.

Zadeh, L. A. (1979). A theory of approximate reasoning. In J. E. Hayes D. Michie, and L. I. Mikulich (eds.): *Machine Intelligence.* New York: Elsevier, 149–194.

Zadeh, L. A. (1981). PRUF: A meaning representation language for natural languages. In E. H. Mamdani and B. R. Gaines (eds.): *Fuzzy Reasoning and its Applications.* New York: Academic Press.

Zadeh, L. A. (1983). The role of fuzzy logic in the management of uncertainty in expert systems. *Fuzzy Sets and Systems,* **11,** 199–227.

21 Use of fuzzy relations in knowledge representation, acquisition, and processing

Ladislav J. KOHOUT and Wyllis BANDLER
Department of Computer Science
Florida State University
Tallahassee, FL 32306, USA

Abstract. This chapter looks at the general aspects of knowledge elicitation, acquisition, and representation, and their impact on the ways of effective knowledge processing when varied aspects of uncertainty appear in this process.

1. FUZZY MATHEMATICAL RELATIONS AS A TOOL FOR ELICITING, REPRESENTING, AND VERIFYING CONCEPTUAL KNOWLEDGE STRUCTURES

In this paper we deal with those aspects of the theory and practice of **fuzzy relational products** and fast fuzzy relational algorithms that are indispensable for the description, representation, and symbolic manipulation of knowledge. This is compatible with the epistemology of expert action, and of knowledge engineering, presented in Section 2 and 3, respectively.

Since 1975 we have been developing the mathematical theory,

computational algorithms, and a systemic methodology of crisp and fuzzy relational products as well as having been engaged in their practical utilization in knowledge engineering, design of knowledge-based systems, information retrieval, analysis of medical and psychological data, and some business applications. In the present review we concentrate mainly on those of our original results that are directly relevant to knowledge engineering, design of knowledge-based systems, knowledge elicitation, and verification of knowledge structures. After outlining the epistemological foundations of our approach, the paper proceeds to deal with the following three issues: (1) mathematical theory, (2) fast relational algorithms, and (3) methodology and applications of fuzzy relational methods in knowledge engineering.

2. ACTIVITY STRUCTURES AS A FOUNDATION OF THE EPISTEMOLOGY OF EXPERT ACTION

Expert reasoning, decision making, and actions have to operate on the background of uncertainty, incompleteness of information and conflicting evidence. These activities involve conceptual structures and dispositions that the experts intuitively use. Understanding these underlying processes is difficult, yet essential in our attempts to aid expert decision making with computing and information processing technology. The reasoning involves a discipline that is two thousand years old and is called logic. The recent development of mathematical logic that started in the nineteenth century and has vigorously continued during the present century has dealt adequately only with abstract form that is devoid of the full referential context of natural languages. Reasoning with uncertainty, incompleteness, and also with conflicting evidence (to be called *reasoning with imperfect information*), on the other hand, cannot be fully devoid of the conceptual structures on which the phenomena of vagueness, uncertainty, incompleteness of information, and conflicting evidence operate. Identification of relevant conceptual structures, frameworks, meta-frameworks, and knowledge contents of individual knowledge domains therefore plays the crucial role in such reasoning with imperfect information. Not only the form of classical Aristotelian and

Chrysippian logic or its modern embodiment into a formal Fregean calculus, but also the semiotic contents and its semantic linguistic features are important. Capturing the richness of the conceptual and linguistic world of a competent expert therefore requires new tools. Thus we have to face the problem of acquisition of relevant, but generally **context-dependent** and **localized** fragments of knowledge, forming a system. Within this system, reasoning with imperfect information would operate. This leads us to the question of knowledge: its epistemological status, its utilization by the experts, its transfer to the computers. One should not neglect the problem of correct use of knowledge once transferred and the maintenance of acquired knowledge sources that is to be done because of the necessary changes in the environment.

2.1. Activities and Dispositions

The question "What is knowledge," has been in the forefront of philosophical debates for thousands of years, yet no fully satisfactory solution has been reached. From a more practical view, however, considerable progress has been made in understanding psychological and logical conditions of decision making, utilizing conceptual and logical formal structures that are abstract embodiments of Gestalt knowledge used by intelligent agents.

In order to achieve this level of universality of knowledge elicitation methodology, the basic principles in which the methodology is grounded ought not to be based on the structure of the knowledge itself, however all-encompassing or general it may be; but rather on the *dispositions* that determine the dynamics and the character of knowledge growth. These dispositions are determined by the potentiality of the intentional acts of the intelligent agent realizing a problem solving process (Kohout, 1990) and acquiring some knowledge.

2.2. Intelligent Agents in a Problem Solving Situation

An intelligent agent in a problem solving situation ought to perform the following activities (cf. Kohout, 1990):

1. **Perception** and **evaluation** of the problem solving situation.
2. **Determining** what the situation *must become* instead of *what it is*.
3. **Deciding:**
   a. *What* must be done;
   b. *How* it must be done;
   c. *What* are the available resources.

Let us call the ability to perform iteratively and/or recursively these activities *the essential problem solving disposition.*

It has been noted that the agent/expert realizing the problem solving strategy consisting of the above activities has to possess the following dispositions (Bandler and Kohout, 1980b):

(i)   cognitive ability
(ii) decision ability
(iii) action ability

The three abilities (i), (ii), (iii) being granted, one can view the competent expert as an intelligent agent capable of goal-oriented intelligent behavior whose repertory of dispositions must also contain the *essential problem solving disposition*. The potentiality to act as an expert implies the ability and intention to apply this essential problem solving disposition as the leading meta-activity in the expert's domain of expertise. This will be reflected in the expert's internal model of the environment as a gradually evolving cognitive model of the domain of expertise. Models of experts' cognitive and problem solving activities can be characterized by a number of general principles (Kohout, 1990):

1. Each expert activity is teleological, i.e., performed for a particular purpose, hence we deal with functional environment structures.
2. The description of knowledge deals with conceptual and formal spaces of different degrees of abstraction, hence a partially ordered family of functional structures has to be employed for the description of the knowledge to be elicited.
3. Each functional conceptual structure imposes specific constraints on the semiotics and dynamics of communication between the expert and the knowledge elicitor.
4. The set of coherent constraints imposed on the knowledge structure possessed by the knowledge elicitor during the

knowledge elicitation process creates additional symbolic or message content (meaning) in addition to that implied by the initial semantic agreement needed for starting a conversation between the expert and the knowledge elicitor.

5. The degrees of abstraction of individual substructures can be defined only in the case that there is a common initial residual semantics shared by the whole functional family of the descriptive functional structures used.

These five points summarize an epistemological view that forms the foundation of our knowledge engineering methodology.

3. EPISTEMOLOGY OF KNOWLEDGE ENGINEERING: KNOWLEDGE ELICITATION VS. KNOWLEDGE ACQUISITION

The Oxford Dictionary defines **acquire** as *come into possession,* whereas **elicit** is defined as *draw forth what is latent.* Indeed, "knowledge acquisition" is a generic term, as it is neutral with respect to the way in which the transfer of knowledge is achieved. The term "knowledge elicitation," on the other hand, implies that because the knowledge is latent, it must somehow be drawn out of its sources, in which it is hidden. The second implication of this term is that we need an active agent that will draw it out. In our case this active agent is a **knowledge elicitor**, a person that actively draws the knowledge from an expert by systematic questioning in a series of well organized interviews, or by active interpretation of texts (e.g., books) or both. The role of the knowledge elicitor is usually taken by a person called a "knowledge engineer," a computer professional trained in the application of computer science techniques in general, and of Artificial Intelligence in particular, to the design of knowledge-based systems (e.g., expert systems with deep knowledge, expert database systems, rule-based expert systems, etc.). The knowledge elicitor, on the other hand, does not need to be a knowledge engineer, but a domain expert working in conjunction with a knowledge engineering team, a communication expert, a psychologist, a linguist, etc.

Once we move from rule-based expert systems (well established but rather narrow in their applicability) to other systems, and as the spectrum of the computer-based knowledge representation schemes that are available broadens, we need to sharply distinguish the process of knowledge elicitation from knowledge representation. The knowledge elicited from the expert by the knowledge elicitor may not be representable within the repertory of available computer knowledge representation schemes. Indeed, the computer structures in which the knowledge will be embedded may be dynamically changing, as may be the case with the community of AI-agents mutually interacting and communicating, which is built of subsystems connected in a distributed network consisting of expert systems, intelligent databases, neural nets, highly parallel adaptive architectures, etc.

But knowledge is dependent on context and environment (Kohout, Anderson, and Bandler, 1991). A knowledge-based system or indeed a neural network that has learned to perform well in one context or environment may badly deteriorate (judged in terms of the appropriateness and correctness of its behavior) once moved to a different context or environment, although it was expected to perform there equally well.

4. FORMAL ASPECTS OF FUZZY MATHEMATICAL RELATIONS

4.1. Mathematical Theory

What is inadequately taught as "relation theory" centers mostly on *equivalence relations* and a couple of kinds (*ordinary* and *strict*) of *order relations*, all of which are characterized in terms of overlapping sets of special properties. Certain other combinations of the elementary properties have an importance that is much less generally understood. This section gives a brief exposition of definitions, and original results concerning these and other special properties, in a form providing a much-needed unification of crisp and fuzzy relational theory (cf. Bandler and Kohout, 1987). It then continues with the discussion of relational compositions of three distinct types, namely *triangle sub-* and *super-product* (Bandler and Kohout, 1978, 1980b, c), and the *square product*. In 1977 Bandler and Kohout introduced the *triangle subproduct* $R \triangleleft S$, the *triangle superproduct* $R \triangleright S$, and *square product* $R \square S$.

4.2. Triangle and Square Types of Relational Products

A binary (2-place) relation R between two sets X and Y is a *predicate* with two empty slots. When an element x of X is put into the first slot and an element y of Y into the second, a grammatical statement ensues, which may be either true or false if the relation is crisp. For a fuzzy relation a degree of truth is assigned to that statement. For any element x_i in X, the *afterset* x_iR is the subset of Y consisting of those elements to which x_i is related via R. Similarly, for any element y_j in Y, the *foreset* Ry_j is the subset of X consisting of those elements related by R to y_j. If R is a crisp relation, these are crisp sets; if R is fuzzy, they are fuzzy sets, with membership degrees given by the degrees of the truth of the relational statement.

Where R is relation from X to Y, and S a relation from Y to Z, a *product relation* $R * S$ is a relation from X to Z, determined by R and S. There are several types of product used to produce product-relations, each distinctive in its *intention* and *use*. But, when the relations are fuzzy, there is a further wide choice of realization for each of the four kinds of products, because of the plethora of the many-valued logic-based candidates for the role of *implication operator* and other connectives. It is hoped that our readers will appreciate the distinctions among the four main *logical types* of products (circle, both triangle types, and the square type), which follow in this section, and the way in which the requirement for an implication operator or an equivalence operator comes in. To see that each product type performs a **different logical action** on the intermediate sets is important, as *each logical type* of the product enforces a *distinct specific meaning* on the resulting product-relation $R * S$.

In order to explain clearly the need for, and the significance of, different logical types of relational products, we begin with crisp relations, and then extend these to fuzzy. The definition specifies each $R * S$, for various $*$, by saying exactly when this product-relation holds between and x and a z.

Definition:

Circle Product:	$x(R \bigcirc S)z \Leftrightarrow xR$ intersects Sz
Triangle Subproduct:	$x(R \lhd S)z \Leftrightarrow xR \subseteq Sz$
Triangle Superproduct:	$x(R \rhd S)z \Leftrightarrow xR \supseteq Sz$
Square Product:	$x(R \square S)z \Leftrightarrow xR = Sz$

To give a simple example of a concept representation scheme, if R is the relation between *patients* and *individual symptoms,* and S a relation between *symptoms* and *diseases,* $R * S$ will quite naturally be a relation between *patients* and *diseases.* It is clear that to make sense it should be conditioned by the intermediate set of concepts, and the observatory and classificatory relations R and S, although these no longer appear in it explicitly.

Where R and S have the clinical meaning as stated, the meanings of these product-relations are as follows:

$x(R \circ S)z$: x has at least one symptom of illness z
$x(R \lhd S)z$: x's symptoms are among those that characterize z
$x(R \rhd S)z$: x's symptoms include all those that characterize z
$x(R \square S)z$: x's symptoms are exactly those of z

These product-relations faithfully reflect aspects of the thought sequence in a diagnostician's mind: $R \circ S$ arouses suspicion; $R \lhd S$ would deepen it but $R \rhd S$ would clinch it, while $R \square S$ is perhaps reserved for the textbook cases.

It is clear that before these products can be of real service in knowledge representation or in any other kind of structural semantic modeling, they must be fuzzified. In order to assist this, it is helpful to express the relational products in their logical form as follows. In the formulas, R_{ij} represents the fuzzy degree to which the statement $x_i R_{yj}$ is true.

$$(R \circ S)_{ik} = \bigvee_j (R_{ij} \wedge S_{jk}) \qquad (R \lhd S)_{ik} = \bigwedge_j (R_{ij} \to S_{jk})$$
$$(R \rhd S)_{ik} = \bigwedge_j (R_{ij} \leftarrow S_{jk}) \qquad (R \square S)_{ik} = \bigwedge_j (R_{ij} \leftrightarrow S_{jk})$$

The customary logical symbols for the logic connectives AND, OR, both *implications* and the *equivalence* in the above formulas represent the connectives of some many-valued logic, **chosen** according to the properties of the products required. Lack of space does not permit us to go into details of the available repertory of various implication operators here; the interested reader will find the definitions of the most useful implication operators used in the triangle products in Bandler and Kohout (1980c, 1986a).

It is important to distinguish from what we call the *harsh* products (defined above), the family of the *mean* products. Given the general formula

$$(R @ S)_{ik} ::= \,\,\neq (R_{ij} * S_{jk})$$

the outer connective denoted $\neq$ is replaced by Σ and the resulting product normalized appropriately. The mean products are very important in some applications (Bandler and Kohout, 1979c), although their mathematical theory does not take such a neat form as that of the harsh products.

4.3. Forming New Relations by Products

Product-relations formed by the relational products represent new entities composed from the original data, with their specific semantics dependent on the conceptual meaning of the original data-relations.

Now, we can go further than that. If R is any relation (perhaps itself a product of other relations) from X to Y, we call R^T the *transposed relation* (often called *converse*, or sometime *inverse*), in which y is related by R^T to x exactly when x is related by R to y. This well-known converse tells us nothing new in itself semantically, but participates in important constructions. In particular, $R * R^T$ is a relation from X to X, and $R^T * R$ a relation from Y to Y. Examples using the specific relations mentioned in Section 2.1 include

$x_i(R \lhd R^T)x_k$: patient x_i's symptoms are among these of x_k
$x_i(R \square R_T)x_k$: patient x_i has exactly the same symptoms as x_k
$y_j(R^T \lhd R)y_l$: whenever symptom y_j occurs, so does y_l (in this
           group of patients)
$y_j(S \square S^T)y_i$: symptom y_j characterizes exactly the same diseases
           as does y_l

The reader can construct others also of considerable utility.

Relations so constructed might exhibit some important relational properties revealing some important characteristics and interrelationships of the source of information from which they were generated. Hence, an important problem of scientific analysis of the computed new constructs is **whether**, and **which**, special *relational properties* various conceptual schemes expressed relationally possess. Suitable methods for testing the presence of these are reviewed in the next section.

4.4. Local Properties of Crisp and Fuzzy Relations

Relational properties, such as reflexivity, symmetry, and transitivity, and classes such as tolerances, equivalences, and partial orders have been studied since the 1940s and are well known for crisp relations. Zadeh (1971) extended these to fuzzy relations in a now classic paper entitled "Similarity relations and fuzzy orderings." From the point of view of applicability of relational methods of analysis of structures, this is a very significant extension, as it allows for approximation of the crisp structures by fuzzy ones. Thus one may identify in data approximate similarities, approximate equivalences, and orders. One essential drawback shared with the crisp theories of relational properties still remains in Zadeh's extension: namely, the properties are *global*, and must be shared by all the elements of a relation. Our contribution was to provide an adequate **definition of locality** for both crisp and fuzzy relations (Bandler and Kohout, 1982, 1987, 1988).

One may ask, why be concerned with local properties, such as local reflexivity, local tolerance, local equivalence, local preorder, etc.? This has good reason behind it. It is very often the case that some of the elements of the universe X fail to participate in the relation of interest, and this should not be allowed to obscure the properties that the relation may have in its *effective domain*. In particular, what is doubtless the best known aspect of relational theory – the isomorphism between *equivalences* and *partitions* on X–has an important generalization in the isomorphism between *local equivalences* and *partitions* in X (Boruvka, 1974), which is of great theoretical interest and of great practical consequence.

Our extension of both the crisp and fuzzy relational properties by introducing the notion of locality is based on the crucial definition of **local equality:**

Definition (Bandler and Kohout, 1982, 1988): *Where R is any fuzzy relation on X, the local equality of R is the relation E_R given by* $(E_R)_{ii} = \vee_j(R_{ij}, R_{ji})$, $(E_R)_{ij} = 0$ *if* $j \neq i$.

This contrasts with the *full equality* E_x which has $E_{ii} = 1$ for all i. In the above definition, the connective $\vee$ is from the logical point of view a suitable many-valued logic-based **OR** connective, or algebraically speaking a conorm.

Using the above definition, **local reflexivity** is defined: R is *locally reflexive* iff $E_R \subseteq R$. All other compound local properties are defined by replacing reflexivity by the local reflexivity thus defined.

The usual way to study a fuzzy relation is through consideration of its α-cuts R_α. Our definitions of the local properties of fuzzy and crisp relations given in Bandler and Kohout (1982, 1987, 1988) are, we feel, justified by the following simple but valuable theorem.

Justification Theorem (Bandler and Kohout, 1982, 1988): *It is true of each of the simple and compound properties P defined (cf. Bandler and Kohout, 1988, sec. 1 and 2), that every α-cut of a fuzzy relation R possesses P in the crisp sense, if and only if R itself possesses P in the fuzzy sense.*

Where *P* is any property that a fuzzy relation *R* on *x* may have or fail to have, the *P-closure* of *R* is defined to be the *least inclusive relation S* containing *R* and possessing *P*. Dually, the *P-interior* of *R* is the *most inclusive relation Q* that possesses *P* and is contained in *R*.

The existence theorem, formal definitions, and other theorems, as well as the details concerning the closures and interiors of the most important local and global relational properties, the interested reader may find in Bandler and Kohout (1988) or in our earlier papers (Bandler and Kohout, 1982, 1987).

Relational properties are important for characterizing the relational structures representing some knowledge, as the local and global properties extract important semantic distinctions between various concepts captured by these structures. Typically, we want to ask which elements of a relation will **participate** in sharing some local properties. For example, the elements possessing the property of local equivalence exhibit their equal status relative to the criteria determined by the *semantic meaning of the intermediate sets* over which the product-relation has been composed.

Bandler and Kohout (1982, 1987, 1988) also contain a number of interesting formulas specifying the equivalent definitions of the composite relational properties. These are very useful in computations, and form bases for the fast relational algorithms (cf. Section 5). A typical example is the following formula for the *local preorder closure*:

locpre clo R = locref clo(tra clo R) = tra clo(locref clo R)

It can be seen that this formula gives two ways of computing the *local preorder closure* that are equivalent mathematically, but may be different from the point of view of computational complexity. A number of such useful formulas for determining the closures and interiors for various compound relational properties can be found in Bandler and Kohout (1982, 1988). This theory forms the necessary prerequisite for design of fast identification algorithms by which we are able to check the presence or absence of various properties in the empirical data, be it the knowledge structures elicited for use in an expert system for medical data analysis, or some commercial data. In all these cases, the identification of local or global preorders, orders, tolerances, or equivalences properties of arbitrary mathematical relations can be used to provide the essential semantic information about the empirical data obtained from various scientific, engineering, medical, and commercial domains. This is further discussed in Sections 5 and 7.

5. METHODOLOGY AND SEMANTICS

In Section 2.1 we emphasized the multiplicity of choice of the implication operators for both triangle types of product, and of equivalence operators for the square type. The triangle and square products may be based on a large variety of many-valued logic implication operators; a practical question then arises, as to which many-valued set or relational theory is the best for a particular application and/or knowledge domain. Evaluation experiments performed in various applications conclusively show how essential it is to select such a fuzzy knowledge representation structure or inference/decision making method so as to appropriately match the data/knowledge structures dictated by a particular application (Bandler and Kohout, 1980c). The most important point that emerges from the empirical studies is that the many-valued implication operators and other connectives that should be employed in a specific application will crucially depend on the nature of data and knowledge involved (Bandler and Kohout, 1980c; Kohout and Kallala, 1987; Stiller et al., 1989; Løvstad et al., 1990; Ben-Ahmeida et al., 1991). Inappropriate choice of the technique (be it probabilistic, Bayesian, or based on a particular fuzzy many-valued logic) may distort results beyond recognition. This applies to our choice of an inference or decision method, as well as that of a formal scheme for knowledge elicitation or representation.

We have asked the question how the choice of the implication operator can influence the structure of the relations extracted from empirical data. This started with the reanalysis of the data of our first applications (Bandler and Kohout, 1978, 1979c, 1980b). The reader interested in comparison will find the details in Bandler and Kohout (1980a, c, 1981). The results of this analysis did show that in some cases the structures of the relational products obtained are very similar, almost identical, differing only in the level of the α-cut for each distinct implication operator used.

Table 21.1. Checklist paradigm of the assignment of fuzzy values

	No for B	Yes for B	Row total
No for A	a_{00}	a_{01}	r_0
Yes for A	a_{10}	a_{11}	r_1
Column total	c_0	c_1	n

Define
$a = r_1/n$

Define
$b = c_1/n$

In other instances there was a more significant difference in some substructures. This led us to a more systematic experimental study of the role of different implication many-valued connectives in this context. We refer the interested reader to a sample of our work and that of our collaborators (Bandler and Kohout, 1980c; Kohout and Kallala, 1987; Løvstad et al., 1990).

In order to understand also theoretically what the individual similarities and differences mean, and to decide on the appropriate use of each operator in practical applications, we had to look more closely at the semantics of each implication operator. To this end we have developed the so-called **checklist paradigm** (Bandler and Kohout, 1980c, 1984b, 1986b), which gives rather startling and unexpected results, shedding light not only on the semantics of the operators discussed, but also on the true methodological importance of fuzzy methods in the analysis of systems and structures.

Let us assume existence of a competent observer/assessor and of an object to be evaluated. Let the *abstract checklist* (Bandler and Kohout, 1986b) consist of n descriptive adjectives (descriptors/terms), expressing some potential features of the object in question, that are relevant to some particular knowledge domain. The observer checks those terms on the checklist that apply to the object being assessed. The assessment of the object is then *summarized* by computing the total score of the object by dividing the "yes" answers by the total number of the questions (i.e., descriptor terms on the checklist). It is natural to interpret the proportion thus scored as a *fuzzy degree of agreement* of the features of the object with the query determined by the checklist.

Now suppose the same checklist is filled out for two objects, or for the same object on two different occasions; to fix the ideas, let us suppose the latter situation. The least we can do is record the observer's two total scores. At the other extreme of detail, we could compare, item by item, the terms on the checklist to which the observer assented on the two occasions. By an excercise of *reduction* we could instead fill in the *contingency template* of Table 21.1, with *A* standing for the first occasion and *B* for the second. The resultant table summarizes the item-by-item information in a way that tells us much more than merely the two scores (which can, however, be read from the margins). **To what extent can the extra information inside the table be reconstructed from a knowledge of the margins?** This is the central question of the paradigm.

Now, consider a single checklist used to give a degree of assent to two different objects *A* and *B*, where these abstract objects *A*, *B* are both some propositions. For the general case, formally, let *F* be any logical propositional function of propositions *A* and *B*. Where *i* and *j* can each take the value 0 or 1, let $f(i,j)$ be the classical truth value of $F(A, B)$ that corresponds to the evaluation *i* for *A* and *j* for *B*; this also must be either 0 or 1. Let $u(i,j)$ be the ratio of the number in the *ij*-cell of the contingency table, to the grand total. Then what we have been agreeing with is that the *fuzzy assessment of the truth of the proposition* $F(A, B)$ is

$$m(F) = \Sigma_{ij} f(i,j) u(i,j)$$

We now have quite a satisfactory way of assigning fuzzy values to compound propositions. But *truth-functionality* has been lost. It has been employed in the construction of the fuzzy assessments of the truth of a compound proposition but it disappears in the outcome.

The four interior cells of the contingency template constitute its *fine structure*; the margins constitute its *coarse structure*. The fine structure gives us the appropriate fuzzy assessments for all propositional functions of *A* and *B*; the coarse structure gives us only the fuzzy assessments of *A* and *B* themselves. Our central question is, *to what extent can the fine structure be reconstructed from the coarse?*

We have shown elsewhere (Bandler and Kohout, 1980c, 1984b, 1985a, 1986b) that the *coarse* structure imposes bounds on the fine structure, without determining it completely. Hence, *associated with the various logical connectives between propositions are their extreme values.* Thus we obtain the inequality restricting the possible values of $m(F)$:

$$contop \geqslant m(F) \geqslant conbot$$

where *con* is the name of connective represented by $f(i, j)$. So there are

16 such inequalities, as there are 16 logical types of *con*, 10 of which are nontrivially two-argument.

Let us look now at some typical results. Choosing for the logical type of the connective *con* the *implication*, and making the assessment of the fuzzy value of the truth of a proposition by the formula

$m_1(F) = 1 - (\alpha_{10}/n)$, we obtain:
$\min(1, 1 - a + b) \geqslant m_1(F) \geqslant \max(1 - a, b)$

We can see that for the *plytop* the checklist paradigm produced the Łukasiewicz implication operator, and the other bound (*plybot*) is the Kleene-Dienes implication operator. Choosing for *con* the connective type AND we get:

$$\min(a, b) \geqslant m_1(F) \geqslant \max(0, a + b - 1)$$

It is interesting to note that this bound (logical type *andtop* and *andbot*) is identical with that of Schweitzer and Sklar (1983) on their so-called *copulas*, which play an important role in their theory of *norms* and *conorms*.

If for *con* type we choose an implication again, but only the evaluation "by performance" (that is, we are concerned only with the cases in which the evaluation of A is 1), we obtain m_2 given by

$$\min(1, b/a) \geqslant m_2(F) \geqslant \max(0, (a + b - 1)/a)$$

where *plytop* is in this instance the well-known G43 implication. Choosing for $m(F)$ yet other functions we obtain a variety of interesting results for implications bounds, the details of which cannot be discussed here. (See Bandler and Kohout, 1980c.)

6. FAST FUZZY RELATIONAL ALGORITHMS

It is in accord with the fuzzy way of looking at things to advance from absolute assertion or denial of a property, to thinking of the *degree to which* a relation possesses the property. But how is one to assess such a degree? For example, one may feel that a particular relation is "very nearly transitive," without quite achieving that property in full, if examination shows only a few arcs in its digraph with lower values than the property requires, or more such arcs but with only slightly too low values, etc. In other words, *comparison of a relation with its closure* shows exactly where it falls short, and gives complete data for filling any suitable formula for the *degree to which* it succeeds or fails.

Dually, *the comparison of a relation with its interior,* for a property for which that exists, shows exactly where the relation has exceeded the restrictions demanded by the property, and so can also underlie a suitable measure of *degree.* Those properties considered in Bandler and Kohout (1988) that have an interior operator also have a closure, and in these cases a comparison of the closure of a relation with its interior, showing the gap within which the original relation lies, can underlie still other measures.

The idea of *comparison of a relation with its closure* and *comparison of a relation with its interior* leads to design and to validity proofs of fast fuzzy relational algorithms that can test various local properties and also automatically discover the cases when the tested properties hold not only locally, but also globally. Fast algorithms for transitive closures, local preorder closures, and preorder closures have been embodied in successful software tools TRISYS (Bandler and Kohout, 1981) and TRIMOD (written in Pascal and MODULA-2, respectively).

7. APPLICATIONS IN KNOWLEDGE ENGINEERING

The triangle relational products and the algorithms discussed above were applied with gratifying results to a number of practical problems in a number of scientific fields. For a general introduction to the approach see Bandler and Kohout (1980b). For examples in the acquisition and analysis of medical diagnostic data and patient management processes see Bandler and Kohout (1979c, 1980c, 1986a) and Kohout et al. (1984); for medical sign and symptom comparison, see Ben-Ahmeida et al. (1991); for information retrieval, Kohout et al. (1984) and Kohout and Bandler (1987b); for handwriting classification, Kohout and Kallala (1986); and for other areas see Kohout (1984); Kohout and Bandler (1985); and Wilcox (1980).

Directly relevant to the mathematics and methodology described in the previous section are our studies in knowledge representation (Kohout and Bandler, 1986b), knowledge elicitation, and *validation* of acquired knowledge structures. Space does not permit us to discuss in detail these issues here. It may, however, be useful to just adumbrate one of the applications that clearly demonstrates the crucial importance of knowledge structures validation as well as an important role the methods outlined in the previous sections play here.

It is usually assumed by the knowledge engineers that knowledge of a specific domain acquired from diverse sources can be freely combined in a single knowledge structure. An example drawn from Ben-Ahmeida et al. (1991) clearly demonstrates that this is not always so. We have selected 22 diseases of the endocrine system from two well known medical sources and constructed classification hierarchies (Kohout, 1975) using the TRISYS algorithm (Bandler and Kohout, 1988). Although our medical expert expected the identical outcome of the analysis from both sources, we found significant differences. Although this was rather startling, the medical expert was able to find the rational explanation of the differences. It was also true that not all the implication (ply) operators were equally suitable for the verification of the structures. Note that the numbering system for the ply operators and the definitions of the all the operators that TRYSIS can employ can be found in the following: Kohout and Bandler (1986b); Bandler and Kohout (1980a, c). For the further details of this analysis and the exposition of related issues the reader is referred to Ben-Ahmeida et al. (1991).

Fuzzy relational products, in particular the triangular ones together with the semantic explanation of their logical meaning afforded by the checklist paradigm, are very useful in other areas of knowledge and data engineering. For examples of eliciting, representing, and manipulating fuzzy relational structures that are used to represent knowledge see Kohout and Bandler (1986a) and Kohout et al. (1991); for examples providing inference mechanisms in knowledge-based systems see Bandler and Kohout (1979c, 1985), and Kohout et al. (1987).

The fuzzy relational methods also play an important role in our approach to design of knowledge-based systems architectures (Kohout and Bandler, 1981, 1987b; Anderson et al., 1985; Kohout et al., 1985; Kohout and Kallala, 1986; Kohout et al., 1991). The general theoretical issues of computer protection as well as some of their practical aspects were analyzed by means of triangle products in Bandler and Kohout (1979a,b, 1980b); Kohout and Bandler (1987a). A general overview of the use of relational products in information processing architectures can be found in Kohout and Bandler (1985).

We can conclude that the triangle and square types of relational products find useful application in knowledge engineering, knowledge representation, and knowledge elicitation, acquisition, and validation. Their worth has also been demonstrated in design of knowledge-based and expert systems architectures, including the design of empty shells and parallel inference engines (Kohout and Bandler, 1985).

BIBLIOGRAPHY

Anderson, J., W. Bandler, L. J. Kohout, and C. Trayner. (1985). The design of a fuzzy medical expert system. In M. M. Gupta, A. Kandel, W. Bandler, and J. B. Kiszka (eds.): *Approximate Reasoning in Expert Systems.* Amsterdam: North-Holland, pp. 689–703.

Bandler, W. and L. J. Kohout. (1978). Fuzzy relational products and fuzzy implication operators. In *International Workshop on Fuzzy Reasoning Theory and Applications,* Queen Mary College, University of London, September.

Bandler, W. and L. J. Kohout. (1979a). Activity structures and their protection. In R. F. Ericson (eds.): *Improving the Human Condition: Quality and Stability in Social Systems (Proc. Silver Anniversary 1979 International Meeting of the Society for General Systems Research).* New York: Springer-Verlag, pp. 239–244.

Bandler, W. and L. J. Kohout. (1979b). Applications of fuzzy logics to computer protection structures. In *Proc. Ninth International Symposium on Multiple-Valued Logic, Bath, England, May 1979.* IEEE 79CH1408-4C, New York, pp. 200–207.

Bandler, W. and L. J. Kohout. (1979c). The use of new relational products in clinical modelling. In B. R. Gaines (ed.): *General Systems Research: A Science, a Methodology, a Technology. Proc. 1979 North American Meeting of the Society for General Systems Research,* Louisville KY, January, pp. 240–246.

Bandler, W. and L. J. Kohout. (1980a). Fuzzy power sets and fuzzy implication operatos. *Fuzzy Sets and Systems,* 4, 13–30.

Bandler, W. and L. J. Kohout. (1980b). Fuzzy relational products as a tool for analysis and synthesis of the behaviour of complex natural and artificial systems. In P. P. Wang and S. K. Chang (eds.): *Fuzzy Sets: Theory and Applications to Policy Analysis and Information Systems.* New York and London: Plenum, pp. 341–367.

Bandler, W. and L. J. Kohout. (1980c). Semantics of implication operators and fuzzy relational products. *Internat. Journal of Man-Machine Studies,* 12, 89–116. Reprinted in E. H. Mamdani, and B. R. Gaines (eds.): *Fuzzy Reasoning and its Applications.* London: Academic Press, pp. 219–246.

Bandler, W. and L. J. Kohout. (1981). The identification of hierarchies in symptoms and patients through computation of fuzzy relational products. In R. D. Parslow (eds.): *BCS'81: Information Technology for the Eighties. Proc. Conf. The British Computer Society, London, July 1981.* London: Heyden & Son, pp. 191–194.

Bandler, W. and L. J. Kohout. (1982). Fast fuzzy relational algorithms. In A. Ballester, D. Cardús, and E. Trillas (eds.): *Proc. of the Second Internat. Conference on Mathematics at the Service of Man,* Las Palmas, Canary Islands, Spain, 28 June–3 July, Universidad Politechnica de las Palmas, pp. 123–131.

Bandler, W. and L. J. Kohout. (1984a). The four modes of inference in fuzzy expert systems. In R. Trappl. (ed.): *Cybernetics and Systems Research,* 2, pp. 581–586. Amsterdam: North-Holland.

Bandler, W. and L. J. Kohout. (1984b). Unified theory of multiple-valued logical operators in the light of the checklist paradigm. In *Proc. of the 1984 IEEE Conference on Systems, Man and Cybernetics*. New York: IEEE, pp. 356–364.

Bandler, W. and L. J. Kohout. (1985a). The interrelations of the principal fuzzy logical operators. In M. M. Gupta, A. Kandel, W. Bandler, and J. B. Kiszka (eds.): *Approximate Reasoning in Expert System*. Amsterdam: North-Holland, pp. 767–780.

Bandler, W. and L. J. Kohout. (1985b). Probabilistic vs. fuzzy production rules in expert systems. *Internat. Journal of Man-Machine Studies, 22*, 347–353.

Bandler, W. and L. J. Kohout. (1986a). A survey of fuzzy relational products in their applicability to medicine and clinical psychology. In L. J. Kohout and W. Bandler (eds.): *Knowledge Representation in Medicine and Clinical Behavioural Science*. An Abacus Book. London and New York: Gordon and Breach, pp. 107–118.

Bandler, W. and L. J. Kohout. (1986). The use of checklist paradigm in inference systems. In C.V. Negoita and H. Prade (eds.): *Fuzzy Logics in Knowledge Engineering*. Köln: Verlag TÜV Rheinland, pp. 95–111.

Bandler, W. and L. J. Kohout. (1987) Mathematical relations. In M. G. Singh (ed.): *Systems and Control Encyclopedia*. Oxford: Pergamon Press, pp. 4000–4008.

Bandler, W. and L. J. Kohout. (1988). Special properties, closures and interiors of crisp and fuzzy relations. *Fuzzy Sets and Systems, 26*, 317–332.

Ben-Ahmeida, B., L. J. Kohout, and W. Bandler. (1991). The use of fuzzy relational products in comparison and verification of correctness of knowledge structures. In L. J. Kohout, J. Anderson, and W. Bandler, (eds.): *Knowledge-Based Systems for Multiple Environments*. U.K. Gower, Aldershot. In press.

Boruvka, O. (1977). *Foundations of the Theory of Groupoids and Groups*. Berlin: VEB Deutscher Verlag der Wissenschaften.

Kohout, L. (1975). Algebraic models in computer-aided medical diagnosis. In Anderson, J. (ed.): *Proceedings of MEDINFO 74*. Amsterdam: North-Holland, pp. 575–579, addendum pp. 1069–70.

Kohout, L. J. (1984). Fuzzy decision making and its impact on the design of expert systems. In *IEEE Technical Digest No. 67*, IEEE, London, May 1984. IEEE Colloquium on Decision Support Aspects of Expert Systems. Reprinted in: *Bulletin of British Computer Society Specialist Group on Artificial Intelligence*, 1984.

Kohout, L. J. (1990). *A Perspective on Intelligent Systems: A Framework for Analysis and Design*. London and New York: Chapman and Hall & Van Nostrand.

Kohout, L. J. and W. Bandler (1981). Approximate reasoning in intelligent relational data bases. In R.D. Parslow (ed.): *BCS'81: Information Technology for the Eighties. Proc. Conf. The British Computer Society, London, July 1981*. London: Heyden & Son, pp. 483–485.

Kohout, L. J. and W. Bandler. (1985). Relational-product architectures for information processing. *Information Science, 37*, 25–37.

Kohout, L. J. and W. Bandler. (1986a). Knowledge representation, clinical action and expert systems. In L. J. Kohout and W. Bandler (eds.):

Knowledge Representation in Medicine and Clinical Behavioural Science. An Abacus Book. London and New York: Gordon and Breach, pp. 1–8.

Kohout, L. J. and W. Bandler (eds.). (1986b). *Knowledge Representation in Medicine and Clinical Behavioural Science.* London: Abacus. New York: Gordon and Breach.

Kohout, L. J. and W. Bandler. (1987a). Computer Security Systems: Fuzzy Logics. In M. G. Singh (ed.): *Systems and Control Encyclopedia.* Oxford: Pergamon Press.

Kohout, L. J. and W. Bandler. (1987b). The use of fuzzy information retrieval techniques in construction of multi-centre knowledge-based systems. In B. Bouchon and R. R. Yager (eds.): *Uncertainty in Knowledge-Based Systems. Lecture Notes in Computer Science, vol. 286.* Berlin: Springer-Verlag, pp. 257–264.

Kohout, L. J. and M. Kallala. (1986). Evaluator of neurological patients' dexterity based on relational fuzzy products. In *Proc. of Second Expert Systems International Conference, London, October.* New Jersey and Oxford: Learned Information, pp. 1–12.

Kohout, L. J. and M. Kallala. (1987). Choice of fuzzy optimal logics for pattern classifiers by means of measure analysis. In *Proc. of Seventh International Congress on Cybernetics and Systems.* London: Imperial College, September.

Kohout, L. J., J. Anderson, and W. Bandler. (1991). *Knowledge-Based Systems for Multiple Environments.* U.K.: Gower, Aldershot.

Kohout, L. J., E. Keravnou, and W. Bandler. (1984). Automatic documentary information retrieval by means of fuzzy relational products. In B. R. Gaines, L. A. Zadeh, and H.-J. Zimmermann (eds.): *Fuzzy Sets in Decision Analysis.* Amsterdam: North-Holland, pp. 383–404.

Kohout, L. J., W. Bandler, J. Anderson, and C. Trayner. (1985). Knowledge-based decision support system for use in medicine. In G. Mitra (ed.): *Computer Models for Decision Making.* Amsterdam: North-Holland, pp. 133–146.

Kohout, L. J., E. Keravnou, W. Bandler, C. Trayner, and J. Anderson. (1984). Construction of an expert therapy adviser as a special case of a general system protection design. In R. Trappl (ed.): *Cybernetics and Systems Research,* **2**, 97–104. Amsterdam: North-Holland.

Kohout, L. J., A. Behrooz, J. Anderson, S. Gao, C. Trayner, and W. Bandler. (1987). Dynamics of localised inference and its embedding in activity structures based IKBS architectures. In *Proc. of Second IFSA Congress,* pp. 740–743.

Løvstad, S., W. Bandler, and V. Mancini. (1990). Hierarchies of urban nodes and constructs. In *Proc. of NAFIPS'90 North American Fuzzy Information Processing Society Conference,* Toronto, Canada, June.

Schweizer, B. and A. Sklar. (1983). *Probabilistic metric spaces.* New York: North-Holland.

Stiller, E., S. Løvstad, W. Bandler, and V. Mancini. (1989). Representing the social dimension: Design and methodology for an urban planning system. In M. B. Fishman (eds.): *Proceedings of Second Florida Artificial Intelligence Research Symposium,* pp. 216–220. Florida AI Research Symposium, St. Petersburg.

Wilcox, T. (1980). The usefulness of fuzzy sets analysis with repertory grids in measure of change in social competence. In G. E. Lasker (ed.): *Applied*

Systems and Cybernetics, volume VI, Fuzzy Sets and Systems, Possibility Theory and Special Topics in Systems Research. New York: Pergamon Press.

Zadeh, L. A. (1971). Similarity relations and fuzzy orderings. *Information Sciences,* **3,** 177–200.

22 Approximate reasoning in diagnosis, therapy, and prognosis

A. F. ROCHA
and M. THEOTO
RANI – Research on Artificial
and Natural Intelligence
Rue Tenente Ary Aps, 172
13200 Jundiai, BRAZIL

C. A.C. OLIVEIRA
Superintendencia Geral
de Automação e Instrumen-
tação
Companhia Siderurgica
27180 Volta Redonda,
BRAZIL

F. GOMIDE
Faculty of Electrical Engineering
UNICAMP
13081 Campinas, BRAZIL

Abstract. A model describing the knowledge net used by the expert to reason about diagnosis, therapy, and prognosis in a variety of fields of human activity ranging from medicine to process control in engineering is presented. Also, a method for acquiring the knowledge involved in this reasoning is described.

1. INTRODUCTION

Expert systems were introduced in medicine as an intelligent tool for diagnosis (Buchanan and Shortliffe, 1985) and it is now widely used in classification tasks in a variety of fields of specialization of human activity. Among these fields, expert systems are now being successfully used for process control in many areas such as blast furnace, chemical plants, oil industry, etc. (e.g., Fujio et al., 1990; Ishii et al., 1990; Yamada and Suzuki, 1990).

The complexity of the structure of expert systems increased in order to accommodate the new demands imposed by their application to control tasks, which may involve at least three main steps: diagnosis, therapy, and prognosis.

The purpose of any process control system is to maintain the operation of the specified process within a certain tolerable range. Thus, the first task of a control expert system is to diagnose any significant deviation from this fuzzy normal state, that is to say, to evaluate the confidence on the existence of pathological states. Whenever confidence on at least one of these pathological states is greater than the confidence about the normal state, a warning is issued, requiring the system to determine the actions (therapy) necessary to bring the process to normal conditions again.

Because recovery is a time-consuming activity, it is necessary to probe whether the pathway of state changes under the chosen therapy will guarantee the normal conditions as the final state. This probing is performed by matching, from time to time, the system's actual state with some of the states of the desirable pathway. These states are called prognostic states. If confidence on the prognostic states is high, there is no need of changing the therapy. Otherwise, the system's actual state is considered a *pathological state* and another warning is issued.

Of interest is the fact that these same steps on process control are the main activities of the physician concerned with the health of his patient. Whenever a disease is diagnosed, a therapy is implemented and its results evaluated by assessing the prognosis (Ingelfinger, 1975; Kassirer and Gorry, 1978).

The purpose of the present paper is to discuss the expert reasoning within this broad scope, pointing out the most important properties of the fuzzy reasoning involved in diagnosing, choosing the therapy, and assessing prognosis. The model presented here was developed by eliciting and analysing knowledge from different medical experts in different fields of medicine and from experts on blast furnace control, using a fuzzy graph tool developed earlier by two of the authors (Leão and Rocha, 1990; Machado, Rocha, and Leão, 1991; Rocha et al., 1989; Rocha et al., 1990; Theoto and Rocha, 1989; Theoto, Rocha, and Machado, 1990; Theoto et al., submitted).

2. EXPERT REASONING

Expertise in a field of human activity like medicine, process control, etc., is the ability to perform correct classification of defined pathological states (diseases, perturbations, etc.) and to choose the adequate therapy (actions) to recover the system to a normal or acceptable state.

2.1. The Knowledge Graph

The first step in any process of expert knowledge acquisition is to characterize these pathological states, because the definition of the normal state requires a complete characterization of all state variables and their respective ranges of normal values, and in most of, if not all, the instances a complete knowledge of the system or process is not available. The characterization of pathological states is easier than that of normal states because the expert may focus attention only a small set from among all the variables. Also, the recovery of normal state may be characterized by verifying that this set of variables reached their normal ranges.

Each pathological state is characterized by asking the expert to furnish the list of data used to support his decision about the classification (Figure 22.1). This list is ordered according to the temporal sequence in which the data are obtained during the diagnosis process, and it is used as the set of terminal nodes of the graph representing the procedural knowledge used to assess the diagnosis (Rocha et al., 1990). This graph is obtained by asking the expert to join the terminal nodes into secondary, tertiary, etc. nodes in the same way the data must be combined to support his decision about the diagnosis. This aggregation process continues until all nodes in the graph converge to a root representing the pathological state.

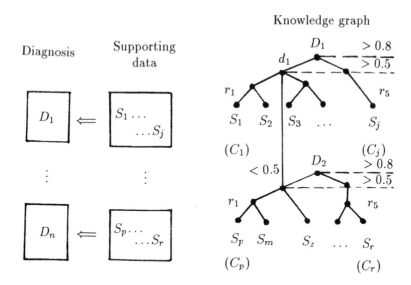

Figure 22.1. Acquiring the knowledge

The reasoning is not a crisp process; on the contrary, it involves at least three different types of uncertainty (Rocha, Machado, and Theoto, 1990; Theoto, Rocha and Machado, 1990):

1. *Confidence* – a measure of the matching between the actual and some prototypical datum supporting a given diagnosis. For example, the actual temperature and the concept of fever required to support a diagnosis about infection.
2. *Relevance* – a measure of the uncertainty about the conditional frequency of the datum and the diagnosis. It measures the importance of each piece of information to support the decision about the classification.
3. *Utility* – a measure of the uncertainty about the cost of obtaining the datum and the amount of information provided by it.

The relevance (r_i in Figure 22.1) in the knowledge graph is represented by the weights assigned by the expert to its arcs. The utility is related with the ranking of the data in the list of the terminal nodes, because in general, if not always, high-cost data are obtained later in the diagnostic process. The confidence (c_i in Figure 22.1) is assessed by means of membership functions provided by the expert to define the linguistic variables (e.g., fever, high pressure, etc.) used in the description of the data (Rocha and Theo, and Theoto and Rocha, submitted).

2.2. The Reasoning Process

The diagnostic process begins when the expert receives some initial data (S_1/S_3 or S_p/S_r in Figure 22.1) about some dysfunction of the system. These initial data are used to trigger some working hypothesis (Eddy and Clanton, 1982; Rocha, Theoto, and Torasso, 1988) according to the relevance of and confidence on these data. Relevance of and confidence on terminal nodes are combined by means of t-norms (in general, the product) to furnish the confidence on the next nonterminal node (Theoto and Rocha, 1989; Theoto, Rocha, and Machado, 1990). In this way, high confidence on highly relevant nodes provides high confidence on the next nonterminal node, while either low confidence or low relevance results in low confidence in the upper nodes. The working hypotheses are chosen as those diagnoses presenting confidence above an acceptance threshold.

The next step in the process is to acquire more data to support or to exclude these initial hypothesis. Thus, if confidence on the triggers is above the acceptance threshold, new information (S_2,..., or S_x in Figure 22.1) is sought by means of physical examination, instrument reading, laboratory tests, etc.

The information obtained in this way is aggregated at specific nodes in the knowledge graph, called *decision nodes* and labeled d_i in Figure 22.1. Confidence $c(d_i)$ on decision nodes is calculated as a geometric averaging of confidence on and relevance of the incoming data (Rocha et al., 1989; Rocha et al., 1990):

$$c(d_i) = (1 - \alpha)(\prod_{i=1}^{n} p_i)e_1 + \alpha(1 - \prod_{i=1}^{n} (1 - p_i))e_2 \qquad (1)$$

$$p_i = c_i r_i \qquad (2)$$

where the product $\prod$ is taken over all the n pieces of information converging on the node d_i from lower terminal nonterminal nodes. Decision nodes are labeled ANDOR nodes by the expert, the degree of andness (or orness) being expressed by α, such that

$$\alpha = 0 \text{ for a true AND and } \alpha = 1 \text{ for a true OR} \qquad (3)$$

If e_i is equal to n, then (1) is the geometric means, otherwise, gain or loss of confidence is allowed during the aggregation.

Decision at these nodes obeys the following:

1. High confidence $c(d_i)$ supports the decision for the diagnosis (D_1 or D_2 in Figure 22.1).
2. Intermediate values (but greater than 0.5) of $c(d_i)$ on the already acquired data maintains the inquiry about other pieces of information according to their utility (Rocha et al., 1989; Roca et al., 1990; Theoto, Rocha, and Machado, 1990).
3. Confidence lower than 0.5 forces the focus of attention to change to another working hypothesis (e.g., from D_2 to D_1 in Figure 22.1).

Decision nodes aggregate knowledge graphs into a knowledge net, and they are key nodes for approximate reasoning with partial data. If confidence is high or low, the expert is able to make a decision without asking for all supporting data. Besides this, decision is made even in presence of contradictory information, if contradiction is related with low relevant data.

3. THE KNOWLEDGE NET

3.1. Choice of Therapy

Expert knowledge involves not only knowledge for doing correct classifications, but also to map diagnoses into therapies. This map may be a very simple one if bijective relations are established between the sets of diagnosis and therapy, but in general the choice of the adequate action to bring the system to a normal state requires a complex reasoning involving also other pieces of information (Figure 22.2). Because the characterization of pathological states is founded over a small set among all the variables defining the actual system's state, the choice of the adequate therapy in many instances is dependent on the actual value of some other variables of the system, such as age, weight, pressure, etc., or even other dysfuntions if the system supports multiple failures.

The reasoning to map diagnosis d_k into therapy is supported by decision nodes (d_k and d_r in Figure 22.2) aggregating the chosen diagnostic and other information about the actual state of the system. The complexity of the decision will be reflected in the complexity of

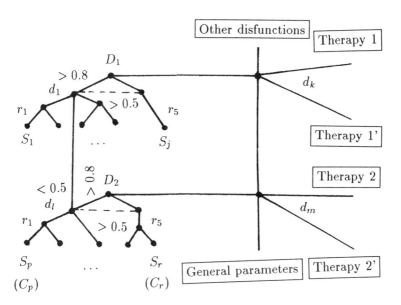

Figure 22.2. Choosing the therapy

the graph used to describe the influences of the other variables of the system on the choice of the therapy (the boxes Other Dysfunctions and General Parameters in Figure 22.2 must be understood as a general representation of such graphs).

In this line of reasoning, the chosen diagnosis is used as a trigger for a reasoning similar to that described in the previous section, to bring different therapies under consideration. The data supporting each therapy is combined into decision graphs similar to those representing the knowledge about the diagnosis, and decision is dependent on how these graphs are navigated.

In this context, a therapy is a set of actions (including the null action) intended to move the system from a specific pathological state toward an acceptable final state. It is desirable that the final state is a normal state, but in some instances it is just more stable than the pathologic state. This final state is reached when the set of variables used to characterize the pathological state reaches specified ranges.

As a set of actions, a therapy is also represented by means of graphs having the actions as the terminal nodes. The navigation in this graph is from the root toward the terminal nodes, thus it is in the opposite

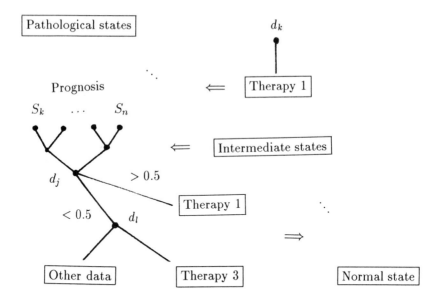

Figure 22.3. Controlling the therapy

direction concerning the previous decision graphs. Besides this, the therapy graph does not contain any decision node, because all the decision was made before. Thus, the therapy graph encodes a descriptive knowledge.

3.2. Controlling the Therapy

The purpose of any therapy is to move the system from a pathological to an acceptable state. This defines a pathway of states, having the pathological state as the initial state and the acceptable state as the final one (Figure 22.3). To evaluate the effect of a therapy is to compare the actual state pathway with a prototypical or intended pathway. The similarity of the two pathways corresponds to the effectiveness of the therapy. The actual pathway is said to describe the prognosis of the therapy, and the prototypical pathway is the best prognosis. Thus, prognosis is defined according to the chosen diagnosis and therapy.

From time to time, the expert evaluates the system's actual state by taking information about some of the variables of the system and processing these data in decision graphs describing some specific state in the prototypical pathway. If confidence on this best prognosis is high, the chosen therapy is maintained, otherwise the outcome of the processing may be viewed as a new diagnosis and a new therapy may be elected by the same reasoning process described in the previous section (Figure 22.3).

The matching between the actual and the prototypical pathways may be also used to control the output of the therapy graph. In this condition, the prognostic states may activate defined pathways in this graph.

4. CONCLUSION

The model presented here describes the knowledge net used by the expert to reason about diagnosis, therapy, and prognosis in a variety of fields of human activity, ranging from medicine to process control in engineering.

The knowledge net is composed by a set of individual graphs linked by means of decision nodes. Each individual graph is either a partial description of a system's state or of a set of actions (therapy) used to bring the system from a pathological to an acceptable state.

Decision is supported by a fuzzy reasoning about three different types of uncertainty: (1) confidence as uncertainty of matching; (2) relevance as uncertainty of frequency, and (3) utility as uncertainty of cost of information.

The expert knowledge about the whole process of diagnosing and treating a system may be acquired with the methodology developed by Rocha, Theoto, and colleagues (Rocha et al., 1989; Rocha et al., 1990; Theoto, Rocha, and Machado, 1990; Theoto et al., submitted) and it was acquired and tested with good results in the case of blast furnace control.

Keywords: fuzzy reasoning, knowledge elicitation, knowledge graph, uncertainty

BIBLIOGRAPHY

Buchanan, B.G. and E. H. Shortliffe. (1985). *Rule Based Expert Systems.* Reading, MA: Addison-Wesley, pp. 3–19.

Eddy, D. and C. H. Clanton. (1982). The art of diagnosis. *New England J. of Medicine,* 21, 1263–1268.

Fujio, I., K. Omura, Y. Tajima, H. Morita, and K. Kawachi. (1990). Application of fuzzy expert systems to PP-Plant. *Proceedings of NAFIPS' 90,* pp. 231–234.

Ingelfinger, F.J. (1975). Decision in medicine. *New England J. of Medicine,* 293 (5), 254–255.

Ishii, K., R. Nakajima, S. Kishimoto, H. Hotta, and M. Sakurai. (1990). Application of artificial intelligence for blast furnace operation. *Proceedings of NAFIPS' 90,* pp. 235–238.

Kassirer, J.P. and G. A. Gorry. (1978). Clinical problem solving: A behavioral analysis. *Annals of Internal Medicine,* 89, 245–255.

Leão, B.F. and A. F. Rocha. (1990). Proposed methodology for knowlege acquisition: A study on congenital heart disease diagnosis. *Methods of Information in Medicine,* 29, 30–40.

Machado, R.J., A. F. Rocha, and B. Leão. (1991). Calculating the mean knowledge representation from multiple experts. In J. Kacprzyk and M. Fedrizzi (eds.): *Multiperson Decision Making Models Using Fuzzy Sets and Possibility Theory.* Dordrecht: Kluwer.

Rocha, A.F. M. Theoto, and P. Torasso. (1988). Heuristic learning expert systems–General principles. In M. M. Gupta and T. Yamakawa (eds): *Fuzzy Logic in Knowledge-Based Systems.* North-Holland, Elsevier, pp. 289–306.

Rocha, A.F., M. Theoto, I. Rizzo, and M. P. R. Laginha. (1989). Handling Uncertainty in medical reasoning. *Proceedings of the Third IFSA Congress,* Seattle, pp. 480–483.

Rocha, A.F., M. P. R. Laginha, R. J. Machao, D. Sigulem, and M. Angão. (1990). Declarative and procedural knowledge: Two complimentary tools for expertise. In Verdegay and Delgado (eds.): *Approximate Reasoning Tools for Artificial Intelligence.* Cologne: Verlag TÜV Rheinland, pp. 229–253.

Rocha, A.F., M. Theoto, and M. Theoto Rocha. Investigating medical linguistic variables. (Submitted.)

Rocha, A.F., R. J. Machado and M. Theoto. (1990). Complex neutral networks. *Proceedings of ISUMA' 90, Maryland,* IEEE Computer Society Press, pp. 497–499.

Theoto, M. and A. F. Rocha. (1980). Fuzzy belief and text decoding. *Proceedings of the Third IFSA Congress,* Seattle, pp. 552–554.

Theoto, M., M. S. Koizumi, L. T. M. Margarido, and A. F. Rocha. Comparing expertise and the expert's data base. (Submitted.)

Theoto, M., A. F. Rocha, and R. J. Machado. (1990). Approximate reasoning with partial data. *Proceedings of ISUMA' 90, Maryland,* IEEE Computer Society Press, pp. 567–572.

Yamada, T. and K. Suzuki. (1990). Fuzzy control of plural hydraulic jacks in an elastic-plastic structural test. *Proceedings of ISUMA' 90, Maryland,* IEEE Computer Society Press, pp. 546–551.

23 Elementary learning in a fuzzy expert system

James J. BUCKLEY
Department of Mathematics
University of Alabama at Birmingham
Birmingham, AL 35294, USA

Abstract. In this paper we consider using weights, which are attached to all data items and rules, in our fuzzy expert shell FLOPS to enable the system to achieve elementary learning. A teacher sets fuzzy goals and FLOPS manipulates the weights on rules (rule-based learning), or on the data items (data-driven learning) in pursuit of maximizing the intersection of the fuzzy goals. Theoretical results are presented, and numerous examples illustrate the methods.

1. INTRODUCTION

The objective of this paper is to show how our fuzzy expert system shell FLOPS, which has been enhanced by the addition of weights attached to all data items and rules, can use these weights to learn how to achieve certain elementary goals. The use of weights in FLOPS is analogous to how weights are employed in neural networks (Rumelhart and McClelland, 1988) to train the network on test data. In this section we will present on overview of the problem and in the next section we review the internal operations of FLOPS with the addition of weights. The third section contains a description of how FLOPS can manipulate its weights to attain fuzzy goals and the last section has a brief summary and our conclusions.

Consider a fuzzy expert system having a set of rules, some initial data, whose job it is to come up with a fuzzy set of conclusions

$$\bar{C} = \left\{ \frac{\lambda_1}{c_1}, \frac{\lambda_2}{c_2}, ... \right\} \tag{1}$$

The c_i are members of $\bar{C}$ with membership value[1] λ_i in $[0,1]$, $i = 1, 2, ...$. FLOPS will be considered an infant, or a very young person, who has a teacher (expert). The teacher, based on the given information, decides on the best values for the λ_i and defines fuzzy goals $\bar{G}_i$ for each element c_i in $\bar{C}$. We will always place a "bar" over a symbol if it represents a fuzzy set. $\bar{G}$ will be a (normalized) fuzzy subset of $[0,1]$ so let $y = \mu(x|\bar{G}_i)$ denote its membership function, $i = 1, 2, ...$. If $\mu(\lambda_i|\bar{G}_i) = 1$, the teacher returns a grade of "good," if $\mu(\lambda_i|\bar{G}_i) \in (0,1)$ the grade is "fair," and $\mu(\lambda_i|\bar{G}_i) = 0$ receives a "bad" grade for c_i in $\bar{C}$, $i = 1, 2, ...$. FLOPS' objective is to maximize $\bar{G} = \bar{G}_1 \cap \bar{G}_2 \cap ...$ and, if possible, get a good grade for all c_i in $\bar{C}$.

If the grade of a c_i in $\bar{C}$ is not good, then FLOPS will change the weights attached to data items in working memory, or those attached to the rules, in order to improve its grade for c_i. Once a good grade is received then FLOPS, if the system is to be data driven, will change the weights on the rules back to their original values and compute new weights for the data items so that given the same, or similar, information (confidence values) it will get a good grade on its first run.

We will say that the learning is data driven (or data based) if FLOPS can change the weights only on the data items in working memory. Learning is rule based (or rule driven) when FLOPS is allowed to vary only the weights attached to the rules. Of course, we may also have a mixed case of changing the weights on some of the rules and being able to vary the weights on certain data items. FLOPS will never decrease a weight for a rule or data item. It is allowed only to increase the weights.

Data items in working memory are of two types: (1) the initial fuzzy sets; and (2) other fuzzy sets, usually starting with no confidence values, whose confidence values and weights are constructed from the rules (see the examples in the third section). If learning is to be data based, then FLOPS can increase the weights attached only to data items within the initial fuzzy sets in working memory.

---

[1] Later we will expand λ_i to a pair (cf_i, wt_i) where cf_i is the confidence value and wt_i is the weight.

FLOPS may not be able to achieve a good grade on all c_i $\bar{C}$ simultaneously. First, FLOPS will attempt to make $\mu(\lambda_i|\bar{G}_i) = 1$ for each $i = 1, 2, \ldots$ separately. If there is an i so that it is impossible to make $\mu(\lambda_i|\bar{G}_i) = 1$ by only changing the weights, then the data and/or rules are not comprehensible enough (FLOPS is too young) for the system to learn the objective. We will discuss this point in more detail below.

Now suppose that individually FLOPS can alter the weights so that it can get a good grade for each c_i in $\bar{C}$. However, it may still be impossible to obtain a good grade for all c_i in $\bar{C}$ simultaneously. That is, FLOPS may be able to pick a set of weights so that $\mu(\lambda_i|\bar{G}_1) = 1$ but then the best it can do is $\mu(\lambda_2|\bar{G}_2) = 0.7$. In this case the goals are conflicting. It is not FLOPS' fault that the teacher has set up conflicting goals and the best it can do for $\bar{G} = \bar{G}_1 \cap \bar{G}_2$ is $\mu(\lambda|\bar{G}) = 0.7$, where $\lambda = (\lambda_1, \lambda_2)$.

Calling FLOPS an infant, or a very young person, means that it is limited in what it can do in pursuit of good grades. FLOPS will not be able to alter in any way[2] its rule set, or create new rules. Changing its rules will be learned later. One can always, as we will discuss in the fourth section, create a new specified rule to get a good grade for any c_i in $\bar{C}$. Special purpose rules are to be avoided in the beginning of the learning process. Also, FLOPS will not be allowed to change confidence values attached to rules nor can it alter directly any confidence value for a data item in working memory. FLOPS can change some confidence values indirectly through using different weights (see the examples in the third section).

We have previously advocated adding weights to a fuzzy expert system. A main problem in the management of uncertainty in a fuzzy expert system is when, and how, to reduce confidence values. In our original system (Buckley, Siler, and Tucker, 1986a) confidence values can never decrease and may only increase (monotonic logic). However, for the system to be able to "change its mind" provision must be made for reducing confidence values (nonmonotonic logic). Weights for rules and data were initially proposed so that FLOPS can update its conclusions when presented with new, and possibly conflicting, data (Buckley, 1990a). The memory update algorithm uses the weights to block certain commands, with low weight, from being processed and hence these commands will not affect working memory. In this paper we expand the memory update algorithm to handle both weights and confidence values in order to completely update working memory for the next round of parallel rule firing.

---

[2] Except the weights attached to the rules.

2. FUZZY EXPERT SYSTEM

In this section we will discuss the pertinent parts of our fuzzy expert system shell FLOPS (Siler and Tucker, 1986; Buckley, Siler and Tucker, 1986a; Buckley, Siler, and Tucker 1986b; Buckley, Siler, and Tucker, 1987a; Buckley, Siler and Tucker, 1987b; Buckley and Tucker, 1988; Buckley and Tucker, 1989) needed for the discussion on learning in the next section. All data items in working memory and all rules have associated with them a confidence value (cf) and a weight (wt). We will first discuss the structure and operation of the rules, secondly the memory update algorithm (MUA), and lastly the structure of data items in working memory.

A rule is of the form

$$\mathbf{R}(\sigma, R, \tau) \quad I F \; X_1 \, AND \, X_2 \, AND \, ... \, AND \, X_m, \, THEN \, Y \qquad (2)$$

where the X_i are patterns, Y is an instruction on how to change (a confidence value in) working memory, σ is the rule's prior wt, R is the rule's prior cf, and τ denotes the rule's thresholding value. R and τ will be numbers in $[0, 1]$ but σ can be any positive integer or zero. Default values for τ and σ are zero but R will default to one.

Patterns are of the form Θ, or Θ (relation)constant, or Θ_a(relation)Θ_b, where the Θ's are attribute values[3] and the relations are fuzzy or binary. When the rule is to execute, all data items, together with their confidences and weights, are inserted into the patterns and the system then determines each pattern's confidence ($\mathrm{conf}[X_i] = \alpha_i$) and weight ($\mathrm{weight}[X_i] = w_i$).

The confidence values attached to data items are numbers in $[0, 1]$, or they are B for "blank." For example, consider a fuzzy set $Size$ in working memory whose members are $small$, $medium$, and $large$. Then we would have[4]

$$Size = \left\{ \frac{(cf_1, wt_1)}{small}, \frac{(cf_2, wt_2)}{medium}, \frac{(cf_3, wt_3)}{large} \right\} \qquad (3)$$

where $\mathrm{conf}[small] = cf_1$ and $\mathrm{weight}[small] = wt_1$, etc. Technically, $Size$ is not a classical fuzzy set because each member has two numbers associated with it with $cf_i = $ its degree of membership in $Size$. However, we will still call $Size$ a fuzzy set. If no information is

---

[3] Members of fuzzy sets in working memory.
[4] We will omit the bar over fuzzy sets defined linguistically.

available on conf[*small*], then the system defaults to $cf_1 = B$. Otherwise, conf[*small*] $\in [0, 1]$. The default value is zero for all weights, but cf-values default to B for data and to one for rules.

Now we will explain how α_i and ω_i are calculated for each pattern X_i. The management of uncertainty in a fuzzy expert system has been discussed in detail in Buckley (1988) or Buckley (1990b). For simplicity we will employ Zadeh's logic of min for AND and max for OR in manipulating confidence values. Therefore, if: (1) $X_i = \Theta$, then $\alpha_i = $ conf$[\Theta]$; (2) $X_i = \Theta$ (relation) constant, then $\alpha_i = \min($conf$[\Theta]$, value of the relation); and (3) $X_i = \Theta_a$ (relation)Θ_b, then $\alpha_i = \min($conf$[\Theta_a]$, value of relation, conf$[\Theta_b]$). For the rationale of using min here, see Buckley (1988), or Buckley (1990b). For the calculation of ω_i we adopt the results in Buckley (1990a), which are: (1) if $X_i = \Theta$, then $\omega_i = $ weight$[\Theta]$; (2) if $X_i = \Theta$ (relation) constant, then $\omega_i = $ weight$[\Theta]$; and (3) if $X_i = \Theta_a$ (relation) Θ_b, then $\omega_i = \max($weight$[\Theta_a]$, weight$[\Theta_b]$). We have assumed that: (1) constants have $cf = 1$ and $wt = 0$; and (2) relations have no confidence values and weight[relation] $= 0$. If conf$[\Theta] = B$, for blank, then the rule will not fire so conf$[X_i]$ need not be computed.

Now we have $\alpha_i = $ conf$[X_i]$ and $w_i = $ weight$[X_i]$ for each X_i in the antecedent part of the rule in equation (2). FLOPS next combines these numbers across all patterns to get

$$\alpha_0 = \min(\alpha_1, ..., \alpha_m) \tag{4}$$

$$w_0 = \max(\omega_1, ..., \omega_m) \tag{5}$$

where α_0 is final antecedent confidence and w_0 is final antecedent weight. We use min for AND to get α_0 and see Buckley (1990a) for the reason why we use max to get w_0.

The thresholding number τ is used as follows: (1) if $\alpha_0 \geqslant \tau$, then fire this rule; and (2) if $\alpha_0 < \tau$, then do not fire this rule. Assuming the rule executes, FLOPS now combines R and α_0 to produce final left-hand side confidence α and combines σ and w_0 to obtain final left-hand side weight w. For these computations (see Buckley, 1988; Buckley, 1990a; Buckley, 1990b) we will use

$$\alpha = \min(R, \alpha_0) \tag{6}$$

$$w = \max(\sigma, w_0) \tag{7}$$

Now the pair (α, w) is assigned to Y in the right-hand side of the rule.

The statement Y in the right-hand side of the rule will not be compound and may be of the form: (1) $\bar{Z}$ is Θ where $\bar{Z}$ is a fuzzy set in working memory and Θ is a member of $\bar{Z}$; or (2) conf$[\Theta] = \lambda \in [0, 1]$.

Y will be simple, not compound like $\bar{Z}_1 = \Theta_1$ AND $\bar{Z}_2 = \Theta_2$..., since FLOPS fires rules in parallel. If Y is $\bar{Z}_1 = \Theta_1$ AND $\bar{Z}_2 = \Theta_2$, then we could make two identical rules one with consequence $\bar{Z}_1 = \Theta_1$ and the other with consequence $\bar{Z}_2 = \Theta_2$ both having simple conclusions. When Y is $\bar{Z} = \Theta$, then (α, w) are assigned to Θ, which then awaits the MUA. A conclusion like $\text{conf}[\Theta] = \lambda$, where Θ is a member of a fuzzy set, is needed in order to be able to reduce confidences (nonmonotonic logic) and will be discussed in the next section. If $Y = [\text{conf}[\Theta] = \lambda]$, then (λ, w) is assigned to Θ, and not (α, w), to await the MUA. Other statements for Y, those that change the rules or create new rules, are possible but will not be considered in this paper.

FLOPS will be operating in its parallel mode, which means that all rules execute, subject to certain restrictions, after every memory update. The restrictions on rule firing are: (1) they must pass threshold; (2) they do not fire on old information; and (3) they do not execute on no information (some $\text{conf}[\Theta] = B$). If the data used in the patterns in the rule has not changed since the last round of rule firing (the old information case), then this rule will fail to fire in the next round of rule firing.

After all fireable rules execute, the system presents all right-hand side attributes Θ, together with their cf and wt-values to MUA. To more easily explain MUA let us consider a specific example of updating (cf_1, wt_1) for $small$ in the fuzzy set $Size$ given in equation (3). Suppose there are K rules whose right-hand side action Y refers to $small$ in $Size$ and further assume that the cf and wt-values computed from these rules are $(\alpha^{(i)}, w^{(i)})$, $1 \leqslant i \leqslant K$. Let $\alpha^{(0)} = cf_1$ and $w^{(0)} = wt_1$. We first compute

$$w^* = \max\{w^{(i)} | 0 \leqslant i \leqslant K\} \tag{8}$$

and only consider

$$\Gamma = \{\alpha^{(i)} | w^{(i)} = w^*\} \tag{9}$$

and disregard all commands Y with $w < w^*$. Then, the new cf for $small$ is[5]

$$\text{new}[cf_1] = \max\{\alpha | \alpha \in \Gamma\} \tag{10}$$

and the new wt for small will be

$$\text{new}[wt_1] = w^* \tag{11}$$

In this way MUA updates all the (cf, wt) pairs for all members of the fuzzy sets in working memory.

---

[5] If the original $cf = B$, and $B \in \Gamma$, then we take the max over the $\alpha \in \Gamma$, $\alpha \in [0, 1]$.

In its normal, forward chaining, operation FLOPS changes *cf* and *wt*-values as described above, finally halting with the construction of the *cf* and *wt*-values of the fuzzy set of conclusions $\bar{C}$. In its new learning mode FLOPS will change the *wt*-values of data and rules, to be described in the next section, halting with its best overall grade with respect to the fuzzy goals. In its learning mode FLOPS will not be allowed to alter any *cf*-values directly, nor change any rules except through their *wt*-values σ.

The organization of FLOPS makes it possible to work with a hierarchy of fuzzy sets where at the highest level we have memory elements. An example of a memory element would be *Animal* whose members include *Size*, *Weight*, *Color*, where each of these are themselves fuzzy sets. All of our fuzzy sets will be like *Size* in equation (3).

The *wt*-values of members of fuzzy sets may represent the element's importance, or reliability, etc. In this case *wt*-values (greater than zero) could be initially supplied by the user or automatically generated by the system. As an example of how the system could generate *wt*-values consider a fuzzy set $\bar{A}$ in working memory given by

$$\bar{A} = \left\{ \frac{x_1}{\bar{a}_1}, \frac{x_2}{\bar{a}_2}, \dots \right\} \tag{12}$$

where $x_i = (cf_i, 0)$, all *i*. Now each $\bar{a}_i$ is itself a fuzzy set with

$$\bar{a}_i = \left\{ \frac{x_{i1}}{a_{i1}}, \frac{x_{i2}}{a_{i2}}, \dots \right\} \tag{13}$$

where $x_{ij} = (cf_{ij}, 1)$. Here information about an a_{ij} is considered more specific than information about only $\bar{a}_i$ and the system assigns a higher *wt*-value of one to each a_{ij} in $\bar{a}_i$. The user can, of course, a priori assign any *wt*-values to the elements of fuzzy sets in working memory and also any σ-values (weights) to the rules.

3. LEARNING

We start this section with a simple example showing how manipulating the weight values can produce elementary rule-based, or data-based, learning.

3.1. Example 1. Tweety the Bird

We have the following fuzzy sets in working memory

$$Animal = \left\{ \frac{(B,0)}{bird}, \frac{(B,0)}{fish}, \dots \right\} \tag{14}$$

$$Bird = \left\{ \frac{(B,0)}{penguin}, \dots \right\} \tag{15}$$

and the fuzzy set of conclusions

$$Movement = \left\{ \frac{(B,0)}{fly}, \frac{(B,0)}{swim}, \dots \right\} \tag{16}$$

We have an object called Tweety and the system is to decide on its movement. The rules are:

$\mathbf{R}_1(0, 0.8, 0)$ If *Tweety* = *bird*, then *Movement* = *fly* $\qquad$ (17)

$\mathbf{R}_2(0, 1.0, 0)$ If *Tweety* = *fish*, then *Movement* = *swim* $\qquad$ (18)

$\mathbf{R}_3(0, 1.0, 0.8)$ If *Tweety* = *penguin*, then *Movement* = *swim* (19)

$\mathbf{R}_4(0, 1.0, 0.8)$ If *Tweety* = *penguin*, then conf $[fly] = 0$ $\qquad$ (20)

All data items have default $cf = B$ and $wt = 0$, all rules have default $wt = 0$, and only $\mathbf{R}_3$ and $\mathbf{R}_4$ have a nonzero threshold value.

We are now presented with the information conf $[penguin] = 1$ and conf $[fish] = 0$. The system automatically sets conf $[bird] = 1$ in *Animal* because penguins are birds. The teacher sets the fuzzy goals $\bar{G}_i$ for the elements in *Movement* to be: (1) $\mu(\lambda_1 | \bar{G}_1) = -5\lambda_1 + 1$ for $0 \leqslant \lambda_1 \leqslant 0.2$, and zero otherwise, where conf $[fly] = \lambda_1$; and (2) $\mu(\lambda_2 | \bar{G}_2) = 5\lambda_2 - 4$ for $0.8 \leqslant \lambda_2 \leqslant 1.0$, and zero otherwise, where conf $[swim] = \lambda_2$. All rules fire producing

$$Movement = \left\{ \frac{(0.8, 0)}{fly}, \frac{(1, 0)}{swim}, \dots \right\} \tag{21}$$

which says that penguins swim and probably fly. Its grade on fly is "bad," on swim it receives "good," with an overall grade of "bad."

FLOPS must reduce conf $[fly]$ since it is now 0.8, which comes from

$$0.8 = \max(0.8, 0) \tag{22}$$

where the 0.8 in equation (22) comes from $\mathbf{R}_1$ and the zero from $\mathbf{R}_4$. The weights do not enter into the computations since they are all zero by default. FLOPS increases the *wt*-value in R_4 to $\sigma = 1$, fires all rules again after setting *Movement* back to its original value in equation (16) and we obtain

$$Movement = \left\{ \frac{(0,1)}{fly}, \frac{(0,1)}{swim}, \dots \right\} \tag{23}$$

with an overall grade of "good."

If learning is to be rule-based, FLOPS is finished. However, if learning is to be data-based, FLOPS first sets the *wt*-value σ back to zero in R_4 and changes the *wt*-value to one for penguin in the fuzzy set *Bird* so now

$$Bird = \left\{ \frac{(B,1)}{penguin}, \dots \right\} \tag{24}$$

In either case FLOPS has learned that penguins do not fly.

3.2. Theory

We first discuss rule-based learning and then data-based learning.

3.2.1. Rule-based Learning

Assume there are three elements c_1, c_2, and c_3 in the fuzzy set of conclusions $\bar{C}$ and FLOPS has received a grade of "fair" or "bad" with respect to each fuzzy goal $\bar{G}_i$, $i = 1, 2, 3$. The objective is to obtain a "good" grade for each c_i. Also, after the first run let

$$\bar{C} = \left\{ \frac{(cf_1, 2)}{c_1}, \frac{(cf_2, 3)}{c_2}, \frac{(cf_3, 2)}{c_3} \right\} \tag{25}$$

In order to simplify the discussion suppose there are only seven rules R_i, $1 \leqslant i \leqslant 7$, with initial weights $\sigma_1 = \sigma_5 = \sigma_6 = 2, \sigma_2 = \sigma_3 = \sigma_4 = \sigma_7 = 1$. Recall, σ_i is the weight attached to rule R_i. Let $\pi = (\sigma_1, \sigma_2, \dots, \sigma_7)$ be a vector of weights where each σ_i is zero or a positive integer.

Next assume that: (1) rules R_1, R_2, R_3 effect c_1; (2) R_3, R_4, R_5 effect c_2; and (3) R_2, R_6, R_7 effect c_3. A rule may effect a c_i directly if its conclusion is $\bar{C} = c_i$ or conf$[c_i] = \lambda$. A rule effects c_i indirectly in one step if its conclusion is $\bar{Z} = \Theta$ or conf$[\Theta] = \lambda$ and Θ is in a pattern in the antecedent of a rule that effects c_i directly. Similarly, a rule may effect c_i indirectly in two steps, three steps, etc. A rule effects a c_i if it

Table 23.1. Rules in learning in Sections 3.2.1 and 3.2.2

Rule	weight $= \sigma$	Antecedent	Consequence
R_1	2	$X_{11} = \Theta_1$ AND $X_{12} = \Theta_2$	$\bar{C} = c_1$
R_2	1	$X_{21} = m$ AND $X_{22} = h$	$\bar{\Theta} = \Theta_1$
R_3	1	$X_{31} = D$ AND $X_{32} = s$	$\bar{\Theta} = \Theta_2$
R_4	1	$X_{41} = l$ AND $X_{42} = \Theta_2$	$\bar{C} = c_2$
R_5	2	$X_{51} = U$ AND $X_{52} = h$	$\bar{C} = c_2$
R_6	2	$X_{61} = U$ AND $X_{62} = \Theta_1$	$\bar{C} = c_3$
R_7	1	$X_{71} = m$ AND $X_{72} = b$	$\bar{C} = c_3$

effects it directly or indirectly in n steps for $n = 1, 2, \dots$. An example of a rule set having these properties is shown in Table 23.1.

We say that $\pi = (\sigma_1, \dots, \sigma_7)$ is a solution for c_j if when rule R_i has weight σ_i, $1 \leqslant i \leqslant 7$, FLOPS gets a "good" grade for c_j. Let SR_i be all solutions for c_i, $i = 1, 2, 3$ and let $SR = SR_1 \cap SR_2 \cap SR_3$. We will assume that $SR_i \neq 0$ for each i. If SR_i is empty for some i, say $SR_2 = 0$, then the data and rule structure is not rich enough for FLOPS to learn the single goal attached to c_2. An example of all SR_i empty will be presented later in this section. If $SR \neq 0$, then any π in SR will do for an overall "good" grade. The goals are conflicting when SR is empty and a compromise solution may be called for. An example of each SR_i nonempty but SR empty will be given further on in this section.

Now let us consider an algorithm to find an SR_i. Any algorithm will do since we are not concerned in this paper with developing a most efficient procedure in computing SR_i. First of all not all positive integers need be considered for a σ_i in π. We need only go to $w^*_i + 1$, with w^*_i given in equation (8), for each c_i. From equation (25) we have $w^*_1 = 2$, $w^*_2 = 3$ and $w^*_3 = 2$.

Now let us concentrate on SR_1. First select a subset of $\{R_1, R_2, R_3\}$, say $\{R_1, R_2\}$, since these are the rules that effect c_1. Next we try $\sigma_1 = 3$, $\sigma_3 = 2$ and $\sigma_1 = 3$, $\sigma_3 = 3$ since $w^*_1 + 1 = 3$, $w^*_3 + 1 = 3$. In each case all the other σ_i numbers are equal to their original values. Suppose $\sigma_1 = 3$ and $\sigma_3 = 2$ gives a basic solution. That is, $\pi = (3,1,2,1,2,2,1)$ is a basic solution for c_1. Since R_4 through R_7 do not effect c_1 we may employ any σ-values for these rules and still have a solution. But, R_2 effects c_1 so we will keep $\sigma_2 = 1$. Hence

$$\pi = (3,1,2,\sigma_4,\sigma_5,\sigma_6,\sigma_7) \tag{26}$$

for $\sigma_4 = 1,2,3,4$, $\sigma_5 = 2,3,4$, $\sigma_6 = 2,3$, $\sigma_7 = 1,2,3$, are all solutions that we put into SR_1. If $\sigma_3 = 3$ and $\sigma_3 = 3$ is also a basic solution we generate solutions π, based on $\sigma_1 = \sigma_3 = 3$, as in equation (26) and place them in SR_1. Then we go back and choose another subset of R_1, R_2, R_3 until we have considered all nonempty subsets. This contructs SR_1 and in a similar manner we build SR_2 and SR_3.

3.2.2. Data-based Learning

We will assume the same information as in the previous section on rule-based learning. Let the initial database contain three fuzzy set $\bar{F}_i$, $i = 1,2,3$ where: (1) $\bar{F}_1$ has members s,m,l; (2) $\bar{F}_2$ has elements U, D; and (3) $\bar{F}_3$ has members b, h. The structure of the rules is given in Table 23.1 and the fuzzy sets $\bar{F}_i$, in initial working memory, are presented in Table 23.2. Θ is another fuzzy set with elements Θ_1 and Θ_2, which is constructed by rules R_2 and R_3. Therefore, FLOPS may only increase the weights of the attributes in the $\bar{F}_i$ in search of a solution.

Let $W = (w_1, \ldots, w_7)$ be a vector of weights for the elements of the $\bar{F}_i$. We see that: (1) attributes, s,m,D,h effect c_1; (2) s,l,U,D,h effect c_2; and (3) m,U,b,h are effect c_3. Let SD_i be all W so that giving the

Table 23.2. Fuzzy sets in working memory for data-based learning in Section 3.2.2

Fuzzy Set	Member	Weight
$\bar{F}_1$	s	$w_1 = 0$
	m	$w_2 = 0$
	l	$w_3 = 0$
$\bar{F}_2$	U	$w_4 = 1$
	D	$w_5 = 1$
$\bar{F}_3$	b	$w_6 = 1$
	h	$w_7 = 1$
$\bar{\Theta}$	Θ_1	0
	Θ_2	0

attributes these weights FLOPS gets a good grade for c_i, $i = 1,2,3$, and let $SD =$ the intersection of the SD_i. We assume that $SD_i \neq 0$ all i.

One algorithm to find SD_1 would be to first choose any subset of $\{s,m,D,h\}$, say $\{m,h\}$. Then we will try $w_2 = 1$, $w_7 = 2$, and $w_2 = 1$, $w_7 = 3$, and ..., $w_2 = 3$, $w_7 = 3$. In all cases all the other w_i are set to their original values. If $w_2 = 2$, $w_7 = 3$ is a basic solution, which is $\mathbf{W} = (0,2,0,1,1,1,3)$, then

$$\mathbf{W} = (0,2, w_3, w_4, 1.w_6, 3) \tag{27}$$

for $w_3 = 0,...,4$, $w_4 = 1,...,4$, $w_6 = 1,2,3$ are all solutions that are placed in SD_1. Do this for all basic solutions gained from the subset $\{m,h\}$ and then consider all other nonempty subsets of $\{s,m,D,h\}$. This defines SD_1. Similarly, we construct SD_2, SD_3 and find SD if it is nonempty.

If $SD \neq 0$, then any $\mathbf{W}$ in SD will do the job. If $SD = 0$, then the goals are conflicting for data-based learning and some compromise solution may be found.

3.2.3. Relationship between the Two Methods

We can first show that if $SD_i \neq 0$, then $SR_i \neq 0$. Let $\mathbf{W} \in SD_i$ and set A to be all the attributes Θ in the fuzzy sets in the initial data in working memory whose weights have been changed in W from their original values. Let B be all the rules that have at least one Θ from A in a pattern in their antecedent. Let R be in B whose final left-hand side weight value is wt^* using $\mathbf{W} \in SD_i$ and whose initial weight is σ. If $\sigma \geqslant wt^*$, then do not change this rule's weight, but if $\sigma < wt_*$ set its new weight to be $\sigma = wt^*$. Then the final left-hand side weight for R is unchanged when we set all the weights of the Θ in A back to their original values. We do the same for all R in B. Then π, with some σ_i set equal to wt_i^*, will be in SR_i.

However, $SR_i \neq 0$ does not imply that $SD_i \neq 0$. To show this consider the following simple example.

Example 2. There are three rules

$$\mathbf{R}_1(0, 1, 0.7) \text{ If } X_{11} = \Theta_1, \text{ then conf}[c_1] = 0 \tag{28}$$

$$\mathbf{R}_2(0, 1, 0.6) \text{ If } X_{21} = \Theta_1 \text{ AND } X_{22} = \Theta_2, \text{ then } \bar{C} = c_1 \tag{29}$$

$$\mathbf{R}_3(0, 1, 0.6) \text{ If } X_{31} = \Theta_2, \text{ then conf}[c_1] = 0 \tag{30}$$

Recall that c_1 is an element (and the only member) in the fuzzy set of conclusions $\bar{C}$ where the teacher has specified that $\mu(\lambda_1 | \bar{G}_1) = 1$ if and only if $\lambda_1 = 0$. That is, FLOPS gets a good grade for c_1 if and only if $\text{conf}[c_1] = $ zero, and a fair or bad grade otherwise. There is only one fuzzy set in working memory, which is

$$\bar{\Theta} = \left\{ \frac{(1,0)}{\Theta_1}, \frac{(0.6,0)}{\Theta_2} \right\} \tag{31}$$

It is easy to get a good grade for rule-based learning since $\pi = (1,0,0)$, $(0,0,1)$, $(1,0,1)$ all belong to SR_1. But $W = (1,0)$, $(0,1)$, $(1,1)$ all produce $\text{conf}[c_1] = 0.6$ and not a good grade. Hence, $SD_1 = 0$.

We may also argue that $SD \neq 0$ implies that $SR \neq 0$. It is usually easier to find an SR_i than its corresponding SD_i. Since SD_i may be empty and its corresponding $SR_i \neq 0$, one may wish to first find the SR_i. Then, for a given SR_i one could transfer some of the changed weights on the rules to changed weights on the attributes obtaining mixed (some rule- some data-driven) learning.

3.3. More Examples

Example 3. This example is a fuzzy expert system that cannot learn anything ($SR_i = 0$ for all i). This would be a special purpose system designed to do a single job with no flexibility to learn goals.

There are two rules

$$\mathbf{R}_1(0, 0.8, 0.5) \text{ If } X_{11} = s \text{ AND } X_{12} = U, \text{ then } \bar{C} = c_1 \tag{32}$$

$$\mathbf{R}_2(0, 0.9, 0.6) \text{ If } X_{21} = l \text{ AND } X_{22} = D, \text{ then } \bar{C} = c_2 \tag{33}$$

and two fuzzy sets in working memory

$$\bar{F}_1 = \left\{ \frac{(1,0)}{s}, \frac{(0.6,0)}{l} \right\} \tag{34}$$

$$\bar{F}_2 = \left\{ \frac{(0.6,0)}{U}, \frac{(1,0)}{D} \right\} \tag{35}$$

The teacher sets the goals: (1) for c_1 $\mu(\lambda_1 | \bar{G}_1) = -5\lambda_1 + 1$ for $0 \leqslant \lambda_1 \leqslant 0.2$, and zero otherwise; and (2) for c_2 $\mu(\lambda_2 | \bar{G}_2) = 5\lambda_2 - 4$ for $0.8 \leqslant \lambda_2 \leqslant 1$ and zero otherwise. Then FLOPS will get a bad grade for both c_1 no matter what values one gives for the weights on the rules.

Table 23.3. Rules in Example 4

Rule	(σ, R, τ)	Antecedent	Consequence
R_1	$(1, 0.8, 0.5)$	$X_{11} = s \text{ AND } X_{12} = D$	$\overline{\Theta} = \Theta_1$
R_2	$(0, 0.8, 0.5)$	$X_{21} = m \text{ AND } X_{22} = U$	$\overline{\Theta} = \Theta_1$
R_3	$(0, 0.8, 0.5)$	$X_{31} = s \text{ AND } X_{32} = U$	$\overline{\Theta} = \Theta_2$
R_4	$(1, 0.8, 0.5)$	$X_{41} = l \text{ AND } X_{42} = D$	$\overline{\Theta} = \Theta_2$
R_5	$(0, 0.9, 0.7)$	$X_{51} = \Theta_1$	$\text{conf}[c_1] = 0$
R_6	$(0, 0.9, 0.7)$	$X_{61} = \Theta_1$	$\text{conf}[c_2] = 1$
R_7	$(0, 0.9, 0.7)$	$X_{71} = \Theta_2$	$\text{conf}[c_2] = 0$
R_8	$(0, 0.9, 0.7)$	$X_{81} = \Theta_2$	$\text{conf}[c_1] = 1$
R_9	$(0, 0.7, 0.5)$	$X_{91} = m \text{ AND } X_{92} = U$	$\overline{C} = c_1$
R_{10}	$(0, 0.7, 0.5)$	$X_{10,1} = l \text{ AND } X_{10,2} = D$	$\overline{C} = c_2$

Table 23.4. Fuzzy sets in working memory in Example 4

Fuzzy Set	Member	(cf, wt)
$\bar{F}_1$	s	$(0.9, 0)$
	m	$(1, 0)$
	l	$(0.5, 0)$
$\bar{F}_2$	U	$(1, 0)$
	D	$(0.6, 0)$
$\overline{\Theta}$	Θ_1	$(B, 0)$
	Θ_2	$(B, 0)$

Example 4. Our next example will show that each SR_i can be nonempty but $SR = 0$. The rules are shown in Table 23.3 and the two fuzzy sets $\bar{F}_1$ and $\bar{F}_2$ in initial working memory are in Table 23.4. There is another fuzzy set $\overline{\Theta}$, with members Θ_1 and Θ_2, that is contructed by the rules. The fuzzy set $\bar{C}$ of conclusions has only two members c_1 and c_2, for which the teacher sets goals so that FLOPS will obtain a good grade if and only if $\text{conf}[c_i] = 0$, $i = 1, 2$.

On the first run rules R_5 though R_8 do not pass threshold so R_9 and R_{10} produce $\text{conf}[c_1] = 0.7$, $\text{conf}[c_2] = 0.5$ and a bad grade. If

$\sigma_2 = 1$, we get $\mathbf{R}_5$ and $\mathbf{R}_6$ passing threshold and producing $\operatorname{conf}[c_1] = 0, \operatorname{conf}[c_2] = 1$ giving a good grade on c_1 and $SR_1 \neq 0$. If $\sigma_3 = 1$, then $\mathbf{R}_7$ and $\mathbf{R}_8$ pass threshold, $\operatorname{conf}[c_2] = 0$ and $\operatorname{conf}[c_1] = 1$, with a good grade on c_2 and $SR_2 = 0$. However, when $\sigma_2 = \sigma_4 = 1$ we obtain $\operatorname{conf}[c_1] = \operatorname{conf}[c_2] = 1$ and a bad grade. Hence, $SR = 0$.

Example 5. Our last example is based on the first example in Buckley and Tucker (1987). Here the rules and data are rich (diverse) enough for FLOPS to learn how to get a good grade. The rule set is presented in Table 23.5 and the fuzzy sets $\bar{F}_i$ in initial working memory are given in Table 23.6. The fuzzy set of conclusion $\bar{C}$ has only two members c_1 and c_2 and the fuzzy goals, determined by the teacher, are: (1) $\mu(\lambda_1 | \bar{G}_1) = 1$ if $1 \leqslant \lambda_1 \leqslant 0.2$, equals $-5\lambda_1 + 2$ between 0.2 and 0.4, and is zero otherwise; and (2) $\mu(\lambda_2 | \bar{G}_2) = 1$ for $0.8 \leqslant \lambda_2 \leqslant 1$, is $5\lambda_1 - 3$ on $[0.6, 0.8]$, and zero otherwise.

Table 23.5. Rules in Example 5

Rule	(σ, R, τ)	Antecedent	Consequence
$\mathbf{R}_1$	$(0, 0.8, 0.6)$	$X_{11} = s \text{ AND } X_{12} = U$	$\bar{P} = P_1$
$\mathbf{R}_2$	$(0, 0.8, 0.6)$	$X_{21} = m \text{ AND } X_{22} = D$	$\bar{P} = P_1$
$\mathbf{R}_3$	$(0, 0.8, 0.6)$	$X_{31} = m \text{ AND } X_{32} = U$	$\bar{P} = P_2$
$\mathbf{R}_4$	$(0, 0.8, 0.6)$	$X_{41} = l \text{ AND } X_{42} = D$	$\bar{P} = P_2$
$\mathbf{R}_5$	$(0, 0.8, 0.6)$	$X_{51} = b \text{ AND } X_{52} = P_1$	$\bar{Q} = Q_1$
$\mathbf{R}_6$	$(0, 0.8, 0.6)$	$X_{61} = h \text{ AND } X_{62} = P_1$	$\bar{Q} = Q_1$
$\mathbf{R}_7$	$(0, 0.8, 0.6)$	$X_{71} = U \text{ AND } X_{72} = P_2$	$\bar{Q} = Q_2$
$\mathbf{R}_8$	$(0, 0.8, 0.6)$	$X_{81} = D \text{ AND } X_{82} = P_2$	$\bar{Q} = Q_2$
$\mathbf{R}_9$	$(0, 0.8, 0.6)$	$X_{91} = m \text{ AND } X_{92} = P_2$	$\bar{Q} = Q_3$
$\mathbf{R}_{10}$	$(0, 0.9, 0.6)$	$X_{10,1} = m \text{ AND } X_{10,2} = Q_1$	$\bar{C} = c_1$
$\mathbf{R}_{11}$	$(0, 0.9, 0.6)$	$X_{11,1} = U \text{ AND } X_{11,2} = Q_1$	$\bar{C} = c_1$
$\mathbf{R}_{12}$	$(0, 0.9, 0.6)$	$X_{12,1} = l \text{ AND } X_{12,2} = Q_2$	$\bar{C} = c_2$
$\mathbf{R}_{13}$	$(0, 0.9, 0.6)$	$X_{13,1} = b \text{ AND } X_{13,2} = Q_2$	$\bar{C} = c_2$
$\mathbf{R}_{14}$	$(0, 0.9, 0.6)$	$X_{14,1} = h \text{ AND } X_{14,2} = Q_3$	$\operatorname{conf}[c_1] = 0$

Table 23.6. Fuzzy sets in working memory in Example 5

Fuzzy Set	Members	(cf, wt)
$\bar{F}_1$	s	$(0.9, 0)$
	m	$(0.3, 0)$
	l	$(1.0, 0)$
$\bar{F}_2$	U	$(1.0, 0)$
	D	$(0.6, 0)$
$\bar{F}_3$	b	$(1.0, 1)$
	h	$(0.6, 1)$
$\bar{P}$	P_1	$(B, 0)$
	P_2	$(B, 0)$
$\bar{Q}$	Q_1	$(B, 0)$
	Q_2	$(B, 0)$
	Q_3	$(B, 0)$

Notice that initially the wt-values of the elements in $\bar{F}_3$ are one, otherwise all wt-values are zero. The cf-values for $\bar{P}$ and $\bar{Q}$ are initially B since these fuzzy sets will be constructed by FLOPS. On the first run we get

$$\bar{P} = \left\{ \frac{(0.6, 0)}{P_1}, \frac{(0.8, 0)}{P_2} \right\} \tag{36}$$

and

$$\bar{Q} = \left\{ \frac{(0.6, 1)}{Q_1}, \frac{(0.8, 0)}{Q_2}, \frac{(0.8, 0)}{Q_3} \right\} \tag{37}$$

That is, weight$[Q_1] = 1$ from $\mathbf{R}_5$ and $\mathbf{R}_6$. Then from $\mathbf{R}_{10}$ through $\mathbf{R}_{14}$ we obtain: (1) $(0.6, 1)$, $(0.6, 1)$, $(0, 1)$ presented to MUA for c_1; and (2) $(0.8, 0)$, $(0.6, 1)$ presented to MUA for c_2. Hence

$$\bar{C} = \left\{ \frac{(0.6, 1)}{c_1}, \frac{(0.6, 1)}{c_2} \right\} \tag{38}$$

and a bad grade for both c_1 and c_2.

One easily finds basic solutions for SR_1 to be $\sigma_{14} = 2$, $\sigma_9 = 2$, and $\sigma_3 = 2$ or $\sigma_4 = 3$. However, $\sigma_3 = 2$ or $\sigma_4 = 2$ is also a basic solution for SR_2 together with $\sigma_{12} = 2$. Hence $SR \neq 0$ since it contains basic solutions $\sigma_3 = 2$ and $\sigma_4 = 2$. Basic solutions for SD_1 and SD_2 are also easily discovered with weight $[1] = 2$ belonging to both and therefore SD is also nonempty.

4. CONCLUSION

In this paper we have shown how our fuzzy expert system FLOPS may increase weights to achieve fuzzy goals. Increasing the weights only on data items in initial working memory was called data-based learning, and rule-driven learning is to increase the weights only on rules. We also briefly mentioned increasing weights on both rules and data giving a mixed learning situation.

FLOPS was never allowed to change the rules (except their weights) nor create new rules. Changing rules is more advanced learning to be accomplished later. FLOPS can always create a new special purpose rule to achieve a fuzzy goal. Consider element c_1 in the fuzzy set of conclusions and the fuzzy goal for c_1 gives value one if the confidence in c_1 is $\lambda_1 \in [0, 1]$. If Θ is some attribute in working memory whose confidence is not B (blank) and M is a large positive integer then the rule

$$\mathbf{R}(M,1,0) \text{ If } X = \Theta, \text{ then conf}[c_1] = \lambda_1 \tag{39}$$

will achieve the fuzzy goal for c_1. Since the threshold value τ is zero and conf$[\Theta] \neq B$, this rule always fires presenting (λ_1, M) to the memory update algorithm for c_1. Now M will be larger than all other weights so the final confidence in c_1 will be λ. Such special purpose rules are not allowed in our automated learning. However, special purpose rules (usually with high threshold) are important in fuzzy expert systems (see Buckley, 1990a) so that system can change its mind given new information.

Future research will be concerned with allowing FLOPS to also alter the rules to learn to meet a fuzzy goal. A more mature FLOPS can manipulate weights and rules in its learning mode. Other topics for future study include: (1) finding a way in which to decrease weights in addition to increasing the weights; (2) mixed learning, being a combination of data-driven and rule-driven; and (3) a more efficient algorithm to find solutions.

Keywords: artificial intelligence, expert systems, learning

BIBLIOGRAPHY

Buckley, J. J. (1988). Managing uncertainty in a fuzzy expert system. *Int. J. Man-Machine Studies*, **29**, 129–148.

Buckley, J. J. (1990a). Belief updating in a fuzzy expert system. *Int. J. Intelligent Systems*, **5**, 265–275.

Buckley, J. J. (1990b). Managing uncertainty in a fuzzy expert system. In B. Graines and J. Boose (eds.): *Machine Learning and Uncertain Reasoning*. London: Academic Press, pp. 191–210.

Buckley, J. J. and D. Tucker. (1987). Extended fuzzy relations: Applications to fuzzy expert systems. *Int. J. of Approximate Reasoning*, 1, 177–196.

Buckley, J. J. and D. Tucker. (1988). The utility of information and risk-taking fuzzy expert system. *Int. J. Intelligent Systems*, 3, 179–197.

Buckley, J. J. and D. Tucker. (1989). Second generation fuzzy expert system. *Fuzzy Sets and Systems*, 31, 271–284.

Buckley, J.J., W. Siler, and D. Tucker. (1986a). Fuzzy expert system. *Fuzzy Sets and Systems*, **20**, 1–16.

Buckley, J. J., W. Siler, and D. Tucker. (1986b). FLOPS, a fuzzy expert system: Applications and perspectives. In C. V. Negoita and H. Prade (eds.): *Fuzzy Logics in Knowledge Engineering*. Verlag TÜV Rheinland, pp. 256–274.

Buckley, J. J., W. Siler, and D. Tucker. (1987a). Functional requirements for a working fuzzy expert system. In E. Sanchez and L. Zadeh (eds.): *Approximate Reasoning in Intelligent System, Decision and Control*. Oxford: Pergamon Press, pp. 69–76.

Buckley, J. J., W. Siler, and D. Tucker. (1987b). A parallel rule firing production system with resolution of memory conflicts by weak fuzzy monotonicity, appplied to the classification of objects characterized by multiple uncertain features. *Int. J. Man-Machine Studies*, **26**, 321–332.

Rumelhart, D. E. and J. L. McClelland. (1988). *Parallel Distributed Processing, Vols. I and II*. Cambridge: MIT Press.

Siler, W. and D. Tucker. (1986). *FLOPS: A Fuzzy Logic Production System User's Manual*. Birmingham, AL: Kemp-Carraway Heart Institute.

24 Fuzzy logic with linguistic quantifiers in inductive learning

Janusz KACPRZYK and Cezary IWAŃSKI
Systems Research Institute
Polish Academy of Sciences
ul. Newelska 6, 01-447 Warsaw, POLAND

Abstract. A new approach to inductive learning under imprecision and errors is proposed. We assume, first, that the classification into the positive and negative examples is to a degree (of positiveness and negativeness), between 0 and 1, second, that the (possibly fuzzy) value of an attribute in an example and in a selector need not be the same allowing for an inexact (fuzzy) matching between a concept description and an example, and third, that errors in the data may exist though their number is not precisely known. A new inductive learning problem is formulated so as to find a concept description that best satisfies, say, almost all of the positive examples and almost none of the negative ones. A fuzzy logic – based calculus of linguistically quantified propositions is employed.

1. INTRODUCTION

Among various machine learning approaches, *inductive learning* (from examples) may be the most natural and easiest to implement in many practical cases (cf. Cohen and Feigenbaum, 1982). Inductive learning is basically a process of inferring a *concept description* (description, classification rule, hypothesis), of a *class* (concept) from a description of some individual elements of the class called *positive examples*; moreover, some *negative examples* are usually used to constrain the search space.

The examples are commonly assumed to be described by a set of "attribute-value" pairs. For instance (cf. Shaw, 1987), in a banking context, the examples (customers) may be described by the attributes: "assets," "total debt," and "annual growth rate," and the concept (class) "good customer" may be described by the following concept description (to be derived via inductive learning):

$$[\text{assets} > \$ 1.000.000] \ [\text{total\_debt} < \$ 250.000] \\ [\text{annual\_growth\_rate} > 10\%] \rightarrow [\text{class : "Good"}] \tag{1}$$

to be read as: IF ("his or her assets exceed $ 1.000.000" and "his or her debt is less than $ 250.000" and "his or her annual growth rate > 10%") THEN ("he or she is a good customer"); in (1) and in the sequel we use for convenience Michalski's (1973, 1983) variable-valued logic (VL) formalism.

The inductive learning procedures for the derivation of concept descriptions are usually evaluated with respect to: (1) *completeness*, i.e., that a concept description must correctly describe (cover) all the positive examples, (2) *consistency*, i.e., that a concept description must not describe any of the negative examples, and (3) *convergence*, i.e., that a concept description is derived after a finite number of steps. Moreover, some additional criteria may be added as, e.g., that a concept description with the least number of attributes should be sought.

This general inductive learning scheme is often inapplicable. First, a *crisp classification* (positive and negative examples) is often artificial, and some *grade of positiveness* and *negativeness*, say between 0 and 1, may be more adequate (e.g., in medicine it is often difficult to classify patients as [fully] ill or [fully] sick). Second, a misclassification is always possible (and difficult to detect and correct).

The purpose of this paper is propose a new approach to inductive learning using fuzzy logic with linguistic quantifiers to overcome the above two difficulties. This approach is an extension of the authors' previous papers (Kacprzyk and Iwański, 1991).

As to some other related approaches, one can mention Bergadano and Bisio (1988), Gemello and Mana (1988), or Raś and Zemankova (1988); none of them makes it possible to jointly handle imprecision and errors as in the present approach.

2. A FUZZY LOGIC–BASED CALCULUS OF LINGUISTICALLY QUANTIFIED PROPOSITIONS

Our notation related to fuzzy sets is standard. A fuzzy set A in $X = \{x\}$, is represented by — and often practically equated with — its *membership function* $\mu_A : X \to [0, 1]$; $\mu_A(x) \in [0, 1]$ is the *membership grade* of x in A, from full membership to full nonmembership through all intermediate values.

For our purposes the following operations on fuzzy sets are relevant:

- the *complement* defined as

$$\mu_{\bar{A}}(x) = 1 - \mu_A(x) \qquad \#\text{for each } x \in X \qquad (2)$$

- the *intersection* defined as

$$\mu_{A \cap B}(x) = \mu_A(x) \ t \ \mu_A(x) \qquad \#\text{for each } x \in X \qquad (3)$$

where t: $[0, 1] \times [0,1] \to [0,1]$ is the so-called t-*norm* defined as, for each $a, b, c \in [0,1]$:

(1) $a \ t \ 1 = a$
(2) $a \ t \ b = b \ t \ a$
(3) $a \ t \ b \geqslant c \ t \ d$ if $a \geqslant c, b \geqslant d$
(4) $a \ t \ b \ t \ c = a \ t \ (b \ t \ c) = (a \ t \ b) \ t \ c$

Some examples of t-norms are: $a \wedge b = \min(a, b)$ which is the most commonly used, ab, and $1 - (1 \wedge ((1 - a)^p + (1 - b)^p)^{1/p}, \ p \geqslant 1$.

- the *union* defined as

$$\mu_{A+B}(x) = \mu_A(x) \ s \ \mu_B(x) \qquad \text{for each } x \in X \qquad (4)$$

where s: $[0, 1] \times [0, 1] \to [0, 1]$ is the so-called s-*norm* (t-*conorm*) defined as, for each $a, b, c \in [0,1]$:

(1) $a \ s \ 0 = a$
(2)–(4) as for a t-norm

Some examples of s-norms are: $a \vee b = \max(a, b)$, which is the most commonly used, $a + b - ab$, and $1 \wedge (a^p + b^p)^{1/p}, \ p \geqslant 1$.

Now we will briefly sketch Zadeh's (1983) calculus of linguistically quantified propositions.

A *linguistically quantified proposition* is exemplified by "most experts are convinced" and may be generally written as

$$Q y\text{'s are } F \tag{5}$$

where Q is a *linguistic quantifier* (e.g., most), $Y = \{y\}$ is a *set of objects* (e.g., experts), and F is a *property* (e.g., convinced).

Importance B may also be added to (5) yielding

$$Q B y\text{'s are } F \tag{6}$$

that is, say, "most of the important experts are convinced."

Basically, the problem is to find either truth $(Q y\text{'s are } F)$ in the case of (5) or truth $(Q B y\text{'s are } F)$ in the case of (6).

In Zadeh's (1983) approach the *fuzzy linguistic quantifier* Q is assumed to be a fuzzy set in $[0, 1]$. For instance, $Q =$ "almost all" may be given as

$$\mu_{\text{"most"}}(u) = \begin{cases} 1 & \text{for } u \geqslant 0.8 \\ 2u - 0.6 & \text{for } 0.3 < u < 0.8 \\ 0 & \text{for } u \leqslant 0.3 \end{cases} \tag{7}$$

Property F is defined as a fuzzy set in Y, $F \subset Y$. If $Y = \{y_1, ..., y_p\}$, then it is assumed that truth $(y_i \text{ is } F) = \mu_F(y_i)$, $i = 1, ..., p$.

Truth $(Q y\text{'s are } F)$ is now calculated using the *(nonfuzzy)* cardinalities, the so-called ΣCounts (defined as: if $F \subset Y$ is a fuzzy set with $\mu_F(y_i)$, then $\Sigma\text{Count } (F) = \sum_{i=1}^{p} \mu_F(y_i)$, in the following two steps:

$$r = \Sigma Count\ (F)/\Sigma Count\ (Y) = \frac{1}{p} \sum_{i=1}^{p} \mu_F(y_i) \tag{8}$$

$$\text{truth } (Q y\text{'s are } F) = \mu_Q(r) \tag{9}$$

In the case of *importance*, B, and $\mu_B(y_i) \in [0, 1]$ is a *degree of importance* of y_i, from definitely important $(= 1)$ to definitely unimportant $(= 0)$, through all intermediate values.

We rewrite first "$Q B y\text{'s are } F$" as "$Q(B \text{ and } F)y\text{'s are } B$" which implies the following counterparts of (8) and (9):

$$r' = \Sigma\text{Count } (B \text{ and } F)/\Sigma\text{Count } (B)$$
$$= \sum_{i=1}^{p} (\mu_B(y_i) \text{ t } \mu_F(y_i)) / \sum_{i=1}^{p} \mu_B(y_i) \tag{10}$$

$$\text{truth } (Q B y\text{'s are } F) = \mu_Q(r') \tag{11}$$

For more details on this calculus, see Zadeh (1983), or Kacprzyk (1987). Another, more sophisticated approach, which is not used here, was proposed by Yager (1983) (see also Kacprzyk, 1987 or Kacprzyk and Yager, 1985).

3. INDUCTIVE LEARNING UNDER IMPRECISION AND ERRORS

Conventionally, *inductive learning (from examples)* is to find a *concept description R* that describes (covers) all the positive examples and none of the negative ones. If $X = \{x\}$ is the set of positive and negative examples, P is the property of being a "positive example," and N is the property of being a "negative example," then we seek an R such that

$$\text{"All } Px\text{'s are } R\text{"} \quad \& \quad \text{"None of the } Nx\text{'s are } R\text{"} \tag{12}$$

i.e., a concept description (R) such that all the positive examples (Px's) are covered by R, and no negative examples (Nx's) are covered by R; notice that "positive" and "negative" are crisp (of "yes-no" type).

Problem (12) may be unsolvable as mentioned in Section 1 due to, e.g., misclassification, errors, difficulty in a crisp determination of positiveness/negativeness, etc.

We "soften" problem (12) by substituting for it the following general formulation of (inductive) learning from examples under imprecision and errors: find a concept description R such that

$$\text{"}Q^+ \ \tilde{P}x\text{'s are } R\text{"} \quad \& \quad \text{"}Q^- \ \tilde{N}x\text{'s are } R \tag{13}$$

where Q^+ is a linguistic quantifier of type "almost all," "most," etc., Q^- is a linguistic quantifier of type "almost none," "(at most) a few," etc., $\tilde{P}$ denotes a "soft" positiveness and $\tilde{N}$ denotes a "soft" negativeness (both to degree between 0 and 1).

Problem (13) may be exemplified by: find an R such that

$$\begin{aligned} &\text{"}almost\ all\text{ of } \tilde{P}x\text{'s are } R\text{"} \\ \& \ &\text{"}almost\ none\text{ of } \tilde{N}x\text{'s are } R\text{"} \end{aligned} \tag{14}$$

to be read as to find a concept description (R), which describes almost all of the ("softly") positive examples ($\tilde{P}x$'s) and almost none of the ("softly") negative examples ($\tilde{N}x$'s). The term "describes" may be meant here (and later on) in a fuzzy sense, i.e., to a degree from 0 to 1.

As in the conventional case, in the new formulation (13) the two main evaluation criteria are now: (1) Q^+ — *completeness*, i.e., that a concept description must correctly describe (in fact, as well as possible) Q^+ (e.g., *almost all*) of the positive examples, and (2) Q^- — *consistency*, i.e., that a concept description must not describe more than Q^- (e.g., *almost none*) of the negative examples.

Notice, first, the inclusion of a "soft" positiveness/negativeness, and, second, a natural accounting for some errors in the classification; since their number cannot be usually known precisely, evaluation like "almost all" and "almost none" are certainly adequate; evidently if we suspect more errors, we may use some "milder" quantifiers as, e.g., "much more than 75%" and "much less than 25%."

The description of an example is in terms of the attribute-value pairs. A single attribute-value pair is called a *selector*, $[A \text{ r } `a']$, where $A$ is an attribute, r is a (possibly fuzzy) relation (e.g., `=', `$\geqslant$', ...), a is a (possibly fuzzy) value, and may be exemplified by: [height = 'high'], [color = 'red'], [temperature $\geqslant$ '150°C'], etc. For notational simplicity, "r" and "a" will be used for both nonfuzzy and fuzzy entities.

For instance, an example x may be described as

$$x = [\text{height} = `190 \text{ cm}'] \ [\text{color} = `\text{reddish}']$$
$$[\text{temperature} \gg `100°C']$$

i.e., that an example x is 190 cm high, is reddish, and its temperature is much more than 100°C.

It is clear that the value of A_i in this selector and in a particular example need not be the same as, e.g., when $s_i = [\text{height} = `\text{high}']$ and $x = [\text{height} = `190 \text{ cm}']$. Since a dichotomous (different–identical) evaluation is certainly too rigid and unrealistic in practice, we allow for a *degree of identity* of the value of attribute A_i in selector s_i and in example x, $\mu_{s_i}(x) \in [0, 1]$, from 0 for definitely different to 1 for definitely identical through all intermediate values; this degree can be obtained using fuzzy matching.

By a *complex*, C_j, we mean the conjunction of a number of different selectors, $s_{j_1}, ..., s_{j_k}$, i.e., $c_j = s_{j_1} \cap ... \cap s_{j_k}$, $k \leqslant n$.

If we have an example $x = s_{i_1} s_{i_2} ... s_{i_l} s_{i_1} ... s_{j_k} s_{m_1} s_{m_2} ... s_{m_w}$, then the *degree of covering* example x by complex $c_j = s_{j_1} \cap ... \cap s_{j_k}$ is defined as

$$\mu_{C_j}(x) = \mu_{s_{j_1}}(x) \wedge ... \wedge \mu_{s_{j_k}}(x) \tag{15}$$

or more generally

$$\mu_{C_j}(x) = \mu_{s_{j_1}}(x) \ t ... t \ \mu_{s_{j_k}}(x) \tag{16}$$

Evidently, $\mu_{C_j}(x) \in [0, 1]$.

The *concept description* R is the alternative of the complexes (say $C_1, ..., C_m$), i.e., $R = C_1 \cup ... \cup C_m$.

The *degree of covering example x* by concept description $R = C_1 \cup ... \cup C_m$ is defined as, for each $x \in X$,

$$\mu_R(x) = \mu_{C_1}(x) \vee ... \vee \mu_{C_m}(x) \tag{17}$$

where $\mu_{C_j}(x)$ is the degree of covering example x by complex C_j defined by (15) or (16); more generally

$$\mu_R(x) = \mu_{C_1}(x) \, s ... s \, \mu_{C_m}(x) \tag{18}$$

Suppose now that imprecision in the classification (into the positive and negative examples) is formalized by using a *degree of positiveness* of example x, denoted $\mu_{\tilde{P}}(x) \in [0, 1]$ such that 1 stands for "definitely positive" and 0 for "definitely not positive (definitely negative)," with all intermediate values. And analogously, a *degree of negativeness* of x is denoted by $\mu_{\tilde{N}}(x) \in [0, 1]$. For technical reasons, we assume $\mu_{\tilde{P}}(x) = 1 - \mu_{\tilde{N}}(x)$. Notice that if $\mu_{\tilde{P}}(x), \mu_{\tilde{N}}(x) \in \{0, 1\}$, then we end up with the conventional case. The $\mu_{\tilde{P}}(x)$'s and $\mu_{\tilde{N}}(x)$'s will be interpreted here in term of degrees of membership in fuzzy sets theory, which is convenient from the viewpoint of a calculus of linguistically quantified propositions to be used.

The problem (cf. (13)) is to find a concept description R^* such that

$$\text{truth (``}Q^+ \, \tilde{P}x\text{'s are } R\text{'' \& ``}Q^- \tilde{N}x\text{'s are } R\text{'')} \rightarrow \max_R \tag{19}$$

i.e., to find a(n) "(sub)optimal" R^* in the sense that (19) is satisfied to the highest possible extent.

In a more extended form, (19) may be written as to find an R^* such that (cf. (11))

$$\text{truth } (Q^+ \tilde{P}x\text{'s are } R) \wedge \text{truth } (Q^- \tilde{N}x\text{'s are } R) =$$

$$= \bar{\mu}_{Q^+}(R) \wedge \bar{\mu}_{Q^-}(R) = \mu_{Q^+}(\sum_{x \in X}(\mu_{\tilde{P}}(x) \wedge \mu_R(x)) / \sum_{x \in X}\mu_{\tilde{P}}(x)) \wedge$$

$$\wedge \mu_{Q^-}(\sum_{x \in X}(\mu_{\tilde{N}}(x) \wedge \mu_R(x)) / \sum_{x \in X}\mu_{\tilde{N}}(x)) \rightarrow \max_R \tag{20}$$

where "$\wedge$" may be replaced by, e.g., a t-norm, $\mu_R(x)$ is given by (17) or (18).

To proceed to an algorithm for solving (19) or (20), we denote for simplicity:

$$\bar{\mu}_{Q^+}(s_i) = \text{truth } (Q^+ \tilde{P}x\text{'s are } s_i) =$$

$$= \mu_{Q^+}(\sum_{x \in X}(\mu_{\tilde{P}}(x) \wedge \mu_{s_i}(x)) / \sum_{x \in X}\mu_{\tilde{P}}(x)) \tag{21}$$

$$\bar{\mu}_{Q^-}(s_i) = \text{truth } (Q^- \tilde{N}x\text{'s are } s_i) =$$
$$= \mu_{Q^-}\left(\sum_{x \in X} (\mu_{\tilde{N}}(x) \wedge \mu_{s_i}(x)) / \sum_{x \in X} \mu_{\tilde{N}}(x)\right) \tag{22}$$

$$\bar{\mu}_{Q^+}(c_j) = \text{truth } (Q^+ \tilde{P}x\text{'s are } c_j) =$$
$$= \mu_{Q^+}\left(\sum_{x \in X} (\mu_{\tilde{P}}(x) \wedge \mu_{c_j}(x)) / \sum_{x \in X} \mu_{\tilde{P}}(x)\right) \tag{23}$$

$$\bar{\mu}_{Q^+}(c_j) = \text{truth } (Q^+ \tilde{N}x\text{'s are } c_j) =$$
$$= \mu_{Q^-}\left(\sum_{x \in X} (\mu_{\tilde{N}}(x) \wedge \mu_{c_j}(x)) / \sum_{x \in X} \mu_{\tilde{N}}(x)\right) \tag{24}$$

where $\mu_{c_j}(x)$ is given by (15) or (16), and $\mu_{s_j}(x)$ is a degree of identity of attribute A's (possibly fuzzy) value in example x and selector s_i.

In the algorithm for solving (20), R is built up iteratively, adding in each iteration a new complex to R, i.e., the number of examples covered by R is not decreasing. Moreover, since we add the complexes in a special way, $\bar{\mu}_{Q^+}(R)$ is increasing as quickly as possible, while $\bar{\mu}_{Q^-}(R)$ is decreasing as slowly as possible. This makes the algorithm more efficient.

We need to introduce first the concept of a *typoid*. Suppose that each example is $x = s_1 \dots s_n = [A_1 = `a_1\text{'}] \dots [A_n = `a_n\text{'}]$, i.e., it contains n selectors. Assume that attribute A_i takes on its (possibly fuzzy) values in a set $\{a_{i_1}, \dots, a_{i_q}\}$. A typoid is defined as an artificial example $\tau = \hat{s}_1 \dots \hat{s}_n = [A_1 = `\hat{a}_1\text{'}] \dots [A_n = `\hat{a}_n\text{'}]$ such that each $\hat{s}_i = [A_i = `\hat{a}_i\text{'}]$ is determined by

$$\sum_{x \in X} (\mu_{\tilde{P}}(x) \wedge (1 - \mu_R(x)) \wedge \mu_{s_i = [A_i = `a_i\text{'}]}(x) \rightarrow \max_{a_i \in \{a_{i_1}, \dots, a_{i_k}\}} \tag{25}$$

i.e., into the typoid we put such consecutive selectors, $\hat{s}_i$, that are "most typical" for the examples that are not described by R (cf. $1 - \mu_R(x)$), and are "most positive" (cf. $\mu_{\tilde{P}}(x)$); $\mu_{s_i}(x) \in [0, 1]$ is a degree of identity of attribute A_i's (possibly fuzzy) value in selector s_i and in example x. The algorithm is now:

Step 1. To initialize, set:

(a) $\mu_{\tilde{P}}(x) \in [0, 1]$, for each example x (evidently, $\mu_{\tilde{N}}(y) = 1 - \mu_{\tilde{P}}(x)$)
(b) $R = \text{"ø"}$ and $C = \text{"ø"}$ meant that the (initial) concept description R contains no complex, and the (initial) complex C contains no selectors.

Step 2. $R := R \cup C$, i.e., "add" to the current R a currently formed complex C, and assume this as the new R.

Step 3. Form a typoid τ as previously described.

Step 4. Find an example $x^* \in X$ that is both most positive and similar to the typoid formed in Step 3, that is,

$$\mu_{\tilde{p}}(x) \wedge \text{sim}(x, \tau) \rightarrow \max_{x \in X}$$

where sim: $X \times X \rightarrow [0, 1]$ is some function expressing the *similarity* between x and τ, from 0 for full *dissimilarity* to 1 for full *similarity* through all intermediate values. For instance:

$$\text{sim}(x, \tau) = (1/n) \sum_{i=i}^{n} \mu_{\hat{s}_i}(x) \tag{26}$$

where the $\hat{s}_i$'s are the selectors included in τ; other forms of sim are also possible.

Step 5. Form a complex C as follows:

Substep 5a. To initialize, set $C =$ "ø", and $a_{\max} = 0$.

Substep 5b. For each s_i^*, $i = 1, \dots n$ (s_i^* is the i-th selector of x^* found in Step 4), such that s_i^* is not in C, calculate

$$h_i^* = h(\mu_{Q^+}(R \cup (C \cap s_i^*)), \mu_{Q^-}(R \cup (C \cap s_i^*))) \tag{27}$$

where h: $[0, 1] \times [0, 1] \rightarrow [0, 1]$ is an averaging operator, e.g., $h(u, w) = (u + w)/2$.

Substep 5c. Find $h^* = \max_i h^*$, and i^* such that $h^* = h_{i^*}^*$.

Substep 5d. If $h^* \geqslant h_{\max}$, then:

(1) $h_{\max} := h^*$
(2) $C := C \cap s_{i^*}^*$
(3) go to Substep 5b; else go to Step 6.

Step 6. If $\min(\mu_{Q^+}(R \cup C), \mu_{Q^-}(R \cup C)) > \min(\mu_{Q^+}(R), \mu_{Q^-}(R))$, then go to Step 2.

Step 7. Output the final result R, and STOP.

Since a typoid is a very good starting point, the algorithm is in general very effective and efficient in practice.

We will now present a simple example to illustrate the consecutive steps of the algorithm.

Example. Suppose that we have two fuzzy attributes, A and B, taking on their fuzzy values in X. Suppose that we have four examples, with their respective $\mu_{\tilde{P}}(.)$'s (evidently, $\mu_{\tilde{N}}(x) = 1 - \mu_{\tilde{P}}(.)$):

$$
\begin{aligned}
x_1 &= [A = \tilde{a}_1]\,[B = \tilde{b}_1] & \mu_{\tilde{P}}(x_1) &= 1.0 \\
x_2 &= [A = \tilde{a}_2]\,[B = \tilde{b}_3] & \mu_{\tilde{P}}(x_2) &= 0.7 \\
x_3 &= [A = \tilde{a}_3]\,[B = \tilde{b}_2] & \mu_{\tilde{P}}(x_3) &= 0.5 \\
x_4 &= [A = \tilde{a}_4]\,[B = \tilde{b}_4] & \mu_{\tilde{P}}(x_4) &= 0.0
\end{aligned}
$$

that is, we have one definitely positive example (x_1), one definitely negative (x_4), one that is positive to a large extent (x_2), and one to which we are indifferent whether it is positive or negative (x_3).

The fuzzy values, assumed to be the trapezoid fuzzy numbers (with piecewise linear membership functions, i.e., represented by four numbers), are defined as follows:

$$
\begin{aligned}
\tilde{a}_1 &= \tilde{b}_1 = (0,\,1,\,9,\,10) \\
\tilde{a}_2 &= \tilde{b}_2 = (1,\,1,\,10,\,11) \\
\tilde{a}_3 &= \tilde{b}_3 = (8,\,9,\,17,\,18) \\
\tilde{a}_4 &= \tilde{b}_4 = (9,\,10,\,18,\,19)
\end{aligned}
$$

We assume that:

$$
\mu_{Q^+}(u) = \begin{cases} 1 & \text{for} & u \geqslant 0.8 \\ 2u - 0.6 & \text{for} & 0.3 \leqslant u \leqslant 0.8 \\ 0 & \text{for} & u \leqslant 0.3 \end{cases}
$$

$$
\mu_{Q^-}(u) = \begin{cases} 1 & \text{for} & u \leqslant 0.2 \\ -2u + 1.4 & \text{for} & 0.2 \leqslant u \leqslant 0.7 \\ 0 & \text{for} & u \geqslant 0.7 \end{cases}
$$

t is "$\wedge$" and s is "$\vee$", and the degree of identity (fuzzy matching) to be given as

$$
M(\tilde{a}_i, \tilde{a}_j) = \frac{\text{Area}\,(\tilde{a}_i \cap \tilde{a}_j)}{\text{Area}\,(\tilde{a}_i \cup \tilde{a}_j)}
$$

where $\tilde{a}_i$ and $\tilde{a}_j$ are fuzzy numbers, and "$\cap$" and "$\cup$" are the set-theoretic intersection and union.

The consecutive steps of the algorithms are now as follows:

Step 1. To initialize, we take the $\mu_{\tilde{P}}(.)$'s as given above and $R := $ "ø" and $C := $ "ø".

Step 2. $R := R \cup C = $ "ø".

Step 3. We obtain for attribute A the following values of the left-hand sides of (25):

- 1.76 for $s_{11} = [A = \tilde{a}_1]$
- 1.63 for $s_{12} = [A = \tilde{a}_2]$
- 0.69 for $s_{13} = [A = \tilde{a}_3]$
- 0.57 for $s_{14} = [A = \tilde{a}_4]$

and similarly for attribute B:

- 1.56 for $s_{21} = [B = \tilde{b}_1]$
- 1.43 for $s_{22} = [B = \tilde{b}_2]$
- 0.89 for $s_{23} = [B = \tilde{b}_3]$
- 0.84 for $s_{24} = [B = \tilde{b}_4]$

Thus, the typoid obtained is $\tau = [A = \tilde{a}_1] [B = \tilde{b}_1]$.

Step 4. We obtain that x_1 is the closest to τ.

Step 5.

Substep 5a. We assume $C := $ "ø", and $h_{max} := 0$.

Substep 5b. We obtain first

$$\mu_{\tilde{P}}(x_1) + \mu_{\tilde{P}}(x_2) + \mu_{\tilde{P}}(x_3) + \mu_{\tilde{P}}(x_4) = 2.2$$

and

$$\bar{\mu}_{Q^+}(R \cup (C \cap [A = \tilde{a}_1])) = \bar{\mu}_{Q^+}([A = \tilde{a}_1]) = \mu_{Q^+}(1.76/2.2) = 1.00$$
$$\bar{\mu}_{Q^-}(R \cup (C \cap [A = \tilde{a}_1])) = \bar{\mu}_{Q^-}([A = \tilde{a}_1]) = \mu_{Q^-}(0.37/1.8) = 0.98$$
$$\bar{\mu}_{Q^+}(R \cup (C \cap [B = \tilde{b}_1])) = \bar{\mu}_{Q^+}([B = \tilde{b}_1]) = \mu_{Q^+}(1.56/2.2) = 0.82$$
$$\bar{\mu}_{Q^-}(R \cup (C \cap [B = \tilde{b}_1])) = \bar{\mu}_{Q^-}([B = \tilde{b}_1]) = \mu_{Q^-}(0.57/1.8) = 0.76$$

Hence

$$h_1^* = (1.00 + 0.98)/2 \simeq 0.99$$
$$h_2^* = (0.82 + 0.76)/2 \simeq 0.79$$

Substep 5c. We obtain $i^* = 1$, i.e., $s_{i^*}^* = [A = \tilde{a}_1]$.

Substep 5d. Since $h_1^* > h_{max} = 0$, then:

(1) $h_{max} = 0.99$
(2) $C := C \cap [A = \tilde{a}_1] = [A = \tilde{a}_1]$

and we go to:

Substep 5b. We obtain:

$$\bar{\mu}_{Q^+}(R \cup (C \cap [\mathbf{B} = \tilde{b}_1])) = \bar{\mu}_{Q^+}([A = \tilde{a}_1][B = \tilde{b}_1]) = 0.40$$
$$\bar{\mu}_{Q^-}(R \cup (C \cap [\mathbf{B} = \tilde{b}_1])) = \bar{\mu}_{Q^-}([A = \tilde{a}_1][B = \tilde{b}_1]) = 1.00$$

and $h_1^* \simeq 0.70$.

Substep 5c. Hence, $h^* = 0.7$ and $i^* = 1$.

Substep 5d. Since $0.70 < 0.99$, then we go to:

Step 6. Since min $(1.00, 0.98) >$ min $(0.00, 1.00)$, then we go to:

Step 2. $R := R \cup C = [A = \tilde{a}_1]$.

Step 3. We obtain the following values of the particular terms of the left-hand sides of (25):

- 0.26 for $[A = \tilde{a}_1]$
- 0.33 for $[A = \tilde{a}_2]$
- 0.63 for $[A = \tilde{a}_3]$
- 0.56 for $[A = \tilde{a}_4]$
- 0.26 for $[A = \tilde{b}_1]$
- 0.33 for $[A = \tilde{b}_2]$
- 0.33 for $[A = \tilde{b}_3]$
- 0.76 for $[A = \tilde{b}_4]$

hence the typoid obtained is $\tau = [A = \tilde{a}_3][A = \tilde{b}_3]$.

Step 4. We obtain:

$$\text{sim}(x_1, \tau) = 0.06$$
$$\text{sim}(x_2, \tau) = 0.13$$
$$\text{sim}(x_3, \tau) = 0.13$$
$$\text{sim}(x_4, \tau) = 0.00$$

and x_2 is chosen as the closest to τ.

Step 5.

Substep 5a. We assume $C := $ "ø", and $h_{\max} := 0$.

Substep 5b. We obtain:

$$\bar{\mu}_{Q^+}(R \cup (C \cap [A = \tilde{a}_2])) = \bar{\mu}_{Q^+}([A = \tilde{a}_1][A = \tilde{a}_2]) = \mu_{Q^+}(0.83) = 1.00$$
$$\bar{\mu}_{Q^-}(R \cup (C \cap [A = \tilde{a}_2])) = \bar{\mu}_{Q^-}([A = \tilde{a}_1][A = \tilde{a}_2]) = \mu_{Q^-}(0.27) = 0.86$$

$$\bar{\mu}_{Q^+}(R \cup (C \cap [B = \tilde{b}_1])) = \bar{\mu}_{Q^+}([B = \tilde{b}_1][A = \tilde{b}_3]) = \mu_{Q^+}(0.83) = 1.00$$
$$\bar{\mu}_{Q^-}(R \cup (C \cap [B = \tilde{b}_1])) = \bar{\mu}_{Q^-}([B = \tilde{b}_1][A = \tilde{b}_3]) = \mu_{Q^-}(0.68) = 0.04$$

and $h_1^* = 0.93$, $h_2^* = 0.52$;

Substep 5c. Hence, $h^* = h_1^*$.

Substep 5d. Since $0.93 > h_{max} = 0$, then:

(1) $h_{max} = 0.93$
(2) $C := C \cap [A = \tilde{a}_2] = [A = \tilde{a}_2]$

and we go to:

Substep 5b. We obtain:

$$\bar{\mu}_{Q^+}(R \cup (C \cap [B = \tilde{b}_3])) = \bar{\mu}_{Q^+}([A = \tilde{a}_1] \cup [A = \tilde{a}_2][B = \tilde{b}_3]) =$$
$$\bar{\mu}_{Q^+}(0.83) = 1.00$$
$$\bar{\mu}_{Q^-}(R \cup (C \cap [B = \tilde{b}_3])) = \bar{\mu}_{Q^-}([A = \tilde{a}_1] \cup [A = \tilde{a}_2][B = \tilde{b}_3]) =$$
$$\bar{\mu}_{Q^-}(0.48) = 0.44$$

and $h_1^* = 0.72$.

Substep 5c. Hence, $h^* = h_1^*$.

Substep 5d. Since $0.93 > 0.72$ we go to:

Step 6. Since min $(1.00, 0.86) <$ min $(1.00, 0.98)$, then we go to:

Step 7. The final result is $R = [A = \tilde{a}_1]$, where $\mu_{Q^+}(R) = 1.00$ and $\mu_{Q^-}(R) = 0.98$.

4. CONCLUSION

The algorithm proposed may be used in a vast spectrum of real-life inductive learning problems in which imprecision, errors in classification, inexact matching, etc. preclude the use of conventional techniques. Our experience, mostly in the field of medicine, is very promising and encouraging, and will be presented in a subsequent paper.

Keywords: machine learning, inductive learning, learning from examples, imprecision, linguistic quantifier, fuzzy logic

BIBLIOGRAPHY

Bergadano, F. and R. Bisio. (1988). Constructive learning with continuous-valued attributes. In B. Bouchon, L. Saitta and R. R. Yager (eds.): *Uncertainty and Intelligent Systems*. Berlin-Heidelberg-New York: Springer-Verlag, pp. 154–162.

Cohen, P.R. and E.A. Feigenbaum. (1982). *The Handbook of Artificial Intelligence*. Vol. 3. Los Altos: Kaufmann.

Dietrich, T. G. et al. (1981). Learning and inductive inference. In P. R. Cohen and E. A. Feigenbaum (eds.): *The Handbook of Artificial Intelligence*. Los Altos: Kaufmann, pp. 323–525.

Gemello, R. and F. Mana. (1988). Controlling inductive search in RIGEL learning system. In B. Bouchon, L. Saitta and R.R. Yager (eds.): *Uncertainty and Intelligent Systems*. Berlin-Heidelberg-New York: Springer-Verlag, pp. 171–178.

Kacprzyk, J. (1987). Towards "human-consistent" decision support systems through commonsense-knowledge-based decision making and control models: A fuzzy logic approach. *Computers and Artificial Intelligence, 6,* 97–122.

Kacprzyk, J. and C. Iwański. (1991). Inductive learning from incomplete and imprecise examples. In B. Bouchon-Meunier, R. R. Yager and L.A. Zadeh (eds.): *Uncertainty and Intelligent Systems*. Berlin-Heidelberg-New York: Springer-Verlag (forthcoming).

Kacprzyk, J. and R. R. Yager. (1985). Emergency-oriented expert systems: A fuzzy approach. *Information Sciences, 37,* 147–156.

Michalski, R. S. (1973). Discovering classification rules using variable-valued logic system VL1. *Proc. of the Third Int. Joint Conference on Artificial Intelligence (IJCAI)*, pp. 162–172.

Michalski, R. S. (1983). A theory and methodology of inductive learning. In R. S. Michalski, J. Carbonell, and T. Mitchell (eds.): *Machine Learning*. Paolo Alto: Tioga Press, pp. 83–133.

Raś, Z. W. and M. Zemankova. (1988). Learning driven by the concepts structure. In B. Bouchon, L. Saitta and R. R. Yager (eds.): *Uncertainty and Intelligent Systems*. Berlin-Heidelberg-New York: Springer-Verlag, pp. 193–200.

Shaw, M. J. (1987). Applying inductive learning to enhance knowledge-based expert systems. *Decision Support Systems, 3,* 319–322.

Yager, R. R. (1983). Quantifiers in the formulation of multiple objective decision functions. *Information Sciences, 31,* 107–139.

Zadeh, L. A. (1983). A computational approach to fuzzy quantifiers in natural languages. *Computers and Mathematics with Applications, 9,* 149–184.

25 On fuzzy neuron models

M. M. GUPTA and J. QI
Intelligent Systems Research Laboratory
College of Engineering
University of Saskatchewan
Saskatoon, Saskatchewan, CANADA S7N 0WO

Abstract. In recent years, an increasing number of researchers have become involved in the subject of fuzzy neural networks in the hope of combining the strengths of fuzzy logic and neural networks and achieving a more powerful tool for fuzzy information processing and for exploring the functioning of human brains. In this paper, an attempt has been made to establish some basic models for fuzzy neurons. First, several possible fuzzy neuron models are proposed. Second, some learning (training) and adaptation mechanisms for the proposed neurons are given. Finally, the possibility of applying nonfuzzy neural networks approaches to fuzzy systems is also described.

1. INTRODUCTION

A typical neural network has multiple inputs and outputs connected by many neurons via weights to form a parallel structure for information processing. The potential benefits of such a structure are as follows: First, the neural network models have many neurons or computational units linked via the adaptive weights arranged in a massively parallel structure. This structure is believed to be essential for building systems with a faster response and a higher performance than the modern sequentially arranged digital computers. In fact, the structure is built after biological neural systems in the hope of emulating and taking advantage of the capabilities of human brains.

Second, because of its high parallelism, problems with a few neurons do not cause significant effects on the overall system performance. This characteristic is also called fault-tolerance. Third, probably the biggest attraction of the neural network models is their adaptive and learning ability. Adaptation and learning are achieved by constantly modifying the weights and other elements.

Neural network models mainly deal with imprecise data and ill-defined activities. The subjective phenomena such as memories, perceptions, and images are often regarded as the targets of neural network modeling. It is interesting to note that fuzzy logic is another powerful tool to model phenomena associated with human thinking and perception. In fact, the neural network approach merges well with fuzzy logic (Cohen and Hudson, 1990) and some research endeavors have given birth to the so-called "fuzzy neural networks," which are believed to have considerable potential in the areas of expert systems, medical diagnosis, control systems, pattern recognition, and system modeling.

The term "fuzzy neural networks" (FNN) has existed for more than a decade. However, the recent resurgence of interest in this area is motivated by the increasing recognition of the potential of fuzzy logic, some successful examples, and the belief that fuzzy logic and neural networks are two of the most promising approaches for exploring the functioning of human brains. Recently, an increasing number of researchers have become involved in the area of fuzzy neural networks. Yamakawa and Tomoda (1989) described an FNN model and applied it successfully to a pattern recognition problem. Kuncicky and Kandel (1989) proposed a fuzzy neuron model in which the output of one neuron is represented by a fuzzy level of confidence and the firing process is regarded as an attempt to find a typical value among the inputs. Kiszka and Gupta (1990) studied a fuzzy neuron model described by the logic equations. However, no specific learning algorithms are given in these three cases. Gupta and Knopf (1990) proposed a fuzzy neuron model similar to the first two cases except that a specific modification scheme was proposed for weights adaptation during learning. Nakanishi et al. (1990) and Hayashi et al. (1989) used the nonfuzzy neural networks approach for the design of fuzzy logic controllers with adaptive and learning ability. Similarly, Cohen and Hudson (1990) used nonfuzzy neural network learning techniques to determine the weights of antecedents for use in fuzzy expert systems. However, no fuzzy neuron models were used.

Some new fuzzy neuron models are proposed in this paper that would overcome some of the weakness of the models mentioned

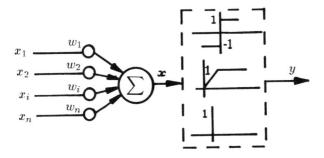

Figure 25.1. A nonfuzzy neuron model

above. Improvements have been made by futher and more reasonable modifications of nonfuzzy neuron models into fuzzy ones and, more importantly, by adding learning algorithms to fuzzy neuron models. A class of weighting operators and aggregation operators are proposed that are also called "synaptic" operators and "somatic" operators, respectively. Basically, two kinds of fuzzy neuron models are discussed. One is the "fuzzification" of nonfuzzy neuron models. The other is where the input-output relations are described by "if-then" rules. Learning algorithms are proposed for both types of fuzzy neurons.

2. BASIC MODELS OF A FUZZY NEURON

Figure 25.1 shows the most popular nonfuzzy neuron model proposed by McCulloch and Pitts more than forty years ago. The neuron has N inputs, which are weighted and then passed on to the node. The node sums the weighted inputs and then transfers the results to one of the three nonlinearities. A neuron hs an internal threshold level, a predetermined value θ, and the neurons fire when the sum of the weighted inputs exceeds the value θ. A mathematical representation of such a neuron is given by:

$$y = f(\sum_{i=0}^{N} x_i w_i - \theta)$$

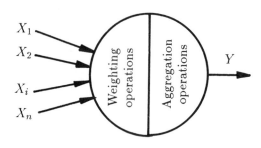

Figure 25.2. A fuzzy neuron model

where y is the output of the neuron, f represents one of the three nonlinearities, x_i and w_i are the i-th input and its corresponding weighting factor, respectively.

The fuzzy neuron is designed to function in much the same way as the nonfuzzy neuron does, except that it reflects the fuzzy nature of a neuron and has the ability to cope with fuzzy information. The basic structure of a fuzzy neuron is described in Figure 25.2. The inputs to the fuzzy neuron are fuzzy sets X_1, X_2, ..., X_n in the universes of discourse U_1, U_2, ..., U_n, respectively. These fuzzy sets may be labeled by such linguistic terms as *high, large, warm*, etc. The inputs are then weighted in ways much different from those used in the nonfuzzy case. The weighted inputs are then aggregated not by the summation but by the fuzzy aggregation operations. The fuzzy output Y may stay with or without further operations depending on specific circumstances. It is also noted that the procedure from the input to the output may not necessarily always be the same.

In the following, detailed discussions of three types of fuzzy neural network models are given. Some possible learning (training) schemes are also proposed.

2.1. A Fuzzy Neuron Described by Logical Equations

In knowledge-based systems, one often uses a set of conditional statements, "if-then" rules, to represent human knowledge extracted

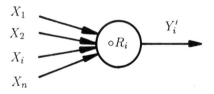

Figure 25.3. Fuzzy neuron I

from human experts. Very often this knowledge is associated with uncertain and fuzzy terms. Therefore, antecedents and consequents in the if-then rules are treated as fuzzy sets. The first fuzzy neuron model we discuss here is described by such rules. In Figure 25.3, a fuzzy neuron with N inputs and one output is shown and the input-output relations are represented by one if-then rule:

If X_{1i} and X_{2i} and ... X_{ni} then Y_i

Here $X_1, X_2, ..., X_n$ are the current inputs and Y_i the current output of the i-th neuron, which is described by the i-th rule of the overall M rules shown in Figure 25.4. This means that each neuron represents one of the M if-then rules.

According to the fuzzy logic theory, the i-th fuzzy neuron can be described by a fuzzy relation R_i, for example

$$R_i = X_{1i} \times X_{2i} \times ... \times X_{ni} \times Y_i$$

or in the general case:

$$R_i = F(X_{1i}, X_{2i}, ..., X_{ni}, Y_i)$$

where F represents an implication function.

Given the current inputs (fuzzy or nonfuzzy) $X_1, X_2, ... X_n$, according to the compositional rule of inference, the i-th rule gives an output as

$$Y_i = X_1 \text{ o } (X_2 \text{ o } (... \text{ o } (X_n \text{ o } R_i)...)$$

where o represents any composition operation, such as sup-T-norm.

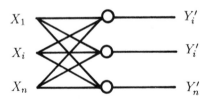

Figure 25.4. An example of fuzzy neural networks

Here, the proposed fuzzy neuron is the one whose inputs are related to its outputs by a fuzzy conditional statement or an if-then rule. The experience of the neuron is stored in a fuzzy relation R_i, and its output is composed from the current inputs and the past experiences R_i. Therefore, it seems that this artificial fuzzy neuron behaves in much the same way as a biological neuron does.

It should also be noted that inputs to the neuron can be either fuzzy or nonfuzzy; crisp values are the special cases of the fuzzy ones.

The learning algorithms for this fuzzy neuron may vary depending on the real-world problems. Here some basic considerations are given about how the fuzzy neuron changes itself during learning and adaptation. This goal may be achieved by synaptic or somatic adaptation. "Synaptic" adaptation means all the inputs are constantly modified and then forwarded to the neuron's body, and the "somatic" adaptation implies modifying the past experience. More detailed discussions are given in the next section.

2.2. A Fuzzy Neuron Given by Direct "Fuzzification" of its Nonfuzzy Counterpart

Unlike the above model, the fuzzy neuron proposed in this section is not described by an if-then rule, rather it is obtained by a direct fuzzification or extension of a nonfuzzy neuron model. Similar to

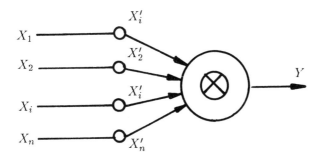

Figure 25.5. Fuzzy neuron II

a nonfuzzy neuron, all the inputs (fuzzy or crisp) of a fuzzy neuron are modified by weighting (or synaptic operations) and then go through an aggregation (or somatic operations) before giving the final results (either a fuzzy set or a membership value). Two fuzzy neuron models as their learning schemes are discussed next.

2.2.1. A Fuzzy Neuron with Crisp Inputs

As shown in Figure 25.5, this fuzzy neuron has N nonfuzzy inputs, and the weighting operations are replaced by membership functions. The result of each weighting operation is the membership value of the corresponding input in a fuzzy set as shown in Figure 25.6. All these membership values are aggregated together to give a single output in the interval of $[0, 1]$, which may be considered as the "level of confidence." The aggregation process represented by $\otimes$ may use any aggregation or somatic operator, such as MIN, MAX and any other T-norm and T-conorm given in Gupta and Qi (1991). A mathematical representation of such a fuzzy neuron is described by:

$$\mu(x_1, x_2, ..., x_n) = \mu_1(x_1) \otimes \mu_2(x_2) \otimes ... \otimes \mu_i(x_i) \otimes ... \otimes \mu_n(x_n)$$

where x_i is the i-th input to the neuron, $\mu_i(.)$ the membership function of the i-th weight, μ the output of the neuron, and $\otimes$ an aggregation operator.

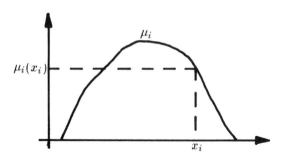

Figure 25.6. Weighting of fuzzy neuron II

2.2.2. A Fuzzy Neuron with Fuzzy Inputs

Figure 25.7 shows another fuzzy neuron that seems to be very similar to a nonfuzzy neuron except that all the inputs and the output are fuzzy sets rather than crisp values. Each fuzzy input undergoes a synaptic operation that results in another fuzzy set. All the modified inputs are aggregated to produce an N-dimensional fuzzy set. Because the output is rather complicated, it may go through further operations. It must be noted that, unlike the one above, the weighting operation here is not a membership function; instead, it is a modifier

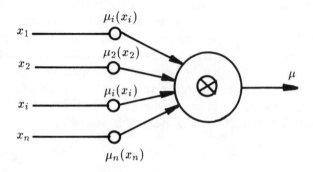

Figure 25.7. Fuzzy neuron III

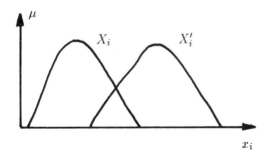

Figure 25.8. Weighting of fuzzy neuron III

to each fuzzy input. As shown in Figure 25.8, the fuzzy set X_i is modified into another fuzzy set X'_1. The aggregation operator $\otimes$ may be the same as the one mentioned above. This fuzzy neuron is mathematically described as

$$Y = X_1 \otimes X_2 \otimes \ldots \otimes X_i \otimes \ldots \otimes X_n$$
$$X_i = G_I(X_i) \; i = 1, 2, \ldots, n$$

where Y is the fuzzy set representing the output of the fuzzy neuron, Y_i and X_i the i-th inputs before and after the weighting operation, respectively, and G_I the weighting operation on the i-th synaptic connection.

2.3. Learning and Adaptation Mechanisms

An adaptive neuron usually goes through the learning and adaptation processes in order to improve its performance. This goal is often achieved by weights modification or synaptic modification. In the fuzzy neuron model, in addition to synaptic modification, one may also utilize the somatic modification, which means making modifications to the structure of a neuron's body. The learning and adaptive mechanisms discussed here are applicable to all the neuron models discussed above.

2.3.1. Synaptic Modification

During a learning or training process, a neuron constantly changes itself to adapt and improve its performance. Synaptic modification is one of the scenarios used to realize this purpose. In a neuron (fuzzy or not), all inputs are modified by weighting or synaptic operations. In the fuzzy case, however, the weighting or synaptic operations are rather complex.

In the case of the fuzzy neuron I, one may also introduce the weighting operations. If so, the fuzzy neurons I and III are considered the same as far as the weights modifications are concerned. In both cases, all the weights simply serve as mapping functions that transform or modify each fuzzy input into another fuzzy set; this modification process continues until the training results are satisfactory. The modifications may vary depending on the practical problems. However, in the case of triangular fuzzy numbers, the following cases shown in Figure 25.9 may occur. Here, the dotted lines represent the fuzzy inputs before modification and the solid ones after modification. In Figure 25.9a the synaptic operation is a shifting process. In Figure 25.9b, the width of the triangular fuzzy number changes, and in Figure 25.9c, the shape of the triangular fuzzy number changes. In the case of fuzzy neuron II, the weights are membership functions that transform numerical inputs into their corresponding membership values as shown in Figure 25.6. However, the above three modification schemes can also be used in the modifications of the membership functions of the weights in this case.

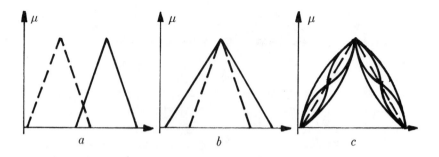

Figure 25.9. Changes of membership functions during learning

2.3.2. Somatic Modification

During a learning or training process, a fuzzy neuron may also change its body's structure rather than modifying its inputs. In the case of fuzzy neuron I, this means changing or updating the past experience, which includes:

1. changing the rules,
2. changing the membership functions assigned to the fuzzy terms in the rules, or
3. changing the way of representing the rules; for example, various implication functions and aggregation operations (Gupta and Qi, 1991) may be considered.

In the cases of fuzzy neurons II and III, many options are available for the aggregation operator $\otimes$, such as T-norms, T-conorms, etc.

2.4. Nonfuzzy Neural Network Approaches to Fuzzy Systems: Fuzzy Logic Controllers and Fuzzy Expert Systems

In the above sections, several models of a fuzzy neuron are proposed in the hope of combining the strengths of fuzzy logic and neural networks and achieving a more powerful fuzzy information processing tool. However, it is also possible to use the well-established nonfuzzy neural networks approach to fuzzy system modeling and construction where the neural networks' ability to learn and to be trained is particularly attractive. For example, in fuzzy logic controllers and expert systems, one often represents expert knowledge by the if-then rules. A membership function is assigned to each fuzzy term in the rules. By using the backpropagation learning algorithm of conventional neural networks, the membership functions for fuzzy terms are learned based on the training data. More recently, the subject starting to attract researchers is fuzzy systems modeling using nonfuzzy neural networks where membership functions involved in input and output models are learned either from the if-then rules extracted from experienced human operators, or from the numerical data obtained by data logging experiments.

3. CONCLUSION

Compared with the conventional neural networks theory, which has been successfully applied to various areas concerning information processing, the fuzzy neural networks approach, which is intended to play the same role in fuzzy information processing, is still in its infancy. This paper is an attempt to contribute to the further theoretical development of fuzzy neural networks theory.

In this paper, three types of fuzzy neuron models are proposed. Neuron I is described by logical equations or the if-then rules; its inputs are either fuzzy sets or crisp values. Neuron II, with numerical inputs, and neuron III, with fuzzy inputs, are considered to be a simple extension of nonfuzzy neurons. A few methods of how these neurons change themselves during learning to improve their performance are also given. Finally, the application of the nonfuzzy neural networks approach to fuzzy information processing is also briefly discussed.

Further research work is underway toward implementing these fuzzy neural models in practical problems.

Keywords: neural networks, fuzzy logic, fuzzy neural networks, learning and adaptation, fuzzy systems

BIBLIOGRAPHY

Cohen, M. E. and D. L. Hudson. (1990). An expert system based on neural network techniques. In I. B. Turksen (ed.): *Proceedings of NAFIP's 90,* Toronto, June 6–8, pp. 117–120.

Gupta, M. M. and G. K. Knopf. (1990). Fuzzy neural network approach to control systems. *Proceedings of international symposium on uncertainty modeling and analysis.* University of Maryland, College Park, Dec. 3–5, IEEE Computer Society Press, pp. 483–488.

Gupta, M. M. and J. Qi. (1991). Theory of T-norms and fuzzy inference methods. *Fuzzy sets and Systems.* In press.

Hayashi, I., H. Nomura, and N. Wakami. (1989). Artificial neural network driven fuzzy control and its application to the learning of inverted pendulum system. *Proceedings of the Third IFSA Congress* (J. C. Bezdek, ed.), Seattle, Washington, Aug. 6–11, pp. 610–613.

Kiszka, J. B. and M. M. Gupta. (1990). Fuzzy logic neural network. *BUSEFAL,* no. 4, pp. 104–109.

Kuncicky, D. C. and A. Kandel. (1989). A fuzzy interpretation of neural networks *Proceedings of the Third IFSA Congress* (J. C. Bezdek, ed.), Seattle, Washington, Aug. 6–11, pp. 113–116.

Lippmann, R. P. (1987). An introduction to computing with neural nets. *IEEE ASSP Magazine*, pp. 4–22.

Nakanishi, S., T. Takagi, K. Uehara and Y. Gotoh. (1990). Self-organising fuzzy controllers by neural networks. *Proceedings of International Conference on Fuzzy Logic & Neural Networks* (Vol. 1), IIZUKA'90, Fukuoka, Japan, July 22–24, pp. 187–192.

Yamakawa, T. and S. Tomoda. (1989). A fuzzy neuron and its application to pattern recognition. *Proceedings of the Third IFSA Congress* (J. C. Bezdek, ed.), Seattle, Washington, Aug. 6–11, pp. 30–38.

5

KNOWLEDGE-BASED SYSTEMS USING FUZZY LOGIC

26 FLISP: representing and processing of uncertain information

Zenon A. SOSNOWSKI *
Knowledge Systems Laboratory
Institute for Information
Technology
National Research Council
of Canada
Ottawa, CANADA K1A 0R6

Witold PEDRYCZ
Electrical & Computer
Engineering Department
University of Manitoba
Winnipeg
CANADA R3T 2N2

Abstract. This paper presents fundamentals and applications of FLISP programming language. Based on LISP, the language is equipped with mechanisms for handling and processing fuzzy sets. Basic software constructs (data structures, links between them, ways of handling, etc.) representing fuzzy sets and their generalizations will be discussed. The entire presentation will be structured around a hierarchy of concepts of fuzzy sets starting from defining objects (fuzzy sets), their operations, and underlying computational structures (linguistic approximation, inference schemes). First it will be revealed how lists creating a basic format of processed information can be enriched by concepts stemming from fuzzy sets. A collection of standard terms used in fuzzy sets (such as "modifiers") will be implemented. We will study implementation issues of reasoning schemes carried out in terms of generalized modus ponens and relational calculus (relational equations). In such a way all components of the language necessary for applications of fuzzy sets in many areas will be covered in depth. For illustrative purposes we will concentrate on functional software specification using fuzzy decision tables, and specification of fuzzy controllers in particular.

* On leave from the Department of Computer Science, Technical University of Białystok, Białystok, Poland.

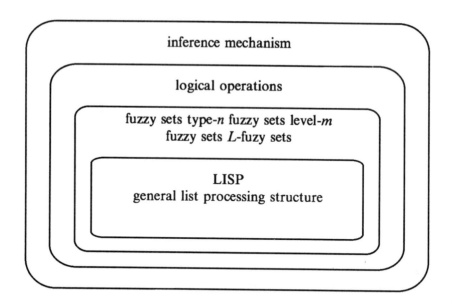

Figure 26.1. FLISP and its layered structure: An overview

1. INTRODUCTION

Witnessing a steady growth of a variety of applications of fuzzy sets one can easily observe an increasing demand for software and hardware realizations, such as those being introduced in Japan (Yamakawa, 1990).

Languages for processing fuzzy sets, fuzzy relations, and related objects can be viewed as inevitable tools for pursuing research and facilitating development, for maintaining and upgrading of software products, and for supporting configuration of underlying hardware structures. It is worthwhile to indicate a wide class of fuzzy controller. In this case the need for a flexible designing platform becomes especially important, in particular at some preliminary stages since a final highly cost-efficient implementation (e.g., carried out in terms of look-up tables) is significantly nonreconfigurable. As such it calls for a very careful and exhaustive analysis at the beginning of the project. In this context PROLOG and usually LISP—two basic languages of artificial intelligence—were considered as good candidates for all possible extensions incorporated in order to carry out the processing of fuzzy sets (Shen, Ding and Mukaidono, 1987; Umano, 1987). PROLOG is extended by excluding two-valued predicates and/or incorporating underlying reasoning mechanisms (backtracking or resolution principle) that are specific for fuzzy sets. In LISP fuzzy sets and all their possible extensions and generalizations are structured into lists, and a collection of related functions are incorporated such that the user can treat all these objects (i.e., fuzzy sets) as if they were standard to the language.

In this paper we will study an extension of LISP, called FLISP, provide its syntax, and study underlying data structures, transformation, and inference mechanisms. The general structure to be analyzed is contained in Figure 26.1.

In addition to all those extensions necessary to cope with fuzzy sets we will investigate FLISP as an interesting tool for software specification of knowledge bases and associated inference mechanisms that equip it with some necessary operations. It will permit us to treat it as a useful designing platform for handling and processing uncertain information.

2. DATA STRUCTURES FOR REPRESENTING FUZZY INFORMATION

Let us recall that in LISP all data structures and functions are represented as lists of elements (McCarthy, 1965). Each element can be a name (which may represent an atom or a name of a standard or user-defined function) or a sublist. There are two ways to represent value of atoms in LISP, i.e., the APVAL indicator and A-list. As our intent is to maintain FLISP as nested in original LISP, we will keep those two standard ways for representing nonfuzzy objects. There are three generic kinds of fuzzy objects in FLISP: fuzzy sets, fuzzy relations, and linguistic variables. Fuzzy data will be stored on property lists of atoms under special indicators. Descriptions of a fuzzy set, a fuzzy relation, and a linguistic variable will be stored under the FSET, the FREL, and the FLV indicators, respectively. As each fuzzy object has a universe of disourse connected with it, we will store the description of the universe of discourse on the property list of a given object under the U indicator. It can be the set of natural numbers (N), the set of real numbers (R), an interval [A, B], or the name of a set of elements defined as a list of atoms.

The representation of fuzzy data is presented below in detail.

2.1. Representation of Fuzzy Sets

Let A be a fuzzy set in a universe of discourse U characterized by a membership function

$$\mu_A : U \to [0.1]$$

which associates with each element x of U a number $\mu_A(x)$ in the interval $[0,1]$, which represents the grade of membership of x in fuzzy set A.

If the grade of membership $\mu_A(x)$ of x in fuzzy set A is a positive number, then it will be represented as a dotted pair $(x \cdot \mu_A(x))$ (or $(x \cdot \mu(x))$).

If a universe of discourse U is a finite set, then a fuzzy set A will be represented as a list

$$((x_1 \cdot \mu_1)(x_2 \cdot \mu_2) \ldots (x_n \cdot \mu_n)) \tag{1}$$

where x_i is an atom from U and μ_i is a number denoting the grade of membership of x_i in the fuzzy set A. In order to achieve a high speed of computation, the list (1) is ordered by the $\leqslant$ relation according to μ_i. This list will be stored on the property list of atom A under the FSET indicator.

It is worthwhile to mention, that any crisp (Boolean) set can be implemented in LISP as a list of elements. This list of elements is stored under the APVAL indicator of the atom describing the given set (Figure 26.2). In the representation of a fuzzy set an element of a set is not expressed as an atom, but as a dotted pair, which contains the nonfuzzy element and its grade of membership in a fuzzy set.

The graphical representation is visualized in Figure 26.3. Two examples given below illustrate the way of handling objects in FLISP.

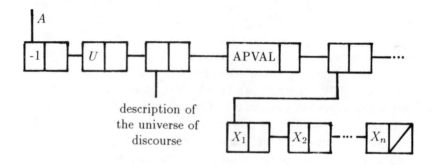

Figure 26.2. List representation of a set in LISP

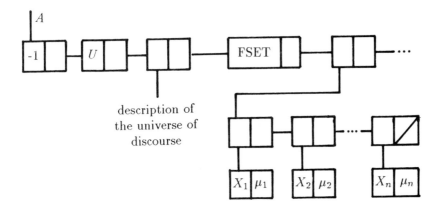

Figure 26.3. The graphical representation of a fuzzy set

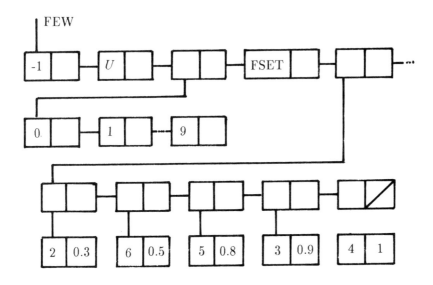

Figure 26.4. The graphical illustration of the fuzzy set FEW

Example 1: Let $U = (0, 1, 2, 3, 4, 5, 6, 7, 8, 9)$. Then a fuzzy set "few" in U may be defined as follows:

$$\mu(0) = 0 \quad \mu(1) = 0 \quad \mu(2) = 0.3 \quad \mu(3) = 0.9 \quad \mu(4) = 1$$
$$\mu(5) = 0.8 \quad \mu(6) = 0.5 \quad \mu(7) = 0 \quad \mu(8) = 0 \quad \mu(9) = 0$$

We can represent this fuzzy set by the following list of singletons:

$$((2 \cdot 0.3)(6 \cdot 0.5)(5 \cdot 0.8)(3 \cdot 0.9)(4 \cdot 1))$$

The graphical representation of the fuzzy set FEW is presented in Figure 26.4.

Besides a list of singletons, a name of the EXPR function that describes a membership function of a fuzzy set can be stored under the FSET indicator.

Example 2: Let $U = [0, 100]$. A fuzzy set "young" in U may be defined by the following continuous membership function:

$$\mu_{young}(x) = \begin{cases} 1 & \text{for } x \leqslant 25 \\ \left(1 + \dfrac{(x - 25)^2}{25}\right)^{-1} & \text{for } 25 < x \leqslant 100 \end{cases} \tag{2}$$

The atom YOUNG represents the EXPR function in LISP that calculates the values of the membership function. The property list of the atom YOUNG is presented in Figure 26.5.

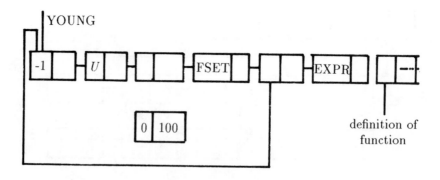

Figure 26.5. The property list of the atom YOUNG

Frequently, it is useful to describe a membership function as one among standard functions s, π, and z (Zadeh, 1975). These functions, as well as their parameters, can be chosen depending on applications. All of them have been implemented and are available in FLISP.

Since Zadeh first formulated the concept of fuzzy sets, some important conceptual extensions have been described, known as L-fuzzy sets (Goguen, 1967), level-m fuzzy sets, and type-n fuzzy sets.

2.1.1. Representation of Fuzzy Sets of Higher Ranks

In this section we will recall two important generalizations of fuzzy sets, level-m and type-n fuzzy sets. A level-m fuzzy set $Y(m = 1,2, ...)$ in a universe of discourse U, characterized by the following membership function

$$
m-1 \begin{cases} & U \\ & \quad \quad \quad [0,1] \\ & \quad \cdot \cdot \\ & [0,1] \\ & [0,1] \end{cases} \tag{3}
$$

$$\mu_Y : [0,1] \to [0,1]$$

will be represented by a list of singletons (1), where x_i is an atom denoting a level-$(m$-1) fuzzy set and μ_i is a number.

Example 3: Assume that $U = \{a, b, c, d\}$ and, for example, for the same U, two fuzzy sets in U are expressed as follows: $Y_1 = 0.9/a + 0.2/b + 0.8/d$, and $Y_2 = 0.6/a + 0.1/c$.

Then, one may have a level-2 fuzzy set Y in U as $Y = 0.8/Y1$ $0.1/Y2$, and represent this as the following list $((Y2 \cdot 0.1) (Y1 \cdot 0.8))$. The graphical representation of Y is shown in Figure 26.6.

Another straightforward generalization refers to generalization performed with respect to a nested structure occurring at a level of grades of membership. A type-n fuzzy set Z $(n = 1,2,...)$ in a universe of discourse U is characterized by the following membership function

$$
n-1 \begin{cases} & [0,1] \\ & \quad \cdot \cdot \\ & [0,1] \end{cases} \tag{4}
$$

$$\mu_Z : U \to [0,1]$$

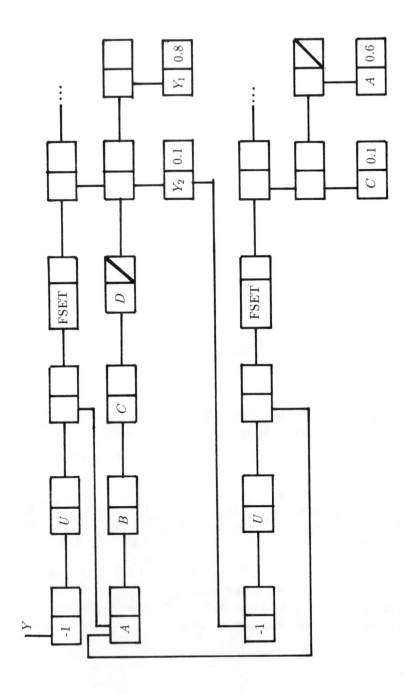

Figure 26.6. An example of level-2 fuzzy set Y

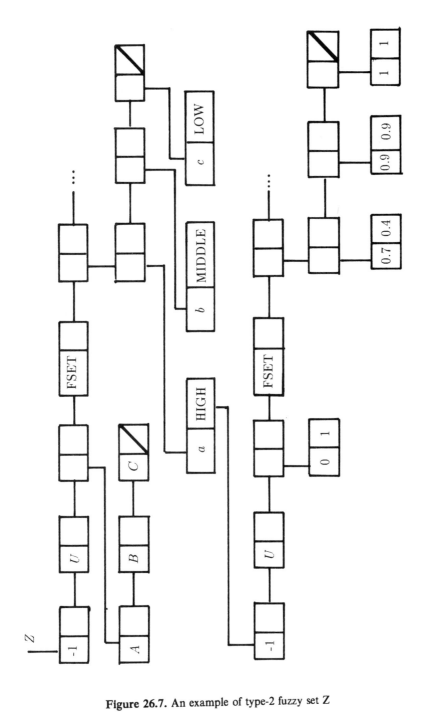

Figure 26.7. An example of type-2 fuzzy set Z

Subsequently it will be represented by a list of singletons (1), where x_i is an atom from U, and μ_i is an atom denoting a type-$(n-1)$ fuzzy set.

For the processing of linguistic variables (Zadeh, 1975), type-2 fuzzy sets are very useful. In these sets a grade of membership of an element is not a number from the $[0,1]$ interval but becomes a fuzzy set in this interval.

Example 4: Consider again a discrete space $U = \{a,b,c,\}$. One may have a type-2 fuzzy set $Z =$ high/a + middle/b + low/c where "high," "middle" and "low" are fuzzy sets and, for example, are expressed as follows: high $= 0.4/0.7 + 0.9/0.9 + 1/1$, middle $= 0.3/0.3 + 1/0.5 + 0.3/0.8$, and low $= 1/0.1 + 0.7/0.2 + 0.3/0.3$.

The type-2 fuzzy set Z can be represented by the list ((c · low) (b · middle) (a · high)). Its graphical representation is summarized in Figure 26.7.

Examples 3 and 4 illustrate a recursive character of the definition of fuzzy sets and their generalizations in FLISP.

2.1.2. Representation of L-Fuzzy Sets

L-fuzzy sets (Goguen, 1967) are a generalization of generic fuzzy sets in a sense such that now grades of membership take values from a lattice L. Note that $[0, 1]$ forms a very particular case of L.

An L-fuzzy set X in U characterized by the following membership function

$$\mu_X : U \to L$$

where L represents a lattice, will be specified by a list of singletons (1), where x_i is an atom from U, and μ_i is a list of values of a lattice. Additionally, the names of sup and inf operations for a lattice will be stored under the L indicator.

Example 5: Assume that $U = \{a,b,c,d\}$. Then, one may have an L-fuzzy set X in U as $X = <0.1,0.9>/a + <0.8,1>/b + <0.9,0>/c$. In this example, L is a lattice $[0,1] \times [0,1]$ ordered by $<u_1, v_1> \leqslant <u_2, v_2>$ iff $u_1 \leqslant v_1$ and $u_2 \leqslant v_2$, where u_1, u_2, v_1, and v_2 are elements of $[0,1]$. Figure 26.8 visualizes the graphical representation of the set X.

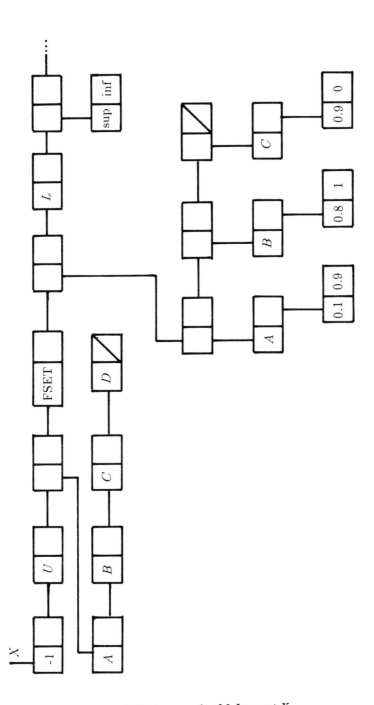

Figure 26.8. An example of L-fuzzy set X

2.2. Representations of Fuzzy Relations

The fuzzy relation in $U \times V$ is characterized by a bivariate membership function

$$\mu_R : U \times V \to [0,1]$$

It U and V are finite sets, then the fuzzy relation R in $U \times V$ is expressed as a matrix

$$R = \sum_{i,j} \mu(u_i, v_j) / <u_i, v_j> = \begin{bmatrix} \mu(u_1, v_1), ..., \mu(u_1, v_n) \\ .... \\ \mu(u_m, v_1), ..., \mu(u_m, v_n) \end{bmatrix} =$$

$$\begin{bmatrix} r_{1,1} \cdots r_{1,n} \\ .... \\ r_{m,1} \cdots r_{m,n} \end{bmatrix}$$

where $u_i (i = 1,2,...,m)$, and $v_j (j = 1,2,...,n)$ represent the elements of U and V, respectively.

The fuzzy relation will be unfolded as the following list of singletons:

$$((v_1 (u_1 \cdot r_{1,1})(u_2 \cdot r_{2,1}) ... (u_m \cdot r_{m,1}))$$
$$(v_2 (u_1 \cdot r_{1,2})(u_2 \cdot r_{2,2}) ... (u_m \cdot r_{m,2}))$$
$$\vdots$$
$$((v_n (u_1 \cdot r_{1,n})(u_2 \cdot r_{2,n}) ... (u_m \cdot r_{m,n})))$$

This list will be stored under the FREL indicator. The U indicator will be applied to store the list $(U V)$ describing the consecutive components of the relation.

Example 6: Let $U = \{a,b,c,d\}$. Then, one may have a fuzzy relation R in $U \times U$ given as

$$R = 0.9/<d,b> + 0.8/<a,d> = \begin{bmatrix} 0 & 0 & 0 & 0.8 \\ 0 & 0 & 0 & 0 \\ 0 & 0 & 0 & 0 \\ 0 & 0.9 & 0 & 0 \end{bmatrix}$$

and represented as a list

$$((a)$$
$$(b (d \cdot 0.9))$$
$$(c)$$
$$(d (a \cdot 0.8)))$$

The graphical representation of the fuzzy relation R is shown in Figure 26.9.

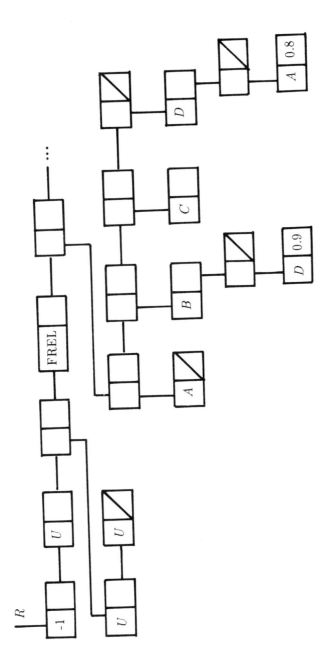

Figure 26.9. An example of fuzzy relation R

2.3. Representation of Linguistic Variables

A linguistic variable has been defined by Zadeh (1975) as a system

$$< L, T(L), X, G, M >$$

where $L, T(L)$ (or shortly T), X, G and M denote respectively:

   L – name of variable;
   T – set of labels of a fuzzy subset of the universe of discourse;
   X – universe of discourse;
   G – syntactic rules, defined as generative grammar, which define the well-formed sentences in T;
   M – semantics, which consists of rules by which the meaning of the sentences in T can be determined.

In FLISP the syntax G and semantics M of a linguistic variable are defined as follows. G is expressed in terms of a grammar:

$$G = <V, \Sigma, P, \partial>$$

The set of its terminal symbols V consists of primary terms t_i, modifiers m_j, logical operators *not* and *or*, and two special symbols "(" and ")". Thus we can write

$$V = \{t_1, t_2, ..., t_n, h_1, h_2, ..., h_k, not, or, (,)\}$$

The semantics M is defined as a mapping that associates with each sentence of the language $L(G)$, generated by the grammar G, its meaning as a fuzzy set in a universe of discourse U. So we can write

$$M : L(G) \rightarrow F(U)$$

A linguistic variable is represented in FLISP in such a way that on the property list of an atom, which represents a given linguistic variable, the following indicators and their values are stored:

1. Indicator U and the description of a universe of discourse;
2. Indicator FLV and the list of primary terms of grammar G;
3. Indicator HEDGES and the list of modifiers that are LISP functions.

Figure 26.10 shows the graphical representation of the linguistic variable in FLISP, completing our discussion on essential constructs of fuzzy sets and their selected generalizations.

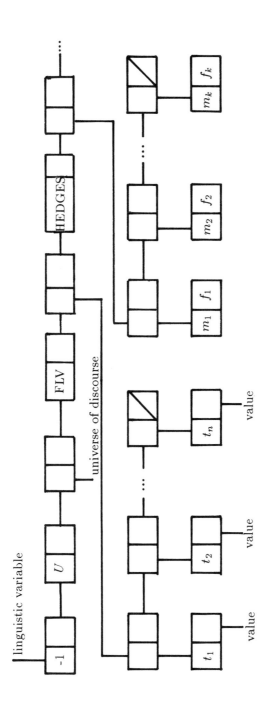

Figure 26.10. Graphical representation of a linguistic variable

3. OPERATIONS FOR PROCESSING FUZZY DATA

In this section, some functions for processing fuzzy objects (or their generalizations) in FLISP are presented. We will then model all logical connectives (both of and- and or-type) with the aid of t- and s-norms. This will allows us to cope with different situations involving a broad range of strength of connectivity (interaction) occurring between the defined objects.

3.1. Basic Operations

Input of fuzzy sets, fuzzy relations, and linguistic variables is realized with the aid of the FSETQ function. This function puts description of a fuzzy object on the property list of a given atom. It will be called as follows:

(FSETQ *name   description of fuzzy object*)

where *name* is a LISP atom that represents the name of the fuzzy object, and *description of fuzzy object* represents a fuzzy set, fuzzy relation, or linguistic variable. Detailed syntax of this function can be found in Sosnowski (1990).

To input the fuzzy set the second argument of FSETQ is as follows:

((*universe of discourse*) (FSET *description of fuzzy set*))

where *description of fuzzy set* can be a list (1) or a name of the EXPR function describing the membership function of a given fuzzy set.

For example the fuzzy set "few" defined in Example 1 can be input as follows:

(SETQ U '(0 1 2 3 4 6 7 8 9))
FSETQ FEW ((U) (FSET ((2 · 0.3) (6 · 0.5) (5 · 0.8) (3 · 0.9) (4 · 1)))))

and the fuzzy set "young" from Example 2 can be input as follows:

(FSETQ YOUNG (((0 · 1)) (FSET YOUNG))

where YOUNG is the following function in LISP

(YOUNG (LAMBDA (X)
  (COND ((LESSP X 25) 1)
    (T (QUOTIENT 25
      (PLUS 650 (TIMES -50 X) (TIMES X X)))))))

To input a fuzzy relation, the second argument of FSETQ must be as follows:

((*list of universe of discourse*)
   (FREL (*description of fuzzy relation*)))

For example, the relation *R* defined in Example 6 can be input as follows:

(SETQ U '(A B C D))
(FSETQ R ((U U) (FREL ((A) (B (D . 0.9)) (C) (D (A . 0.8))))))

When we input the description of a linguistic variable the second argument of FSETQ is as follows:

((*universe of discourse*)
   (FLV (*list of values*) (HEDGES (*list of hedges*))))

where the *list of values* and *list of hedges* are list of dotted pairs. The left element of a dotted pair of the *list of values* is a string in the sense of LISP and it describes the name of value of a linguistic variable. The left element of a dotted pair of the *list of hedges* is also a LISP string. It represents the name of hedge. The right element describes the name of the LISP function connected with this hedge.

Example 7: A linguistic variable "height" will be defined as the following structure:

$$< L, T(L), U, G, M >$$

where

L = height
$T(L)$ = {small, high, medium, very high, more or less medium, ...}
U = [140,210]
G = syntax of a linguistic variable, which has the form of a grammar for generating the names of values of the variable.
M = semantics of a linguistic variable for associating with each linguistic value its meaning, which is a fuzzy set of U.

It is realized accordingly:

(FSETQ HEIGHT ((140 · 210)
   (FLV (("LOW" · (Z 180 170 160))
      ("MIDDLE" · (PI 15 170))
      ("HIGH" · (S 165 175 185))
      (HEDGES (("MORE OR LESS" · SQRT)
         ("VERY" · SQR))))))

The list of operations available in FLIP is presented in Tables 26.1 and 26.2.

Table 26.1. Fuzzy-set operations available in FLISP

Fuzzy-Set Operation	Arguments	Remarks
(FCOMPLEMENT A)	A-a fuzzy set	Complement
(FCON A)	A-a fuzzy set	Concentration
(FDIL A)	A-a fuzzy set	Dilation
(FCINT A)	A-a fuzzy set	Contrast intensification
(FBLR A)	A-a fuzzy set	Contrast reduction
(FPROD A B)	A, B-fuzzy sets	Product
(FASUM A B)	A, B-fuzzy sets	Algebraic sum
(FSC C A)	C-a scalar A-a fuzzy set	Scalar multiplication
(FCUT ALFA A)	ALFA $\in$ [0,1] A-a fuzzy set	α-level set
(FADIF A B)	A, B-fuzzy sets	Absolute difference
(FBSUM A B)	A, B-fuzzy sets	Bounded sum
(FBDIF A B)	A, B-fuzzy sets	Bounded difference
(FMAXG A)	A-a fuzzy set	Maximum grade
(FNROM A)	A-a fuzzy set	Normalization
(FCARD A)	A-a fuzzy set	Cardinality
(FSUB A B)	A, B-fuzzy sets	Inclusion
(FEQ A B)	A, B-fuzzy sets	Equality
(FUNION A B S)	A, B-fuzzy sets S-an s-norm	Union
(FINTERSECTION A B TT)	A, B-fuzzy sets TT-a t-norm	Intersection

Table 26.2. Fuzzy relation operations

Fuzzy-Relation Operation	Arguments	Remarks
(FRU R1 R2 S)	R1, R2- fuzzy relations S-an s-norm	Union of relation
(FRI R1 R2 TT)	R1, R2-fuzzy relations TT-a t-norm	Intersection of relation
(FCOMPOSE R1 R2)	R1, R2-fuzzy relations	Composition
(FCP B TT)	A, B-fuzzy sets TT-a t-norm	Cartesian Product
(FIMAGE A R)	A-a fuzzy set R-a fuzzy relation	Image
(FCIMAGE R A)	A-a fuzzy set R-a fuzzy relation	Converse image

3.2. A Conditional Statement Involving Fuzzy Predicates (FCOND)

A conditional statement FCOND of FLISP is an analog of COND statement of LISP. FCOND is a base for implementing methods of fuzzy reasoning for which all pieces of knowledge are represented by conditional propositions containing fuzzy statements.

$$\text{if } A \text{ is } \underline{X} \text{ then } B \text{ is } U \tag{5}$$

where $\underline{X}$ and U are fuzzy labels expressed by a fuzzy relation and a fuzzy set, respectively.

The task accomplished by FCOND is to aggregate the above conditional propositions (5):

prop. 1. if $(A_1$ is X_{11} and A_2 is X_{12} and ... and A_k is $X_{1k})$ then B is U_1

prop. 2. if $(A_1$ is X_{21} and A_2 is X_{22} and ... and A_k is $X_{2k})$ then B is U_2 $\qquad$ (6)

$\vdots$

prop. n. if $(A_1$ is X_{n1} and A_2 is X_{n2} and ... and A_k is $X_{nk})$ then B is U_n

where A_i ($i = 1,2,...,k$) are the names of linguistic variables that can take their values as fuzzy sets X_{ji} ($j = 1,2,...,n$), B is the name of a linguistic variable that can take its value as U_1, U_2, ..., U_n.

The set of propositions in (6) may be viewed as a part of a knowledge base of an expert system with incomplete and/or uncertain information or interpreted as control rules of a fuzzy controller (Mamdani and Assilian, 1981).

The syntax of the FCOND statement is the following:

(FCOND   *name*   *format of rules*   (*list of rules*))

where *name* is the name of the relation that aggregates the rules, and *format of rules* is a list of linguistic variables used in antecedent and consequence part of the rules.

3.3. Fuzzy Inference Mechanisms (FIMPLY)

FIMPLY is a function for fuzzy inference. This function realizes the generalized modus ponens for the sequence of statements (6) and the additional presumption

$$A_1 \text{ is } X_1' \text{ and } A_2 \text{ is } X_2' \text{ and } ... \text{ and } A_k \text{ is } X_k' \tag{7}$$

where X_1', X_2', ..., X_k' are the values of variables A_1, A_2, ..., A_k.

According to modus ponens we will be interested in deriving a linguistic value of variable B.

The form of FIMPLY is as follows:

(FIMPLY *name of linguistic variable*
    FROM name of relation FOR antecedent)

where: *name of linguistic variable* denotes a name of variable B, *name of relation* denotes the relation calculated by FCOND for sequence of statements (6), and *antecedent* denotes the value of presumption (7).

The function FIMPLY is based upon the compositional rule of inference proposed by Zadeh. According to this rule, FIMPLY calculates the composition of the rules with the given fact. Thus

$$U' = \underline{X}' \circ R$$

where $\underline{X}' = X_1' \times X_2' \times ... \times X_k'$.

An original method proposed by Mamdani (1981) aggregates all conditional statements (6) as the union of Cartesian products of subconditions R and takes the max-min composition to derive the result of reasoning.

Following some basic findings in the theory of fuzzy relations calculus (Pedrycz, 1985), there was proposed an alternative method in which for the fuzzy relation R computed as previously the inference process takes the Gödel implication (α-operator).[1] Bearing this in mind, a global variable FIMPL can be introduced to implement both the cases.

Depending on its value, U' is calculated as follows:

- If FIMPL is equal "EHM", then
$$U' = \underline{X'} \circ R$$

where $\mu_{U'}(u) = \max_{x \in X} (\min(\mu_{X'}(x), \mu_R(x, u))$, for each $u \in U$.

- If FIMPL is equal "WP", then
$$U' = \underline{X'} \alpha R$$

where $\mu_{U'}(u) = \min_{x \in X}((\mu_{X'}(x) \alpha \mu_R(x, u))$, for each $u \in U$.

4. ANALYSIS OF QUALITATIVE DECISION TABLES – STUDIES ON FUNCTIONAL SPECIFICATIONS OF SOFTWARE

In this section we will present results of experimental studies completed in the analysis of decision tables using FLISP. Decision tables are often found among formal methods of software specification (Fairley, 1985). As constructs handling a declarative facet of a variety of specifications, they should be carefully analyzed with respect to their completeness and consistency. Recall that in their generic format all rules forming a decision table are summarized by listing all involved conditions and action stubs. In its essence fuzzy controllers (sometimes referred to as fuzzy logic controllers) can be perceived as a sort of functional specification of a software construct that will interact with environment to achieve a given control target. This target is given implicitly in terms of control rules. All of these rules form a decision table. For a single input variable–single output variable controller a condition part usually consists of two stubs such as an error and a change of error. Before proceeding with any further implementation such as look-up tables or VLSI chips it is necessary

---

[1]
$$a \alpha b = \begin{cases} 1 \text{ for } a \leqslant b \\ b \text{ for } a > b \end{cases} \quad a, b \in [0,1]$$

to complete analysis of the table (i.e., individual rules) to discover some potential discrepancies or inconsistencies. It should be emphasized here that this type of analysis must be carried out at a "logical," that is, fuzzy-set level (manifesting in the functional specification of the controller) rather than on a purely numerical level occurring in its implementation (Pedrycz, 1985).

For illustrative purposes this analysis is carried out studying the fuzzy controller used by Mamdani to control a boiler. Two input variables are the heat to the boiler and the throttle opening of the input of the engine cylinder.

Furthermore, two output variables are the speed of the engine and the steam pressure in the boiler. An ultimate requirement is to stabilize values of the output variables. A collection of actions that should be taken involves their error and change of error. A complete decision table pertaining to the throttle change consists of rules (conditional statements) contained in Table 26.3.

Tabela 26.3. Decision table containing software specification of the fuzzy controller; see description in text

Condition \ Rule		1	2.1	2.2	2.3	3.1	3.2	4	5.1	5.2	5.3	5.4	5.5	5.6	6	7.1	7.2	8.1	8.2	8.3	9
SE	NB	Y	N	N	N	N	N	N	N	N	N	N	N	N	N	N	N	N	N	N	N
	NM	N	Y	Y	Y	N	N	N	N	N	N	N	N	N	N	N	N	N	N	N	N
	NS	N	N	N	N	Y	Y	N	N	N	N	N	N	N	N	N	N	N	N	N	N
	NO	N	N	N	N	N	N	Y	N	N	N	Y	Y	Y	N	N	N	N	N	N	N
	PO	N	N	N	N	N	N	N	N	N	N	N	N	N	Y	N	N	N	N	N	N
	PS	N	N	N	N	N	N	N	N	N	N	N	N	N	N	Y	Y	N	N	N	N
	PM	N	N	N	N	N	N	N	N	N	N	N	N	N	N	N	N	Y	Y	Y	N
	PB	N	N	N	N	N	N	N	Y	Y	Y	N	N	N	N	N	N	N	N	N	Y
CSE	NB	Y	N	N	N	N	N	N	N	N	N	N	N	N	N	N	N	N	N	N	Y
	NM	Y	N	N	N	N	N	N	N	N	N	N	N	N	N	N	N	N	N	N	Y
	NS	N	N	N	N	N	N	N	N	N	Y	N	N	Y	N	N	N	N	N	N	N
	NO	N	N	N	N	N	N	N	N	N	Y	N	N	Y	N	N	N	N	N	N	N
	PS	N	N	N	Y	N	N	N	Y	N	N	Y	N	N	N	N	N	N	N	Y	N
	PM	N	N	Y	N	N	Y	N	N	N	N	N	N	N	N	N	Y	N	Y	N	N
	PB	N	Y	N	N	Y	N	Y	N	N	N	N	N	N	Y	Y	N	Y	N	N	N
Action TC	NB	N	N	N	N	N	N	N	N	N	N	N	N	N	N	N	N	N	N	N	Y
	NS	N	N	N	N	N	N	N	N	N	N	N	N	N	Y	Y	Y	Y	Y	Y	N
	NO	N	N	N	N	N	N	N	Y	Y	Y	Y	Y	Y	N	N	N	N	N	N	N
	PS	N	Y	Y	Y	Y	Y	Y	N	N	N	N	N	N	N	N	N	N	N	N	N
	PB	Y	N	N	N	N	N	N	N	N	N	N	N	N	N	N	N	N	N	N	N

Here the abbreviations for linguistic terms for speed error (SE) and change in speed error (CSE) are the following:

PB = *Positive Big*
PM = *Positive Medium*
PS = *Positive Small*
PO = *Positive Zero*
NO = *Negative Zero*
NS = *Negative Small*
NM = *Negative Medium*
NB = *Negative Big*

For example, the input of the linguistic variable TC (throttle change) with two modifiers *very* and *more or less* can be done as follows:

(FSETQ 'TC' ((–2 –1 0 1 2))
(FLV (PB · ((1 · 0.5) (2 · 1)))
    (PS · ((2 · 0.5) (0 · 0.5) (1 · 1)))
    (NO · ((1 · 0.5) (–1 · 0.5) (0 · 1)))
    (NS · ((0 0.5) (–2 · 0.5) (–1 · 1)))
    (NB · ((–1 · 0.5) (–2 · 1))))
(HEDGES (("MORE OR LESS" · SQRT)
        ("VERY" · SQR)))))

Two linguistic modifiers *very* and *more or less* are constructed in a standard form by using the sqr and sqrt function.

The control algorithm is considered as a sequence of rules

if (SE *is* SE$_i$ *and* CSE *is* CSE$_i$) *then* TC *is* TC$_i$

where TC, SE and CSE are linguistic variables and for $i = 1,2,...,9$, SE$_i$, CSE$_i$ and TC$_i$ are values of linguistic variables in the i-th rule.

In addition to the original collection of rules specified in Mamdani and Assilian (1981) we have now distinguished some subrules (e.g., the original rule 2 is rewritten as three subrules 2.1, 2.2, and 2.3) to get a format required by decision table techniques.

As we have indicated (Pedrycz, 1985), in the structure of a controller two primordial design aspects should be reflected:

- a mechanism of creation of the relation that aggregates the rules into a format of a fuzzy relation

$$(SE_i \times CSE_i \rightarrow TC_i) \quad i = 1,2,...,9$$

- a method of reasoning

$$\{(SE' \times CSE'); [(SE_i \times CSE_i) \rightarrow TC_i]_{i=1,2,\ldots,9}\} \rightarrow TC' \qquad (8)$$

where SE' and CSE' are fuzzy values describing the input data.

First we utilize the reasoning method found in most implementations of fuzzy controllers as introduced by Mamdani and Assilian (1981). There the rules are aggregated by the formula (Cartesian product)

$$R = \bigcup_{i=1}^{9} (SE_i \times CSE_i \times TC_i) \qquad (9)$$

and the compositional rule of inference applied afterwards takes the max-min convolution

$$TC' = (SE' \times CSE') \circ R \qquad (10)$$

where $\times$ denotes the Cartesian product, and $\circ$ denotes the max-min composition.

We will also consider two other approaches (Pedrycz, 1985) that address the question of coherence of logical connection between the mechanisms of creation of the relation which aggregates all the rules, and the method of reasoning. Here we summarize a method used first in Pedrycz (1985). We will refer to this scheme of reasoning as "WP."

1. The relation is created according to the formula:

$$R' = \bigcap_{i=1}^{9} ((SE_i \times CSE_i) \,\alpha\, TC_i) \qquad (11)$$

while the method of reasoning is described by formula:

$$TC' = (SE' \times CSE') \circ R' \qquad (12)$$

2. In the sequel the relation of the controller is created according to (9) and the method of reasoning is described by the formula:

$$TC' = (SE' \times CSE') \,\alpha\, R \qquad (13)$$

For example, the aggregation of rules of throttle change described by (11) can be calculated in FLISP as follows:

```
(SETQ SELECT "WP")
(FCOND RWP (CSE SE TC)
    ((IF (SE IS NB AND CSE IS NOT (NB OR NM)) THEN TC
        IS PB)
```

(IF (SE IS NS AND CSE IS PB OR PM OR PS) THEN TC IS PB)

(IF (SE IS NS AND CSE IS PB OR PM) THEN TC IS PS)

(IF (SE IS NO AND CSE IS PS) THEN TC IS PS)

(IF (SE IS PB OR NO AND CSE IS PS OR NS OR NO) THEN TC IS NO)

(IF (SE IS PO AND CSE IS PB) THEN TC IS NS)

(IF (SE IS PS AND CSE IS PB OR PM) THEN TC IS NS)

(IF (SE IS PM AND CSE IS PB OR PM OR PS) THEN TC IS NS)

(IF (SE IS PB AND CSE IS NOT (NB OR NM)) THEN TC IS NB)))

Once the decision table is constructed it should be tested with respect to its consistency. A standard and very useful way is to study the performance of the table in cases (rules) already covered by the table. Briefly speaking for an already developed reasoning scheme one completes inference making use of a given condition stubs covered by the decision table itself. The obtained result should be as close as possible to a relevant action part summarized in the table. If it does not hold, then it strongly suggests a need to reanalyze corresponding entries of the table and modify them to achieve a higher consistency.

Two different avenues are usually exploited:

i. The first one expresses a degree of difference (such as an appropriate distance function) between a fuzzy set of action existing in the table and the one inferred from the rules and the given set of conditions. This in turn implies some confidence intervals that can be associated with a fuzzy set of action and therefore reflect a confidence associated with it. In other words, it imposes some interval-valued fuzzy set of action.

   In an ideal situation of perfect consistency all confidence intervals reduce to points yielding genuine fuzzy sets.

ii. Another approach to express consistency is to perform an appropriate linguistic approximation of an original action stub in order to minimize a distance function between this approximated set and the corresponding result of inference.

Following (ii) we will minimize the following expression

$$\min_{m \in M} \sum_{j=1}^{n} |TC'_i(x_j) - TC^m_i(x_j)| \qquad i = 1,2,...,9$$

Table 26.4. Results of linguistic approximation. Method 1 refers to Mamdani's approach; method 2 and method 3 were implemented using (11) and (12) and (9)–(13), respectively

Rule	TC	Method$_1$	Method$_2$	Method$_3$
1	PB	more or less PB	PB	PB
2	PS	PS	PS	PS
3	PS	PS	PS	PS
4	PS	PS	PS	PS
5	NO	NO	NO	NO
6	NS	NS	NS	NS
7	NS	NS	NS	NS
8	NS	NS	NS	NS
9	NB	more or less NB	NS	NS

where M denotes the set of possible modifiers of TC. Table 26.4 presents the results of linguistic approximation applied to outcomes of inference using two modifiers *more or less* and *very* defined in example of the definition of the linguistic variable TC.

5. CONCLUSION

By introducing extended list structures, FLISP has been developed to capture basic components of fuzzy set theory such as fuzzy sets, fuzzy relations, fuzzy sets of higher types and orders, linguistic variables, and inference mechanisms. It is characterized by a clear programming structure. Furthermore, if necessary, new functions can be also easily introduced.

Several inference mechanisms have been proposed including those based on fuzzy relational equations.

An example of utilization of FLISP as a functional software specification tool performed with the aid of decision tables is provided. It implies another look at fuzzy logic controller as a software product being completely described by its decision table with entries formed as fuzzy sets.

FLISP was originally implemented in LISPF3 on the ODRA 1305 computer (compatible with the ICL 1900). It also runs under SUN Common LISP on SUN workstations.

Acknowledgment

Support from the Natural Sciences and Engineering Research Council of Canada is greatly appreciated.

Keywords: fuzzy information, LISP, software specifications, logic-oriented validation of knowledge bases, artificial intelligence

BIBLIOGRAPHY

Fairley, R. E. (1985). *Software Engineering Concepts,* New York: McGraw Hill.

Gougen, J. A. (1967). L-fuzzy sets. *J. Math. Anal. Appl.,* **18,** 145–174.

Mamdani, E. H. and S. Assilian. (1981). An experiment in linguistic synthesis with a fuzzy logic controller. In E. H. Mamadani and B. R. Gaines (eds.): *Fuzzy Reasoning and its Applications.* New York: Academic Press, pp. 311–323.

McCarthy, J. (1965). *LISP 1.5 Programmer's Manual.* Cambridge, MA: MIT Press.

Pedrycz, W. (1985). Application of fuzzy relational equations for methods of reasoning in presence of fuzzy data. *Fuzzy Sets and Systems,* **16,** 163–175.

Shen, Z., L. Ding, and M. Mukaidono. (1987). Demonstration on the fuzzy prolog system. *Preprints of Second IFSA Congress,* Tokyo, pp. 844–847.

Sosnowski, Z. A. (1990). FLISP – A language for processing fuzzy data. *Fuzzy Sets and Systems,* **37,** 23–32.

Umano, M. (1987). Fuzzy-set manipulation system in LISP. *Preprints of Second IFSA Congress,* Tokyo, pp. 840–843.

Yamakawa, T. (ed.). (1990). *Proceedings of Int. Conf. on Fuzzy Logic and Neural Networks,* Iizuka '90, July 22–24, Iizuka, Japan, vols. 1 and 2.

Zadeh, L. A. (1975). The concept of a linguistic variable and its application to approximate reasoning. *Inform. Sci.,* **8,** 199–249.

27 Structured local fuzzy logics in MILORD

J. AGUSTÍ,* F. ESTEVA,* P. GARCIA,*
L. GODO,** R. LÓPEZ DE MÁNTARAS,**
J. PUYOL,* and C. SIERRA*
Centre d'Estudis Avançats de Blanes (CSIC)
Blanes (Girona), SPAIN

L. MURGUI
Aliança Mataronina Hospital
Mataró, SPAIN

Abstract. The MILORD language is described emphasizing two important characteristics: its modularity and the use of local logics attached to the different modules. The need of communication among modules with different local logics during the problem solving process puts some requirements on the different local uncertainty calculi. These requirements are analyzed and a solution is proposed. The paper also proposes a solution to the problem of complex communication between modules, i.e., a communication not restricted to just the certainty values of predicates.

1. INTRODUCTION

MILORD (Sierra, 1989) is a currently working expert system shell oriented to classification tasks. The most relevant features are its

---

* Research partially supported by the SPES project, CICYT id. 880j382

** Research partially supported by the ESPRIT-II Basic Research Action DRUMS.

multilevel architecture and the management of linguistically expressed uncertainty based on fuzzy logic. In this paper we describe a modular extension of the MILORD system. This modular extension addresses two main characteristics of human problem solving: the adequation of general knowledge to particular problems, and the dependence of the kind of management of uncertainty on the particular subtasks. In this paper we mainly focus on the role uncertainty plays in this modular system: (1) as part of local deductive mechanisms, and (2) in the interaction between modules. This interaction will be analyzed and a new communication mechanism will be proposed. This new type of communication between modules with different uncertainty calculi has led us to analyze the requirements that a correspondence between the different uncertainty calculi must fulfill.

1.1. Modularity: Knowledge Adequation and Knowledge Transfer

The use of modularization techniques in expert system design (Agustí-Cullell and Sierra, 1989) is due to the need of adequating the general and spread knowledge in a knowledge base (KB) to specific subtasks. Specific subtasks generally make use only of a subset of the whole KB. For instance, the suspicion of a bacterial disease will rule out all knowledge referring to virus diseases, or a patient in coma will make useless all the knowledge units that need patient's answers. Moreover, this adequation determines the universe of discourse, and this is made by means of selecting certain units of the KB, which should be of a variable granularity depending on the problem. However, in any case, the level of granularity will never be as fine as reducing the universe of discourse to an elementary KB object (a rule). These considerations lead to define structured KBs, which are represented by a hierarchy of modules.

In the hierarchy modules interact when they communicate to each other the results of their logical inferences. This interaction is explicitly defined in the *export* interface of a module. The only predicates available to other modules are, of all the predicates either obtained from the user or deduced inside the module, those declared in the Export declaration (see Section 2.2.2). However, different ways of communicating the results of the deduction of a predicate are imaginable. Some of them are analyzed in the rest of the section by means of an example. The simplest one is the communication of the certainty value obtained in the deduction of a predicate. In this case, the usual communication procedure between modules is:

(1st) Module M' asks a question to module M, for example, P?
(2nd) Module M uses its deductive and control knowledge to find a certainty degree for P.
(3rd) Module M gives this certainty value back to module M'.

Looking carefully at how experts communicate to each other their knowledge, and at their problem solving procedures, we can find much more complex communication mechanisms. Sometimes experts cannot reduce their interaction only to the communication of certainty values of predicates. For instance, when experts in medical diagnosis communicate, they also need:

(1) *To condition their answers.* Suppose that it is not known if a patient is allergic to penicillin. A module deducing the possibility of giving penicillin can answer: *Penicillin is a good treatment from a clinical point of view if there is no allergy to it.* From a logical point of view, the answer could be:

{if no(allergy_penicillin) then Penicillin is very_possible}

(2) *To give conclusions that have to be considered with the answer.* If in a culture of sputum pneumococcus has been isolated then it is strongly suggested to make an antibiogram to the patient.

{Pneumococcus_isolation is sure, Make_Antibiogram is sure}

(3) *To give conditioned conclusions to be considered with the answer.* A treatment with ciprofloxacine is not recommended for breast-feeding women. However, if a woman is on lactation period, then the treatment can be done if the woman stops breast-feeding.

{Cipro is very_possible, if lactation then stop_lactation is sure}

(4) *To give a more general answer.* Imagine that Gram positive coccus is detected. An answer to the predicate pneumococcus is at that moment too precise and cannot be given, but at least the morphological classification can be answered, i.e.: {coccus is sure}

These types of communication can be modeled by the next schematic sets of formulas.

The possible sets of answers to question p? can be:

1. $\{(c_1 \wedge c_2 \wedge \ldots c_n) \to p\}$
2. $\{p, c_1, c_2, \ldots c_n\}$
3. $\{p, ((c_{11} \wedge c_{12} \wedge \ldots c_{1_{n_1}}) \to r_1), \ldots, ((c_{m1} \wedge c_{m2} \wedge \ldots c_{mn_m}) \to r_m)\}$
4. $\{c_1, c_2, \ldots, c_n\}$

To model such communication protocols, we need to extend the module answering procedure. What we need is to answer a given question with a set of formulas (rules and facts). To answer the question, the rules considered are those in deductive paths to and from the question. The facts in the answer are those that have been obtained in the application of such rules. The rules in the answer are those rules that could not be applied because they used unknown knowledge. We consider only the rules in the deduction tree of the question because we assume that when a module makes a question it expects only an answer to it, and eventually all the relevant information associated with that answer.

Example 1: Consider a module M with the following set of rules:

> Rules = {**if** Gram_negative_rods **then** Treatment_with_ciprofloxacine **is** possible,
> **if** Treatment_with_ciprofloxacine **and** lactation **then** Stop_lactation **is** definite,
> **if** Bacterian_infection **and** Gram_negative_rods **then** Treatment_with_ceftriaxone **is** very_possible}

and the following set of facts

> Facts = {Gram_negative_rods **is** definite, lactation **is** definite, Bacterian_infection **is** definite}

given the question *Treatment_with_ciprofloxacine?* made by another module M′ we can see the different answers obtained by a classical procedure and by the proposed one:

> Classical answer = {Treatment_with_ciprofloxacine **is** very_possible}

> Proposed answer = {Treatment_with_ciprofloxacine **is** possible, Stop_lactation **is** definite}

The mechanism of computing classical answers is to look for a proof to the question. This proof will trivially be obtained by a modus ponens application:

if Gram_negative_rods then Treatment_with_ciprofloxacine is possible
Gram_negative_rods is definitive

Treatment_with_ciprofloxacine is possible

In our proposal, the set of rules related to Treatment_with_cipro-
floxacine is obtained first:

{if Treatment_with_ciprofloxacine and lactation then Stop_lactation is
definitive
if Gram_negative_rods then Treatment_with_ciprofloxacine is poss-
ible}

then using the set of known facts, rules will be partially evaluated to
obtain the reduced final set of formulas:

{Treatment_with_ciprofloxacine is possible, Stop_lactation is definite}

Example 2: Consider the same set of rules from the previous example
and the following set of facts:

Facts = {Gram_negative_rods is definite, lactation is unknown, Bac-
terian_infection is definite}

then the classical and proposed answers will be:

Classical answer = {Treatment_with_ciprofloxacine is very_possible}

Proposed answer = {Treatment_with_ciprofloxacine is possible, if lactation then Stop_lactation is definite}

In this second case the classical evaluation provides the same result as
in the previous example but in our proposal a different final set of
formulas will be provided. This set is different because the fact
lactation is unknown and then the third rule cannot be applied:

{Treatment_with_ciprofloxacine is possible, if lactation then Stop_
lactation is definite}

Finally, we have to remark that the set of formulas computed in
a module M as an answer to a question can eventually be evaluated in
the module M' that receives them. To do it safely, it is necessary to
have:

1. A mechanism of renaming formulas that avoids undesired
   crashings of symbols of both modules (M and M').
2. An inference preserving relation between the different local
   logics of modules M and M'.

These points will be developed in this paper. In Section 2 a description of the modular MILORD language is presented. Particularly we show how to define local logics. The desired communication behavior of modules is obtained by an algorithm based on partial evaluation of rules. The overall description of this algorithm will be presented in Section 3. Section 4 is devoted to the analysis of the inference preserving relation between local logics. In the rest of this section we point out the need of having different local logics associated to modules and we introduce some general requirements that mappings between local logics should fulfill.

1.2. Uncertainty Management in Modular Systems: Local Logics

Psychological experiments (Kuipers et al., 1988; Fox, 1989) show that human problem solvers do not use numbers to deal with uncertainty and that the way they manage it is situation dependent. These requirements were partially satisfied in the MILORD system in the sense that the treatment of uncertainty was based on different operators defined over a set of linguistic terms describing the global verbal scale the experts use to express degrees of uncertainty (Godo et al., 1989). However, the modular structure of the MILORD extension, together with this approach to uncertainty management, allows us to define in a natural way local uncertainty calculi attached to each module, in such a way that the knowledge adequation process can also be applied to the uncertainty management. The interest in having different uncertainty calculi in a KB becomes clearer when expert systems involving several human experts have to be built.

On the other hand, the need of communication among modules with different local uncertainty calculi has led us to analyze the requirements that a correspondence between uncertainty calculi must fulfill. Uncertainty calculi can be considered as inference mechanisms defining logical entailment relationships. Therefore the correspondences (or communications) between different calculi can be analyzed as mappings between different entailment systems. This issue is introduced below.

1.3. Mappings between Different Local Logics

Let M and M' be two modules and $(L, \vdash)$ and $(L', \vdash')$ their corresponding logics, L and L' standing for the languages and $\vdash$ and

$\vdash'$ for the entailment relations defined on L and L', respectively. To establish a correspondence from module M to module M', a mapping $H: L \to L'$ relating their languages is needed. In the following we will analyze some natural requirements for the mapping H with respect to the entailment system $\vdash$ and $\vdash'$. Henceforth, Γ and e will denote a set of formulas and a formula of L, respectively.

RQ-1: *If $\Gamma \vdash e$, then $H(\Gamma) \vdash' H(e)$*

With this requirement we assure that for every formula deducible from a set of formulas Γ in M, its correspondent formula in M', by the mapping $H(e)$, will also be deducible in M' from the correspondent formulas of $H(\Gamma)$. In other words, there is no inferential power lost when translating from M to M' through a mapping H satisfying **RQ-1**. Nevertheless, the main drawback of requirement **RQ-1** is that it does not forbid to deduce from $H(\Gamma)$, in M', formulas that are not translations of any formula deducible from Γ in M. The property means that, in the case of modules representing different experts, an expert E' related to M', using knowledge coming from an expert E related to M, will be able to deduce the same facts as E, but not only those facts.

RQ-2: *If $H(\Gamma) \vdash' H(e)$, then $\Gamma \vdash e$*

This is the inverse requirement of **RQ-1**. So, in this case all deductions in M' involving only translated formulas from M are translations of deductions in M, or equivalently if a fact is not deducible in M, then its correspondent fact in M' will not be deducible from the translated knowledge.

RQ-3: *If $H(\Gamma) \vdash' e'$, then there exists e such that $\Gamma \vdash e$ and $H(e) \vdash' e'$*

This requirement assures that every formula deducible from $H(\Gamma)$ in M' must be in agreement with what can be deduced from Γ in M. This requirement is slightly different from **RQ-2**, in the sense that it is not necessary that e' be exactly a translation of a deducible formula e from Γ, but only something deducible from such a translation. In the framework of logics for uncertainty management, e' can be interpreted as "weaker" from of e, i.e., a formula expressing more uncertainty than e.

It is worth noticing that, if C denotes the consequence operator with respect to an entailment system $(L, \vdash)$, that is, $C(\Gamma) = \{e \in L \mid \Gamma \vdash e\}$ for all sets of formulas Γ, then the requirements **RQ-1** and **RQ-2** can be rewritten in the following way:

RQ-1: $H(C(\Gamma)) \subset C'(H(\Gamma))$

RQ-2: $C'(H(\Gamma)) \subset H(C(\Gamma))$

C' being the consequence operator associated to the entailment system $(L', \vdash')$.

2. MILORD MODULAR LANGUAGE

In this section we describe two main components of the MILORD language. First, the king of fuzzy logics associated to MILORD'S uncertainty management system. Second, the modular organization of KBs. A more detailed description of the modular system can be found in (Sierra and Agustí–Cullell, 1991).

2.1. Uncertainty Management in MILORD: A Fuzzy Logic Approach

The uncertainty management approach used in MILORD has the following characteristics:

1. The expert defines a set of linguistic terms expressing uncertainty that will be the verbal scale he will use to weight facts and rules.
2. The set of linguistic terms is supposed to be at least partially ordered according to the amount of uncertainty they express, with the Boolean "true" and "false" as their maximum and minimum elements, respectively.
3. The combination and propagation of uncertainty is performed by operators defined over the set of linguistic terms, basically the conjunction, disjunction, negation and detachment operators. A method for the elicitation of these operators from the expert has been proposed in López de Mántaras et al. (1990). The main difference of this approach with respect to previous ones is that no underlying numerical representation of the linguistic terms is required. Linguistic terms are treated as mere labels. As it has been already pointed out, the only a priori requirement is that these labels should represent an ordered set of expressions about uncertainty. For each logical connective, a set of desirable properties of the corresponding operator is listed. Nevertheless,

many of these properties are a finite counterpart of those of the uncertainty calculi based on t-norms and t-conorms, which are in turn the basis of the usual $[0,1]$-valued systems underlying fuzzy sets theory. The listed properties act as constraints on the set of possible solutions. In this way, all operators fulfilling them are generated. Finally, the expert may select the one he thinks fits better his own style of uncertainty management in the current task. This approach has been implemented by formulating it as a constraint satisfaction problem.

These three characteristics make clear that the logics associated to the MILORD uncertainty management are a class of finite multiple-valued logics (Rescher, 1969), taking the linguistic terms as truth-values and the operators as the interpretations of the logical connectives. In other words, each linguistic term set together with its set of operators defines a truth-values algebra and thus a corresponding multiple-valued logic. In Agustí-Cullell et al. (1990), these logics have been analyzed and formalized from the semantic point of view in a more general framework.

Following this line, the MILORD multiple-valued logics are defined by:

- An **algebra of truth-values**: a finite algebra
  $A = \langle A_n, 0, 1, N, T, I \rangle$ such that:

  (1) The set of truth-values A_n is a chain[1] represented by

  $$0 = a_0 < a_1 < ... < a_{n-1} = 1,$$

  where **0** and **1** are the common minimum and maximum elements of all chains respectively.

  (2) The negation operator N is a unary operation such that the following properties hold:

  N1: *if* $a < b$, *then* $N(a) > N(b)$

  N2: $N^2 = $ Id, i.e. $N(N(a)) = a$

  The only negation operator satisfying N1 and N2 is defined by $N(a_i) = a_{n-1-i}$.

---

[1] Usually the set of truth-values A_n stands for a totally ordered set of linguistic terms that the expert uses to express uncertainty, but nothing changes if it is only partially ordered.

(3) The "and" operation T is any binary operation such that the following properties hold:

T1: $T(a, b) = T(b, a)$
T2: $T(a, T(b, c)) = T(T(a, b), c)$
T3: $T(0, a) = 0$
T4: $T(1, a) = a$
T5: if $a \leqslant b$, then $T(a, c) \leqslant T(b, c)$, for all c

Note that in the unit interval these properties define t-norms if we add the condition of continuity.

(4) The implication operator is defined by residuation with respect to T:

$$I(a, b) = \text{Max} \{c \in A_n : T(a, c) \leqslant b\}$$

i.e., I is the finite counterpart of an R-implication generated by a t-norm.

- A set of **Connectives**: not ($\neg$), and (&), implication ($\rightarrow$).
- A set of **Sentences**: a sentence is a pair of classical-like propositional sentences and an interval of truth-values. The classical-like propositional sentences are built from a set of atomic symbols and the above set of connectives. However, the sentences used in MILORD are of the following types only:

  (p_1, V)
  $(p_1 \& p_2 \& \dots \& p_n, V)$
  $(p_1 \& p_2 \& \dots \& p_n \rightarrow q, V)$

  where $p_1, \dots, p_n$ are literals (an atom or the negation of an atom), q is an atomic sentence, and V is an interval of truth-values. For each truth-values algebra A, L_A will stand for the set of sentences with intervals of truth-values belonging to A.
- **Models**: are defined by valuations, i.e., mappings ρ from the first components of sentences to A_n provided that:

  $\rho(\neg p) = N(\rho(p))$
  $\rho(p_1 \& p_2) = T(\rho(p_1), \rho(p_2))$
  $\rho(p \rightarrow q) = I(\rho(p), \rho(q))$

- **Satisfaction Relation**: between models and sentences is defined by:

$M\rho \models (p, V)$ if and only if $\rho(p) \in V$,

where $M\rho$ stands for the model defined by a valuation ρ.

- **Entailment system**: the minimal entailment determined by

(1) the following set of axioms:

(A-1) $((p_1 \& p_2) \& p_3 \rightarrow p_1 \& (p_2 \& p_3), 1)$
(A-2) $(p_1 \& (p_2 \& p_3) \rightarrow (p_1 \& p_2) \& p_3, 1)$
(A-3) $(p_1 \& p_2 \rightarrow p_2 \& p_1, 1)$
(A-4) $(\neg\neg p \rightarrow p, 1)$

(2) the following inference rules, which are sound with respect to the satisfaction relation (Agustí-Cullell et al., 1990):

(RI-1) WEAKENING: $\Gamma, (p, V) \vdash (p, V')$, where $V \subseteq V'$ and Γ is a set of sentences,

(RI-2) NOT-introduction: $(p, V) \vdash (\neg p, N(V))$,

(RI-3) AND-introduction: $(p_1, V_1), (p_2, V_2) \vdash (p_1 \& p_2, T(V_1, V_2))$,

(RI-4) MODUS PONENS: $(p_1, V_1), (p_1 \rightarrow q_1, V_2) \vdash$
$\vdash (q_2, MP(V_1, V_2))$, being for each a and b of A_n

$$MP(a, b) = \begin{cases} \Phi, & \text{if } a \text{ and } b \text{ are inconsistent} \\ [a, 1] & \text{if } b = 1 \\ T(a, b), & \text{otherwise} \end{cases}$$

where a and b are said to be inconsistent if there exist no c such that $I(a, c) = b$.

Note that these inference rules are the only ones that the inference engine will need when working on sets of sentences of the above specified types, very common in rule-based ES. However, instead of rule RI-4, the MILORD inference engine uses the following inference rule:

(RI-4') MILORD MODUS PONENS: $(p_1, V_1), (p_1 \rightarrow q_1, V) \vdash$
$\vdash (q_2, T(V_1, V_2))$

Notice that, although it is correct for instance in the common case of upper intervals of truth values, from a logical point of view this inference rule is not sound in general with respect to the semantics defined above. Nevertheless, it is well known that from the cognitive point of view detachment operators share the same properties as those required for conjunction operators (Bonissone, 1987). These arguments together with self-evident computational reasons have led us to implement the inference rule RI-4' instead of RI-4. Therefore, from now on, given a truth-values algebra A we will denote by $(L_A, \vdash_A)$

the local fuzzy logic whose language is L_4 and its entailment relation is the minimal one determined by the axioms A-1, A-2, A-3 and A-4, and inference rules RI-1, RI-2, RI-3 and RI-4'.

The disjunction operator needed for parallel combination is obtained from the negation and conjunction by duality using the De Morgan laws. For these reasons, and from the deductive point of view, only the ordered set of truth-values (linguistic terms) and the conjunction operator should be specified in the local logics declaration of a module (see Section 2.2). In the case of a not totally ordered set of truth-values, the negation operator should also be specified.

Although MILORD's multiple-valued logics allow an expert to represent uncertainty by assigning intervals of truth values to rules and facts, in most cases this expressive power is not necessary from the point of view of experts. This expressive power is fully exploited in the definition of mappings between local logics (see Section 4). The intervals assigned to rules and facts in MILORD are represented by pairs of linguistic terms, or example [*moderately possible, very possible*]. In most cases experts use degenerated intervals, for example [*very possible, very possible*], which can be represented by a single truth value, i.e., *very possible*. This is the case with the examples used throughout the paper.

2.2. Modules

As it has already been mentioned, the basic KB units written in MILORD are the modules. These are hierarchically organized, and are composed of a set of importation, exportation, rule, control, meta-rule and submodule declarations. The Import/Export interface establishes the input/output behavior of the module and the declaration of the submodules settles the hierarchic structure of the KB. The declaration of submodules is identical in every aspect to the declaration of the modules (see the modules in Table 27.1 and their declaration as submodules in Table 27.3). To access the exported facts of a submodule a prefix mechanism is used. An exported fact of a submodule is identified by three components: (1) a path of module names indicating how to access the fact in the hierarchy of modules, (2) a slash "/", and (3) the name of the fact, i.e.: $name_1 / name_2 / ... / name_n / fact\_name$ (see for instance R001 in module Gram in Table 27.3).

Table 27.1. Module definitions in MILORD

```
Module Respiratory_Diagnosis =
  Begin
      Import Bact_Pneumonia,Influenz_superinf, Aspiration_Pn, Cronic_Pn
      Export Bact_Pneumonia,Influenz_superinf, Aspiration_Pn, Cronic_Pn
      Deductive knowledge
          Dictionary: not defined here
          Inference system:
              Truth values = (false, true)
                  Connectives:
                      Conjunction: ((false, false) (false, true))
                      Disjunction: ((false, true) (true, true))
      end deductive
  end

Module Type_of_Infection =
  Begin
      Import Nosocomial, Extrahospitalary
      Export Nosocomial, Extrahospitalary
      Deductive knowledge
          Dictionary: not defined here
          Inference system:
              Truth values = (false, true)
                  Connectives:
                      Conjunction: ((false, false) (false, true))
                      Disjunction: ((false, true) (true, true))
      end deductive
  end
```

The language provides three basic mechanisms of module manipulation:

1. Composition of modules through the declaration of submodules,
2. Refinement of modules, and
3. Composition of modules through operators defined by the user via generic modules definition.

Module refinements is a mechanism that allows to incrementally construct knowledge bases (Sierra and Agustí-Cullell, 1991). This paper addresses the locality and communication aspects of different uncertainty calculi, but not the incremental construction of knowledge bases. Therefore the refinement mechanism is not explained.

Intuitively, the semantics of a module is a module identifier that can be referenced by the other modules and a piece of code whose main functionalities are shown below. The most basic elements are the same as in previous versions of MILORD (Godo et al., 1987; Sierra,

1989), i.e., facts of order $0+$, production rules, and meta-rules. Table 27.2 exemplifies the primitive declarations outlined in this section.

2.2.1. Import Declarations

Imported facts are those whose values are obtained at run time from the user. These facts are declared by:

Import $fact_1$, $fact_2$, ..., $fact_n$

The values of these facts are obtained when needed in the evaluation of a rule. With this declaration we define the input interface of the module that contains it. The code of a module containing an import declaration will be allowed only to ask for values of imported facts. They will be obtained from the user.

2.2.2. Export Declarations

Exported facts are those facts that can be used by other modules. All exported facts must be conclusions of rules in the module or else be imported by the module. They are declared by:

Export $fact_1$, $fact_2$, ..., $fact_n$

Conclusions of rules and imported facts not mentioned in the export declaration are hidden to the rest of the modules, i.e., they cannot be used in the body of the rest of the modules. This is the only mandatory declaration in the construction of a module. A module with no exported facts is meaningless. The code of a module containing an export declaration will provide means to answer questions about the values of the exported facts only. Also visible submodules will provide code with the same characteristics that will be added to the code of the module that contains them.

Table 27.1 contains two modules that just import predicates (asking to the users) and export them. These modules will be used later on in the examples of the paper.

2.2.3. Kernel Declarations

The kernel of a module is made up of two components called *deductive knowledge* and *control knowledge*. Deductive knowledge

Table 27.2. Module with a nonempty deductive component

```
Module Previous_Treatment =
  Begin
    Import Prev_Treat
    Export Penicilin, Tetracycline
    Deductive knowledge
      Dictionary: not defined here
      Rules:
        R001 If Prev_Treat = (Peni) then conclude Penicilin is sure
        R002 If Prev_Treat = (Peni) then conclude Tetracycline is impossible
      Inference system:
        Truth values = (impossible, sure)
          Connectives:
            Conjunction: (  (impossible,  impossible)
                            (impossible,  sure))
            Disjunction: (  (impossible,  sure)
                            (sure,        sure)
    end deductive
  end
```

includes the rules and local logics declarations. Control knowledge is represented by means of a meta-language, which acts by reflection over the deductive knowledge and the module hierarchy. The current implementation of the meta-language allows the definition of meta-rules and the definition of some control parameters (*evaluation type*). These components of MILORD are explained in Sierra and Agustí-Cullell (1991). Table 27.2 shows an example of module definition containing rule and logic declarations.

2.2.4. Local Logics Declarations

In the deductive knowledge of a module it is possible to define three main components of an *inference system*. This declaration defines (1) the set of linguistic certainty terms used in weighting facts, rules, and meta-rules, (2) a renaming mapping between the term set of the module and the term sets of its submodules, if any, and (3) the connective operators used to combine and propagate the linguistic terms when making inference. A more complete description can be found in Sierra and Agustí-Cullell (1991) and Agustí et al. (1991). In Table 27.3 there is an example of module definitions showing how local logics are defined. Module *Gram* contains several renaming functions. Each one relates the logic of a submodule with the local logic of *Gram*. To distinguish the different functions we use the same

Table 27.3. Example of module local logic declarations in MILORD

```
Module Gram_of_Sputum =
  Begin
      Import Sputum_clas, Sputum_Gram
      Export End, Gram_yes, DCGP, CGPC, CGPR, BGN, CBGN
      Deductive knowledge
      Dictionary: not defined here
      Rules:
          R001 If Sputum_clas = (Grup_1 or Grup_2 or Grup_3)
                  then conclude Sputum_ok is true
          R002 If Sputum_clas = (Grup_4 or Grup_5 or Grup_6)
                  then conclude Sputum_not_ok is true
          R003 If Sputum_ok then conclude Gram_yes is true
          R004 If Sputum_not_ok then conclude End is true
          R005 If Sputum_Gram = (DCGP_MC)
                  then conclude DCGP is true
          R006 If Sputum_Gram = (DCGP_MC)
                  then conclude CGPC is unlikely
          R007 If Sputum_Gram = (CGPC_MC)
                  then conclude CGPC is likely
          R008 If Sputum_Gram = (CGPC_MC)
                  then conclude DCGP is unlikely
          R009 If Sputum_Gram = (CGPR_MC)
                  then conclude CGPR is true
          R010 If Sputum_Gram = (BGN_MC) then conclude BGN is likely
          R011 If Sputum_Gram = (CBGN_MC)
                  then conclude CBGN is likely
      Inference system:
          Truth values = (false, unlikely, may_be, likely, true)
          Connectives:
          Conjunction:
          (   (false,     false,     false,     false,     false)
              (false,     false,     unlikely,  unlikely,  unlikely)
              (false,     unlikely,  may_be,    may_be,    may_be)
              (false,     unlikely,  may_be,    may_be,    likely)
              (false,     unlikely,  may_be,    likely,    true))
          Disjunction:
          (   (false,     unlikely,  may_be,    likely,    true)
              (unlikely,  may_be,    may_be,    likely,    true)
              (may_be,    may_be,    may_be,    likely,    true)
              (likely,    likely,    likely,    true,      true)
              (true,      true,      true,      true,      true))
      end deductive
  end
```

Module Gram =
  Begin
      Module D = Resiratory_Diagnosis
      Module T = Type_of_Infection
      Module P = Previous_Treatment
      Module S = Gram_of_Sputum
      Export Pneumococcus, Haemophilus, Staphylococcus, Enterobacteria
      Deductive knowledge
        Dictionary: ; *not defined here.*
      Rules:
          R001 **If** S/DCGP **then conclude** Pneumococcus **is** possible
          R002 **If** S/DCGP **and**D/Bact_Pneumonia
              then conclude Pneumococcus **is** very_possible
          R003 **If** S/BGN **and** D/Aspiration_Pneumonia **and** T/Nosocomial
              then conclude Enterobacteria **is** quite_possible
          R004 **If** S/CBGN **and** P/Penicilin
              then conclude Haemophilus **is** sure
      Inference system:
        Truth values = (impossible, few_possible, sligh._possible, possible,
                  quite possible, very possible, sure)

        Renaming =
          D/False   ⇒ impossible
          D/True   ⇒ sure
          T/Flase   ⇒ impossible
          T/True   ⇒ sure
          P/impossible ⇒ impossible
          P/sure   ⇒ sure
          S/false   ⇒ impossible
          S/unlikely   ⇒ [impossible, possible]
          S/may_be   ⇒ possible
          S/likely   ⇒ [possible, sure]
          S/true   ⇒ sure
      Connectives:
      Conjunction:
((impossible,impossible,impossible,impossible,impossible,impossible,impossible)
(impossible,few_possible,few_possible,few_possible,few_possible,few_possible,
few_possible)
(impossible,few_possible,sligh._possible,sligh._possible,sligh._possible,sligh._
_possible,sligh._possible,sligh._possible)
(impossible,few_possible,sligh._possible,possible,possible,possible,possible)
(impossible,few_possible,sligh._possible,possible,quite_possible,quite_possible,quite
_possible)
(impossible,few_possble,sligh._possible,possible,quite_possible,very_possible,very_
posible)
(impossible,few_possible,sligh._possible,possible,quite_possible,very_possible,sure))
        Disjunction:
((impossible,few_possible,sligh._possible,possible,quite_possible,very_possible,sure)
(few_possible,few_possible,sligh._possible,possible,quite_possible,very_possible,
sure)

```
(sligh._possible,sligh._possible,sligh._possible,possible,quite_possible,very_possible,
  sure)
(possible,possible,possible,possible,quite_possible,very_possible,sure)
(quite_possible,quite_possible,quite_possible,quite_possible,quite_possible,very_
  possible,sure)
(very_possible,very_possible,very_possible,very_possible,very_possible,very_
  possible,sure)
(sure,sure,sure,sure,sure,sure,sure))
        end deductive
    end
```

prefixing mechanism used for exported facts. Connectives operators are matrices defined on the linguistic certainty terms and they are represented by the list of their rows.

2.3. Generic Modules

The definition of generic modules opens to the user the possibility of defining specific operations of composition. This standard technique consists of isolating a piece of a program, or module, from its context and then abstracting it by specifying:

1. Those modules that the abstracted module may depend on (requirements or import interface).
2. The contribution of the abstracted module to the rest of the program (results or export interface). The internal definition of this abstracted module is made in terms of the import interfaces.

The obvious example of this technique is functional programming, where such abstractions form the basic program units. The functional body defines how to compute the output (results) in terms of the input (requirements). For modular programming we abstract encapsulated sets of the underlying language primitive declarations. Such abstractions are in fact program-valued functions and are called parametric or generic modules (the parameter type being the import interfaces). When applied to particular modules that satisfy their import interfaces, they result in a new module that satisfies their export interface. Generic modules represent the reusable components of an expert system. For instance, the methods used to decompose a task in its subtasks can be represented by generic modules. Then, large KB systems can be built from a library of generic modules by applying them to nongeneric ones.

An example of definition of generic modules is shown in Table 27.4. Imagine we make an abstraction of the module *Gram* in Table 27.3 on

Table 27.4. Example of generic module definition

```
Module Sample =
  Begin
       Export End, Gram_yes, DCGP, CGPC, CGPR, BGN, CBGN
  End
Module Global_Gram (X : Sample) =
  Begin
       Module D = Respiratory Diagnosis
       Module T = Type_of_Infection
       Module P = Previous_Treatment
       Export  Pneumococcus, Haemophilus, Enterobacteria
       Deductive knowledge
          Rules:
             R001 If X/DCGP then conclude Pneumococcus is possible
             R002 If X/DCGP andD/Bact_Pneumonia
                    then conclude Pneumococcus is very_possible
             R003 If X/BGN and D/Aspiration_Pneumonia and T/Nosocomial
                    then conclude Enterobacteria is quite_possible
             R004 If X/CBGN and P/penicilin
                    then conclude Haemophilus is sure
       Inference system:
          Truth values = (impossible, few_possible, sligh._possible, possible,
                          quite_possible, very_possible,sure)
             Renaming =
                 D/False       ⇒ impossible
                 D/True        ⇒ sure
                 T/False       ⇒ impossible
                 T/True        ⇒ sure
                 P/impossible  ⇒ impossible
                 P/sure        ⇒ sure
                 X/false       ⇒ impossible
                 X/unlikely    ⇒ [impossible, possible]
                 X/may_be      ⇒ possible
                 X/likely      ⇒ [possible, sure]
                 X/true        ⇒ sure
             Connectives:
                 Conjunction: ; the same table defined in Table 3.
                 Disjunction: ; the same table defined in Table 3.
  end
```

the submodule S. We build a parametric module applicable to any module that satisfies the same output interface that module S satisfies (call this interface module *Sample*). The operation ":" which appears in the example of Table 27.4 checks the satisfaction of interfaces by modules. Table 27.4 shows a generic module and it can be seen that the module *Gram* of Table 27.3 can be obtained now by the application of the generic module *Global_gram* to the module *Gram_of_sputum* in the declaration:

Module Gram = Global_Gram(gram_of_sputum)

3. PARTIAL EVALUATION OF MODULES

In this section we shall consider how the deduction mechanism of a module is affected when a complex communication with another module, such as the one described in Section 1.1, is required. When a question is made to a module, the interpreter goes through an iterative process until it has gathered enough information from the user and/or from other modules to answer it. Each step of the iteration starts with a question to the user or to a submodule. The answer to this question is obtained by the interpreter using the same deduction mechanism on the asked submodules. The answer obtained is then translated from the local logics of the answering module to the local logics of the asking module. The translation uses the local logics renaming function of the asking module to change the certainty values and the syntax of the answered formulas. Some details are given in the example below. Once the translated answers are incorporated to the asking module, this module is partially evaluated taking into account the answers. We use partial evaluation (Venken, 1984; Gallagher, 1986) to reduce a module depending on a given question to a new module where the dependencies have been solved using the answers given to that question. After each partial evaluation the iteration proceeds with the next question. To finally answer the initial question the interpreter selects from the last partial evaluation made the subset of formulas that are in a deductive path starting from or going to the initial question. Next, we explain the algorithm by means of an example.

Example: Let's consider the module *Global_culture* in Table 27.5.

Suppose that the question *Pneumococcus_isolation*? is asked to the module *Global_culture*. Below we exemplify the iterative process of questions, translations, partial evaluations, and the final selection of the answer. For the sake of clarity we will not cover the recursive call of the algorithm on the submodules.

Table 27.5. Simplified module *Global_culture* from the Bacter-IA expert system

---

Module global_culture =
  Begin
    Module G = Gram
    Module D = Respiratory_diagnosis
    Module C = Culture_of_sputum
    Export Pneumococcus_isolation, Haemophilus_isolation,
            Staphylococcus_isolation, No_microorganism_isolation,
            antibiogram
    Import Multiresistant_microorganism
    Deductive knowledge
      Dictionary:
        Predicates:
        ; only an extract of the dictionary is presented
        More_incubation = **Name:** "more time of culture incubation is
                     recommended until discarc is negative"
        Antibiogram = **Name:** "Make appropriate antimicrobial tests
                  because of the high prevalence of resistant
                  microorganisms to antibiotics in our country"
        Selective_report = **Name:** "Antimicrobial agents should be reported
                   only selectively"
        Physician_contact = **Name:** "Contact with physician for appropriate
                   antimicrobial therapy."
      Rules:
        R001 **if** G/Pneumococcus **and** C/Pneumococcus
            then conclude Pneumococcus_isolation **is** sure
        R002 **if** G/Haemophilus **and** C/Haemophilus **and** D/Chronic_
            Bronchitis **then conclude** Haemophilus_isolation **is** sure
        ...
        R0025 **if** C/no isolation
            then conclude No_microorganism_isolation **is** very_possible
        R0026 **if** no_microorganism_isolation
            then conclude more_incubation **is** sure
        R0027 **if** Pneumococcus_isolation
            then conclude Antibiogram **is** sure
        R0028 **if** Haemophilus_isolation **then conclude** Antibiogram **is** sure
        R0029 **if** Antibiogram **and** Multiresistant_microorganism
            then conclude Physician_contact **is** sure
    Inference system:
      Truth values = (impossible, few_possible, sligh._possible, possible,
                quite_possible, very_possible, sure)
      Renaming =
        D/False   ⇒ impossible
        D/True   ⇒ sure
        C/False   ⇒ impossible
        C/True   ⇒ sure
        G/impossible   ⇒ impossible

G/few_possible   ⇒ few_impossible
G/sligh._possible ⇒ sligh._possible
G/possible   ⇒ possible
G/quite_possible ⇒ quite_possible
G/very_possible   ⇒ very_possible
G/sure   ⇒ sure
Connectives:
Conjunction: ; *the same table defined in Table 3.*
Disjunction: ; *the same table defined in Table 3.*
end deductive
end

Initial set of rules:

R001 if G/Pneumococcus and C/Pneumococcus
    then conclude Pneumococcus_isolation is sure
R002 if G/Haemophilus and C/Haemophilus and D/Chronic_
    Bronchitis then conclude Haemophilus_isolation is sure
...
R0025 if C/no isolation
    then conclude No_microorganism_isolation is very_possible
R0026 if no_microorganism_isolation
    then conclude more_incubation is sure
R0027 if Pneumococcus_isolation
    then conclude Antibiogram is sure
R0028 if Haemophilus_isolation then conclude Antibiogram is sure
R0029 if Antibiogram and Multiresistant_microorganism
    then conclude Physician_contact is sure

First question: G/Pneumococcus
Answer: {G/Pneumococcus is possible}
Translation: {G/Pneumococcus is possible}
Partial evaluation: Rules affected by partial evaluation are {R001}

G/Pneumococcus is possible
R001 if C/Pneumococcus
    then conclude Pneumococcus_isolation is possible
R002 if G/Haemophilus and C/Haemophilus and D/Chronic_
    Bronchitis then conclude Haemophilus_isolation is sure
...
R0025 if C/no isolation
    then conclude No_microorganism_isolation is very_possible
R0026 if no_microorganism_isolation
    then conclude more_incubation is sure
R0027 if Pneumococcus_isolation
    then conclude Antibiogram is sure
R0028 if Haemophilus_isolation then conclude Antibiogram is sure
R0029 if Antibiogram and Multiresistant_microorganism
    then conclude Physician_contact is sure

Second question: C/Pneumococcus
Answer: {C/Pneumococcus is true}
Translation: {C/Pneumococcus is sure}
Partial evaluation: Rules affected by partial evaluation are {R001, R0027, R0029}

> G/Pneumococcus is possible
> C/Pneumococcus is sure
> Pneumococcus_isolation is possible
> Antibiogram is possible
> R002 if G/Haemophilus and C/Haemophilus and D/Chronic_
>   Bronchitis then conclude Haemophilus_isolation is sure
>
> ...
> R0025 if C/no isolation
>   then conclude No_microorganism_isolation is very_possible
> R0026 if no_microorganism_isolation
>   then conclude more_incubation is sure
> R0028 if Haemophilus_isolation then conclude Antibiogram is sure
> R0029 if Antibiogram and Multiresistant_microorganism
>   then conclude Physician_contact is possible

Selection:

> Pneumococcus_isolation is possible
> Antibiogram is possible
> if Multiresistant_microorganism
>   then conclude Physician_contact is possible

In Table 27.6, other questions to the *Global_culture* and possible answers obtained by partial evaluation are shown:

Table 27.6. Questions and possible answers obtained by partial evaluation of module *Global_culture*

Questions	Possible answers
Pneumococcus_isolation?	{ Pneumococcus_isolation is sure, antibiogram is sure }
Staphylococcus_isolation?	{ Staphylococcus_isolation is very_possible }
Haemophilus_isolation?	{ if Global_culture/G/Haemophilus and Global_culture/C/Haemophilus and Global_culture/D/Chronic_Bronchitis then conclude Haemophilus_isolation is sure if Haemophilus_isolation then conclude is sure if Antibiogram and Multiresistant_ microorganism then conclude Physician_ contact is sure }

4. RELATING MILORD'S LOCAL LOGICS

As it has already been noted, to establish communication between the modules is necessary to consider which kind of relation between their corresponding uncertainty logics is required. Some possible requirements to relate such logics as entailment systems have been proposed in the introductory Section 1.3. On the other hand, the different uncertainty calculi that can be defined in the modular extension of MILORD have been described and defined (Section 2.1) as the minimal entailment systems determined by four axioms (A-1, A-2, A-3, A-4) and four inference rules (RI-1, RI-2, RI-3, RI-4') which depend on the particular truth-value algebras. In this section we will focus on the analysis of which conditions have to be asked to the module renaming functions (in the local logics declarations) in order to satisfy the above mentioned requirements to map different MILORD entailment systems.

Remember that a truth-value algebra $A = \langle A_n, 0, 1, N, T, I \rangle$ is composed by an ordered set of linguistic terms expressing uncertainty together with a negation, a conjunction and an implication operator. However, as long as the implication operator is not needed explicitly (but only implicitly in the modus ponens) in the formulation of the above mentioned inference rules, from now on we will consider truth-value algebras only with negation and conjunction operators.

Let $A = \langle A_n, 0, 1, N, T \rangle$ and $A' = \langle A_m, 0, 1, N', T' \rangle$ be two truth-value algebras. Let $(L_A, \vdash_A)$ and $(L_{A'}, \vdash_{A'})$ be their corresponding local logics as defined in Section 2.1. We are interested in mapping the entailment system $(L_{A'}, \vdash_A)$ into the entailment system $(L_A, \vdash_{A'})$ by means of module renaming functions (see Section 2.2.4) between linguistic terms sets. This means that we will only consider those mappings translating sentences from L_A to $L_{A'}$ that only involve translations of truth-values, i.e., any mapping $G: L_A \to L_{A'}$ will be defined as $G((e, V)) = (e, g(V))$, where g translates subsets of values of A_n to A_m, i.e., g is a mapping from 2^{A_n} to 2^{A_m}. However, if the natural condition $g(V) = \cup \{g(v), v \in V\}$ is required, then it is sufficient to have mappings $g: A_n \to 2^{A_m}$. In order to map the Boolean values into themselves, such a mapping g must fulfill $g(0) = 0$ and $g(1) = 1$. Moreover, it can be a natural requirement that $g(A_n) \subseteq I(A_m)$, where $I(A_m) = \{[a, b] \mid a, b \in A_n\}$, $[a, b] = \{x \mid x \in A_n, a \leqslant x \leqslant b\}$, is the set of intervals of A_m, that is, the translation of a value of A_n is not any subset of A_m but an interval. Note that $A_m \subseteq I(A_m)$ if we identify every element a of A_m with the interval $[a, a]$ of $I(A_m)$. It is also suitable to consider mappings g that preserve the uncertainty ordering of the linguistic term sets, i.e., $g(a) \leqslant^* g(b)$ if $a \leqslant b$, where the order in $I(A_m)$ is defined as

$$I_1 \leqslant^*_{DEF} I_2 \text{ iff for all } a \in I_1 \text{ and for all } b \in I_2, a \leqslant b$$

It is worth noticing that $(I(A_n), \leqslant^*)$ is only a partialy ordered set. Next we give a small example of an algebra of intervals generated by a truth-value algebra of four elements.

Example: Let $A = \{0 < a < b < 1\}$ be a chain of four elements. Then the set of intervals of A is $I(A) = \{[0, a], [0, b], [0, 1], [a, b], [a, 1], [b, 1], [0, 0], [a, a], [1, 1]\}$. Identifying every interval $[x, x]$ with the element x of A, the order relation on A and $I(A)$ can be represented by the graphs shown in Figure 27.1.

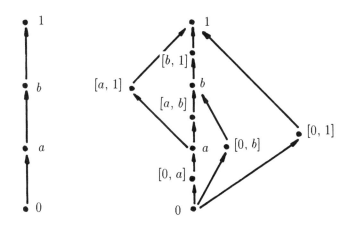

Figure 27.1.

In particular, from now on, given an order preserving mapping $h: A_n \rightarrow I(A_m)$ such that $h(0) = 0$ and $h(1) = 1$, we will denote by H the mapping $H: L_A \rightarrow L_{A'}$ defined by $H((e, V)) = (e, h(V))$, using the same notation for h and its extension from 2^{A_n} to 2^{A_m}. Observe that if $f: A_m \rightarrow A_n$ is an order preserving onto mapping, then it generates an order preserving mapping $h_f: A_n \rightarrow I(A_m)$ defined by $h_f(a) = f^{-1}(a)$.

Taking into account that deductions are performed by applying a finite sequence of inference rules RI-1, ..., RI-4', it is easy to observe that an entailment such as

$$(p_1, V_1), \ldots, (p_n, V_n) \vdash (e, V)$$

holds if and only if there exists $G = (G_1, G_2)$ such that $e = G_1(p_1, \ldots, p_n)$ and $V \supseteq G_2(V_1, \ldots, V_n)$, where G is a term representing the transformation by inference rules RI-2, RI-3 and RI-4' on the sentences in the premise. Thus, G_2 only involves the N and T operators. For instance, the deduction

$$(p, V_1), (r, V_2), (p \rightarrow q, V_3) \vdash (\neg r \,\&\, q, V_4)$$

has associated the following term G:

$$G[(p, V_1), (r, V_2), (p \rightarrow q, V_3)] \equiv \text{RI-3}\,[\text{RI-2}[(r, V_2)],$$

$$\text{RI-4'}\,[(p, V_1), (p \rightarrow q, V_3)]]$$

and thus,

$$G_1[p, r, p \rightarrow q] = \neg r \,\&\, q$$

and

$$G_2[V_1, V_2, V_3] = T(N(V_2), T(V_1, V_3))$$

Using this result, the next theorems give conditions for the mappings H to satisfy the requirements RQ-1, RQ-2, and RQ-3 (see Section 1.3).

Theorem 1: The mapping H satisfies the requirement RQ-1 if and only if the mapping h fulfills the following conditions:

1. $h(T(V_1, V_2)) \supseteq T'(h(V_1), h(V_2))$
2. $h(N(V)) = N'(h(V))$

Corollary 1: If $h(a) \in A_m$ for every a of A_n, then the mapping H satisfies the requirement RQ-1 if and only if the mapping h is a morphism with respect to the negation and conjunction operators.

Theorem 2: The mapping H satisfies the requirement RQ-2 provided that the mapping h fulfills the following conditions:

1. if $h(V_1) \subseteq h(V_2)$, then $V_1 \subseteq V_2$
2. $h(T(V_1, V_2)) \subseteq T'(h(V_1), h(V_2))$
3. $h(N(V)) = N'(h(V))$

Corollary 2: If $h(a) \in A_m$ for every a of A_n, then the mapping H satisfies the requirement RQ-2 provided that the mapping h is a monomorphism with respect to the negation and conjunction operators.

Corollary 3: Let $f: A_m \to A_n$ be an exhaustive order preserving mapping and let $h(a) = f^{-1}(a)$. Then the mapping H satisfies the requirement RQ-2 provided that the mapping f is a morphism with respect to the negation and conjunction operators.

Theorem 3: The mapping H satisfies the requirement RQ-3 provided that the mapping h fulfills the following conditions:

1. $h(T(V_1, V_2)) \subseteq T'(h(V_1), h(V_2))$
2. $h(N(V)) = N'(h(V))$

Corollary 4: If $h(a) \in A_m$ for every a of A_n, then the mapping H satisfies the requirement RQ-3 provided that the mapping h is a morphism with respect to the negation and conjunction operators.

From these results it is clear that if the mapping h is a morphism from A_n to A_m then requirements RQ-1 and RQ-3 are satisfied, and if h is a monomorphism then the requirement RQ-2 is also satisfied.

As an example, let's consider the renaming function from module *Gram_of_Sputum* to module *Gram* given in Table 27.3 (Section 2.2.4). If 0, 1, 2, 3 and 4 stand for *false, unlikely, may_be, likely* and *true*, respectively, and 0', 1', 2', 3', 4', 5' and 6' stand for *impossible, few_possible, slight_possible, possible,quite_possible, very_possible,* and *sure*, respectively, the conjunction operators T and T' are given by the following matrices:

T	0	1	2	3	4
0	0	0	0	0	0
1	0	0	1	1	1
2	0	1	2	2	2
3	0	1	2	2	3
4	0	1	2	3	4

T'	0'	1'	2'	3'	4'	5'	6'
0'	0'	0'	0'	0'	0'	0'	0'
1'	0'	1'	1'	1'	1'	1'	1'
2'	0'	1'	2'	2'	2'	2'	2'
3'	0'	1'	2'	3'	3'	3'	3'
4'	0'	1'	2'	3'	4'	4'	4'
5'	0'	1'	2'	3'	4'	5'	5'
6'	0'	1'	2'	3'	4'	5'	6'

Let's consider the algebras $A = \langle \{0, 1, 2, 3, 4\}, 0, 4, N, T \rangle$ and $A' = \langle \{0', 1', 2', 3', 4', 5', 6'\}, 0', 6', N', T' \rangle$ which are the algebras of truth-values of the local logics of modules *Gram_of_Sputum* and *Gram*, respectively. It can be checked that there is no morphism from

A to *A'*. However, the renaming function given in the module *Gram* declaration, that is, the mapping *h* defined by:

$$h(0) = 0'$$
$$h(1) = [0', 3']$$
$$h(2) = 3'$$
$$h(3) = [3', 6']$$
$$h(4) = 6'$$

fulfills the conditions required in Theorem 3, and thus the requirement RQ-3 for the communication between those modules is satisfied.

5. CONCLUSION

We have presented the modular MILORD language whose main characteristic is its modularity allowing to build structured knowledge bases by means of a hierarchy of modules. Such modularity allows us to associate different local uncertainty calculi to modules performing different subtasks. The interaction between modules with different uncertainty calculi has been analyzed and solutions are given to problems, including those due to interaction between modules involving not only the communication of certainty values but more complex communications of knowledge.

Keywords: modular languages, uncertainty management, fuzzy logics, expert systems

BIBLIOGRAPHY

Agustí-Cullell, J., F. Esteva, P. Garcia, and L. Godo. (1990). Formalizing multiple-valued logics as institutions. Short version in *Proceedings of Third International IPMU Conference,* Paris, pp. 355–357. Full version will appear in *Lecture Notes on Computer Science* in June 1991.

Agustí-Cullell, J. and C. Sierra. (1989). Adding generic modules to flat rule-based languages: A low cost approach. *Methodologies for Intelligent Systems,* Amsterdam: North Holland, pp. 43–52.

Alsina, C., E. Trillas, and L. Valverde. (1983). On some logical connectives for fuzzy set theory. *Journal of Mathematical Analysis and Applications,* 93, 15–26.

Bonissone, P. P. (1987). Summarizing and propagating uncertain information by triangular norms. *International Journal of Aproximate Reasoning*, 1, 71–101.

Dubois, D. and H. Prade. (1988). An introduction to possibilistic and fuzzy logics. In P. Smets et al. (eds.): *Non-Standard Logics for Automated Reasoning*. New York: Academic Press, pp. 287–326.

Fox, J. (1989). Symbolic decision procedures for knowledge based systems. In H. Adeli (ed.): *Knowledge Engeneering*. New York: McGraw Hill.

Gallagher, J. (1986). Transforming logic programs by specializing interpreters. In *Proc. of ECAI'86*. Brighton, July 1986, pp. 109–122.

Godo, L., R. López de Mántaras, C. Sierra, and A. Verdaguer. (1989). MILORD: The architecture and management of linguistically expressed uncertainty. *Int. Journal of Intelligent System*, 4, 471–501.

Kuipers, B., A. J. Moskowitz, and J. P. Kassirer. (1988). Critical decisions under uncertainty: Representation and structure. *Cognitive Science*, 12, 177–210.

López de Mántaras, R. (1990). *Approximate Reasoning Models*. Chichester: Ellis Horwood.

López de Mántaras, R., L. Godo, and R. Sangüesa. (1990). Connective operators elicitation for linguistic term sets. *Proc. Intl. Conference on Fuzzy Logic and Neural Networks*. Iizuka, Japan, pp. 729–733.

Rasiowa, H. (1974). *An Algebraic Approach to Non-Classical Logics*. Amsterdam: North Holland.

Rescher, N. (1969). *Many-valued Logic*. New York: McGraw-Hill.

Sierra, C. (1989). MILORD: Arquitectura multi-nivell per a sistemes experts en classificació. Ph. D. Universitat Politècnica de Catalunya, Barcelona.

Sierra, C. and J. Agustí-Cullell. (1991). COLAPSES: A methodology and a language for knowledge engineering. In *Proceedings Avignon'91*, in press.

Venken, R. (1984). A Prolog meta-interpreter for partial evaluation and its application to source transformation and query optimization. In *Proc. of ECAI'84*, Pisa, pp. 81–100.

Verdaguer, A. (1989). PNEUMON-IA; desenvolupament i validació d'un sistema expert d'ajuda al diagnòstic mèdic. Ph.D. Thesis, Universitat Autònoma de Barcelona.

28 Management of uncertainty in knowledge-based medical systems

M. E. COHEN
California State University
Department of Mathematics
Fresno, CA 93749, USA

D. L. HUDSON
University of California,
San Francisco
School of Medicine
Fresno, CA 93793, USA

Abstract. The handling of uncertainty in knowledge-based systems has progressed from the *ad hoc* techniques, which were originally incorporated into these systems fifteen years ago, to the incorporation of sophisticated techniques of approximate reasoning. Many issues remain, including theoretical concerns over the most advantageous approaches, as well as practical concerns in the actual implementation of these techniques in functioning expert systems. In this article, we will discuss several approaches to the handling of uncertainty in knowledge-based systems, and will emphasize problems encountered in the adaptation of these techniques to medical decision making. Specific examples of all techniques will be provided, along with their theoretical foundations.

1. INTRODUCTION

The introduction of the knowledge-based system in the 1970s represented a dramatic departure from traditional computer applications, which focused on computational, algorithmic structures (Armitage and Gehan, 1974; Patrick, 1970). This new symbolic approach offered a new paradigm for the establishment of computerized decision making systems that resembled human reasoning (Buchanan, Sutherland, and Feigenbaum, 1969). This approach caught almost immediate attention in medical applications (Shortliffe, Davis, Buchanan, and Feigenbaum, 1979) since, in general, medical decision making systems up to this point were less than satisfactory (Gorry, 1973; Blois, 1980). Along with these new symbolic representation systems, a new problem arose almost immediately– that of handling uncertain information. In fact, this aspect occupied much of the research for the implementation of the MYCIN, the first knowledge-based system in medicine (Shortliffe, 1976). The solution in MYCIN was the use of certainty factors to capture the idea that decisions, or in fact, contributing pieces of information, were not absolute (Shortliffe, 1975). The certainty factor approach, although giving good approximations in the MYCIN system, was based on an ad hoc approach. The development of the knowledge-based system at that time was in the domain of artificial intelligence research (Winston, 1977).

At approximately the ame time, work was progressing on the theoretical aspects of fuzzy logic (Zadeh, 1983), after the introduction of Zadeh's (1965) seminal paper. Initially, researchers in this field had little contact with this work on knowledge-based systems. In the last decade, these two fields have finally come together, with promising results (Yager, 1984; Bouchon, 1987; Dubois and Prade, 1989; Whalen and Schott, 1983). Well-founded theoretical techniques are now incorporated into knowledge-based systems to handle the inevitable uncertainty (Anderson, Bandler, Kohout, and Trayner, 1982; Adlassnig, 1982; Vila and Delgado, 1983; Esogbue and Elder, 1983).

A final problem remains to be solved in order to build knowledge-based systems that deal with uncertainty and are capable of dealing with practical problems. All approaches to dealing with uncertainty, whether they be ad hoc techniques such as certainty factors, or techniques incorporating fuzzy logic or other methods of approximate reasoning, require the determination of numerical parameters for certainty factors, degrees of membership, thresholds of substantiation, etc. In practice, determination of these factors proves to be quite difficult (Hudson and Cohen, 1987). In this article, methods for obtaining these factors are described (Cohen, Hudson, and Anderson, 1989b). Three cases are considered: the rule-based expert system, the connectionist expert system, and a combined system approach. These approaches are then illustrated with examples from medical decision making.

2. RULE-BASED EXPERT SYSTEMS

In the traditional expert system, there are a number of areas in which uncertainty must be handled, including the certainty with which the given rule is presumed to be applicable, the degree to which each antecedent of the rule is substantiated, and the degree to which each antecedent contributes to the substantiation of the rule. The original certainty factor approach attempted to address some, but not all, of these potential problems. These sources of uncertainty can be divided into two categories: uncertainties in the knowledge base itself, and uncertainties in the information provided for each case under analysis.

2.1. Uncertainty in the Knowledge Base

In order to get a comprehensive solution, the standard production rule format must be changed. Traditionally, all antecedents are assumed to contribute equally. In practice this is rarely true. Thus some kind of weighting must be defined that indicates the relative importance of each antecedent. Once this is accomplished, binary logic is no longer applicable, and techniques of approximate reasoning must be employed. A number of workers have addressed this problem (Kacprzyk, 1989; Yager, 1989; Zadeh, 1985) from a theoretical point of view. In general, some type of aggregating of information must be performed that determines to what degree the rule should be substantiated. Then it must be decided if the degree is sufficiently high to activate the rule. This in fact is an ideal application of fuzzy logic and fuzzy set theory. Many practical fuzzy control systems have been developed based on the use of fuzzy production rules (Togai, 1987), although most do not consider the unequal contribution of antecedents.

Sample Rule (Threshold. 75)

IF	Forced vital capacity is high	.7
	Bronchoscopy results are positive	.2
	Local symptoms are present	.1
THEN	Surgery is probably appropriate	
UNLESS	(Threshold .4)	
	Metastasis is present	.5
	Contraindications to surgery exist	.5

Figure 28.1. Modified production rule format

A modified production rule would take the form shown in Figure 28.1 Note that this production rule format also accommodates rules containing an UNLESS clause. Although a number of theoretical techniques are available for dealing with this structure, there are some practical considerations to be addressed. First, how are the relative weights of the antecedents determined? Second, how does one determine a suitable threshold for substantiation of the rule? No totally suitable solution has been found for this problem. An approach will be presented in Section 4.

2.2. Uncertainty in Case Data

Assuming issues pertaining to uncertainty in the knowledge base have been resolved, issues remain in the handling of uncertainty in case data. This includes degrees to which each premise is substantiated, which is connected to the degree to which symptoms may be present. A number of approaches have been taken to solve this problem, including definition of exhaustive sets of fuzzy numbers for each application (Sanchez and Bartolin, 1989). Again, apart from the theoretical issues, the problem remains of defining these values for each new application.

2.3. Model for Handling Different Sources of Uncertainty

A model for handling all of the above areas of uncertainty has been discussed by the authors (Hudson and Cohen, 1988). In order to handle weighting of antecedents and partial presence of symptoms, the following is used:

Let Q be a type 1 linguistic quantifier, and proceed from the statement

$$\text{``}QV\text{'s are } A\text{'' to ``}Q_1(Q_2V\text{'s) are } A\text{''} \tag{1}$$

The truth of the proposition is then determined by assuming there exists some subset C of V such that (1) the number of elements in C satisfies Q, or (2) each element in C satisfies the property A. The degree to which P is satisfiedy by c

$$V_p(C) \text{ is given by } V_p(C) = \max_{C \in 2^A} \{V_p(c)\} \tag{2}$$

Then

$$V(P) = \max\left[\left(Q_1 \sum_{i=1}^{n} c_i \wedge r_i\right) \wedge \min_{i=1,\ldots,n} \left(a_i^{c_i \wedge r_i}\right)\right] \qquad (3)$$

where Q_1 is a type 1 quantifier, $c_i \in \{0,1\}$ indicates membership status, r_i is the weighting factor for the ith antecedent, and a_i is the degree of presence of the ith finding.

In summary, a number of theoretical approaches are available for handling uncertainty in rule-based systems. In practice, the implementation of these approaches presents difficulties. In the next section, an alternative solution to this problem is presented through the use of neural networks, which produce connectionist expert systems.

3. CONNECTIONIST EXPERT SYSTEMS

Neural network techniques, a field which has been essentially dormant since the 1960s (Rosenblatt, 1961; Newell, 1983), has seen renewed interest in the last few years (Gallant, 1988; Rummelhart and McClelland, 1986; Takaji and Hayashi 1988), including the development of connectionist expert systems. This approach, as opposed to the traditional rule-based approach, has fundamental differences in the source of information used for the knowledge base. Rule-based systems rely almost exclusively on information supplied by one or more experts in the field of application. By comparison, information in connectionist expert systems is derived entirely from accumulated data. The pertinent information is extracted from the database through the use of a learning algorithm that operates on data of known classification. In the process, parameters that are important in the decision making process are identified, along with their relative degrees of importance. In previous work of the authors (Hudson and Cohen, 1989), a nonlinear, nonstatistical learning algorithm has been developed. This learning algorithm is outlined in the next section.

3.1. Neural Network Learning Algorithm

The potential function approach has its basis in pattern classification. The goal is to develop decision functions that generate partition boundaries to separate one class from another. The process involves weight-adjusting training algorithms, which use patterns in data of known classification to determine the final weights. The potential function for any sample pattern x, which is a vector composed of contributing features, is given by

$$P(\mathbf{x}, \mathbf{x}_k) = \sum_{i=0}^{\infty} \lambda_i^2 \varphi_i(\mathbf{x}) \, \varphi_i(x_k) \tag{4}$$

where $\varphi_i(x)$, $i = 1, 2, \ldots$ are orthonormal functions. The selection of these functions will be discussed later.

The supervised learning proceeds iteratively, until a separation of the data into correct categories is accomplished. In the process, weights are adjusted for each of the features. The decision hypersurface takes the form

$$D(\mathbf{x}) = \sum_{i=1}^{m} w_i x_i + \sum_{i=1}^{m} \sum_{j=i, i \neq j}^{m} w_{i,j} x_i x_j \tag{5}$$

In network form, the w_is would provide weighting factors for connections of nodes x_1 and x_2 while the $w_{i,j}$ s would be the weighting factors for the interaction for these nodes. All weights in equation (5) are with respect to the same output node; thus the weighting factors indicate the originating node only, for simplicity of notation.

Once weighting factors have been determined, in the decision making model, equation (5) produces a numerical value. The larger the absolute value, the more certain one can be that the vector belongs to the indicated category. In order to normalize these values, the following method is used.

The maximum and minimum values for the decision surface $D(x)$ must be determined. Let $A_i = \{m_1, \ldots, m_k\}$, the set of all values which x_i can assume, where $m_i > 0$ for all i. Then, to obtain the maximum value $D_{max}(x)$, we use the following general rule:

$$\text{If } w_i > 0, \text{ let } x_i' = \max[A_i] \tag{6}$$

$$\text{If } w_i < 0, \text{ let } x_i' = 0$$

for all $i = 1, \ldots, n$; w_i is the currently computed value. Then

$$D_{max}(\mathbf{x}) = \sum_{i=1}^{m} w_i x_i' + \sum_{i=1}^{m} \sum_{j=i, i \neq j}^{m} w_{i,j} x_i' x_j' \tag{7}$$

Similary, $D_{min}(\mathbf{x})$ is obtained by the following:

If $w_i > 0$, let $x_i' = 0$ (8)

If $w_i < 0$, let $x_i' = \max[A_i]$

and by the application of equation (8). All decisions are then normalized by

$$D_n(\mathbf{x}) = \begin{cases} D(\mathbf{x})/D_{max}(\mathbf{x}) & \text{if } D(\mathbf{x}) > 0 \quad (\text{class 1}) \\ D(\mathbf{x})/|D_{min}(\mathbf{x}) & \text{if } D(\mathbf{x}) < 0 \quad (\text{class 2}) \\ 0 & \text{if } D(\mathbf{x}) = 0 \quad (\text{indeterminate}) \end{cases} \quad (9)$$

The result is a value between -1 and 1, inclusive, which gives a degree of membership in that category. The values are then shifted to give an answer between 0 and 1, inclusive by

$$V(\mathbf{x}) = [1 + D_n(\mathbf{x})]/2 \quad (10)$$

The interpretation of the $V_n(\mathbf{x})$ for each individual case is the certainty with which the condition is present.

3.2 Selection of Potential Functions

The potential functions utilized in this procedure are chosen from either the class of Cohen one-dimensional orthogonal functions or multidimensional orthogonal functions (Cohen and Hudson, 1988). Both of these general classes of functions are capable of generating nonlinear polynomial decision hypersurfaces, but can also produce functions in which each paarameter contributes to fractional powers. This latter feature allows the tailoring of decision surfaces to the specific application under consideration.

4. COMBINED DECISION SYSTEMS

The most promising systems are those using a combination of the two technologies outlined above (Cohen, Hudson, and Anderson, 1989a). The advantage of combining both approaches is that all sources of potential information can be tapped, since the rule-based approach extracts information from experts, while the neural network approach extracts information directly from data. The resulting expert system can be presented to the user as a comprehensive decision making tool.

In addition to using both approaches directly, the neural network approach can be used to augment the rule-based approach in another way. Neural network models can be utilized to determine relative weighting factors for antecedents, as well as threshold values of substantiation of the rules, two of the major problems inherent in the implementation of fuzzy reasoning approach to expert systems.

4.1. Determination of Antecedent Weightings

Antecedent weightings are determined in the following manner. A neural network model is set up separately for each rule, with each antecedent representing one symptom. The model is then run on accumulated data using the supervised learning algorithm. In the process, weights are assigned, according to equation (5), without the hidden layer. The result is an equation of the form

$$D(x) = \sum_{i=1}^{m} w_i x_i \tag{11}$$

The weights a_i are then

$$a_i = w_i / \sum_{j=1}^{m} w_j x_j \tag{12}$$

A practical example is shown in Section 5.

4.2. Determination of Threshold Levels

The threshold for each rule is obtained in a similar manner. The neural network is run separately for each rule, as described above. The value of $D(\mathbf{x})$ is normalized according to equations (6)–(10). $V_n(\mathbf{x})$ in equation (10) then becomes the threshold value for that rule. See Section 5 for an example.

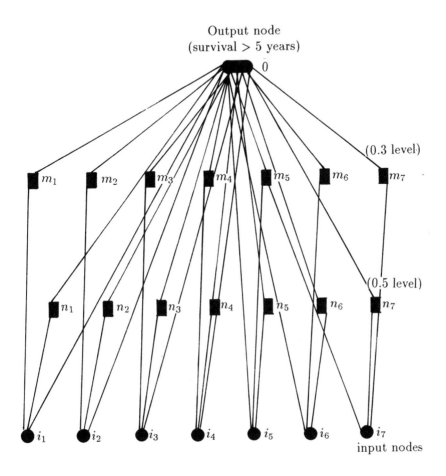

Figure 28.2. Neural network for melanoma prognosis

5. MEDICAL DECISION SUPPORT SYSTEMS

The combined approach discussed in the previous section is illustrated here in an expert system for determination of prognostic factors in malignant melanoma. The goal is to determine what factors are important predictors of the survival of patients for five years or longer, with a goal of directing possible therapies accordingly. Initially, this problem was approached purely as a neural network problem. The network configuration is shown in Figure 28.2.

The database consisted of 1756 cases accumulated at the Melanoma Clinic at University of California, San Francisco, under the direction of the late M. S. Blois, Ph.D., M.D. There were 109 variables that were examined. The model reduced this to seven Variables (Cohen and Hudson, 1990a), which were:

x_1: Thickness of tumor
x_2: Clark's level
x_3: Gender of the patient
x_4: Skin thickness
x_5: Location on body
x_6: Lymph node involvement
x_7: Mitotic rate

As an interesting addition to this system, recent work has established the importance of chromatographic analysis of urine for

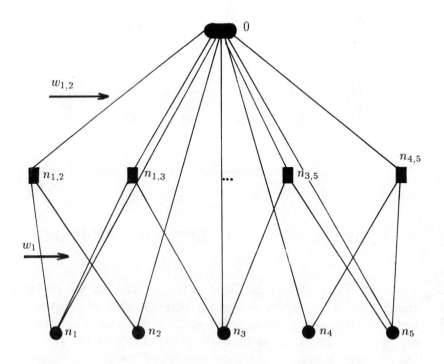

Figure 28.3. Sample neural network for chromatographic analysis

patients with melanoma for determination of the presence of metastasis (Cohen, Hudson, and Anderson, 1989b). This information was derived through a separate neural network model, which is shown in Figure 28.3. The nodes in this model represent the degrees of presence of five known constituents in the urine samples. The five constituents were:

y_1: Dihydroxyphenylacetic acid
y_2: Vanillactic acid
y_3: Homovanillic acid
y_4: 2-S-Cysteinyldopa
y_5: Dihydroxyphenylalanine acid

In the following consultation, if a yes/no response is indicated, a number between 0 and 10, inclusive, may be entered instead to indicate a degree of presence of the symptom. A value of 0 corresponds to no; a value of 10 corresponds to yes.

Name of patient: RW
Age (years): 47
Thickness of tumor (mm): 2.5
Level (1,2,3,4,5) :3
Gender (M/F): F
Skin thickness (MM): 1.8

Using the codes   1: Upper extremities
                  2: Lower extremities
                  3: Lower back or chest
                  4: Abdomen
                  5: Head or neck
Location on body: 5

Lymph node involvement (y/n): y
Mitotic rate (1,2,3): 1

Do you have a urine chromatogram for this patient? N

It is recommended that a urine chromatogram be obtained at this time.

Figure 28.4. Sample consultation

Some rules, however, cannot be obtained directly from the data. The model can then be supplemented by user-supplied rules, as shown in the consultation in Figure 28.4. It should be noted that for these rules, relative importance of premises can be determined through separate neural network models. Also, it should be noted that in the consultation presented to the user, it is not evident what underlying technology is used to arrive at the decision.

As an example of the determination of weighting of antecedents, consider the rule:

Rule 010:
> IF   level is greater than 2, AND
>   location is head, neck, or upper back, AND
>   lymph nodes are involved
> THEN   chromatography results should be considered

If the neural network algorithm is run for this rule, the following type of decision surface equation is obtained:

$$D(\mathbf{x}) = 7.1x_1 + 13.3x_2 + 2.4x_3 \tag{13}$$

where

> x_1: level
> x_2: location
> x_3: lymph node involvement

Normalizing the above, the weights become (.31, .58, .11).

The threshold value is obtained by running the entire training set of data through the neural network for this single rule. In the process the division surface is adjusted to produce the correct classification for each case in the training set. $D(\mathbf{x})$ is then normalized, producing $V_n(\mathbf{x})$ as the threshold value, which in this case is 0.55. The rule then takes the form:

Rule 010 (Threshold .55)
> IF   level is greater than 2   .31
>   location is head, neck, or upper back   .58
>   lymph nodes are involved   .11
> THEN   chromatography results should be considered

6. CONCLUSION

Choice of the proper aproach to automated decision making depends on the problem. If a small amount of concrete data is available, the rule-based approach utilizing expert-derived knowledge is the best solution. On the other hand, if few general guiding principles are known, but data exist or can be collected, then the neural network approach makes sense. In most instances, the only way to take advantage of all available sources of information is through a combination of approaches. Even if the same amount of data exists, it can be successfully utilized to obtain information for a pure knowledge-based system in the form of degrees of importance, and levels of substantiation.

The nonstatistical approach to neural network learning described here accommodates all types of data, including continuous, binary, and categoric, and removes problems of dealing with dependent variables. In the rule-based portion of the systems, the approximate reasoning techniques employed permit handling of uncertain information, both in the knowledge base itself, and in the data for each patient case.

The combined system approach is currently being tested for a number of applications. In addition to determination of prognosis in malignant melanoma, systems have been established for chest pain analysis and diagnosis, staging, and treatment in carcinoma of the lung.

Keywords: degrees of membership, rule-based systems, neural network models

BIBLIOGRAPHY

Adlassnig, K. P. (1982). A survey on medical diagnosis and fuzzy subsets. In M. M. Gupta, and E. Sanchez (eds.): *Approximate Reasoning in Decision Analysis.* Amsterdam: North-Holland, pp. 203–217.

Anderson, J., W. Bandler, L. J. Kohout, and C. Trayner. (1982). The design of a fuzzy medical expert system. In M. M. Gupta, A. Kandel, W. Bandler, and J. B. Kiszha (eds.): *Approximate Reasoning in Expert Systems.* Amsterdam: North-Holland, pp. 689–793.

Armitage, P. and E. A. Gehan. (1974). Statistical methods for the identification and use of prognostic factors. *Int. J. Cancer,* 13, 16–36.

Blois, M. S. (1980). Clinical judgment and computers. *New England Journal of Medicine,* **303,** 192–197.

Bouchon, B. (1987). On the management of uncertainty in knowledge-based systems. In A. G. Holzman, A. Kent, and J. G. Williams (eds.): *Encyclopedia of Computer Science and Technology.* New York: Dekker.

Buchanan, B., G. Sutherland, and E. Feigenbaum. (1969). Heuristic DEN-DRAL: A program for generating explanatory hypotheses in organic chemistry. In *Machine Intelligence,* **4,** New York: Elsevier.

Cohen, M. E. and D. L. Hudson. (1988). The use of fuzzy variables in medical decision making. In M. Gupta and T. Yamakawa (eds.): *Fuzzy Computing: Theory, Hardware Realization and Applications.* North Holland, pp. 263–271.

Cohen, M. E. and D. L. Hudson. (1990). A medical decision aid based on neural network model. In B. Bouchon and R. Yager (eds.): *Information Processing and Handling of Uncertainty in Knowledge-Based Systems,* **3,** 178–180.

Cohen, M. E., D. L. Hudson, M. F. Anderson. (1989a). Combination of a neural network model and a rule-based expert system to determine testing efficacy. *Proceedings, IEEE Engineering in Medicine and Biology,* Y. Kim and F. A. Spelman (eds.): 1989, **11,** pp. 1991–1992.

Cohen, M. E., D. L. Hudson, and M. F. Anderson. (1989b). A neural network learning algorithm with medical applications. In L. C. Kingsland (ed.): *Computer Applications in Medical Care.* IEEE Computer Society Press, **13,** 307–311.

Dubois, D. and H. Prade. (1989). A typology of fuzzy IF...THEN rules. *Proceedings, Third Congress of International Fuzzy Set Association,* pp. 782–785.

Esogbue, A. O. and R. C. Elder. (1983). Measurement and valuation of a fuzzy mathematical model for medical diagnosis. *Fuzzy Sets and Systems,* **10,** 223–242.

Gallant, S. (1988). Connectionist expert systems. *Comm ACM,* **31,** 152–169.

Gorry, G. A. (1973). Computer-assisted clinical decision making. *Method. Inform, Med.,* **12,** 45–51.

Hudson, D. L. and M. E. Cohen. (1987). Management of uncertainty in a medical expert system. *Lecture Notes in Computer Science,* **286,** B. Bouchon and R. Yager (eds.): Berlin-Heidelberg-New York: Springer-Verlag, pp. 283–293.

Hudson, D. L. and M. E. Cohen. (1988). An approach to management of uncertainty in an expert system. *International Journal of Intelligent Systems,* **3,** 45–58.

Hudson, D. L. and M. E. Cohen. (1989). Use of neural network techniques in a medical expert system. *Proceedings of Third Congress, of International Fuzzy Set Association,* pp. 476–479.

Kacprzyk, J. (1989). Approximate reasoning based on belief qualified if-then rules represented by compatibility relations. *Proceedings of Third Congress of International Fuzzy Set Association,* pp. 709–812.

Newell, A. (1983). *Intellectual Issues in the History of Artificial Intelligence.* F. Machlap, et al. (eds.): New York: Wiley.

Patrick, E. A. (1970). Pattern recognition in medicine. *IEEE Trans. on Systems, Man, and Cybernetics, SMC-6,* 173–178.

Rosenblatt, F. (1961). *Principles of Neurodynamics, Perceptrons, and the Theory of Brain Mechanisms.* Washington: Spartan.

Rummelhart, D. E. and J. L. McCelland, and the PDP Research Group. (1986). *Parallel Distributed Processing, Vols. 1 and 2.* Cambridge: MIT Press.

Sanchez, E. and R. Bartolin. (1989). Fuzzy inference and medical diagnosis, a case study. *First Annual Meeting, Biomedical Fuzzy Systems Association,* pp. 1–18.

Shortliffe, E. H. (1975). A model of inexact reasoning in medicine. *Math. Bioscience,* **23,** 251–279.

Shortliffe, E. H. (1976). *Computer-Based Medical Consultations, MYCIN.* New York: Elsevier/North-Holland

Shortliffe, E. H., R. Davis, B. Buchanan, and E. Feigenbaum. (1979). Knowledge engineering for medical decision making: A review of computer-based clinical decision aids. *Proc. IEEE,* **67,** pp. 1207–1224.

Takagi, H. and I. Hayashi. (1988). Artificial neural network-driven fuzzy reasoning. *International Workshop on Fuzzy Systems Aplications,* pp. 217–218.

Togai, M. (1987). The fuzzy logic chip and fuzzy inference accelerator. *IEEE Conference on Decision and Control.*

Wila, M. A. and M. Delgado. (1983). On medical diagnosis using possibility measures, *Fuzzy Sets and Systems,* **10,** 211–222.

Whalen, T. and B. Schott. (1983). Alternative logics for approximate reasoning in expert systems. *International Journal of Man-Machine Studies,* **19,** 57–71.

Winston, P. (1977). *Artificial Intelligence.* Reading, MA: Addison-Wesley.

Yager, R. R. (1984). Approximate reasoning as a basis for rule-based expert systems. *IEEE Trans. on Systems, Man, and Cybernetics, SMC-14* 636–643.

Yager, R. R. (1989). Decision analysis in uncertain environments. *Proceedings of Third Congress of International Fuzzy Set Association,* pp. 404–407.

Zadeh, L. A. (1965). Fuzzy sets. *Information and Control,* **8,** 338–353.

Zadeh, L. A. (1983). A computational approach to fuzzy quantifiers in natural languages. *Comp. and Mach. with Applications,* **9,** 149–184.

Zadeh, L. A. (1985). Syllogistic reasoning in fuzzy logic and its application to usuality and reasoning with dispositions. *IEEE Trans, on Systems, Man, and Cybernetics, SMC-15* 754–763.

29 The use of fuzzy logic for the management of uncertainty in intelligent hybrid systems

Abraham KANDEL
Department of Computer
Science and Engineering
University of South
Florida
Tampa, FL 33620, USA

Moti SCHNEIDER
Department of Computer
Science
Florida Institute
of Technology
Melbourne, FL 32901, USA

Gideon LANGHOLZ
AMU/FSU College of Engineering
Tallahassee, FL 32306, USA

Abstract. Intelligent hybrid systems represent a new field of artificial intelligence research concerned with the integration of the computational paradigms of expert systems and neural networks. The integration of these complementary techniques of knowledge representation is imperative to the process of developing effective robust intelligent systems for a large number of important applications. Since many applications involve human expertise and knowledge, which are invariably imprecise, incomplete, or not totally reliable, fuzzy inferencing procedures are becoming increasingly important to the process of managing uncertainty. Fuzzy inferencing is discussed in the first part of this paper (Sections 1–4), where we consider the theory and algorithms involved in the design of a fuzzy inference architecture. In the second part of the paper (Section 5), we discuss briefly the fuzzy intelligent hybrid system (FIHS) approach, in which the fuzzy expert system is integrated with a neural network. By integrating neural network learning mechanisms with fuzzy inferencing, we can enhance considerably the ability of intelligent autonomous systems to learn in imprecise environments. These learning techniques enable the fuzzy expert system to modify and enrich its knowledge structure autonomously. Potential real-time FIHS applications are also outlined.

1. INTRODUCTION

Uncertainty management (Zadeh, 1983) is one of the most important characteristics of any intelligent system. Proper handling of fuzzy knowledge and data brings any intelligent system in general, and an expert system in particular, one step closer to better emulating experts in their decision-making process.

Several types of fuzzy parameters must be considered in the implementation of any rule-based fuzzy expert system:

(1) **Confidence in a given rule.** Production rules have the following general format:

IF P THEN C

Two questions must be considered. First, what confidence do we have in the given rule and to what extent does it contribute to the solution of the overall problem? We address this question by means of a confidence factor referred to as the *rule certainty* (*RC*).

The second question has to do with the relation between the premise (P) and the conclusion (C) of the rule. Given that the premise has some truth, to what extent is the conclusion true? For example, if we have a rule "If it is cold then wear a coat," we can ask: "Given that it is cold, how certain are we that wearing a coat will make us more comfortable?" This question is addressed by a parameter called the *conclusion certainty* (*CC*).

(2) **Rule priority.** The relative importance of a rule in the process of solving (or participating in solving) the problem is indicated by a parameter called the *rule priority* (*RP*). For example, when

someone has a scratch on his arm, the physician will first attempt to prescribe some medicine, and only when that fails will the physician consider other options. This example illustrates that the activation of rules should be *prioritized*. Thus, the rules associated with the treatment of scratches have to be ranked in the order in which they will be executed.

(3) Confidence in the given data. Often, the user may provide data in which he has no complete confidence. For example, the user may say "I think that the length of the fiber is 7 inches, but I am not sure." To handle such cases, we assign a grade of confidence to the given data, to indicate the extent of our belief in the data. We call this parameter the *data certainty (DC)*.

(4) Fuzziness in data and knowledge descriptions. In many cases, the knowledge and/or data are described in fuzzy terms; for example, "John is more or less old" or "The range to the target is between 20 and 24 yards." The fuzzy expert system must allow for the implementation of reasoning under such fuzzy descriptions.

(5) Fuzzy matching. Often, the data provided to the expert system do not completely match the knowledge base. We have, therefore, to resort to a *matching process* that will evaluate the consistency between the incoming data and the knowledge base and will allow the implementation of reasoning under such uncertainty.

To deal with these issues, we developed a fuzzy inference engine that forms part of our *fuzzy expert system tools* (FEST). The fuzzy engine incorporates the fuzzy parameters mentioned above, and generates conclusions *even when the data and the knowledge are fuzzy.* In other words, inferencing can still be carried out even when the data and the knowledge base do not match completely.

The user provides the expert system with the four confidence factors:

- Rule Certainty (*RC*)
- Conclusion Certainty (*CC*)
- Data Certainty (*DC*)
- Rule Priority (*RP*)

The expert system then matches the clauses and evaluates the overall confidence in any given conclusion. To accomplish that, the fuzzy inference engine executes the following tasks:

1. Parse each clause and interpret the fuzzy description if it is included in the clause.
2. Match the given data and the knowledge base and compute the *matching factor M (RD)*, where R is the premise clause and D is the data clause.
3. Use the confidence factors RC, CC, DC, and RP, as well as the matching factor $M(D, R)$, to find the overall certainty of the conclusion.

FEST forms an integral part of the *fuzzy intelligent hybrid system* (FIHS) approach, which is outlined in Section 5. The FIHS integrates the fuzzy expert system with a neural network into a single intelligent unit. The neural network provides FIHS with learning capabilities that enable the system to overcome the knowledge acquisition bottleneck, and to allow for dynamic environments by changing knowledge whenever this becomes necessary.

In the following sections we consider the theory and algorithms involved in the architectural considerations of FEST's fuzzy inference engine and outline the rationale behind our fuzzy intelligent hybrid system approach. Parsing is dealt with in Section 2, and the matching process is introduced in Section 3. The algorithm for computing the certainty factor of a conclusion is detailed in Section 4. Section 5 outlines the fuzzy intelligent hybrid system approach, and Section 6 provides a brief summary.

2. PARSING

In this section we introduce the process of parsing modifiers and negation in FEST. These operators play an important role in the fuzzy matching process described in Section 3.

The general structure of a clause is of the form:

"X is Y"

where "Y" can be either a word, a single number, or an interval, and can be modified and/or negated. As we will see shortly, "Y" is associated with two intervals, denoted by [LB1, UB1] and [LB2, UB2], where LB and UB, respectively, designate a lower bound and an upper bound.

Since we are concerned with two operators, we have to consider four types of clauses: "X is Y," "X is MOD Y," "X is NOT Y," and "X is NOT MOD Y." We parse each one of these clauses as follows:

(1) "X is Y." In this case, both the negation (NOT) and the modifier (MOD) are off. Thus,

- If "Y'''" is a *word*, then $LB1 = UB1 = 1$.
- If "Y'''" is a *single number* (N), then $LB1 = UB1 = N$.
- If "Y'''" is an *interval* $[N1, N2]$, then $LB1 = N1$, and $UB1 = N2$.

Thus, in the first interval associated with "Y," $[LB1, UB1]$, both $LB1$ and $UB1$ are assigned certain values, whereas the second interval $[LB2, UB2]$ remains undefined.

(2) "X is MOD Y." Since the modifier modifies "Y," we use a procedure COMPUTE_RANGE (MOD, NUM, LB, UB) that takes as inputs the modofier (MOD) and some number (NUM), and generates the interval $[LB, UB]$.

For example, let $MOD = $ *more-or-less* and $NUM = 20$, and assume that *more-or-less* will generate the interval $[NUM-10\%, NUM + 10\%]$. The procedure COMPUTE_RANGE (MOD, NUM, LB, UB) will therefore generate the interval $[18, 22]$ so that $LB = 18$ and $UB = 22$. We assign these values in accordance with Case 1 above, so that $LB1 = 18$ and $UB1 = 22$. Here, too, the second interval $[LB2, UB2]$ remains undefined.

(3) "X is NOT Y." In this case we have to negate the interval generated in Case 1. Let α be the smallest possible number in the domain of "Y" and let β be the largest possible number in that domain. Then, the negation of Y will generate two intervals: $[\alpha, LB1 - \varepsilon]$ and $[UB1 + \varepsilon, \beta]$, where $\varepsilon > 0$ is an arbitrarily small number. In other words, NOT "Y" generates two distinct intervals (Weiss and Kulikowski, 1984) where:

$$LB1 = \alpha, UB1 = LB1 - \varepsilon, LB2 = UB1 + \varepsilon, UB2 = \beta$$

Note that using an arbitrarily small positive number is imperative to the process of parsing "X is NOT Y" in order to prevent an overlap between the original interval (Case 1) and its negation. Otherwise, without ε, some data may be included in both the original interval and its negation.

(4) "X is NOT MOD Y." Here, we apply the procedure outlined for Case 2 to the first interval and then the procedure of Case 3 to the interval resulting from Case 2.

3. FUZZY MATCHING

Proper matching between two clauses is a major task of the inference engine. There are two types of matching algorithms: (1) the Boolean matching process, which succeeds only if the clauses to be matched are identical, and (2) the fuzzy matching process that does not require a one-to-one matching between the clauses. In this section, we describe the fuzzy matching procedure, explain its features, and provide examples to illustrate it.

FEST prompts queries about the truth of each clause and assigns the certainty factor accordingly. For example, if the knowledge base contains the rule:

IF John is between 20 and 30 **THEN** John is young

FEST will ask: "What is the certainty factor that John is between 20 and 30?" The user may then input a number between 0 and 1, say 0.8. Then, only if that number is greater than or equal to some *threshold*, the rule will fire and the conclusion will be "John is young" with a certainty factor (*CF*) of 0.8.

Some expert systems assign the certainty factor to the conclusion but nevertheless require complete matching between clauses. This means that, if the clauses match, the certainty factor of the conclusion is assigned a priori, and if the clauses do not match, the rule does not fire. For example, let the rule be:

IF John is between 20 and 30 **THEN** John is young with $CF = 0.9$

It the user provides data that matches the premise of the rule, then, provided that the premise has been evaluated positively, the conclusion will be activated with a confidence of 0.9; otherwise, the confidence will be zero.

FEST, on the other hand, recognizes the fact that we do not always have a one-to-one matching between the premise of the rule and the data and, therefore, utilizes a procdedure that evaluates the *extent* of similarity between the two clauses. The extent to which two clauses are matched is called the certainty factor (Negoita, 1985; Schneider, 1990; Schneider and Kandel, 1988; Schneider et al., 1990; Kandel, 1982, 1987; Waterman, 1985).

To introduce the matching process, assume that we have defined a certain syntax for the grammar to be used by the expert system and by the user. We utilize the parsing procedure described in Section 2 to parse the relevant knowledge and data, and to produce a structure that is used by the inference engine. The inference engine then utilizes the following algorithm:

1. The inference engine places the parsed user-entered data on the blackboard.
2. The premise of each rule in the knowledge base is matched against the blackboard.
3. The conclusion of a rule becomes true if and only if the matching process generates a *matching factor* that is greater than or equal some *threshold*.
4. If the conclusion of a rule is rendered true (i.e., the threshold is exceeded), then that rule is "fired" and its conclusion is placed on the blackboard.
5. Steps 1–4 are repeated until no more rules are fired.

To illustrate the steps involved in the matching algorithm, consider a knowledge base consisting of the single rule:

IF John is not more-or-less 20 **THEN** John is happy

and assume that the user enters the following data:

John is almost 19

The question is "Is John happy?"

First, we parse the clause "John is almost 19." Let us assume that some function maps the statement "almost 19" into the interval [18, 19]; namely, John is 18 to 19 years old, but not quite 19. This result is placed on the blackboard in the form:

"John" $[18, 19 - \varepsilon]$

where $\varepsilon > 0$ is an arbitrarily small number (see Section 2, Case 3).

Next, we parse the premise of the rule in the knowledge base. Assume that the statement *"more-or-less 20"* is mapped into the interval [18, 22]. Since it is John's age we are dealing with, let $\alpha = 0$ and $\beta = 120$. Hence, as shown in Section 2, Case 3, the negation of the interval [18, 22] due to the **NOT** operator will generate the two intervals: $[0, 18 - \varepsilon]$ and $[22 + \varepsilon, 120]$. Therefore, we have to match the interval $[18, 19 - \varepsilon]$ against the two intervals $[0, 18 - \varepsilon]$ and $[22 + \varepsilon, 120]$. As will be seen later, if we set the threshold at 0.5 for this example, the resulting matching factor would be less than the threshold and, therefore, the rule will not fire.

It is important to note that we *always match the rule against the blackboard*. Since we have to match two clauses, and since each clause may be associated with two distinct intervals, we may have to consider up to four intervals: two that are associated with the clause on the blackboard, and two that are associated with the clause in the premise of the rule.

The matching process generates a *matching factor* between two clauses according to the following formula:

$$M(x,y) = \frac{\text{INTERSECT }(A,C) + \text{INTERSECT }(A,D) + \text{INTERSECT }(B,C) + \text{INTERSECT }(B,D)}{C + D} \qquad (1)$$

where A and B are the sizes of the two possible intervals associated with clause (x) in the premise of the rule, and C and D are the sizes of the two possible intervals associated with the blackboard clause (y). The INTERSECT procedure calculates the overlapping size of any two given intervals (Zimmermann, 1985) and is illustrated in the following examples, which demonstrate the process of computing the matching factor.

Example 1. The premise is: "John is **NOT** between 20 and 30," and the user-entered data is: "John is 10 to 50." Since we have to match ages, let $\alpha = \beta = 120$ (see Section 2, Case 3). Parsing the data, we place the interval $[10, 50]$ on the blackboard. Since the premise contains the keyword "NOT," parsing the clause generates two intervals: $A = [0, 20 - \varepsilon]$ and $B = [30 + \varepsilon, 120]$. The blackboard, on the other hand, contains only a single interval $C = [10, 50]$. For simplicity, we will ignore ε since, in this example, it will not affect the outcome of the calculations.

We now apply equation (1). Since D is not defined in this example (the blackboard clause does not contain the **NOT** operator), equation (1) reduces to:

$$M = [\text{INTERSECT }(A, C) + \text{INTERSECT }(B, C)]/C$$

The intersection of the intervals A and C results in 10 and the intersection of the intervals B and C produces 20. The size of the interval C is 40. Hence:

$$M = (10 + 20)/40 = 0.75$$

Therefore, the extent to which the two clauses match, the *matching factor*, is 0.75.

The matching process in Example 1 can also be illustrated graphically, as shown in Figure 29.1. As can be seen, two overlapping areas are created by intersecting A and C, and B and C. The

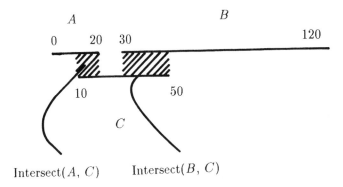

Figure 29.1. Graphical illustration of the matching process

intersection of A and C is 10 and the intersection of B and C is 20. The combined intersection of the intervals in which the overlapping occurs is 30, and the size of the interval C is 40.

Example 2. Let the blackboard contain a single interval: $C = [70, 150]$, and assume that the parsed premise also contains a single interval: $A = [50, 100]$. Therefore, we have to match only two intervals. Since both B and D are undefined, equation (1) reduces to:

$$\underline{M} = \text{INTERSECT}(A, C)/C = 30/80 = 0.375$$

This result can be interpreted to say that in 30 out of 80 possible cases the data matches the premise of the rule. Once again, since the data contains an interval that is not covered by the premise of the rule, the extent of our belief that the conclusion of the rule is true is proportional to the extent that the premise and the data match.

Example 3. The blackboard contains the number 70 and the premise is associated with the interval $[50, 100]$. Here, too, we have only two intervals: $C = [70, 70)$, and $A = [50, 100]$. However, in this case, INTERSECT $(A, C) = 70$ and the size of C is also 70 so that the resulting matching factor is $\underline{M} = 1$. Indeed, since the data is within the range of the premise, we have a complete matching between the blackboard and the premise. Clearly, the data will always be covered for all possible ranges of the rule, resulting in a complete matching between the premise and the data.

Example 4. Let $A = [20,30]$ and $C = [50, 80]$. Equation (1) produces $\underline{M} = 0$ since the two intervals do not intersect and, therefore, do not match.

4. COMPUTING THE CERTAINTY FACTOR OF A CONCLUSION

In this section we provide a procedure for evaluating the certainty factor of any concluding rule.

In Section 1, we introduced the following fuzzy parameters: *rule priority (RP)*, *rule certainty (RC)*, and *conclusion certainty (CC)*. We can now integrate these parameters into the process of computing the certainty factor of any concluding rule. Since each of these parameters may have a different impact on the decision-making process, we assign each of them a *weight*. Thus, let W_{RP}, W_{RC}, and W_{CC} be the weights associated with *RP*, *RC*, and *CC*, respectively.

The algorithm for computing the certainty factor (*CF*) of a conclusion consists of the following steps:

1. Evaluate the certainty factor of any clause x in the premise:

$$CF_x = M(x,y)*CF_y \qquad (2)$$

where y is either a user-entered data clause or any conclusion clause, and $M(x,y)$ is the matching factor (1).

2. Evaluate the certainty factor CF_{PI} of the *entire* premise of rule i, using any one of the following equations as applicable:

$$CF_{Pi} = not\ a = 1 - a \qquad (3)$$
$$CF_{Pi} = a\ and\ b = MIN\ (a,\ b) \qquad (4)$$
$$CF_{Pi} = a\ or\ b = MAX\ (a,\ b) \qquad (5)$$
$$CF_{Pi} = a \qquad (6)$$

where a and b are the certainty factors of the two clauses.

3. Evaluate the certainty factor of any clause x in a conclusion:

$$CF_{Cx} = MIN\ (CF_{Pi},\ W_{Ri}) \qquad (7)$$

where W_{Ri} is the *weighted average* of *RP*, *RC*, and *CC* associated with rule i:

$$W_{Ri} = \frac{W_{RP}\ RP + W_{RC}\ RC + W_{CC}\ CC}{W_{RP} + W_{RC} + W_{CC}} \tag{8}$$

To illustrate this algorithm, assume a knowledge base consisting of the following two rules:

R1: IF a THEN b
R2: IF b^* and c THEN d

Our *objective* is to fire rule 2 and compute the certainty factor of the conclusion d.

The user provides the input data a^* and c^*, and their associated *data certainties* (*DC*) (Section 1), say 0.95 and 0.85, respectively. (It should be noted that this example allows for the possibility that the data and the premise of the rule will not match one-to-one.) In addition, the user also supplies the following parameter values: For the first rule (**R1**), $RP = 1$, $RC = 0.9$, and $CC = 0.9$, and for the second rule (**R2**), $RP = 1$, $RC = 0.95$, and $CC = 0.85$.

We note that a, a^*, b, b^*, c, c^*, and d are clauses and assume that a and a^*, b and b^*, and c and c^* are matchable, with corresponding matching factors $M(a, a^*) = 0.8$, $M(b,b^*) = 0.9$, and $M(c,c^*) = 0.75$. Finally, let $W_{RP} = 0.9$, $W_{RC} = 0.95$, and $W_{CC} = 1$, and assume that the *threshold* is set to 0.5.

First, we place the input data provided by the user on the blackboard:

blackboard $= \{[a^*, 0.95], [c^*, 0.85]\}$

We now attempt to fire the first rule (**R1**). Using (2) (Step 1 in the algorithm), we get:

$$CF_a = M(a,a^*)^*CF_{a^*} = 0.8^*0.95 = 0.76$$

Next, we utilize (6) to calculate the certainty factor of the *entire* premise of **R1** (Step 2 in the algorithm). Thus:

$$CF_{P1} = CF_a = 0.76$$

Since $0.76 > 0.5$ (0.5 is the threshold value), **R1** fires and we can compute the certainty factor of its conclusion b (Step 3 in the algorithm):

$$CF_{Cb} = \text{MIN}\ (CF_{R1}, W_{R1}) = \text{MIN}(0.76, 0.95) = 0.76$$

Note that in order to compute CF_{Cb}, first we had to calculate W_{R1} using (8):

$$W_{R1} = (0.9*1 + 0.95*0.9 + 1* 0.95)/(0.9 + 0.95 + 1) = 0.95$$

Since **R1** fired, we place its conclusion on the blackboard, so that now:

$$\text{blackboard} = \{[a^*,0.95], [c^*,0.85], [b,0.76]\}$$

We now attempt to fire the second rule (**R2**). Using (2) (Step 1 in the algorithm), we get:

$$CF_{b'} = M(b,b^*)*CF_b = 0.9*0.76 = 0.68$$

and

$$CF_c = M(c,c^*)*CF_{c'} = 0.75*0.85 = 0.64$$

Using (6) to calculate the certainty factor of the *entire* premise of **R2** (Step 2 in the algorithm), yields:

$$CF_{P2} = \text{MIN}(CF_{b'},CF_c) = 0.64$$

Since $0.64 > 0.5$ (0.5 is the threshold value), **R2** fires and we can compute the certainty factor of its conclusion d (Step 3 in the algorithm):

$$CF_{Cd} = \text{MIN}(CF_{R2},W_{R2}) = \text{MIN}(0.64,0.93) = 0.64$$

Note that in order to compute CF_{Cd}, first we had to calculate W_{R2} using (8):

$$W_{R2} = (0.9*1 + 0.95*0.95 + 1*0.85)/(0.9 + 0.95 + 1) = 0.93$$

We have now reached our stated objective for this example: **R2** has fired, resulting in:

"d is true with $CF = 0.64$"

5. FIHS–FUZZY INTELLIGENT HYBRID SYSTEM

5.1. Overview

In the preceding sections we introduced the theory and algorithms underlying FEST's fuzzy inference architecture. FEST forms an integral part of our *fuzzy intelligent hybrid system* (FIHS) approach which involves the integration of the computational paradigms of fuzzy expert systems and neural networks.

Expert systems and neural networks represent complementary approaches to knowledge representation: The logical, cognitive, and mechanical nature of the expert system versus the numeric, associative, and self-organizing nature of the neural network.

The fuzzy expert system component of FIHS reflects the fact that human expertise embedded in the knowledge base of the expert system is imprecise, incomplete, or not totally reliable. It offers knowledge-based techniques for gathering and processing information coupled with methods of approximate reasoning to better emulate human decision-making processes. Using fuzzy logic to manage uncertainty provides a systematic framework for dealing with fuzzy quantifiers. Fuzzy logic subsumes both predicate logic and probability theory and makes it possible to deal with different types of uncertainty within a single conceptual framework (Kandel, 1987).

Neural networks (Dayhoff, 1990; Simpson, 1990) consist of densely interconnected simple nonlinear devices, called *processing elements* (or *neurons*). The knowledge of a neural network resides in the interconnections between these elements and in the strengths (weights) of the interconnections. Collectively, neurons with simple properties, interacting according to simple rules, can accomplish complex functions such as generalization, error correction, information reconstruction, pattern analysis, and learning. Neural networks provide a greater degree of robustness, or fault tolerance, than conventional von-Neumann sequential machines. Indeed, damage to a few neurons or interconnections, and/or minor variabilities in the characteristics of neurons, do not impair overall network performance significantly. In addition, neural networks also possess the ability to gracefully handle inconsistencies or conflicts in the data.

The ability of the neutral network to learn in an imprecise environment enables the expert system to modify and enrich its knowledge structures autonomously. Consequently, FIHS can overcome some of the major drawbacks of convential expert systems: (1) their reliance upon consultation with human experts for knowledge acquisition (the knowledge acquisition bottleneck); (2) their inability to synthesize new knowledge; and (3) their inability to allow for dynamic environments by changing knowledge whenever this becomes necessary.

It is, therefore, of paramount importance to develop methodologies for integrating the computational paradigms of fuzzy expert systems and neural networks, and for exploring the similarities between the underlying structures of these two methods of knowledge representation. Such hybrid architecture, which allows for imprecise information and/or uncertain environments, is more powerful than either of its components standing alone. The importance of this field of research is clearly attested to by the fairly large number of recent publications (Kandel and Langholz, 1992; Hall and Romaniuk, 1990; Gallant, 1988; Fu, 1989; Hudson et al., 1989; Bigus and Goolsbey, 1989; Bochereau and Bourigne, 1990; Bradshaw et al., 1989; Touretzky and Hunton, 1985, 1988; Yang and Bhargava, 1990; Kunicky, 1990; Hruska et al., 1991).

5.2. Organization and Knowledge Transfer

The FIHS functionally organized in two separate units: the fuzzy expert system and the neural network. It allows for a *bidirectional* (transparent) transfer of knowledge between its two components. Initially, the fuzzy expert system is invoked with a base of knowledge that is necessarily incomplete. The neural network takes the knowledge from the fuzzy expert system and modifies it through learning. (Since the fuzzy expert system supplies the metaknowledge to begin the learning process, learning in the neural network is implemented more efficiently.) Based on the information acquired from the neural network, the fuzzy expert system can modify certainty factors, modify existing rules, or infer new rules.

The transfer of knowledge from the fuzzy expert system to the neutral network is accomplished by decomposing the rule base clauses into three classes:

1. Clauses requiring input from the user;
2. Clauses that yield the final output decisions; and
3. Clauses that do not fall into either category.

These classes result in a neural network that consists of an input layer, an output layer, and hidden layers. The interconnections between the layers result from the chaining in the fuzzy expert system. The certainty factors are identified with interconnection weights in the neural network, and antecedents and consequents are associated with processing elements. The different rule-base operations (conjunctions, disjunctions, and negations) result in different types of processing elements, each having distinct combining and activation functions.

5.3. FIHS Applications

The FIHS is very attractive in a large number of applications involving human expertise and knowledge that are invariably imprecise, incomplete, or not totally reliable. To illustrate the applicability of the FIHS approach, we will briefly outline two important applications: Automatic target identification (ATI) and intelligent robot control systems. Both areas are distinguished in that a variety of *unintegrated* expert system and neural network solutions have already been proposed to tackle some of their unique problems.

ATI involves the extraction of critical information from fuzzy data for which traditional solutions of either artificial intelligence or pattern recognition have been unable to provide satisfactory solutions (Hsu and Psaltis, 1988; Mead and Mahowald, 1988; Stoll and Lee, 1988). The problem is difficult because a complete and robust system must consider many different image variations including: position, scale, orientation, contrast, perpsective, background occlusion, and noise. The ultimate goal is to develop a flexible system that can classify objects in varying positions, orientations, and dimensions in the image plane, as well as to tolerate a certain degree of random variations in the shape.

Roth (1990) has recently surveyed some of the preliminary work on the applicability of neural network technology to ATI. Neural network models offer several advantages over traditional recognition techniques, such as:

1. High computation rates provided by massive parallelism.
2. Noise and error tolerance.
3. Adaptability to changing environments due to their learning abilities during dynamic data cycles.

Machine intelligence and robot control systems are also related technologies. An autonomous intelligent control system requires significantly enhanced capabilities to achieve real-time operational responses when the decision-making process is based on incomplete information, uncertainty, and competing constraints. However, conventional control systems design techniques are usualy inadequate when a representative model describing the dynamic system to be controlled is difficult to obtain due to uncertainty, nonlinearity, time dealy, saturation, time-varying parameters, and overall complexity.

On the other hand, control systems based on neural network models (Narenda and Parthasarathy, 1990) offer several advantages over traditional control techniques, such as:

1. Fast decision making and control, since computations are done in parallel.
2. Fast adatation to a large number of parameterers (Hopfield, 1984; Hopfield and Tank, 1985).
3. Adaptation to parameter variations over continous and discrete time domains.
4. Since learning can be done through examples, the controll laws do not have to be stated explicitly (Carpenter and Grossberg, 1987).
5. Fault tolerance and graceful degradation.
6. Robustness to unmodeled parameters and uncertainty.

In contrast with the neural-based approaches to both ATI and intelligent robot control, the FIHS approach offers an integrated tool in which FEST provides a mechanism to handle a priori fuzzy knowledge, whereas the neural network offers powerful collective-computation techniques as well as learning capabilities in uncertain environments. It would thus facilitate autonomous knowledge acquistion via learning and continous refinement to improve the performance of the system.

6. CONCLUSION

In this paper, we introduced the theory and algorithms involved in the design of a fuzzy inference architecture and outlined its integration into the fuzzy intelligent hybrid system FIHS. It has been shown that the procedure for fuzzy matching between two clauses is completely general and can accommodate cases where the information provided by the user is fuzzy or incomplete. This information can be in the form of a rule in the knowledge base or user-entered data. The generality and simplicity of the proposed fuzzy inferencing procedure provide a very useful tool in designing fuzzy expert systems.

The integration of fuzzy inferencing procedures within the FIHS framework shows great promise for real-time applications involving autonomous systems. By integrating neural network learning mechanisms with fuzzy inferencing, we can enhance considerably the ability of the intelligent autonomous system to learn in an imprecise environment. The FIHS is based on the bidirectional transfer of knowledge between the fuzzy expert system and the neural network and takes advantage of FEST's uncertainty management techniques to provide potentially powerful solutions to a variety of real-time applications within uncertain environments. Two such applications, automatic target identification and intelligent robot control, were briefly outlined.

Keywords: fuzzy logic expert systems, uncertainty management, neural networks, intelligent hybrid systems.

BIBLIOGRAPHY

Bigus, J. and K. Goolsbey. (1989). Integrating neural networks and knowledge-based systems in a commercial environment. *Proc. Int. Joint Conference on Neural Networks,* Vol. II, pp. 463–466, Washington, D.C. June 18–22.

Bochereau, L. and P. Bourgine. (1990). Rule extraction and validity domain on a multilayer neural network. *Proc. Int. Joint Conference on Neural Networks,* June 17–21, San Diego, CA, Vol. I, pp. 97–100.

Bradshaw, G. R., R. Fozzard, and L. Ceci. (1989). A connectionist expert system that actually works. In D. S. Touretzky (ed.): *Advances in Neural Information Processing Systems,* San Mateo, CA: Morgan Kaufmann, pp. 248–255.

Buchanan, B. G. and E. H. Shortliffe (eds.). (1984). *Rule-based Expert Systems.* Reading, MA: Addison-Wesley.

Carpenter, G. A. and S. Grossberg. (1987). A massively parallel architecture for a self-organizing neural pattern recognition machine. *Computer Vision, Graphcs, and Image Processing,* 37, 54–115.

Dayhoff, J. (1990). *Neural Network Architectures.* New York: Van Nostrand Reinhold.

Dubois, D. and H. Prade. (1988). *Possibility Theory.* New York: Plenum.

Fu, L. M. (1989). Integration of neural heuristics into knowledge-based Inference. *Cognition Science,* 1 (3).

Gallant, S. I. (1988). Connectionist expert system. *Comm. ACM,* 31, 152–169.

Hall, L. and S. G. Romaniuk. (1990). **FUZZNET**: Toward a fuzzy connectionist expert system development tool. *Proc. Int. Joint Contference on Neural Networks,* Jan. 15–19, Washington, D.C., Vol. II, pp. 483–486.

Handelman, D. A., S. H. Lane, and J. J. Gelfand. (1989). Integration of knowledge-based system and neural network techniques for autonomous learning machines. *Proc. Int. Joint Conference on Neural Networks,* June 18–22, Washington, D.C., Vol. I, pp. 683–688.

Handelman, D. A., S. H. Halne, and J. J. Gelfand. (1990). Integrating neural networks and knowledge-based systems for intelligent robotic control. *IEEE Control Systems Magazine,* 10, 77–87.

Hopfield, J. J. (1984). Neurons with graded response have collective computational properties like those of two-state neurons. *Proc. Nat. Acad. Sci.,* 81, 3088–3092.

Hopfield, J. J. and D. W. Tank. (1985). Neural computation of decision in optimization problems. *Biol. Cybern.*, **52**, 141–152.

Hruska, S. I., D. Kuncicky, and R. C. Lacher. (1991). Learning in acyclic expert networks. *Proc. WNN-AIND'91*, SPIE Vol. 1515, pp. 181–186.

Hsu, K., and D. Psaltis. (1988). Invariance and discrimination properties of the optical associative loop. *Proc. IEEE Int. Conf. Neural Networks*, pp. 395–402.

Hudson, D. L., M. E. Cohen, and M. F. Anderson. (1989). Use of neural network techniques in a medical expert system, *Proc. Third Congress of the International Fuzzy Systems Association.*

Kanal, L. N. and J. F. Lemmer (eds.). (1986). *Uncertainty in Artificial Intelligence.* Amsterdam: North-Holland.

Kandel, A. (1982). *Fuzzy Techniques in Pattern Recognition.* New York: Wiley.

Kandel, A. (1987). *Fuzzy Mathematical Techniques with Applications.* Reading, MA: Addison-Wesley.

Kandel, A. and G. Langholz (eds.). (1992). *Intelligent Hybrid Systems.* To be published by CRC Press.

Kunicicky, D. C. (1990). The transmission of konwledge betweeen neural networks and expert systems. *Proc. WNN-AIND'90*, Feb. 1990, pp. 311–319.

Mead, C. A. and M. A. Mahowald. (1988). A silicon model of early visual processing. *Neural Networks*, 1, 91–97.

Narendra, K. S. and K. Parthasarathy. (1990). Identification and control of dynamical systems using neural networks. *IEEE Trans. Neural Networks*, 1, 4–27.

Negoita, C. V. (1985). *Expert System and Fuzzy Systems.* Reading, MA: Benjamin Cummings.

Roth, M. W. (1990). Survey of neural network technology for automatic target recognition. *IEEE Transactions on Neural Networks*, 1, 28–43.

Schneider, M. and A. Kandel. (1989). *Cooperative Fuzzy Expert Systems–Their Design and Applications in Intelligent Recognition.* Cologne: Verlag TÜV Rheinland, Cummings.

Schneider, M., D. Clark, and A. Kandel. (1990). On the matching process in fuzzy expert system. *Proc. Third International IPMU Conference*, July 2–6, 1990, Paris, France, pp. 46–48.

Schneider, M., E. Shnaider, and A. Kandel. (1990). Applications of the negation operator in fuzzy production rules. *Fuzzy Sets and Systems*, **34**, 293–299.

Simpson, P. K. (1990). *Artificial Neural Systems.* New York: Pergamon Press.

Stoll, H. M. and L. S. Lee. (1988). A continuous-time optical neural network. *Proc. IEEE Int. Conf. Neural Networks*, II, pp. 373–384.

Touretzky, D. and G. Hinton. (1985). Symbols among the neurons: Details of a connectionist inference architecture. *Proc. Ninth International Joint Conference of Artifical Intelligence*, Aug. 18–23, Los Angeles, CA, pp. 238–243.

Touretzky, D. and G. Hinton. (1988). A distributed connectionist production system. *Cognitive Science*, **12**, 423–466.

Waterman, D. A. (1985). *A Guide to Expert Systems.* Reading, MA: Addison-Wesley.

Weiss, M. and C. A. Kulikowski. (1987). *Designing Expert Systems*. Rowman and Allanheld.

Yand, Q. and V. K. Bhargava. (1990). Building expert systems by a modified perceptron network with rule-transfer algorithms. *Proc. International Joint Conference on Neural Networks*. June 17–21, San Diego, CA, Vol. 11, pp. 77–82.

Zadeh, L. A. (1983). The role of fuzzy logic in the management of uncertainty in expert systems. *Fuzzy Sets and Systems*, 11, 199–227.

Zimmermann, H. (1985). *Fuzzy Set Theory and Its Applications*. Dordrecht: Kluwer-Nijhoff.

30 The validation of fuzzy knowledge-based systems

Ana M. CHANG
Honeywell Inc., MavD
11601 Roosevelt Blvd.
St. Petersburg
FL 33716-2202, USA

Lawrence O. HALL
Department of Computer
Science and Engineering
University of South Florida
Tampa, FL 33620, USA

Abstract. Expert system validation is defined as demonstrating that the expert system performs the functions it is required to perform (e.g., diagnose, predict, instruct, explain, etc.) and is useful for the intended purposes. Because of the increasing interest in expert systems as a way of solving problems and the seriousness of some expert system applications, these functions must be performed correctly without danger of reaching erroneous or illogical conclusions that may lead to disastrous effects such as the loss of life and money. This paper presents some of the approaches developed for expert system validation. The importance of validation is detailed, the evolution of expert system validation is described, and some developed methodologies are discussed. An extension of validation methods for fuzzy expert systems is given. Rule-based expert systems are emphasized. The techniques will be directly applicable to the broader field of knowledge-based system validation.

1. INTRODUCTION

Although validation methods have been developed for regular procedural software, there are problems to be faced when applying them to expert systems. Some of these are due to the separation of inference from knowledge and the nonprocedural nature of expert systems:

1. It is sometimes impossible to know exactly what the system does until it is actually built, especially if the initial objective is vague, or the requirements keep changing through the development.
2. The fact that the resulting code of an expert system does not resemble the actual execution sequence, as does that of conventional software, makes the number of possible conclusion states difficult to predict. In addition, this number may be so large that exhaustive testing becomes infeasible.
3. It is difficult to obtain an ideal set of domain-representative test cases that may test all states and justly represent the domain.
4. There are questions as to what part of the system to validate, when to validate each part, and what to validate against: known results or expert performance. The consensus is to validate the inference engine, knowledge acquisition facility, and explanation facility first, since these are the most procedural parts of the system and conventional methods apply. The performance of the system, as will be shown, depends mostly on the validity of the knowledge; thus validation of the knowledge must begin when sufficient knowledge is present in the knowledge base so that complete reasoning paths may be tested. This process must continue through the life of the system when knowledge is modified or added. Finally, as to what to validate against, it would be ideal to always validate against expert performance, but he or she is seldom available and unfortunately also perishable. For this reason, test cases with known results are often used.

There are other issues that pose problems such as controlling the cost of validation, determining who should be responsible for performing the validation such that several types of bias are eliminated, and even how to validate a validation methodology.

In addition to the above problems, it has been found that knowledge representation plays an important role in the task of validation and it poses another set of problems:

1. In attempts to achieve greater representational power, several methods of representing knowledge are being developed as a result of the ongoing research in the area. Unfortunately, these

efforts are not equaled by those made in the field of expert system validation. The fact that knowledge representation schemes continue to emerge, while validation of such knowledge is neglected, is an important factor behind the lack of public belief in expert systems.

2. Methods for representing uncertainty are often misunderstood and therefore may be defectively implemented and wrongly interpreted by a validation tool.

3. Finally, in many knowledge bases, domain-level knowledge, meta-level knowledge, and control knowledge, are combined using the same representation scheme, thus confusing the validation analysis process. This makes it necessary to incorporate into the validation tool a way of distinguishing the various types of knowledge in order to validate them separately.

The validation of fuzzy rule-based expert systems will be a generalization of validation for *traditional* rule-based systems. After the discussion on validation for rule-based systems and a discussion of example validation systems, we will identify the differences in validating fuzzy rules. An approach to validating fuzzy rule-based expert systems will be suggested.

2. APPROACHES TO EXPERT SYSTEM VALIDATION

It has been found that most, if not all, of the work done on this subject concentrates only on the validation of rule-based knowledge. This is clearly an indication that the task of expert system validation is far from mature and is also lagging behind since the efforts in the field don't parallel those efforts made in other areas of expert system research. The software world in now faced with changing its gears toward the new and not widely accepted method of software design, which is object-oriented analysis and design (OOA and D). Some argue it is only a "fad" and that this approach applies only to certain problem domains giving rise to another new issue of "domain analysis." Nevertheless, all this is present also in the AI world in the form of object-oriented knowledge representations such as structured objects and frames, and object-oriented versions of languages for building expert systems. Some work on frame-based knowledge validation has been done (Cheng and Hall, 1990).

2.1. Primitive Approaches

In the paper "Validating expert system performance" (Balci et al., 1987), the authors expose some qualitative and quantitative approaches to validation.

2.1.1. Qualitative Approaches

These approaches originate from approaches for validating regular procedural software.

Face Validation: Project team members, potential expert system users, and domain experts compare expert system performance against a selected human expert, and determine whether it performs within a "performance range" established prior to development.

Predictive Validation: The expert system is driven by input from test cases, and its performance is compared with that of the expert. This is the traditional approach that poses the problem of difficulty in finding the cause of failure and correcting it.

Turing Tests: Validating the expert system against a human expert's performance without knowing the performer's identity eliminates pro- or con- computer bias as well as the bias that results from validating against an expert that is biased in his or her domain of expertise (called *expert bias*).

Field Tests: Placing prototypes of the system in the field and letting the end users do the testing has the implicit advantage that the required performance range can be obtained once the users stop reporting problems with the way the system works. This approach eliminates the bias that results when the developers perform the validation without regard to their familiarity with the system (called *developer bias*).

Sensitivity Analysis: This applies to validating the knowledge base. It consists of changing input variable values and parameters, and observing the effects on the system's performance. It has proven to be one of the most powerful methods available.

Visual Interaction: Visually animating the expert system's reasoning allows the developer to interact by changing parameters, modifying the knowledge base, and visually perceiving the system's workings.

The emergence of the above approaches shows that steps are being taken to formalize validation, but there are no consistencies among them. For example, not all can be applied during development, which still delays validation to the last stages. Most approaches don't provide a way of correcting the failures, they only indicate whether any exist.

2.1.2. Quantitative Approaches

These approaches employ statistical techniques to compare an expert system's performance to a human expert's or to performance stored in test cases with known results. Given an acceptable performance range, a formal hypothesis test is used to determine whether the performance lies within the predetermined performance range. The hypotheses are of the type:

HO = The expert system is valid for the acceptable performance range under the prescribed input domain.

or

H1 = The expert system is invalid for the acceptable performance range under the prescribed input domain.

Paired T-tests, Hotelling's one-sample T-test, simultaneous confidence intervals, and other statistical techniques (Balci et al., 1987) are used to test hypotheses. None of these quantitative methods help localize the cause of failure or correct it. They simply result in a numeric evaluation of the system's performance.

2.1.3. An Iterative Development Methodology

This is an approach described in the paper "Verification and validation of expert systems" (Geissman and Schultz, 1988), which incorporates validation to the development process. It consists of the following six steps:

1. *Development of an initial prototype of a subset of the problem:* This prototype is iteratively enhanced to deal with a larger portion of the problem until a system that can be delivered is obtained. From this stage, clear and testable expert system requirements are formed. This is a solution to one of the important problems in validation cited earlier.

2. *Design in terms of formal paradigms:* That is, determining the one or several inference mechanisms used by the system, and testing them separately to see whether each complies with the knowledge representation used.
3. *Certifying the inference engine:* That is, making sure it correctly carries out the inference mechanisms in step 2.
4. *Design for verification:* This refers to verifying that the design correctly conforms to the requirements in step 1.
5. *Verify the knowledge base:* By checking the correctness of the knowledge (rules, facts, objects, etc.), and confirming that it conforms to the inference paradigms.
6. *Perform formal validation, which includes:*

   - Determining validation criteria such as accuracy, adaptability, reliability, sensitivity, Turing tests, and others.
   - Specifying inputs for which the system must work.
   - Developing a library of test cases for testing when the knowledge is modified.
   - Developing testing drivers for automatic testing.
   - Comparing with other existing expert systems.
   - Recording information on performance throughout the life of the system

This approach has similarities with regular procedural software development and validation methodologies, and it attempts to be well guided, but the steps are sometimes redundant. It has the advantage that a failure can be localized to a stage in development, but finding its place in the body of the system an correcting it is still an unsolved problem.

2.2. Broader Approaches

2.2.1. SEEK

Seeing the above, it would be desirable to have a method that would not only detect problems, but also suggest experiments for modifying the knowledge base in order to solve them. This approach would also require the support of a (complete, domain-representative) set of test cases stored with their correct conclusions. It should also be able to simulate the expert system's reasoning. Lastly, it would require a set of functions to analyze previous and current performance, and from this analysis, suggest the mentioned experiments. This process of relying on experience and observation defines what is called empirical analysis for the verification and validation of expert systems.

One of the most successful efforts in expert system validation is the development of SEEK (System for Empirical Experimentation with Expert Knowledge) (Politakis, 1985). It is an interactive system that offers advice on rule refinement during the design of a diagnostic rule-based expert system model whose domain is connective tissue diseases. It can validate the model over an entire set of test cases, or one test case in particular, and suggest experiments for modifying the rules when the model's results and the known results don't match.

SEEK makes use of two knowledge sources: (1) expert knowledge in the form of rules, and (2) experience in the form of test cases with known conclusions. It simulates the inference process, and detects regularities in performance when cases are misdiagnosed.

The system suggests two classes of rule refinement experiments:

1. Generalization or weakening of rules, thus making a rule easier to satisfy or making its impact on decision making carry more weight. This can be done by removing conditions from the premise of the rule, or by increasing its confidence level, respectively.
2. Specialization or strengthening of rules, thus making a rule more difficult to satisfy or making its impact on decision making carry less weight. This is done by adding conditions to the premise, or by decreasing its confidence level, respectively.

The process of suggesting experiments on misdiagnosed cases consists of gathering rule-refinement statistics from previous and current examples. Some of these include figures such as: the number of satisfied components in the rules, number of components needed for satisfaction, number of cases in which rules are used to reach to correct and incorrect conclusions, number of cases suggesting the generalization or specialization of a rule, a list of candidate rules for modification, etc. These are then examined in the premises of a set of heuristic rules (meta-knowledge) to determine and suggest the actual modification. The knowledge engineer has the choice of either accepting or rejecting the suggested experiment, and he or she may base this decision on a measure of closeness to correcting the case(s) obtained from the above analysis.

The SEEK approach to validation not only detects failures in the system but also localizes them and suggests ways to correct them. This was not true of any of the approaches previously explored.

2.2.2. EVA

Another successful project in expert system validation is the development of EVA (Expert System Validation Associate) (Chang et al., 1987), a meta-knowledge-based system whose purpose is to define and develop automated tools to validate the structural, logical, and semantic integrity of rule-based knowledge-based systems. The AI engineers in this project recognize the difficulty of applying conventional validation methods to knowledge-based and expert systems, so they propose a tool that uses domain-independent metaknowledge in the form of meta-predicates, meta-rules, and meta-facts, to represent and enforce semantic and integrity constraint information. This makes it possible to detect errors in the facts and rules of any rule-based expert system, to do this automatically, and to offer advice on how to ensure the knowledge's validity.

EVA has two component sets of modules. The first consists of conversion algorithms to translate the application (the knowledge of the expert system being validated) and its validation and control statements into a format that can be understood by EVA's second set of modules, the validation modules. This set includes the following:

- *Logic Checker:* It checks whether the rule base of an application is consistent and numerically complete. Direct inconsistency refers to cases in which two rules have mutually exclusive conclusions and equivalent premises. Indirect inconsistency is when more than two rules are involved, e.g., if A then B, if B then C, if A then C. Numeric incompleteness refers to gaps in numeric information, e.g., if $A \leqslant 5$ then B, if $A \geqslant 7$ then C. For this case, the logic checker should suggest the insertion of a new rule for the condition $5 < A < 7$ into the knowledge base, if one does not exist.
- *Structure Checker:* It takes the rules and facts of the application and builds a directed graph, where the edges between nodes represent a match between a clause in the conclusion of the source rule and a clause in the premise of the destination rule. It then uses graph theory algorithms to locate errors such as unreachable and dead-end nodes, redundancy (duplicate or equivalent rules), recursiveness, and irrelevancy.
- *Semantics Checker:* Its purpose is to detect errors in ranges, legal values for variables, value compatibility, and data types.
- *Omission Checker:* It detects omissions in the application knowledge, e.g., is-a (man, person), is-a (woman, person), father-

-off(person, man). For this case, the omission checker would suggest the insertion of a new relation that relates person to woman, namely mother-of, into the knowledge base, if one does not exist.

- *Rule proposer:* It's an "intelligent" debugger used to make the rules fit, given test cases, by suggesting the application of the generalization or specialization operations to the rules. Out of all the modules in the EVA project, the rule proposer module shows the greatest similarity to the approach used in SEEK. We could say that the part of SEEK's empirical analysis portion is equivalent in function to EVA's rule proposer.

The EVA project is a continuing effort and additional validation modules are in development (Chang et al., 1990).

Both SEEK and EVA ease the task of knowledge-base validation and correction through simulation and thorough analysis of the knowledge elements. Both efforts are aimed at rule-based knowledge validation, but present two different contexts for validation. SEEK validates the correctness of the expertise, requiring the support of test cases with known results, and a model of the inference process with additional statistics gathering and analysis capabilities. EVA validates the integrity of the knowledge with techniques that apply only to the encoded knowledge. It is essential that knowledge be valid in both contexts in order to have a valid expert system.

3. AN IDEAL APPROACH: GENERIC EXPERT SYSTEM VALIDATION

It would be desirable to extend facilities such as those of SEEK and EVA to expert systems of any type, existing or in development. We could have a "generic" validation tool to build expert systems and validate them in both contexts, during their development as well as throughout their lives. If this tool is to be used on any expert system, then it is necessary to have translating programs to change the expert system's knowledge representation into the one used by our tool and back again since it has its own knowledge representation for which validation statements and refinement advice are generated. The tool should also be able to model the expert system's inference mechanism. These two notions, especially the latter one, seem somewhat infeasible considering that as the field of expert systems evolves, newer and more sophisticated methods of representing knowledge and of inferencing on that knowledge continue to emerge, but we are very far from finding a knowledge representation scheme that encompasses all expert systems. Such a knowledge representation scheme could be called the "generic" knowledge representation scheme. Alternatively, tools to perform validation could be included with each developed expert system shell (or base level expert system). This would require fitting the known validation tools to the chosen knowledge representation.

4. VALIDATING FUZZY RULES

There are two approaches, using fuzziness, which may be taken in expert system development. One method is to provide fuzzy truth values to rules and conditions in their premises, which is one way to address nonprobabilistic uncertainty. The second approach to using fuzziness is to handle uncertainty and imprecision with linguistic quantifiers and the use of fuzzy terms in the conditions. For example, the fuzzy rule in Table 30.1 contains two imprecise conditions in its premise. The two approaches can be combined into one system, if needed. The problems posed for validation are similar. We will concentrate on the second approach.

Table 30.1. Fuzzy rule with two conditions and nonfuzzy conclusion

IF the water level of the river is **high** and the water level of the river is **rapidly rising**
THEN prepare to open the gates to the bypass canal

In the case of the rule in Table 30.1, the fuzzy sets **high** and **rapidly rising** must be correctly defined in the domain (flood control) of discourse. There will be no uniform definition for these sets across domains. The fuzzy set **high** would have a distinctly different definition for airplanes' cruising altitudes from what it would have for river height. The sets will be derived by the domain expert or possibly from writings about the domain. They can be graphically presented to the expert for validation and/or presented as discrete sets in the cases where the latter is reasonably possible. Ensuring that the fuzzy sets defined by linguistic terms are reasonable will be crucial to the validation of fuzzy expert systems.

Intuitively, it seems likely that different definitions for terms (in a specific domain of discourse) such as **high** might be obtained. Slight differences will probably be acceptable, as these are imprecise concepts. There will be a "range" of possible definitions that will allow the system to function correctly. Hence, the focus must not be on an exact definition for a fuzzy set, but on one that is acceptable in the expert system. A fuzzy expert system is not expected to be extremely sensitive to small changes in the definitions of the sets.

4.1. Matching

A fuzzy conclusion, such as **inventory is very high,** provides information on the condition **inventory is high**. However, using nonfuzzy validation techniques the possibility of chaining the two rules involved might be missed. This is because there is not an exact match between the two conditions. By simply removing the fuzzy quantifier there will be a match. The format may be different in specific fuzzy expert systems, but the expert and/or the knowledge engineer will necessarily be aware of the fuzzy correspondences between terms. This information will need to be communicated to the validation tool(s).

Table 30.2. Fuzzy rule with fuzzy conclusion

IF inventory is **very high**
THEN slow production

Information on the fuzzy correspondences between terms will be used in determining dead-end rules (those rules that are not concluding rules and lead nowhere). The fuzzy matching will also enable redundant conditions and unused conditions to be identified in the validation process. For example, a rule could be written as:

IF the water level is **high** and the water level is **very high**
THEN move to **higher** ground

Only the second condition is needed in the above rule. However, without removing the **very**, the two may appear different to currently used validation rule checkers.

The strength of the quantifiers must also be considered in doing matching. For example, one would not match conditions containing **very high** with one containing **almost high** though they both contain the fuzzy set **high**. The validation system will need to know which of the possible imprecise matches are valid and which are invalid, after quantifiers are removed. It can also be the case that a conclusion will be fuzzily quantified. If for example, a rule is as shown in Table 30.2, and we are given **inventory is slightly high,** a conclusion of **slightly slow production** may be reached. This may now exactly (or inexactly) match a condition in some other rules premise. In order to perform validation, the range of quantifiers that may be applied to a conclusion will need to be known.

4.2. Testing the Fuzzy System

In the course of testing a fuzzy expert system it will be natural for the answers to be imprecise in some cases. When they are precise, validating that they are correct defaults to the crisp or previously discussed case. In the cases where the conclusions are fuzzy, validation will require that the strength of the conclusion be appropriate in addition to embodying the correct recommendation. The conclusion must not be quantified such that it is too weak or requires a fuzzy action that only partially sloves the problem. Also, the fuzzy set defined by the conclusion must be within the acceptable bounds of its possible range. The expert must be able to clearly identify the conclusion, as defined, to be correct.

The other major difference in testing a fuzzy expert system (as opposed to one without uncertainty or imprecision) is that the information entered into the system can be uncertain or imprecise. When the inputs are certain and match the conditions of rules it is clear that an answer will be expected of the system. However, the inputs to the system may be fuzzy and then the difficulty is in determining when the appropriate rules should fire. Also, as the strength of information given to the expert system declines, the strength of the systems' conclusions will (in general) decline.

A method to tackle the problem of varying strength inputs is to use the concept of α-cuts (Kandel, 1984) above which designated conclusions should be made. The α-cuts may involve linguistic quantifiers applied to specific terms instead of the usual numeric membership values. For a given set of quantifiers and any stronger quantifiers applied to designated inputs, it will be determined that a conclusion should fire with some minimal strength and bounded by a maximal strength. Sets of quantified inputs will be matched with the appropriate conclusion and its appropriate strength(s). Clearly, if exhaustive testing of the expert system is to be undertaken and the system is very large, the concept of using α-cuts will prove to be expensive. It is not hard to imagine a case in which exhaustive testing is not feasible.

The number of test cases needed will be larger with a fuzzy expert system. This will tend to lengthen the validation process and is probably one indication that the use of imprecision in the expert system should be limited to where it is essential. However, fuzzy rules tend to cover a larger space than nonfuzzy ones. This means that a smaller number of fuzzy rules may cover the decision space making the validation process easier. In validation, the concentration needs to be on the most pervasive conlusions and the most likely sets of inputs that bear on them. The α-cut concept can be used to validate as the inputs become fuzzy. As in the case where there is no fuzziness, it will not always be feasible to test for every possible situation. Careful testing on the major possible scenarios with "reasonable" coverage of other possible cases for the expert system will provide a system that is generally reliable. The validators in conjunction with the domain expert will have to determine what level of testing is necessary before confidence in the system is justified. There will clearly be different levels of testing necessary, for example, in controlling a nuclear reaction and in recommending (returnable) clothing outfits.

5. SUMMARY

The major part of expert system validation lies in the validation of the knowledge. The inference engine and its additional facilities may be validated using more familiar techniques such as those for conventional procedural software.

Knowledge can be validated in two separate contexts: the validation of the integrity of the knowledge and the validation of the correctness of the expertise. The first applies only to the contents of the knowledge base, while the second requires a model of the inference engine that implements additional statistical and heuristic analysis functions, as well as a domain-representative set of test cases stored with known results.

There are several methods of representing knowledge, and many more are being developed. Unfortunately, these efforts are not equaled by those in the field of expert system validation. The fact that knowledge representation schemes continue to emerge while the validation of knowledge in such schemes is neglected is an important factor behind the lack of public belief in and acceptance of expert systems.

The issues of knowledge representation, knowledge acquisition, and knowledge transformation are all relevant to the issue of expert system validation. This paper concentrates solely upon rules as a knowledge representation. To have fully validated expert systems, they must acquire knowledge correctly. Also, the selection of a representation scheme may have crucial effects on the complexity and effectiveness of the validation methodology. If these two criteria are not met, knowledge transformation may provide a bridge to validating the knowledge by translating it to a representation scheme for which effective validating techniques exist, and translating it back to its original scheme. However, maintaining the semantics can be difficult (Chang, 1990).

The incremental validation of the knowledge through the life of the system should be conducted with minimum effort. If changes are made or knowledge is added to the knowledge base, the validation process should involve the new knowledge and any old knowledge that may be affected. Still, the knowledge must be validated in both contexts. Validating the integrity of the knowledge requires that domain parameters referenced in the new knowledge be identified so that the integrity checking techniques may be applied only to a subset of the entire knowledge. On the other hand, validating the correctness of the expertise should be performed using only test cases that apply to the new/modified knowledge. If the new knowledge is the result of a new test case, this test case must be added to the validation set.

The validation of rule-based expert systems has been examined. The validation of these systems in the case of fuzzy rules is viewed to be an extension or generalization of the process for nonfuzzy systems. The discussion on fuzzy systems has centered on the use of fuzzy terms and fuzzy quantifiers; for fuzzy truth values the problems and solutions will be similar. The definition of the fuzzy terms and fuzzy quantified terms must be correct, but need not be exact. The testing process in a fuzzy expert system may require more effort than in a nonfuzzy system, but can be made relatively straightforward by using ranges or α-cuts for quantifiers above which a conclusion will hold with some desired precision.

The process of performing validation on expert systems is undergoing evolution. The techniques presented here are some of the best current validation techniques and can be applied to successfully validate fuzzy expert systems.

Acknowledgments

This research is partially supported by a grant from the Systems and Research Center of Honeywell, Inc.

Keywords: fuzzy expert systems, validation, rules

BIBLIOGRAPHY

Aikins, J. S. (1983). Prototypical knowledge for expert systems. *Artificial Intelligence,* **20.**

Balci, O., R. M. O'Keefe, and E.I. Feigenbaum. (1981). *The Handbook of Artificial Intelligence,* Vol. I, II and III. Los Altos: Morgan Kaufmann.

Bundy, A. (1987). How to improve the reliability of expert systems. *Proceedings of Expert Systems '87. Seventh Annual Technical Conference of the British Computer Society Specialist Group on Expert Systems.* Cambridge University Press, December.

Buchanan, B. G. and E. H. Shortliffe. (1981). *Rule based expert programs: The MYCIN Experiments of the Stanford Heuristic Programming Project.* Reading, MA: Addison-Wesley.

Chang, C. L. and R. A. Stachowitz. (1988). *Verification and Validation of Expert Systems.* Tutorial, SP2 - AAAI - 88.

Chang, C. L., J. Combs, and R. A. Stachowitz. (1990). *A Report on the Expert Systems Validation Associate (EVA).* Technical Report, Software Information Exchange A-54, Lockheed Software Technology Center.

Chang, C. L., and R. A. Stachowitz, and T. B. Combs. (1987). Validation of knowledge-based systems. *Proceedings of Second AIAA/NASA/USAF Symposium on Automation, Robotics, and Advanced Computing,* March.

Cheng, A. (1990). *Expert System Validation as it Applies to Expert Systems Utilizing a Frame-Based Knowledge Representation.* Master's Thesis, Computer Science Department, University of South Florida, Tampa.

Cheng, A. and L. O. Hall. (1990). Expert system validation as it applies to expert systems utilizing a frame-based knowledge representation. *Proceedings of the Second Annual Florida A.I. Research Symposium,* Orlando, April.

Geissman, J. R. and R. Schultz. (1988). Verification and validation of expert systems. *AI Expert,* February.

Ginsberg, A., S. M. Weiss, and P. Politakis. (1988). Automatic knowledge base refinement and classification systems. *Artificial Intelligence,* **35,** June.

Hall, L. O. and A. Kandel. (1989). On the validation and testing of fuzzy expert systems. *IEEE Transactions on Systems, Man and Cybernetics.*

Hayes, P. J. (1985). *The Logic of Frames, Frame Conceptions and Text Understanding.* In J. Brochman (ed.): *Readings in Knowledge Representation.*

Jackson, P. (1990). *Introduction to Expert Systems,* Second ed. Reading, MA: Addison-Wesley.

Kandel, A. (1984). *Fuzzy Mathematical Techniques with Applications.* Reading, MA: Addison-Wesley.

Lundsgaarde, H. P. (1987). *Evaluating Medical Expert Systems. Soc. Sci. Med.,* **24.**

Minsky, M. (1981). A Framework for Representing Knowledge. MIT Press. Also in Brachman (ed.): *Readings in Knowledge Representation,* New York: De Gruyter, 1985.

Neches, R., W. R. Swartout, and J. Moore. (1985). Enhanced maintenance and explanation of expert systems through explicit models of their development. *IEEE Transactions on Software Engineering,* Vol. SE-11, no. 11.

Nguyen, T. A., W. A. Perkins, T. J. Laffey, and D. Pecora. (1987). Knowledge base verification. *AI Magazine,* Summer.

O'Keefe, R. M. (1987). Validating expert system performance. *IEEE Expert,* **2,** 81–90.

O'Leary, D. E. (1988). *A Fuzzy Set Approach to Analyzing the Validation of Expert Systems.* Technical Report, Graduate School of Business, University of Southern California, Los Angeles, July.

Politakis, P. G. (1985). *Empirical Analysis for Expert Systems.* London: Pitman, Advanced Publishing Program.

Rothman, P. (1988). Knowledge transformation. *AI Expert,* November.

Scott, A. C., E. H. Shortliffe, and M. Suwa. (1982). An approach to verifying completeness and consistency in a rule-based expert system. *AI Magazine,* Fall.

Self, K. (1990). Designing with fuzzy logic. *IEEE Spectrum,* November, pp. 42–44.

Thuraisingham, B. (1989). From rules to frames and frames to rules. *AI Expert,* October.

Turksen, I. B. (1984). Production control with a linguistic rule-based system. *Proc. First International Conference on Fuzzy Information Processing,* (Hawaii, USA).

6

FUZZY LOGIC FOR INTELLIGENT DATABASE MANAGEMENT SYSTEMS

31 A survey of conceptual and logical data models for uncertainty management

A. YAZICI, R. GEORGE, B. P. BUCKLES,
and F. E. PETRY
Center for Intelligent and Knowledge-Based
Applications
Department of Computer Sciences
Tulane University
New Orleans, LA 70118, USA

Abstract. File systems gave way to database systems in the early 1960s due to the need for data integrity and independence. The first generation of databases consisted of the network and hierarchical data models. The relational model, developed in the early 1970s, dominated the research scene in the 1980s. The first research involving fuzzy databases took place in the late 1970s and was, for a time, preoccupied with the relational model, although uncertainty mechanics were retrofitted to the first generation models. Directions taken with the relational model included simply adding a membership attribute to each relation, allowing data values to be possibility distributions, and the substitution of similarity for equality in the application of query terms and relational operations. Languages were designed that corresponded to the relational algebra and relational calculus. In the 1980s there began a new research direction in databases with the objective of overcoming the obstacles of scientific databases, i.e., complex objects and large amounts of data. Initially, this took the form of semantic data models which emphasized representation but not behavior. More recently, this has taken the form of three distinct schools of thought regarding the form of the next generation of database: object-oriented databases, third-generation concepts exemplified by non-first normal form databases, and deductive databases. Thus far, little or nothing has been done in the area of fuzzy deductive databases. Object-oriented databases involve many issues such as inheritance and relationships between objects. Thus far, fuzzy set research in both object-oriented and non-first normal form databases has concentrated solely on data representation. These present trends as well as past developments are reported here.

1. INTRODUCTION

Database management systems have traditionally modeled a precise universe, where all values are known and unambiguous. However, more often real-world data values are imprecise with fuzzy connotations and are sometimes even missing. ANSI/X3/SPARC, for instance, defines 14 types of null values alone. Fuzzy data (predicate values or numbers) can arise whenever subjective judgments or evaluations are part of the stored data. Such data cannot be discarded or forced to conform to precise values, since that would result in a loss of important information. What are required, however, are data models capable of representing real-world situations, with no loss of manipulation power (vis-à-vis "crisp" data models).

The extension of data models to incorporate fuzzy and imprecise information has important benefits. First, as detailed above it would constitute a more accurate representation of the database universe. Second, it gives the user considerably more flexibility in data manipulation, allowing, for instance, retrieval based on "similarity" of data values. (It should be noted that all these approaches to imprecision modeling consider crisp data as a special case of fuzzy data.) There is yet another advantage that arises out of this property. There has, in recent years, been an interest in the coupling of artificial intelligence and database systems specifically to improve the functionality and applicability of the systems. Proposals for such a coupling (Buckles and Petry, 1982; George et al., 1991; Yazici et al., 1992) have called for databases of higher semantic content, capable of managing impreciseness, to increase the cohesiveness, and reduce the coupling between the integrated systems.

Database management systems evolved out of generalized file management systems. The second generation of databases were the network and the hierarchical models. The lack of physical independence of these models was soon apparent and they were superseded by the relational model (third generation), which became the de facto standard of database systems by the mid-1980s. The growing complexity of data modeling requirements forced a reappraisal of the relational model, leading to the definition of extended relational models and the semantic database model. In the last few years, the success of the object-oriented paradigm in producing high quality, reusable software, has resulted in ongoing work on the object-oriented data models. The commercial release of a number of object-oriented database systems marks the genesis of the fourth generation of data models. In this paper we survey three different categories of data models that have been extended to incorporate fuzzy and imprecise data-conceptual models, such as the entity-relationship and the IFO models, Navigational models, specifically the network and object-oriented data models, and relational models represented by the first normal form (1NF) and the non-first normal form models (Non-1NF).

The information stored within a database depends on the data model and this also affects the type and nature of the imprecision represented. The first maintains the standard data model and has imprecise queries, and the second retains the standard language (SQL in the case of the 1NF), and extends the data model (Motoro, 1990). In this paper we concentrate on the latter approach.

Typically, the approaches to modeling uncertainty in databases have focused on the theory of fuzzy sets (Buckles and Petry, 1982; Shenoi and Melton, 1989), which associates each member of a set of elements with a value in the unit interval [0, 1], denoting the grade of membership in the set. The model may have heterogeneous or homogeneous attribute values. The homogeneous approach ensures all instances of an attribute are of the same type while in the heterogeneous model they may be of different types such as range values, nulls, or possibility distributions. The homogeneous approach is more consistent with normative database theory and is the subject of our study.

In the similarity model (Buckles and Petry, 1982), the concept of identity is replaced with that of pairwise similarity. The similarity relationship, s, has the following properties:

$$s(x, y) = 1 \qquad \text{[reflexivity]}$$
$$s(x, y) = s(y, x) \qquad \text{[symmetry]}$$
$$s(x, y) \geqslant \max_{z \in D} [\min (s(z, y), s(z, y))] \qquad \text{[transitivity]}$$

The only overhead is explicitly maintaining a similarity matrix within the system.

2. FUZZINESS AT THE CONCEPTUAL DESIGN LEVEL

An SDM (Semantic Data Model) description can serve as a conceptual model in the database design process. The primary goal of SDMs is to provide the user and designer of a database a precise and clear description. In addition, an SDM serves as a formal specification mechanism for capturing and expressing much of the meaning associated with data in a database. In particular, a new user of a large, complex database should be able to determine from the SDM schema what information and semantics are contained in the database. . That is, an SDM description enhances the effectiveness and usability of database systems. In order to describe the semantics of an application environment, SDMs provide a collection of high-level modeling primitives.

There are many applications where attributes deal inherently with imprecise, incomplete, or vague data, or with data that is qualitative rather than quantitative, or the exact values of attributes are not known, but there exists partial knowledge of possible data values distribution. Since fuzzy information is part of many real-world applications, it is important to have the capability of representing such information in a high level design, where we seek a precise representation of the semantics of a database. By incorporating the notion of information imprecision and incompleteness at conceptual design (SDM), we can establish a better communication channel between database users and designers. We do this by adding high-level constructs and including the domain (value set) of the imprecise or incomplete attributes as part of the SDM.

There are two existing approaches for describing the specification and documentation of an application invironment whose attributes are not assumed to be precise and exact. Zvieli and Chen (1986) extended the entity-relationship (E/R) model for representing and processing fuzzy data. The other approach consists of an extended IFO model, which supports a systematic representation and extended NF^2 relations as the implementation level for processing fuzzy information.

Since the degree of represented information and the notations for these approaches are different, we describe them separately. However, we include the fuzzy set constructors in the representation of E/R model with the same notation used in the representation of the extended IFO model for uniformity.

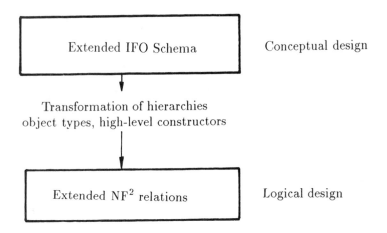

Figure 31.1. Overall structure of the methodology

2.1. Extended IFO Model

The extended IFO model approach (Yazici et al., 1992) to representing uncertainty in database design starts from a very high-level
design (conceptual) and terminates in the implementation database
model (logical design), which consists of NF^2 relations. The transformation of the high-level constructs of the conceptual design into NF^2
relations is done by applying a translation algorithm similar to one
described (George et al., 1990). The overall structure of the methodology is shown in Figure 31.1.

An extended IFO scheme is a directed graph with various types of
vertices and directed edges, representing atomic types, constructed
types, constructed types, functions, and ISA relationships.

1. There are three kinds of atomic types: printable, which are also
   called predefined types, abstract atomic types, which have no
   underlying structure, and free atomic types, which correspond
   to entities. The graphical representation of the atomic types is
   shown in Figure 31.2.
2. Constructed types are built by using four high-level constructs.

One of the four mechanisms for constructing nonatomic types is
the grouping constructor, which is used to form (finite) sets of objects
of a given structure type. Each member of the set necessarily and
precisely belongs to the set. This constructor is also called the M-set

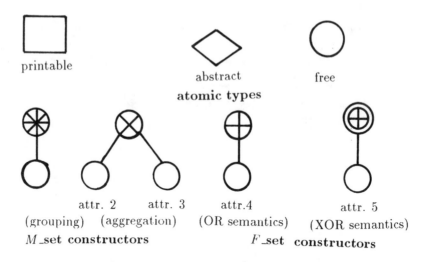

Figure 31.2. The atomic types and constructors of the extended IFO model

constructor (Yazici, 1990), which defines a set with AND semantics among its members. More specifically, the membership degree of each element of the set can only be one (1). For example, assume that in a Library information system, shown in Figure 31.3, some books are written by a set of authors, which are specified in the Author attribute. Each attribute in this set belongs precisely to the set and there is an AND semantics among the author values in the set.

Another *M*-set constructor, called the Cartesian product (or aggregation constructor), is used to construct new types out of existing ones. The object associated with a type with an aggregation mechanism is viewed as an ordered pair of the attribute types that are used to construct the new type.

Two high-level primitives are added to the IFO Model (Abiteboul and Hull, 1987) to describe the meaning associated with imprecise and incomplete data in conceptual design. These constructors are called F-set constructors and form sets with OR or XOR semantics. The representation of attribute values that they construct is shown with $F = [f_j, f_{j+1}, ..., f_i]$, where $[f_j, f_{j+1},...f_i]$ denotes a nonempty subset of $\{f_1, f_2, ...f_n\}$ the domain of attribute A and $2 \leqslant i \leqslant n$. As they are shown in Figure 31.2, whenever these constructors are used, the domain of the attributes is attached to them at conceptual design stage.

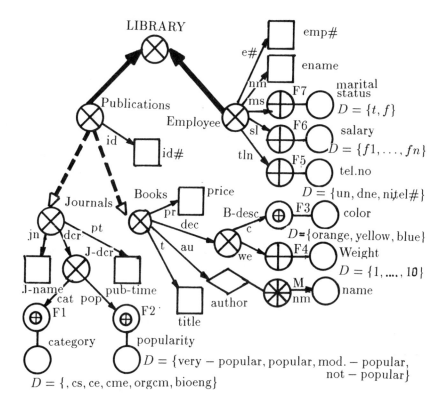

Figure 31.3. Library example represented with the extended IFO model

One of these F-set constructors (Figure 31.2) defines a set with the semantics that exactly one element of the set is the true value. This constructor is interpreted as XOR and used to represent incomplete information, such as range values and null values. For example, the Weight attribute of a books may not be precisely known, but only as a range between 1 and 10 lb, which may be represented as $F = [1,...,10]$.

Another F-set constructor constructs sets among whose elements there exists imprecise relationships. This kind of relationship can be interpreted as OR semantics. Referring to Figure 31.2, the attribute corresponds to a set of data values of attribute 5. In other words, the membership degree of each element in the set is in the interval [0, 1]. This set constructor is used to represent imprecise information, which may be inherent in the domain attributes. For example, assume that the Books database has an attribute called Popularity and the value of this inherently imprecise attribute is in the set {very-popular, popular, moderate-popular, not-popular}. Based on the similarity value among the values of the set and the interpretation of the threshold value specified by the user, the elements of the set that belong to the set are determined.

Since we assume that fuzziness may occur only in values of an attribute type, there is no need to apply F-set constructors recursively. However, the grouping constructor and aggregation constructor can be applied recursively in any order, as described in Yazici et al. (1990).

   3. Functional relationships between two objects in the IFO model are expressed with functions.
   4. ISA relationships indicate that each object associated with subtype is associated with the supertype.

Because of the interplay between object structures and ISA relationships, two types of ISA relationships are distinguished in the IFO model: specialization and generalization. The specialization relationship is used to define occurrences and properties of members of a given type; that is, object type is inherited downwards. In contrast, the generalization relationship is used to define situations where distinct types are combined to form new virtual types. Object types are inherited upwards in this ISA relationship.

An example of each of the items mentioned is given in Figure 31.3. This scheme includes printable objects (Person, id #, etc.), free objects (Author, color, etc.), grouping constructor, also called set constructor, (M), aggregation constructor, also called Cartesian product constructor (Journals, Employee, etc.), F-set constructor with OR semantics (F1, F2, F3) and F-set constructor with XOR semantics (F4, F5, F6, F7), function (the edge from Employee to emp#, and so on), specialization (the edge from Publications to Books and Journals) and generalization (the edge from Publications and Employee to Library).

For the manipulation of fuzzy information represented in the conceptual design, first of all, the extended IFO structures are transformed into the extended NF^2 relations. The algorithm developed for this purpose preserves data semantics during the transformation. Processing of either imprecise or precise data is by means of an extended relational algebra for NF^2 relations, developed and presented in Yazici et al. (1992).

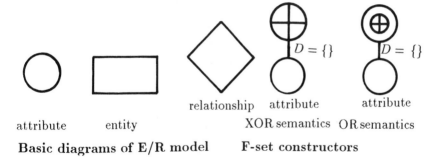

Basic diagrams of E/R model   F-set constructors

attribute   entity   XOR semantics   OR semantics

relationship   attribute   attribute

Figure 31.4. Diagrams and constructors used in E/R model

2.2. Entity-relationship modeling of fuzzy data

This approach employs the E-R model to describe databases. The approach proposed in Zvieli and Chen (1986) considers fuzziness at three levels. In the first level, the fuzziness arises during database design, or design modifications of the database conceptual scheme. At this level, an entity set, a relationship set, or an attribute set may be fuzzy. The second level of fuzziness may occur in the specific occurrences of entities or relationships. In the third level, attributes of specific entities or relationships may be fuzzy. Here, the domain of a fuzzy attribute is emphasized as part of the E/R diagram. Since the frequent source of fuzziness is the values of attributes, we discuss only this latter level. Interested readers may consult Zvieli and Chen (1986) for detailed information on the other levels.

A conceptual database structure can be constructed using the following entity-relationship diagrams (Figure 31.4):

1. Rectangles, which represent entity sets.
2. Diamonds, which represent relationship sets; they are linked to their constituent entity sets by directed edges.
3. Circles, which represent attributes; they are linked to the entity sets or relationships by directed edges (from entity/relationship sets to attributes) and linked to F-set constructors.

For example, consider a library database with the entity set Books, B-Description, and Author. The relationships are: Books are "described by" B-Desc, written by Author. Attributes of the Books entity

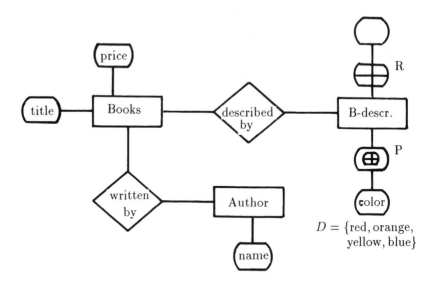

Figure 31.5. Books entity in a library database represented with E/R model

are "title" and "price," the imprecise and incomplete attributes of
B-desc are "color" and "weight." Figure 31.5 represents this situation.

In Zvieli and Chen (1986), fuzzy objects are shown in the E/R
diagram by a contour made of wavy lines. In order to be uniform with
the previous schemas, we alter here the representation of fuzzy
attributes by using F-set constructors and emphasizing the domain.

The generalized fuzzy E/R algebra pertains to fuzziness at levels
two and three. Fuzziness in the first level may be dealt with by
designer before implementing the database. The output of a query
written in the fuzzy E/R algebra is a fuzzy set. In the query,
membership function $\mu_A(x)$ is used to map elements of the universe
into the set [0, 1]. The value of μ_A for the argument x indicates
whether x is a member of A.

3. RELATIONAL MODELS

Primarily, attempts at uncertainty management in database systems
have concentrated on the 1NF relational model. We present a general

overview of the work done in this area in Section 3.1. The demand for models with higher representational capability led to the interest in extending relational technology. We present a non-first normal form database capable of representing imprecise information in Section 3.2.

3.1. 1NF Models

The conceptual (or user-level) view of a 1NF relational database is simple. It consists of one or more two-dimensional tables called relations. The relation columns are called attributes, thus each row (called a tuple) is a sequence of attribute values.

The relational model has broad applicability. One natural application that has been considered is the representation of bibliographic data (Crawford, 1981). Tables 31.1 and 31.2 illustrate such an ordinary relational database having two relations. The key for relation BOOKS consists of attributes TITLE and AUTHOR, YEAR, and PUBLISHER. The key for relation PUBLISHERS consists of the attributes of PUBLISHER.

The distinguishing characteristic of an ordinary relational database (or ordinary databases of other forms) is the uniformity or homogeneity of the represented data. For each attribute, there is a prescribed set of values, called the domain, from which values may be selected. Further, each element of the domain set has the same structure, e.g., integers, real numbers, or character strings. Attributes

Table 31.1. Relation: BOOKS

Title	Author	Year	Publisher
Dynamic Information & Library Processing	Salton	1975	Prentice-Hall
Automatic Inf. Organization & Retrieval	Salton	1968	McGraw-Hill
Principles of Database Systems	Ullman	1982	Comp.Sci.Press
Computer Database Organ.	Martin	1977	Prentice-Hall

Table 31.2. Relation: PUBLISHERS

Publisher	City	State
Prentice-Hall	Englewood Cliffs	NJ
McGraw-Hill	New York	NJ
Comp. Sci.Press	Rockville	MD

for which the domain set is not homogeneous are "unrepresentable" within the ordinary database context such as a relation consisting of a borrower and a borrowed item (Maier, 1983). The borrowed item may range from a book (represented by author and title) to an automobile (rpresented by model, year of production, and serial number).

The earliest extensions of the relational data model that permitted nonhomogeneous domain sets did not utilize fuzzy set theory. Rather, they were attempts to represent null values and intervals. The ANSI/X3/SPARC report of 1975, for instance, notes more than a dozen types of null. At one end of this spectrum, null means the valid value is completely unknown. For example, a null value in the current salary of an employee could mean the actual value is any one of the permissible values for the salary domain set. At the other end, null may mean that no domain value is valid.

Approaches to representation of inexact information that we will consider here include fuzzy membership values, similarity relationships, and possibility distributions. The simplest form for a fuzzy database is the use of a membership value (numeric or linguistic) in each tuple. This allows retention of homogeneous data domains and strongly typed data sets, but the semantic interpretation of the fuzzy membership domain must be known to the query processor. Table 31.3 illustrates two distinct semantics for the membership domain. In

Table 31.3. Relations with fuzzy membership domains

Name	Sport	Fuzz-Mem
Tim	Baseball	0.8
Mary	Soccer	1.0
Sam	Ping-Pong	0.6
Juan	Croquet	0.5

a: Relation: ATHLETE

Title	Author	Type	Fuzz-Mem
Lincoln	Vidal	Biography	0.75
Abraham Lincoln	Sandburg	Biography	1.0
Burr	Vidal	Biography	0.5
Iacocca	Iacocca	Business	0.8

b: Relation: BOOK-CLASSIFICATION

the first relation, ATHLETE, the membership value denotes the degree to which the tuple belongs within the relation. In the relation BOOK-CLASSIFICATION, the membership value denotes the strength of the dependency between the key, TITLE, and the attribute TYPE. (Buckles and Petry, 1982).

Other approaches (Anvari and Rose, 1984; Buckles and Petry, 1982) maintain homogeneity of data domains and also import little semantics in the query interpretation process. That is, little knowledge beyond symbol manipulation is required to implement the mechanics of querying. The major characteristic of the two data models is the existence of fuzzy measures that, within each domain set, describe for each pair of values of the degree of similarity or distinguishability. Table 31.4 illustrates the major components of this model in the context of the similarity-based formulation.

To more directly represent uncertainty within attribute values requires departure from homogeneity of representation. Possibility theory is frequently the medium employed in this context. This approach allows a straightforward unification of interval-valued attributes and "non applicable" attribute values (i.e., all values are impossible).

Among query methods, most frequently cited nonfuzzy approaches are those by Codd (1970) and Lipski (1979). Codd proposes

Table 31.4. Relations with domain similarity conditions

Title	Popularity
Lincoln	moderate
Iacocca	{extreme, high}
Abraham Lincoln	{moderate, high}
Citizens	{low, medium}

a: Relation: BOOK-POPULARITY

extreme	1.0	0.81	0.81	0.75	0.25
high	0.81	1.0	0.90	0.75	0.25
moderate	0.81	0.90	1.0	0.75	0.25
medium	0.75	0.75	0.75	1.0	0.25
low	0.25	0.25	0.25	0.25	1.0

b: Similarities

a three-valued logic using T, F, and $\bot$ (null in the sense of unknown) in conjunction with the following predicates:

$X \Theta Y \equiv \bot$ if x or y is null and Θ is $<$, $<$, $=$, $\neq$, $>$, $>$
$\bot \in S \equiv \bot$ for any set S
$\{\bot\} \subseteq S = 1$ for any set S

The logic is based on the truth tables shown in Table 31.5

Table 31.5. Truth tables for three-valued logic

$\wedge$	F	$\bot$	T		$\vee$	F	$\bot$	T		$\neg$	
F	F	F	F		F	F	$\bot$	T		F	T
$\bot$	F	$\bot$	$\bot$		$\bot$	$\bot$	$\bot$	T		$\bot$	$\bot$
T	F	$\bot$	T		T	T	T	T		T	F

Although Codd embeds these semantics into the relational algebra syntactic form, here Boolean queries will be sufficient to clarify the important issues.

Lipski does not assume a relational database form (or any other) but, for illustration, one will be used here. Assume a relation EMPLOYEE with domains NAME and AGE. The database object $T = <\text{Bob } 30-35>$ could represent six real-world objects (one for each year in the age range). Query Q places each database object in one of three categories.

$T \in \{\text{surely-set}\}$ if $\|Q\| \supseteq \|T\|$,
$T \in \{\text{possible-set}\}$ if $\|Q\| \cap \|T\| \neq \emptyset$
$T \in \{\text{eliminated-set}\}$ if $\|Q\| \cap \|T\| = \emptyset$

For instance, the query

EMPLOYEE [AGE > 32]

places T in possible-set while

EMPLOYEE [AGE > 25] L EMPLOYEE [AGE < 40]

places T in surely-set.

Query evaluation for typical fuzzy data models has two basic steps: (1) evaluation of matching or comparison predicate(s); and (2) calculation of the result set or relation based on results of the comparison. For systems that use a relational algebra query language, the JOIN operation is used for illustration:

JOIN $R1$ and $R2$ where $A1$ is about the same as $A2$

where $A1$ and $A2$ are attribute names in $R1$ and $R2$. In any representation, the fuzzy expression, "is about the same," must be given a concrete interpretation relative to the data representation. In general, this becomes more complex as the homogeneity of the data model decreases.

Consider first the data model in which a membership value denotes the degree of belonging to the relation (Table 31.3). Here, attributes to be joined are nonfuzzy, and so "about the same" is just equal and thus the evaluation is identical with an ordinary JOIN. The second step in this case requires the determination of fuzzy membership and is often computed as the minimum of the membership values.

For a representation using similarity tables, the comparison is specified in the query by a clause

LEVEL $(D) = a$

In the first step of query evaluation, the JOIN of the relations is carried out by the following process: $t1_i$ in $R1$ and $t2_j$ in $R2$ are joined over the compatible attributes with domain D if $x, y \in D$ are the values in $t1_i$ and $t2_j$ respectively, and SIMILARITY $(x, y) > a$.

The second step involves merging the redundant tuples that have been formed by the JOIN. The redundancy of tuples is determined, for a given domain, by the similarity threshold THRES(D), which is just the minimum similarity over all values in the attributes. The ultimate form of the result is obtained by merging as many tuples as possible without violating the constraint

THRES $(D) >$ LEVEL (D)

With the use of explicit possibility distributions, query evaluation is somewhat more complex. For example, tuples may be assigned membership values that may be possibility distributions over a set of membership values, and also ordinary attribute values may be singletons or possibility distributions.

Now, consider the term "is approximately equal," which is realized in Umano (1983) by the specification of a fuzzy predicate $P(D1_i, D2_j)$, where the values in the domains are possibility distribution. In this specific data model, a membership value is required for each tuple, where the value may be a possibility distribution. Thus the last step in forming the result is the computation of the membership value possibility distribution. This value is calculated by ANDing the predicate possibility distribution and the two original membership distributions: if $t1_i$ in $R2$ are joined over the compatible domain D, and x, y are values in $t1_i$, $t2_j$, respectively, then

$$\mu = P(x, y) \wedge \mu_{t1_i} \wedge \mu_{t1_j}$$

3.2. Non-1NF Model

A non-first normal form (NF^2) relation is simply an unnormalized relation scheme and an instance over this scheme. This form was first suggested by Makinouchi (1977) who relaxed the 1NF assumption to allow attributes to be set-valued. In recent years, a number of researchers (Abiteboul and Bidoit, 1984; Ozsoyoglu et al., 1987; Roth et al., 1987; Schek and Scholl, 1986; Thomas and Fischer, 1986) generalized the NF^2 database model by allowing components of a tuple to be either atomic or set-valued, and even subrelations. The NF^2 data model can be considered a generalized relational data model that treats flat relations and hierarchical structures uniformly.

Definition: A *relation scheme* is a collection of rules of the form $R = (A_1, A_2, ..., 1_n)$. $D_1, D_2, ..., D_n$ are the corresponding *domains* from which values for $A_1, A_2, ..., A_n$ are selected. R and A_i, $1 \leq i \leq n$, are called *attributes*. An A_i that does not occur on the left side of some rule is called a *zero-order attribute*.

An NF^2 scheme may contain any combination of zero- or higher-order attributes on the right side of the rules. Values of zero-order attributes may be atomic or set-valued. A 1NF scheme contains only zero-order, attributes and attribute values are atomic. An instance, r, of scheme R consists of attributes A_i and an A_i value for each tuple. If A_i is a higher-order attribute, then $A_i = (A_{i1}, A_{i2}, ..., A_{i_m})$ and a corresponding value of A_i is an element of $2^{Di1} \times 2^{Di2} \times ... \times 2^{Dim}$. If A_{ij} is zero-order then null values are allowed by an explicit symbol (usually "unk" for unknown, "dne" for do not exist, or "ni" for no information) incorporated in D_{ij}.

Operators exist to transform a 1NF relation into a NF^2 relation and vice versa in addition to extensions to the ordinary relational algebra. NEST and UNNEST (Roth et al., 1987; Schek and Scholl, 1986; Thomas and Fischer, 1986; additionally, PACK and UNPACK in Ozsoyoglu et al., 1987) are commonly cited as the classical schema redefinition operators.

Table 31.6. An example of an extended NF^2 relation

Books					
id #	title	B-desc		price	Author
		color	weight		name
id1	t1	red	w1	p1	{a1, a2}
id2	t2	orange	w1	p1	
id3	t3	blue	w2	p2	{a1, a3, a8}
id8	t8	[red, orange]	w2	p1	{a5, a8}

Table 31.7. The relation books-um after unmerging Books

Books-um					
id #	title	color	weight	price	name
id1	t1	red	unk	p1	a1
id2	t2	orange	w1	p1	a1
id1	t1	red	unk	p1	a2
id2	t2	orange	w1	p1	a2
id3	t3	blue	w1	p1	a1
id3	t3	blue	w1	p1	a3
id3	t3	blue	w1	p1	a8
id8	t8	[red, orange]	w4	p3	a5
id8	t8	[red, orange]	w4	p3	a8

We defined two restructuring operators, namely, MERGE and UNMERGE in Yazici (1992). The MERGE operator is defined in a manner that can be considered a combination of NEST (Thomas and Fischer, 1986; Schek and Scholl, 1986) and PACK operators (Ozsoyoglu et al., 1987). It may also interact with similarity relationships to manipulate imprecise information. That is, it can change the levels of nesting in a relation as the NEST operator does, and also deals with uncertain data. The functionality of the UNMERGE operator defined here is the same as that of the UNNEST operator (Roth et al., 1987; Thomas and Fischer, 1986; Schek and Scholl, 1986).

Example: Consider an example of a database shown in Table 31.6. If we restructure the relation by grouping "color" and "weight" attributes under a relation-valued attribute called "B-desc," and "name" attribute under "Author," then the resulting relation will be the one shown in Table 31.7. To do this, we would perform the MERGE operation:

MERGE (Books) [{color, weight}-. B-desc]

The UNMERGE operation inverts this operation and results in the relation shown in Table 31.7:

UNMERGE (Books) [B-desc]

Example: Assume a flat version of relation Books, where BOOKS = (BNO, AUTHOR, TITLE, PRICE, WGT, DECR) is given in Table 31.8. WGT means "weight" and DECR means "description." Assume that the similarity relation of each attribute of BOOKS is an identity relation.

If we apply the MERGE, NEST, and PACK operators to all the attributes of the relation BOOKS, we get the relation BOOKS2 shown in Table 31.9.

BOOKS2
= MERGE (BOOKS) [ ]   WITH Level (AUTHOR, TITLE, PRICE, DECR) = 0.0,
Level (BNO, WGT = 1
= NEST BNO-.BNO, AUTHOR-.AUTHOR, TITLE-.TITLE, PRICE-.PRICE, WGT.WGT, DECR-.DECR
= PACK (BOOKS) BNO, AUTHOR, TITLE, PRICE, WGT, DECR

Table 31.8. A book inventory flat relation

BOOKS					
BNO	AUTHOR	TITLE	PRICE	WGT	DECR
1	A1	T1	P1	W1	D1
1	A2	T1	P1	W2	D2
1	A1	T1	P1	W2	D2
1	A2	T1	P1	W1	D1
2	A2	T1	P2	W1	D1
2	A2	T1	P2	W3	D2
3	A1	T2	P1	W2	D1
3	A1	T2	P1	W1	D2
3	A1	T2	P1	W3	D3

Table 31.9. Relation BOOKS2 after applying the MERGE operator to relation BOOKS

BNO	AUTHOR	TITLE	PRICE	WGT	DECR
{1}	{A1, A2}	{T1}	{P1}	{W1}	{D1}
{1}	{A1, A2}	{T1}	{P1}	{W2}	{D2}
{2}	{A2}	{T1}	{P2}	{W3}	{D1}
{2}	{A2}	{T1}	{P2}	{W1}	{D2}
{3}	{A1}	{T2}	{P1}	{W2}	{D1}
{3}	{A1}	{T2}	{P1}	{W1}	{D2}
{3}	{A1}	{T2}	{P1}	{W3}	{D3}

BOOKS2

Table 31.10. Relation BOOKS3 merging similar tuples of relation BOOKS

BNO	AUTHOR	TITLE	PRICE	WGT	DECR
1	{A1, A2}	{T1}	{P1}	{W1, W2}	{D1, D2}
2	{A2}	{T1}	{P2}	{W1, W2}	{D1, D2}
3	{A1}	{T2}	{P1}	{W1, W2, W3}	{D1, D2, D3}

BOOKS3

Note that the final form of relation BOOKS2 is obtained by merging all tuples that do not violate the constraint where the threshold value is equal to or less than the Level value specified in MERGE; that is, the LEVEL value is the minimum threshold value. Also, note that we used Level (AUTHOR, TITLE, PRICE, DECR) = 0.0 instead of Level (AUTHOR) = 0.0, Level (TITLE) = 0.0, Level (PRICE) = 0.0, Level (DECR) = 0.0. This is done only for convenience.

Until now, the examples have been cases in which the results of these operators also allows us to combine similar tuples utilizing similarity relations. Therefore, there are relations generated by the MERGE operator that cannot be generated by any sequence of NEST and PACK operators. Table 31.10 shows this sort of relation.

BOOKS3
= MERGE (BOOKS) WITH Level (AUTHOR, TITLE, PRICE, WGT, DECR) = 0.0

The above example shows that the MERGE operator as defined here is more general and flexible than the PACK and the NEST operators. This additional capability of MERGE allows us to operate on imprecise information using similarity relations. Below we give an example to show how this additional property of the MERGE operator is useful in applications such as library information systems, where some attributes may be imprecise, hospital information systems, where personal evaluation is needed, etc. Here, we use the BOOKS relation with a modified attribute set as an example, which is shown in Table 31.11 and the similarity relation for attribute COLOR and its domain, shown in Table 31.12.

Table 31.11. Relation BOOKS' as a book inventory used in library information systems

BOOKS'				
BNO	AUTHOR	TITLE	PRICE	COLOR
1	A1	T1	P1	RED
1	A2	T1	P1	RED
1	A1	T1	P1	RED
1	A2	T1	P1	RED
2	A1	T2	P2	LIGHT-RED
2	A1	T2	P2	LIGHT-RED
3	A1	T3	P3	ORANGE
3	A1	T3	P3	ORANGE
3	A1	T3	P3	ORANGE
4	A2	T4	P4	BLUE

Table 31.12. The similarity relation for attribute COLOR

	Red	Redish	Orange	Light-red	Blue
Red	1	0.8	0.4	0.6	0
Redish	0.8	1	0.5	0.5	0
Orange	0.4	0.5	1	0.3	0
Light-red	0.6	0.5	0.3	1	0
Blue	0	0	0	0	1

Let us assume the following query using the relation BOOKS:

Query: "Print the titles of the books which are red or close to red and written by author A2."

> BOOKS″ = MERGE (BOOKS′) [ ] WITH Level (COLOR) ⩾ 0.6,
> Level (BNO, PRICE) ⩾ 0.0, Level (AUTHOR, TITLE) = 1.0.

We can now use the SQL-like extension for the extended NF^2 data model to answer the query.

> SELECT TITLE FROM BOOKS″
> WHERE AUTHOR {A2} AND COLOR = {RED}

The resulting relation is shown in Table 31.13 and the answer to the query is {T1, T2}. Of course, how "close to" should be interpreted may change from one user to another. But, it is clear that we are looking for a book which is "red," so we give the minimum threshold value as 0.6, which is an a priori fixed value. If one chooses a minimum threshold value of 0.3 as the interpretation of "close-to," then the result may be different. In this case, as it can be seen from the intermediate relation depicted in Table 31.14, {T1, T2, T3} would be the answer to the query:

> BOOKS″ = MERGE (BOOKS′) WITH Level (COLOR) ⩾ 0.3,
> Level (BNO, PRICE) ⩾ 0.0, Level (AUTHOR, TITLE) = 1.0.

Table 31.13. The BOOKS‴ relation, where similar tuples are merged and level value of attribute COLOR = 0.6

BNO	AUTHOR	TITLE	PRICE	COLOR
		BOOKS‴		
[1, 2]	{A1, A2}	{T1, T2}	[P1, P2]	[RED, LIGHT-RED]
[3]	{A1}	{T3}	[P3]	[ORANGE]
[4]	{A2}	{T4}	[P4]	[BLUE]

Table 31.14. The BOOKS‴ relation, where similar tuples are merged and level value of attribute COLOR = 0.3

BNO	AUTHOR	TITLE	PRICE	COLOR
		BOOKS‴		
[1, 2, 3]	{A1, A2}	{T1, T2, T3}	[P1, P2, P3]	[RED, LIGHT-RED, ORANGE]
[4]	{A2}	{T4}	[P4]	[BLUE]

Note that we use two different brackets to designate attribute values. We call "[ ]" F-set and "{ }" M-set. We should give here an aspect of F-set and M-set, namely the relationship between the level values and the sets.

Definition: "{ }" is a multivalued expression (M-set), which uses AND semantics among its elements. By AND semantics we mean that the membership degree of each element of the set is one (1). This means that each member of the set necessarily and precisely belongs to the set.

Definition: "[ ]" is a fuzzy expression (F-set), which has elements with imprecise relationship among them. This relationship may be interpreted as XOR or OR. The OR semantics says that the membership degree of each element in the set is exactly equal to one (1), or between one (1) and zero (0). This means that an element of the set, or a subset of the set, or all elements of the set possibly belong to the set; that is, the relationship among the elements of the set is not precise. In case of XOR, exactly one element of the set can possibly belong. Here we interpret F-set as XOR.

Even though an attribute may be prime (i.e., part of the key), we still can permit level value zero (0) so that any pair of tuples can potentially merge. When an attribute ocurs in a query term with a precise or static match value, we must use level value one (1), otherwise we may get an incorrect result. Also, we use level value zero (0) for attributes for which the query does not directly apply and a level value between 0 and 1 to attributes for which imprecise outcomes are allowed.

The algebra, presented in Yazici et al. (1990), consists of the basic operators of the relational algebra, i.e., selection, projection, Cartesian product, union, and difference, along with the two restructuring operations, merge und unmerge. Extended NF^2 algebra has all the capabilities of the relational algebra. In addition, set comparisons and uncertain data manipulation are allowed.

4. NAVIGATIONAL MODELS

Extensions to the network mode (Buckles et al., 1990) and the object-oriented data model (Buckles et al., 1991; George et al., 1991) that allow them to model and manipulate uncertainty are presented here. Of the two, the OODM, is a *navigational model* in only the broadest sense, and data retrieval in this model is not tied to the physical storage as in the network model.

4.1. Network Data Models

Network data models have not received the level of attention accorded to relational models in fuzzy database research. The DBTG network data model is widely used but is not frequently the subject of research regarding imprecision. This is partly due to the lack of formality in its description, which is particularly evident when compared with the relational model. Here, a formal definition of the record interrelationships is presented together with a concise logical description of the constraints enforced by the DBTG network databases. Three approaches for incorporating imprecision of semantics are discussed in Buckles et al. (1990).

The most extensive specification of a network data model, the DBTG data model, is the 1971 report published by the Data Base Task Group of the Conference on Data Systems Languages (CODA-SYL, 1971). The objective of the original report was, in general, to specify facilities of a DBMS and, in particular, to propose a facility for embedding this DBMS into COBOL. We discuss only those aspects of the proposal related to data modeling.

The DBTG network data model (CODASYL, 1971) consists of:

i. A set of record types $\{R_A, R_B, ..., R_N\}$. A record type is used to represent entities.
ii. A set of named links $\{L_{IJ}\}$ connecting one record of type R_I to zero or more records of type R_J. Links are used to represent the relationship between two entities.
iii. Every link is functional in at least one direction.
iv. No link of the form L_{II} is allowed.

Unfortunately, a named 1:N link, L_{IJ}, between two different record types is called a set in the DBTG proposal. To avoid the obvious confusion with the more common mathematical concept of a set, we refer to links as DBTG sets. Record R_i is called the owner record type and R_j is called the member record type in a link. The collection of one owner record and zero or more member records belonging to a set

type is referred to as an occurrence of the set type. From conditions
(iii) and (iv) we have:

i. The same record cannot be more than one set occurrence.
ii. The same record type cannot be an owner and member of the
same set type.

4.1.1. Formal Representation

Let R_A and R_B be two record types $(R_A \neq R_B)$ and also denote sets of
records of types A and B. Then the set type S_{AB} between the record
types R_A and R_B is

$$S_{AB} \subseteq R_A \times P(R_B) =$$
$$= \{ <A_i, \beta_i > | \text{ for each } j \neq i, A_i \neq A_j \wedge \beta_i \cap \beta_j = \varnothing \}$$

where A_i is a record of type R_A and β_i is a set of records of type R_B.
$P(R_B)$ represents the powerset of R_B.

Each occurrence is an ordered pair of an instance of the owner
record R_A and a subset of member records of type R_B. In general for
records of type C, we use C to denote its role as owner and c for the
role of member. Further, we impose the usual constraints that the
owner of each set occurrence must be unique and a member cannot
belong to different set occurrences (functionality condition) of the
same type.

4.1.2. Fuzzy Alternatives

Among the alternatives for the utilization of fuzzy set theory in the
DBTG framework, the first that might occur is to allow the DBTG set
to be a fuzzy set. For example, the DBTG set BUILD with two
occurrences, *Obese* and *Lean,* could be viewed as shown in Figure
31.6.

The drawback is that one can conceive of a situation in which
a member record is present in two occurrences of the same set type
and thus violates the functionality condition. This can be represented
by

$$S_{AB} \subseteq R_A \times P(R_B) = \{ <A_i, \beta_i > | \text{ for each } j \neq i, A_i \neq A_j \}$$

where $\beta_i = \{ b_{il} / \mu_i(b_{il}), ..., b_{ik} / \mu_i(b_{ik}) \}$, $b_{il}, ..., b_{ik} \in b_i$, $\mu_i(b_{ik}) \in [0, 1]$.
$P(R_B)$ denotes the set of fuzzy subsets defined over B and $\mu_i(b_{ik})$

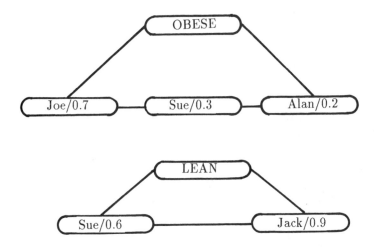

Figure 31.6. DBTG Set BUILD with two occurrences, Obese and Lean

represents the membership value of b_{ik} in β_i. In the case of set type BUILD, the owner records, A_i's, are *Obese* and *Lean,* and the b_i's are sets of people that are member records. However, because β_i and β_j are fuzzy subsets defined over the same universe, generally $\beta_i \cap \beta_j \neq \emptyset$. This violates the functionality condition of the DBTG network data model. Clearly this situation cannot be modeled directly within the DBTG framework.

One way to overcome this problem is to insist that each occurrence of set type S_{AB} form a separate singular set type. In other words, each instance of record type R_A is viewed as a separte record type, i.e., $|S_{AB}| = 1$. So S_{AB} is just $<A, \beta>$ where β is a fuzzy subset over record type B. Hence, we have overcome the problem of $\beta_i \cap \beta_j \neq \emptyset$ simply by ensuring that there is only one fuzzy subset β. If we consider the earlier example in this light, the records *Obese* and *Lean* are singular sets over the member type person. With this the fuzzy subsets *Obese* and *Lean* can be viewed as a fuzy restriction (i.e., a unary fuzzy relation that acts as a fuzzy constraint) on the values that can be assigned to a variable (a person record in the example) or an implied attribute of the person (the person's weight in the example). The variable (or the implied attribute) ranges over the entire universe of discourse (the set of all people records). This is parallel with the approach taken in fuzzy relational models in which tuples are assigned membership values denoting the degree to which the tuple belongs to the relation.

A shortcoming here is that the hierarchical structure of the network model has been diluted to overcome the possibility of a member record being present in multiple set occurrences. As a result, one might have to scan all records instead of only a subset of the record type.

Now let us consider alternative approaches. Since a DBTG set represents a named 1:N link among record types an M:N relationship is represented with the aid of dummy records. The drawback of considering a DBTG set as fuzzy is the situation in which a member record is in more than one fuzzy subset. In other words, the relationship between the owner and member records is M:N. By introducing a dummy set type we can represent the fuzzy set type as two ordinary set types. The dummy link approach allows a set type to be represented in which the owner is a fuzzy set over the members using two DBTG sets. This approach retains the hierarchical structure and the functionality restriction. The price is an intervening dummy record.

Next, from the mathematical representation of set type, it is evident that the DBTG set type is an ordinary binary relation with domains owner record type and the power set of the member record type (subject to certain conditions). So another approach would be to consider a set type as a fuzzy binary relation.

Directly representing a set type as a fuzzy binary relation within the DBTG limitations allows all conditions necessary in a DBTG framework to be retained. Namely, the uniqueness of the owner record an the notion of a functional link are preserved. The membership value represents the degree to which the set of member records "belongs" to an owner record occurrence. This degree of membership can be maintained as a field in the owner record. This representation is possibly too restrictive for real applications.

Relaxing the condition that each member belongs to exactly one owner, the same set of member records might have membership values corresponding to different owner occurrences. Because the functionality condition is violated, this representation cannot be modeled directly in the DBTG framework. To accommodate the functionality condition of the DBTG framework a dummy record type must again be introduced.

To summarize, more direct methods of applying fuzzy set theory are hampered by the functionality condition. Two alternatives are proposed. One preserves the hierarchical structure at the expense of more complex query specification and the other dilutes the hierarchical structure in order to maintain a simpler query specification.

The chief conclusion is that the greatest obstacle to incorporating fuzzy set concepts in the DBTG data model is the condition that the owner-to-member link must be functional in at least one direction. Hence, more general network models (Bonzeck, 1984) that directly allow M:N relationships would enable a more natural representation of imprecision.

4.2. The Object-Oriented Data Model

The object oriented approach (to data modeling) views the universe as consisting of a collection of interacting objects, where each object represents an entity or an event or interest. An object is completely specified by its identity, behavior, and state. The state of the object consists of the values of its attributes and the behavior is specified by the set of methods that operate on the state. An object identifier maintains the identity of an object, thereby distinguishing it from all others. Object identity facilitates data sharing: two different objects can reference the same data and yet remain distinct. The use of object identifiers permits three different types of object equality (Khoshafian, 1986):

1. **Identity** ($=$): the identity predicate corresponds to the equality of references or pointers in conventional languages.
2. **Shallow equality** (se): two objects are shallow equal if their states or contents are identical, i.e., corresponding instance variables need not be the same object; contents must be identical objects.
3. **Deep equality** (de): this ignores object identities and checks whether two objects are instances of the same class (i.e., same structure or type) and the values of the corresponding base objects are the same.

It can be seen that identity is stronger than shallow equality and shallow equality is stronger than deep equality. If identity holds, the same can be said of shallow and deep equality, and if shallow equality holds so does deep equality.

The most powerful aspect of an OODM is its ability to model inheritance. Similar objects are grouped together into a type. A type may be completely specified by its structure and a set of methods.

A type with its extension (data) constitutes a class. A class may inherit all the methods and attributes of its superclass. If a class inherits from one superclass it is classified as single inheritance. If a class inherits from more than one superclass, it is classified as multiple inheritance and the inheritance structure form a lattice. The class-subclass relationships form a class hierarchy similar to a generalization-specialization relationship. Every attribute takes values from a domain. An attribute value may be simple — integer, real, Boolean, etc. — or may be composite — i.e., have attributes themselves that fall into a class. This leads to a hierarchy that can/may originate at an attribute: the class composition hierarchy (Kim, 1989). The class composition hierarchy is distinct and orthogonal to the class hierarchy. Object-oriented databases offer considerable representational capability with respect to fuzzy information. Two levels of impreciseness may be represented: (1) the impreciseness of object membership in class values, and (2) the fuzziness of object attribute values (George et al., 1991). Note that the improved representational capability arises out of the modeling power of the object-oriented paradigm.

4.2.1. A Fuzzy Class Hierarchy

We assume the following as given:

1. A finite set of domains, $D_1, D_2, ..., D_n, n \geqslant 1$.
2. A countable set of attributes A.
3. A countable set ID of identifiers, which are used as object identifiers.

Definition [Class]: A class is characterized by structure, methods and extension. A class is a pair $C_i = (t_i, \text{ext}(t_i))$ where t is a type. Let Φ be a set of consistent objects such that for all methods $m_i \in \text{Methods}(t_i)$, m is defined on struct (t_i).

Definition [Subclass relationships]: C_i is a subclass of C_i' $(C_i \subseteq_s C_i')$ iff:

1. The structure of C_i' is less equally defined (more general) in comparison to C_i.
2. A class possesses every method owned by its superclasses although the methods themselves may be refined in the class.

A class hierarchy models class-subclass relationships and may be represented as follows:

$$C_i \subseteq_s C_{i+1} \subseteq_s C_n$$

In this notation C_n represents the root (basic) class and C_i is the most refined (leaf) class. Note that this notation represents a path in the hierarchy and it is possible to have a number of such paths originating at various "leaf" classes and terminating at the root class. Analysis of class-subclass relations indicates that they can be very broadly divided into two different types:

i. specialization subclass (also referred to as partial subclass or object-oriented subclass) where the subclass is a specialization of its immediate superclass, i.e., computer science is a specialization of engineering.
ii. subclass that is a subset of its immediate superclass, i.e., the class of employees is a subset subclass of the class of persons.

A fuzzy hierarchy exists whenever it is judged subjectively that a subclass or instance is not a full member of its immediate class. Consideration of a fuzzy representation of the class hierarchy should take into account the different requirements and characteristics of the class-subclass relations. We associate a subclass with a grade of membership in its immediate class, i.e., assuming $C_i \subseteq_s C_{i+1}$, C_i possesses a grade of membership in its immediate superclass C_{i+1}, which is represented as $\mu_{C_i}(C_{i+1}) \in [0, 1]$. In other words the class hierarchy is generalized to include the concept of membership. A subclass is represented now by a pair $(C_i, \mu(C_{i+1}))$, the second element of which represents the membership of C_i in its immediate class C_{i+1}; for notional simplicity, we write $\mu(C_{i+1})$ instead of $\mu_{C_i}(C_{i+1})$. Note that the leaf node is always an object that also has to be represented as part of the hierarchy. The class hierarchy can now be generalized as

$$(o_i, \mu(C_i)) \subseteq_s (C_i, \mu(C_{i+1})) \subseteq_s (C_{i+1}, \mu(C_{i+2})) \subseteq_s \cdots \subseteq_s (C_n, \mu(C_{n+1})) \quad (1)$$

Note $\mu(C_{n+1})$ is for positional convenience only, since the root class does not have membership in any other class.

In the case of subset hierarchies no distinction is made between the subset subclass and the homomorphically embedded subclass (e.g., the set of integers is a subclass of the set of reals) in the development of a subset hierarchy theory. In this hierarchy each subclass is a crisp member (i.e., one with a membership grade of one) in its superclass. In other words, $\mu_{C_i}(C_{i+1}) = 1$. Notationally, the hierarchy may be represented as $(o_i, 1) \subseteq_s (C_i, 1) \subseteq_s (C_{i+1}) \subseteq_s \cdots \subseteq_s (C_n, 1)$. Since the grade of membership of a class in its immediate superclass is 1, the subset hierarchy behaves similarly to the nonfuzzy OODM.

The nature of class-subclass relationships also depends on the type of ISA links existing between the two. It is possible to have strong and weak ISA relationships between a class and its subclass. In a weak ISA relationship the membership of a class in its superclasses is monotonically nonincreasing while for the strong ISA link the membership is nondecreasing. A fuzzy hierarchy possesses the following properties:

1. Membership of an instance/subclass in any of the superclasses in its hierarchy is either constant, monotonically nonincreasing, or monotonically nondecreasing. If the membership is constant the hierarchy is a subset hierarchy, if nonincreasing, a weak ISA specialization hierarchy, and if nondecreasing, a strong ISA specialization hierarchy.
2. For a weak ISA specialization hierarchy and a strong ISA specialization hierarchy, $\mu_{C_i}(C_n) = f(\mu_{C_i}(C_{i+1}), \mu_{C_{i+1}}(C_{i+2}), \ldots, \mu_{C_{n-1}}(C_n))$. The function that is application dependent may be a product, min, max, etc.
3. For two objects o and o' such that o, o' $\in$ ext (C_i), if o de o' or o se o', then $\mu_o(C_i) = \mu_{o'}(C_i)$. In other words, two objects have the same membership in a class (and all its superclasses) if they are value equal.

We have prescribed a fuzzy hierarchy in which each instance/subclass is described as a member in its immediate superclass with a degree of membership, and described the membership of an instance in a class as function of the membership of the instance in the immediate classes that lie between the instance and the class of interest. However, this may not be possible because the hierarchies are not always "pure" and mixed hierarchies are more the rule. In some applications it might therefore be necessary to assume that the membership of an object (class) in its class (superclass) is list directed.

Thus equation (1) can be generalized to account for the different types of links that can exist within an object hierarchy:

$$(o_i, \{\mu(C_i), \mu(C_{i+1}), \ldots, \mu(C_n)\} \subseteq_s (C_i, \{\mu(C_{i+1}), \mu(C_{i+2}), \ldots, \mu(C_n)\})$$
$$\subseteq_s \cdots \subseteq_s (C_n, \mu(C_{n+1}))$$

4.2.2. The Fuzzy Class Schema

The object-oriented data model permits data to be viewed at different levels of abstraction based on the semantics of the data and their interrelationships. By extending the model to incorporate fuzzy and imprecise data we allow data in a given class to be viewed through another layer of abstraction — this time based on data values. This ability of the data model to chunk information further enhances its utility. In developing the fuzzy class schema, the merge operator is defined, which combines two object instances of a class into a single object instance, provided predefined levels values are achieved. The merge operator at the same time maintains the membership relationship existing between the object/class and its class/superclass.

Assume for generality two object members of a given class C_i with list directed class/superclass memberships:

$$o = (i, < a_{k1}:i_{k1}, a_{k2}:i_{k2}, ..., a_{kj}:i_{kj}, ..., a_{km}:i_{km} >, < \mu_0(C_i), \mu_0(C_{i+1}),$$
$$..., \mu_0(C_n) >)$$
$$o' = (i', < a_{k1}:i'_{k1}, a_{k2}:i'_{k2}, ..., a_{kj}:i'_{kj}, ..., a_{km}:i'_{km} >,$$
$$< \mu_{0'}(C_i), \mu_{0'}(C_{i+1}), ..., \mu_{0'}(C_n) >)$$

Definition [Extension]: The extension of a fuzzy class C_i is a subset of the set cross product of the domains of the attributes:

$$\text{ext}(C_i) \subseteq \text{dom}(a_{k1}) \times \text{dom}(a_{k2}) \times ... \times \text{dom}(a_{kj}) \times ... \times \text{dom}(a_{km})$$

Definition [Fuzzy Object]: o is a fuzzy object in C_i if $o \in \text{ext}(C_i)$ and $\mu_0(C_i)$ takes values in the range $[0, 1]$.

Definition [Similarity Threshold]: Assume attribute a_{kj} of class C_i with a noncomposite domain D_j. By definition of fuzzy object, the domain of $a_{kj}, d_{kj} \subseteq D_j$. The threshold of D_j is defined as $\text{Thresh}(D_j)$ $= \min_i \{\min_{x,y \in D_{jk}} [s(x, y)]\}$, where $o \in \text{ext}(C_i)$ and x, y are atomic elements.

The threshold of a composite object is undefined. A composite domain is constituted of simple domains (at some level) each of which has a threshold value, i.e., the threshold for a composite object is a vector.

The threshold value represents the minimum similarity of the values an object attribute may take. If the attribute domain is strictly atomic for all objects of the class (i.e., cardinality of a_{ij} is 1), then the threshold $= 1$. As the threshold value tends to 0, larger chunks of information are grouped together and the information conveyed about the particular attribute of the class decreases. A level value given a priori determines which tuples may be combined by the set union of the respective domains. Note that the level value may be specified via the query language with the constraint that it may never exceed the threshold value.

Definition [Merge]: For object o_i and $o_{i'}$ assume that for each a_{kj}, $\text{dom}(a_{kj})$ is noncomposite, then:

$$o_{i''} = \text{merge}(o_i, o_{i'}) = (i'', < a_{k1} : i''_{k1}, a_{k2} : i''_{k2}, ..., a_{kj} : i''_{kj}, ..., a_{km} : i''_{km}$$
$$>$$
$$< \mu_{o''}(C_i), \mu_{o''}(C_{i+1}), ..., \mu_{o''}(C_n) >)$$

where

$$o''_{kj} = (i''_{kj}, \{i_{kj}, i'_{kj}\})$$

and

$$\mu_{o''}(C_m) = \text{fx}((C_m), (C_{m'})) \text{ for each } m, m = 1, ..., n$$

such that

for each $\text{val}(i_{kj})$, $\text{val}(i'_{kj}) \in d_{ij} \cup d'_{ij}$: $\min[s(\text{val}(i_{kj}), \text{val}(i'_{kj})) >$
$$\text{Level}(D_j)]$$

and

$$\text{Level}(D_j) \leqslant \text{Thres}(D_j)$$

The merge operator permits a reorganization of the objects belonging to a class scheme by grouping them according to the similarity of one attribute object to another. As in the definition of threshold, this definition can be extended to composite objects.

Two objects in a OODBMS can be nonredundant even if they are shallow equal. By introducing fuzziness into the model, however, we weaken this property. Two objects that are shallow equal are redundant as are objects exhibiting deep equality. But equality alone does not determine redundancy.

Lemma: Two objects o_i and $o_{i'}$ are redundant if for each $j, j = 1, 2, ...,$ m, and Level (D_j) given a priori

for each $\text{val}(i_{kj})$, $\text{val}(i'_{kj}) \in d_{ij} \cup d'_{kj}$: $\min[s(\text{val}(i_{kj}), \text{val}(i'_{kj})) >$
$$\text{Level}(D_j)]$$

The property of redundancy is directly responsible for the property of value abstraction exhibited by the fuzzy database. It also ensures that the results of database operations are unique.

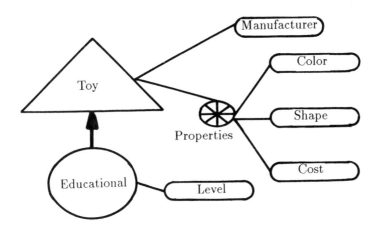

	cheap	moderate	high
cheap	1.0	0.8	0.6
moderate	0.8	1.0	0.6
high	0.6	0.6	1.0

Similarity matrix for price

	red	orange	yellow
red	1.0	0.85	0.55
orange	0.85	1.0	0.55
yellow	0.55	0.55	1.0

Similarity matrix for color

Figure 31.7. Schematic representation for a database of toys with the similarity matrices for Price and Color

We assume the following instances of Toys in Figure 31.7:

$$o_1 = (i_1, < \text{manufacturer}:i_{11}, \text{properties}:i_{12}>,<1>)$$
$$o_2 = (i_2, < \text{manufacturer}:i_{11}, \text{properties}:i_{13}>,<1>)$$
$$o_3 = (i_1, < \text{manufacturer}:i_{14}, \text{properties}:i_{15}>,<1>)$$
$$o_4 = (i_4, < \text{manufacturer}:i_{14}, \text{properties}:i_{16}>,<1>)$$
$$o_5 = (i_{12}, < \text{shape}:i_{17}, \text{color}:i_{19}, \text{cost}:i_{22}>)$$
$$o_6 = (i_{13}, < \text{shape}:i_{18}, \text{color}:i_{20}, \text{cost}:i_{22}>)$$
$$o_7 = (i_{15}, < \text{shape}:i_{17}, \text{color}:i_{19}, \text{cost}:i_{22}>)$$
$$o_8 = (i_{16}, < \text{shape}:i_{18}, \text{color}:i_{21}, \text{cost}:i_{22}>)$$

$$o_{23} = (i_{23}, < \text{manufacturer}: i_{11}, \text{properties}: i_{12},$$
$$\text{level}: i_{27}>, <0.95, 1>)$$
$$o_{24} = (i_{24}, < \text{manufacturer}: i_{11}, \text{properties}: i_{13},$$
$$\text{level}: i_{28}>, <0.75, 1>)$$
$$o_{25} = (i_{25}, < \text{manufacturer}: i_{14}, \text{properties}: i_{15},$$
$$\text{level}: i_{29}>, <0.9, 1>)$$
$$o_{26} = (i_{26}, < \text{manufacturer}: i_{14}, \text{properties}: i_{16},$$
$$\text{level}: i_{30}>, <0.8, 1>)$$

$o_9 = (i_{11}, \text{'Kiddy Kars}^{TM}\text{'})$ $o_{10} = (i_{14}, \text{'Tinker Toys}^{TM}\text{'})$
$o_{11} = (i_{17}, \text{'spheroid'})$ $o_{12} = (i_{18}, \text{'parallelopiped'})$
$o_{13} = (i_{19}, \text{'red'})$ $o_{14} = (i_{20}, \text{'orange'})$ $o_{15} = (i_{72}, \text{'red'})$
$o_{16} = (i_{21}, \text{'yellow'})$ $o_{17} = (i_{22}, \text{'cheap'})$
$o_{27} = (i_{27}, \text{'sophomore'})$ $o_{28} = (i_{28}, \text{'junior'})$
$o_{29} = (i_{29}, \text{'freshman'})$ $o_{30} = (i_{30}, \text{'senior'})$

Query: Retrieve educational toys that are red in color

Red-Toys = Merge (Toys) with Level (Toy. Properties. Color) $\geqslant 0.85$
Level (Toy. Manufacturer) $\geqslant 0.0$, Level (Toy. Properties. Shape) $\geqslant 0.0$,
Level (Toy. Properties. Cost) $\geqslant 0.0$, Membership (Toys. Educational) $\geqslant 0.85$.

giving the new objects

$$o_1' = (i_1', < \text{manufacturer}: i_{11}', \text{properties}: i_{12}', \text{level}: i_{27}' >,$$
$$<0.95, 1>)$$
$$o_{12}' = (i_{12}', < \text{shape}: i_{13}', \text{color}: i_{14}', \text{cost}: i_{15}' >)$$
$$o_{13}' = (i_{13}', \{i_{11}, i_{31}\}) \quad o_{14}' = (i_{14}', \{i_{51}, \ i_{61}\}) \quad o_{15}' = (i_{15}', \{i_{52}, i_{62}\})$$
$$o_{27}' = (i_{27}', \{i_{27}, i_{29}\})$$

The query asks for toys that are "near" red in color with the corresponding values of manufacturer, shape, and cost being immaterial. The red and the educational levels are based on the attribute level and object membership grade values supplied. We assume the combination function used for object membership levels is max. The result of the query supplies the answer that the manufacturers are "Kiddy Kars^{TM}" and "Tinker Toys^{TM}", the toys are "parallelopiped" and "spherical" in shape and they are all "cheap" in price and they are suitable for the educational levels of "freshman" and "sophomore." Note that the new membership has the maximum of the individual object membership levels.

5. CONCLUSION

Many nontraditional applications in the areas of science, engineering, and office automation have common objects that are usually large, very often complexly structured and may even deal with imprecise, incomplete, or vague information. Research has been conducted into various approaches to represent and deal with complex objects with (possibly) imprecise and incomplete attributes. Some of these techniques, developed at a conceptual design level, describe the meaning associated with data in a database, and others, developed at a logical level, concentrate on processing the data. There also exist some approaches, i.e., NF^2 and object-oriented models, which are powerful enough both to describe and process the complex objects along with uncertain features.

In this paper, we elaborated on the issue of uncertainty management in the conceptual, logical, and navigational data models. Two different approaches to the conceptual modeling were examined: the extended IFO model and the extended E/R model. These models can represent complex objects with uncertainty in the attribute values chiefly with their powerful abstraction mechanism. The logical models, specifically the 1NF model, which has been the subject of more thorough inquiry, and the non-1NF data model (also called NF^2 Model) were also discussed in detail. Finally, the question of representing and manipulating impression in navigational models, i.e., network and object-oriented data models, was considered.

Keywords: fuzzy databases, semantic data models, non-first normal form databases, query languages

BIBLIOGRAPHY

Abiteboul, S. and N. Bidoit. (1984). Non-first normal form relations: An algebra allowing data restructuring. Rapports de Recherche no. 347, INRIA, France.

Abiteboul, S. and R. Hull. (1987). A formal semantic database model. *ACM Trans. on Database Systems,* 12, 525–565.

Anvari, M. and G. F. Rose. (1984). Fuzzy relational databases. *Proc. of Int. Conf. on Fuzzy Information Processing,* Hawaii.

Bertino, E. and L. Martino. (1990). Object-oriented database management systems: Concepts and issues. *IEEE Computer,* April.

Bonzeck, R. (1984). *Micro Database Management.* New York: Academic Press.

Buckles, B. P. and F. E. Petry. (1982). A fuzzy representation of data for relational databases. *Fuzzy Sets and Systems*, 7, 213–226.

Buckles, B. P. and F. E. Petry. (1985). Uncertainty models in information and database systems. *Journal of Information Science*, 11.

Buckles, B. P., F. E. Petry, and J. Pillai. (1990). Network data models for representation of uncertainty. *Fuzzy Sets and Systems*, 38.

Buckles, B.P., R. George, and F. E. Petry. (1990). Towards a fuzzy object-oriented data model. *Proc. of NAFIPS Workshop on Uncertainty Modelling in the 90's*, May.

CODASYL (1971). *Data Base Task Group Report Conference on Data System Languages*. New York: ACM Press.

Codd, E. R. (1970). A relational model of data for large shared databases, *Comm. ACM*. 13 (6).

Crawford, R. (1981). The relational model in information retrieval. *JASIS*, 30 (1).

George, R., B. P. Buckles, and F. E. Petry. (1991). Integrating artificial intelligence and database systems — where do we manage uncertainty. *Proc. of IJCAI '91, Workshop on Integrating AI and DBMS*, August.

George, R., A. Yazici, and B. P. Buckles. (1990). Preserving data semantics: A semantic data model approach utilizing NF^2 relations. *Proc. of the Fifth Int. Symp. on Computer and Information Sciences*, October.

Kim, W. (1989). A model of queries for object-oriented databases. *Proc. of the Fifteenth Int. Conf. on Very Large Databases*.

Khoshafian, S. N. and G. P. Copeland. (1986). Object identity. *Proc. of the OOPSLA '86 Conference*, pp. 406–416, September.

Lipski, W. (1979). On semantic issues connected with incomplete information databases. *ACM Trans. on Database Systems*, 4 (3).

Maier, D. (1983). *The Theory of Relational Databases*. Rockville, MD: Computer Science Press.

Makinouchi, A. (1977). A consideration on normal form and not necessarily normalized relations in the relational data model. *Proc. of the Third Int. Conf. on Very Large Databases*, Tokyo, pp. 447–453.

Motoro, A. (1990). Accommodating imprecision in database systems: Issues and solutions. *SIGMOD RECORD*, 19 (4), December.

Prade, H. (1985). A computational approach to approximate and plausible reasoning with applications to expert systems. *IEEE Trans. on PAMI*, 7 (3).

Ozsoyoglu, G., Z. M. Ozsoyoglu, and V. Matos. (1987). Extending relational algebra and relational calculus with set-valued attributes and aggregate functions. *ACM Trans. on Database Systems*, 12, 566–592.

Roth, M. A., H. F. Korth, and D. S. Batory. (1987). SQL/NF: A query language for non-1NF relational databases. *Information Systems*, 12, 99–114.

Roth, M. A., H. F. Korth, and A. Silberschatz. (1985). Null values in non-1 NF relational databases. *Res. Rep. TR – 85 – 32*, Dept. of Computer Science, University of Texas, Austin.

Shenoi, S., and A. Melton. (1989). Proximity relations in the fuzzy relational database model. *Fuzzy Sets and Systems*, 31 (3).

Schek, H. J., and M. H. Scholl. (1986). The relational model with relational-valued attributes. *Information Systems*, 1, 137–147.

Tsichritzis, D., and F. Lochovsky. (1977). *Database Management Systems.* New York: Academic Press.

Thomas, S. J., and P. C. Fisher. (1986). Nested relational structures. *Advances in Computing Research*, 3, JAI Press, pp. 269–307.

Umano, M. (1983). Retrieval from fuzzy database by fuzzy relational algebra, *Proc. of IFAC Conf. on Fuzzy Information, Knowledge Representation and Decision Processes*, Marseille.

Yazici, A. (1990). Representing imprecise information in NF^2 relations, *IEEE Southeast '90 Proceedings*, vol. 3, pp. 1026–1030.

Yazici, A., B. P. Buckles, and F. E. Petry. (1990). A new approach for conceptual and logical design of databases. *Proc. of the Fifth Int. Symp. on Computer and Information Sciences*, October.

Yazici, A., B. P. Buckles, and F. E. Petry. (1992). Database Architecture for knowledge intensive applications. *Proc. of the Sixth Int. Symp. on Computer and Information Sciences*, Antalya, March.

Zadeh, L. A. (1971). Similarity relations and fuzzy orderings. *Information Sciences*, 3, 177–200.

Zvieli, A., and P. P. Chen. (1986). Entity-relationship modelling and fuzzy databases. *Proc. of the Int. Conf. on Data Engineering*, Los Angeles, pp. 320–327.

32 Fuzzy querying in conventional databases

P. BOSC and O. PIVERT
IRISA/ENSSAT
22305 Lannion Cédex, FRANCE

Abstract. In this paper, various approaches for introducing flexibility inside queries addressed to a database are presented. A special emphasis is put on systems founding the interpretation of imprecise queries on the fuzzy sets theory. The principal features of a language extending SQL and the norm for database querying are outlined, as well as some considerations concerning the implementation of such database systems.

1. INTRODUCTION

The database domain is presently subject to many evolutions. Initially (in the 1970s and early 1980s) the main objective was to design and implement systems intended for data about the management of the enterprises. The research topics now turn to more general applications and thus more general types of data and user needs, which will lead to a new (third) generation of database management systems (DBMS). In this context, one can imagine storing imprecise or uncertain data in a database, especially in the scope of large knowledge-base management systems (cf. Yazici et al., 1992). In the context of ordinary databases where precise data are stored, another field of evolution concerns the facilities and capabilities of querying the user is provided with. One cannot avoid noticing the available DBMSs suffer from a *lack of flexibility*. Consequently, several research works have been undertaken to oercome this problem, especially in the area of user interfaces.

One important point to notice is that the word "flexibility" covers several different meanings. Basically, the use of a DBMS (for querying purpose) implies several requirements as shown in Motro (1989). The user has at least to know the data model, the contents of the base, and the query language, and must have a well-defined retrieval goal expressible in terms of a Boolean query. So a more flexible system is any that relaxes some of these constraints, for instance, in introducing: (1) the automatic correction of some syntactic or semantic errors, (2) browsing capabilities as suggested by D'Atri and Tarantino (1989), (3) some kind of cooperation as proposed by Janas (1981), Kaplan (1982), and Gal (1988) in particular in order to avoid empty responses, (4) a qualitative distinction among the answers, and (5) imprecise or vague terms or predicates in the condition part of a query (as we shall see in the next section).

We now make precise the meaning of "flexibility" assumed in the following. A system is flexible in so far as it allows imprecise terms in user queries. Consequently, it becomes necessary to determine to what extent a certain element matches more or less the query more than another element, which leads to a classification or ranking of the selected elements. According to this definition, we are essentially concerned with items 4 and 5 of the above list. However, since very often an implicit objective is to avoid empty answers, the approaches reported hereafter are also connected with cooperative answers.

Several approaches allowing imprecision in user queries can be imagined and some of them have been proposed and implemented in research prototypes. One idea is to consider queries made of two parts: a Boolean qualification selecting elements and an imprecise condition intended for the ranking of these elements. Another approach is to allow imprecise queries. Then, two main cases appear depending on the interpretation of imprecise conditions. As a matter of fact, we can imagine translating an imprecise condition into a Boolean one expressing intervals of acceptance and such that some kind of "distance" is computed for each selected element. An alternate view is to use fuzzy sets as a basis for the evalution of imprecise conditions. Here again, some kind of distance is computed for each element, but this framework is more general than the previous one. In fact, we shall see that the central point of a system depends on whether or not it is based on the Boolean logic.

The remainder of the paper is organized as follows. In Section 2, we successively present methods and/or systems that illustrate at least partially the three approaches we mentioned. We shall see that none of them offers a complete framework for imprecise querying if we refer to the characteristics of usual relational languages. So, the third section is devoted to a survey of the extension of the SQL language that we propose. This language, called SQL^f, was designed in order to introduce fuzzy querying capabilities wherever possible. In the next section, we deal with the problem of query processing. Although not explicitly stated, it seems that efficiency is the reason for coming down to the Boolean logic. We therefore present some implementation mechanisms likely to support some of the features of the language suggested in Section 3. Finally, some concluding remarks are given.

2. APPROACHES FOR IMPRECISE QUERYING

As mentioned before, three main categories (see Figure 32.1) of solutions can be found in order to introduce imprecision inside user queries. As we shall see, the first two methods are basically founded on the usual logic and their objective is clearly to adapt an existing system to handle some (limited) kind of imprecision. On the other hand, the third class relies on fuzzy sets and is illustrated by two proposals suggesting some features for an imprecise query language. Although specific, the suggestions made there have been retained at least partly in SQL^f.

2.1. Deduce 2

This system, described in Chang (1982), is an extension of a deductive DBMS and offers a predicate calculus language for the expression of user queries. A query comprises mainly two components connected by an AND: a Boolean condition ($F1$) and an optional imprecise condition ($\%F2$). F2 involves terms like "old," "around 45," etc. that are combined using the two usual connectors: AND, OR. The semantics of such a query may be stated as follows: "find the elements satisfying $F1$ and rank them according to $F2$."

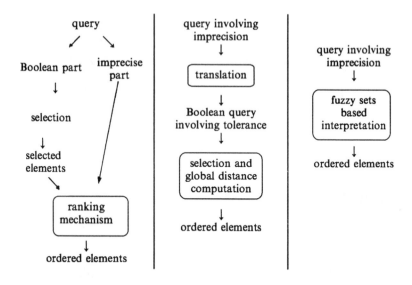

Figure 32.1. The three approaches for imprecise querying

Now we describe the ranking mechanism. Let us consider the case where F2 is only one imprecise term T. Chang assumes that T is a monotonic function of one attribute A that is either a base attribute (present in a relation), or a derived one (computed from attributes of relations), for instance such that: $a_1 > a_2 \Rightarrow T(a_1) > T(a_2)$. The adequation with respect to T can then be measured by a decreasing sort of the considered relation on attribute A (the higher A, the more T is satisfied). More generally, when $F2$ involves conjunctions and disjunctions the following principles apply: for a conjunction T_1 AND T_2, each tuple of the relation is assigned a rank R_1 according to the sort on A_1, and a rank R_2 according to the sort on A_2, and the final rank is max (R_1, R_2). Conversely, for a disjunction, the final rank is obtained by min (R_1, R_2).

To undestand how the system works, let us take an example. Consider the relation EMPLOYEE (num, name, salary, age, city) and the query "find the name of employees living at San Diego who are *well-paid* and whose age is *around 40*." The imprecise part of the query is: *well-paid* (increasing function of salary) AND age *around 40* (decreasing function of |age − 40|). If we assume that the relation EMPLOYEE contains the three tuples: *t1* < 17, Smith, 11000, 38, San Diego >, *t2* < 26, Jones, 30000, 37, San Diego > and *t3* < 8, Perkins, 10000, 39, San Diego >, we obtain the results: *t1*(2,2), *t2*(1,3), *t3*(3,1) and therefore Smith is the best, Jones and Perkins are second. This result does not match the intuition for which Jones would have been the first. This situation can be explained by the fact that a sort can only order two values but cannot express the semantic difference between them.

If this solution is easy to implement since it is based on sorts, the results returned are not necessarily satisfactory. Moreover, the allowed queries are not general since (1) the imprecise part is intended only for ranking, and (2) any imprecise term must be supported by a monotonic function. We must mention a system called PRE-FERENCES (Lacroix and Lavency, 1987), that has some analogy with DEDUCE. This system suggests also a mechanism to distinguish among the elements selected by a usual condition, but without referring to imprecision. The principle is to state additional conditions called preferences, and the system returns first the elements satisfying most of them.

2.2. ARES and VAGUE

These two systems are in fact very close and VAGUE (Motro, 1988) can be considered an improvement of ARES (Ichikawa and Hirakawa, 1986). The common objective is to prevent the user from a tedious iterative querying mechanism to adjust the number of returned answers. Their common principle is to allow for a new operator called "similar to" ($\approx$), thus relaxing the strict equality condition.

First, we briefly present ARES and then point out its specific drawbacks. In ARES, the meaning of the imprecise predicate A $\approx$ a is based on the notion of *similarity* between couples of values. Depending on the domain of A, this similarity is measured either as sim ($|v_1 - v_2|$) or sim (v_1, v_2). A query may involve terms like $A \approx a$ called *ambiguous selections* and $A_1 \approx A_2$ called *ambiguous joins*. One purpose of the paper is to present very clearly how these new operations can be translated into usual relational operations using similarity relations. For example, let us consider that the similarity on domain (A) is represented by the relation sim $A (v1, v2, s)$ where s is close to 0 if $v1$ and $v2$ are very similar. Given an acceptance threshold t, the selection $A \approx a$ on the base relation R becomes as shown in Figure 32.2.

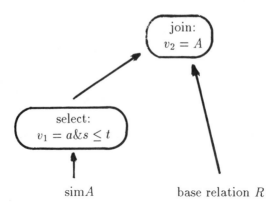

Figure 32.2.

Given a query involving ordinary and imprecise predicates connected by ANDs, the following process takes place. First of all, the user is asked to determine the value of the acceptance threshold for each imprecise predicate. Then the system starts the translation into a Boolean query (the Boolean predicates are left unchanged). This query is then run and each element satisfying the various thresholds is associated with a global similarity that is in fact the sum of the elementary similarities found for each impreise condition. Finally, the elements are sorted in decreasing order on the global similarity.

The major question arising with ARES is about the semantics of the queries. As a matter of fact, the values of similarities are not normalized and one may wonder whether the thresholds assigned by the user are intended to normalize or to weight each imprecise component. Moreover, the meaning of the global similarity is not quite obvious and is acceptable only under the assumption that the terms are connected by ANDs. The majority of these points have been solved in the system called VAGUE that is now briefly presented.

In VAGUE, Motro (1988) proposes the same new operator ($\approx$) standing for similarity rather than equality. One or several *data metrics* (similarity measures) are tied to each domain, which allows different users to have different interpretations of the term $A \approx v$. Moreover, a data metric for a domain D is a function $M: D \times D \to R$ such that: $M(x, y) \geq 0$, $M(x, y) = 0 \iff x = y$, $M(x, y) = M(y, x)$, $M(x, y) \leq M(x, z) + M(z, y)$. It has a *radius r* used to define neighborhoods. Given x, any value y such that $M(x, y) \leq r$ is said to be close to x and the imprecise predicate $x = y$ is satisfied. Moreover, the value $M(x, y)/r$ yields a normalized measure (i.e., that does not depend on the domain), which makes sense for future combinations of such values. The interpretation of a query can be explained as a two-step process. First, the imprecise predicates are translated into Boolean conditions ($A \approx a$ becomes $M(A, a) \leq r$) and the obtained query is run against the database. Then, a ranking machanism takes place based only on imprecise predicates for which *adjusted distances* are computed. If d is the initial distance attached to $A \approx a$, and w its importance (defined by the user), the adjusted distance is $(d/r) \times w$. The distance associated with a disjunction is the smallest distance and the distance for a conjunction is the root of the sum of the squares. So doing, each selected tuple receives a global distance and can then be ordered.

It is obvious that VAGUE brings more convenient results and answers our previous remarks. However, we believe that these two systems present a couple of common weaknesses. First of all, the new operator proposed here extends only the equality and queries calling on other kinds of comparisons (much greater than, salary very high, ...) are not supported. The second point is more fundamental and concerns the reference to the Boolean interpretation of queries. In this approach, the usual predicate $A = a$ is replaced by $A = a \pm r$ and a *discontinuity* appears again around the points $a + r$ and $a - r$ instead of around the single point a. Consequently, when predicates are mixed, it is possible that rejected tuples would have been better than some of those selected. The major advantage of these two systems resides in the ease for implementing the proposed extensions. It is clear that they can be inserted inside an existing (commercial) DBMS and that the response time will not increase significantly. To end up with this approach, let us mention the approach known as "best match query" (Rivest, 1976) or "nearest neighbors" (Friedman et al., 1975). A query is the description of an ideal object and here also, the system calculates a distance for each tuple of the base.

2.3. Fuzzy Sets–Based Approaches

We have seen that the preceding proposals were strongly tied to the Boolean logic. At the end of the 1970s, a very different approach has been proposed by Tahani (1977), based on the idea that fuzzy sets (Zadeh, 1965) could be used to interpret simple imprecise queries. In

Kacprzyk and Ziółkowski (1986), and Kacprzyk, Zadrożny and Ziółkowski (1989) another class of imprecise queries is defined. In both cases, an imprecise predicate bears on individual tuples. Finally, most of these suggestions along with additional original features, in particular concerning sets of tuples (Bosc et al., 1988) have been gathered into the SQL language (Section 3).

The originality of Tahani's (1977) proposal was to define the concept of a fuzzy relation in a DBMS in associating a grade of membership μ with each tuple. A relation R defined on a set of domains $X = \{X_1,...,X_n\}$ is $R = \{x/\mu \mid x \in X, \mu$ is the extent to which x belongs to $R\}$. So doing, a usual relation is a fuzzy relation where $\mu = 1$ for each tuple. A fuzzy relation is generated from an ordinary one by means of fuzzy predicates that involve *linguistic variables* such as new, recent, expensive, around 40, more or less young, very old, etc., and also new operators like much more ... than, much less ... than, etc., represented by fuzzy sets. Let R be a relation (possibly fuzzy) defined on a set of domains denoted $X = \{X_1,...,X_n\}$. The result, denoted Res, of the restriction of R by the predicate P is defined as:

$$\text{for each } x \in X, \mu_{Res}(x) = \min(\mu_R(x), \mu_P(x)) \tag{1}$$

The usual set-oriented operations over relations can also be extended according to the following definitions:

$$\mu_{R \cup S}(x) = \max(\mu_R(x), \mu_S(x)) \tag{2}$$
$$\mu_{R \cap S}(x) = \min(\mu_R(x), \mu_S(x)) \tag{3}$$
$$\mu_{\bar{R}}(x) = 1 - \mu_R(x) \tag{4}$$
$$\mu_{R-S}(x) = \min(\mu_R(x), 1 - \mu_S(x)) \tag{5}$$

A user can mix Boolean and fuzzy predicates inside a query and the connectors AND and OR are canonically extended in terms of intersection and union. Referring to E in our previous relation EMPLOYEE, the following compound predicate will restrict E: city = "Los Angeles" AND age = "very young" AND salary = "around 100K." So doing, the semantics of simple queries is defined: the more a tuple of the considered relation matches a fuzzy predicate, the higher the grade it receives. In his approach, Tahani (1976, 1977) defined in fact an extension of the usual relational algebra (except the division), which is sufficient from a theoretical point of view but does not provide a query language for the end user.

On their own behalf, Kacprzyk and Ziółkowski (1986), and Kacprzyk, Zadrożny and Ziółkowski (1929) desired to define the meaning of a set of queries involving the previous ones (called direct) and the so-called *quantified queries*. The query: "find the employees such that *almost all* out of {salary is very large, age is young but not very young, ...} match" is an illustration. The question is: how do we interpret such queries? First of all, we can distinguish *absolute* (around 3, a dozen) and *relative* (all, a few, several, almost all) *fuzzy quantifiers*. They are represented by a fuzzy set defined over **R** or **N** (the set of real and natural numbers, respectively) for the former and over [0,1] for the latter. Let us consider a relation R defined on a set of attributes $\{A_1,...,A_p\}$ and an extension of R made of a set of tuples $\{t_1,...,t_n\}$. The idea is to consider that the determination of the extent to which a tuple satisfies: "<quantifier> out of $\{A_1$ <comp$_1$> $v_1,...,A_m$ <comp$_m$> $v_m\}$ match" and the determination of the truth of the proposition "<quantifier> tuples of R satisfy $(A_j$ <comp> $v)$" both rely on the same calculus. In the first case, the quantifier applies to a set of *horizontal* values (issued from a same tuple by several fuzzy predicates), whereas in the other case the quantifier refers to a set of *vertical* values (issued from various tuples by the same fuzzy predicate). An interpretation for the second kind of sentence has been suggested in (Zadeh, 1983). Basically, the truth v of "<relative quantifier Q> tuples of R satisfy the fuzzy predicate P" is given by:

$$v = \mu_Q \left(\frac{1}{n} \sum_{i=1}^{n} \mu_P(t_i) \right) \qquad (6)$$

and the extent g to which a tuple t satisfies "<relative quantifier Q> out of $\{P_1,...,P_m\}$ match" is:

$$g = \mu_Q \left(\frac{1}{m} \sum_{i=1}^{m} \mu_{P_i}(t) \right)$$

We must mention the existence of queries derived from the previous ones by introducing an importance for each tuple (respectively predicate). If $\mu_i \in [0,1]$ denotes the importance of the predicate P_i, the extent g' to which a tuple t satisfies "<relative' quantifier Q> out of $\{P_{1/\mu_1},...,P_{m/\mu_m}\}$ match" is:

$$g' = \mu_Q \left(\sum_{i=1}^{m} \min(\mu_{P_i}(i), \mu_i) / \sum_{i=1}^{m} \mu_i \right)$$

We shall see in the next section that the concept of quantified proposition can be introduced into a query language in order to allow the *selection of sets of tuples* rather than individual tuples. The major interest of fuzzy sets–based interpretations is the fact that there is a continuity between the full match and the full mismatch.

3. AN OVERVIEW OF AN EXTENDED SQL-LIKE LANGUAGE

3.1. Introduction: A Look at SQL

The preceding systems suggest specific and partial extensions to improve database querying capabilities. In this section, we present an overview of an extension of a database query language, namely SQL derived from SEQUEL (Chamberlin et al., 1976). The new language, called SQL^f, is in fact a more complete version of a previous language that we proposed earlier (Bosc et al., 1988). SQL has the property that the same need can be expressed through several queries, which gives rise to an equivalence phenomenon. Our two main objectives were to introduce fuzzy predicates into the language wherever possible while ensuring that the equivalences remain valid. First, we recall the principal features of SQL and then we present the extensions.

An SQL query is made of one or several base blocks and is founded on the tuple relational calculus. The fundamental construct is the base block that specifies the structure of the resulting relation by means of the *select clause*, the concerned relation(s) of the database in the *from clause*, and the condition to satisfy in the *where clause*. When several relations are involved, one can consider that they are mixed into a single relation (using the Cartesian product) to which the condition applies. This construct has thus at least the power of selection, projection, and join in the relational algebra.

Rather than putting all relations into a single block, often but not always (it depends only on the relations involved in the select clause), a user can express his or her query by means of several nested blocks (also called subqueries). The connection between two blocks can be achieved by several operators: (i) set membership ([NOT] IN), (ii) set existence ([NOT] EXISTS), (iii) existential or universal quantification (ANY, ALL), (iv) scalar comparison if the inner block results in a single value using aggregates (MIN, SUM, ...). In cases (i) – (iii) the inner block (subquery) is seen as a set and the considered predicate (IN, ...) compares the value of the current tuple of the outer block with it. If we consider a base consisting of the relations EMPLOYEE (num, name, salary, job, age, city, depart), DEPART (nd, manager, budget, location), the query "find the number and name of the employees who work in a department located in their own city" can be expressed:

(a) single block: **select** num, name **from** EMPLOYEE DEPART **where** depart = nd **AND** city = location

(b) nesting (i): select num, name **from** EMPLOYEE E **where** depart **IN** (**select** nd **from** DEPART **where** location = E. city)

(an employee is selected if his or her department belongs to the set delivered by the subquery)

(c) nesting (ii): select num, name **from** EMPLOYEE E **where** **EXISTS** (select *from DEPART **where** nd = E. depart **AND** location = E. city)

(an employee is selected if the subquery contains at least an element).

It must be noticed that queries (b) and (c) are such that the condition appearing in the subquery refers to the current (and is evaluated for each) tuple of the outer block.

Two blocks can also be combined using the UNION set operator. It can be shown that one can do without the intersection and the difference and that is the reason why they do not belong to the SQL norm even if they are supported in some commercial systems. For instance, the difference between the two relations R and S defined on a single attribute A can be expressed: **select** A **from** R **where** A NOT IN (**select** A **from** S).

The last important feature of SQL concerns the operations allowed on sets of tuples. As a matter of fact, it is possible to partition a relation into subsets using a *group by* clause, mainly in order to select some subsets using a *having* clause made of set-oriented predicates usually calling on aggregate functions (MIN, AVG: average, ...). The query: "find the departments in which the mean salary of clerks is over 1400" would be:

select depart **from** EMPLOYEE **where** job = "clerk" **group by** depart **having** AVG (salary) > 1400

In the next subsections, we shall review the various constructs and present how they can be extended to support fuzzy querying capabilities.

3.2. Single Block Queries in SOL^f

The objective is to introduce some fuzziness in the base block of SQL. This can be achieved at two principal levels: in the predicates and in the way they are combined (connectors). First of all, we assume that a fuzzy condition *fc* delivers a fuzzy relation *fr* in the sense given in Section 2.3 and that the result of a query must be a usual relation, more precisely the "best" elements of *fr*. So, it becomes neccessary to provide the user with an output regulation machanism that can be either the number *n* of desired responses for a quantitative calibration or $t \in [0,1]$ for the *t*-cut of *fr* in case of a qualitative calibration. So doing, the new formulation for a simple base block is:

> **select** $<n/t>$ $<$attributes$>$ **from** $<$relations$>$ **where** $<$fuzzy condition$>$

Sometimes, as in the examples below, we omit this element of a query without loss of generality. Basically, a fuzzy condition applying to individual tuples is composed of Boolean and fuzzy predicates (as proposed by Tahani, 1977) and connectors. We have previously mentioned a canonical extension of the two usual connectors AND and OR. However, they are only a subset of interesting operators. Especially, it is sometimes useful to allow a compensation effect between two (or more) predicates. This can be done using new operators that have no counterpart in usual queries. For instance, let us mention the geometric mean:

$$gm(x, y) = \sqrt{x\,y} \tag{7}$$

and the *weighted mean*:

$$wm(x, y) = \frac{px + qy}{p + q} \tag{8}$$

such that $p = q = 1$ gives the arithmetic mean. All these operators differ in the way they gather their arguments and their use depends on the desired interaction (Dubois and Prade, 1985).

Just as in an ordinary query a predicate can express a join between two relations, it is possible to connect two relations by means of a fuzzy predicate. The following example illustrates this:

select ... **from** $R\ S$ **where** ... more or less equal $(R.A,S.B)$ ...

Finally, we must specify the meaning of the select clause that in SQL looks like an algebraic projection. In fact, it is possible that two tuples selected by the condition have the same value on the specified attributes but have different grades of membership. We shall assume from here on that only the one with the highest grade is retained (specific operators can be designed if other strategies are needed). To finish this section, let us remark that the semantics of a query are mainly based on formula (1). Formulas (2), (3), and those similar to (7) or (8) are used to compute the grade of membership of a tuple when several predicates appear. Formula (4) gives the interpretation of the negation of a predicate (NOT).

3.3. Using Subqueries

The objective is to define the semantics of operators like IN, etc., when fuzzy relations are involved, and to extend them if necessary. Consider the query "find the 10 best young employees earning about the same as another employee of the same department who is rather well-paid." Using a multirelation block, we have:

select $E1$.num, $E1$.name **from** EMPLOYEE $E1$, EMPLOYEE $E2$
where $E1$.age $=$ "young" **AND** $E1$.num $<>$ $E2$.num **AND** $E1$.salary $\approx E2$.salary
AND $E2$.salary $=$ "well-paid" **AND** $E1$.depart $=$ $E2$.depart

The grade of an employee $e1$ (before projection and calibration) is given by:

$$\mu(e2) = \min\left(\mu_{young}(e1),\ \sup_{e2\in EMPLOYEE}\min\mu_{<>}(e1.\text{num},\ e2.\text{num}),\ \mu_{\approx}(e1.\text{salary},\ e2.\text{salary}),\ \mu_{=}(e1.\text{depart},\ e2.\text{depart}),\ \mu_{well-paid}(e2.\text{salary})\right)$$

Using a subquery, one can express the query:

> select num, name **from** EMPLOYEE E **where** age = "young" AND E1.depart **IN** (select depart **from** EMPLOYEE **where** salary = "well-paid" AND num <> E. num AND salary ≈ E.salary)

In this case, if SQ denotes the inner block, the grade of an employee e is:

$$\mu(e) = \min(\mu_{young}(e), \mu_{IN}(e.\text{depart}, SQ))$$

The grade of a department d of an employee e' of SQ is:

$$\mu(e'.d) = \min(\mu_{well-paid}(e'.\text{salary}), \mu_{<>}(e'.\text{num}, e.\text{num}), \mu_{\approx}(e'.\text{salary}, e.\text{salary})).$$

The equivalence is obtained if the IN predicate is defined as:

$$\mu_{IN}(a, SQ) = \sup_{b \in support(SQ)}(\min(\mu_{=}(a, b), \mu_{SQ}(b))) \qquad (9)$$

That means that if $fc(R)$ stands for a fuzzy condition applying to R, it remains legal to use equally:

> select R.* **from** RS **where** $fc1(R)$ AND $fc2(S)$ AND $R.A = S.B$

or

> select* **from** R **where** $fc1$ AND A **IN** (select B **from** S **where** $fc2$)

But, one could also think of a formulation where the ≈ comparator gives rise to a subquery connection. To this end, a new predicate IN_f is necessary. Its semantics is directly depending on that of ≈. If $A \approx B$ means A is more or less equal to B, then the predicate $(x \, IN_f \{y\})$ means that x belongs more or less to the set $\{y\}$. It can be shown that the equivalence between:

> select R.* **from** S **where** $fc1(R)$ AND $fc2(S)$ AND $R.A \approx S.B$

and

select* from R where $fc1$ AND A IN$_f$ (select B from S where $fc2$)

is guaranteed as long as IN$_f$ is defined as:

$$\mu_{IN_f}(a, SQ) = \sup_{b \in support(SQ)}(\min (\mu_\approx (a, b), \mu_{SQ}(b)) \qquad (10)$$

where SQ denotes the result of the subquery, $\mu(a) = \min(\mu_R(a), \mu_{fc1}(a))$ and $\mu_{SQ}(b) = \min(\mu_S b), \mu_{fc2}(b))$. In fact, it is not mandatory to retieve all the attributes of R (specified by*). In the following examples and formula, we shall assume that only for notational convenience. In general, the query **select** A **from** R **where** fc results in a set of A values and we have to define the grade of membership of any a in dom (A) that is:

$$\mu(a) = \sup_{x \in support(R)}(\min (\mu_R (x)) \mid x.A = a)$$

According to the example given in Secion 3.1, we have to consider (when it is meaningful) the case of a fuzzy query involving the EXISTS predicate equivalent to a query expressed using a single block. Two kinds of interpretations are a priori possible for the predicate EXISTS (select...): a quantitative one based on the cardinality of the considered fuzzy set (resulting from the select) and a qualitative one based on the determination of the extent to which at least one element belongs to this set. This second interpretation has been retained since it preserves the equivalence between:

select $R.$ * from RS where $fc1$ (R) AND $fc2$ (S) AND $R.A \approx S.B$

and

Select * from R where $fc1$ AND EXISTS (select * from S where $fc2$ AND $B \approx R.A$)

as long as we have for any subquery SQ:

$$\mu_{EXISTS}(SQ) = \sup_{x \in support(SQ)}(\mu_{SQ}(x)) \qquad (11)$$

The last nesting mechanism concerns the quantifiers (ALL, ANY). Here again, the objective is to allow the use of these quantifiers together with fuzzy comparisons. Here again, some attention must be paid to the equivalences. For instance, the term $R.A = $ ANY (select B from S ...) is equivalent to $R.A$ IN (select B from S ...). More generally, the predicate (A <comp> ANY Q), where <comp> is a (possibly fuzzy) comparator and Q a subquery delivering a set of values compatible with A, looks for (at least) one element y of Q such that A <comp> y matches at best. Consequently, the following equivalence holds:

> **select * from R where** $fc1$ **AND** $A \ominus$ **ANY (select B from S where** $fc2$)

is equivalent to:

> **select * from R where** $fc1$ **AND EXISTS (select B from S where** $fc2$ **AND** $A \ominus B$)

if the extended ANY is interpreted as:

$$\mu_{\ominus ANY}(a, SQ) = \sup_{b \in support(SQ)}(\min(\mu_\ominus(a, b), \mu_{SQ}(b)))$$

Similarly, the semantics of ALL can be defined by:

$$\mu_{\ominus ALL}(a, SQ) = 1 - \sup_{b \in support(SQ)}(\min(1 - \mu_\ominus(a, b), \mu_{SQ}(b)))$$

3.4. Set Operators

As we said before, the SQL norm contains only the union operator. Its extension when the relations result from fuzzy selections such as in

> **select * from R where** $fc1$ **UNION select * from S where** $fc2$

is given by:

$$\mu(x) = \max(\min(\mu_R(x), \mu_{fc1}(x)), \min(\mu_S(x), \mu_{fc2}(x)))$$

Since the intersection and difference operators must generally be transformed into queries involving joins (intersection) or NOT IN, NOT EXISTS (difference), we must ensure that the equivalence is still valid in the context of the definitions adopted in (9)–(11). The general proof is beyond the scope of this paper, but we provide the way to express an intersection in SQL^f. Let us assume that R and S are defined on the same set of attributes $\{A_i\}$ and we desire to formulate:

select * from R **where** *fc1* **INTER select * from** S **where** *fc2*

The resulting fuzzy relation RES is such that:

$$
\begin{aligned}
\mu_{RES}(x) &= \min\left(\min\left(\mu_R(x), \mu_{fc1}(x)\right), \min\left(\mu_S(x), \mu_{fc2}(x)\right)\right) \\
&= \min\left(\mu_R(x), \mu_{fc1}(x)\right), \mu_S(x), \mu_{fc2}(x)) \tag{12}
\end{aligned}
$$

With a multirelation query we have:

select $R.*$ **from** $R\,S$ **where** *fc1* **AND** *fc2* **AND** $R.A_1 = S.A_1$
AND $... RA_n = S.A_n$

which produces exactly the same result since:
$$
\mu_{RES'}(x) = \min\left(\mu_{fc1}(x)\right), \mu_{fc2}(x), \min\left(\mu_R(x), \mu_S(x)\right))
$$

is the same as μ_{RES} defined in formula (12).

3.5. Partitioning and Quantification

We saw in SQL that it is possible to apply conditions to sets of tuples issued from a given relation. In SQL^f, our intention is to extend this capability in allowing fuzzy conditions for sets of tuples in a having clause. The first extension is directly derived from SQL using aggregates whereas the second relies on fuzzy quantifiers as described in Section 2.3. These two mechanisms can obviously be mixed in the same query.

In SQL, the selection of a partition is arrived at using a predicate involving one or several aggregate functions. This kind of feature has been slightly adapted in the context of SQL^f according to two directions. The aggregates are still used but their result can be a parameter of a fuzzy predicate. Moreover, the various conditions can be linked by the generalized connectors presented in Section 3.2. The following example, searching for the 10 best departments with respect to the condition "the mean salary of clerks is around 1600," illustrates this possibility:

select 10 depart **from** EMPLOYEE **where** job $=$ "clerk"
group by depart **having** AVG (salary) $=$ "around 1600"

A second way for qualifying partitions relies on the use of fuzzy quantifiers and has no counterpart in SQL. These quantifiers (see Section 2.3) allow the expression of fuzzy constraints on the sum or the proportion that characterizes the absolute or relative cardinality of a fuzzy set (Zadeh, 1983). Let us recall that absolute (based on the absolute cardinality of a fuzzy set: several, about 5,...) and relative (based on the relative cardinality of a set: none, a few of, most of,...) quantifiers can be used. In the context of SQL^f, such quantifiers are used to determine the extent to which the different partitions of a relation satisfy a proposition. The general syntax is:

> select ... from ... where ... group by ... having ... < quantified proposition > ...

Two kinds of basic predicates are possible: (1) Qf are fc, where Qf is an absolute quantifier applying to the number of tuples of a partition that satisfy the fuzzy condition fc, and (2) $Qf[fc2]$ are $fc2$, where Qf is a relative quantifier that applies to the proportion of tuples of a given partition that satisfy $fc2$ with respect to those that satisfy $fc1$ (all if $fc1$ is omitted). If we want to retrieve the 10 best departments with respect to the condition "most of the young employees are well-paid," we can write:

> select 10 depart from EMPLOYEE group by depart having most-of (age = "young") are "well-paid"

It must be noted that it would be also possible to select partitions by means of fuzzy sets comparisons seen in terms of indices as proposed in Dubois and Prade (1982). This point is not detailed here and the interested reader can refer to (Bosc et al., 1988).

4. FUZZY QUERY PROCESSING

4.1. Introduction

In conventional relational DBMSs, query processing is a somewhat open problem, since given a query, it is not possible in general to define the optimal way to process it. However, there is an agreement on the fact that this process is made of three levels. The first one concerns the available algorithms to implement the basic operations (selection, join, sort,...). For each operator, the system is provided with algorithms that depend mainly on the implementation of the operand relation(s) such as indexes, links, and clusters. The second level deals with the decomposition of the query into an (at least partly) ordered set of the previous elementary operations. This point is the crucial one and there are many possible strategies for a general query (Jarke and Koch, 1984). The third level is a concern of semantic analysis in order to find equivalent queries that will be evaluated more efficiently.

In the context of a DBMS allowing fuzzy querying capabilities, there is no basic difference from what we just described. In fact, the process becomes even a little more complex since: (1) the available access paths cannot be directly used, and (2) a larger number of tuples is selected by fuzzy conditions with respect to Boolean ones. Consequently, it is of prime importance to design methods that are expected to afford realistic performances.

In the remainder of this section, we first present an extension of a usual index in order to be able to have an associative access to a relation via a fuzzy value. Then, we point out an original strategy for the evaluation of project-select-join (PSJ) fuzzy queries so that a conventional DBMS could be used. The last point is devoted to more general queries especially comprising quantifiers.

4.2. Indexing Fuzzy Predicates

In ordinary DBMSs, the creation of indexes is intended to provide the access to those tuples of a relation whose value on a given attribute is known. Unfortunately, when fuzzy predicates are used, this kind of access path is unusable since the predicate does not refer to entry values of the index. So, the solution derives from the technique adopted in some information retrieval systems. The idea is to design an index per fuzzy predicate tied to an attribute (which gives rise to many indexes for the same attribute) similar to that suggested in Tahani (1976) and Radecki (1982). The principle of the extended index is to associate each grade of a fuzzy predicate with the list of tuples that satisfies the predicate at the considered grade. In fact, it is not necessary to define an index per predicate since all predicates issued from the same fuzzy *primary term* using modifiers (more or less, very, ...) can use the same index. In order to limit the amount of data on secondary storage and to facilitate database updates, it is possible to take into account the existence of a usual index. The approach

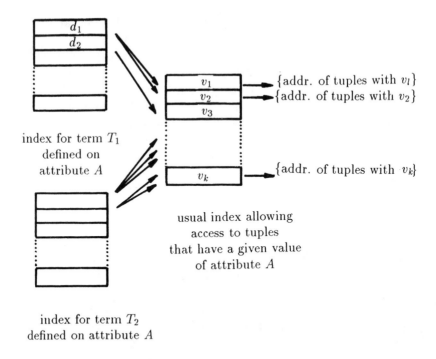

Figure 32.3.

consists in providing an access on grades of membership to a given primary term referring only to existing values of the concerned attribute. Consequently, an additional level is added into the index for each primary term according to the schema given in Figure 32.3.

If such a structure is available, it becomes easy to answer queries involving only restrictions in which fuzzy predicates are connected by ANDs and at least one is indexed as we propose in Bosc and Pivert (1989).

4.3. Simple Queries and Derivation Principle

Here we consider SQL^f queries involving a single base block without grouping and aggregates, known as *PSJ queries*. Very often a user is interested in only a very small number of tuples in the answer. Let us assume that a threshold t is given and we want to retrieve the elements whose grade is greater than this threshold. The idea is to use an ordinary DBMS to first select a small subset of tuples that will then be scanned by the fuzzy query. During the first step, tuples whose degree is small will be discarded, which is expected to restrict severely the size of the input relation for the second step. It would be ideal if we could determine exactly those tuples that are the desired t-cut; unfortunately it is not generally possible.

The principle adopted is to construct a Boolean query called *envelope* that will characterize the previous set, by means of a derivation from the initial fuzzy PSJ query. The envelope related to the query Q and the threshold t is denoted $Q\,[d \geqslant t]$. It delivers at least all the tuples whose grade d is over t. We can design a set of transformation (derivation) rules to construct it. Basically, the objective is to express the envelope for Q as a Boolean combination of those of the components of Q (selection or join predicates and connectors). A rule says that we can replace expression A by expression B and two cases occur depending on whether the set of tuples selected by A is the same as or a superset of those selected by B. In the first situation, we have a *strong* rule denoted $A \to B$, otherwise the rule is said to be *weak* and is written $A \sim\,\sim\, > B$. This point is obviously important since in the worst case, step by step, there is a risk for the method to deliver the entire relation if only weak rules are applied. In the following, we give an overview of the available rules; more information can be found in Bosc and Galibourg (1988).

We first consider the transformation rules for the connectors (binary or n-ary). The problem is to replace a combination of fuzzy terms with an expression where the individual envelopes are connected by the Boolean AND/OR operators. Due to the definition given earlier, the fuzzy and^f and or^f give rise to the rules:

$$(P \, and^f \, Q)\,[d \geqslant t] \to P\,[q \geqslant t]\ \text{AND}\ Q[d \geqslant t]$$
$$(P \, or^f \, Q)\,[d \geqslant t] \to P\,[q \geqslant t]\ \text{OR}\ Q[d \geqslant t]$$

When compensations are expressed using means, only weak rules apply based on the fact that for any mean m, the inequality $m(x, y) \leqslant \max(x, y)$ holds. Therefore, an expression involving the arithmetic mean is subject to the rule:

$$am\,(P, Q)\,[d \geqslant t] \sim\,\sim\, > P\,[d \geqslant t]\ \text{OR}\ Q\,[d \geqslant t]$$

However, more specific rules may be discovered and this can be illustrated by a rule related to the weighted mean $\mathrm{wm}(P_1,...,P_n)$ $= w_1p_1 + ... + w_np_n$ such that $\Sigma w_i = 1$:

$$\mathrm{wm}(P_1,...,P_n)[d \geqslant t] \sim \sim > P_1[d \geqslant \max(((t + w_1) - 1)/w_1, 0)$$
$$\mathrm{AND} ... \mathrm{AND}$$
$$P_n[d \geqslant \max(((t + w_n) - 1)/w_n, 0)$$

The unary operators are often called hedges or modifiers and they apply to a primary term to change its meaning. A typical example is the negation for which the following rule works:

$$(\mathrm{NOT}\, P)[d \geqslant t] \to P[d \leqslant (1 - t)]$$

Different authors have different definitions, but the interesting point is the fact that applicable rules exist anyway. For instance, if we consider exponential operators h defined as: $\mu_{hP}(x) = (\mu_P(x))^n$, we have the general rule:

$$(hP)[d \geqslant t] \Longrightarrow P[d \geqslant t^{1/n}]$$

For instance, if "very" corresponds to $n = 2$, the expression "very well-paid $[d \geqslant t]$" can be equivalently replaced by "well-paid $[d \geqslant \sqrt{t}]$."

Now let us have a look at the primary fuzzy terms. If we assume that they are modeled by a parametrized base function as suggested in Zadeh (1978), it is possible to express the t-cut S_t as one or a union of intervals. If the Boolean expression that characterizes S_t is written $<S_t>$, the rule $P[d \geqslant t] \to <S_t(P)>$ is valid. For example, if μ_p is an increasing function, $<S_t(P)>$ is the interval defined as $\{u \mid u \geqslant \mu_P^{-1}(t)\}$ where μ_P^{-1} is the inverse function of μ_P. When a primary term refers to a join, a similar process works in so far as the join predicate P between the two attributes A and B agrees on:

$$\text{for each } (a, b) \in \mathrm{dom}(A) \times \mathrm{dom}(B), \mu_P(a, b) = f(a - b)$$

The join predicates "much taller than" and "almost equal to" are illustrations of such predicates and the Boolean criterion will express whether $(a - b)$ belongs to one or several intervals. If μ_P is an increasing function f, the final Boolean join predicate will have the form: $a \geqslant b + f^{-1}(t)$.

Finally, let us consider an example of the transformation process on the condition $fc =$ (very young and well-paid) $[d \geqslant 0.64]$ where the membership functions:

$$\mu_{young}(x) = \begin{cases} \dfrac{1}{1 + \left(\dfrac{x-25}{7}\right)^2}, & \text{if } x > 25 \\ 1 \text{ otherwise} \end{cases}$$

$$\mu_{well-paid}(x) = \begin{cases} 0, \text{if } x \leqslant 4000 \\ 2 * \left(\dfrac{x-4000}{4500}\right)^2, & \text{if } x \in [4000, 6500] \\ 1 - 2 * \left(\dfrac{x-8500}{4500}\right)^2, & \text{if } x \in [6500, 8500] \\ 1, \text{if } x \geqslant 8500 \end{cases}$$

$fc \rightarrow$ young $[d \geqslant 0{,}64^{1/2}]$ AND well-paid $[d \geqslant 0.64]$
$\rightarrow\; < S_{0.8}$ (young) $>$ AND $< S_{0.64}$ (well-paid) $>$
$\rightarrow$ age < 29 AND salary > 6600

In the process presented earlier the threshold value must be known and the process is adapted for a qualitative calibration but not so for a quantitative one, which is likely to happen with end users. To deal with this problem, two main solutions can be proposed: (1) some statistical information is available to transform a number of desired responses into a threshold, and (2) several thresholds are tried and therefore several envelopes are built and finally submitted to the DBMS. To cope with efficiency, it would be interesting to process all these queries in a single database scan, which is a matter of future research.

4.3. Complex Query Evaluation

If we consider a general SQL^f query and we desire to process it without calling on a conventional DBMS, we must at least define algorithms to perform all the basic operations: selections, joins, etc. This work has already been undertaken and here we limit ourselves to exhibiting an algorithm in the case of quantifiers. A fuzzy quantifier is defined in terms of a fuzzy set allowing for an imprecise constraint on the cardinality of a fuzzy set (Zadeh, 1983).

Let us consider the query: **select * from** R **group by** A **having** Qf **are** fc. If Qf is an absolute quantifier, one must determine the absolute cardinality of fc in each partition E of R: Σ count $(fc) = \Sigma_{x \in E}(\mu_{fc}(x))$. The condition Qf are fc can be replaced by $Qf(\text{sum}(\mu_{fc}(x)))$ for each x of E. Thus, it is shown that the tuples whose grade equals zero are not useful and R can be restricted to the convenient subset before partitioning takes place. The evaluation process may be broken down into three parts: (i) restriction of R by fc producing the intermediate relation $R1$, (ii) grouping of the tuples of $R1$ according to A and creation of a binary relation $R2(A, B)$ where B is the sum of μ_{fc} for the tuples of a partition, and (iii) restriction of $R2$ according the condition $\mu_{Qf}(B) \geqslant t$, if t represents the threshold applying to the query.

If the quantifier is relative, Qf will apply to the relative cardinality of fc in a given partition E: Σ count $(fc \mid E) = \Sigma_{x \in E}(\mu_{fc}(x))/n$ where $n = \text{card}\{x \in E\}$. Since the calculation of n requires all the tuples of a partition, the initial relation R cannot be restricted here. The criterion Qf becomes: $Qf(\text{sum}(\mu_{fc})/\text{count}(*))$ where count $(*)$ counts the elements of a partition. The evaluation process comprises only steps (ii) and (iii), and during step (ii) B is computed as: $\text{sum}(\mu_{fc})/\text{count}(*)$. In both cases, the quantifier may be considered a fuzzy criterion bearing on the result of usual aggregate functions, which will not differ significantly from what is done for usual having clauses. When conditions looking like $Qf fc1$ are $fc2$ are dealt with, the major difference relies on the fact that the quantity to compute is the proportion of tuples of a partition that satisfy $fc2$ among those that satisfy $fc1$:

$$\Sigma count\,(fc2 \mid fc1) = \frac{\Sigma count\,(fc2\ and\ fc2)}{\Sigma count\,(fc1)} = \frac{\Sigma_E \min\,(\mu_{fc1}(x), \mu_{fc2}(x))}{\Sigma_E \mu_{fc1}(x)}$$

5. CONCLUSION

In this article, we have presented various approaches aiming at more flexible relational database management systems. We have especially focused on the capability of these systems to support imprecise conditions. Three different methods for the interpretation of imprecise conditions have been illustrated. Two of them, implemented in the context of the systems DEDUCE and ARES / VAGUE, are based on a transformation of imprecise conditions into Boolean conditions comprising the notion of interval of tolerance. Hovever, they basically rely on the Boolean logic, so discontinuities may still appear and they allow for only a limited kind of imprecision. The third approach is founded on the fuzzy sets theory and offers a general framework to deal with imprecise conditions. Some previous proposals, such as those made by Tahani (1976, 1977) and Kacprzyk and Ziółkowski (1986), and Kacprzyk, Zadrożny and Ziółkowski (1989), illustrate the possibilities of fuzzy sets even if no complete language is defined. The lack of a relational language allowing for imprecise querying led us to suggest an extension of the SQL norm, called SQL^f. One of the goals was to introduce imprecise capabilities wherever possible and moreover to adopt an extension so that most of the usual equivalences in SQL (in particular between single block and nested block queries) remain valid in SQL^f. The extended language has the same structure as SQL and it is possible to apply imprecise conditions to individual tuples as well as to sets of tuples issued from partitioning. In this latter case, conditions involving fuzzy quantifiers are allowed and they have no counterpart in SQL.

An important topic related to the support of additional capabilities concerns the performances. In the context of relational systems, the key point is the way the system determines an algorithm (how) starting from a nonprocedural query expressing what to retrieve. It seems that a reason why some methods do not rely on fuzzy sets is some ease in the implementation that is very close to usual systems so that no additional complexity appears. In the context of a system intended for supporting the querying capabilities of SQL^f, specific strategies are necessary. To this end, we have suggested an extension of the usual indexes in order to provide an associative access through a fuzzy predicate. Moreover, for a subset of imprecise queries, a method based on the derivation of a Boolean query that is expected to select a small subset that comprieses all the desired tuples has been suggested. The ultimate goal of our current work is to determine to what extent the introduction of fuzzy queries influences the performances.

Keywords: imprecise queries, fuzzy relations, query processing

BIBLIOGRAPHY

Bosc, P. and M. Galibourg. (1988). Flexible selection among objects: A framework based on fuzzy sets. *Proc. SIGIR Conf.*, Grenoble, F.

Bosc P. and O. Pivert. (1989). Algorithms for flexible selections in relational databases. *Proc ASLIB Conf.*, York, GB.

Bosc P., M. Galibourg, and G. Hamon. (1988). Fuzzy querying with SQL: Extensions and implementation aspects. *Fuzzy Sets and Syst.*, **28**, 333–349.

Chamberlin et al. (1976). SEQUEL 2: A unified approach to data definition, manipulation and control. *IBM Jour. of Res. and Dev.*, **20** (6), 560–575.

Chang, C. L. (1982). *Decision Support in an Imperfect World*. Research Report RJ3421, IBM, San José, CA. USA.

D'Atri, A. and L. Tarantino. (1989). From browsing to querying. *Data Eng. Bull.*, **12** (2), 47–53.

Dubois, D. and H. Prade. (1982). A unifying view of comparison indices in a fuzzy set theoretic framework. In R. Yager (ed.): *Recent Advance in Fuzzy Set and Possibility Theory*. New York: Pergamon Press.

Dubois, D. and H. Prade. (1985). A review of fuzzy set aggregation connectives. *Inf. Sc.*, **36**, 85–121.

Friedman, J. H., F. Baskett, and L. J. Shustek. (1975). An algorithm for finding nearest neighbors. *IEEE Trans. on Comp.*, 1001–1006.

Gal, A. (1988). *Cooperative Responses in Deductive Databases*. Technical Report CS-TR-2075, Department of Computer Science, University of Maryland, MD.

Ichikawa, T. and M. Hirakawa. (1986). ARES: A relational database with the capability of performing flexible interpretation of queries. *IEEE Trans. on Soft. Eng.*, **12** (5), 624-634.

Janas, K. (1981). On the feasibility of informative answers. In H. Gallaire, J. Minker, and J.-M. Nicolas (eds.): *Advances in Database Theory*. New York: Plenum.

Jarke, M. and J. Koch. (1984). Query optimization in database systems. *ACM Comp. Surv.*, **16**, 2.

Kacprzyk, J., S. Zadrożny, and A. Ziółkowski. (1989). Fquery III: A "human-consistent" database querying system based on fuzzy logic with linguistic quantifiers. *Information Systems*, **14**, 443–453.

Kacprzyk, J. and A. Ziółkowski. (1986). Database queries with fuzzy linguistic quantifiers. *IEEE Trans. on Syst., Man and Cyber.*, **16** (3), 474–478.

Kaplan, S. (1982). Cooperative responses from a portable natural language database query system. In M. Brady (ed.): *Computational Models of Discourse*. Cambridge: MIT Press.

Lacroix, M. and P. Lavency. (1987). Preferences: Putting more knowledge into queries. *Proc. of the Thirteenth VLDB Conf.*, Brighton, GB.

Motro, A. (1988). VAGUE: A user interface to relational databases that permits vague queries. *ACM Trans. on Off. Inf. Syst.*, **6** (3), 187–214.

Motro, A. (1989). A trio of database user interfaces for handling vague retrieval requests. *Data Eng. Bull.*, **12** (2), 54–63.

Radecki, T. (1982). Generalized Boolean methods of information retrieval. *Int. Jour. of Man-Mach. Stud.*, **18.**

Rivest, R. L. (1976). Partial match retrieval algorithms. *SIAM Jour. of Comp.*, **5** (1), 19–50.

Tahani, V. (1976). A fuzzy model of document retrieval systems. *Inf. Proc. & Manag.*, **12,** 177–187.

Tahani, V. (1977). A conceptual framework for fuzzy query processing: A step toward very intelligent database systems. *Inf. Proc. and Manag.*, **13,** 289–303.

Yazici, A., R. George, B. P. Buckles, and F.E. Petry. (1992). A survey of conceptual and logical data model for uncertainty management. In L. A. Zadeh and J. Kacprzyk (eds.): *Fuzzy Logic for the Management of Uncertainty.* New York: Wiley.

Zadeh, L. A. (1965). Fuzzy sets. *Information and Control*, **8,** 338–353.

Zadeh, L. A. (1978). PRUF: A meaning representation language for natural languages. *Int. Jour. of Man-Mach. Stud.*, **10,** 395–460.

Zadeh, L. A. (1983). A computational approach to fuzzy quantifiers in natural languages. *Comp. Maths with Appl.*, **9,** 149–183.

INDEX